CONSTITUTIONAL DEVELOPMENT OF THE WEST INDIES: 1922-1968

A Selection from the Major Documents

The CARIBBEAN HISTORY BIBLIOGRAPHICAL
AND DOCUMENTARY SERIES
is published by
Caribbean Universities Press
on behalf of
the Department of History at
the University of the West Indies.

Other titles in the series:

Source Material relating to Caribbean Commonwealth Countries in U.S. and Canadian Repositories

Other history series being developed are:

MONOGRAPHS
REPRINTS
CHAPTERS
PAMPHLETS
THE JOURNAL OF CARIBBEAN HISTORY
(twice yearly, May and November)

Constitutional Development of the West Indies

1922–1968

A SELECTION FROM THE MAJOR DOCUMENTS

Ann Spackman

Department of Government, University of the West Indies

CARIBBEAN UNIVERSITIES PRESS
in association with the
BOWKER PUBLISHING COMPANY
1975

ISBN 0 85474 030 9

First published in 1975 by Caribbean Universities Press
Devon House, Rockley New Road, St. Lawrence 4, Barbados
in association with the Bowker Publishing Company, Epping, Essex, England

Printed in Belgium

To my parents

ACKNOWLEDGEMENTS

My major debt of gratitude is to Mr G.E. Mills, Head of the Department of Government, Mr A. McIntyre, Director of the Institute of Social and Economic Research (both of the University of the West Indies) and the Ford Foundation for making it possible for me to be relieved of teaching duties for the academic year 1969-1970. For assistance, financial and otherwise, in the location and copying of documents I wish to thank again Mr Mills, Dr F.R. Augier, the Ford Foundation, the staff of the University Library at Mona, and the staff of the Attorney General's Library, Government of Jamaica. In this respect I am particularly indebted to Mrs Catherine Levy, formerly of the University Library, Mona. Extremely useful have been critical readings of the manuscript by G.E. Mills, A. McIntyre, K. Lawrence, T. Munroe and Louis Lindsay. I would also like to record my gratitude to Mrs D. Phillibert and Mrs D. Tucker for their help in typing the manuscript. However, my thanks for constant stimulation of ideas can never be adequately expressed to all my colleagues, staff and students, with whom I have worked in the University of the West Indies, and for his very helpful comments I should like to mention Mr Louis Lindsay in particular.

A. S.

University of the West Indies,
Mona,
Jamaica.

TABLE OF CONTENTS

* In this work Guyana will be referred to as British Guiana in the pre-independence period and as Guyana in the post-independence period.

C The Jamaican Constitution of 1944 and documents leading to its adoption.

(i) Extracts from the Report of the Select Committee of the Legislative Council appointed to prepare and draft a political constitution for Jamaica.

(ii) Extracts from the Minority Report of the Select Committee of the Legislative Council appointed to prepare and draft a political constitution for Jamaica.

(iii) Extracts from the Despatch from the Secretary of State for the Colonies to the Governor of Jamaica, dated 7th March 1941.

(iv) Extracts from the Despatch from the Secretary of State for the Colonies to the Governor of Jamaica, dated 5th January 1942.

(v) Extracts from the Proposals for a new constitution of Jamaica, 20th July 1944.

(vi) Extracts from the Despatch from the Secretary of State for the Colonies to the Governor of Jamaica, dated 10th February 1943.

(vii) Extracts from the Jamaica (Constitution) Order in Council, 1944

D The coming of universal adult suffrage and elected majorities in the legislatives of territories other than Jamaica.

(i) Extracts from the Report of the Committee to examine the extension of the franchise, 1944.

(ii) Extracts from a statement made in the House of Commons by the Secretary of State for the Colonies on British Guiana (Franchise), 4th October 1944.

(iii) Constitutional Reform. Windward and Leeward Islands.

(iv) Extracts from the Report of a Committee appointed to consider constitutional reform held at Government Office on Monday, 8th August 1949.

(v) Extracts from the Antigua Constitution and Elections Ordinance, 1951.

E Further increases in the number of elected members of the legislature and the development of bi-cameralism. Also related developments in the office of Speaker and reductions of the Governor's powers.

(i) Extracts from the Despatch from the Secretary of State for the Colonies to the Governor of Trinidad and Tobago, dated 7th January 1949.

B The nominated Executive Council with only a limited right to be consulted by the Governor.

(i) Extracts from the Leeward Islands Letters Patent, dated 11th November 1936.

(ii) Extracts from Royal Instructions to the Governor of the Leeward Islands, dated 17th November 1936.

C The introduction of elected members to the Executive Council, but with no change in its powers or functions.

(i) Extracts from Royal Instructions to the Governor of the Windward Islands, dated 10th August 1951.

(ii) Extracts from the Address by the Governor to the General Legislative Council of the Leeward Islands, 15th October 1951.

D The committee – system experiment.

(i) Extracts from the Address by the Governor to the General Legislative Council, 6th January 1953.

(ii) Announcement by the Acting Administrator of Grenada as President of the Legislative Council, 20th December 1954.

E The development of the Executive Council as the chief instrument of policy and the quasi-ministerial system.

(i) Extracts from the Report of the Select Committee of the Legislative Council appointed to draft a political constitution for Jamaica, 1939.

(ii) Extracts from the Proposals for a New Constitution, published 1944.

(iii) Extracts from the Despatch from the Secretary of State for the Colonies to the Governor of Jamaica, dated 5th January 1942.

(iv) Extracts from the Despatch from the Secretary of State for the Colonies to the Governor of Jamaica, dated 10th February 1943.

(v) Extract from a Message to the Legislative Council from the Governor of Jamaica, 20th September 1944.

(vi) Extracts from the Jamaica (Constitution) Order in Council, 1944.

(vii) Extracts from the Despatch from the Secretary of State for the Colonies to the Governor of Trinidad and Tobago, dated 7th January 1949.

PREFACE

This volume is intended to present to students of West Indian history and politics selections from the major official documents relating to constitutional development from 1922-68. The period covered is one during which there was a mass manufacture of constitutions for the colonies. In the earlier inter-war years there was obvious uncertainty about the Empire – as the white dominions were formally recognized as sovereign states in 1931 earlier grandiose ideas of an Imperial Federation were abandoned, the idea of the Commonwealth emerged, never to be really clarified. The cash value and the moral value of a dependent Empire came to be questioned, but the abandonment of British rule over the colonies was still seen as a possible development in the remote future. Its continuation for an indefinite period was increasingly justified by questioning the fitness of nations to rule themselves. The Colonial Office and the Colonial Service formulated ideas of trusteeship, partnership and 'the capacity for self government', ideas which depended on the ethnocentric judgement that whiteness was in some way related to responsibility and an insight into government and rule.

However, liberal democratic ideas and the doctrine of the right to self-determination did have their impact, and some advances in constitutional position were made during the inter-war years. It is in the post Second World War period that the Colonial Office really began to pour out so-called constitutions for the colonies. The pace of change accelerated and the end product of self-government came more and more into the immediate future. It is during this period that the unreality of the question of capacity or readiness to govern becomes apparent. What stage of development had been passed through, which made British Guiana 'ready' for universal adult suffrage in 1953 when it was not ready in 1944? Were the Windward and Leeward Islands two years more advanced than British Guiana in this respect? Power to control local police forces would be withheld one year and granted the next, and so forth.

The idea of a constitution embodying a country's fundamental law, which establishes and defines the structure and functions of the major institutions of government and their inter-relationships, entails not only some regularity in government but also some permanence. Constitutions in the West Indies were mere halts along a path of development which not even the Colonial Office seemed to have clearly mapped out. Because a false question of fitness to rule was being asked (although this did include a real question about the viability of small states) one can say that these constitutions were false constitutions and that the development from one stage to the next was also false in that often no real political change had taken place in the interim which affected the 'capacity to rule'.

Given this situation the value of examining the formal constitutions and the official documents relating to them can clearly be questioned, and it is not the intention of this book to overstress their importance. Indeed it is the author's opinion that they only have importance insofar as they illustrate certain aspects of a process of change and suggest influences and relationships within the political arena of the West Indies. These documents illustrate, for example, the reality of the power relationship between the metropolis and the colonies, with the subordination of the colonial political system to that of Britain; the growth of local political demands which itself illustrates the growth of political consciousness and articulate nationalism; the difficulty of defining the nation in the West Indian context and the different definitions which were given; the reluctance of Britain's gradual withdrawal in response to local demands, and later the speed with which she attempted to solve 'the problem of the smaller territories' by the questionable formula of association.

These documents also show the essentially authoritarian nature of a colonial political system and its domination by the executive. It is significant that this is a feature of the current West Indian constitutions of independent and associated states which is perpetuated.

A selection from official documents cannot of itself put forward explanations of change: why the British Empire disintegrated during these years; why nationalism and political consciousness developed within the West Indies during this period. However, it is the author's opinion that these documents do contain a wealth of illustrative material which suggest certain hypotheses about past, present and future developments.

Chapter I is an introductory chapter which seeks to put the constitutional changes which were taking place in a broader political and social context.

Chapter II uses the Colonial Office Lists of 1922 to present the constitutional position in that year together with extracts from the Report of the Hon.

E.F.L. Wood on his visit to the West Indies and British Guiana, 1922 (referred to hereafter as the Wood Report).

The Lists and the Wood Report clearly illustrate the considerable variety of colonial constitution in the West Indies, from the survival of the Old Representative System in Barbados and the Bahamas through a number of variations on the basic Crown Colony type.

These extracts also give clear illustration of the subordinate position of the colonial legislature, even under the Old Representative System, the autocratic power of the Governor within the colony and the over-riding authority of the Imperial government.

In this extract from the Wood Report a theme is illustrated which is further developed in the Introduction to this volume: that is the influence of external factors on the political development of the West Indies. Wood refers to the forces, greatly influenced by the First World War, which set in motion a 'wave of democratic sentiment' creating a demand for representative government which Wood felt would in the long run be irresistible. In this context he also clearly recognized the importance of the rise of an educated middle-class, articulate, self-aware, and seeking representation for itself in the institutions of government.

Wood also points to the long history of representative institutions in the West Indies which only came to an end for most of the territories in the late 19th century.[1] Whilst accepting the relevance of this, indeed given the nature of later demands by men like J.A.G. Smith of Jamaica for a return to the old constitution the relevance cannot be denied, nevertheless it should be pointed out that this experience of representative institutions was restricted to a very narrow elite, differentiated from the mass by race-colour as well as by wealth, and that even where there was this limited experience of representation there had been no development of responsible government.

Also of significance in this extract from the Wood Report is the illustration of the importance of example. Wood points out that the approval in principle of the election of a minority of members to the Grenada Legislative Council had led to similar demands being made in all the other territories which lacked elected members. The demonstration effect illustrated here is to be repeated frequently in West Indian political development. In the 1930s riots, associated with serious labour unrest, swept through all the territories; later in the post-war period as one territory acquired some new institutional form so demands

1 British Guiana did not lose its old constitution until 1928. Jamaica and Montserrat lost theirs in 1866; the British Virgin Islands in 1867; British Honduras became a Crown Colony in 1870; St Vincent lost its old constitution in 1876; Grenada in 1877; St Christopher/Nevis in 1878; and Antigua and Dominica in 1898.

and similar grants were made in the other colonies; currently in the late 1960s and 1970 each West Indian territory is experiencing new political demands, sometimes accompanied by demonstration and violence, which can broadly be called 'black power' and are in direct line with earlier attempts to create real popular control over government.

Chapter III includes some familiar material to students of the history of the British Empire. It serves to show the legal limitations which existed to the legislative competence even of the Dominions up to 1931. Of course for most of the period covered by this volume the West Indies were controlled, as colonies, by imperial legislation. One of the most important pieces of legislation in this respect was the Colonial Laws Validity Act, 1865, reproduced here in its entirety. As can be seen, this act was originally intended to be a clarification and expansion of the powers of colonial legislatures although later it was seen as representing the stigma of colonial status and the subordinate nature of colonial legislation.

The documents in this chapter also define the powers of disallowance, reservation, assent, the incompetence of colonial legislature to make law with extra-territorial effect and with regard to merchant shipping. However, this chapter does not illustrate the power of the Governor in Crown Colonies, when he has lost his official majority in the Legislative Council, to legislate against the wishes of the colonial legislature by exercising his power of certification.

Chapter IV contains the largest and perhaps the most significant collection of documents in this volume. The documents relate to the formal constitutional advance of the majority of West Indian territories from Crown Colony status through the various stages prescribed by the Colonial Office to the status of full internal self-government. Even the earliest documents reveal that the Colonial Office had already accepted the principle of constitutional advance towards more representative and responsible government. The principle was explicitly affirmed in the 1920s and later documents show that this was an underlying assumption of the Colonial Office. However, the acceptance of the principle of advance did not involve any clear idea of how far this advance should go, or how quickly it should take place. The compromise solution of associated statehood at the present time shows that, at least for the smaller territories the question of how far advance should go remains unsettled.

This chapter also provides illustrative material, related to the specific West Indian context, of the reality of the subordination of the colony to the Imperial centre. Illustration of this point has already been made in Chapter III of this volume in the documents relating to colonial and dominion status. One of the harshest, but not the least accurate, judgements made of the colonial situation appears in the Memoranda prepared by the elected members of the Combined Court of British Guiana in reply to the Report of the British Guiana Commission, 1927.[2] The elected members state that within the colony 'the right to govern is interpreted as being the right of a bureaucratic autocracy to introduce measures and force them upon a subservient legislature, without the usual legislative enquiries and safeguards'.

In addition to providing much descriptive material these documents contain a wealth of formal legal analysis of the theory and practice of representative and responsible government along Westminster-Whitehall lines. They also show in operation the assumptions behind a whole school of political thought which relates political development to the administrative capacity to maintain law and order, and to govern neutrally and rationally. At the same time they provide some examples of the political thinking which would put more positive emphasis upon the importance of broad-based participation in government. The selections from the Waddington Report show that this was one of the most sophisticated statements of the Westminster-Whitehall view of the political universe, and it includes more explicitly than other documents a theory of the relationship between formal institutions of government and political parties.

The documents in this chapter have been selected to provide ample illustration of the stages of constitutional development from Crown Colony to full internal self-government, as well as the attitudes towards that development in the colonies and the metropolis. The development of the Bahamas and Barbados has not been illustrated in much depth for two major reasons, first, since they were exceptional in retaining the Old Representative System they are not typical of the West Indies as a whole, and secondly in Barbados particularly considerable advance was made by conventional rather than by formal legal means and therefore there is not the wealth of public documents relating to change which is found for the other territories.

The early documents relate to the pure form of Crown Colony government where the Governor, appointed from and by the Imperial centre was supreme. With a few exceptions, for example Lord Olivier and Sir Hugh Foot, these were undistinguished men concerned primarily with narrow administrative ends and not the political development of the territories, and furthermore they were almost entirely of a class which would make them even more remote from the West Indian masses than their colour and British nationality made inevitable. The political structure of the Crown Colony system pushed the powerful Governors even further away from the people. The Legislative Councils were wholly nominated with official majorities[3] and although they

2 Cmnd. 3047/1927. Chapter IV, Part I, document D(ii), p. 95.

3 While this is true of pure Crown Colony government is should be remembered that by 1922 when this selection of documents begins Jamaica and British Guiana had elected members in their respective legislatures.

participated in the legislative process it was the Governor who was vested with the responsibility to make laws for the peace, order and good government of the territories. The Executive Councils[4] were also nominated bodies either with official majorities or were entirely official and they had only advisory functions, the Governor being able to reject their advice. Furthermore, and this is a feature of colonial government until full internal self-government, the Governor was solely responsible for the civil and military services.

The first advance from pure Crown Colony government was the addition of some elected members to the Legislative Council. The official majority was retained and the elections took place on the basis of a narrow franchise. Sometimes the official majority would be secured by the vote of the Governor who was also President of the Council. Where this was the case, the Governor rarely had to use his vote, for even when the official side balanced the unofficial side, the unofficial nominated members, nominated by the Governor, normally identified and voted with the official members. Indeed for the most part the elected members themselves, coming from a narrow elite class, were only infrequently in conflict with the Governor.[5]

The next stage would be the creation of an unofficial majority, normally created by balancing the number of elected members with the number of nominated unofficials and official members combined. The Governor would again be able to exercise his vote to break a deadlock, and for the reasons given above relating to identity of interest and viewpoint he rarely had to exercise his casting vote. However, with the creation of an unofficial majority there existed the obvious possibility of the official side being outvoted in the Council. Since at this stage of development there was no question of the Governor relinquishing or even sharing his total responsibility for 'peace, order and good government' within the colony, it is at this point that the Governor was given the additional reserve power of certification – that is the power to pass as law, bills which were rejected by the Council. This would be in addition to his powers to assent to bills, to reserve them for His Majesty's pleasure and to the power of the Imperial government to disallow legislation which had been given the Governor's assent.[6]

From this point onwards a number of different developments take place relative to greater increases in both representative and responsible government. For convenience, the developments in responsible government will be treated separately although it should be remembered that they were taking place

4 Sometimes called Executive Committees.

5 There were some exceptions to this: Captain A.A. Cipriani; T.A. Marryshow, J.A.G. Smith.

6 See Chapter III.

simultaneously with changes in representativeness. Along with pressure for elected majorities in the Legislative Councils came demands for universal adult suffrage, and this was the next step. It should be noted here that the pace-setter, Jamaica, asked for and was given a bicameral legislature at the same time as universal adult suffrage, and the short-lived constitution of British Guiana in 1953 also made provision for a bicameral legislature with a wholly elected popular chamber. Barbados and the Bahamas of course did not lose their bicameral legislatures. In the other territories bicameralism was a much later development, but where it was introduced the Westminster pattern was followed of having a weak, non-popular second chamber.[7]

Where unicameral, mixed Legislative Councils were retained universal adult suffrage and the years following its introduction saw the gradual reduction in the number of official and unofficial nominated members – the Attorney General being the last of the three *ex officio* members (Chief Secretary, Finance Secretary and Attorney General) to remain in the Council before independence or associated statehood.

Also during these years came a change in the officer who presided over the legislature. As has already been noted the Governor was also President of the Council, but even before he ceased to hold that office the Governor would often give the task to the Deputy President who would be elected from within the Council. The next formal advance would be the appointment by the Governor of a Speaker from outside the Council, who would also have an elected Deputy. The final development would be the election of the Speaker himself from among the elected members of the Council.[8]

As the legislatures of the West Indies became more formally representative so their powers increased. The right to legislate became exercisable by the Governor 'with the advice and consent of the Legislative Council' and finally, following the United Kingdom, the constitutions state that 'There shall be a Parliament of . . . which shall consist of Her Majesty, a Senate and a House of Representatives'. Other changes which followed from increases in representativeness were the gradual removal of the Governor's reserve powers over legislation, so that by the time full internal self-government was achieved he had lost his power of certification, and his discretion to assent. He could reserve for Her Majesty's pleasure only those classes of bills which were specified in the constitution that is, those relating to external affairs, defence, amendment of the constitution, and the royal prerogative, and these bills he must reserve.

7 See Ann Spackman, 'The Senate of Trinidad and Tobago' *Social & Economic Studies,* vol. 16, no. 1 (March 1967).

8 It should be noted here that the West Indies have not followed the unusual British practice of developing conventions which remove the Speaker from the realm of political controversy.

Also the Imperial government's power of disallowance related only to bills which affected Government Stock. Although of course the Imperial government retained the right to approve or disapprove legislation reserved by the Governor.

Simultaneous with these changes in the representative element in legislation there were changes in the exercise of the executive power. Even where the Executive Council remained nominated and only advisory in function the Governor might try to identify the 'people' with the Council by appointing some elected members from the Legislative Council, but it should be remembered that at this stage election would be on the basis of a restricted franchise. Also with these initial advances the Governor might be obliged to consult the Executive Council in the normal exercise of his duties. This represented no real diminution of his authority since he could reject the advice given at his discretion and he did not have to consult the Council if by doing so he would, in his opinion, run the risk of injuring the interests of the Imperial government, or if the matter was too urgent or too trivial. However, if he did not consult the Council on these grounds he was obliged to get the Secretary of State's approval first or, if this was impossible, report his actions with reasons.

As the Legislative Councils became more representative the Governor would be obliged to appoint to the Executive Council some elected members, who were elected from the legislature. Their appointments could be revoked by a two-thirds majority vote, and usually at this stage the official element remained in a majority. This stage was usually associated with the tutelary experiment of the committee system, and there would be no significant change in the Governor's powers.

When the Executive Council became the chief instrument of policy the number of elected members increased (but not necessarily to constitute a clear majority and their manner of being appointed remained unchanged) and the Governor would normally be obliged not only to consult but to act on the advice of the Council. However, he retained the discretion (as outlined above) to not consult and to reject the advice given to him. Although if he did reject the advice a dissenting member now had the right to record his dissent and the reasons for it in the minutes of the Council, which would be sent to the Secretary of State.

At this stage, also, the elected members would be 'associated with the work of departments'. In other words, they would be allocated subject areas by the Governor, and it would be their job to propose policy within that area and to speak on such policy in the legislature. However, they would not be the responsible heads of departments – these remained the career officials who were responsible directly to the Governor and were for the most part expatriate.[9]

9 And with whom elected Ministers often clashed, to the point of sometimes opposing in the legislature what had been approved in Executive Council.

Following more or less naturally from this in the imperial scheme of things came the semi-responsible form of government where elected members would form a clear majority in a still mixed Executive Council. They would still be elected from the legislature but they would have responsibility for the administration of their departments. The penultimate step, before full internal self-government, was the appointment of a Chief Minister, following British conventions, and the establishment of collective responsibility with the Chief Minister presiding at Cabinet meetings (nomenclature changed at this stage as well). The Governor retained his discretionary powers and he could summon a meeting of the Cabinet and preside at it, but this would be exceptional.

Other changes associated with this stage and the establishment of full internal self-government were: the constitution of service commissions which would perform most of the Governor's functions as head of the public service, disciplinary matters alone would remain in his hands until the establishment of full internal self-government;[10] the official Financial-Secretary would give way to a Minister of Finance; the Chief Secretary would lose most of his functions to a Minister of Home Affairs, but internal security would only be handed over with full internal self-government.

As the phrase suggests full internal self-government means that the Imperial government gives over all responsibility for internal affairs to the colonial government and the conventions of Westminster-Whitehall are more or less faithfully copied in the constitutional instruments. External affairs, defence and constitutional amendment alone remaining in the hands of the Imperial government.

The documents selected to illustrate these changes also deal at length with the common problems of colonial government once it ceases to be a straightforward autocracy. These problems can be identified as (a) that of the divorce of power and responsibility, and related to this central conflict in colonial institutions; (b) the electeds, especially after universal adult suffrage, forming themselves into a permanent opposition to the government and (c) the difficulty of operating 'mixed' executives when at the same time some of the conventions of collective responsibility are expected. This last problem was given vivid expression by Mr Bustamante in his Montego Bay speech in 1947,[11] but the most obvious example of the underlying instability of this arrangement is most clearly seen in Appendix A in documents which relate to the suspension of British Guiana's constitution in 1953. The first and most serious problem of colonial constitutions 'on the move', the divorce of responsibility from real power is clearly seen for the first time with the

10 Public Service Commissions did exist before this stage but with advisory functions only.
11 Col. no. 218/1948. Chapter IV, Part III, document A(ii), p. 195.

introduction of a representative element into the formal institutions of government. Wood's justification of the Governor's power of certification illustrates the point: the Governor is still the real government of the colony and therefore must possess the power to enforce his will in the last analysis. Under responsible government in the United Kingdom and Dominions, law and convention ensure that the government has a working majority in the legislature. It therefore possesses the power necessary for government. In a colony, where the Governor is not popularly chosen and where he has lost his official majority, there is no political mechanism – legal or conventional – which would ensure this identity between government and a majority in the legislature. Therefore, since it was altogether too radical a thought to introduce popular executives with legislative support, the Governor had to be given the necessary power to enforce his will and push through a bill despite elected opposition.

Furthermore it is the author's opinion that these documents frequently reveal, better than many subsequent analyses, the attitudes and prejudices prevailing during the period covered, although since they are public documents the bias is clearly towards official opinion. Particularly in the earlier documents there are those examples from British spokesmen which clearly illustrate the now almost incredible self-confidence and self-satisfaction which is perhaps a necessary prerequisite for imperial rule. As Weber suggests, to rule requires a belief in one's own right to rule. To this one can surely add that to rule over an empire of different racial make-up requires the development of belief in racial superiority. The Hon. E.F.L. Wood in his report seems to suggest that the coloured or racially mixed sections of the populations of the West Indies owe their capacities in some way to 'a large infusion of European blood'.[12] The Report of the British Guiana Commission, 1927, states quite explicitly that the European 'class' was needed for responsibility in politics and stability, a point of view which was met by a straight accusation of racial prejudice in the reply from the elected members of the Combined Court.[13] Even as late as the Moyne Report[14] one finds that the problem of racial prejudice referred to is not that of the history of the oppression of the blacks and the indignities which the majority continued to suffer. On the contrary the problem referred to was that of open hostility being shown to expatriate white officials who continued to man most of the senior public offices.

Expressed in the early documents but by the 1930s increasingly supplanting clear statements of belief in racial superiority were the complex of

12 Wood Report. See below Chapter V, Part I document A, p. 268. See also Chapter IV, Part I, document B, p. 89.
13 Chapter IV, Part I, documents D(i) and D(ii), p. 90, 95.
14 Chapter IV, Part I, document E, p. 100.

attitudes which went into the making of the British Imperial idea of trusteeship. As the British Guiana Commission commented of the old constitution: 'At present the elected members are in the position of a minor who can overrule his own trustee'. Self-government was pictured as something which could only be effectively performed after a tutelary period where certain lessons were taught on the operation of the Westminster-Whitehall system of government, examinations had to be set and passed before a certificate, in the form of an 'independence' Act, could be given. The concept of 'fitness to rule' was used, as was a vague idea of 'maturity'. Until West Indians became fit and mature persons Britain had the moral duty to continue to rule over her Caribbean possessions. To the challenge of Bustamante in 1947 that 'we as Jamaicans are adults, we are quite prepared to throw our burden on our shoulders and face the dangers of independence',[15] the reply was 'not yet!' Unfortunately, behind these self-serving attitudes of imperialist politicians and administrators were real problems of poverty and smallness which remain unsolved and the fragmentation of the Caribbean as a whole, along with its poverty, is one of the more disastrous colonial legacies.

Another thread running through the documents was the British concern to appease capital. In referring to Trinidad and Tobago, the Hon. E.F.L. Wood made specific reference to the heavy investment in the oil industry which should not be frightened by any premature grant of responsibility to the local population. In the same extract it can clearly be seen that by responsible public opinion Wood meant only local merchants, planters, professional men and the expatriate officials.[16] As a final illustration of this point a despatch from the Secretary of State to the Governor of Trinidad and Tobago can be quoted: in arguing for the retention of the nominated element in the Legislative Council the Secretary of State upheld that this was necessary to maintain 'confidence in the economic and financial stability of the colony, on which the prosperity and therefore the welfare and standard of living of the people depend'.[17]

Some of the most important political developments taking place during the years 1922-68 are only glimpsed in these documents. The Imperial self-confidence waned as Britain's economic and military position in the world declined. At the same time changing values with regard to the role of government speeded up the process of popularising colonial government which must also be associated with the retreat from Empire. In this selection of documents the earliest indication of commitment to more positive government action is seen in the Report of the British Guiana Commission, 1927.[18]

15 Chapter IV, Part III, document A(ii), p. 155.
16 Chapter IV, Part I, document A, p. 76.
17 Chapter IV, Part II, document E(i), p. 153.
18 Cmnd. 2841/1927. Chapter IV, Part I, document D(i), p. 90.

However, the most significant statement, indicative of a real change of approach to governmental duty, is usually taken to be that of the Moyne Commission Report.[19] Government is seen as having to deal with social reconstruction and economic advance rather than law and order alone. Once the area of government concern is enlarged then the crude authority structure of the pure Crown Colony system, with its divorce of government from the people, becomes completely inadequate. As the Moyne Report itself argues, any attempt at serious social or economic change would need to involve the majority of the people; certainly in the West Indies, it would be necessary to involve in the decision-making process organized labour, which, from the time of the area-wide disturbances in the 1930s, was a politically powerful force.

The Imperial government was weakening; ideas relating to government were developing which demanded more popular representation; it could be argued that popular representation would, in a relatively short run, spell the end of Imperial rule; added to all these was the crucial factor in the development of the region away from the institutional control by Britain: the growth of nationalism and political awareness among West Indian peoples. These documents contain echoes of this growing consciousness and the passions aroused by it. They show the reluctant but progressively speedier retreat of Britain before the demands formulated in these and other colonies.[20] However, it is because the documents only provide remote illustration of some of these developments that the Introduction has been used to fill in some of the gaps.

Chapter V deals with the various experiments with federation, amalgamation etc. which have been attempted or simply considered in the West Indies – including the failed federation itself.

Part I deals with the early consideration of possible forms of union up to 1946, and starts with the West Indian Conference – the origin of which lies in the initiative taken by the Associated Chambers of Commerce of the area and their chairman Sir Edward Davson. The conference was intended to be a purely functional meeting of representatives of the territories, along the lines of the Imperial Conference. It would examine fruitful areas for co-operation such as communications and discuss trade, customs, education, and medical problems. However, the Conference was to be a conference only and was to have no authority to act for the region as a whole, nor was it to have a continuous life.

19 Chapter IV, Part I, document E, p. 100.
20 See especially developments in Grenada and Dominica in the early years; the reply of the elected members of the British Guiana Combined Court, 1927 Chapter V, Part I, D(ii); the documents relating to the Jamaican constitutional changes of 1944; the Waddington Commission Report Chapter IV, Part II, E(v) p. 160, and Appendix A.

Although it was never intended to have and never developed any governmental status early documents relating to the Conference are included because they are illustrative of a number of points. First they give evidence of early attempts at co-operation at an official governmental level – since the Conferences were meetings of official and unofficial members of territorial governments and legislatures. The documents also contain references to specific areas where consultation and co-operation were taking place. Secondly, the documents show that even at a time when elected representation was minimal and the franchises were limited throughout the West Indies there was nevertheless a linking of ideas of regional co-operation with ideas of popular representation, even though at the time this had a much narrower meaning than it did later. Thirdly, the documents give early evidence of the tension within the region created by a recognition on the one hand of certain common problems which called for common solutions, of the reality of shared experiences and similar histories, and on the other hand by a recognition of the differences, the insularity, the insecurity which refuses to abandon a separate identity. The documents also show the appalling communications between the West Indies: so bad were they that the Secretary of State could say in 1926 that London was still the most convenient meeting place *in* the West Indies!

The importance of separation and poor communications in holding back the development of federation is repeated in many of the documents in Part I of this chapter. However, it was not always realized that the 'problem' of separation was only a problem because of the barrier of poor communications – a point which was recognized by the Governor of the Leeward Islands in 1931.[21] It appears as if there was, and one suspects that there still is a belief that because the geographic separation of the West Indies is natural so also is the lack of contact between the peoples of the region. It should be pointed out here that historically water transport, by sea and river, was a more important link between peoples than over-land transport, and that in its early development Australia relied very heavily on sea links along the coast – involving vast distances. The Caribbean Sea only divided the West Indies because there was a failure over the centuries on the part of the metropolitan government to develop links between the colonies.

However, the problem of a lack of a sense of unity created by poor communications was clearly recognized. This recognition is expressed throughout these documents in the reiteration of the need to wait on the development of strong local opinion before moving towards closer union.[22] There was a certain ambiguity however as to the identity of the public which was to express

21 See Chapter V, Part I, document B(v), p. 283. Also Gordon K. Lewis, *The Growth of the Modern West Indies* (London, 1968), p. 371.
22 For example see Chapter V Part I, documents A(i), B(i) and B(x), p. 268, 277, 291.

this opinion. Although it is not clearly stated one can nevertheless assume that it did not involve any attempt to ascertain the views of the mass of the population since they were expressly denied any access to government by way of genuinely popular representation.[23]

Furthermore the documents show that during the inter-war years there was a lack of clear ideas on the nature of the association which was to be sought, the territories which were to be associated, and whether association would actually involve any 'savings' for the imperial country or for the colonies themselves. The Governor of Barbados at the West Indian Conference of 1929 said that there was no desire to abandon 'our independence and sacrifice our right to individual management of our own affairs' apparently quite unaware of the irony of speaking of 'our independence' in a colony. One finds on the one hand the recommendation of association so as to save the British taxpayer money, and on the other hand the rejection of association because it would involve too much expense. Sometimes association means nothing more than a sharing of Governors – an idea which was usually strenuously resisted in the Eastern Caribbean since colonies which existed in a purely client relationship with the metropolis wanted their own Governor since he was the crucial link with the British Government.

A much clearer idea of a form of real federation is apparent in the Roseau Conference,[24] and despite the fact that the report to which the recommendations of the Roseau Conference were appended[25] was much more limited in its vision, recommending only the merging of the Governorships of the Leeward Islands, Windward Islands and Trinidad and Tobago, nevertheless it was the Roseau Conference of West Indian unofficial members of their various legislatures which was to be the herald of later discussions.

This summary of some of the points raised in the documents in Part I of Chapter V would not be complete without referring to the significance of the despatch from the Secretary of State for the Colonies to the Governors of the Leeward Islands and Windward Islands, dated 14th March 1946. The despatch dimly recognizes two major dangers in the path of federation: first, that of allowing the individual territories to pursue constitutional advance without linking this to federation (although the Secretary of State sees this mainly as an inconvenience for legal draftsmen in Britain); and secondly, the failure to achieve unification among the Leeward Islands and the Windward Islands so as to reduce the number of tiny legislatures within the area, and create units

23 Neither did it involve any attempt to inform or influence the mass of the people in the issues involved. Federation was to remain a sometimes polite sometimes impolite discussion at an elite level.

24 Chapter V, Part I, document B(viii), p. 288.

25 Chapter V, Part I, document B(vii), p. 284.

which could federate with Jamaica and Trinidad without being completely dwarfed.

The desire to pursue individual constitutional advance is seen clearly in Part II of this chapter in the speech of Alexander Bustamante to the Montego Bay Conference of 1947.[26] Mr Bustamante sounded a warning note for the future of the federation, expressing real suspicion with regard to British motives in encouraging the idea of federation and the fear that unless federation and self-government came together then Jamaica, Barbados and to a lesser extent Trinidad and Tobago would be held back in their constitutional advance, a consequence which would be quite unacceptable. In the same extract from the report on the Montego Bay Conference Mr Albert Gomes of Trinidad and Tobago pointed out that to allow 'the system of graduating single isolated units in varying stages towards self-government . . .' would be to encourage the already strong centrifugal tendencies within the West Indies. Despite these warnings the Montego Bay Conference agreed that the political development of the 'several units of the British Caribbean territories . . . must be pursued as an aim in itself, without prejudice and in no way subordinate to progress towards the federation', a principle which was reaffirmed in the Report of the Standing Closer Association Committee, 1950.[27]

These documents still point out the real differences between the territories: social, economic and constitutional,[28] the latter being heavily stressed by Mr Bustamante in his speech at Montego Bay, to which we have already referred. They also reiterate the problems confronting the West Indies which are illustrated in the earlier documents in Part I of this chapter. In 1945 the Secretary of State was still dubious as to whether there was sufficient popular support for federation,[29] and Mr Bustamante referred not only to the absence of such support but also the widespread ignorance on the subject of federation and the dangers of encouraging popular support by, in effect, trading on this ignorance and picturing federation as some kind of panacea for the ills of the West Indies. There are continuing references to poor communication and the lack of inter-territorial trade.[30] A further problem referred to in these documents is the need for continued financial assistance from the United Kingdom.[31] The Report of the Standing Closer Association Committee argued that financial dependence curtailed any real enjoyment of full political

26 Chapter V, Part II, document B, p. 306

27 Col. no. 255/1950. Chapter V, Part II, document D, p. 316,

28 See especially Chapter V, Part II, documents A(iii), B and D, pp. 303, 306, 316.

29 Chapter V, Part II, document A(i), p. 299.

30 Chapter V, Part II, document A(i) and Mr Bustamante's speech in Chapter V, Part II, document B, pp. 299, 306.

31 Chapter V, Part II, documents A(i) and D, pp. 299, 316.

independence, and went on to argue that the necessary financial and economic stability which independence required could not be achieved on a unit basis. Federation was the only hope, although it would not make the achievement of economic viability easy.

Thus one finds that although problems in the way of federation are outlined, the view was expressed and repeated that in the modern world the small territorial units of the West Indies could not survive separately. Independence 'cannot be achieved without some form of federal association', 'the sheer force of circumstances of the modern world makes independence on a unit basis a mirage'.[32] Thus in the late 1940s and early to mid-1950s one finds a broad acceptance of the need for federation at the expressed official governmental level in the West Indies and the United Kingdom. At the same time the nature of that federation remained unclear. Initially it was hoped that the federation would include all the territories of the English-speaking Caribbean, preferably with the Leeward and Windward Islands joining together to form a single unit. However, the Bahama Islands declined to join as early as 1947 to be followed by British Guiana and British Honduras; the status of the British Virgin Islands was uncertain but because of the failure to unite the Leeward and Windward Islands the British Virgin Islands were left out of the federation. In 1945 the British Government was still hoping to use the closer union of 'the small islands' as a testing ground for the larger federation,[33] but by 1947 the Secretary of State felt that West Indian public opinion was ready for federation, with or without the experiment of closer union of the Leewards and Windwards.[34] However, the Minister also felt that such closer union ought to be pursued in its own right to prevent the very small territories being swamped within the federation and thereby denied full and equal participation in it. This union of the smaller territories was never achieved, partly because it was overtaken by the negotiations for the larger federation and, possibly, partly because separately they could wield more votes during those negotiations.

Another question with regard to the nature of the federation which was to prove crucial, was whether it would start its life as an independent, or at least self-governing, member of the Commonwealth. Here again Mr Bustamante's speech at Montego Bay must be referred to: 'Federation can come, but I cannot see the advisability of federation without self-government . . .'. In 1945 the Secretary of State put the achievement of full internal self-government

32 Chapter V, Part II, document D, p. 316. See also the Secretary of State's speech at the Montego Bay Conference 1947. Chapter V, Part II, document B, p. 306, and Document A(iii), p. 303.
33 Chapter V, Part II, document A(i), p. 299.
34 Chapter V, Part II, document A(ii), p. 302.

(not independence) as the ultimate aim of His Majesty's Government.[35] By 1948-49 the Report of the Standing Closer Association Committee said that the aim of policy was the shortest path to independence.[36] However, the authors of that Report were clearly contemplating the initial federation as being not even fully self-governing with regard to internal affairs. In the event federation did not bring full internal self-government when it was established, and indeed did not achieve that position until 1960. This meant that the federation started its life with a less advanced constitution than some of its units, and as Mr Bustamante had warned, this was felt to be holding back the constitutional advance of Jamaica, Barbados, and Trinidad and Tobago. Furthermore it should be pointed out that one of the serious sources of weakness in the federal government was that it was the government of a colony. Wherever there are federations the central government is given, as its real source of power, the conduct of external affairs and defence; a colony by definition has no external relations except with the metropolis and so during its short life the government of the federation was denied the functions which above all make federations meaningful political organizations.

Whilst stressing the importance for its collapse of the colonial status of the federation, one can see in these documents the erosion of the power of the central government and the problems which held up federation and eventually destroyed it:[37] the co-ordination of fiscal, customs and tariff policy (especially incentives to encourage investment and the protection of infant industries); a customs union; freedom of movement of persons throughout the federation; the choice of a capital site; the financing of the federal government, especially whether it should be granted an independent taxing power; the raising of loans by federal and unit governments; the representation of the territories in the federal legislature. In trying to seek solutions to these problems it was nearly always the powers of the federal government which were eroded until what was projected as a weak federal centre (with residual powers going to the units) became, in affect, confederal, and then collapsed.[38]

Part III of this chapter of documents on federal experiments deals with the attempt to salvage something from the collapse of the Federation with the

35 Chapter V, Part II, document A(i), p. 299.
36 Chapter V, Part II, document D, p. 316.
37 To trace the chronology of these problems see Chapter V, Part II, documents, C, D, E, F, J, K and L, pp. 312-332, 344-352. See also Sir John Mordecai, *The Federal Negotiations* (London, 1968) for a valuable and detailed commentary on the problems, and a blow by blow account of how they were dealt with, or not dealt with in many cases.
38 For further reading see, especially, G.K. Lewis, op. cit., Chapter XV; Sir John Mordecai, op. cit., and R.L. Watts, *New federations: experiments in the Commonwealth* (Oxford, 1966).

withdrawal of Jamaica and Trinidad and Tobago. The first document (A) is an extract from the Report of the Conference on the East Caribbean (Cmnd. 1746/1962) and it outlines the dissolution of the old Federation and the beginning of a search for a new federal formula for Barbados, the Leewards and Windwards. The desire for such a federation undoubtedly appeared to be present, at least in official opinion, and the British Government was of the opinion that an East Caribbean Federation 'appeared to offer the best solution to the problems of the area.'

However, as can be seen in the documents the attempt at finding a solution in federal terms for the smaller region was beset by almost the same problems as the larger – despite the fact that the East Caribbean appears to form a more integrated unit than the Commonwealth Caribbean. The actual membership of the projected union was put in doubt almost immediately after the Barbados Conference in 1962. New elections in Grenada brought a change in government and the new government decided to withdraw from the discussions on federation and explore the offer of Trinidad and Tobago for unitary statehood. The draft plan for federation was scarcely published in an 'agreed' form before one by one the disagreements were voiced and the same pattern of attempting to reduce the powers of the central government emerged – only this time the largest unit, Barbados, defended a strong central government while the smaller units attacked the idea. Previously Jamaica had played a different role but this could be explained by the fact that Barbados would more easily dominate the central government of the East Caribbean Federation than Jamaica could have dominated that of the defunct Federation of the West Indies. The form of the constitution came under attack; the unification of the public service; the establishment of a loan council; the financing of central government, especially whether it should be given power to levy income tax; police; agriculture; postal services; customs union – the list of areas of disagreement grew as negotiations went on, so that eventually by 1965 even the placing of the capital site in Barbados was being challenged by the new government of St Lucia and by Montserrat.[39]

The documents clearly show that one of the major areas of uncertainty was whether the new federation should be independent from the outset.[40] The British Government wanted to postpone independence but the island governments wavered, led by Barbados they sometimes insisted on immediate independence but nearly all the Leewards and Windwards changed their position on this point at least once. The Barbados Government at least had no doubt as to where real responsibility for the uncertainty lay: at the door of

39 For details of disagreements see especially Chapter V, Part III, document H, p. 368.

40 See Chapter V, Part III, documents C, D, E and H, pp. 357-365, 368.

the United Kingdom Government.[41] The really crucial issue for the establishment and survival of the East Caribbean Federation was United Kingdom financial assistance. Demands for assurances from the islands were met by evasions by the British. Uncertain of their financial survival if they entered a poor but independent union,[42] the islands hesitated to leave their colonial but grant-aided status. Britain refused to accept the argument of Barbados that she had a moral responsibility to make reparations. Indeed looking back at the Report of the Standing Closer Association Committee, Col. no. 255/1950,[43] the attitude of the United Kingdom Government on this question could be discerned: rather than accepting any responsibility for the poverty of the West Indies, the British Government adopted the tone of moral condemnation of the administrator of poor relief who sees poverty as a sure sign of idleness.

Given this crucial weakness the negotiations simply fell apart as one by one the smaller territories, fearful of independence without financial guarantees from Britain, withdrew from the scene until Barbados brought the entire process to a halt, recognizing the futility of proceeding any further under the circumstances and deciding to 'go for independence' alone. 'The Barbados White Paper, 1965'[44] ends with a spirited justification for the existence of 'mini-states' countering the view that 'sheer force of circumstances of the modern world makes independence on a unit basis a mirage.'[45]

Chapters VI, VII and VIII, contain documents which illustrate current constitutional arrangements in the independent and the associated states of the West Indies. The documents in Chapter VI give a clear picture of the nature of the association between these states and the United Kingdom. In this Preface it is only necessary to point out that the relationship is not an equal one as has sometimes been claimed.[46] With the United Kingdom controlling external affairs and defence, the associated states are really colonies with full internal self-government, but unlike other colonies they have the legal power to amend their own constitutions, and to terminate their association with the United Kingdom. However, a point which should be noted here is that since those territories are in receipt of aid from the United Kingdom Treasury, they are in reality less free than larger and richer states which, when colonies, did not have any legal right to amend their constitutions or terminate their relationship with the United Kingdom.

41 Chapter V, Part III, document H, p. 368.
42 Documents E and H, Chapter V, Part III, refer to Dr Carleen O'Laughlin's estimates that the islands would need at least a ten year guarantee of assistance from the United Kingdom.
43 Chapter V, Part II, document D, p. 316.
44 Chapter V, Part III, document H, p. 368.
45 Chapter V, Part II, document D, p. 316.
46 See, for example, Chapter VI, documents A(i), A(ii), B(i) and B(ii), pp. 375-387, 389-403.

The extracts from the current constitutions of the West Indies, independent and associated, show that the thinking behind them was in line with the tradition of thought which places value on the establishment of limited government. Two major assumptions are made, one relating to the nature of social reality, the other more of an evaluative judgement. The first assumption in theories of limited government is that the institutional structure affects the nature of decisions made and the power relationships within a political community. This is not necessarily a simple theory of constitutionalism assuming that if certain institutional arrangements are introduced then certain results – tyranny and oppression or democracy and liberty will follow. However, a concern with constitutional arrangements does assume that there is a complex relationship between formal rules and social forces as both causes and effects of each other.[47] The second assumption is that the government does not express a Rousseauesque sovereign general will of perfect morality, identical with the will of the organic society. If the government is assumed to express only a partial will which is not always moral and not always perfectly identified with the public interest then it ought to be limited in its exercise of power and forced to be responsible to the larger society. The author, like the creators of the West Indian constitutions, shares these assumptions. The question remains open as to whether the institutional arrangements adopted in these constitutions are the most appropriate for the societies of which they are the fundamental law.

The constitutional arrangements which are illustrated in this volume clearly belong in the Western, and more specifically British tradition. Attempts have been made to establish limited government by forcing government itself to operate within a framework of law, by instituting the British version of modified separation of powers, with some additional checks and balances.[48]

In looking at the constitutions in greater detail the point which needs to be made first is that even for the independent states the constitutions are not autochtonous. K.C. Wheare defines a constitution as autochtonous when it has the force of law 'through its own native authority and not because it was enacted or authorised by the parliament of the United Kingdom; that it is, so to speak, 'home grown', sprung from their own soil, and not imported from the United Kingdom . . . being constitutionally rooted in their own native soil'.[49] Although the preambles of the Guyanese and Trinidad and Tobago constitutions do invoke the authority of the people, all these constitutions

47 M.J.C. Vile, *Constitutionalism and the separation of powers* (Oxford, 1967), p. 312.
48 For further elaboration see Vile, op. cit.
49. K.C. Wheare, *The constitutional structure of the Commonwealth* (Oxford, 1960).

remain orders in council enacted under the authority of acts of the British Parliament. Despite the fact that the elected members of the legislatures participated fully in the process of drafting these constitutions, so long as they derive their legal force from metropolitan rather than local law, they must remain as reminders of the long colonial history of the territories.

To elaborate on all the features of these constitutions which point to a colonial past would be unnecessary in what are intended to be only prefatory remarks. However, it is necessary to point to their existence and as illustration the following examples will suffice: (1) the retention of a nominated element in all the legislatures apart from the National Assembly of Guyana, and more especially the retention of nominated members in the unicameral legislatures of the associated states, a mixed legislative council being one of the hallmarks of a colonial legislature; (2) the monarchic form retained in all the states, again with the exception of Guyana. However, even in Guyana the President has the same functions as a Governor General. Of course it could well be argued that in providing for a ceremonial rather than an executive head of state the West Indian countries are breaking with the gubernatorial tradition of colonial government. However, although a purely ceremonial head of state is not a feature of colonial government nevertheless these countries are remaining faithful to the Westminster pattern; and finally (3) the extremely important part played in the judicial process of the territories by the Judicial Committee of the Privy Council. In addition to these three features to which specific reference has been made there is the overall fidelity of these constitutions to the British pattern of Cabinet government.

One departure from the British, but not from Commonwealth, tradition is the supremacy of these constitutions. The governments of the West Indies are not bound only by ordinary statute law but also by their constitutions which define the structures and functions of government, implementing in law the theories of separation and checks referred to above. Further, statute law itself is subordinate to the law of the constitution. It remains to be seen whether the West Indian courts will create a tradition of judge-made constitutional law or whether they will follow the restricted sphere traditionally occupied by the British judiciary. The area where the courts would be most able to act positively in the limitation of executive authority and the broad interpretation of the constitution is in cases related to the protection of fundamental rights and freedoms. As can be seen from these documents there are no sweeping grants of inalienable rights under the West Indian constitutions. Most of the rights given are easily alienated – executive power is effectively unchecked and the chapters which embody these rights are more expressions of pious intention than grants of positive freedoms which can be used as protection against executive acts. However, in spelling out the conditions under which these rights can be invaded the phrases used are: 'reasonably justifiable', 'reasonably suspected', 'reasonable suspicion', 'reasonably required' etc. The invoking of the 'reasonable man' is as old as the common law itself; however, the embodiment of these bills of rights in supreme law is an innovative step.[50] Clearly the West Indian courts could continue to follow their own and British precedents and allow that the executive does have good reason to act, even if this means the invasion of citizens' rights, except where there is a clear illegality, or they could move more in the direction of the Supreme Court of the United States of America, and make substantive decisions as to what is reasonably justified in the public interest. Either course of action has its attendant dangers: the one leaves the executive free to follow expediency rather than genuine public interest in its invasion of citizens' rights; the other gives to an unrepresentative body a positive role in defining the public interest, and the public is left with no means of making the courts accountable to it.

In seeking to preserve the independence of the judiciary with elaborate safeguards the West Indian constitutions follow the British pattern, where the separation of powers is most strictly enforced with regard to the preservation of a separate and independent judiciary. They also follow Britain in establishing a fusion of executive and legislature in that the members of the chief executive, policy-forming body, the Cabinet, are chosen from the majority in the legislature. As in Britain, it is this principle of responsible government, conceived initially as a means of parliamentary control over the King's Ministers, which ironically provides the basis for the executive domination of government. The Prime Minister and his Cabinet can proceed in the knowledge that given any normal party-political situation they have complete control over the legislature: where there are second chambers the constitution itself guarantees a government majority; and the need to select as Prime Minister the man best able to command a majority in the representative house gives him control over that house in all normal circumstances. During the long five-year life of a

50 It should be emphasized here that it is the introduction of bills of rights into the constitutions which is innovative in the West Indian context, and not the principle of the supremacy of the constitution. In that the constitutions of the West Indies derived from imperial law, and that under the Colonial Laws Validity Act, 1865, all colonial law was null and void insofar as it conflicted with imperial law which extended to the colony, the constitutions of the West Indian colonies were always supreme law, and their courts have never operated on the assumption of sovereign legislatures. Indeed the concept of a sovereign legislature in a colony is a contradiction in terms. This point is emphasized because the view has recently been expressed that the supremacy of the constitution is a new principle of law in the West Indies. See Urias Forbes, 'The West Indies Associated States: constitutional arrangements', *Social and Economic Studies,* vol. 19, no. 1 (March 1970).

legislature the Cabinet would only lose control of the legislature in the event of either (a) an extremely unlikely back-bench revolt within the majority party or (b) the development of a multi-party system leading to coalition or minority governments, an eventuality which is clearly not impossible but would appear to run counter to past and present trends in West Indian political life.

Given this control over the legislature and leadership of the permanent bureaucracy, the Prime Minister and his Cabinet are for the most part politically unchecked unless they act outside the law. Whilst this latter is obviously an important limitation, given the growth of executive discretion under ordinary statute law and the wide area of discretion granted by the constitutions,[51] the executive is left in an extremely dominating position. However, some recognition of this is made in all these constitutions in their attempts to introduce checks to executive power in sensitive areas. A review of the documents shows, however, that, in putting in a variety of checks and balances, the creators of these constitutions relied very heavily on the elite principle of nomination: nominated Service Commissions, Privy Councils, Elections Commissions, Delimitation Commissions, Auditors General, Directors of Public Prosecutions, second chambers, and the Ombudsman of Guyana. Furthermore, in all these cases, to a greater or lesser extent, the Prime Minister or Premier plays a predominant role in making the nominations to the bodies which are presumably created in order to check the improper exercise of executive power.

For these reasons it can be argued that despite the importance of some of these checks, and the need to run for re-election, and the presence of political oppositions (both formal parties and more or less informal movements), the borrowing of the Westminster model has tended to create constitutional situations, not unlike the colonial experience, where the executives are so dominant that it is difficult, within the framework of the constitutions, to hold them to account.

It should be noted that all footnotes in the documents are the editor's unless otherwise stated.

51 See above the arguments relating to the chapters on fundamental rights and freedoms.

CHAPTER 1

INTRODUCTION

In this chapter an attempt will be made to place in a broader political, social and economic context the constitutional changes outlined in the Preface and illustrated by this collection of documents.

Historically the West Indies[1] were colonized as part of the first British Empire, an outward movement initially motivated largely by the desire for plunder, a motive which was rapidly replaced by the desire to settle and to trade, but not to trade freely. On the contrary the mercantilist ideas of this period led to monopolies, to the use of the newly centralized state power to regulate trade between colony and metropolis very strictly, and to prohibit manufacturing in the colony. As described some time ago by Hugh E. Egerton: 'The dominant policy of the time was well exemplified by the West Indies. In these every encouragement was given to the cultivation of sugar. A practical monopoly was secured in the home market, and the slave trade, which secured a regular supply of labour for the planters, was the object of special solicitude. The interests of the British manufacturers forbade that the colony should refine their own sugar, and the industry was, so far as possible, confined to the mother country.'[2]

The search for lands to settle, to conquer and exploit for agricultural and mineral raw materials led to heavy military commitments, and since modern

1 By the term West Indies I refer to all the territories of the Caribbean which were in British hands after the Napoleonic Wars, including the Bahamas and the two mainland territories of British Guiana and British Honduras.
2 Hugh Egerton, 'Colonies and the Mercantile System', in George H. Nadel and Perry Curtis (eds), *Imperialism and Colonialism* (New York, 1964) pp. 58-60. See also Michael Barratt-Brown, *After Imperialism* (London, 1963), Chapter 2, passim.; Ernst Mandel, 'Contemporary Imperialism', *New Left Review,* no. 25 (May-June 1964), p. 16.

empires, with the exception of the Russian, have been overseas empires, there was also the establishment of colonies as strategic bases securing the sea routes which were a vital part of the trading empire. It was from this base that the European industrial revolution took off, and from this base that large profits have continued to accrue to individual, influential capitalists and firms in the metropolis.[3]

The French Revolution, the American War of Independence and the Napoleonic Wars form the watershed between the First and Second British Empires. During these turbulent years the West Indian territories were tossed between the warring European powers. One effect of this period was that the colonies of conquest were added to the original colonies and with them was introduced into the West Indies the Crown Colony form of direct administrative control. However until the late 19th century the original colonies retained the Old Representative System, a system which kept alive the early idea, never completely abandoned in the British Empire, that colonies were '. . . individual societies with their own lives to lead within the imperial matrix'.[4] The question of the dual nature of societies within the imperial matrix is one to which we shall have to return. At this stage it is necessary only to point to the phenomenon. William Friedman in 1943 referred to the imperial centres in the following manner: 'Such national States as Great Britain, France, Holland and Spain had a double nature. At home they were and are national States, but internationally they are the nerve-centres of empires.'[5] This duality is also imposed on the colony which is neither an administrative unit of a nation state nor a state in itself.[6]

Through the revolutionary years of the late 18th and early 19th centuries only Haiti in the Caribbean succeeded in throwing off imperial rule and establishing itself as an independent state. The West Indies remained colonies, and unlike the other old colonies of the New World or the new colonies of settlement such as New Zealand and Australia, they were not a part of the 19th century movement towards dominion status and increasing self-rule. On the contrary, Jamaica and after her all the other territories except Barbados and the Bahamas, lost the limited powers of self-regulation which they had under the Old Representative System and became Crown Colonies. This was largely

3 For further discussion on the aims of and motivations for imperialism see, in addition to the classic works of Hobson and Lenin, The Royal Institute of International Affairs, *The Colonial Problem*: a report by a study group of members of the Royal Institute of International Affairs (London, 1937); Barratt-Brown, op. cit; Nadel and Curtis (eds), op cit; and George Lichtheim, 'Imperialism in this Century', *Commentary*, vol. 49, nos. 4 and 5 April and May, 1970.

4 Nadel and Curtis (eds), op. cit., Introduction, p. 20.

5 W. Friedman, *The Crisis of the National State* (London, 1943), p. 57.

6 See below, p. 27-29. (Discussion on systems.)

because, although they were established as colonies of settlement, the West Indies were never settled by many white people. The plantation system of agriculture which was early introduced into the territories depended on slave labour and not on free settler labour. The populations of the West Indies were thus drawn mainly from Africa and later, under the indenture system, from Asia. Only a very small minority of ruling white colonists remained. Thus, whilst historically one of the objects of the colonizing drive of Europe after the Middle Ages, the West Indies shared an important characteristic with the later colonies of Britain: their populations were predominantly black or brown.

The inextricably linked features of plantation agriculture and non-European populations undoubtedly contributed to the fact that while America removed itself, and Canada, Australia, Newfoundland and New Zealand were moving, with official blessing, towards greater self-government, the West Indies either stood still or actually moved towards greater control by the government at Westminster. This phenomenon of divergence as the white areas of the Empire moved ahead while the black areas stagnated or declined is repeated in social and economic affairs as well as political. Michael Barratt-Brown points out that all white areas of the Empire, metropolis or colony, benefited from the adverse terms of trade for primary products throughout the 19th and 20th centuries.[7]

The result of this very long period of colonial rule, together with the institutions of slavery and indenture, and the economics of exploitation have had extremely debilitating effects on political, social and economic life in the area. To this must be added the erection of social barriers and the openly expressed contempt by whites for the black population, supported, long after slavery and even into the current period, by 'theories' of racial superiority whereby black people were made to feel inferior in all ways except physical labour – which was itself considered degrading in the perverted culture of the plantation.

Much has been written about the beneficial effects of colonization, from the very earliest land empires to the sea empires of modern Europe. Imperial rule is seen as the carrier of new ideas, new techniques and of superior civilizations thus meriting 'the title of world revolution', 'a gigantic adventure which in a bare half-millenium changed the face of the world unrecognizably, tore entire continents from isolation, transported populations, plants and animal races around the globe, peopled millions of square miles of virgin lands of both hemispheres, and for the first time made it possible to think of mankind

7 Barratt-Brown, op. cit., p. 68. See also J.A. Hobson, *Imperialism* (London, 1948 edition), pp. 6-7.

as a single whole, and of history as universal history'.[8] Alongside this catalogue of imperial adventure and achievement a string of islands and continental territories have been left with impoverished, dependent economies, without any strong political tradition, and with large numbers of their populations doubting their own value as men and women.

Economic background

An understanding of past and present political reality in the West Indies depends very heavily on knowledge of the economic base of these societies. And the most important single economic fact was the 'seventeenth century transformation of a flourishing yeoman agricultural colony (Barbados) into one enormously socially degraded plantation'.[9] Plantation agriculture for the production of sugar for export became the pattern throughout the West Indies 'thus making it an integral part of the general American plantation regime which, as a massive socio-economic system, developed its characteristic institutions and social forms from Brazil to the United States of America'.[10] Many of the difficulties facing the West Indies derive from the fact that many of the characteristics of that system continue in the present.

The large-scale production of sugar gave the territories modern economies from the beginning in the sense that this was basically factory production, 'highly capitalised' and 'linked to a complex commercial organisation in which credit played a part of primary importance'.[11] However, largely because the basis of this capitalistic development was not free labour but slave labour, one finds that alongside the modern characteristics of the economies were trends, quite uncharacteristic of highly capitalized production. There was, for example, a failure to invest except in the purchase of more and more slaves since labour

8 Herbert Luthy, 'Colonization and the Making of Mankind' in Nadel and Curtis (eds), op. cit. p. 27. The view of the civilizing mission of empire is too frequently expressed by its apologists to need further recording. It is, however, necessary to note that it was also a view held by opponents of the bourgeois capitalist state: see, for example, Karl Marx, 'British Rule in India' and F. Engels, 'A Defence of Progressive Imperialism in Algeria' both reproduced in Lewis Feuer (ed.), *Marx and Engels: Basic Writings on Politics and Philosophy* (New York, 1959).

9 Sidney Mintz, Forward to Ramiro Guerra Y Sanchez, *Sugar and Society in the Caribbean* (New Haven and London, 1964), p. xii.

10 Gordon K. Lewis, *The Growth of the Modern West Indies* (London, 1968), p. 16.

11 Elsa Goveia, *Slave Society in the British Leeward Islands at the End of the Eighteenth Century* (New Haven, 1965), p. 105. See also H.O. Patterson, *The Sociology of Slavery* (London, 1967), p. 34 and R. Pares, 'Merchants and Planters', *Economic History Review*, Supplement 4, passim.

was treated as capital investment.[12] This false capital investment diverted funds from improvement in techniques of production. In addition to the sums that were poured into the purchase of slaves (the most unproductive form of labour) much money went into high levels of consumption rather than being ploughed back into the productive process. Moreover the high propensity to import, characteristic of the West Indies throughout history, meant that these levels of consumption did nothing to stimulate the local economy. Professor Goveia speculates that this conspicuous consumption and the associated failure to invest arose in part from the unstable character of the economy, the need to remove oneself as far as possible from the slave and the low status overseer by a pattern of consumption characterized by waste, and from the absence of the Puritan ethic which, as Professor Goveia points out, is not suited to a slave oligarchy.[13]

Failure to invest, failure to effect technical improvements in production, wasteful consumption, absenteeism, and poor management led to the failure of the slave based economies of the West Indies. By the time of emancipation large numbers of estates were encumbered and bankrupt. The vast capital grant which 'compensated' the planters for the loss of their slave 'property' had to be paid out for the most part to clear debts. Even had the planters had the inclination there was little money left to mechanize and improve industry, and so the West Indies continued to be capitalist, money economies but short of capital, tied to export agriculture, and with a high propensity to import. They were therefore extremely vulnerable, entirely dependent on a world market which they could not control. For example there was crisis throughout the sugar industry of the West Indies 1846-50. This crisis was associated with the loss of protected markets as the British government implemented free trade policies, and with a commercial crisis which racked the British-based West Indian merchants. However, as W. K. Marshall suggests, the crisis was only exacerbated by the events in Britain; the real weakness was in the structures of these economies which had failed to develop any effective internal base, and were characterized by indebtedness, encumbered estates, inefficient farming and manufacture, and bad labour relations.[14]

The failure to develop market links within and between the territories, which is one of the most serious consequences of the colonial plantation system, is itself linked to the failure of the post-emancipation period and is a

12 Patterson (op. cit., p. 51) also makes this point.

13 Goveia, op. cit., p. 109.

14 W.K. Marshall, 'The Social and Economic Development of the Windward Islands, 1838-1865'. Ph.D. thesis, St John's College, Cambridge, 1963). See also D.G. Hall, *Free Jamaica* (New Haven, 1959 and London, 1969) Appendix 2.

feature of the current situation.[15] This failure is partly a reflection of the rigidity in social, economic and political forms developed during slavery. This rigidity created fixed ideas which in emancipation would lead to a failure to innovate and a continued, unwavering belief that the West Indies depended on export agriculture, plantation produced, and that the survival of the plantations depended upon a supply of servile labour.

The planters constituted in Marshall's words 'a massive element of reaction in a revolutionary social situation'.[16] The policy they pursued involved the deliberate use of coercion, the law, and the introduction of indentured labour, all with the aim of inhibiting the development of an independent peasantry and guaranteeing a cheap supply of dependent labour.[17] The effect was to prevent the development of an internal market with a demand for and supply of domestic products, such as led to the development of the North American economy. Instead the West Indies continued to export what they produced and to import what they consumed, which meant not only that the economies remained vulnerable but that the societies failed to develop a network of social links around economic exchanges. Had a free peasantry been allowed to emerge and fully realize its potential it would have softened the harsh social divisions within the West Indian societies, it could have led to more dynamic, broader based economies, mixed both in crops and in type of farm and less dependent on King Sugar (a pattern which did indeed begin to emerge in the Windward Islands, Jamaica and Trinidad and Tobago where some peasant development did take place).[18]

Another tragedy for the West Indian economies associated with the failure of slavery and the post-emancipation period is that the plantation system, slavery, and later attempts to crush the free peasantry did nothing to create good husbandry and innovation at the level of the labourer (slave or free) or the post-emancipation small farmer. As Professor Goveia points out slaves could be forced 'to work hard and for long hours, but no compulsion could force them to work well'.[19] So from plantation to small farm or provision ground techniques of farming remained primitive depending very heavily on

15 For most of the following analysis I am indebted to W. K. Marshall who allowed me to read his unpublished doctoral thesis (see footnote 14 above).
16 Marshall, op. cit., p. 50.
17 Marshall, op. cit., p. 157; Elsa Goveia, *A Study of the Historiography of the British West Indies* (Mexico City, 1956); Philip Curtin, *Two Jamaicas: the role of ideas in a tropical colony, 1830-1865* (Cambridge, Mass., 1955), p. 15 et seq; D. Wood, *Trinidad in Transition* (London, 1968), p. 62 et. seq.
18 Marshall, op. cit., p. 364 et seq; Curtin, op. cit., p. 111.
19 Goveia, *Slave Society in the British Leeward Islands*, p. 129. See also C.S. Salmon, *Caribbean Confederation*, p. 68; Barratt-Brown, op. cit., p. 26.

manual labour, a characteristic of slave economy which has still not been removed from the West Indies.

Indeed one finds that most of the significant economic features of the past are retained in the present. The economies remain export oriented with a very narrow productive base, relying on a small range of products for export which are either only partially processed, or not processed at all, within the West Indies. Much of what is consumed locally is still imported, so that one still finds the characteristic paradox of plantation economies where predominantly agricultural societies import much of their foodstuffs.[20] The economies therefore remain peculiarly vulnerable to outside influences and shifting terms of trade, particularly the apparently permanent adverse terms of trade for primary products which is a feature of world trade throughout most of the 19th and 20th centuries. There is still the need to diversify agricultural production with an increased percentage of output being produced for domestic consumption thus providing more stable economies with greater capacity to withstand outside forces. As Dr Beckford argues, the very protection provided by the United Kingdom for West Indian products, which is usually hailed as the saviour of these economies, itself results in the perpetuation of much of these basic weaknesses in the economies. By protecting uneconomic production and insulating the West Indies from competition with low cost producers the solution to fundamental economic problems is postponed and not provided. The artificially high prices paid for export crops and their assured market in Britain skews agricultural production in favour of export rather than the home economy, and often leaves producers at the mercy of foreign-owned shippers.[21]

The presence of largely mono-crop plantation agriculture also led in the past and in the present, to a few very large economic units in farming occupying much of the arable land, with land hunger being characteristic of the bulk of the rural population.[22] For example Dr Beckford gives figures on land

20 It should be noted here that in Jamaica the manufacturing sector has overtaken other sectors in contribution to gross national product, whilst bauxite mining in Guyana and Jamaica and oil mining in Trinidad make major contributions to G.N.P. However, if one takes the West Indies as a whole, or if one uses indices of the percentages of the populations directly or indirectly dependent on agriculture, it would still be true to say that we are looking at predominantly agricultural societies.
21 G. Beckford, *The West Indian Banana Industry,* Studies in Regional Economic Integration, vol. 2, no. 3. (Institute of Social and Economic Research, University of the West Indies, Kingston, 1967.)
22 For an analysis of how the sugar plantation squeezed out the small and middle-sized farmer in Cuba and the consequences of this development see R. Guerra Y Sanches, op. cit.

holdings in banana cultivation, traditionally thought of as the Jamaican peasant crop: 67 per cent of growers have plots of 0.1 acres and they occupy 17 per cent of the total acreage of bananas producing 4 per cent of the crop; 0.1 per cent of growers have farms of over 100 acres, occupy 16 per cent of the total acreage and produce 20 per cent of the crop.[23] Arising out of this situation is the need for radical agrarian reform to satisfy the land hunger of the mass of the rural population and provide a more egalitarian base for these societies. In the 1930s W.M. Macmillan pointed out in his *Warning from the West Indies*[24] the dangers of having a landless proletariat in a rural economy. The depressed level of most of the population created a situation where there was a failure to generate sufficient internal demand to maintain dynamic economies.

The absence of a real internal dynamic for growth is both caused by and leads to a continued shortage of capital. Lack of domestic capital coupled with a need to develop some industrial base to the economies has led to the encouragement of an inflow of foreign capital throughout the West Indies, particularly in the larger territories. Furthermore, because the governments have established protective tariffs for local industry wherever possible, foreign companies seek to export capital rather than goods, so that they can then benefit from monopoly positions in the local market, with tax holidays and other benefits. As Eric Armstrong writes: 'The Government (of Trinidad and Tobago) had to compete with other Governments, particularly Puerto Rico and Jamaica, for the establishment of new industries; consequently the concessions offered had to be more and more attractive as the situation changed to compete with these territories.'[25] This competition for foreign capital by way of incentive legislation is clearly wasteful, only benefits the foreign investor and clearly works against future economic integration in the region.[26] Furthermore by giving generous tax holidays the governments fail to make foreign capital pay its way, the fear of frightening it away to other more welcoming countries leads to the pursuit of policies which place the burden of taxation on the salaried and the poor, a point which was again clearly seen by W.M. Macmillan in 1936.[27] Furthermore the repatriation of profits by the

23 Beckford, op. cit., p. 8.
24 W.M. Macmillan, *Warning from the West Indies* (London, 1936).
25 Eric Armstrong, *An Evaluation of Incentive Legislation in Trinidad and Tobago,* Studies in Regional Economic Integration, vol. 2, no. 5, part A., p. 3. (Institute of Social and Economic Research, University of the West Indies, Kingston, 1967.)
26 H. Brewster and C.Y. Thomas, *The Dynamics of West Indian Economic Integration,* Studies in Regional Economic Integration, vol. 1, p. 30. (Institute of Social and Economic Research, UWI, Kingston, 1967.)
27 Macmillan, op. cit., p. 191.

foreign investors means that the West Indies remains short of domestic capital for investment, and investment in manufacturing and mining has failed to generate enough jobs to seriously touch the enormous problem of unemployment, while the high level of unemployment itself contributes to the failure of the domestic economies to generate savings for investment.[28]

If the influx of foreign capital has failed to generate new domestic capital, has failed to solve the problem of unemployment, and has led to wasteful competition, hindering further economic integration in the region, then clearly one is forced to ask why the governments of the region continue to pursue the policy of encouraging foreign investment. The answer is complex but the reasons probably have to do firstly with the fact that 'industrialisation by invitation' was part of the orthodoxy of economic theorists such as Sir Arthur Lewis – if you have no capital of your own then you must use foreign capital to establish the necessary industrial base for economic 'take-off' – an orthodoxy which is now seriously questioned by economists but not yet by many politicians in the West Indies; and secondly the foreign investment which has taken place has led to very rapid growth in certain sectors of the economy particularly mining, manufacture and construction,[29] which growth continues to make the policy appear successful.

However, as Dr Jefferson shows in his article on the Jamaican economy,[30] average figures of growth can give a very false picture of development: a distortion which can be shown by using other criteria such as the employment rate, distribution of income between both individuals and sectors of the economy, and the extent of autonomy in local decision-making for the economy. Indeed Jefferson suggests that Jamaica's heavily skewed distribution of income is getting worse, unemployment is certainly not getting less, and there is a serious sluggishness in agriculture in a country which is still heavily agricultural (and yet imports a high percentage of its basic foods). Dr Jefferson also points out that the presence of high wage enclaves such as bauxite and tourism in a situation of generally high unemployment, creates the much commented upon situation of men refusing to work for the very low agricultural wage and thus there is some shortage of labour in agriculture where there are

28 Eric Armstrong (op. cit., pp. 9-10) discusses the capital-intensive nature of the new industries. By adopting inappropriate technology the new industrial development has failed to create many new jobs: a point which is further developed by O. Jefferson, 'Some Aspects of the Post-War Economic Development of Jamaica', *New World Quarterly*, vol. 3 (1967), p. 3.
29 Jefferson, op. cit., p. 1.
30 Ibid., passim; also E. Ahiram, 'Income Distribution in Jamaica and Trinidad and Tobago', in F.M. Andic and T.G. Matthews (eds), *The Caribbean in Transition Papers on Social, Political and Economic Development,* Second Caribbean Scholars Conference, Mona, Jamaica, 1964 (Puerto Rico, 1965).

nevertheless high levels of unemployment.

While there are real differences between the territories of the West Indies it would be true to say that the general picture as outlined for Jamaica is much the same for all,[31] although the pattern in some of the smaller islands is simpler and more depressed, being little more than impoverished plantations. Their dependence on Britain is more marked, American investment only having seriously entered the tourist fringe where there is one, and their dependence is more complete since most are still in receipt of grants to enable them to balance their budgets.

A startling feature of the 20th century is the extent to which old and new resources (sugar, oil and bauxite) are controlled by the American or British based multi-national corporation. Ernst Mandel writing of imperialism generally argues that from the end of World War I to the fifties Empire and Commonwealth became 'a means whereby big vertically-integrated oligopolistic trusts could preserve their private sources of raw materials and private markets, in the face of competition from other capitalistic powers'. He goes on to argue that imperialism 'in the sense of domination by monopoly capitalism of under-developed countries' is still real, and that aid to those countries, in that it often creates a demand for heavy equipment, 'is in one sense a huge permanent subsidy to the heavy equipment manufacturers of the imperialist countries themselves'.[32]

Undoubtedly the West Indies has always tended to absentee ownership of resources, from slavery to the present, but the 20th century has seen the takeover of many local plantations by Tate and Lyle and Bookers', and the discovery of oil and bauxite has seen the entry of the giant North American multi-national corporations, thus increasing the direct control of resources by foreign interests and both speeding up and increasing the percentage loss of income overseas.[33]

The West Indies therefore continue to be characterized by vulnerable, dependent and poor economies. L. Stepanov, a Soviet economist, gives the following criteria of dependence: (a) the extent of mono-culture or a small number of exports; (b) the degree of foreign capital in the economic structure, leading to withdrawal of profits and unfavourable terms of trade; (c) the participation by an underdeveloped country in the currency zone of the metropolis; (d) the existence of special economic agreements between the underdeveloped country

31 See for example Ahiram, op. cit.

32 Mandel, op. cit., pp. 17-18.

33 See N. Girvan, *The Caribbean Bauxite Industry,* Studies in Regional Economic Integration, vol. 2, no. 4. (Institute of Social and Economic Research, U.W.I., Kingston, 1967.)

and the metropolis; and (e) the use of aid as a foreign policy lever.[34] The West Indies more than satisfy all these criteria of dependence.

The economic problems of not only the West Indies but the entire Caribbean area cry out for an end to the fragmentation of these economies and some form of meaningful economic integration.[35] However, as Brewster and Thomas argue, 'Because of this company structure, the "integration" of resources which occurs does so via the metropolitan area. Furthermore it creates a situation in which the disposition and utilization of the resources of these sectors are guided by the *global* considerations of these companies and their search for private profit over their entire operations, which are in most cases vertically integrated into their final manufacture activities located in the metropolitan area. In many instances this branch system stands in striking conflict with the national interests of the West Indies.'[36] There are therefore extremely powerful interests who would be opposed to any meaningful horizontal integration of the economies of the West Indies. Whether these interests will be overcome is more a political than an economic question.

Social background

It would be inappropriate in an introductory chapter of this nature to present more than an impressionistic overview of those aspects of West Indian society which appear to be most directly relevant to an explanation of political movement. For this reason no consideration will be given, for example, to family structure, not because the author is of the opinion that it is not an important aspect of social structure but because it is difficult to demonstrate its direct impact on political life.

We shall, therefore, examine first those aspects of social structure and then those cultural values which appear to have explanatory value for the political events which were the dynamic of constitutional change during the period covered by this book.

The most obvious feature of West Indian social structure persisting from slavery is the hierarchical ranking of society by colour and race.[37] Clearly

34 L. Stepanov, 'The Problem of Economic Dependence' (1962) in T.P. Thornton (ed.), *The Third World in Soviet Perspective* (Princeton, New Jersey, 1964).
35 See all the Studies in Regional Economic Integration (I.S.E.R., U.W.I., Kingston, 1967.)
36 Brewster and Thomas, op. cit., p. 25.
37 Much has been written on this subject. See Lloyd Braithwaite, 'Stratification and Pluralism' in *Social and Cultural Pluralism in the Caribbean, Annals of the New York Academy of Sciences,* vol. LXXXIII, no. 5 (1960); and 'Social Stratification in Trinidad', *Social and Economic Studies,* vols. II and III (October 1953); F. Henriques, *Family and Colour in Jamaica* (London,

based on the slave plantation, the ranking of society by race and colour has continued into the 20th century supported by an economic system which is still largely dominated by white-owned capital. The ranking operates objectively against the black mass of the society who are socially at the lowest point of the hierarchy and are economically extremely depressed.

Not only is the social distance between the depressed black mass and the top of the hierarchy considerable but, from the first emergence of the monocrop plantation, there has been a paucity of effective mediating structures which would soften the harshness of the social divisions. The development of the plantation squeezed out of the society the 'small' whites – peasants, craftsmen, artisans, servants, labourers – leaving a situation where there was no economically significant group between the oligarchs and the slaves.[38] This remains a relatively accurate generalization throughout the period of slavery despite the emergence of the free coloureds. Although this last-named group outnumbered the whites in Jamaica by 1830, they had no role to play in the only significant economic unit, the plantation, and although occupying a mid-position in the society, could not soften the harshness of divisions on the plantation itself. Philip Curtin points out where there was any such shading off at all it was provided by the high-status slaves, especially the driver, in their contact with the overseers and the slaves under their command. However, the society retained an almost caste-like separation.[39] As Elsa Goveia illustrates, the whites, free coloureds and slaves were ranked *within* each caste but there was no significant shading-off between them.[40]

Emancipation and the subsequent development of both an urban middle class, largely based on the early free coloureds, and an independent peasantry based on the freed slaves, did see a softening of the absolute nature of social divisions under slavery. However, the independent peasantry did not emerge in all the territories, for example Barbados and the Leeward Islands continued with a virtually unmodified plantation system, and where it did establish itself it was with extreme difficulty. The white plantocracy, as is shown most clearly

1953); H. Hoetink, *The Two Variants in Caribbean Race Relations* (London, 1967); M.G. Smith, *A Framework for Caribbean Studies* (Mona, Jamaica, 1955); 'Social and Cultural Pluralism' in *Social and Cultural Pluralism in the Caribbean, Annals of the New York Academy of Sciences,* vol. LXXXIII, no. 5 (1960); 'The Plural Framework of Jamaican Society', *British Journal of Sociology,* vol. XII, no. 3 (September 1961); and *The Plural Society in the British West Indies* (Berkeley, 1965).

38 Goveia, *Slave Society in the British Leeward Islands,* p. 86 et seq.; Ramiro Guerra y Sanches, op. cit., Part One; and Patterson, op. cit., p. 34.

39 Curtin, op. cit. p. 23.

40 Goveia, op. cit., Chapter IV.

by Curtin and Marshall, failed to accommodate itself to a free labour situation and used '. . . contract labour, rent manipulation, class legislation and direct taxation to bear heavily on the small settler . . .'[41] Thus, despite the obvious social importance of the growth of a peasantry and a middle class, Curtin would still argue that even in the 1860s there were basically only two Jamaicas and that they were growing further apart, '. . . not only separate in caste and race, but to varying degrees had separate economies, separate religions, and separate cultures'.

The late 19th and 20th centuries have witnessed a decline in the economic importance of the plantation and a growth of the towns of the West Indies. The societies, particularly of the larger territories are now far more complex – merchant, professional middle class, urban proletariat, a growing urban 'lumpen proletariat', planter, agricultural labourer, subsistence farmer (often working on the plantations during crop time), small farmer, middle-sized farmer/planter, bauxite worker, oil worker, etc. The hierarchy remains but the divisions, no longer supported by the law, are not hard and fast. A white man, except to a limited extent in Barbados and the Bahamas, is almost inevitably high in the ranking order of the society, but black men do hold high status positions. However, a white in the same occupation with the same qualifications and wealth as a black would normally be accorded higher status than the black by nearly all members of the society, and the vast majority of black people find themselves where they have always been – in the most depressed and oppressed segment of the society – and it is of course a segment which makes up the mass of the populations of all the West Indian territories.

M.G. Smith is the scholar whose name is most closely associated with the idea that the societies of the West Indies are plural by nature, and whether or not one accepts the predictive aspects of the theory of the plural society it remains a valuable descriptive concept for the West Indies.[42] As Smith and many others show, the West Indian societies are characterized by segmentation where different segments show very marked variation in cultural values,

41 Curtin, op. cit., p. 131; also Marshall, op. cit., p. 421 et seq.
42 See footnote 37 and also Bertram Collins, 'The Civil Service of British Guiana in the General Strike of 1963', *Caribbean Quarterly,* vol. X, no. 2 (June 1964); Leo Despres, *Cultural Pluralism and Nationalist Politics in Guyana* (New York, 1967); J.S. Furnivall, *Colonial Policy and Practice* (Cambridge, 1948) and *Netherlands India* (Cambridge, 1939); Ernst Halperin, 'Racism and Communism in British Guiana', *Journal of Inter-American Studies,* vol. VII, no. 1 (January 1965); H.I. McKenzie, 'The Plural Society Debate: Some Comments on a Recent Contribution', *Social and Economic Studies,* vol. XV, no. 1 (March 1966); Peter Newman, *British Guiana, Problems of Cohesion in an Immigrant Society* (London and New York, 1964); R.T. Smith, *British Guiana* (London, 1962).

social organization, family structure, educational patterns and occupational interests, and that this is true not only where there has been a significant importation of indentured Indian labour, as in Trinidad and Guyana, but in all the societies of the West Indies. O.W. Phelps writes: 'Beyond these (whites, coloureds, Syrians, Chinese) was the great underlying proletariat of African descent – mainly agricultural, propertyless, destitute, semi-literate, and insecure, separated from both their coloured and white neighbours by the institutions of marriage and the church, by opportunities in education and in business, and restrained by law, force, and custom from organization for protest or revolt.'[43] Indeed as Mervyn Alleyne argues there remains a serious problem in basic communication between the elite and the mass. In some West Indian territories a different language system is used, for example in St Lucia and Dominica where the mass speak a Creole derived from French while the elite speak English, but even where the root language is the same there is a considerable gulf between the elite and the mass, the former speaking a version of Standard English, the latter a Creole form. Even where the elite can speak Creole it is not used on formal occasions and so the mass are removed from understanding and identifying with the governmental processes of the society. While emphasizing the seriousness of this gulf Alleyne does hypothesize that the bi-lingual mulatto group would have an important communicative role to play, thus mediating between elite and mass.[44]

The overall picture of cultural segmentation is, of course, even more obvious where other ethnic types are present such as the Chinese, Syrians, Portuguese and Amerindians, and the most significant of the ethnic groups other than the West Indian of African descent is the West Indian of Indian descent. Indians were brought as indentured labourers to the West Indies in the latter half of the 19th and early years of the 20th centuries. Though present in other territories they are most significant numerically in Trinidad and Guyana. The integration of Indians into Creole society was, and to a large extent still is, hindered as Donald Wood argues, by ignorance on both sides, by a failure even up to the Second World War to develop education among the Indians, by endogamous marriage patterns by the Indians, and a tendency for both groups to view the other as being sexually unattractive.[45] Despite the facts that the number of urban Christian Indians has increased; that the use of Indian languages is rapidly declining as are many Indian customs; and that the Indian rice farmers make a major contribution to intra- and inter-territorial

43 O.W. Phelps, 'Rise of the Labour Movement in Jamaica', *Social and Economic Studies,* vol. IX, no. 4 (December 1960), p. 417.

44 Mervyn Alleyne, 'Communications between the elite and the mass', in Andic and Matthews (eds), op. cit.

45 Donald Wood, *Trinidad in Transition: The Years after Slavery* (London, 1968), pp. 137-9.

trade, there are still deep divisions between Indian society and the Creole society in which they live but of which they are still not a fully integrated part.[46] Obviously part of the problem is to be found in the fact, already dealt with, that Creole society is itself not a fully integrated social system.

Given these divisions within the society, and its hierarchic structure, with mass unemployment and poverty, as Gordon Lewis states, one does not have to accept all the reasoning of the plural society theory in order to reject a consensus model for West Indian countries.[47]

In addition to the existence of cultural segments sharing little in common, the West Indies are characterized by another kind of fragmentation – in this case the existence of essentially similar social structures which nevertheless have little contact with each other. Again this fragmentation finds its roots in the original purely plantation system of slavery. Orlando Patterson writes of Jamaica during slavery: 'Jamaica is best seen more as a collection of autonomous plantations, each a self-contained community with its internal mechanisms of power, than as a total social system.'[48] The essentially export-oriented, open nature of these economies has created a situation where each productive unit is linked with the metropolitan market, and the absence of a developed internal market linking production and consumption has tended to maintain this fragmentation into the 20th century. Where new crops have been developed, or new raw materials such as oil and bauxite extracted, there has been no tendency to create real economic or social linkages within the West Indies.

The fragmentation which exists within each territory, acutely evident in the plantations and the company towns, is even more obvious between the individual territories. The colonies were kept apart for three centuries,[49] trade and transport links between them were not developed, and most routes led to the United Kingdom. Thus one finds the paradoxical situation of very small societies, with essentially the same history, with social structures which follow the same pattern (what variations there are are probably no greater than those regional variations that exist in the United Kingdom), geographically in the same area, linked by the same sea but where the very basis of the similarity – the plantation-based export economy – has served only to keep them apart economically and politically.

A structural feature of the West Indies in the 20th century, particularly in the post Second World War period, has been an increase in social mobility and

46 Lloyd Braithwaite, 'Social Stratification in Trinidad', *Social and Economic Studies,* vol. II, nos. 2 and 3 (October 1953); Despres, op. cit.; I. Oxaal, *Black Intellectuals Come to Power: The Rise of Creole Nationalism in Trinidad and Tobago* (Cambridge, Mass., 1968), especially p. 85 et seq.

47 Lewis, op. cit., p. 35 et seq.

48 Patterson, op. cit., p. 70.

49 See Lewis, op. cit., p. 18.

an expansion of the urban middle class. Opportunities for upward mobility have accrued as a result of the expansion of manufacturing in the larger islands, tourism, mining, the service sectors of the economy, and as the result of the declining percentage of expatriates employed in both the public and private sectors of these economies. Given the traditional rigidity of social divisions based on ascriptive status criteria one might assume that increased mobility would ease social tension. However, there has always been a contradiction in the West Indies between values based on individualism and achievement and those based on ascription. Status among the whites in slavery was based on achievement of wealth rather than on birth. The profit motive ruled supreme, more especially a version of 'get rich quick' where the intention was to make one's fortune in the colonies and then return to the United Kingdom and live off the plantation as an absentee owner. Thus, although white society in slavery was ranked, mobility occurred within it and economic success was highly valued, and yet the total society had to stress not the values associated with achievement but those of ascription which alone justified the enslavement of the black man.

In the 20th century upward mobility and high status is no longer completely restricted to one segment of society but there is still a conflict of values. As pointed out earlier, while considerably modified, the ranking of society is still based on race and colour, but now social leaders stress at all times the importance of values based on achievement: poverty is a sign of failure; upward mobility is sought; success in the school system is urged; and increasingly some formal qualification is demanded for entry into the middle classes. Morley Ayearst points out that where there is this conflict between the acceptance of achievement and ascriptive values there can be an actual increase in social tension as mobility increases, particularly where although mobility has increased, opportunity for advancement is still both limited and very unevenly distributed within the society.[50] As the author writes elsewhere: 'The old expatriate elite was largely removed from the scene, particularly in government positions. Upward mobility had to occur but this does not mean . . . that equality of opportunity increased significantly.'[51]

Another aspect of these societies which is derived from slavery and still persists in part is absenteeism, both physical and spiritual. Orlando Patterson has argued that absenteeism was inherent in the slave system of the West Indies and he gives the figure of nine-tenths of all land under cultivation in Jamaica before emancipation being absentee owned.[52] Of course this figure

50 Morley Ayearst, *The British West Indies: The Search for Self-Government* (London, 1960), p. 57.
51 Ann Spackman, 'The Senate of Trinidad and Tobago', *Social and Economic Studies,* vol. XVI, no. 1 (March 1967), p. 84.
52 Patterson, op. cit., p. 37 et seq.

varied from territory to territory with Barbados having a much larger settler population and almost no absentee ownership. Today the absentee owners are not the individual *grandees* of the slave period but foreign based companies: Tate & Lyle, Bookers, Alcan, Texaco, etc. However, many of the effects are the same – economically the export of profits, socially the lack of commitment to the societies by the owners of the means of production, distribution and exchange. The aim of the economic elite, with the limited exception of Barbados, has been to extract as much profit as possible and then leave. If an industry declines or an individual enterprise shows a falling-off in profitability there has been no concern to innovate, to create new industries with capital accumulated and retained within the territories, neither has there been a concern with the development of culture or education, except for very limited purposes.

Philip Curtin argues that it was this absenteeism which was the principal cause of 'cultural and intellectual poverty'.[53] Concerned with the profit motive and characterized by conspicuous consumption the privileged classes of the West Indies have exhibited a certain decadence throughout the history of these societies. Absenteeism led to the failure until the 20th century to establish a good education system even for the privileged, since where they sought education at all they did so in the metropolitan society.

This means that the entire burden of carrying the cultural life of the West Indies fell on those whose energies had to be expended, for the most part, on mere survival and who were until very recently denied education. Patterson and Curtin both point to some real strengths in the cultural life of the depressed mass of the West Indies,[54] and clearly it is on these that survival and development depend. However, a serious weakness is the absence of a culture of science and technology[55] where this is essential for the capacity to adapt one's economy. The mass of the West Indian people have a vigorous culture but one which is still based in mysticism and magico-religious beliefs, and the economic elite are not concerned with innovation except insofar as it contributes to their interests which are essentially metropolitan based.

Absenteeism among the elite has therefore led to another form of dependence in the West Indies – cultural and intellectual dependence. Techniques, forms of organization, ideas, concepts have tended to be imported from outside which clearly means that they will not always be appropriate to the society and even where appropriate will still tend to perpetuate dependence on outside initiative.[56] It is significant that real innovation within the West

53 Curtin, op. cit., p. 15.
54 Patterson, op. cit., p. 93, and Curtin, op. cit., p. 25 et seq.
55 Brewster and Thomas, op. cit., pp. 334-5.
56 See L. Best, 'Economic Planning in Guyana' in Andic and Matthews (eds), op. cit.; K. Boulding, 'Social Dynamics in West Indian Society', *Social and Economic Studies*, vol. X, no. 1 (March 1961).

Indies has tended to be limited to art forms, especially music and literature, and that perhaps the most original of the West Indian novelists, Wilson Harris, writes works which are characterized by mysticism and fantasy.

Finally on structure, one must refer to the fact that these societies were colonies for centuries – power and prestige rested in the imperial centre, and the social life of the elite revolved around transient Governors, thus reinforcing the pre-eminence of the outside world and the unsettled nature of the elite.

In turning to a consideration of those values and attitudes which one associates with the social structure in the West Indies we shall again be concerned with those which appear to be most directly relevant to political life. However, despite a considerable amount of agreement in the literature one is not on very strongly established ground since there is not an extensive or very rigorously established body of work on the subject.[57] Nevertheless certain tentative generalizations can be made.

The institutions of slavery and colonialism called for and received certain reinforcing values in order to support social structures which depended upon the oppression of one race by another. Out of these institutions came elaborate racial myths of superiority and inferiority.[58] The black man was not enslaved because Europeans had superior weapons and an economic need for a mass of cheap labour for their plantations, but because he was naturally a slave, less than human. Such attitudes were born in slavery but continued long after emancipation both because they had been very firmly implanted and because they continued to justify not only colonial rule but, within the West Indies, the rigidity of the social hierarchy. Thus one finds Lord Milner in 1903 stating that: 'The white man must rule, because he is elevated by many, many steps above the black man . . .'[59] In 1924 the distinguished constitutional lawyer A. Berriedale Keith could exhibit a crude form of prejudice and racial superiority, arguing that self-rule for 'native races' was at best 'a distant goal' owing to their proved 'political incapacity'.[60] In 1940 Lord Lloyd, Secretary of State for the Colonies, addressing new recruits to the Overseas

57 However the following are extremely useful: Lloyd Braithwaite, 'Social Stratification in Trinidad', *Social and Economic Studies,* vol. II, nos. 2 and 3, October 1953; Madeleine Kerr, *Personality and Conflict in Jamaica* (Liverpool, 1952); A.W. Singham, *The Hero and the Crowd in a Colonial Policy* (New Haven and London, 1968); and M.G. Smith, *The Plural Society in the British West Indies* (Berkeley, 1965).

58 Elsa Goveia argues that such racial myths are functional in a slave society. Goveia, *Historiography of the British West Indies,* p. 87.

59 Quoted in George Bennett, *The Concept of Empire* (London, 1953), p. 343.

60 A. Berriedale Keith, *The Constitution, Administration and Laws of the Empire* (London, 1924), pp. 120-2.

Civil Service, said: 'Think of the opportunity. In what other task can you have so much power so early? You can at the age of twenty-five be the fathers of your people: you can drive the road, bridge the river, and water the desert; you can be the arm of justice, and the hand of mercy to millions. You can, in fact, serve England. You can, indeed, in this vital moment serve something that is greater than England itself. You can serve and secure the cause of Christian civilization.'[61] A sentiment which was shared by a later Secretary of State, Arthur Creech-Jones when he wrote: 'These men and women of the Colonial Service are extending the frontiers of civilization.'[62]

Whether expressing the outright belief in imperialism or later ideas of trusteeship and partnership these attitudes were (and still are) clearly and firmly embedded in racist values, values which were part and parcel of the political formula which legitimised slavery and imperialism, so that until very recently demands for self-government by black people had to appear at best premature and at worst simply absurd. Gordon Lewis suggests that, in the West Indies, fear of the black masses and the idea of their incapacity 'lay at the heart of British policy'.[63]

If the racial myth of the naturally superior white and naturally inferior black expressed important supporting values for British colonial policy, it was even more obviously necessary within the West Indies to support the social order. Firmly held by the local elite and reinforced from outside by the prestigious 'men and women of the Colonial Service', it was conveyed by the formal churches, by schools, by economic and social relationships to the majority of the West Indian population, and more especially to the largely coloured middle class. So that Austin Clarke writing in the Barbados Independence Issue of *New World Quarterly* can say with bitterness '. . . we are all cockroaches in the same closet pit'.[64] For the black man the obvious consequence of internalizing the racial myth is self-denigration and even self-hatred. Another possibility, not necessarily to be found in different men, is aggressive competitiveness. For example, Austin Clarke in the same essay writes: 'I was left then with nothing but aggression and ambition, which I could use as antidotes to my poverty. I sometimes wonder, from my new mental safety in Canada, whether fate alone divided those who writhed a shitty living out of their poverty, and those who were buried in shit and poverty. I cannot yet understand how I escaped its death knell. Perhaps it was my aggressiveness . . .

61 Quoted in Sir Charles Jeffries, *Partners for Progress: The Men and Women of the Colonial Service* (London, 1949), pp. 17-19.
62 Ibid, Foreward by Arthur Creech-Jones, p. 3.
63 Lewis, op. cit., p. 107.
64 Austin Clarke, 'Harrison College and Me', *New World Quarterly*, vol. III, nos. 1 and 2, Barbados Independence Issue (Dead Season 1966 and Croptime 1967), p. 32.

'. . . But I had to shine. And I chose to shine at athletics. For me, athletics was a more acceptably aggressive way of fighting back, than coming first in Latin Unseen . . .', but finally, for Clarke and many other West Indian artists, 'I had to leave'.[65]

It is however likely, though not proved, that this extreme of contempt for oneself and one's situation and the repressed aggression are most often found among those in closest contact with the elite – the middle class and those few from poor origins recruited into the middle class through the elitist education system. Orlando Patterson argues that many of the pure black slaves did not lose their race pride.[66] Paul Bogle called on his followers to 'Cleave to the black', Marcus Garvey based his political movement on pride in blackness, the dignity and worth of the black man, and found enormous support, and the latest radical movements in the West Indies, following in these distinguished footsteps, are building on a West Indian version of black consciousness and black power.

However, inevitably a social system based on fear, coercion, deference and rigid ranking produced attitudes of ambivalence to authority and to racial types.[67] Authority is both feared and therefore submitted to, and hated and therefore on occasions violently attacked, or at least evaded wherever possible. The white man becomes for the black man the object of overt adulation and covert hatred.[68] Similarly the white and light coloured viewed the black both as a dangerous and violent threat because of his fear of the oppressed mass, and as a happy, simple child because this picture could justify his position and at the same time make oppression appear less oppressive.

One of the most obvious physical expressions of these attitudes was, and to a considerable extent still is, violence. Harsh laws enforced in a punitive spirit are characteristic of much of West Indian history, as are violent uprisings of the mass in an explosion of their aggressive feelings towards the elite and the system which operates so much against them both spiritually and materially. Beginning on the actual slave ships, going throughout slavery, into the emancipation period, the riots of the 1930s and the, so far, milder Black Power demonstrations of the current period, the history of the West Indies has always been punctuated by violent uprisings.

Another expression, illustrating the ambivalence of values in the West Indies, has been, on the other hand extreme deference to white, and more particularly, British values. Again this is probably, but not proven, most commonly found among the middle class, and can be illustrated by some of the

65 Ibid.

66 Patterson, op. cit., p. 64.

67 Braithwaite, op. cit., p. 148; Kerr, op. cit., pp. 156-60; Lewis, op. cit., p. 66; Singham, op. cit., pp. 149-52.

68 Patterson, op. cit., p. 170 et seq.

statements of a man who was nevertheless in the forefront of the West Indian struggle for self-government, T.A. Marryshow. In an article in the Jamaican *Daily Gleaner* in 1953 Marryshow wrote under the headline 'The Coming of the Queen' – 'That the Queen is coming after all makes me feel that another of my dreams has come true', and later in the same article, 'I see no other way before us now than in building British, and this, at least, for a long, long time to come.'[69] While using these quotations from Mr Marryshow the author does not want to imply that he was in any way unique, or more thoughtlessly deferential than others. On the contrary, Marryshow was chosen precisely because he has an important place in the history of West Indian nationalism, the movement for self-government, and the questioning of the colonial *status quo.*

Clearly out of this highly impressionistic view of West Indian culture showing rigidity, status ranking, racial stereotyping, self-denigration, deference to outside values, aggressiveness often repressed, violence, come many of those character traits which have been linked together under the single term *authoritarian.* Again the absence of rigorous research on the subject of personality structure in the West Indies, and some uncertainty in the literature of psychology as to the validity of the concept of the authoritarian personality, make one hesitant to arrive at any certain conclusion. However, the evidence is highly suggestive and clearly of significance in the political sphere, since if the West Indian personality structure is commonly *authoritarian* this would clearly reinforce any existing tendency in the political sphere towards non-participation in government by the mass of the people, towards inflexible government, and towards an emphasis on coercion and control.

Political background

This section of the Introduction is intended to elaborate on the nature of the political systems of the West Indies and the occurrence of events, in order to place in context the formal constitutional changes which are dealt with in this volume.

It is a theoretical assumption of this work that the nature of the political system is dependent upon the social, economic and constitutional structures. It has been argued so far that the two most important structural features of West Indian societies and economies are that they are internally inegalitarian and externally dependent. The Preface and the actual documents selected in this work give adequate illustration of the constitutional subordination of the West Indies throughout the colonial period. It is necessary therefore to examine to what extent that subordination has ended for Barbados, Guyana, Jamaica, and Trinidad and Tobago with independence, and to what extent

69 *Daily Gleaner,* Monday, 14th September 1953.

the political systems exhibited inegalitarian characteristics, if at all.

Clearly slave societies are purely inegalitarian in their political structures. Not only are political rights necessarily denied to slaves but so also are most forms of legal rights. An added factor in the West Indies was that during slavery, free coloureds were also denied political and some legal rights.

The post-emancipation period saw the granting of legal rights to all in a purely formal sense, but the continued restriction of political rights together, of course, with extreme social and economic inequality. The vote, awarded on the basis of property and income qualifications which affectively ruled out the mass of the population, was therefore exercised by a handful of men, who chose representatives from an even more restricted group of property-owners.[70] The Imperial Government which retained ultimate responsibility in its own hands and placed executive power in the hands of its appointed Governors, nevertheless failed to assert its authority in the post-emancipation period,[71] leaving power in the hands of the Assemblies of oligarchs who had no responsibility for government but had power over legislation and finance. W.K. Marshall points to the unreality of much of the political life of this period in the Windward Islands, which can be generalized to the West Indies as a whole. The Assemblies were obstructive, irresponsible, and apathetic – totally incapable of dealing with the new and potentially revolutionary situation created by emancipation.[72]

However, particularly in Jamaica and the Windward Islands there was a rising middle class of coloureds and blacks who by the second half of the 19th century were poised to challenge the hegemony of the white planters. At the same time, particularly in Jamaica, a depressed peasantry was ready to revolt. It was the peasantry, led by Paul Bogle, who rose up to challenge the existing order in 1865 at Morant Bay. Having savagely put down the peasant revolt the Imperial Government and the local plantocracy agreed to a constitutional measure which was directed, not against the peasants who had not yet entered the formal political institutions, but against the coloured and black middle class. The agreement reached was for the withdrawal of the old constitution and the introduction of Crown Colony government. Significantly, although Morant Bay was a Jamaican event and a limited revolt in terms of numbers and area, all the West Indian islands where a similar challenge presented itself gave up their constitutions before the end of the century – to quote W.K. Marshall: '. . . the planters accepted constitutional retrogression rather than face the implications of political advance which might result from progressive

70 This only refers to those territories with the Old Representative System. The Crown Colonies, acquired finally during the Napoleonic Wars had no representative institutions.

71 Curtin, op. cit., p. 97.

72 Marshall, op cit., p. 456 et seq.

extension of the francise'.[73] Interestingly it was the Bahamas and Barbados who retained their old constitutions where the white hegemony was not threatened until the 20th century.[74]

One finds therefore in the post-emancipation period the emergence of a new middle class, beginning to demand and in certain individual cases receive political rights, but having their demands frustrated by a rigid and short-sighted plantocracy. It is a fairly well-established view that the stability and legitimacy of a political system over time depends upon its capacity to accommodate the rise of a new class articulating demands for entry into the formal structures of the system.[75] In the late 19th century the systems of the West Indies showed that they were incapable of such accommodation.

This rigidity of thinking is well illustrated by W.K. Marshall when he quotes a Report of the Registrar General of St Vincent in 1865: '. . . a little expenditure for the care of infant life might yield a large return many times more profitable than the introduction, at such heavy expense, of Coolies . . .'[76] However, the planters could not perform such simple accounting. Their calculations could go no further than that the West Indies depended upon sugar; sugar had to be grown on plantations; plantations needed servile labour, and therefore they demanded indentured labour. That their request was granted and that they were assisted in their importation of 'coolies' is one of the clearest pieces of evidence that Crown Colony government, despite its paternalistic theory, was essentially elitist by nature and governed in the interests of the plantocracy. The introduction of semi-slave labour was directly opposed to the interests of the mass of the existing population, it was not even in the interest of the urban middle class, but was only in the perceived interest of the plantocracy.

Thus Crown Colony government was introduced as a result of two separate but linked factors: the irresponsibility and obstructiveness of the Assemblies and the fear of opening representative political institutions to coloured and black men. It is not surprising therefore to see that this was essentially a conservative step to preserve the *status quo ante*. Firstly the mobility of the

73 Ibid., p. 480, and see also Douglas Hall, op. cit., p. 7, where Dr Hall points out that the (white) Country Party of Jamaica was already threatened in the Assembly by the (coloured) Town Party, and preferred to see an extension of the Governor's powers than the Town Party in control of the Assembly.

74 British Guiana did not lose its Dutch constitution until 1928, and the circumstances were somewhat different. See Chapter IV, Part I below.

75 S.M. Lipset, *Political Man* (London, 1963), p. 79 et seq., and Robert Dahl, *Modern Political Analysis* (New Jersey, 1970, 2nd ed.), Chapter VII passim.

76 Marshall, op. cit., p. 501.

coloured population was held back[77] by encouraging essentially static economic policies, by recruiting for public and private sector jobs in the metropolis, as well as by closing the doors of the representative assemblies. Secondly the operation of Crown Colony government ensured that much power was retained at the local level where the plantocracy could still control most of the countryside.[78]

This was despite the paternalistic theory which suggested that Crown Colony government was necessary to better protect the interests of the black masses of the West Indies. To some extent the system did replace the outright selfishness of the planter oligarchs with something more like a legal-rational political system. However, it only tempered some of the excesses of the early system and forced men to operate within a more rigid framework of law. Socially the Governors were obviously only in contact with the white population of the colonies and were therefore within the local context primarily concerned with its interests, although obviously they first had to serve the Imperial interest. The practice of trusteeship was in fact very far from paternalistic theory and was in fact rule in favour of the elite,[79] and here of course one should point out that even had the paternalism been more benevolent it is an essentially debilitating situation for those being 'protected'.

Furthermore one finds that throughout the Crown Colony period the governments were essentially concerned with law, order and bureaucratic efficiency. Welfare legislation was not seriously considered until after the Royal Commission (Moyne) Report and neither was the possibility of creating a participant democracy. The British, insofar as they pursued a policy of political development at all, were concerned in later years with the development of a trained elite, thus contradicting any argument that they were attempting to develop the colonies towards a Westminster model with real checks and balances to the exercise of bureaucratic power with a participating electorate embracing the entire adult population. The concern was with creating what Whitehall would consider efficient government and here one must note again the high bureaucratic involvement in the political process at all stages,[80] and the significance of the title, Administrator, given to the Heads of the Presidencies of the Leeward and Windward Islands.

An observation of C.S. Salmon in the 1880s deserves further consideration here, where Salmon argued that in Crown Colony government Britain had

77 Hall, op. cit., p. 263.
78 W.K. Marshall, 'Peasant Movements and Agrarian Problems in the West Indies. Part I: Aspects of the Development of the Peasantry'. (Unpublished paper, Department of History, UWI, Mona, November, 1969, Mimeo) p. 17.
79 Lewis, op. cit., p. 104.
80 See above: Preface to this work.

created 'irresponsible, bureaucratic systems'.[81] Until the 1950s it could be argued that there was no real change in the irresponsible nature of government in the West Indies. The governments, for most of this period, contained no elected members and were therefore in no way answerable to the legislatures and the electorates. Even when the system was modified by the introduction of some elected members and later by the creation of quasi-ministers responsible for policy decisions, real power remained with the bureaucrats who were still in control of departmental administration and in the person of the Governor were still ultimately responsible, to the Imperial government, for policy decisions. Indeed given the operation of the British imperial system the responsibility of the Governors to the Secretary of State was not very immediate since much emphasis was put on the importance of the 'man on the spot'. As J.M. Lee shows particularly in the early years the Governors were far more important than the Secretaries of State, the power of reservation being used far more often than the power of disallowance and the really crucial powers being those of certification and the right to ignore the advice of the Executive Council. It was only when the move to self-government started seriously that the Secretary of State became more important since the decisions taken involved legislative action in London.

Furthermore one finds that the Secretary of State himself was to a greater extent than most other Ministers not immediately responsible to the Imperial Parliament for his administration. Many of the powers he exercised derived from the royal prerogative, for although the 17th century saw the establishment of the right of Parliament to legislate for the colonies, nevertheless power and control of the colonies stayed effectively in the hands of the Crown – thus one finds that legislation was largely by Order in Council and Letters Patent, and the Imperial final court of appeal was the Judicial Committee of the Privy Council. Attempts were made during the period under review to increase the answerability of the Secretary of State to the British Parliament, especially by establishing a Parliamentary Committee for Colonial Affairs but these efforts were finally abandoned in 1959.[82]

Given the absence of effective legal responsibility in colonial political systems until the achievement of ministerial government it is not surprising to find that the bureaucratic system was not responsive to most of the demands made of it. Efficiency, which in a state bureaucracy involves responsiveness, was usually confused with the capacity to keep proper accounts, collect taxes and to perform certain other supporting functions. Means were confused with

81 C.S. Salmon, *The Caribbean Confederation.*
82 Lee, op. cit., p. 60 et seq; David Goldsworthy: 'The Debate on a Parliamentary Committee for Colonial Affairs', *Parliamentary Affairs,* vol. XIX, no. 2 (Spring 1966).

ends – an error which could be said to follow from the fact that the controlling bureaucrats were serving a society other than that which they were servicing. However much the degree of responsiveness in government followed from the nature of the colonial political system, one should point out that West Indian society contributed to this failure. W. Richard Jacobs in his thesis on labour movements in Trinidad gives many examples of the Imperial bureaucracy either failing to respond to the demands of both labour and the middle class, or responding too late, and argues that the fragmentation of the society, the gulf between the elite and the mass and the close association of Governor and local elite, meant that the authorities were unable to anticipate demands or the nature of the unrest likely to occur because there was no real communication taking place.[83] Indeed even the addition of elected members to the Legislative and Exeçutive Councils did not really end this situation until universal adult suffrage and responsible local Ministers were introduced. In fact until these later changes the elected formed yet another irresponsible element in the system.

However, the Crown Colony system did bring to the West Indies a modern form of bureaucracy, even if it did not bring the idea of the purpose of bureaucracy being to serve the people of the country. Rational procedures were introduced, rules and regulations were applied in orderly fashion, recruitment to the service was by merit – although local men were not deemed to have sufficient merit for senior positions until quite late in the Crown Colony period. Of course it can be argued that to introduce the forms of modern bureaucracy without arriving at any idea of its real function is to run the risk of creating a machine which serves its own ends – indeed which becomes an end in itself, form is confused with substance, and reform becomes even more difficult.

Finally as Trevor Munroe argues, the Crown Colony system, even where elected members were still a minority in the Legislative Council, did familiarize men with the procedures of parliament and with the ideas of Government and Opposition.[84] Obviously whether this was valuable depends on whether what was learned was that opinions contrary to one's own should be heard, that possible alternative policies exist, that one's own policy might have weaknesses; or that what was learned was a ritualized form, an automatic response of 'for' or 'against' and the view that the country is necessarily divided along partisan lines.

The elitist nature of the West Indian colonial political system, its remoteness, its lack of concern and responsiveness to the desperate problems of the

83 W. Richard Jacobs, 'The Role of Some Labour Movements in the Political Process in Trinidad, 1937-1950'. (Unpublished M.Sc. thesis, Department of Government, U.W.I., Mona, 1969) pp. 39-40.

84 Trevor Munroe, 'Political Change and Constitutional Development in Jamaica, 1944-1962'. (Unpublished D.Phil. thesis, Oxon, 1969) p. 23.

majority of people, has 'left behind a popular suspicion of all government, so that the West Indian today is almost a natural anarchist'.[85] Suspicion of and alienation from government are characteristic of people's response to the colonial political system, and although there is no objective evidence, a subjective assessment suggests that these characteristics have survived into the independence/associated statehood period. Historically Morant Bay and the response to it, the Federation Riots in Barbados, the 1903 riots in Port-of-Spain because of 'a simple expedient by the government to conserve the island's water resources',[86] the 1905 strike of dock workers in British Guiana and the response of government, the riots of the 1930s throughout the West Indies, all testify to the deep suspicion of government, the failure of communication and of access to government at any level for most people. Within the colony government was remote from the people because of social distance, economic differences of interest and the lack of a language of communication; outside the colony there was no direct access to the political institutions of the metropolis which controlled their destiny.

Clearly the result of this combination of factors has been a low level of political involvement, even where the franchise has been granted, and a pattern of resistance to authority. Resistance to authority has not been an exclusively black phenomenon in the West Indies – slavery and the post-emancipation period saw many examples of white resentment and resistance; today evasion of the law particularly with respect to taxation or regulation of trade and industry carries little moral disapprobation, but resistance expressed with violence has, not surprisingly, been a black phenomenon of frequent occurrence.

Having examined some aspects of the nature of the colonial political system in the West Indies, some further discussion is needed on the basic contradictions of that system. The most important is that the colonial political system is a subordinate system, being controlled from the metropolis in most aspects of its economic and political life, and some of the more important aspects of its social life. The colony is penetrated at all levels of decision-making by the metropolis and is strongly influenced by the metropolis in less formal areas.[87] However, despite this subordination and inter-linking the colony is neither an integral part of the metropolis nor of any other colony. Each colony exists, as an identifiable social system, with its own institutions,

85 Lewis, op. cit., p. 66.

86 F.A. Hoyos, *The Rise of West Indian Democracy: the Life and Times of Sir Grantley Adams* (Bridgetown, 1963), p. 9.

87 For penetration of colony by metropolis see: Lloyd Braithwaite, 'Social Stratification in Trinidad', p. 42 et seq.; Singham, op. cit., pp. 303-5; H.V. Wiseman, *A Short History of the British West Indies* (London, 1950), pp. 110-11.

structures and values. It is potentially autonomous but is not. To be absorbed into a land empire as an integral unit might be painful but does not involve the inherent contradiction in the position of a colony in an overseas empire of the later European variety. Unlike the functional sub-systems of a total social system which are abstract categories and are therefore incapable of existing alone (indeed it is meaningless to talk of an economic sub-system existing outside the social system as a whole), the metropolis and colonies of an imperial system are concrete categories which are capable, theoretically and to varying degrees practically, of autonomous existence. So that, although an imperial political system cannot survive the loss of a metropolis or all its colonies, it can survive the loss of individual colonies, and retain the characteristic of empire which is the domination of one polity by another. Similarly the colony can survive its severance from the metropolis. Thus, a colony can either be described as a subordinate system: 'A subordinate system, then, is a special case of a system in general, as opposed to a sub-system',[88] or as a 'system part' with a high degree of functional autonomy: 'Operationally speaking, we might say that the functional autonomy of a system part is the probability that it can survive separation from the system.'[89]

Overseas empires therefore – whether following the British pattern of a high degree of formal devolution of authority or the more highly centralized Continental European pattern – would be cases of systems where the parts (metropolis and colonies) had high functional autonomy, and that, without violence to the facts, these empires could be considered as sets of closely related systems, each system capable of being viewed as a system in its own right.

However, connected with any idea of a social system is the presence of structures performing the function of authoritative decision-making – in older and less precise terminology – of the political sovereign. In strictly numerical terms it is true that most authoritative decisions for a colony were and are taken within that colony, albeit under the Crown Colony system by an expatriate official from the metropolis, but these decisions could be overridden by the Imperial government. Ultimate decision-making rested outside the colony. The individual colony shared the same 'sovereign' with other colonies but was itself not normally bound by all the decisions of that sovereign, only being bound by those which specifically extended to it.[90] The overseas empire is therefore a curious type of system where there is a decision-making centre in the metropolis whose decisions rarely bind all parts of the Empire.

88 Singham, op. cit., p. 303.
89 Alvin Gouldner, 'Reciprocity and Autonomy in Functional Theory', in Llewellyn Gross (ed.), *Symposium on Sociological Theory* (Evanston and New York, 1959), p. 354.
90 Colonial Laws Validity Act, 1865.

This then is the basic contradiction of the colonial polity: it has identifiable structures of its own; it often has a sense of community, creating loyalty to the colony itself and not to other parts of the empire, but it is legally unable to make decisions for itself, and its economy and society are penetrated by metropolitan structures and values. Inevitably movements develop seeking to put an end to the contradiction by shifting the locus of decision making to the local government. More simply, as A.W. Singham puts it, there is a 'basic antagonism between colonized and colonizers'.[91] The economic interests of colonized and colonizers are opposed, but because of their dominance the colonizers are able to impose their will on the colonized. The structural contradiction is therefore a reflection of a real conflict of interest.

In addition to this basic conflict and the conflict of values already referred to above, the West Indies has always seen a tension created between values for and against equality. Elsa Goveia points out that the earliest demands for representative assemblies in the slave societies of the West Indies were based on the idea of the equality of all subjects of the English Crown, but they were expressed in a situation which not only denied all rights to slaves, but also violated the foundations of the common law system by denying political and some legal rights to free subjects who happened also to be coloured.[92]

Emancipation was pushed forward ideologically on grounds of the equality of men. But the post-emancipation period saw the persistence of gross inequalities in all spheres of life, with no effort being made to change this by the same Imperial government which had passed the Emancipation Act.

The 19th century in Britain saw the growth of ideas of liberty, equality, self-rule and participation in government, but it also saw the denial of these values in the tropical colonies and an expansion of colonial rule in Africa. Even the ancient, inegalitarian value that voters and representatives should have a 'stake' in the country, which was strongly held in Britain, was denied in the colonies where the supreme representative – the Governor – not only had no stake in the country he governed but was only a salaried official from another country.

However, these ideas – essentially destructive to imperial rule – could not be kept out of the colonies. This is partly because ideas can never be completely contained and partly because the British were themselves involved in a contradiction: on the one hand was the desire to keep firm control over the colonies; on the other hand was a need to train the local elite to fill some of the state offices from the colony itself. Not only did this mean that some education had to be provided, but given the British belief in the role of liberal arts as a training for administrators, it meant that the colonized were exposed

91 Singham, op. cit., p. 306.

92 Goveia, *Historiography of the British West Indies*, pp. 124-5.

to many of these ideas by the colonizers. Thus education led men to question the validity of the system and it also created a class whose interests would be directly served by freeing all local offices for local men, an object which could eventually only be achieved by constitutional independence.

Thus one finds that out of the subordination of the colony; the gross inequalities within; the lack of responsiveness of the authorities; the changing economic structure creating towns, a peasantry, a middle class and an urban proletariat to join the existing agro-proletariat of the estates; and the development of education both to create an elite and to equip the mass for the more complex tasks of a changing economy, came a number of inter-related movements and related ideas. The more important of these movements can be said to be middle class nationalism, the labour movement, and black nationalism, and the ordering ideas being those of nationalism, racial-consciousness and some form of 'socialism', which in the West Indies as elsewhere ranged from a mild idea of reform to Marxism-Leninism.

It is impossible to treat separately the strands of nationalism, black consciousness and labour movements, for in West Indian history of this period they are all inextricably linked together in the surge which produced political movements leading to formal constitutional change. Although the early demands of the 1920s and 1930s were for increased representation for the middle class, these did have 'implications for broadening the constitutional order',[93] and as Sir Charles Jeffries of the Colonial Service argued, once modified the Crown Colony system cannot long survive.[94] Furthermore one finds that the more radical demands of later years for full self-government and for universal adult suffrage were often couched in socialist language and were often associated with demands for radical economic and social change. For example F.A. Hoyos in his biography of Sir Grantley Adams shows how the Barbadian moved from support of Asquithian Liberalism to support for a far more radical position in the late 1930s. At the 1938 meeting of the British Guiana and West Indies Labour Congress in Port-of-Spain, Adams supported resolutions calling for the nationalization of the sugar industry, the break-up of estates, and the creation of a peasant society.[95] At the Caribbean Labour

93 Munroe, op. cit., p. 25.
94 Sir Charles Jeffries, *Transfer of Power* (London, 1960), pp. 33, 44 et seq. Sir Charles argues that once the Colonial Office accede to middle class demands for elected representation in the Legislative Council then the Crown Colony system, like the Old Representative system, is involved in its own contradiction created by the divorce of responsibility from power: a contradiction which can only be resolved by moving to a point where responsibility and power are again shared, but this time being held by new men – the local politicians.
95 Hoyos, op. cit., p. 97 et seq.

Congress of 1945 Adams 'put the case for a new series of textbooks for the West Indies *written from the Socialist viewpoint* in order that pupils of the schools and students of the West Indian University should be brought up in a socialist environment',[96] and at a meeting of his party in Barbados in 1946 the crowds sang the Red Flag and carried the hammer and sickle.[97]

A much commented upon characteristic of West Indian politics is the merger of party and trade union, the trade union acting as the organizational base for the party which is often, but not by any means invariably, middle class led.

It is similarly difficult to treat separately the other, perhaps most powerful idea in West Indian politics, that of black consciousness, or the reassertion of race pride in the face of centuries of systematic denigration. For example Marcus Garvey, whose name is obviously pre-eminent in this connection, always stressed the vital importance of organization for political purposes, and in 1930 the first plank of the programme of his People's Political Party was 'To secure representation in the Imperial Parliament for a larger modicum of self-government for Jamaica.'[98]

Thus one finds in the early years that the demands of the nationalists, articulated by men like Marryshow of Grenada, Dr O. Neale of Barbados, J.A.G. Smith of Jamaica, by British Guiana's Progressive Party, were often ignored or only partially met because, in English official opinion, they only represented a self-seeking minority and were not supported by responsible opinion: that is the opinion of merchants, planters, and expatriate officials of the state and established church. This response, short-sighted from the point of view of English self-interest, forced the middle class nationalists to think in terms of recruiting a mass base of support. At the same time men like Critchlow of British Guiana, Cipriani of Trinidad and Tobago, and Coombs of Jamaica had not only been thinking in terms of more self-government but had been engaged in attempts to organize labour. And Garvey, following in the footsteps of his Jamaican precursors, Bogle, Love and Bedward, was stressing the dignity of his race. Drawing very strongly on Judaeo-Christian tradition and its Messianic belief in the Saviour coming to lead his people back to the Promised Land, Garvey was not only much closer to the mass, developing a real popular feeling, but as mentioned before he also recognized the importance of organization. Garvey not only established his party in Jamaica but

96 Ibid., p. 101. Italics added.

97 It is ironic that in 1953 Adams took up the West Indies wide attack on Jagan in British Guiana. Here F.A. Hoyos (p. 194) says that 'Grantley was never in any doubt as to where he should take his stand in the Guianese affair. He had confidence in the man who was then Governor of British Guiana, Sir Alfred Sharpe.'

98 Amy Jacques Garvey, *Garvey and Garveyism* (New York, 1970, 1st ed. in Collier Books), p. 207.

also spread his United Negro Improvement Association (UNIA) throughout the West Indies. The information at the moment is fragmentary but, for example, in the 1920s when the British Guiana Labour Union (BGLU), led by Hubert Critchlow, fought but failed to resist wage cuts because of high unemployment, it received large support from the local UNIA.[99] Also the Democratic League, founded in Barbados 1923-4, received some of its support from Garveyites[100] And in the 1930s a Garveyite, Hubert Seale, attempted to radicalize the Barbados labour movement.[101]

One can therefore argue that the early challenge was real but as Gordon Lewis says of the men who made it: 'They fought, generally, the abuses of colonialism rather than the idea of colonialism.'[102] However, during these years they were bound to be frustrated: if they tried to move on a mass front they came up against the wall of a high franchise; if they tried to organize labour they were confronted by archaic legislation and the united opposition of local capital and the Imperial interest; and if they tried to remain elitist, arguing like gentlemen for their rights, they could be very easily handled by the Colonial Office and Colonial Service.

However, the presence of these men during the 1920s and early 1930s did present a foundation for the challenge to the colonial system – by preparing the middle class to think in terms of the constitutional changes which would improve its position, and by preparing the mass in providing organization and the articulation of some of its most deeply-felt ideas.

It was, of course, the riots of the middle and late 1930s which produced the real dynamic for change and raised the question, not yet adequately answered, of the entry of the mass of the people into the political system. Many factors contributed to the rioting which swept through the West Indies. The Great Depression created even worse poverty than the colonies had experienced before, wages were cut, unemployment soared, the cost of living went up as the prices for West Indian primary products on the world market declined. Social services were either appalling or non-existent.[103] Avenues of emigration were closed and workers returned from Costa Rica and Panama adding to the already high numbers seeking employment.[104] There already

99 Ashton Chase, *A History of Trade Unionism in Guyana, 1900-1961 with an Epilogue to 1964* (Ruimveldt, Demerara, 1964), p. 65.

100 Ayearst, op. cit., p. 89.

101 Hoyos, op. cit., pp. 86-7.

102 Lewis, op. cit., p. 279.

103 See, for example, Macmillan, op. cit.; T.S. Simey, *Welfare and Planning in the West Indies* (Oxford, 1946); *Report of the Commission on the Trinidad and Tobago Disturbances* (Cmnd. 5641/1938); *Report on Labour Conditions in the West Indies* by Major G.St.J. Orde-Browne (Cmnd. 6070/1939); *Report of the West India Royal Commission* (Cmnd. 6607/1945).

104 Hoyos, op. cit., p. 60; Munroe, op. cit., p. 29

existed large concentrations of labour on the plantations – what has been called the agroproletariat of the West Indies, and the growth of the urban centres created further concentrations of labour and high unemployment. Added to this was the fact that, amidst this evidence of distress and governmental neglect of basic services, the governments of the larger territories announced budgetary surpluses. Furthermore the Italo-Abyssinian War, the teachings of Marcus Garvey, and in Trinidad the presence of South African staff on the oil fields[105] created an explosive racial situation.

The distress was basically economic and the riots were largely a spontaneous outburst against an intolerable situation. Neither the leaders nor their followers were radically challenging the system which had created these conditions. Whilst the riots themselves appear to have been largely leaderless, a new style of leader did emerge during this turbulent period. These men were more radical in manner, often contemptuous of constitutional niceties, more prone to direct action, and more immediately in touch with the masses. These were men such as Bustamante, Butler, Bradshaw, Bird and later Joshua and Gairy. But their basic concern was with 'bread and butter' issues. They delighted the masses because of their irreverent behaviour, their activist image and their oratory, but they were not in any radical conflict with the colonial system.

The authorities and the workers' leaders having successfully negotiated with each other and defused the situation, the most spectacular result of the 1930s and the most immediate was the mushrooming of trade unions, for the most part of the blanket union type.[106] However, it is important to point out that most of these unions were the product of the riots and not their organizers. After the riots the need for organization was apparent, the economic base for unions was there, and legislative reform, shocked out of the authorities, created the legal basis for modern trade unionism.

An important development during these years was the linking of trade union with political party. The Colonial Office fought hard to depoliticize the unions, attempting to instil the idea that the proper role of unions was restricted to limited industrial action and ought not to be involved in politics. However, their efforts were only really successful in Trinidad and Tobago, where, for additional reasons, there has not been an effective merger between party and trade unions.[107] Elsewhere in the West Indies parties and unions were inextricably linked. Hoyos quotes Grantley Adams as saying: 'It is impossible to dissociate politics from the trade union movement. So far as colonial

105 Jacobs, op. cit., p. 37.

106 Trinidad and Tobago is an important exception to this. The unions of Trinidad remain based on trade and industry and have resisted all attempts at mergers.

107 Ibid., p. 64 et seq.

territories are concerned, a trade union cannot be strong unless it has political power and it is for the people to make their union strong.'[108] Adams should have added that it was also difficult for the party to achieve power without the union, for when he resigned from the Barbados Workers' Union in 1954, observing the British idea of constitutional niceties, he lost his trade union base and eventually his voter support.

The trade unions therefore provided the real organizational base for mass politics in the West Indies. Their efforts, the shock of the riots, the emergence of political parties and the effective demands of the middle class led to the grant of universal adult suffrage in the 1940s and early 1950s, thereby providing the constitutional means for that mass participation. However, the leadership was essentially accommodating rather than radically challenging the authorities, and the outburst in rioting was not an expression of real political consciousness on the part of most of the participants. It was rather a cry of despair.

In discussing political leadership in the West Indies, A.W. Singham says: 'On the one hand there is the middle class hero, claiming that he has sacrificed his career for the sake of helping the people; . . . On the whole, this type of leader has tended to stress constitutional advance. On the other hand, there is the hero who comes from humble origins and bases his claims to political leadership on his role as a trade union leader. In spite of the differences in their class origins and their leadership style, however, these two types share certain similarities: they tend to develop personal organizations which are essentially authoritarian.'[109] They also tend, in the West Indies, to be essentially accommodative: bargaining and negotiating according to the rules. If they broke the rules, as Gairy did, the Colonial Office was very quick to act, but did so, for the most part, mistaking the nature of the challenge which was directed more to style than to substance.

Thus one must agree with Trevor Munroe when he states that the real outcome of the 1930s was the strengthening of middle-class reformist nationalism,[110] despite the dramatic emergence of labour movements, political parties and new leaders who were more radical in style than their predecessors. This was an outcome made almost inevitable by the alienation and relatively low political consciousness of the majority of West Indians; the nature of the colonial system; the specific actions of the Colonial Office and the espousal of negotiation and concession by both labour leaders and the politically active middle class. Thus the turmoil of the 1930s only set the stage for the relatively smooth move forward by these political leaders to self-government and the

108 Hoyos, op. cit., p. 167.
109 Singham, op. cit., p. 152.
110 Munroe, op. cit., p. 33 et seq.

acceptance of British institutional forms for the West Indies in which they could fill the important offices, using the mass electorate and the unions as the base of power for their movement.[111] Even at the height of the disturbances most of the leaders attempted to defuse the situation and move it rapidly from one of confrontation to one of negotiation.[112] Hoyos quotes Grantley Adam's speech to the protesters in Barbados when he said:'I ask you, instead of forming a procession to Government House, to come and tell us every single grievance and let the procession be that of the Progressive League to a seat at the conference table.'[113] This illustrates very clearly the basically elitist view of the mediating and controlling role of the leaders, which was to be directed towards the politics of *politesse* and not of radical action. At the same time only radical action could achieve what the BG and WILC, supported by Adams, had called for in 1938: the nationalization of the sugar industry, the break-up of the estates and the establishment of a peasant society.

It would appear that the real aim of most of the influential political leaders of the time was a share in a constitutional form of government. In *The Process of Independence* Fatma Mansur writes: 'The colonial powers were greatly helped by this attitude, since the control of any territory could thus be made easier because only a handful of men had to be made conscious of the excellence of the existing order . . . It is this group which demanded concessions and received them.'[114] It could be argued that in the West Indies the task of the Colonial Office was made all the easier because of an absence of a strong nationalist entrepreneurial bourgeoisie with a direct interest in freeing their economy from foreign control and diverting profit to themselves. The West Indian middle class was largely based in white collar and professional work, and was therefore primarily concerned with office. Furthermore given the inherited social system they were primarily concerned with status, and the maintenance of high consumption patterns (of largely imported items), and were without the self-confidence which is so often the characteristic of the middle class in industrial societies. On the contrary the West Indian middle class was and is peculiarly prone to self-doubt, to contempt for its 'darker' side and to admire what is white and external to its own society.

The political parties which emerged from this situation had a mass base in their union following and often had radical or socialist overtones in their early days, but because of the factors outlined above they lost their radicalism. The parties became domesticated and non-agitational long before they achieved

111 See for example: ibid, p. 33 et seq.

112 Ibid., Chapter IV, passim, and Ken Post, 'The Politics of Protest in Jamaica, 1938', *Social and Economic Studies*, vol. XVIII, no. 4 (December 1969).

113 Hoyos, op. cit., p. 88.

114 Fatma Mansur, *The Process of Independence* (London, 1962), p. 67.

their goal of independence. Instead they spent long years *in statu pupillari,* accepting the role of the Colonial Office as a benign tutor who made sure that they had acquired the necessary skills before they were allowed to govern themselves.

Two clear examples of parties throwing off or being forced to throw off their early radicalism are firstly the purge of the PNP in the 1950s, when the party expelled its so-called Marxist wing in order to gain respectability, and Forbes Burnham's break from the Marxist Jagan in 1956.

The political parties which continue to compete with each other in the West Indies are found to be almost indistinguishable from each other in policies. The post-war period and independence are seeing the fulfilment of the bourgeois demands which were frustrated in 1866. However, the straightforward conservative parties such as the JDP of Jamaica, the PoPPG of Trinidad and Tobago, and even the later UF of Guyana, were electorally defeated.[115] Since these were parties of employers they could not acquire the mass voting support which in the West Indies has tended to be given by the trade unions. However, the parties which were union based were unable to finance themselves from inadequate union funds. As a result the financing of the mass based parties has tended to come from private capitalist sources. Consequently the policies of the parties, in or out of office, have tended to support private capital both local and foreign, since local capitalists in the West Indies are frequently agents for foreign business interests.[116]

Despite this convergence in policy the party political situation in the West Indies remains one of intense rivalry and partisanship. This is encouraged, for example, in Trinidad and Guyana by racial divisions within the society, and in Jamaica by the existence of two competing unions which encourage competition and conflict within the working class rather than between the working class and the owners of capital. The intensity of this rivalry is also partly explained by the situation of scarcity. Jobs, houses, access roads, schools, clinics are all within the patronage of the party which wins at election time. It therefore becomes a 'life and death' struggle as to who will carry the prize. Obviously one of the many consequences of this division of the working class is that, despite a relatively high level of partisanship at election time, there remains a lack of real political consciousness and a continued concern with very immediate issues.

Political participation in the West Indies tends to be further discouraged by the personalism of politics. The quotation above[117] taken from Singham's

115 Jamaica Democratic Party, Party of Political Progress Groups, United Force.

116 See for example Munroe, op. cit., p. 133.

117 See above p. 34.

The Hero and the Crowd in a Colonial Polity refers to this development of 'personal organisations that are essentially authoritarian', and developed throughout his book is the theme that there is an absence of real organization: the 'hero' is essentially supported by a 'crowd' rather than by organized supporters.

Thus one finds that although the post-war period saw important constitutional changes taking place, including the formation and dissolution of the Federation, and the achievement of formal independence or associated statehood, there was no real involvement of the mass of the people in this process, despite the fact that it was their eruption in the 1930s which, if it did not start this movement, certainly speeded it along its way.

After the war the Colonial Office made it clear that some advance would be permitted, and as it became obvious that this would lead to some form of self-government the political leaders, for the most part, were prepared to accept that constitutional change could be reduced to problems of timing and drafting. And except for the brief moment of the referendum on federation in Jamaica this is largely what it was reduced to. Much of the effort of the post-war period was directed towards proving to the British that West Indians were adept at learning how to work the almost unworkable constitutions of the 'transition period', and that therefore they deserved to be advanced further along a predetermined path.

Not only did most West Indian leaders not really try after they took office to get mass involvement in the process of changing the constitution, but they even lost mass interest. When independence came although there was momentary pleasure there was no wild enthusiasm. Bustamante, Manley, Barrow, Adams, Williams, Jagan, Burnham had all been in politics for a long time and as far as the ordinary man was concerned they had always been the most powerful political figures in his society. The real change had come years before with universal adult suffrage, and this had brought no significant improvement in either his social or economic condition. The little step by little step advances which had taken place since then could not really engage his emotions, and the process had gone on for so long that he had, for the most part, lost interest.

If one can argue that the radical potential of the 1930s was in part stifled by the victory of essentially conservative middle class nationalism, one could also say that it is in the break-up of the Federation that that nationalism met its greatest defeat.

The aim of nationalism in the West Indies was, as elsewhere, the establishment of an independent nation state. However, a phenomenon found throughout the Third World was also present in the West Indies: the difficulty of identifying the nation which was seeking self-conscious expression in its political institutions. Most West Indian political leaders in the 1930s, 1940s and

1950s recognized the impossibility of creating independent states on the basis of the minute territories, but they were confronted with the problem that it was precisely at the territorial level that people identified most strongly. As has been recognized for a long time by writers on nationalism, the nation is only realized by consciousness.[118] It has no objective reality without the subjective identification with the community – the national community being capable of commanding the loyalty of its members above all other communities. Certain objective conditions such as shared language, race, history, political institutions, etc., are likely to create this sense of shared nationality; but it is the subjective identification which makes the nation and not the presence or absence of certain objective conditions. However, the individual and the group can operate at a number of different levels of consciousness. So far in the West Indies the strongest identification has been at the territorial level: the territories being those defined by the colonial or ex-colonial power. However, the case of Anguilla and its self-assertive break from the unitary state of St Kitts/Nevis/Anguilla, illustrates that where the territory is a grouping of islands, territorial identification can break down, and a purely insular consciousness takes over. Even so, at a larger level there is an idea, albeit a variable one, of West Indian identity, and also an idea, probably stronger at the mass level, of shared identity with all black men: an idea which recurs throughout American history generally and has its most recent expression in the various forms of black power movements.

Given this possibility of differing levels of conscious identification with differing potential national communities, it is clear that the political histories of peoples can, for long periods of time, exhibit considerable confusion as to what actual end nationalism is seeking. Despite the current withdrawal to the territorial community, the West Indies, throughout the period covered by this work and into the present, exhibit elements of problems created by the difficulty of determining the identity of the nation: is it territory, race, the West Indies, or possibly in the future, the Caribbean?

The problem of nationalism was clearly recognized in the early days of the international socialist movement by Rosa Luxemburg who, despite her Polish origins, always opposed the Bolshevik strategy of encouraging the resistance of national minorities to imperialism. Luxemburg argued that the potential for fractionalism in nationalism outweighed any advantages which it might have as an immediate strategy.[119] The problem is very clearly illustrated in the West Indies especially at the level of the smaller territories where the

118 For a recent Third World expression of this see Franz Fanon, *Toward the African Revolution: Political Essays* (New York, 1967), p. 43 of essay on 'Racism and Culture'.

119 J.P. Nettl, *Rosa Luxemburg* (London, 1966), p. 700 and Appendix 2 'The National Question' especially pp. 844-7.

imperial government has been unable to resist demands for self-government but where there is no real base for a national society.

Articulate nationalism in the West Indies for much of the period 1922-68 was directed towards the achievement of a federal union of the West Indies which, alone of the possible communities of these years, had some potential for the establishment of a nation state. However, the movement was frustrated by many factors not the least of which were the very poverty and smallness of the societies which made union desirable. An additional problem was the failure, particularly in the largest unit of Jamaica, to involve the mass of the people in the federal idea and therefore to pursue an essentially elitist policy of negotiating with the Colonial Office which itself was actively involved in encouraging federation but without encouraging mass participation.[120] Furthermore the whole history of federalism and federal experiments in the West Indies shows two very destructive fears operating: the small islands' fear of being completely dominated by the larger territories owing to the considerable differences in size, resources and sophistication, and the large islands' fear – which is directly related to their own poverty – that they would have to carry the dependent economies of the small islands which still depend on budgetary assistance from Britain.

Another weakness of the federal movement, which would have to overcome the stronger identification at the territorial level, was the absence of immediate and strong incentives to unite, particularly the absence of any direct military threat from a source which the West Indies could hope to effectively resist. West Indian nationalists such as Marryshow, Cipriani, Manley, Adams, Gomes and Williams did believe that there were real gains in federation: namely, economic, political and constitutional. However, the gains were not obvious except for those of constitutional advance, and the Colonial Office considerably weakened the importance of this incentive by first of all allowing constitutional advance to continue at the territorial level whilst negotiations for federation were taking place, by insisting that the Federation of the West Indies be established as a non-self-governing territory with less responsibility for its own affairs than was enjoyed by some of its constituent units (namely Jamaica, Trinidad and Tobago, and Barbados), and finally of course the Colonial Office passed the death sentence on its own federal policy by conceding that Jamaica possessed in itself the criteria for independence. The short-sighted policy of the Colonial Office effectively removed the one clear incentive for federation, namely that if the units did not federate they could not advance to formal independence.

120 Lewis, op. cit., p. 352; Sir John Mordecai: *The West Indies: The Federal Negotiations* (London, 1968), p. 218 et seq; Munroe, op. cit., p. 189 and Chapter IV passim.

One finds that throughout the Third World there have been strong thrusts towards regional movements. This has often been an acknowledgement of the weakness of the state structures and economies of the individual states. The nationalist leaders in the West Indies, with obvious exceptions, did seek strength in unity but were undoubtedly hampered because the union would itself not be truly strong. Enthusiasm for union declined as leaders perceived that they might find themselves giving up control over a poor, small, internationally weak territory only in order to share control, or lose it altogether, in a federation which in real world terms would remain poor, small, and internationally weak. Further R.L. Watts argues in *New Federations: Experiments in the Commonwealth*, that the instability of many new federations is the result of a widespread trend against liberal-democratic forms of government, whilst federations are essentially liberal-democratic in their constitutional forms.[121] It is possible to argue that in the West Indies, where political control at the territorial level has tended to be strongly authoritarian, this style of political leadership and control would be far more difficult to exercise at a federal level, thereby creating further tension and instability.

However, while admitting the importance of the factors mentioned in contributing to the break-up of the federation, it will be argued that the most important single factor was the pursuit, by the middle class policy makers of the West Indies, of an economic strategy which was in contradiction to their political nationalism. This was the policy of industrialization by invitation: the direct encouragement of further foreign control over the separate economies of territories rather than attempting to diminish that control. Given the economic poverty of the region and its structural dependence on metropolitan countries, together with the colonial status at the time, it might well have been impossible to pursue any other line. Nevertheless, whether one takes the situation as being determined or not, the particular solution chosen was very much a class solution and it was opposed to the nationalist objective of federation.

The economic policy of incentives for and invitations to foreign capital to establish branch plants in the West Indies has so far failed to create jobs for the mass of the people. On the contrary, the introduction of capital-intensive techniques with new industries and their increasing adoption in the more traditional fields of agriculture has significantly increased the number of unemployed who, for the most part, have migrated to the cities. In other words it has not been a policy designed to satisfy the demand for work on the part of labour. On the other hand the policy has created employment opportunities for the middle class, but in their historic role as administrators, brokers

121 R.L. Watts, *New Federations: Experiments in the Commonwealth*. (Oxon, 1966), pp. 4-5.

and merchants rather than producers. There has, in fact, been rapid expansion in certain sectors which has had the effect of increasing the consumption possibilities of the middle class.

That this policy was, and still is, antithetic to the nationalist aim of a federation, is best illustrated by the arguments of Kari Levitt in her article 'Canada: Economic Dependence and Political Disintegration'.[122] Dr Levitt argues that 'The new pattern of North-South trade and investment based on resource development and branch plant manufacturing, does not require a strong central government. There is a Balkanization of the country. Regional government is concerned with regional prosperity. It cannot be the function of regional government to preserve national unity.'[123] She later writes: 'Political fragmentation on regional lines coincides with the interests of the corporations operating in resource and manufacturing industries. If provincial governments were to negotiate greatly increased shares of corporation tax, there could ensue a competitive scramble of incentives to entice foreign industry which could benefit nobody but these corporations.'[124]

Dr Levitt is describing the economic relationships which she perceives to be weakening the existing political framework of a federation which has been in existence for over a century. The Balkanization which is the result of the establishment of branch-plant economies was already present in the West Indies before the federation was established. To encourage more and more economic ties between the local economies and the metropolitan countries was to directly reduce the need for a united federation. Add to this the actual competition between the larger territories in incentives to foreign capital and the fissiparous tendencies of this policy are made clear. The Canadian federation is being strained by these relationships: the West Indies federation, which could be said to have never really got started, broke under the strain. The larger territories were committed by their leadership to pursuing an economic policy which increased the level of participation and control by foreign capital of their respective territories. A federation could only hinder the pursuit of this policy.

It is for this reason that this Introduction has argued that middle class nationalism, which saw the need for a federation to establish a national base for independence, was defeated by the pursuit by the same middle class of what they perceived to be in the economic interest of their class. Politically they sought unity, but a class-dictated economic policy forced them to follow a path which would perpetuate and even intensify the fragmentation which

122 Karie Levett, 'Canada: Economic Dependence and Political Disintegration', *New World Quarterly*, vol. IV, no. 2 (1968).

123 Ibid., p. 136.

124 Ibid., p. 137.

had characterized the region since its initial settlement.

To argue as many do today[125] that the federal venture was a mistake from beginning to end is to confuse failure with mistake. The federation was an undoubted failure, and its failure has long-term consequences for the future of independent government for the West Indies as a whole. To say that federation was a mistake is either to see some national sense in the fragmentation which exists at the moment; or to accept that there is no real independence for the West Indies and that the immediate interests of the middle class are in some way identifiable with the interests of the whole; or to look forward to a larger (and more perfect?) union of the Caribbean as a whole, and in addition to argue that this future union would in some way be inhibited by the existence of the Federation of the West Indies. However, for the fragmented West Indies to enter into a union, as separate units, with the other territories of the Caribbean which would include Cuba, the Dominican Republic, Haiti and Puerto Rico, could lead to some of the same tensions which existed between the larger and smaller territories in the defunct Federation. It has been argued that the Federation would have had a firmer footing had the Leeward/Windward group been amalgamated prior to union, so as to create greater parity between the federating units. In the same way it could be argued that a larger Caribbean Union would be better constituted with the English-speaking West Indies, especially of the Eastern Caribbean, forming a single unit.

The argument has been developed in this Introduction that the political background to constitutional change saw the establishment of the middle class either directly in positions of constitutional authority, or supporting trade union leaders. That, furthermore, in return for office and formal authority the political leaders of the West Indies were for the most part content to leave economic power in the hands of foreign capital, and that for aid in the consolidation of their broader class position they were even prepared to increase the control which foreign capital exercised – often through them as agents. In all this the middle class and the political leaders whom it controlled, and who cannot therefore be distinguished from the middle class, were clearly assisted by the Colonial Office, the United States government and private foreign economic interests.

Furthermore, despite the riots of the 1930s which briefly promised some real mass participation in politics, the new leaders operated in an essentially conservative and elitest role, perpetuating the authoritarian and personalist tradition of West Indian politics.

A critical event in West Indian history during this period was the suspension of the constitution of British Guiana in 1953. More clearly than any other occurrence this dramatically illustrates the real constraints which

125 In 1971

operated to limit the range of possibilities open to the political leaders of the colonies during this period. Prior to the suspension of the constitution all the evidence suggests that the People's Progressive Party (PPP) ministers were trying to precipitate a constitutional crisis to demonstrate that the half-way house of quasi-ministerial government was not really workable, unless the Guyanese leaders were prepared to leave all real initiative with the Governor and the British Government. They sought to invalidate the British view articulated by the Governor in his Speech from the Throne when he spoke of the need 'to prove to the world that the Constitution can not only work but will operate adequately and successfully. Only by doing so we can [sic] prove British Guiana's fitness for a further forward step towards full self-government.[126] The Guyanese ministers were of the firm opinion that they and only they were capable of ruling their country in its own best interest and that the divorce of responsibility from power, characteristic of transitional colonial constitutions, made such constitutions unworkable except on terms, laid down by Britain, which they were not prepared to accept.

The actual events which preceded the suspension of the constitution were firstly a sweeping victory by the PPP in the first election under universal adult suffrage in April 1953. Secondly a strike for bargaining rights was called by the PPP-led trade union, the GIWU. The strike was sufficiently effective to demonstrate that the GIWU did have a strong claim to the recognition which was denied by the sugar producers who were supported by the Governor. The PPP also proceeded to use their ministerial offices to introduce legislation which, while not especially radical, fell well within the imperial definition of unacceptable colonial radicalism.[127] Lastly the Minister of Communications, Mr Sidney King, launched a campaign to get signatures for a 'Patriotic Appeal to the Queen' to amend the constitution: hardly the clandestine action of a revolutionary intent on overthrowing the regime by violent, extra-legal means. Indeed the amendments being sought were remarkably modest: (1) the abolition of the nominated State Council, (2) the curtailment of the Governor's reserve powers, (3) the election of the Speaker of the House and (4) the removal of *ex-officio* members from the House. In fact these rather commonplace amendments, and the means adopted to achieve them, were far more reminiscent of the middle class reformism of other West Indian leaders than of Soviet communism. However, *The Times* of 5th October 1953 stated that 'These amendments if permitted would leave the colony open to single party rule by the People's Progressive Party.' Of course by the end of the decade African states were starting to get independence despite clear indications that what would follow would be single party rule.

126 Reported in *The Sunday Chronicle*, 31st May, 1953.

127 For the details of legislation and other events see the documents in Appendix A of this volume.

There was no evidence of disturbances or an attempted *coup d'etat.* Indeed, by early October there were reports of an orderly return to work. However, on 7th October 1953 *The Times* headlines read 'Danger of Communist Coup in British Guiana – Troops sent to Avert Risk of Bloodshed'. The news report following this quoted a Colonial Office announcement 'that if present developments there continued unchecked, *an attempt might be made,* by methods which were familiar in some parts of the world, to set up a Communist dominated state, and that this would lead to bloodshed'.[128] At the same time reports were of calm in Georgetown. There were no demonstrations and the PPP leaders were advising their followers to stay calm – calling for a boycott strike, non-fraternization with British troops and a boycott of British goods. Significantly J. Carter, leader of the conservative United Democratic Party (UDP) which had been routed in the general election, was quoted as saying that given eighteen months his party could fill the vacuum and that 'British officials hope that the PPP can gradually be deprived of mass support'.[129]

The Constitution was suspended and over six hundred troops despatched to British Guiana, and *The Times* tacitly admitted the weakness of any evidence suggesting a coup and that the real aim of British action was to suspend the Constitution in order to break the PPP. The newspaper reported that the troops were sent 'not so much to prevent any specific Communist coup as to prevent any outbreak of disorder and incendiarism when the decision to suspend the constitution was made known'. This highly dubious action was supported by the Conservative Party of Britain, by many of the British Labour Party, by the West Indian press and by all leading West Indian politicians who saw themselves as 'cold war warriors'.

However, the Guyanese newspapers saw quite clearly that the PPP was not threatening a Communist coup, nor even threatening the overthrow of the Constitution, but that they were endangering the favourable atmosphere for capital. An editorial of the *Sunday Argosy* months before the suspension of the Constitution argued that the PPP '*cannot radically change the Constitution, "nationalise" industry, or institute a revolution . . .*'[130] but that it could 'damage the Colony's credit', impede 'the progress of industry' and 'hamstring commerce'.[131] And with fine, unconscious irony the *Daily Argosy* of 13th May 1953 declared that 'All true Guianese have long enjoyed the democratic way of life and would not exchange it for another': this in a colony which had had an election under universal adult suffrage for the first time in its history only one month before, and which, prior to the suspension, had a

128 Italics added.
129 *The Times*, 12th October, 1953.
130 Italics in original.
131 *Sunday Argosy*, 22nd March, 1953.

constitution which still gave all real responsibility for government to the Imperial authorities.

The same newspaper (*The Daily Argosy*) wrote in an editorial of 6th October prior to the suspension, that an attempt to revoke the Constitution at this time would be 'both unjustified and unwise'. *The Argosy* continued to argue this even after the suspension – but it was the manner rather than the fact of revocation with which they disagreed. Their position was that only a crisis could justify suspension of the Constitution and the use of troops, that no crisis existed, and that therefore the Governor should have provoked a crisis by dismissing the PPP ministers, and then act. What emerges from this is that within British Guiana it was clearly recognized that there was no threatened coup, no real danger of the PPP ministers acting illegally but that, on political grounds, the PPP had to be pushed out of office – even if this meant resorting to questionable tactics.

The conservative opposition to the PPP was exemplified by the capitalist-owned newspapers of British Guiana, but their attitudes were echoed throughout the West Indies by political leaders who feared that the PPP action would affect their own chances for controlled constitutional advance and for receiving foreign capital.

The example of British Guiana in 1953 shows that within the context of the time any attempt at radicalism, any break with the conservative reformism of the other West Indian political leaders, could not succeed without the resort to what could only be a self-defeating violence, given the absence of arms of the size which would give the capacity for successful revolt. The People's National Party (PNP) of Jamaica showed a clear appreciation of the real limitations existing in colonial politics. In commenting on the crisis the PNP praised Kwame Nkrumah of the Gold Coast for putting aside his Marxism and working 'to develop his country, to lay a sound foundation for its political future and to win the right to a larger measure of self-government by a far-sighted understanding of the political realities of his own situation', and they blamed the PPP for 'not working their new Constitution for a future freedom which they could win by that work but could never hope to win by a force and a power they did not possess'.[132]

Whilst the PPP leaders could with some justice feel betrayed by their West Indian colleagues it is clear that their attempt at radicalism was premature given the fact that they did not have the capacity nor the intention to lead a war of national liberation. In this sense the conservative policy of other West Indian political leaders was right, but at the same time they created a situation where independence could bring only the shadow of self-determination and not its substance.

132 *Daily Gleaner*, 16th October, 1953.

So far this analysis has been concerned with political movements in the West Indies outside the international context. However, the events in British Guiana show that the international context is extremely relevant. In fact the action of the British government in 1953 is not really explicable except in the context of the cold war hysteria of the time. The Western powers were engaged in an intense power struggle with the Soviet bloc and, for the most part, the battlefronts were in the Third World. 1953 saw the fall of Dr Moussadeq in Iran after his attempt to nationalize the oil companies and overthrow the Shah at the same time; the Mau Mau were fighting in Kenya; the Viet Minh in Indo-China; Senator Joe McCarthy and John Foster Dulles were powerful in the USA, and in the same country the Rosenbergs were executed for treason with the unfortunate coincidence that this was Mrs Janet Jagan's maiden name; the Korean War was taking place; Italy and Yugoslavia were struggling over Trieste; Archbishop Wyscynsky was arrested in Warsaw; Communist insurgency was only just being brought under control in Malaya; Stalin died; and in Egypt the recent coup led to doubts over the future of the Suez Canal and the Sudan.

In this situation it was clearly impossible for Britain or the United States to tolerate, in the name of liberal democracy, the possibility that Dr Jagan might try to take British Guiana into the Soviet sphere of influence.

However, in outlining the political background to constitutional development in the region facts of the international scene, other than the cold war, have to be taken into account. First among these is the change of British colonial policy during this period – moving through ideas of trusteeship, to ideas of partnership and finally to acceptance of independence. Undoubtedly through much of the period 1922-68 Britain dragged its feet on the question of constitutional advance. However, the decline of the power of Western Europe *vis-à-vis* the rest of the world, speeded up by two wars; the forced recognition of the autonomy of the Dominions, and especially the struggles in India and Ireland; the loss of British power in the Middle East; the growth of colonial nationalism generally; the experiences of France in Indo-China and especially in Algeria; the failure to maintain law and order wherever aggressive nationalism was present, all contributed to the end of empire, and undoubtedly the West Indian nationalist movements benefited from this change of imperial climate. On the other hand it must be recognized that the strategic importance of these countries in the Caribbean and the Cuban revolution has meant that the granting of formal independence has not opened up the possibility of these territories pursuing genuinely independent policies.

Another question which needs to be considered is how far the internal politics of the West Indies were affected by international events. Clearly most of the dynamic was generated internally by the conditions of the mass of the people and the frustrations of the middle class. However, two world wars exposed West Indians, especially their soldiers, to new and radicalizing experiences. For example Cipriani was undoubtedly radicalized by the discrimination shown against his regiment in the First World War, and at the same time men were exposed to a less rigidly racially determined situation, to ideas of socialism, the evils of capitalism and the unity of the international proletariat.

Furthermore out of the First World War came the public affirmation of the idea of the right to self-determination of peoples. Russia claimed the right for herself and the Austro-Hungarian Empire was dismantled, while the anti-colonialism of the United States was, at this time, quite vocal. As Alfred Cobban wrote: 'It did not occur to the Allied governments that the propaganda they employed against the Central Empires would affect their own empires fundamentally, or that by proclaiming the principle of self-determination they had laid the axe at the roots of their own colonial domains.'[133]

During the same years, and clearly spurred on by the Bolshevik Revolution, there was the growth of international socialism and its anti-imperialism. This affected the West Indies directly especially through its intellectuals, and indirectly through the effect that these ideas had on opinion in Britain. Thus one finds the British Labour Party as the close ally of Marryshow, Cipriani, Critchlow, Adams and Manley. Clearly the wisdom of linking colonial movements with a metropolitan political party is very much in doubt. However, the Labour Party, especially its left wing, was truly radical, if not revolutionary, and during the inter-war years the West Indian national movements desperately needed some voice for there was a restricted franchise at home and very limited constitutions.

Also of direct importance to the development of West Indian nationalism were events taking place throughout the old empires – especially the British. First, the formal recognition of the Dominions as independent states within the Commonwealth in 1931 was of symbolic importance to the dependent Empire. Then the struggles for freedom in Ireland, India, Cyprus, the Middle East, Burma, the Philippines, Central America and the Caribbean were reported in the West Indies very widely – especially events in Ireland and India – and clearly provided encouragement, if not the original inspiration, to some movements. It is significant that Marcus Garvey's opening words in his address to the first UNIA convention in New York were those from a telegram being sent from the convention to De Valera, greeting him as President of the Irish Republic.

Thus world ideas and movements of nationalism, socialism and liberal democracy had their impact in the West Indies. How they were translated into movements can only be understood in the local context but their importance should not be overlooked, for together with the dynamic provided

133 Alfred Cobban, *National Self-Determination* (London, 1945), p. 124.

from within they led the territories to formal independence or associated statehood.

However, constitutional reality does not always coincide with political reality. Even the four independent territories of the West Indies still exhibit characteristics of rigidly stratified societies with gross inequalities of wealth and status, an alarming and growing rate of unemployment, overall poverty and economic dependence. The economies are still controlled from outside and therefore important decisions on the use of resources, the distribution of wealth, foreign policy are also controlled from outside. The institutions of government still have their legal basis in Orders in Council of the British Government. The political parties are still controlled by the middle class, being financed by private capital and only using as voting support the mass of the people, who are still basically apathetic and alienated from government. One finds that much of government time is still taken up with policing the community – the suppression of literature, the banning of individuals, and the withdrawal of passports. Guyana already has preventive detention legislation. In 1970 Barbados introduced legislation to control public meetings, some of the smaller islands followed suit, Trinidad and Tobago attempted to do the same and in Jamaica the same end is achieved by using existing police power.

Recently there has been a resurgence and development of black consciousness, most clearly exhibited in the Trinidad disturbances in 1970. Marcus Garvey had demonstrated that this was the most potentially powerful idea in West Indian politics. However, there is evidence that the old idea is being reinterpreted in the West Indian context as a world idea expressing the unity of all colonial peoples in a more coherent framework of theory than it previously had.

However, given the authoritarian tendencies in West Indian politics, the rigid and divided nature of their societies, the poverty and dependence of their economies, and the tendency towards extreme centralization in decision-making there is a clear danger that a premature eruption of the black masses, without further development of their political awareness, could lead to a fascist dictatorship of the left, whilst its more likely defeat could reinforce the more pronounced fascist tendencies exhibited on the right.

The most immediate danger in the author's opinion is that, given the factors mentioned above and the real insecurity of the West Indian 'broker' middle class, when that class perceives its position to be threatened from below, it will react in much the same way as did the plantocracy in 1866. In other words the middle class will voluntarily give up some of their existing constitutional rights, which are in any case rather weakly protected by the constitutions, to a completely authoritarian government either military or bureaucratic, in order to preserve their economic position.

CHAPTER 2

CONSTITUTIONAL POSITION IN 1922

A Extracts from Regulations for His Majesty's Colonial Service: Chapter I – Constitutions. (Colonial Office List. HMSO, London, 1922.)

1 Colonies and Protectorates

1 The British Colonies and Protectorates may be classified as follows:-

I Colonies possessing responsible government, now known as the self-governing Dominions, in which the Crown has only reserved the power of disallowing legislation and the Secretary of State for the Colonies has no control over any public officer except the Governor. In all matters affecting the internal affairs of such a Colony the Governor acts on the advice of Ministers who are responsible to the Legislature. These Colonies fall constitutionally into two groups:-

(i) Dominion of Canada, Dominion of New Zealand, Union of South Africa, Newfoundland

(ii) The Australian Commonwealth and its six component States.

II Colonies not possessing responsible government, in which the administration is carried on by public officers under the control of the Secretary of State for the Colonies; and Protectorates similarly controlled.

(i) Colonies possessing an elected House of Assembly and a nominated Legislative Council:-
Bahamas, Barbados, Bermuda.

(ii) Colonies possessing a partly elected Legislative Council, the constitution of which does not provide for an official majority:-
British Guiana, Cyprus.

(iii) Colonies possessing a partly elected Legislative Council, the constitution of which provides for an official majority:-

Ceylon, Fiji, Jamaica, Leeward Islands, Malta, Mauritius.

(iv) Colonies and Protectorates possessing a Legislative Council nominated by the Crown:-

British Honduras, East Africa Protectorate, Falkland Islands, Gambia, Gold Coast, Grenada, Hong Kong, Nyasaland Protectorate, St Lucia, St Vincent, Seychelles, Sierra Leone, Southern Nigeria, Straits Settlements, Trinidad.

In all the above Councils, except British Honduras, the constitution provides for an official majority.

The Legislative Councils of Gambia, Sierra Leone, and Southern Nigeria have power to legislate for the following Protectorates respectively:-

Gambia Protectorate, Sierra Leone Protectorate, Southern Nigeria Protectorate.

(v) Colonies and Protectorates without Legislative Council:-

Ashanti, Basutoland, Bechuanaland Protectorate, Gibraltar, Northern Nigeria, Northern Territories of the Gold Coast, St Helena, Somaliland, Swaziland, Uganda, Weihaiwei, Islands included under the Western Pacific High Commission.

In all these Colonies and Protectorates, except Bahamas, Barbados, Bermuda, British Honduras, and the Leeward Islands, the Crown has the power of legislating by Order in Council.

The territories in South Africa which are under the control of the British South Africa Company are not included in the above classification.

2 *The Governor*

2 In the case of Colonies, the officer appointed by the Crown to administer the Government is styled either:-

Governor-General and Commander-in-Chief,
Governor and Commander-in-Chief, or
Captain-General and Governor-in-Chief . . .

In these regulations the term "the Governor" includes all officers appointed to administer Governments, however styled . . .

4 The Governor is the single and supreme authority responsible to, and representative of, His Majesty. He is, by virtue of his Commission and the Letters Patent constituting his office, entitled to the obedience, aid and assistance of all military and civil officers . . .

13 The powers of every officer appointed to administer the government of a Colony or Protectorate are conferred, and his duties are defined, by His Majesty's Commission and the Instructions with which he is furnished. The following is a general outline of the nature of his powers and duties, subject to the special laws of each Colony:-

He is empowered to grant a pardon or respite to any criminal convicted in the colonial Courts of Justice and to remit any fines, penalties or forfeitures which may accrue to the King. It is his duty to transmit to the Secretary of State by the earliest opportunity a report on each case in which, after sentence of death, a pardon is granted or the capital sentence is remitted.

The moneys to be expended for the public service are issued under his warrant.

He has the power, in the King's name, of issuing writs for the election of Representative Assemblies and Councils, and of convoking, proroguing and dissolving legislative bodies.

He appoints, suspends and dismisses public servants in the Colony.

He is empowered to administer the appointed oaths to all persons, in office or not; whenever he may think fit, and particularly the oath of allegiance provided by 31 & 32 Vict. c. 72, s. 2.

He has the power of granting or withholding his assent to any Bills which may be passed by legislative bodies, but he is required, in the case of certain Bills, to reserve them for the signification of His Majesty's pleasure or to assent to them only if they contain a clause suspending their operation until they are confirmed by the Crown . . .

3 Councils and Assemblies

14 Legislative Councils nominated by the Crown generally consist in part of the principal executive officers of the Colony and in part of private persons appointed by name; the former being termed Official, and the latter Unofficial Members.

15 Legislative Councils which are partly elected, generally consist of Official and Nominated Members, appointed as in the preceding regulation, and of members elected by the inhabitants of the Colony.

16 The numbers respectively of Official, Unofficial or Nominated, and Elected Members are prescribed by the Letters Patent and Instructions to Governors . . .

18 Every law, vote or resolution the object or effect of which may be to dispose of or charge public revenue must be proposed by the Governor or with his consent.

19 A law comes into operation immediately on receiving the Governor's assent, unless some other date is prescribed by the law itself. The Crown, however, retains power to disallow it, and if this power be exercised the law ceases to have operation from the date at which notification of such disallowance is published in the Colony.

20 His Majesty's pleasure with regard to a law is signified through a Secretary of State, or by Order in Council where the constitution of a Colony so prescribes . . .

22 In Colonies possessing responsible government the Governor is empowered to appoint and remove members of the Executive Council, it being understood that Councillors who have lost the confidence of the local legislature will tender their resignation to the Governor or discontinue the practical exercise of their functions in analogy with the usage prevailing in the United Kingdom.

23 In other Colonies the Executive Council consists of certain principal officers of the Government with or without the addition of unofficial members. These Executive Councillors are either the holders of offices specified in the Governor's instructions or persons appointed in pursuance either of a Royal Warrant or of instructions from the Crown signified through a Secretary of State. The Governor may in cases of vacancies make provisional appointments, subject to the confirmation of the Crown. Members of the Executive Council can be dismissed by the Crown alone, but in case of urgency may be suspended by the Governor, who must, however, at once report fully to the Secretary of State the grounds of his action.

24 In such Colonies the Executive Council has the duty of assisting the Governor with its advice, and the Governor is required by his instructions to consult the Council in all matters of importance, except in cases of urgency (when it is his duty at the earliest practicable period to communicate to the Council the measures which he may have adopted with the reasons therefor), and in cases of such a nature that in his judgment the King's service would sustain material prejudice by consulting the Council thereon. Unless otherwise provided in any particular case by law or by his instructions, the Governor may act in opposition to the advice of the Council, but he is then required to report the reasons for his action to the Secretary of State by the first convenient opportunity.

B A description of the constitution of the Bahamas (Colonial Office List, HMSO, London, 1922, pp. 99-100.)

The Executive Council Government is conducted, under Letters Patent, by the Governor, aided by an Executive Council not exceeding 9 members. The Legislative authority resides in the Governor, a Legislative Council, nominated by the Crown, and a Representative Assembly of 29 members, elected for 15 districts by persons owning land of the value of £5, or occupying houses of the rental value of £2 8s. in New Providence, or half that amount in the Out Islands. The qualifications of electors are full age, a residence of 12 months, with land value £5; or being a house-holder of premises value £2 8s. in New Providence, or £1 4s. elsewhere, for six months. The qualification of Members is possession of an estate of real or personal property of the value of £200.

The Executive Council is composed partly of official and partly of unofficial Members who have a seat in one of the branches of the Legislature. In the absence of the Governor the Senior Member of the Executive Council (nominally the Colonial Secretary, *ex officio*) administers the Government.

C A description of the constitution of Barbados (Colonial Office List. HMSO, London, 1922, p. 110.)

The Colony possesses representative institutions, but not responsible Government. The Crown has only a veto on legislation, but the Home Government retains the appointment and control of public officers, except the Treasurer, who is an officer of the House of Assembly. The Legislature consists of a Governor, a Legislative Council, consisting of nine members appointed by the King, and a House of Assembly, having twenty-four members elected annually on the basis of a moderate franchise. The qualifications of members and electors are regulated by a Franchise Act, which became law in April, 1884, and which repeals all previous legislation on the subject. By this act a liberal extension of the franchise was granted, and 2,004 electors were registered under its provisions, the number previous to its enactment being only 1,641. This and other Acts relating to the franchise was consolidated by the Representation of the People Act, 1901. The only change made was the extension of the franchise to persons enjoying a pension of 50L. a year or more. The number of registered electors for the year 1920 was 2,308. The Executive part of the Government is vested in the Executive Council appointed by the Crown and consists of the Governor, the Colonial Secretary, the Attorney-General *ex officio,* . . . [the] Speaker of the House of Assembly, and . . . [the] President of the Legislative Council, and such other persons as may be nominated by the King, and the Executive Committee consisting of the members of the Executive Council *ex officio,* one member from the Legislative Council, and four members of the House of Assembly nominated annually by the Governor. This body introduces all money votes, prepares the estimates, and initiates all Government measures. The Governor of Barbados was for many years the Governor-in-Chief of the Windward Islands, consisting of Barbados, St Lucia, St Vincent, Grenada, and Tobago, but in 1885, by Royal Letters Patent, Barbados was separated from the other Windward Islands, and made a distinct Government.

D A description of the constitution of British Guiana (Colonial Office List. HMSO, London, 1922, p. 115.)

The Constitution, as it existed up to 1891, may be summed up very briefly. It consisted of a Governor, Court of Policy, and a Combined Court. The unofficial members of the Combined Court and Court of Policy were chosen by a College of Electors. The functions of an Executive and Legislative Council and House of Assembly were performed by the Governor and Court of Policy, except as regards taxation and finance, which were and still are dealt with by the Combined Court, composed of the Governor and Members of the Court of Policy, combined with the six Financial Representatives. The Court of Policy passes all laws and ordinances, except the Annual Tax Ordinance, which is passed by the Combined Court.

During 1891 an Act was passed, which came into force in 1892, effecting a considerable change in the constitution. By this Act the administrative functions of the Court of Policy were transferred to an executive council and the duties of the former became purely legislative.

The College of Electors was abolished, and the unofficial members have since been elected by the direct vote of the whole body of electors.

The Combined Court has the power of (1) imposing the Colonial taxes and auditing the public accounts; and (2) discussing freely and without reserve the items on the annual estimates prepared by the Governor in Executive Council; it can reduce or reject, but not increase, any item. The first of these powers is the birthright of the Combined Court, having been bestowed in 1796, when Governor Beaujon called the financial representatives into being, "with a right of voting only for the raising of colonial taxes and not further"; while the second is conferred periodically by His Majesty's Order in Council after each renewal of the Civil List and is coexistent with the Civil List. The Civil List has recently been renewed for five years from the 1st January, 1918.

The Court of Policy, under the new constitution, consists of the Governor, seven official members, and eight elected members. It may be prorogued or dissolved at any time by the Governor and in any case is dissolved at the end of five years, and a general election must be held within two months of the date of dissolution. The number of financial representatives, who with the Court of Policy form the Combined Court, remains unchanged (6).

The qualifications for members and electors are now contained in Ordinance 24 of 1909, and are too complex to be recapitulated here.

E A description of the constitution of British Honduras (Colonial Office List. HMSO, London, 1922, p. 124.)

. . . The settlement was declared a Colony on the 12th May, 1862, and a Lieutenant-Governor was appointed subordinate to the Governor of Jamaica. In 1870 the Legislative Assembly was abolished by a local enactment, and a Legislative Council substituted therefor, consisting of five official, and not less than four unofficial, members, with the Lieutenant-Governor as President. Since 1913 the Council contains five official and seven unofficial members. On the 31st October, 1884 Letters Patent were proclaimed constituting the office of Governor and Commander-in-Chief, which rendered the Colony independent of Jamaica. These were renewed by Letters Patent proclaimed on the 10th September, 1909.

The English Common Law and all statutes of the Imperial Parliament "in abrogation or derogation or in any way declaratory of the Common Law" passed before 1899 extend to the Colony as far as local circumstances render such extension suitable to, and subject to modification by Colonial ordinances. . . . Appeals to His Majesty in Council be regulated by Chapter 16 of the Consolidated Laws.

The Executive Council consists of the Governor, and six members, three of whom are *ex officio*, the other three appointed members.

F A description of the constitution of Jamaica (Colonial Office List. HMSO, London, 1922, p. 230.)

(In 1854) an Executive Committee was established. The latter was to act as a sort of Cabinet, especially as regards financial matters.

After the suppression of the rebellion in 1865, Governor Eyre, at the meeting of the Legislature, urged the unsuitability of the then existing form of Government to meet the circumstances of the community, and the necessity of making some sweeping change, by which a strong Government might be created. The Legislature responded by abrogating all the existing machinery of legislation, and left it to Her Majesty's Government to substitute any other form of Government which might be better suited to the altered circumstances of the Colony.

Accordingly a Legislative Council was, by Orders in Council of the 11th June, 1866, and 11th November, 1869, established, consisting of such numbers of official and unofficial members as Her Majesty might think fit. The numbers of each were six until 1878, when they were enlarged to eight, and a ninth was added in 1881.

By Order in Council dated 19th May, 1884, and Amending Order of

3rd October, 1895, the constitution was fixed in the following manner:-

The Council to consist of the Governor (with only a casting vote) and five *ex officio* members, viz: the Senior Military Officer, the Colonial Secretary, Attorney-General, Director of Public Works and Collector-General, and such other persons, not exceeding ten in number, as Her Majesty may from time to time appoint, or as the Governor may from time to time provisionally appoint, and fourteen persons to be elected as therein provided. The Council shall be dissolved at the end of five years from the last preceding general election, if it shall not have been previously dissolved.

There is also a Privy Council, with the usual powers and functions of an executive council. It consists of the Lieutenant-Governor, if any, the Senior Military Officer in command, the Colonial Secretary, and Attorney-General and such other persons as may be named by the King, or provisionally appointed by the Governor subject to the approval of His Majesty, but the number of members is not to exceed eight. The Governor is to preside at each meeting. and the Governor and two members form a quorum.

A special feature of this constitution is that nine elected members can carry any financial measure, while the unanimous vote of the whole fourteen elected members on other matters cannot be overridden by the other votes unless the Governor declares that such a decision is of paramount importance in the public interest.

G A description of the constitution of the Leewards Islands Federation (Colonial Office List. HMSO, London, 1922, p. 251.)

By "The Leeward Islands Act, 1871," one Executive and one Legislative Council, under one Governor, were constituted for the six (now five) presidencies. As reconstituted by the Federal Act No. 1 of 1899, the Legislative Council now consists of eight official and eight elective members. Three elective members are chosen by the unofficial members of the Legislative Council of Antigua, two by those of the Legislative Council of Dominica, and three by those of the Legislative Council of St Kitts and Nevis. They must be and continue members of their respective island councils. The official members are the Governor, the Colonial Secretary, the Attorney-General, the Auditor-General, the Administrators of St Kitts-Nevis and Dominica, and the Commissioners of Montserrat and the Virgin Islands.

The Legislative Council has concurrent legislative powers with the local legislatures on certain subjects specified in the Act, such as matters of property, mercantile and criminal law, the law relating to status, the maintenance of a general police force and a common convict establishment, quarantine, postal and telegraph affairs, currency, audit, weights and measures, education and the care of lunatics, all matters relating to immigration, copyright and patents, and its own constitution and procedure. Any island legislature is, in addition, competent to declare other matters to be within the competency of the general legislature. Any island enactment on such subjects is void if repugnant to an enactment of the general legislature, or may at any time be repealed or altered by one.

The Council meets at least once a year, at a place notified by proclamation, and no Council lasts more than three years. The session usually lasts for about one week.

The expenses of the federal establishments are voted by the Council, and apportioned among the Presidencies.

The Council has power to alter its constitution by an ordinary Act, to be reserved for the King's pleasure, and the King has power, by Order in Council, at any time to include any other West Indian Island in the federation, upon joint addresses from the Legislative Body of such island, and from the Council, on such terms and conditions in each case as are in the addresses expressed. This power has not actually been exercised, and the inclusion in the Colony of Sombrero, which had no legislative body, was effected as above mentioned under a different Act.

H A description of the constitution of Antigua (Colonial Office List. HMSO, London, 1922, pp. 253-4.)

On the 22nd March, 1898, the Legislative Council, which was previously partly elected and partly nominated by the Governor, passed an Act abrogating itself and substituting the Crown Colony System. The new Council consists of sixteen members, eight official and eight non-official, all nominated by the Governor under Royal Letters Patent. The Governor presides. By Ordinance No. 7, of 1910, the duration of the Council is limited to three years.

I A description of the constitution of St Christopher-Nevis (Colonial Office List. HMSO, London, 1922, pp. 256-7.)

In 1878 the single chamber constitution was repealed in St Kitts and in Nevis, and the Crown Colony form of government adopted in its stead, and in 1882 these two islands, with Anguilla, were united into one Presidency.

The office of Lieutenant-Governor, which existed until 1870, has been abolished, and the Presidency, in the absence thereform of the Governor, is under the immediate supervision of an Administrator, acting under his instructions.

There is one Executive Council for the Presidency, consisting of the Governor, the Administrator, certain *ex officio* members, and such other persons as His Majesty may from time to time appoint. The Legislative Council consists of six official and six nominated unofficial members, besides the Governor and the Administrator. Of the unofficial members not more than five shall be from among the people of St Kitts and Anguilla, and one at least from among the people of Nevis. The Governor, or, in his absence, the Administrator, or, in the absence of both of them, a member of the Council appointed in writing, presides, and the President of the Council enjoys an original and a casting vote. The Council meets at the town of Basseterre in St Kitts.

J A description of the constitution of Dominica (Colonial Office List. HMSO, London, 1922, p. 261.)

The Local Government is administered by an Administrator, aided by an Executive Council of 5 members. In July, 1898, the Legislative Assembly, which was previously partly elected and partly nominated, passed an Act abrogating itself, and substituting the Crown Colony system. The new council consists of twelve members, six officials and six non-officials, all nominated by the Governor under Royal Letters Patent. The Administrator presides in the absence of the Governor from the Presidency.

K A description of the constitution of Montserrat (Colonial Office List. HMSO, London, 1922, p. 263.)

Montserrat possessed a Legislative Council and Assembly as early as 1668. In 1861, these were replaced by a single Chamber of eight elected and four nominated members.

By an act of the Legislative Assembly, dated 24th December, 1866, and confirmed by Order in Council 26th February, 1867, this Chamber was replaced by a Legislative Council of not more than six nominated members. By Act No. 2, of 1902, which rescinded these Acts, the number of members was limited to four. Ordinance No. 4 of 1909 repealed No. 2 of 1902 and limited the tenure of office of the members of the Council to three years. Ordinance No. 2 of 1911 amended No. 4 of 1909 and increased the number of members to six.

L A description of the constitution of the Virgin Islands (Colonial Office List. HMSO, London, 1922, p. 265.)

In April, 1867, an Ordinance was passed to amend the Constitution of the Virgin Islands. It was enacted that a Legislative Council should be constituted, to consist of the Colonial Secretary and the Colonial Treasurer, and not more than three unofficial members, to be nominated by the Administrator of the Government. This Ordinance was repealed May 1st, 1902, under which the Governor of the Leeward Islands ordains the laws. There is also an Executive Council.

M A description of the constitution of Trinidad and Tobago (Colonial Office List. HMSO, London, 1922, p. 417.)

The Government is administered by a Governor, with an Executive Council of seven members. The legislative body is the Legislative Council of Trinidad and Tobago, which was reconstituted in 1898, and now consists of the Governor, the Colonial Secretary, the Attorney-General, the Solicitor-General, the Auditor-General, the Inspector-General of Constabulary, the Director of Public Works, the Surgeon-General, the Protector of Immigrants, the Receiver-General, and the Collector of Customs, and of such other persons (unofficial members) as the Governor may appoint. The unofficial members hold their seats for five years, and are at present eleven in number.

N A description of the constitution of the Windward Islands (Colonial Office List. HMSO, London, 1922, p. 441.)

Each Island retains its own institutions, and, when the Governor is absent, is presided over by a resident Administrator, who is also Colonial Secretary. There is no common legislature, nor common laws, revenue, or tariff. A Windward Islands Court of Appeal was set up in 1850 (13 & 14 Vict. c. 15), and abolished in 1920 by an Act (9 & 10 Go. V. c. 47), which set up a Court of Appeal for the West Indies, consisting of the chief justices of the several West Indian Islands except Jamaica. There is also a common audit system instituted in 1889.

O A description of the constitution of Grenada (Colonial Office List. HMSO, London, 1922, p. 443.)

Crown Colony Government was established in December, 1877. The Legislative Council now consists of six official members besides the Governor, and seven unofficial members nominated by the Crown. The members hold their seats for three years from the date of their appointment.

On the 17th March, 1885, letters patent were passed constituting anew the office of Governor of the Windward Islands, and on 1st June, 1885, Grenada became the headquarters of the Government, which includes the colonies of St Lucia and St Vincent.

P A description of the constitution of St Lucia (Colonial Office List. HMSO, London, 1922, p. 446.)

The Government is now conducted by an Administrator (who is subordinate to the Governor of the Windward Islands), aided by an Executive Council. The Legislature consists of the Administrator and a Council composed as the King may direct. Law is administered by a Chief Justice, from whom in civil cases there is an appeal to the West Indian Court of Appeal, and two magistrates, whose decisions are liable to review by the judge. In criminal cases tried in the Superior Court facts are decided upon by a jury of twelve as in England.

Q A description of the constitution of St Vincent (Colonial Office List. HMSO, London, 1922, p. 450.)

But this constitution [the Old Representative System] also was abrogated by an Act of the Local Legislature (confirmed by an Imperial Act, 39 and 40 Vict. c. 47), by which the future modelling of the constitution was left to the Crown. The Legislative Council now consists of official and unofficial members nominated and appointed by the Crown.

The several courts of the Colony, were, by an Ordinance of the Local Legislature passed in 1880, consolidated into one court, styled the Supreme Court of Judicature. The Chief Justice of the Colony is the sole Judge of this court.

Constitutional Position in 1922

R Extracts from Report of the Hon. E.F.L. Wood, M.P., on his visit to the West Indies and British Guiana, 1922 (Cmnd. 1679/1922.)

Chapter I – Constitutional

A The lines of Constitutional Development in the West Indies

Any investigation into the constitutional development of the West Indies reveals not only marked difference in the evolution of a common type, but also a singular variety of the type itself. In Barbados and in British Guiana, this variety of type is the product of historical circumstances, and in present conditions the Constitutions of these Colonies, with their qualities and defects, may be left out of consideration . . . British Honduras is also omitted from consideration, and therefore when reference is made to the West Indian colonies it implies Jamaica, the Leeward Islands, the Windward Islands and Trinidad.

At the present time, with the exception of Jamaica, all these colonies are administered under a system of pure Crown Colony Government i.e. by a legislature composed of:

1 an official majority, controlled by the Governor, responsible to the Secretary of State, and,

2 an unofficial element nominated by the Governor.

Of recent years a demand has been growing for a measure of elective representation, i.e. for the inclusion in the legislature of a number of persons chosen by direct election, and Lord Milner recently approved this principle in the case of Grenada, where however the change has not yet been brought into operation. The consession of this privilege to Grenada has been not unnaturally the occasion for similar demands from all the other islands and Colonies.

Jamaica is far advanced along the road of effective "representative" development, towards which the other Colonies are only just beginning to feel their way; but, in spite of these differences of growth, the main features of the problem affecting all West Indian communities are identical. Several reasons combine to make it likely that the common demand for a measure of representative government will in the long run prove irresistible. The wave of democratic sentiment has been powerfully stimulated by the War. Education is rapidly spreading, and tending to produce a coloured and black intelligensia, of which the members are quick to absorb elements of knowledge requisite for entry into learned professions, and return from travel abroad with minds emancipated and enlarged, ready to devote time and energy to propaganda among their own people. Local traditions of representative institutions reinforce these tendencies. In British islands these go back to the early days of European settlement; . . . among British colonies there is the present example of Jamaica with its powerful elective section and of Grenada about to enter upon the enjoyment of the first instalment of similar privileges . . .

In the British West Indies politics have not yet become in any way associated with "party". Each elective or nominated unofficial is still a unit. Collectively they form the "critics" of the Government but not in any sense an organised opposition.

CHAPTER 3

IMPERIAL DOCUMENTS - DEFINITION OF COLONIAL AND DOMINION STATUS

A The Colonial Laws Validity Act, 1865 c. 63. U.K. Public General Acts

(i) Extracts from the Report of the conference on the operation of Dominion Legislation and Merchant Shipping Legislation, 1929. (Cmnd. 3479/1929.)

5 Colonial Laws Validity Act, 1865.

45 The circumstances in which the Colonial Laws Validity Act, 1865, came to be enacted are so well known that only a brief reference to them is necessary in this Report.

46 From an early stage in the history of Colonial development the theory had been held that there was a common law rule that legislation by a Colonial Legislature was void if repugnant to the law of England. This rule was apparently based on the assumption that there were certain fundamental principles of English law which no Colonial law could violate, but the scope of these principles was by no means clearly defined.

47 A series of decisions, however, given by the Supreme Court of South Australia in the middle of the nineteenth century applied the rule so as to invalidate several of the Acts of the Legislature of that Colony. It was soon realized that, if this interpretation of the law were sound, responsible Government, then recently established by the release of the Australian Colonies from external political control, would to a great extent be rendered illusory by reason of legal limitations on the legislative power which were then for the first time seen to be far more extensive than had been supposed. The serious situation which thus developed in South Australia led to an examination of the whole question by the Law Officers of the Crown in England, whose opinion, while not affirming the extensive application of the doctrine of repugnancy upheld by the South Australian Court, found the test of repugnancy to

be of so vague and general a kind as to leave great uncertainty in its application. They accordingly advised legislation to define the scope of the doctrine in new and precise terms. The Colonial Laws Validity Act, 1865, was enacted as the result of their advice.

48 The Act expressly conferred upon Colonial Legislatures the power of making laws even though repugnant to the English common law, but declared that a Colonial Law repugnant to the provisions of an Act of the Parliament of the United Kingdom extending to the Colony either by express words or by necessary intendment should be void to the extent of such repugnancy.

(ii) The Colonial Laws Validity Act, 1865

An Act to remove Doubts as to the Validity of Colonial Laws
(29th June, 1865)

Whereas Doubts have been entertained respecting the Validity of divers Laws enacted or purporting to have been enacted by the Legislatures of certain of Her Majesty's Colonies, and respecting the Powers of such Legislatures, and it is expedient that such Doubts should be removed:

Be it hereby enacted by the Queen's most Excellent Majesty, by and with the Advice and Consent of the Lords Spiritual and Temporal, and Commons, in this present Parliament assemblied, and by the Authority of the same, as follows:

1 The Term 'Colony' shall in this Act include all of Her Majesty's Possessions abroad in which there shall exist a Legislature, as hereinafter defined, except the Channel Islands, the *Isle of Man*, and such Territories as may for the Time being be vested in Her Majesty under or by virtue of any Act of Parliament for the Government of *India*:

The Terms 'Legislature' and 'Colonial Legislature' shall severally signify the Authority, other than the Imperial Parliament or Her Majesty in Council, competent to make Laws for any Colony:

The Term 'Representative Legislature' shall signify any Colonial Legislature which shall comprise a Legislative Body of which One Half are elected by Inhabitants of the Colony:

The Term 'Colonial Law' shall include Laws made for any Colony either by such Legislature as aforesaid or by Her Majesty in Council:

An Act of Parliament, or any Provision thereof, shall, in construing this Act, be said to extend to any Colony when it is made applicable to such Colony by the express Words or necessary Intendment of any Act of Parliament.

The Term 'Governor' shall mean the Officer lawfully administering the Government of any Colony:

The Term 'Letters Patent' shall mean Letters Patent under the Great Seal of the United Kingdom of *Great Britain* and *Ireland.*

2 Any Colonial Law which is or shall be in any respect repugnant to the Provisions of any Act of Parliament extending to the Colony to which such Law may relate, or repugnant to any Order or Regulation made under Authority of such Act of Parliament or having in the Colony the Force and Effect of such Act, shall be read subject to such Act, Order or Regulation, and shall, to the Extent of such Repugnancy, but not otherwise, be and remain absolutely void and inoperative.

3 No Colonial Law shall be or be deemed to have been void or inoperative on the Ground of Repugnancy to the Law of *England*, unless the same shall be repugnant to the Provisions of some such Act of Parliament, Order or Regulation as aforesaid.

4 No Colonial Law, passed with the Concurrence of or assented to by the Governor of any Colony, or to be hereafter so passed or assented to, shall be or be deemed to have been void or inoperative by reason only of any Instructions with reference to such Law or the Subject thereof which may have been given to such Governor by or on behalf of Her Majesty, by any Instrument other than the Letters Patent or Instrument authorising such Governor to concur in passing or to assent to Laws for the Peace, Order, and good Government of such Colony, even though such Instructions may be referred to in such Letters Patent or last-mentioned Instrument.

5 Every Colonial Legislature shall have, and be deemed at all Times to have had, full Power within its Jurisdiction to establish Courts of Judicature, and to abolish and reconstitute the same, and to alter the Constitution thereof, and to make Provision for the Administration of Justice therein; and every Representative Legislature shall, in respect to the Colony under its Jurisdiction, have, and be deemed at all Times to have had, full power to make Laws respecting the Constitution, Powers, and Procedure of such Legislature; provided that such Laws shall have been passed in such Manner and Form as may from Time to Time be required by any Act of Parliament, Letters Patent, Order in Council, or Colonial Law for the Time being in force in the said Colony.

6 The Certificate of the Clerk or other proper Officer of a Legislative Body in any Colony to the Effect that the Document to which it is attached is a true Copy of any Colonial Law assented to by the Governor of such Colony, or of any Bill reserved for the Signification of Her Majesty's Pleasure by the said Governor, shall be *prima facie* Evidence that the Document so certified is a true Copy of such Law or Bill, and, as the Case may be, that such Law has been duly and properly passed and assented to, or that such Bill has been duly and properly passed and presented to the Governor; and any Proclamation purporting to be published by Authority of the Governor in any

Newspaper in the Colony to which such Law or Bill shall relate, and signifying Her Majesty's Disallowance of any such Colonial Law, or Her Majesty's Assent to any such reserved Bill as aforesaid, shall be *prima facie* Evidence of such Disallowance or Assent.

B. Extracts from the Summary of Proceedings of the Imperial Conference, 1926. (Cmnd. 2768/1926.)

(i) The Status of Great Britain and the Dominions

We refer to the group of self-governing communities composed of Great Britain and the Dominions. Their position and mutual relation may be readily defined. *They are autonomous Communities within the British Empire, equal in status, in no way subordinate one to another in any aspect of their domestic or external affairs, though united by a common allegiance to the Crown, and freely associated as members of the British Commonwealth of Nations.*

(ii) The Position of the Governor-General

In our opinion it is an essential consequence of the equality of status existing among the members of the British Commonwealth of Nations that the Governor-General of a Dominion is the representative of the Crown, holding in all essential respects the same position in relation to the administration of public affairs in the Dominion as is held by His Majesty the King in Great Britain, and that he is not the representative or agent of His Majesty's Government in Great Britain or of any Department of that Government.

It seemed to us to follow the practice whereby the Governor-General of a Dominion is the formal official channel of communication between His Majesty's Government in Great Britain and His Governments in the Dominions might be regarded as no longer wholly in accordance with the constitutional position of the Governor-General. It was thought that the recognised official channel of communication should be, in future, between Government and Government direct.

(iii) The Operation of Dominion Legislation

Our attention was also called to various points in connexion with the operation of Dominion legislation, which, it was suggested, required clarification. The particular points involved were:

(a) The present practice under which Acts of the Dominion Parliaments are sent each year to London, and it is intimated, through the Secretary of State for Dominion Affairs, that His Majesty will not be advised to exercise his powers of disallowance, with regard to them.

(b) The reservation of Dominion legislation, in certain circumstances, for the signification of His Majesty's pleasure which is signified on advice tendered by His Majesty's Government in Great Britain.

(c) The difference between the legislative competence of the Parliament at Westminster and of the Dominion Parliaments in that Acts passed by the latter operate, as a general rule, only within the territorial area of the Dominion concerned.

(d) The operation of legislation passed by the Parliament at Westminster in relation to the Dominions. In this connexion special attention was called to such Statutes as the Colonial Laws Validity Act. It was suggested that in future uniformity of legislation as between Great Britain and the Dominions could best be secured by the enactment of reciprocal Statutes based upon consultation and agreement . . .

On this point we propose that it should be placed on record that, apart from provisions embodied in constitutions or in specific statutes expressly providing for reservation, it is recognised that it is the right of the Government of each Dominion to advise the Crown in all matters relating to its own affairs. Consequently, it would not be in accordance with constitutional practice for advice to be tendered to His Majesty by His Majesty's Government in Great Britain in any matter appertaining to the affairs of a Dominion against the views of the Government of that Dominion.

The appropriate procedure with regard to projected legislation in one of the self-governing parts of the Empire which may affect the interests of other self-governing parts is previous consultation between His Majesty's Ministers in the several parts concerned.

On the question raised with regard to the legislative competence of members of the British Commonwealth of Nations other than Great Britain, and in particular to the desirability of those members being enabled to legislate with extra-territorial effect, we think that it should similarly be placed on record that the constitutional practice is that legislation by the Parliament at Westminster applying to a Dominion would only be passed with the consent of the Dominion concerned . . .

[We recommend that a Committee be set up] with terms of reference on the following lines:

'To inquire into, report upon, and make recommendations concerning:-

(i) Existing statutory provisions requiring reservation of Dominion legislation for the assent of His Majesty or authorising the disallowance of such legislation.

(ii) (a) The present position as to the competence of Dominion Parliaments to give their legislation extra-territorial operation.

(b) The practicability and most convenient method of giving

effect to the principle that each Dominion Parliament should have power to give extra-territorial operation to its legislation in all cases where such operation is ancillary to provision for the peace, order, and good government of the Dominion.

(iii) The principles embodied in or underlying the Colonial Laws Validity Act, 1865, and the extent to which any provisions of that Act ought to be repealed, amended, or modified in the light of the existing relations between the various members of the British Commonwealth of Nations as described in this Report.'

(iv) The Appeal to the Judicial Committee of the Privy Council

Another matter which we discussed, in which a general constitutional principle was raised, concerned the conditions governing appeals from judgements in the Dominions to the Judicial Committee of the Privy Council. From these discussions it became clear that it was no part of the policy of His Majesty's Government in Great Britain that questions affecting judicial appeals should be determined otherwise than in accordance with the wishes of the part of the Empire primarily affected. It was, however, generally recognised that, where changes in the existing systems were proposed which, while primarily affecting one part, raised issues in which other parts were also concerned, such changes ought only to be carried out after consultation and discussion.

C. Extracts from the Report of the Conference on the operation of Dominion Legislation and Merchant Shipping Legislation, 1929 (Cmd. 3479/1929.)

(i) The Disallowance and Reservation of Dominion Legislation.

(a) Disallowance.

18 The power of disallowance means the right of the Crown, which has hitherto been exercised (when occasion for its exercise has arisen) on the advice of Ministers in the United Kingdom, to annul an Act passed by a Dominion or Colonial Legislature.

19 The prerogative or statutory powers of His Majesty the King to disallow laws made by the Parliament of a Dominion, where such powers still subsist, have not been exercised for many years, and it is desirable that the position with regard to disallowance should now be made clear . . .

22 A distinction must, of course, be drawn between the existence of these provisions and their exercise. In the early stages of responsible government cases of disallowance occurred not infrequently merely for the reason that

the legislation disallowed did not commend itself on its merits to the Government of the United Kingdom. This practice did not however long survive, for it was realised that under the conditions of self-government the power of disallowance should only be exercised where grave Imperial interests were concerned, and that such intervention was improper with regard to legislation of purely domestic concern. In fact the power of disallowance has not been exercised in relation to Canadian legislation since 1873 or to New Zealand legislation since 1867; it has never been exercised in relation to legislation passed by the Parliaments of the Commonwealth of Australia or of the Union of South Africa.

23 The Conference agree that the present constitutional position is that the power of disallowance can no longer be exercised in relation to Dominion legislation. Accordingly, those Dominions who possess the power to amend their Constitution in this respect can, by following the prescribed procedure, abolish the legal power of disallowance if they so desire. In the case of those Dominions who do not possess this power, it would be in accordance with constitutional practice that, if so requested by the Dominion concerned, the Government of the United Kingdom should ask Parliament to pass the necessary legislation.

(b) Reservation.

26 Reservation means the withholding of assent by a Governor-General or Governor to a Bill duly passed by the competent Legislature in order that His Majesty's pleasure may be taken thereon.

27 Statutory provisions dealing with reservation of Bills passed by Dominion Parliaments may be divided into (1) those which confer on the Governor-General a discretionary power of reservation and (2) those which specifically oblige the Governor-General to reserve Bills dealing with particular subjects . . .

31 The power of reservation had its origin in the instructions given by the Crown to the Governor of a Colony as to the exercise by him of the power to assent to Bills passed by the colonial legislative body . . . . Its exercise has involved the intervention of the Government of the United Kingdom at three stages – in the instructions to the Governor concerning the classes of Bills to be reserved, in the advice tendered to the Crown regarding the giving or withholding assent to Bills actually reserved, and in the forms in use for signifying the Royal pleasure upon a reserved Bill. Reservation found a place naturally enough in the older colonial system under which the Crown exercised supervision over the whole legislation and administration of a Colony through Ministers in the United Kingdom. In the earlier stages of self-government supervision over legislation did not at once disappear, but it was exercised in a constantly narrowing field with the development of the principles and practice of responsible government. As regards the Dominions, it gradually came

to be realised that the attainment of the purposes of reservation must be sought in other ways than through the use of powers by the Government of the United Kingdom . . .

32 Applying the principles laid down in the Imperial Conference Report of 1926, it is established first that the power of discretionary reservation if exercised at all can only be exercised in accordance with the constitutional practice in the Dominion governing the exercise of the powers of the Governor-General; secondly, that His Majesty's Government in the United Kingdom will not advise His Majesty the King to give the Governor-General any instructions to reserve Bills presented to him for assent, and thirdly, as regards the signification of the King's pleasure concerning a reserved Bill, that it would not be in accordance with constitutional practice for advice to be tendered to His Majesty by His Majesty's Government in the United Kingdom against the views of the Government of the Dominion concerned.

33 In cases where there is a special provision requiring the reservation of Bills dealing with particular subjects, the position would in general fall within the scope of the doctrine that it is the right of the Government of each Dominion to advise the Crown in all matter relating to its own affairs and that consequently it would not be in accordance with constitutional practice for advice to be tendered to His Majesty by His Majesty's Government in the United Kingdom in any matter appertaining to the affairs of a Dominion against the views of the Government of that Dominion.

34 The same principle applies to cases where alterations of a Constitution are required to be reserved.

35 As regards the continued existence of the power of reservation, certain Dominions possess the power by amending their Constitutions to abolish the discretionary power and to repeal any provisions requiring reservation of Bills dealing with particular subjects, and it is, therefore, open to those Dominions to take the prescribed steps to that end if they so desire.

36 As regards Dominions that need the co-operation of the Parliament of the United Kingdom in order to amend the provisions in their Constitutions relating to reservation, we desire to place on record our opinion that it would be in accordance with constitutional practice that if so requested by the Dominion concerned the Government of the United Kingdom should ask Parliament to pass the necessary legislation.

(ii) The Extra-Territorial Operation of Dominion Legislation.

37 In the case of all Legislatures territorial limitations upon the operation of legislation are familiar in practice. They arise from the express terms of statutes or from rules of construction applied by the Courts as to the presumed intention of the Legislature, regard being had to the comity of nations and other considerations. But in the case of the legislation of Dominion

Parliaments there is also an indefinite range in which the limitations may exist not merely as rules of interpretation but as constitutional limitations. So far as these constitutional limitations exist there is a radical difference between the position of Acts of Parliament of the United Kingdom in the United Kingdom itself and Acts of a Dominion Parliament in the Dominion.

38 The subject is full of obscurity, and there is conflict in legal opinion as expressed in the Courts and in the writings of jurists both as to the existence of the limitation itself and as to its extent. There are differences in Dominion Constitutions themselves which are reflected in legal opinion in those Dominions. The doctrine of limitation is the subject of no certain test applicable to all cases, and constitutional power over the same matter may depend on whether the subject is one of a civil remedy or of criminal jurisdiction. The practical inconvenience of the doctrine is by no means to be measured by the number of cases in which legislation has been held to be invalid or inoperative. It introduces a general uncertainty which can be illustrated by questions raised concerning fisheries, taxation, shipping, air navigation, marriage, criminal law, deportation, and the enforcement of laws against smuggling and unlawful immigration. The state of the law has compelled legislatures to resort to indirect methods of reaching conduct which, in virtue of the doctrine, might lie beyond their direct power but which they deem it essential to control as part of their self-government.

39 It would not seem to be possible in the present state of the authorities to come to definite conclusions regarding the competence of Dominion Parliaments to give their legislation extra-territorial operation; and, in any case, uncertainty as to the existence and extent of the doctrine renders it desirable that legislation should be passed by the Parliament of the United Kingdom making it clear that this constitutional limitation does not exist.[1]

40 We are agreed that the most suitable method of placing the matter beyond possibility of doubt would be by means of a declaratory enactment in the terms set out below passed, with the consent of all the Dominions, by the Parliament of the United Kingdom . . .

43 After careful consideration of possible alternatives, we recommend that the clause should be in the following form:

> 'It is hereby declared and enacted that the Parliament of a Dominion has full power to make laws having extra-territorial operation.' . . .

(iii) Merchant shipping legislation.

91 Our general conclusions on the Operation of Dominion Legislation, including the recommendations regarding extra-territorial effect of Dominion

1 See Keith, *Responsible Government in the Dominions* (1928), p. 321-38 (Footnote in the original).

laws, the Colonial Laws Validity Act, 1865, reservation and disallowance, are applicable to the constitutional position of legislation affecting merchant shipping.

92 When these conclusions are given effect to, and the restrictions imposed on Dominion Parliaments by Sections 735 and 736 of the Merchant Shipping Act, 1894, are removed by the Parliament of the United Kingdom, which we recommend should be done, there will no longer be any doubt as to the full and complete power of any Dominion Parliament to enact legislation in respect of merchant shipping, nor will Dominion laws be liable to be held inoperative on the ground of repugnancy to laws passed by the Parliament of the United Kingdom.

93 The new position will be that each Dominion will, amongst its other powers, have full and complete legislative authority over all ships while within its territorial waters or engaged in its coasting trade; and also over its own registered ships both intra-territorially and extra-territorially. Such extra-territorial legislation, will, of course, operate subject to local laws while the ship is within another jurisdiction . . .

D. The Statute of Westminster, 1931 c. 4 U.K. Public General Acts.

An Act to give effect to certain resolutions passed by Imperial Conferences held in the years 1926 and 1930. (11 December, 1931.)

Whereas the delegates of His Majesty's Governments in the United Kingdom, the Dominion of Canada, the Commonwealth of Australia, the Dominion of New Zealand, the Union of South Africa, the Irish Free State and Newfoundland, at Imperial Conferences holden at Westminster in the years of our Lord nineteen hundred and twenty-six and nineteen hundred and thirty did concur in making the declarations and resolutions set forth in the Reports of the said Conferences:

And whereas it is meet and proper to set out by way of preamble to this Act that, inasmuch as the Crown is the symbol of the free association of the members of the British Commonwealth of Nations, and as they are united by a common allegiance to the Crown, it would be in accord with the established constitutional position of all the members of the Commonwealth in relation to one another that any alteration in the law touching the Succession to the throne or the Royal Style and Titles shall hereafter require the assent as well of the Parliaments of all the Dominions as of the Parliament of the United Kingdom:

And whereas it is in accord with the established constitutional position that no law hereafter made by the Parliament of the United Kingdom shall extend to any of the said Dominions as part of the law of that Dominion otherwise than at the request and with the consent of that Dominion:

And whereas it is necessary for the ratifying, confirming and establishing of certain of the said declarations and resolutions of the said Conference that a law be made and enacted in due form by authority of the Parliament of the United Kingdom:

And whereas the Dominion of Canada, the Commonwealth of Australia, the Dominion of New Zealand, the Union of South Africa, the Irish Free State and Newfoundland have severally requested and consented to the submission of a measure to the Parliament of the United Kingdom for making such provision with regard to the matters aforesaid as is hereafter in this Act contained:

Now therefore, be it enacted by the King's most Excellent Majesty by and with the advice and consent of the Lords Spiritual and Temporal, and Commons, in this present Parliament assembled, and by the authority of the same, as follows:-

1 In this Act the expression 'Dominion' means any of the following Dominions, that is to say, the Dominion of Canada, the Commonwealth of Australia, the Dominion of New Zealand, the Union of South Africa, the Irish Free State and Newfoundland.[2]

2(1) The Colonial Laws Validity Act, 1865, shall not apply to any law made after the commencement of this Act by the Parliament of a Dominion.

(2) No law and no provision of any law made after the commencement of this Act by the Parliament of a Dominion shall be void or inoperative on the ground that it is repugnant to the Law of England, or to the provisions of any existing or future Act of Parliament of the United Kingdom, or to any order, rule or regulation made under any such Act, and the powers of the Parliament of a Dominion shall include the power to repeal or amend any such Act, order, rule or regulation in so far as the same is part of the law of the Dominion.

3 It is hereby declared and enacted that the Parliament of a Dominion has full power to make laws having extra-territorial operation.

4 No Act of Parliament of the United Kingdom passed after the commencement of this Act shall extend, or be deemed to extend, to a Dominion as part of the law of that Dominion, unless it is expressly declared in that Act that that Dominion has requested, and consented to, the enactment thereof.

5 Without prejudice to the generality of the foregoing provisions of this Act, sections seven hundred and thirty-five and seven hundred and thirty-six of the Merchant Shipping Act, 1894, shall be construed as though reference therein to the Legislature of a British possession did not include reference to the Parliament of a Dominion.

2 Each time a colony becomes independent the Statute of Westminster is amended by the addition of the new state to the list of Dominions. Newfoundland is, of course, no longer listed since it became a province of Canada.

6 Without prejudice to the generality of the foregoing provisions of this Act, section four of the Colonial Courts of Admiralty Act, 1890 (which requires certain laws to be reserved for the signification of His Majesty's pleasure or to contain a suspending clause), and so much of section seven of that Act as requires the approval of His Majesty in Council to any rules of Court for regulating the practice and procedure of a Colonial Court of Admiralty, shall cease to have effect in any Dominion as from the commencement of this Act.

[Sections 7, 8 and 9 deal specifically with Canada, Australia and New Zealand.]

10(1) None of the following sections of this Act, that is to say, sections two, three, four, five and six, shall extend to a Dominion to which this section applies as part of the law of that Dominion unless that section is adopted by the Parliament of the Dominion, and any Act of that Parliament adopting any section of this Act may provide that the adoption shall have effect from the commencement of this Act or from such later date as is specified in the adopting Act.

(2) The Parliament of any such Dominion as aforesaid may at any time revoke the adoption of any section referred to in subsection (1) of this section.

(3) The Dominions to which this section applies are the Commonwealth of Australia, the Dominion of New Zealand and Newfoundland.

11 Notwithstanding anything in the Interpretation Act, 1889, the expression 'Colony' shall not, in any Act of Parliament of the United Kingdom passed after the commencement of this Act, include a Dominion or any Province or State forming part of a Dominion.

12 This Act may be cited as the Statute of Westminster, 1931.

CHAPTER 4

THE DEVELOPMENT OF REPRESENTITIVES AND RESPONSIBLE GOVERNMENT

It was decided to arrange the documents of this chapter under the headings of the development of representative institutions and the development of responsible institutions. This obviously corresponds with the division between legislative and executive functions of government. It also corresponds very roughly with the chronology of development of colonial constitutions in the West Indies, advances in representation, such as increases in the proportion of elected members in the legislature and the broadening of the franchise, preceding grants of greater responsibility for executive decisions.

There are however, overlappings both in time and in relationship: limited grants of responsibility often preceding grants of fully representative legislatures (in this work meaning universal adult suffrage with at least one house of the legislature being wholly elected); and the linking of grants of responsibility with greater representation in the minds of both metropolitan and colonial politicians. For these reasons neither a simple division between legislature and executive nor a chronological presentation of documents was appropriate. In any case chronology could not be maintained since the many territories did not have, and still do not have, the same type of constitution at the same point of time. Therefore chronological sequence is not adhered to in either of the main sections, and a third section is introduced using sources which show that the development of responsibility for the conduct of government is related to increases in representation.

PART I
THE RELATIONSHIP BETWEEN RESPONSIBLE AND REPRESENTATIVE GOVERNMENT

A. Extracts from the Report of the Hon. E.F.L. Wood, M.P., on his visit to the West Indies and British Guiana, 1922. (Cmnd. 1679/1922.)

Mr. Churchill,

My voyage to the West Indies on your behalf was undertaken, as you will recollect, in consequence of representations made to you from the House of Commons in the course of last summer, which in turn expressed the growing demand in several of the West Indian colonies for the bestowal of a measure of representative government . . .

Diverse as they [the West Indies] are in almost every other respect, there is no difference in the matter of loyalty to the Throne and to the person of His Majesty the King. This sentiment pervades everything, and finds expression in every form and on all occasions. It is the feature of our tour which stands out in boldest outline, and which I recall with the greatest satisfaction. The effect of it is constantly to direct the gaze of the West Indian communities towards Britain and towards the visible symbol of unity that the person of the Sovereign affords. The worth of such an influence in maintaining Imperial solidarity and in counteracting the possible growth of other tendencies can hardly be placed too high, and it is well that citizens of the United Kingdom should appreciate it . . .

The whole history of the African population of the West Indies inevitably drives them towards representative institutions fashioned after the British model. Transplanted by the slave trade or other circumstances to foreign soil, losing in the process their social system, language and traditions, and, with the exception of some relics of obeah, whatever religion they may have had, they owe everything that they have now, and all that they are, to the British race that first enslaved them, and subsequently to its honour restored to them their freedom. Small wonder if they look for political growth to the only source and pattern that they know, and aspire to share in what has been the peculiarly British gift of representative institutions.

Further, it must be borne in mind that in the West Indies there is a considerable population of mixed stock who while coloured in appearance, possess a large infusion of European blood. Those of mixed race throw up not a few individuals of somewhat exceptional capacity and intelligence, who play a prominent part in the public life of their communities. We shall be wise if, with these facts before us, we take steps to build upon the foundation of the remarkable loyalty to the Throne by which these peoples are inspired, and avoid the mistake of endeavouring to withhold a concession ultimately inevitable until it has been robbed by delay of most of its usefulness and of its grace . . .

. . . It should be stated at once that neither in Jamaica nor elsewhere, is there any demand for responsible government in the strict sense of the word, nor within measurable distance of time could such a demand rightly be conceded. Though not the only ones there are four principal considerations that are prohibitive. Notably in Trinidad, but to a considerable extent also in the other islands, the population is of various colour, religion and race. Great blocks of it are backward and politically undeveloped. For all this mosaic of humanity the Crown, through the Secretary of State, is in the position of responsible Trustee: a responsibility of which it cannot morally divest itself until it is satisfied that it can delegate the charge to hands of not less certain impartiality or integrity than its own. Coloured and black well-wishers of their own kind will tell you that that time is not yet.

Secondly, the absence of a class of leisured citizens who could take an active part in political life makes it necessary for the constitution to contain an element such as the official services supply, independent of localities and providing that detachment of outlook necessary for the effective conduct of the services controlled by Government. The comparative smallness and isolation of many of the islands make it questionable whether the experiment of responsible government would be practicable without a greater change in their economic position than their physical conditions seem to allow. However the conditions referred to involve the further risk, which is no small one, that the only effect of granting responsible government might be to entrench in power a financial oligarchy, which would entirely dominate the Colony and use their position for the sole purpose of benefiting one class instead of the community as a whole.

Thirdly, the controlling influence of the Secretary of State is essential for securing some uniformity of administration among these adjacent colonies, whose actions must directly act and react on one another. If the fullness of time should ever lead to West Indian federation or anything analogous, this argument will disappear; but hitherto, the attempts to encourage West Indian unity have been slow and halting.

A fourth factor which makes "responsible government" out of the question at the present stage of political development is the small proportion of the electorate who in fact exercise the franchise. Even in Jamaica, where interest in politics is most widely diffused, and where the press is efficiently conducted, the number of registered voters who actually go to the poll is comparatively small. The majority of the Jamaican electors are coloured or negro small peasant proprietors, for the bulk of whom politics do not yet appear to be a matter of much concern. This limitation is even more forcibly evidenced in islands where the diffusion and standard of education are less advanced . . .

Given then on the one hand that the control of the Secretary of State must continue in effective form, and on the other that the movements towards elective representation must be met, it would seem clear that this can best be done by following existing precedents and including in the Legislatures a certain number of members chosen by direct election . . .

. . . the main stages of such evolution may be briefly suggested.

1 The first stage would be on the basis approved for Grenada by such adjustment of numbers as will, while leaving the official "bloc" in a clear majority, give place to "elected members" by reducing the number of nominated unofficials.

2 The next stage would appear to be the adjustment of numbers with the effect of transferring the majority held by the official "bloc" to the hands of the elected and nominated elements conjointly. Such a redistribution of numbers, under which, of course, the nominated unofficial element would retain complete liberty of voting as it liked – a liberty which it now possesses in all colonies save Jamaica – would at the same time afford reasonable likelihood that on grave matters the responsible element in the community represented by the nominated members would be found in support of the Government, and thus furnish a majority if, on the most unfavourable hypothesis, the elected members were unanimously against it. In this connection it is worthy of note that it is desirable to establish definitely the liberty of nominated unofficial members in Jamaica to vote as they like. Only in this way is it possible to relieve nominated members of the stigma, which detracts so much from their usefulness both in the community and in debate, that they are mere dummies under the thumb of the Governor to whom it is useless to appeal by discussion or by argument.

It may be that in due course further developments in accordance with these principles may be possible, necessary and desirable. In some respects Jamaica, if the general suggestions advanced for the treatment of the Jamaica problem are approved, will furnish an example of a more advanced type of constitutional structure. But the conditions of Jamaica may be said to be exceptional, and proposals to those conditions may not necessarily be the best for universal application. Every measure of constitutional advance must call for prudent and deliberate action, and a careful review of all the circumstances of the time. It is unwise therefore where we have little experience to guide us, to attempt prophesies in the still distant future. On the lines of 1 and 2 above, it will be possible to meet the just demands for a measure of elective representation, and to take the first steps in associating the people directly with the task of their own government. What I have seen of the elected members of the Legislative Council of Jamaica, taken as a whole, gives me no reason to doubt the essential sanity of the electorate in their choice of representatives. Speaking generally, the body of elected members appeared to be animated by a high sense of public duty, and a full consciousness of their responsibilities as a partner in the business of government. Moreover, the share which they take in carrying out their functions establishes a direct link between the Government and the people which is of great value in promoting mutual confidence and general political interest.

But in every case it is for reasons above given essential to preserve unimpaired the ultimate control of the Secretary of State. In state 2 where the Government would no longer control an unofficial majority, this can best be done by entrusting the Governor with the power of carrying in the last resort by the votes of *ex-officio* and nominated official members only, measures or votes declared to be "essential to the good Government of the colony", such action to be matter of reference for confirmation or disallowance by the Secretary of State. In every case also it will be for obvious reasons desirable to retain in the Governor's hands the power of nomination up to whatever may be the appropriate number, in order to secure the due representation of elements in the community that might otherwise be excluded. Within these limits it should be the constant object of reforms to associate the power that attaches to the elected element from popular choice with as great a measure of responsibility as possible. Not the least of the causes that tend to clog the wheels of government in Jamaica is the complete divorce of responsibility from power in the case of the fourteen elected members. It is, therefore, suggested that in order to bridge the gulf between responsible government which is, *ex hypothesi*, impossible on the one hand and representative government with no sense of responsibility on the other, it should be clearly laid down in a public despatch to all Governors that, except in cases of extreme urgency, whenever all the elected members of the Council are unanimous in opposition to a Government proposal, such proposal should be referred, along with a statement of the dissentients' case, to the Secretary of State for his decision.

No attempt has been made to discuss the question of including elected representatives in the Executive Councils. In the main the functions of those bodies are purely advisory, and where they are composed jointly of official and nominated unofficial members, there is nothing to prevent a Governor from nominating one or more of the elected members to serve upon them. It must be recognised that, desirable as it may be, as political experience matures, to initiate the elected element by progressive stages into the inner work of government by including some of their members on the Executive Council, the position of an elected member on an Executive Council with the majority of which he perpetually disagrees, or alternatively the position of executive councillors perpetually over-riding by a majority the elected members sitting there, would rapidly become impossible. The only remedy, i.e. that of collective responsibility of a Cabinet through Parliament to a single authority, the electorate is ruled out by the denial of responsible government; and it therefore becomes a question of balance of advantage. Does the gain to be expected from the inclusion of elected members in an Executive Council outweigh the possible disadvantages arising from the admission of political opponents into the sanctum of government . . .

JAMAICA

. . . I will summarise a scheme for reform which we discussed confidentially with the Governor and the Attorney General and which received their general assent.

1 *The Central Government*

(a) The Privy Council to remain constituted as at present.

(b) A new Executive Committee to be set up (the necessary alterations being made in the instruments to effect the requisite constitutional change). This Committee to be "advisory" to the Governor and to deal with such matters, financial or other, that he may desire to bring before it. In practice it may be anticipated that all financial matters, and projected legislation, will be referred to this body.

This new Executive Committee to be composed as follows:

(1) The Governor.

(2) The Officer Commanding the Troops, the Colonial Secretary, and the Attorney General – i.e. three senior officials ex officio, and two other officials who would usually be the Collector General and the Director of Public Works, but the Governor should have power to select whichever two officials he might consider at the time to be personally most suitable, provided that one of the two is a financial officer.

(3) Two persons who at the time of their nomination are nominated non-official members of the Legislative Council, to be selected by the Governor for three years, with power to re-nominate for one further period of three years, but no longer until a further period of three years had elapsed.
(NOTE: It is important that the Governor should be able to get in fresh blood without appearing to imply censure by changing a nomination of this kind.)[1]

1 The Acting Governor of the Leeward Islands: "We have to welcome a number of new faces on the unofficial side, as a ruling of the Secretary of State,

(4) Four elected members of the Legislative Council to be selected by the Governor from a panel of seven elected, at the commencement of each new Council, from amongst their number by the fourteen elected members by proportional representation, and to serve on the Committee for the term of the Legislative Council.

(c) The Legislative Council to consist of:-

(1) The Governor with original and casting vote.

(2) The O.C. Troops, the Colonial Secretary and the Attorney General, ex-officio.

(3) Two other official members who should usually be the Collector General and the Treasurer, but the Governor should have power to choose whichever head of the more important departments he considered personally most suitable, one at least being a financial officer.

(4) Five nominated non-officials to be nominated by the Governor for the life of the Council, eligible for re-nomination in a new Council and free to vote as they please.

(5) Fourteen elected members as at present.

If this constitution is adopted the special power of the "nine" elected members in finance and the "unanimous" power in legislation should be abolished,[2] and all the questions decided by majority vote . . .

undoubtedly a wise ruling, has declared that henceforward at regular intervals there shall be changes of personnel in the Council; but while we realise that the underlying principle is a sound one we cannot but regret that the inevitable result has been that we have suffered the loss of members some of whom have given loyal, devoted, and valuable service for more than half a lifetime. It is for the new members to keep up the traditions that have been so worthily established by those who have now retired, and this I have no doubt they will do, for we have been so fortunate as to secure the services of five gentlemen who are eminent in the agricultural and industrial life of the community, and who have always shown themselves zealous for the advancement of this fair island of Antigua." (From his address to the Legislative Council of Antigua, on 26th April, 1923. *Leeward Islands Gazette,* 1923, p. 111.)

2 When united, nine elected members of the Legislative Council could veto any financial measure before the Council, and a similar power over ordinary legislation existed when all fourteen elected members were unanimous in their opposition. The veto of the elected members could only be over-ridden by the Governor declaring the matter to be of "paramount importance to the public interest". If the Governor exercised this power then he was constitutionally bound to forward immediately a detailed account of the circumstances to the Secretary of State for the Colonies. See Ronald V. Sires, "The Jamaica Constitution of 1884", *Social and Economic Studies,* vol. 3, no. 1 (June 1954), and Arthur E. Burt, "The First Instalment of Representative Government in Jamaica, 1884", *Social and Economic Studies,* vol. 11, no. 3 (September 1962).

This will place the elected members in a majority in the Council and by itself would leave the Governor with only six votes at his command, without counting his casting vote. However important the matter might be, he would be unable to carry measures which in his judgment were essential to enable him properly to discharge his duty as the responsible head of the administration. On the other hand the majority of the Council cannot effectively assume responsibility for the results of their action. Under responsible government the ministry of the day, ex hypothesi, commands a majority on all vital questions; if it does not it makes way for a ministry which does. Under representative government no such direct combination of power with responsibility is possible. It is, therefore, essential that there should be in the responsible head of the administration a reserve power to carry into effect the official policy in matters of first rate importance. This power is not irresponsible. It is exercised subject to the directions and control of the Secretary of State as the authority ultimately responsible for the administration of the Colony. In view of these considerations, it is usual in colonies not possessing responsible government to give power to the Governor, in grave matters and in the last resort, to put into effect measures which he and the Secretary of State consider essential for the well-being of the Colony, when public order or public faith or other first essentials of good government are in question. This object would be secured if in the Order in Council power is reserved to the Governor, when he is of the opinion that the passing of any bill, or any clause of it, or any amendment to any such bill, or of any resolution or vote, is essential to the good government of the colony, to make a formal notification to that effect, and if it were provided that, upon such formal notification, only the votes of ex-officio members and nominated official members shall be recorded, and that the bill etc. shall be deemed to have been passed by the Council if a majority of the votes of such ex-officio and official members shall be recorded in its favour. It should be laid down by way of general instruction to the Governor that resort should not be had to the exercise of this reserve power except when a serious issue or an important question of principle is at stake, and the Governor should also be instructed in every case in which he exercises his reserve power to report to the Secretary of State his reasons for doing so, and to afford the unofficial members an opportunity of stating at the same time their view of the matter for the Secretary of State's information. It may confidently be anticipated that, except in case of real urgency, no Governor will exercise the reserve power without first consulting the Secretary of State. On the other hand, to lay on him any formal obligation to do so in advance might fatally hamper the Colonial Government at a critical moment. Of course, any exercise of the reserve power will be subject to disallowance by the King, acting on the advice of the Secretary of State, in the same way as any legislative measure; and, in addition, it will be open to the Secretary of State, if he thinks fit, to give executive directions to the Governor to amend, repeal, or otherwise alter the action taken by him. If before any vote is taken the Governor declares that he intends to utilise this reserve power, he should have the right to adjourn the debate without question put, either for the purpose of referring the matter to the Secretary of State or for the purpose of local conference. Ordinarily, however, it may be anticipated that the declaration will be made after the votes of the elected and nominated non-official members have actually been given in the Council, though before they have been recorded in the minutes.

The reduction of the number of officials in the Council will necessitate authority being given to the Governor to summon to the Council any officials who are not members of the Council to defend and explain the policy of the Government; but not being members they will, of course, have no right to vote. It will be noticed that it is proposed that the Treasurer should ordinarily be a member of the Legislative Council. This is in order that Government may be strongly represented on the important question of finance . . .

LEEWARD ISLANDS

The question of representative government in the Leeward Islands has not hitherto attained the same relative importance as in the other Colonies, and today arouses less political interest than the issue of defederation. With the introduction of representative government, the constitutional question summed up in the word defederation could hardly fail to become more difficult, and it appears to me on *prima facie* grounds, undesirable to submit such a far-reaching question of constitutional order to popular vote at this juncture or before the future character of the federation has been removed from the sphere of present controversy.

ST. KITTS-NEVIS

The demand for representative government in this Presidency was raised for the first time in 1919. On the occasion of our visit it was presented to me by the St. Kitts-Nevis Representative Government Association, which claimed to speak on behalf of the whole community except the planters. They pleaded for some form of representative government with a limited franchise, and for the control of finance . . . On the other hand the Agricultural and Commercial Society of St. Kitts stated that they were opposed to any form of election of members of Council. They denied the claim of the Representative Government Association to speak on behalf of the commercial community, stating that the most prominent merchants were represented on the Agricultural and Commercial Society . . .

In reply to the Representative Government Association, I told them plainly that I could not recommend the concession, unless the demand was supported by the general weight of responsible opinion in the islands; and my general conclusion on leaving St. Kitts-Nevis was that this condition was not fulfilled.

ANTIGUA

. . . the demand for representative government came only from certain elements in the community, and those not the most substantial; and after giving the most careful consideration to the representations in support of it, I do not advise that the demand should be conceded.

MONTSERRAT

. . . having regard to the views which I have expressed as to St. Kitts-Nevis and Antigua, it is clearly unnecessary that you should take any action in regard to Montserrat.

DOMINICA

Apart from the more emphatic demands regarding defederation that are expressed in Dominica, there is a strong feeling that, the whole conditions of the island being so different from the rest of the Leeward Islands, Dominica has something of the character of a separate entity, and should accordingly be treated in a different way from other members of the Colony . . .

As compared with the other islands, therefore, conditions favour the peasant owner in Dominica, and the separation of classes is less pronounced. In Antigua and St. Kitts-Nevis the substantial elements of the population were unanimously opposed to any concession in the matter of representative government; in Dominica the same elements were largely in favour of it . . .

. . . whatever may be the result of further discussion of the problem, I think it should be made clear from the outset that an official majority must be assured in the Council . . .

WINDWARD ISLANDS

ST. LUCIA

. . . There is no reason to doubt that there is a substantial body of enlightened and responsible opinion in favour of the concession [of representative government] . A few people expressed opinions privately against it. On the other hand, both the Acting Administrator (Mr. Laborde) and the Governor support it. In these circumstances I have no hesitation in recommending that it should be granted, and the only questions which remain are questions of detail as to the number of seats constituencies and the like. After discussion with the Governor, I advise that you should concur in the suggestion that two or three unofficial members of the Council should be elected, stipulating that the island should be divided into constituencies in which candidates for election should reside or possess property of a clear annual value not less than that now laid down in Jamaica, and that the exact number of members subject to the stated maximum of three, and all other details should be considered by a local commission, as has been done in Grenada.

ST. VINCENT

. . . When we were in the Colony, the demand was pressed upon me by the Citizen's Committee, which spoke for all classes and pointed out that included in the deputation were large landed proprietors, members of Council, leading merchants and professional men of the island and the principal clergy of the different denominations. The petition presented in support of the demand made two requests – (1) that the unofficial members of the Council, or at least a moiety of them, should be elected by popular vote, and be represented in fair transpose on the Executive Council; (2) that such elective members should be given an effective voice in measures affecting the revenue and expenditure of the Colony . . .

We discussed the question both with the Administrator and with the Governor on arrival in Grenada. Both are now in favour of the grant of the measure of representative government. The Administrator stated that probably only a small minority of the population were directly interested in the question, but that it was quite certain that there was no class objection. The Governor recommended . . . that two or three members of the Legislative Council should be elected by popular vote . . . I have no hesitation in accepting the Governor's recommendation, and in advising you to authorise him to proceed accordingly.

At this stage I am not prepared to make any recommendation regarding the appointment of elected members of the Executive Council. Recommendations for such appointments must remain in the discretion of the Governor. As regards the second demand of the Citizens' Committee, I consider that the fact of appointment to the Legislative Council will give elective members the weight that is demanded on their behalf.

GRENADA

In Grenada we were met with a difficult situation. Here the principle of representative government had already been conceded by Lord Milner, and the only matters awaiting consideration were certain details still outstanding. The gentlemen we interviewed on this subject were the Representative Government Association and representatives of the combined District Boards.

The first named were disposed to express dissatisfaction with the concession that had already been given, but I had little difficulty in persuading their more responsible members that such a view was both unreasonable and unwise. The representatives of the combined District Boards asked that the unofficial section of the Council be wholly elective, or that unofficial nominees, if retained, should be selected from names submitted by the joint nomination of the District Boards, and that the number of the elective and nominees together should form the majority of the Council.

I informed the deputation of the Representative Government Association that I should be prepared to recommend that if the principle of a single constituency for the whole island, as hitherto proposed, were given up, the Colony should be allowed to elect five members of the Council instead of four, as had previously been agreed. This is the obvious number of divisions into which the island naturally falls, and to the condition a ready assent was given by the Association. There is no doubt that the objection which can be made to an increase in the size of the Council is less weighty than the advantage to be gained by substituting separate constituencies for the system of a single constituency. Under the new proposal of separate constituencies, any candidate putting himself up for election will be required to possess residential or property qualifications in the constituency, as in the case of Jamaica, and it is satisfactory to have secured local assent to this proposal. It may be added that, on investigation, the local committee were unable to divide the island into four convenient constituencies, and that such a division into five is readily practicable, owing to the existing parochial organisation. The Governor is in entire agreement with this view, and I would recommend it for acceptance. It will be necessary, in order to retain official control in the Council, to increase the official members by one, making the total numbers of the Council sixteen instead of fourteen as at present.

TRINIDAD AND TOBAGO

The question of representative government in Trinidad is more difficult than in any other Colony . . . Trinidad is the one community which appeared largely to lack any homogeneous public opinion. Socially it is divided into all kinds of groups which have very few relations with one another . . . With a population so constituted, Trinidad is exceptionally cosmopolitan. It is the only one of the West Indian Islands which contains mining enterprises, on any substantial scale, and considerable capital has been embarked in asphalt and oil development by outside corporations. It is, accordingly, important that no action should be taken which would disturb the confidence felt by such capital in the stability of the local Government.

. . . The views expressed to us privately were conflicting. The weight of official opinion was in favour of granting a measure of representation, subject to adequate safeguards, and we ourselves arrived at the same conclusion. There is considerable driving force behind the present movement, and it is accentuated by social inequalities. Even the opponents of change recognise this fact. Moreover, it is impossible in the long run to withhold from Trinidad a concession which has been granted to Grenada, however much the conditions may otherwise differ in the two Colonies . . .

The composition of the official side (now consisting of ten officials holding specified offices besides the Governor with an original and a casting vote) should be altered so as to enable the Governor to nominate (apart from the official members of the Executive Council, who should, of course, all possess seats on the Legislative Council) not the holders of particular offices, but the heads of departments as he may think are personally most suitable for inclusion on the Council.

Assuming that Tobago would wish to be included in the scheme of representation,[3] the number of elected members should be seven, and of nominated members six, and the official side of the Council should be increased by two . . . the official majority will be preserved as now by means of the Governor's casting vote. Thus the Government will still be able to pass through the Council financial and other measures, which are regarded as "essential to the good government of the Colony", and it will be unnecessary to make any provision in the constitution for the retention of a reserve of power in the Governor's hands to pass measures of this description . . .

. . . I have not adopted the system of the election of members by particular interests or any system of communal representation. We came to the conclusion that the objections to the first were insuperable on the ground of the difficulties of determining what the constituency would be and of drawing the line between bodies which should, or should not, be represented. Moreover, the concession would not satisfy those who are clamouring for a change. As regards communal representation, apart from the objection that this arrangement would be opposed by the chief advocates of constitutional change, there would again be great difficulty in deciding what the constituencies were to be, and, moreover, it would accentuate and perpetuate the differences which, in order to produce a homogeneous community, it should be the object of statesmanship to remove. The East Indians are an important element in the community, and it would be a great misfortune if they were encouraged to stand aside from the main current of political life instead of sharing in it and assisting to guide its course. Finally, if a concession of this kind were granted to the East Indians, there would be no logical reasons for withholding it from persons of French, Spanish or Chinese descent, a situation which would become impossible. By retaining the system of nomination by the Crown, it

3 Tobago was included.

will always be possible to secure representatives on the Council of races or important interests not otherwise adequately represented by direct election . . .

NOTE ON THE USE OF THE OFFICIAL MAJORITY IN THE LEGISLATIVE COUNCIL OF THE LEEWARD AND THE WINDWARD ISLANDS, AND IN THE COURT OF POLICY OF BRITISH GUIANA[4]

In the three Presidencies of the Leeward Islands, and in the three Windward Island Colonies, considerable misconception seemed to exist as to the reason why, when the unofficial members of Council were unanimous in opposition to Government proposals, the executive should retain the constitutional power in the last resort to override them. In British Guiana where the executive exercise a similar control in matters other than financial through the Governor's casting vote in the Court of Policy, the same question was also raised. Unofficial members and, in some cases, the general public inclined to take the view that, when there was unanimous unofficial opposition to a proposal of the Government, such unanimity was tantamount to evidence that the proposal was either unreasonable or, under local conditions, inexpedient.

I took pains in every Colony in which the question was raised, to point out that under every type of government some machinery must exist in the event of deadlock between the different elements of the constitution. The machinery existed automatically under a system of pure Crown Colony government, and it also existed under a system of responsible government. In the former case the Governor could overrule the opposition; and in the latter the Government disappears, and a new Government, which can command the necessary majority in the legislature, takes its place. I pointed out that so long as the responsibility for the administration of the Colonies rested with the Secretary of State it was essential that the Secretary of State should have this ultimate power, in order to preserve the executive from being rendered impotent. I further pointed out that, where you had the power to-day, there was no case which would justify you in agreeing to so great a change as to deprive you in the last resort of the power to carry measures which you regarded as essential for the sound conduct of administration. As none of the islands were prepared to argue that they were in a condition to receive responsible government, the only recommendation which I could make to you, was that in such circumstances the utmost consideration should be given to the views of unofficial members of Councils. With this object I said that I would advise that a general despatch should be sent to the Colonies concerned, laying down that

4 In reply to a question put by A.A. Cipriani the Governor of Trinidad and Tobago stated that the same principles would apply in that Colony. See Debates of the Legislative Council of Trinidad and Tobago, 1925, p. 256.

when there was such unanimous opposition on the part of all unofficial members of Council, the Governor should refrain from bringing the contested measures into operation until further reference had been made to the Secretary of State. In cases of urgency, however, or when the Secretary of State had already given instructions in the matter and no new material was brought forward, the Governor should be empowered to take immediate action, but in these circumstances the matter should be at once reported to the Secretary of State for confirmation. In either case the dissentient should have the right to simultaneously forwarding to the Secretary of State, through the Governor, a statement of their views which they might themselves desire to prepare, provided that such statement were forwarded without undue delay. If this is done, it must be distinctly understood that financial measures such as taxation ordinances, must always be treated as urgent when there is any possibility of evasion by forestallment or of serious loss of revenue by delay . . .

B. Extract from a speech made in the House of Commons by the Hon. E.F.L. Wood, Under-Secretary of State for the Colonies, 1922. (Parliamentary Debates (Commons) vol. 156, 1922, c.c. 234-235.)

There is one consideration which I think Hon. Members would like to bear in mind. If it be important, as I am satisfied it is important, to maintain in these colonies as a condition of progress and stability a European element, the presence of that European element depends upon the prosperity of the sugar industry, and that is a consideration which should not be lost sight of. I also endeavoured to appraise the force of the movement for representative government as it exists in different islands and to discuss the conditions under which and the limits within which it is in my judgment right at the present day to meet the demand that has been made. I am quite satisfied that while you have, as you have there, the universal foundations of loyalty, confidence in British administration, and good will, this is the time to meet the demands to the utmost legitimate extent. I am extremely pleased that that course of action has been approved by my Hon. Friend. It is possible that as time goes on wisdom may suggest and events may warrant further advances along these lines. That is for the future. For the present and for so long a future as I personally can foresee, I deem it is essential to maintain in some form or other the ultimate control that is exercised on behalf of Parliament by the Secretary of State for the Colonies over these growing and developing communities, and I have made suggestions how that security can be maintained in conformity with constitutional growth and evolution.

C. Extract from a speech made in the House of Commons by Mr Ormsby-Gore, Under Secretary of State for the Colonies, 1923. (Parliamentary Debates (Commons) vol. 167, 1923, c.c. 491-492.)

With regard to the West Indies, I would like, first, to welcome the appointment at long last of a Parliamentary Committee of this House and the other House to take an interest in our oldest and most historic colonies . . . these ancient colonies, which we govern by officials and other representatives, had felt from time to time that their interests for which we are responsible did not receive the attention that they should receive from us. The Committee, I am sure, will be useful. During the past year the necessary steps have been taken to carry out the recommendations of my right hon. Friend the President of the Board of Education as the result of our tour with regard to constitutional reform, and we are now ready for the final issue of Letters Patent, etc., in connection with new Constitutions for Grenada, St. Lucia, St. Vincent, Trinidad and Jamaica. The Dominica discussions are still proceeding. Though it was not recommended in the Report, we subsequently decided to introduce an elected element and a franchise for the first time in the island of Dominica.

D. Documents dealing with the introduction of Crown Colony Government in British Guiana, 1928.

(i) Extracts from the Report of the British Guiana Commission, 1927. (Cmd. 2841/1927.)

CHAPTER VII

CONSTITUTION

British Guiana can be classified as a Colony not possessing responsible government with a partly-elected Legislature not providing for an official majority. The distinctive feature of the constitution is its division of the legislative power between two bodies, the Court of Policy and the Combined Court. To the Court of Policy, consisting of the Governor, seven officials and eight elected unofficial members, and constituted with the Governor's casting vote to secure an official majority, belongs the power of legislation in matters not fiscal; to the Combined Court, that is to say the Court of Policy combined with six more elected members known as Financial Representatives, belongs the power of imposing taxes and in practice the right to control the appropriation of public monies. In the Court of Policy the Government majority is subject to a potential veto which can be exercised by the elected members inasmuch as if seven of them abstain from attending they can prevent the formation of the quorum required. In the Combined Court, on the other hand, and consequently in matters of taxation or involving expenditure, the elected members possess a majority, and the only limitation to their powers is that they cannot increase, though they can reduce or reject, any item on the annual estimates which are prepared by the Governor in Executive Council. Thus this nominally two-chamber system is in fact merely a method of dividing the subjects of legislation into two classes, financial, in which the elected members possess a majority, and non-financial, over which they can only exercise a negative control.

The origin of this constitution is of some practical importance as well as historical interest. Up to the close of the Dutch occupation the Court of Policy was the only legislative body for Demerara and Essequebo. On this Chamber the planters, after a prolonged period of friction with the West India Company, obtained equal representation with the officials through the intervention of the Dutch Government, who in 1789 sent out a commission armed with a "plan of redress", defining the future political system of the Colony. After the fall of the old Dutch Government in Europe in 1795 the planters took advantage of the interregnum to secure a larger measure of control over taxation on lines which crystallised, a few months after the British occupation of 1796, into the present Combined Court. This innovation was guaranteed by the terms of capitulation granted to the Colony when it was reoccupied by the British in 1803 and, together with the other political institutions of Demerara and Essequebo, was extended to Berbice when the Colonies were amalgamated in 1831. It is not clear whether this guarantee was given and acquiesced in by inadvertence or through indifference, it not then being possible to foresee that the Colony would remain permanently in British hands. As to its effects, however, there can be no doubt, in view of the reply given in 1840 by the Law Officers of the Crown to the question whether it was within the power of the Crown-in-Council to raise a revenue in British Guiana and to determine its appropriation:-

> "We are of the opinion that such a power cannot be legally and constitutionally exercised by Her Majesty. British Guiana does not appear to us to be in the situation of a conquered Colony, in which the Crown has supreme legislative authority. By the capitulation of the 19th September, 1803, it was stipulated that 'the law and usages of the Colony should remain in force and be respected; that the mode of taxation then in use should be adhered to; and that no establishment should be introduced without the consent of the Court of Policy, as the Legislature of the Colony.' This capitulation is binding in good faith upon the Crown, and even in strict law we conceive that the sanction of the Crown since the cession of the Colony to the political institutions in existence, has given the same force to those institutions as if they had been established by

an express grant from the Crown, like the legislatures in Colonies settled by British subjects."

The Constitution thus established has survived without substantial structural alteration until the present day. The Combined Court has acquired the right of controlling expenditure, which it did not possess at the time of the capitulation, in return for an arrangement, which still applies, under which it makes statutory provision for the salaries of certain officials for a fixed period of years. The franchise, till 1891 confined by a curious process of indirect election and a high property or income qualification to a small oligarchy of planters, has been extended to anyone with an income of $300 (£62.10s.) and the electorate now is principally composed of the black and coloured population and numbered at the last elections about 11,000 out of an adult male population of some 86,000.

At no time can this remarkable constitution be said to have worked satisfactorily . . .

The disadvantages of this system have not vanished now that the control of the political machine has passed to a wider and more numerous but necessarily, in a racially composite community, when the great majority of the population are too indifferent or too ignorant to exercise their political rights, to a relatively narrow and also inexperienced electorate. Indeed under the new order the practical difficulty of working the old constitution is increased. The Government in British Guiana have never been able to govern. This situation was possible so long as the function of administration was confined to attempting to prevent mis-government. It is not possible when the Government are expected to take a direct and active part in the development of the country and the improvement of the condition of the people.

In Colonies of the constitutional status of British Guiana it is a normal and necessary feature of the political system that power, in the last resort, should reside in the Governor under the control and direction of the Secretary of State . . .

. . . the justification of a reserve power rests on the proposition, which is also a platitude, that under any political system it is desirable that the government should be able to govern.

In British Guiana, as we have said, no Government has ever been in this position. The result in the past has been deadlocks, sometimes culminating in a total stoppage of supplies, when the policy of the Imperial Government came into collision with the views or interests of the represented classes on questions of public policy such as emancipation, immigration, or free trade . . .

The practical consequences of this lack of ultimate control are chiefly to be seen in the financial system of the Colony . . . At present the elected members are in the position of a minor who can overrule his own trustee . . .

Provision for ultimate control is also desirable on grounds of political psychology. The divorce of responsibility from power, which is so marked a feature of the constitution, places the elected members as well as the Government in a false position. The elected members tend to be placed in the position of a permanent opposition, unrestrained by experience or prospect of office. Though we do not wish to press the anology too closely, the position of the Government, under such conditions, might in some respect be compared to that of a ministry without a majority, a state of affairs not tending to inspire respect or promote efficiency and highly detrimental to morale. This is particularly unfortunate in a Colony like British Guiana, which depends so much on the energy and abilities of its officials. There can be no question that the existence of ultimate control would act as a constitutional safety valve, useful not primarily for carrying measures but as an ultimate guarantee and for its psychological effects.

For these reasons we are definitely of opinion that in the present stage of political, economic, and cultural development it is not merely desirable but essential that the authorities finally responsible for the government of the Colony should have power in the last resort to carry into effect measures which they consider essential for its well being . . .

A serious cause of friction is the absence of any link between the executive and the elected members. In the absence of such a link it is easy to imagine that decisions may be taken by the Government of which the elected members, if consulted in advance, might have given notice of their disapproval and that in consequence measures may be rejected without adequate consideration or full knowledge of the facts. Instances of both these cases were brought to our attention, and the suggestion was made that they might be avoided by admitting an elected element to the Executive Council. This body was set up in 1891 to take over from the Court of Policy its executive duties, which included the preparation of the annual estimates. It is constituted by Letters Patent to advise the Governor, who is bound to consult with it in the execution of the powers and authorities granted him by the Crown, except where the matter is too urgent or unimportant or where the King's Service would thereby sustain material prejudice. With the exception of two ex officio members, the Colonial Secretary and the Attorney General, it consists of such persons as may be appointed by the King or provisionally appointed by the Governor subject to confirmation or disallowance. In the past this body has contained representatives of the elected members, but for some years this has not been the case and the present Council consists of five officials and three un-officials, none of the latter being a member of the Legislature, with the result that on the one hand the Executive Council includes no exponent of popular opinion and on the other that the Legislature contains no unofficial exponent of the Government point of view. With a view to promoting greater mutual confidence and co-operation, and on the general principle that responsibility is in itself a good thing, we are in favour of admitting to the Executive Council one or more of such selected members as the Governor may see fit to recommend, for appointment, for the usual period of five years, to His Majesty the King.

It is also for consideration whether the time has not come for considering on its merits the question of importing a nominated element into the Legislature. It is a general phenomenon in tropical colonies that the extension of the electorate and the greater frequency of contests makes it extremely and increasingly difficult for anyone who is not able and prepared to embark more or less whole time on the career of a politician to enter the Legislature by the avenue of the constituencies. The result is the loss to public life of no inconsiderable portion of those who are best qualified for it, or in other words, of the small but extremely important European class which still controls the principal agricultural and commercial activities of the Colony. This is especially regrettable in British Guiana, where all parties unite in desiring to encourage by every means the advent of the capital and business enterprise which is essential to development. It is also regrettable that agriculture should be markedly under-represented in the Legislature of a colony which still depends almost entirely on that industry for its economic existence. In these circumstances we are of opinion that the Colony would be wise to consider whether the time has not come for providing by means of a nominated element for the representation on the Legislature of classes and interests inadequately represented by the process of direct election.

The question of replacing the Court of Policy and the Combined Court by a Legislative Council containing an official, an elected, and a nominated element raises the question of the number of the Council and of its various ingredients. On this we are not prepared to express an opinion, but fourteen members for a registered electorate of some 11,000 means an average constituency of less than 800, and this low figure is exaggerated by the great differences between the strength of the electorates of the various constituencies . . . Clearly some readjustment of the electoral districts is desirable, and at the same time it might be considered whether the representation of the Colony might not be adequately secured by a reduced number of elected members . . .

(ii) Extracts from the Memoranda prepared by the Elected Members of the Combined Court of British Guiana in reply to the Report of the British Guiana Commission. (Cmnd. 3047/1927.)

CHAPTER VII

CONSTITUTION (G)

Section 1

G1 The objections made by the Parliamentary Commissioners to the form of the existing Constitution may be classified under three heads, viz:-

(a) That the Government does not possess a nominated majority in the Combined Court, and is therefore unable to govern; and that political control has passed to the black and coloured portion of the population of the Colony.

(b) That the Colony's finances are in so parlous a condition that they can only be re-adjusted if and when Government is placed in a position to carry into effect its policy against the united opposition of the elected representatives of the people.

(c) That there have been such gross and flagrant abuses of the present Constitution as to reduce it to a scandal of the British Empire, thereby precluding the European elements in the community from taking part in the political life of the Colony.

G2 In so far as the first of these reasons is concerned, the Commissioners have fallen into the fatal error of confusing the Executive Administration with the Government. The Government of British Guiana is not, as in England, a Government by a party in power watched by an official Opposition, which may be called upon at any moment to assume the responsibilities of Government. The form of our local Government aims essentially at achieving the ancient ideal that the Government of a country shall be constituted by the Governor and the Legislature acting as a composite whole, and not by alternate sections of the Legislature separately led.

G3 Unfortunately from the year 1891 up to the present it has been the policy of successive administrators more and more to divorce the Executive from the Legislative Assembly. The Executive, by entirely excluding elected members from enjoying the confidence of the administration, have caused them – to adopt the language employed by the Commissioners themselves – "to be placed in the position of a permanent opposition unrestrained by experience and prospect of office."

G4 When the Constitution Ordinance came into operation in 1891, for some time after the Governor continued to select some of his unofficial Executive advisers from among the elected members of the Legislature. When the unofficial members of the Executive Council were so recruited – as they ought always to have been from the Legislature – those elected members who had been so promoted to what may be regarded as the equivalent to Cabinet rank in England felt themselves more or less responsible in the Combined Court for the Executive policy, and were invariably to be found voting on the Government side. The Executive then shared and enjoyed the confidence of both Government and governed.

G5 Gradually, however, as the local representatives and attorneys of the sugar estate proprietors – chiefly absentee landlords, who have always "had special means of influencing the Government of the different Colonies and of putting pressure on the Home Government to secure attention to their views and wishes" – failed to obtain the support of the electorate of the polls, and their seats in the local Legislature were secured by men of equal ability and equal culture, though not of the same caste, successive Governors abstained from continuing the practice of nominating elected members of the Legislature to the Executive Council, but chose instead from those whose policy had been rejected at the polls with the obvious result that a certain amount of hostility and opposition to Executive policy became increasingly manifest in the Legislature. But this state of affairs was unchallengably the fault of Government, and one that was capable of being easily remedied.

G6 It will be obvious from what we have stated that one way of securing support for Government policy would be for the Government to endeavour to create a majority in its favour in the Legislature by inviting over to the Government side, and attracting to their counsels such members who, by their ability and the confidence reposed in them by the electorate, are entitled to share in the confidences of Government; for it may be urged as more than a truism that if Government is unable to win the support of its own unofficial advisers in the Executive Council before a measure is introduced into the Legislature, and still more so the support of no elected member in the Combined Court, it may be safely assumed that that policy is either not sufficiently appreciated or is unworthy of support. If the former then the measure should obviously be withdrawn until it can be accepted; if the latter, then it should be incontinently rejected as we contend respectfully that the people of the Colony and the elected representatives thereof are those best fitted to determine either the Colony's capacity to pay for the measure in dispute, or its final usefulness.

G7 We are dealing at some length with the theories advanced by the Commissioners, as we are not prepared to concede that the Government has never been able to carry out any policy designed for the progress or development of the Colony, because of the opposition of the elected members. As a matter of fact it is a very rare occurrence indeed for the Government to be unsuccessful, in matters of any importance whatever in securing a division in its favour in the Combined Court. In such instances, there must have been a full attendance of all the electives, and the issues must have been clearly repugnant as to have encouraged the unanimous adverse vote of the fourteen elective members of the Combined Court.

G8 It must be borne in mind that there is no system of "pairing" between absent Government officials and the Electives. The Government maintains its numerical strength in the Legislature by the aid of making acting appointments thereto and this with a cast iron rigidity. Some of the Electives on the other hand are frequently absent from the deliberations therein either through absence from the Colony, through illness, or owing to professional engagements elsewhere. As a consequence, fourteen members are seldom to be found in their places and even when they are – each being free to vote with the Executive – the Government has only to convince three out of the fourteen members – not one of whom is under any party discipline – not to vote with Government, to secure a majority vote.[5]

G9 Further, it has never occurred in the history of the present Constitution that the Legislature consisted of no representatives of "that small but extremely important European class which controls the agricultural and commercial activities of the Colony", and who, according to the Commissioners, may presumably be always expected to vote with Government. It will, therefore, be observed from the foregoing that it is, in a large measure, untrue and inaccurate to say that the Executive Government has never been able to govern, unless the right to govern is interpreted as being the right of a bureaucratic autocracy to introduce measures and force upon a subservient legislature, without the usual legislative enquiries and safeguards . . .

G56 Amongst the lesser complaints of the Commissioners is the allegation that it is difficult for "the small but extremely important European class which still controls the principal agricultural and commercial activities of the "Colony" to enter the Legislature through the avenues of the constituencies, because of the extension of the Electorate and of the great frequency of contests. It is asserted by them that this is a general phenomenon in tropical

5 A similar point could be made with regard to the power of the "nine" and the unanimous opposition of the elected members in the Jamaican Legislature, as well as with regard to the reference of matters to the Secretary of State for the Colonies when the elected members were in unanimous opposition. (See Wood Report, Note on Use of the Official Majority, Chapter IV, Part I, document A.)

Colonies. However true this statement may be of other tropical possessions, it is not so of British Guiana. There has been in this Colony no great frequency of elections, as the members hold their seats for a period of five years, as against those of the House of Assembly in Barbados for a period of one year. It is seldom that a vacancy occurs to necessitate even a by-election during this period.

G57 The class for which the Commissioners are so solicitous now represents less than 2 per cent of the entire population of the Colony – to be accurate, 1.11 per cent . . .

G58 So far as British Guiana is concerned, the reason why a greater number of this class do not seek political honours are both manifold and obvious. Firstly, because of the knowledge which they possess – and which is universally admitted – that the legislature as a body is impotent to mould or control the policy of Government to any great extent; and secondly, because to adopt the words of the Royal Commission of 1897, they feel that they "have special means of influencing the Government and putting pressure on the Home Government to secure attention to their views and wishes." If the Executive Council were recruited from members of the Legislature – a proposal which we strongly recommend – it would be the means, we feel sure, of attracting a greater number of the more conservative elements among us to seek legislative honours. There is a third reason which may be cited, and that is that the members of the European class, not being for the most part proprietors themselves, but the salaried employees of absentee proprietors, have not the same leisure to devote to public affairs as has the ordinary individual; nor would they be always free to exercise that freedom of speech that one looks for in public representatives.

(iii) Extracts from a speech made in the House of Commons
by the Secretary of State for the Colonies
during the Second Reading of the British Guiana Bill, 1928.
(Parliamentary Debates (Commons) vol. 214, 1928, c.c. 989-999.)

The Bill which I have to bring before the House this afternoon is a permissive Bill. It is one which gives the authority of this House to the Crown to enable it, by Order in Council, to modify the constitution of the Colony of British Guiana. The constitutions of His Majesty's Colonies are very frequently changed by Order in Council, but that form of action is impossible in the present case, owing to certain legal considerations, arising out of the form of the original Capitulation of 1803 under which British Guiana became a British Colony . . . Consequently there is no legal method of altering the constitution in British Guiana except through the intervention of the authority of Parliament.[6]

There is no question here of a going back on self-government in the British Empire. The last few years have, in many parts of the British Empire, seen a substantial advance towards fuller representation, in many cases towards a more responsible form of Government, as in the island of Malta, for instance, where a Constitution with precisely the same kind of weakness of divided responsibility had to be modified in 1903. That modification made way 15 years later for that wide measure of responsible Government that is enjoyed today. The question is not one of progress to or from self-government, but rather of enabling the car of government to back out of the *cul de sac* into which it has run, on to the straight high road of constitutional development. The present Constitution of British Guiana is a dead end, out of which there is no outlet for either political or economic development. My hope is that by establishing a Constitution which will lay the final responsibility for Government on the Governor of the Colony, subject to the ultimate authority of the Secretary of State and this House, you will create a condition of things under which the spirit of responsible co-operation and the progress of the Colony will enable the new Legislature to pave the way, in the fullness of time, for further constitutional developments, which are, I am afraid, clearly precluded by the present financial and general situation of the Colony.

(iv) The British Guiana Act 1928.
U.K. Public General Acts c.5.

An Act to make provision for the Government of the
Colony of British Guiana (28th March 1928)

Be it enacted by the King's most Excellent Majesty, by and with the advice and consent of the Lords Spiritual and Temporal, and Commons, in this present Parliament assembled, and by the authority of the same, as follows:-

1 (1) It shall be lawful for His Majesty in Council to create and constitute, in substitution for the existing legislature, a legislature for the Colony of British Guiana in such form and with such powers as His Majesty in Council may determine, and from time to time to alter and amend the constitution of the legislature and any powers thereof; and any such Order in Council may provide that, notwithstanding the powers conferred on the legislature thereby, there

6 It is interesting to note that during the 1950s and early 1960s, when demands were being made for reform in the Bahama Islands (particularly with respect to broadening the franchise, introducing one man, one vote and redelimiting constituency boundaries) this argument was used in the House of Commons against the propriety of the intervention of the Imperial Parliament.

shall be reserved to or conferred on His Majesty full power by Order in Council from time to time to make laws for the peace, order, and good government of the Colony of British Guiana.

(2) Before any such Order in Council creating and constituting such legislature or altering the constitution of powers thereof is made, a draft thereof shall be laid before each House of Parliament for a period of not less than twenty-one days on which that House has sat, and if either House of Parliament before the expiration of that period presents an address to His Majesty against the Order or any part thereof, no further proceedings shall be taken on the draft, without prejudice to the making of a new draft Order.

2 This Act may be cited as the British Guiana Act, 1928.

E. Extracts from the Report of the West India Royal Commission 1938-39. (Cmnd. 6607/1945.)

CHAPTER V

THE ADMINISTRATIVE BACKGROUND

1 Brief Description of Constitutions

3 The details of the political constitutions of the various territories differ considerably. In all there are representative institutions but none has yet reached the stage of responsible government. The nearest approach to this is found in Barbados where the representative element in both the legislative and executive parts of Government is considerable.[7] The former consists of the Legislative Council of nine members appointed by the Crown and the House of Assembly of 24 members elected annually. The executive part of the Government is vested in a Council, appointed by the Crown and composed at present with a majority of officials, and in a Committee which consists of the Executive Council, one member from the Legislative Council and four members nominated by the Governor from the House of Assembly. All money votes are introduced in the legislature and all Government measures initiated

7 Barbados and the Bahama Islands retained the Old Representative System. However, the Bahamas have lagged behind other West Indian territories in constitutional development, while Barbados as this Report indicates, tended to be ahead. The advances in Barbados, because of the nature of the Old Representative System, were able to take place largely by convention (as they did at an earlier date in the original Dominions). For this reason there are few official documents which could be used in this selection to illustrate development in Barbados.

there by, and with the advice of, the Executive Committee, but the executive has no means of ensuring the passage of legislation, or the provision of funds, by the wholly elected House of Assembly whose members therefore have a vital place in the scheme of government.

4 In British Guiana the position until 1928 was not unlike that now obtaining in Barbados, but a new constitution was then introduced as the result of recommendations by two Commissions, of which the first went out from this country, and the second was appointed locally . . . The local Committee reported in favour of a change of the constitution and under instruments made in 1928 a Legislative Council was created on which the nominated element (including officials) has a bare majority over the elected members. The Executive Council which was established at the same time is composed of two *ex-officio* members, not more than four other nominated official members and not more than five nominated unofficial members. Under the existing constitution no legislation may be enacted which was not proposed to the Council by, or with the sanction of the Governor, and the initiation of all money votes is subject to a similar limitation. In addition the Governor has a reserve power under which he, in Executive Council, may decide any matter requiring a vote or enactment to the Legislative Council in a sense contrary to the vote of a majority of the legislature; the exercise of this power is, however, limited to matters in regard to which the Governor declares in writing that his decision is, in his opinion, necessary in the interest of public order, public faith, or other first essentials of good government. Though the Governor is bound by the constitution to consult his Executive Council before using his reserve power, he need not accept their advice.

5 It is not our intention to examine here the constitutional position in the West Indies (to which we return in Chapter XXII) in any greater detail than is necessary for our present purpose of discussing the relationship between the executive and legislative authorities. It may suffice, therefore, to say that while the position in the other Colonies not so far mentioned in this Chapter varies on details, such as the relative proportions of component elements of the Councils, from that in British Guiana, it is similar in essentials, though in the case of Jamaica the elected members have certain special powers of vote . . .

2 *Relation of Executive and Legislature*

6 We have already remarked on the fact that the elected House of Assembly in Barbados may bar the passage of any legislation and has complete freedom to withhold the provision of money votes moved by the executive. The system appears on the whole to have worked reasonably well; although it was represented to us in evidence that the absence of certain social legislation and

services was due to opposition by the Assembly, an official witness assured us that there had been no recent evidence of obstruction, on the part of either branch of the legislature, to any social measure which the Government had introduced, and we received no indication of any wish, on the part of the executive, for a reform of the constitution of Barbados. Any uneasiness that may be felt about the power of the legislature to impede the pursuit in Barbados of a policy designed to improve social and economic conditions throughout the possessions of the Crown in the Caribbean area would, we consider, be met if, after the local inquiry suggested in Chapter XXII of this Report, the franchise in the island is widened.

7 The other Colonies are still administered under what is known as "the Crown Colony system". That is neither an autocracy nor a democracy. It is true that, as we have shown, the Governor can impose his will in the interest of public order, public faith or other first essentials of good government and, in the last resort, the decision whether these vital needs are affected rests with him alone. In practice, however, the force of public opinion can effectively prevent arbitrary decisions and the known unpopularity of the reserve power is a safeguard against its frequent use. It should be – and, we believe, that in the West Indies it is – the aim of every administrator under the Crown Colony system to give full weight to the expressed views of all responsible sections of public opinion, the more so in that some of these may have no share in any sphere of government, and to balance carefully the claims of every interest before a decision is reached and executive action is taken. The weakness of the system, as it operates in most of the West Indian Colonies, seems to us to lie not, as is so often alleged, in the autocracy which it apparently involves but in the opposition which it engenders between Government, on the one hand, and on the other, those, among whom must often be counted elected members of the Legislative Council, who so vehemently and constantly criticise Government in speeches and in the Press. Even these critics recognise that the Governor is not an autocrat, inasmuch as they will usually admit that he and his administration are open to influence; the complaint most frequently heard is, rather, that Governments are dominated by vested interests and that only the representatives of such interests are successful in exercising their influence.

8 Before considering the effects of the position which we have described upon individual officers and upon their relations with the public, we should mention another defect which – so we were told in evidence – is inherent in the Crown Colony System. This point of view was put by a witness whose opinion is the more valuable by reason of his knowledge and experience of several Colonies. He told us that not only are the people, when they became politically conscious, compelled through that system to resort to permanent

opposition to Government, and their elected representatives forced into the position of vehement and continual critics of Government, but those representatives are left with no responsibility for practical alternative measures and their criticism, when it becomes perpetual and irresponsible, often leads to a static position and prevents constructive action by the executive . . .

4 Colour Prejudice and Colour Discrimination

12 The question of racial feeling raises issues which fall outside the scope of a discussion strictly limited to the background of administration in the West Indies, but, in some of its phases, it is connected with the problems described immediately above and it has, as we will show, an important bearing on the relationship between Government and the people.

13 These witnesses whom we questioned on the point were practically unanimous in the view that racial feeling had intensified during recent years, though by one of them a good point was made when he said: "If one is comparing the economic interests of the workers with the economic interests of the employers of labour it can always be interpreted to be promoting ill-will among the different classes". Where people of one colour are predominant among employers and the workers are found almost wholly from those of another colour, it is perhaps inevitable in times of labour troubles that racial and economic issues should be confused. Be that as it may, there is ample evidence, in the form of Press articles, memoranda of evidence submitted to us by unofficials and information received from Governments, that in all responsible quarters in the West Indies there is a widespread feeling that colour prejudice is seriously on the increase. The causes of this are economic, social and political. The desire for a higher standard of life can lead to strikes for improved labour conditions and these, as we have indicated above, may come to, or be represented as, a clash of colour interests. In the social sphere the spread of education has opened the way to greater contact between the white people and the better informed among the coloured sections of the community and we feel that it is essential that Governors should do their utmost to break down old barriers and should not limit to formal occasions the hospitality which they extend to the leading unofficials of mixed or coloured descent. Finally, on the political side, increasing racial prejudice arises from the position, with which we have already dealt, whereby the executive is dominated by officials and it frequently takes the particular form, which is discussed later in this section, of antagonism to, and bitter attacks on, white officers appointed to the service from outside the West Indies . . .

15 Reference has been made above to the resentment frequently caused by the appointment of officials from elsewhere to the public service in the West

Indies. Even the most hostile opponents of such appointments will usually admit that in present circumstances Governors, Colonial Secretaries and other senior administrative staff must generally be found from outside the group. Their claim is that with these few exceptions, all official posts in the West Indies can be filled satisfactorily by local candidates who should have priority of claim to all vacancies for which they are qualified. It is indisputable that of two candidates who are equally suitable for an appointment one of West Indian origin should be given preference over one of other extraction. But the proper organisation of Government services in a world of increasing administrative and technical complexity clearly demands that experience shall be pooled and that the selection for any vacancy shall be the one which is best on grounds of qualifications and merit alone. The application of these tests in making promotions within the Colonial Service has, in fact, resulted in the move to other Colonies of many Officers of West Indian origin, some of whom have gone far in the Service. The fact that they have been of white or mixed descent is not to be taken as implying a rigid colour prejudice but reflects the absence, from most branches of the Service, of coloured officials with qualifications equal to those of officers entering from this country. In so far as colour is a bar to the entry of well qualified West Indian candidates to the Colonial Service outside the Caribbean area it is only reasonable that every opportunity should be given to them to secure suitable appointments within that area . . .

17 It cannot be too strongly stressed that irresponsible and unmeasured criticism of imported officers, whether on ground of colour or as part of a political campaign, detracts from their usefulness, takes up in the answering of it time which should be more profitably employed on constructive work and is a potent cause of that racial prejudice which was so strongly deprecated by all with whom we discussed it . . .

5 Other Criticisms of Administration

19 Complaint was made in evidence that senior officers in the service of West Indian Governments are often inaccessible to private individuals of position and influence . . .

CHAPTER XXII

CONSTITUTIONAL PROBLEMS

1 Reasons for considering these Problems

2 . . . Rightly or wrongly, a substantial body of public opinion in the West Indies is convinced that far-reaching measures of social reconstruction depend,

both for their initiation and their effective administration, upon greater participation of the people in the business of government. Many adherents to this view are prominent in political movements, some of which would not be content with any constitutional change falling short of self-government; others are interested in local politics only in so far as they regard these as the readiest means to the securing of the end of social reform which is their real concern. But all are firmly persuaded that their feeling on the constitutional issue is a correct one, and no amount of argument would change their convictions. An examination of the social and economic problems of the West Indies which, however exhaustive, took no account of this point of view, would therefore be regarded by some section of public opinion in the Caribbean area as having failed in a primary purpose. However, we are satisfied that the claim so often put before us that the people should have a larger voice in the management of their affairs represents a genuine sentiment and reflects a growing political consciousness which is sufficiently widespread to make it doubtful whether any schemes of social reform, however wisely conceived and efficiently conducted, would be completely successful unless they were accompanied by the largest measure of constitutional development which is thought to be judicious in existing circumstances. We felt bound, therefore, to extend our inquiry to the issues which we are now to consider . . .

2 *Composition of Executive and Legislative Councils*

4 Suggestions made to us in evidence varied from one for the grant of immediate and complete self-government, based on a universal franchise, to a proposal that the authority of Governors should be widened in a way which would come near to converting the existing system into the autocracy which it is so often alleged to be. We cannot support either of these extreme points of view. The claim for independence is irreconcilable with that control which, though not necessarily in its present form, must continue to be exercised, in the interests of the home taxpayer, over the finances of Colonies receiving substantial assistance from funds provided by Parliament. On the other hand, any considerable reduction of the powers of an elected body would be difficult to justify, except as a temporary measure in an emergency, unless it was intended to assist the pursuit of a common policy in the West Indies. That apart, while variation in the numbers and composition of the Executive and Legislative Councils may from time to time be found desirable, any fundamental change in the parts which they play in the public affairs of these Colonies is, we consider, to be avoided. The initiative in formulating policy should remain with the Governor in Executive Council but the representatives of popular opinion can be given more opportunity to influence policy, and some of them may perhaps be converted from criticism to co-operation, if an arrangement can be made whereby they are more closely associated with the

work of the executives. At present there is everywhere an unofficial element in the Executive Council but this is normally composed of persons nominated by the Governor who need not have a seat in the Legislative Council. Of only one Executive Council in the West Indies can it be said that it contains any representative of the interests of labour; we consider that, when selecting individuals for nominated appointments on those bodies, Governors should bear carefully in mind the desirability of broadening the basis of their Executive Councils and giving, as far as is possible, representation thereon to all important sections of the community. The question of the appointment to Executive Councils of persons who are elected members of the Legislative Council is one which deserves careful consideration. There may be difficulties in some cases, but we are impressed with the desirability of thus securing the co-operation of the elected members in the work of the executive, and, wherever the difficulties can be overcome, such appointments should be made. In addition – and this we regard as the more important change – some form of committee system[8] should be adopted in the larger Colonies to give unofficial members of the Legislature, particularly elected members, an insight into the details of administration. These Committees should be advisory and not executive bodies, but should be given statutory sanction. Their range should be wide enough to cover all major branches of Government activity in the Colony. Heads of Government Departments, even if they are not members of the Legislative Council, should be appointed to the appropriate Committees; that apart, their composition would vary but in general it is desirable that the representatives of elected members of the Legislature, chosen by them, should be in a majority on each Committee, the Chairman of which would be nominated by the Governor.

7 . . . We consider that the nomination of heads of Departments as members of the Legislature should be exceptional and that normally the Colonial Secretary, the Treasurer and the Attorney-General should be the only officials on that body. Between them these three officers should be able to explain the policy and represent the point of view of Government, and all questions should be addressed to the Colonial Secretary who would answer them, on behalf of the Government, unless they raised issues with which one of the two other official members could deal more appropriately and effectively. Not only would heads of other Departments thus be relieved of a distasteful task, but through the release from long hours of attendance during which they are often required only to record their votes, many of them would be able to give much more time to their proper duties.

8 The Report points out the similarity of this institution of the committee system to that introduced in Ceylon by the "Donoughmore" Constitution, 1931.

8 Before we pass on to the question of filling the places on the Legislature which would be vacated by the removal of officials, it is necessary to refer to the functions of that body under the Crown Colony system. The most important of these are the discussion of policy, the passing of legislation and the voting of monies to finance the administration. So far as the first of these is concerned there is much to be said for widening the scope of unofficial representation on the Councils and for increasing its numbers; the two other purposes can be secured, when there is an unofficial majority in the Council, by some such constitutional device as giving the Governor the power to declare any matter to be of paramount importance and to decide it in a sense contrary to the vote of a majority of the Council if he is satisfied that such a decision is necessary in the interest of first essentials of good government. The use of these powers, however, invariably results in popular outcry. To increase unofficial representation in the Council, even to the extent of making it wholly an elected body, without at the same time relinquishing control by the executive, or dispensing with the Governor's special powers, would do little to satisfy political aspirations in the West Indies. The time for self-government, as we have already said, has not yet come. So long as the need for financial control continues, constitutional reform, apart from the changes recommended earlier in this Chapter, ought to be directed towards making the Legislative Councils more fully representative of all important sections of the community. This can be secured through the wise use of the power to nominate members of the Council. In selecting them the first consideration must, of course, be the enlistment of the help of the individuals, of any race or class, most fitted to offer useful advice on public policy, but the principle of broadening the composition of the Council should be accepted and recognised as second only to that. We will give one example. Women are just beginning to take part in public affairs in the West Indies and, as will be clear from other passages in this report, many reforms are needed on which their advice might be of considerable value. Where representation of these interests has not been secured through the elections to the Legislative Council, the Governor should bear carefully in mind the possibility of nominating a woman to that body.

9 It will be clear from the preceding paragraph that we attach more importance to the representative character of the Legislative Councils than to any more fundamental change in their composition which, unless accompanied by the executive control not practicable in present conditions, could not satisfy those who most pressed for it in evidence before us. It follows therefore that, in our opinion, any appointments to the Council to make good the removal of officials should normally be filled by nomination and not by election. We are anxious, however, that this expression of opinion should not be used as an argument against all other constitutional reform. We understand

that proposals for such changes are being, or may be, put forward by some Governors and we wish it to be understood that any reasonable progressive measures would command our support provided that they satisfy two conditions. The first is that they must be consistent with what is, in our view, the primary need of wider representation on the Legislative Council; the second is that they should give the people an increased share in their government without impairing the essential financial and other control by the executive.

3 Extension of the Franchise

11 Although these qualifications are not high by standards which prevailed in the country when similar tests were applied, they are high in relation to average incomes in the West Indies and in consequence only a small portion of the population is everywhere registered as voters. For example, at the time (January, 1938) of the last election held in Trinidad the registered electorate totalled 30,911 which is only 6.6 per cent of the estimated population of the Colony, and the corresponding figure for Barbados in the same year was 6,359 or 3.3 per cent of the estimated population. Even if, as we were told in several Colonies, a number of people who are eligible to be registered as voters either do not understand, or for other reasons fail to comply with, the formalities of enrolment, the figures given above clearly indicate that the present qualifications have had, as they were no doubt intended to have, the effect of restricting the electorate to the comparatively well-to-do.

12 We questioned many witnesses about their views on the extension of the franchise and from most of them received a favourable reply. In some Colonies it may be true that, as stated by opponents of any change, the lowering, or removal, of the qualifications for the exercise of the vote is not at present a live political issue. Nevertheless, the point clearly deserves serious consideration on its merits. The case for an extension of the franchise is founded mainly on the claim that the people of these Colonies have now reached a stage at which they must either stagnate politically, or move one more step in their progress towards that self-government which is the avowed aim of British Colonial policy. The opponents of concession argue that the changes which have taken place, and are still taking place, in labour and other conditions in the West Indies are so far undermining the existing social structure that any step which today might accelerate the pace of that process should at least be postponed until the West Indian peoples have had time to adjust themselves to the new circumstances brought about by these changes. Between these two extremes lie many varying shades of opinion, of which only one need be mentioned here. It is the view that the franchise should be extended, but made subject to some form of literacy test from which all voters now registered would be excused. This suggestion is superficially

attractive, but experience elsewhere has shewn that such tests may be abused, and we understand that it was not considered desirable to adopt them when an extended franchise was introduced a few years ago in India, where the percentage of illiteracy is higher than that of the West Indies.

13 Some of us hold that the time has already come for the introduction of universal adult suffrage throughout the West Indies. We are not all satisfied that this is the case but we are unanimously of the opinion that universal suffrage should be the ultimate goal.

14 Those of us who feel that it would be premature to adopt at once so wide a measure of enfranchisement recommend that the Colonial Governments should give early and earnest consideration to the subject with a view to reducing the present qualifications so as to enlarge the electorate to as great an extent as local conditions make possible or prudent.

15 It is suggested that a fully representative committee should be appointed in each Colony to undertake this duty and that those various committees should consult with each other in order to secure the maximum possible degree of uniformity in the qualifications required throughout the islands – a point of some importance in connection with a possible future Federation.

16 In this connection the position of women should come under review. At present, in some Colonies women are debarred from registration as electors, while in others the age at which women become eligible for the vote differs from that prescribed for men.

17 All such discrimination between the sexes should certainly be abolished but even the grant of votes to women on the same terms as to men would not, in the circumstances prevailing in the West Indies, result in the enfranchisement of any large number of women. This is one of the considerations which have influenced these members of the Royal Commission who advocate the immediate introduction of universal suffrage. Those of us who dissent from that proposal consider that the situation can be met to some extent by the grant of a vote to the wives of registered electors.[9]

9 Universal adult suffrage was introduced into Jamaica in 1944, Trinidad and Tobago 1946, Barbados 1950, Leeward Islands 1951, Windward Islands 1951, British Guiana 1953, British Honduras 1953 and the Bahama Islands 1962.

CHAPTER XXV

CONCLUSIONS AND RECOMMENDATIONS . . .

Constitutional and Closer Union

53 We do not support either of the extreme proposals put before us for the grant of immediate and complete self-government based on universal suffrage, or for a wide increase of the authority of.Governors which would convert the existing system into a virtual autocracy; the one because it would render impossible the financial control necessary if, as we consider to be inevitable, substantial assistance is to be afforded by Your Majesty's Government through the West Indian Welfare Fund and otherwise; the other because it would be politically a retrograde step. More, and not less, participation by the people in the work of government is a real necessity for lasting social advancement. At the present stage, we attach more importance to the truly representative character of Legislative Councils than to any drastic change in their functions.

54 As stated in paragraph 18 of this Chapter, political federation is not of itself an appropriate means of meeting the pressing needs of the West Indies. Nevertheless, it is the end to which policy should be directed.

55 There is no doubt that the representation of West Indian as of Colonial interests generally at Westminster is inadequate. The pressure of business on Parliament makes it impracticable to provide for this within the framework of present Parliamentary procedure, e.g., by the appointment of colonial representatives to the House of Commons, even if, as is desirable, more Parliamentary time were to be devoted to colonial business. A more hopeful plan would be the association of colonial delegates with the work of any standing Parliamentary Committee which may be created to consider colonial affairs.

56 We recommend:-

(a) That care should be taken to ensure that all important sections and interests of the community receive adequate representation in the Executive Councils (Chapter XXII, paragraph 8);
(b) That consideration should be given to the adoption of a Committee System on an advisory basis to give elected representatives an insight into the practical details of government (Chapter XXII, paragraphs 4-6);
(c) That official representation in Legislative Councils should be confined to the Colonial Secretary, the Treasurer and the Attorney General, and the resulting vacancies filled by nominations in the spirit recommended in (a) above (Chapter XXII, paragraph 7);
(d) That in order to secure that the elected element in Legislative

Councils shall be as truly representative as possible, the object of policy should be the introduction of universal adult suffrage. Some of us held that this should be introduced forthwith; others that it should be reached by gradual stages and to this end recommend the appointment of local committees to consider the extension of the franchise, both for local and for central government . . . (Chapter XXII, paragraphs 12-17);

(e) That in all West Indian Colonies a careful examination should be made at an early date of the possibility of reducing substantially the margin between the qualification for registration as a voter and those for membership of the Legislative Council the latter being in many cases unnecessarily high (Chapter XXII, paragraphs 18 and 19).

PART II
THE DEVELOPMENT OF REPRESENTATION

A. Official majority in the Legislative Council with restricted franchise.

(i) The Dominica Constitution, 1924.

(a) Despatch from the Secretary of State for the Colonies to the Governor of the Leeward Islands dated 29th June 1922.

Sir,

I have the honour to acknowledge the receipt of your despatch No 29 of the 24th of January and to inform you that the petition praying for a measure of representative Government and for the withdrawal of Dominica from the Leeward Islands Confederacy has been laid before the King.

2 By His Majesty's command I have given the requests contained in the petition careful consideration and they are fully discussed in the report of the Honourable E.F.L. Wood which has been laid before Parliament and of which a copy is enclosed.

3 I am addressing you in a separate despatch upon the question of defederation. So far as representative Government in Dominica is concerned, I wish to state emphatically that the conditions in the island are not such as to enable one to agree to any proposal which would deprive the Executive of the ultimate control now exercised through the official majority in the Legislative Council.

(b) Extracts from the Dominica Constitution Ordinance, 1924.[10]
(No: 21 of 1924. Ordinances of Dominica.)

4 From and after the date to be fixed by the Governor under the preceding Section there shall be a Legislative Council in and for the Presidency of Dominica composed of the Governor, the Administrator, six official members, two nominated members and four elected members. Provided that the proceedings of the Council shall not be invalid on account of any vacancies therein.

5 The Official Members shall be persons holding office in the public service of the Presidency and shall be such as His Majesty may from time to time appoint by any Instruction or Warrant under the Royal Sign Manual and Signet, or as the Governor in pursuance of instructions from His Majesty through one of His Majesty's Principal Secretaries of State may from time to time appoint under the Public Seal of the Presidency. If any Official Member of the Council shall cease to hold office in the public service of the Presidency, his seat upon the Council shall thereupon become vacant.

6 The Nominated Members shall be persons not holding any office in the public service of the Presidency and shall be such as His Majesty may from time to time appoint by any Instruction or Warrant under the Royal Sign Manual and Signet or as the Governor in pursuance of instructions from His Majesty through one of His Majesty's Principal Secretaries of State may from time to time appoint under the Public Seal of the Presidency. If any nominated member of the Council shall accept any office in the public service of the Presidency the seat of such member shall become vacant.

7 The Elected Members shall be persons to be elected as hereinafter provided . . .

9 . . . No person shall be capable of being elected a Member of the Council for any electoral district, or having been elected, shall sit or vote in the Council, unless he

(a) possess a clear annual income of £200, or
(b) owns real property in the Presidency of the value of at least £500 above all charges and encumbrances affecting the same, or
(c) is in occupation of lands in the Presidency of an annual rental value of at least £50, and either has resided in that electoral district for 12 months preceding the date of election or is the owner of real

10 Although Crown Colonies the Leeward Islands retained the right to legislate for the constitutions of their Legislative Councils under the Leeward Islands Act, 1871.

property situate in that electoral district of the value of at least £500 above all charges and encumbrances affecting the same or is in the occupation of lands situate in that electoral district of an annual rental value of at least £50 . . .

21 Every person shall be entitled to be registered as a voter for any one electoral district, and, when registered, to vote at the election of a member of the Council, for such district, who is qualified as follows, that is to say:-

(1) Being a man, has attained the age of twenty-one years, or being a woman, has attained the age of thirty years,

(2) Is under no legal incapacity

(3) Is a British Subject

(4) Has resided in the Presidency for twelve months at least previous to the date of registration or is domiciled in the Presidency and is resident therein at the date of such registration, and in either case, possesses some one of the following qualifications:-
(a) has a net income of at least thirty pounds per annum,
(b) is the owner of real property within the Presidency of the value of at least one hundred pounds above all charges and encumbrances affecting the same,
(c) is paying rent in respect of real property situate within Presidency of at least twelve pounds per annum,
(d) being resident in the district has paid direct taxes in the previous year to an amount of at least fifteen shillings.

Provided

(i) That no person shall be registered as a voter or be entitled to vote for the election of a Member of the Council who has been convicted of perjury in any Court in His Majesty's Dominions or who has been sentenced by any such Court to death, or penal servitude, or imprisonment with hard labour for a term exceeding twelve months, and has not either suffered the punishment to which he was sentenced or such other punishment as by competent authority may have been substituted for the same or received a free pardon from His Majesty.

(ii) That no person shall be registered as a voter who has within twelve calendar months immediately proceeding the first day of January in any year in which a register of voters is prepared received any relief from public or parochial funds.

(iii) That no person shall be registered as a voter unless he or she shall with his or her own hand have subscribed his or her name to his or her claim to be registered and written thereon the date of such subscription.

(ii) Extracts from the Saint Vincent (Legislative Council) Order in Council, 1924.
(S.R. & O./1924.)

III There shall be in and for Saint Vincent a Legislative Council, constituted as hereinafter mentioned.

IV The Council shall consist of the Governor, of four *ex-officio* Members, of one Nominated Member and of three Elected Members.[11]

The *ex-officio* Members shall be the persons for the time being lawfully discharging the functions of the respective offices of Colonial Secretary, of Attorney-General, of Treasurer, and of one other office to be from time to time designated by His Majesty by an Order in His Privy Council, or through a Secretary of State.

(iii) Extracts from the Report of the Franchise Committee of Trinidad and Tobago, 1923.[12]
(Trinidad and Tobago Council Paper No: 90 of 1923.)

We, the Commissioners appointed by Your Excellency's Commission dated the 30th October, 1922, to consider and make recommendations upon the following matters, that is to say:

I The qualifications necessary for election to the Legislative Council;

II The qualifications necessary for the right to vote at an election of a member of the said Legislative Council;

11 Sometimes referred to as a "balanced legislature" this type of composition of the Legislative Council is included here since the Governor's original vote creates an official majority.

Qualifications for elected membership in the Legislative Council and for the right to vote were roughly the same as those for Dominica in 1924, but were slightly more restricted.

12 In 1924 the Legislative Council of Trinidad and Tobago was reconstituted by Letters Patent and an Order in Council came into operation on 21st August, 1924. The newly constituted Legislative Council contained elected members for the first time. The composition of the Council was the Governor (with an original and a casting vote), the Colonial Secretary, the Attorney General, the Treasurer, not more than nine other official members, not more than six nominated unofficials and seven elected members. An official majority was thus achieved by the Governor having an original and casting vote.

III The manner in which the Colony should be divided into seven Constituencies;

have the honour to report as follows:-

3 Your Excellency's Commission to us recites as one of the recommendations of the Under Secretary of State that candidates for election to the Legislative Council should be British subjects and should be resident in their constituencies. We were informed however by our Chairman that he was authorised to state that Your Excellency would be willing to consider with a view to submitting to the Secretary of State any recommendation of the Commissioners with regard to relaxing the residence qualifications so far as to permit the alternative of substantial real property interest if in the opinion of the Commissioners candidates thoroughly representative of districts would be secured. Your Excellency will observe that our recommendations under the head of "Members Qualifications" provide that a candidate for election in respect of an electoral district in which he does not reside shall be qualified only by virtue of substantial real property interest in that district. We are satisfied that this provision as an alternative to a residence qualification will ensure efficient representation for the various electoral districts.

4 We now submit the following recommendations upon the matters referred to us –

1 MEMBERS' QUALIFICATIONS

No person shall be qualified to be elected a Member of the Legislative Council or, having been elected, to sit or vote in the Council unless –

(a) he is of the male sex and is entitled to be, and is in fact registered as a voter;
(b) he is able to read and write English; and
(c) he possesses in his own right one or more of the following qualifications, namely:-
 (i) Real estate of the value of at least £2,500 above all charges and encumbrances affecting the same, or from which he derives a clear annual income of not less than £200; or
 (ii) A clear annual income of over £400 arising from any source.

Provided that

(1) A person shall not be entitled to be elected or to be a member of the Legislative Council for any electoral district unless he is resident in that district and has resided therein for the twelve months immediately preceding the date of election, or possesses in that electoral district real

estate belonging to him in his own right of the value of at least £5,000 above all charges and encumbrances affecting the same, or from which he derives a clear annual income of not less than £400.

(2) A person shall not be entitled to be elected or to be a member of the Legislative Council if he is the holder of any office of emolument under the Crown or under the Government of the Colony, or is a Minister of Religion.

II VOTERS' QUALIFICATIONS

Every person shall be entitled to be registered as a voter in any one electoral district, and, when registered, to vote at the election of a member of the Legislative Council for such district, who is qualified as follows:-

(a) being a man, has attained the age of 21 years, or being a woman has attained the age of 30 years;
(b) is under no legal incapacity;
(c) is a British subject by birth or naturalization;
(d) has resided in the Colony for at least two years prior to the date of such registration, or is domiciled in the Colony and is resident therein at the date of such registration;
(e) is able to satisfy the registering officer that he or she can understand the English language when spoken;

and is, in the electoral district in which he or she claims to be registered at the date of such registration, and has been for at least twelve months immediately prior to such date, also possessed of one or more of the following qualifications, namely:

(1) is in occupation, as owner, of premises assessed to any house rate, or taxes under section 3 of the Lands and Building Taxes Ordinance, 1920, at an annual rateable value of not less than £12.10s.0d, in Port-of-Spain or any Borough and £10 elsewhere, or is in occupation, as tenant, of premises in respect of which he or she really and *bona fide* pays rent at a rate not less than £12.10s.0d. per annum in Port-of-Spain or any Borough, and £10 per annum elsewhere; or
(2) is in occupation, as a lodger, of lodgings, and as such lodger has paid during the preceding twelve months not less than £12.10. for rent alone, or not less than £62.10s.0d. for rent and board combined; and has also resided in such lodgings during the whole of such period; or
(3) is in occupation, as owner, or as tenant under agreement in writing for one year or upwards, of land or of land and house thereon, assessed to taxes under section 3 of the Lands and Buildings Taxes Ordinance, 1920, and in respect of which not less than 10/- a year is payable in such taxes or

(4) is in receipt of an annual salary of not less than £62.10s.0d.

Provided that –

(a) When the qualifying property in (1) is jointly occupied by more persons than one, then each of such occupiers shall be entitled to be registered in respect of such property, if the annual rateable value at which the property is assessed to the house rate or taxes is an amount which, when divided by the number of occupiers shall give not less than £12.10.0. or £10, as the case may be for each such occupier.
(b) When the qualifying property in (3) is jointly occupied by more persons than one, then each of such occupiers shall be entitled to be registered in respect of such property if the amount payable in taxes in respect of such property is an amount which, when divided by the number of occupiers, shall give not less than 10/- a year for each occupier.

No person shall be entitled to be registered if –

(a) he or she has, within the six months immediately preceding the date of registration, received poor relief from public funds, or
(b) he or she has been sentenced by any Court in the Empire to death or to penal servitude or to imprisonment with hard labour for any term exceeding 12 months, and has not either suffered the punishment to which he or she was sentenced or such other punishment as by competent authority was substituted for the same, or received a free pardon from His Majesty.[13]

B. Unofficial majority in the Legislative Council with restricted franchise.

(i) Extract from the Address of the Governor to the Legislative Council of the Leeward Islands, 1935.
*(*Leeward Islands Gazette, *Supplement to Gazette No. 10, of 1935.)*

NEW CONSTITUTIONS

You will probably all be interested to know what is going to happen with regard to the suggested altering of the Constitutions of the several Presidencies. As you know, the Secretary of State left it to the unofficial members of the various Legislative Councils to express their own unhampered views, as representing public opinion generally, on the broad questions (subject to

13 The qualifications for members of the Legislative Council and for voters as recommended by this Report were accepted.

certain safeguards) of the abolition of the official majority and of the election of unofficial members. Antigua, Dominica and Montserrat expressed themselves in favour of these suggestions, and St. Kitts, by a majority of one, rejected them. All the replies are now with the Secretary of State, and I expect at any moment to have a decision from him.[14] Four years ago I publicly declared at a meeting of this Council that I considered that the people should have a larger voice in the management of their own affairs, as it was a natural path of progress, and I still adhere to that view. I shall therefore welcome any measure that brings this Colony into line with the modern trend of a rational and progressive form of Government. But I think it would be expected that the people who are to take a part in the burdens and care of administration, whether as electors or elected members, should be of sufficient education and standing to appreciate fully the nature of their new liabilities. And I am thankful to say there are no lack of such, irrespective of race, class or creed, in this Colony.

(ii) Extracts from the Despatch from the Secretary of State for the Colonies to the Governor of the Windward Islands, dated 2nd June 1935.

I am prepared to agree to the new Council in Grenada being composed as follows:-

The Governor (with a casting vote only).
3 *ex officio* members (the officer performing the duties of Colonial Secretary, the Treasurer and the Attorney General).
4 nominated unofficial members.
7 elected unofficial members.

I appreciate the desire which is felt by the unofficials in the present Legislative Council that the Chamber of Commerce and the Agricultural Association should be represented among the nominated unofficial members of the new Council, and I am willing that these bodies should have the right to put forward names of their members for consideration by the Governor. It should be clearly understood, however, that my approval of this arrangement must not be held in any way to imply that the Governor is bound to accept such recommendations, and his discretion in the appointment of nominated members must remain quite unfettered.

In the case of each of the three Legislatures I desire that, in accordance with the recommendations made by the Closer Union Commissioners on page 20 of their Report (Cmd. 4383), the Governor (or Administrator) should have power to summon to the Council the head of any government department,

14 Unofficial majorities were introduced into the Legislatures of the Presidencies in 1936, but not into the General Legislative Council of the Leeward Islands Federation until 1951 when an elected majority was introduced.

when the business before the Council renders the presence of that officer desirable, on the understanding that while for the occasion he would sit as a member of the Council and would take part in its proceedings, he would not exercise any vote.

As regards the question of voters' qualifications, I consider that, in accordance with the recommendations in the Closer Union Commission's Report, the qualifications already in force in Dominica for voters at the elections should be adopted in all three Islands.

In so far as qualifications for elected membership of the Legislature are concerned, these also should, I consider, conform in the three Islands to the provisions of the Dominica constitution. But, if unofficial opinion in the Islands so desires, (a) the qualification in respect of residence in the electoral district and (b) the alternative qualification, viz. the occupation of land in the electoral district of an annual rental value of at least £50, need not be adopted. As indicated in my despatch of the 21st of February under reference, women should retain their eligibility for membership of the several Legislative Councils.[15]

(iii) Extracts from the Grenada (Legislative Council) Order in Council, 1936. (S.I. 1371/1936.)[16]

3 There shall be in and for Grenada a Legislative Council constituted as hereinafter mentioned.

4 The Council shall consist of the Governor, three *ex officio* Members, four Nominated Members and seven Elected Members . . .

5 The Governor may summon to the Council the person for the time being performing the functions of Head of any Government Department in the Island notwithstanding that such person may not be a member of the Council, when in the opinion of the Governor the business before the Council

15 The only major difference between the new constitution of the Windward Islands was that the composition of the legislatures of St. Lucia and St. Vincent, unlike that of Grenada, was the Governor, three *ex-officio*, three nominated and five elected members.

16 This Order in Council is being used to illustrate the changes made in the constitution of the legislatures of the Windwards and Leewards in the mid-1930s. It is followed by the Dominica Order in Council (Document no. B. iv), which was not passed until 1939 because of the problems created by that island's detachment from the Leeward Islands' Federation and its joining the Windward group.

Trinidad and Tobago did not get an unofficial majority in the Legislative Council until 1941.

renders the presence of such person desirable. Any person so summoned shall be entitled to take part in the proceedings of the Council relating to the matter in respect of which he was summoned but shall not thereby become a Member of the Council and shall not have the right to vote in the Council . . .

7 No person shall be capable of being elected a Member of the Council, or, having been elected, shall sit or vote in the Council, who at the time of election –

(1) Is the holder of any office or emolument under the Crown, or under a Municipal Corporation within Grenada; or
(2) Is a minister of religion; or
(3) Is a returning officer of the district for which the election is held; or
(4) Is not entitled to vote at the election of a Member of the Council for some electoral district; or
(5) Does not
  (a) possess a clear income of £200 per annum; or
  (b) own real property in the Island of the value of at least £500 above all charges and encumbrances affecting the same . . .

18(1) Every person shall be entitled to be registered as a voter for any one electoral district, and, when registered, to vote at the election of a member of the Council, for such district, who is qualified as follows, that is to say:-

(a) Has attained the age of twenty-one years,
(b) Is not a lunatic so found or declared under any law in force in the Island,
(c) Is a British Subject,
(d) Has resided in the Island for twelve months at least previous to the date of registration or is domiciled in the Island and is resident therein at the date of such registration, and in either case, possesses any one of the following qualifications:-
  (i) has a clear income of at least thirty pounds per annum,
  (ii) is the owner of real property within the Island of the value of at least one hundred pounds above all charges and encumbrances affecting the same,
  (iii) is paying rent in respect of real property situate within the Island at the rate of at least twelve pounds per annum,
  (iv) being resident in the district has paid direct taxes in the previous year to an amount of at least fifteen shillings.

Provided that –

(i) No person shall be registered as a voter or be entitled to vote for the election of a Member of the Council who has, in any part of

His Majesty's dominions or any territory under His Majesty's protection, been convicted of perjury or been sentenced to death, or penal servitude, or imprisonment with hard labour or for a term exceeding twelve months, and has not either suffered the punishment to which he was sentenced or such other punishment as by competent authority may have been substituted for the same or received a free pardon from His Majesty.

(ii) No person shall be registered in any register of voters who has, within twelve calendar months immediately preceding the first day of January in the year in which that register is prepared, received any relief from public or parochial funds except such special relief as may be declared by any law for the time being in force not to be relief for the purposes of this proviso.

(iii) No person shall be registered as a voter unless he shall with his own hand have subscribed his name to his claim to be registered and written thereon the date of such subscription or, if he is incapacitated by blindness or other physical cause from so doing, such subscription and writing shall be performed on his behalf by the officer charged with the duty of registering voters . . .

37 It shall be lawful for the Governor, by and with the advice and consent of the Council, to make laws for the peace, order and good government of Grenada.

38 Subject to the provisions contained in the following section all questions proposed for decision in the Council shall be determined by a majority of votes of those present and voting. The Governor shall not have an original vote on any question, but he shall have a casting vote if the votes shall be equally divided. In the absence of the Governor from the Council the member presiding shall have an original vote and a casting vote if the votes shall be equally divided. The votes of Members of the Council shall be taken in the inverse order of their precedence.

39 If the Governor shall consider that it is expedient in the interests of public faith or of good government (which expressions shall, without prejudice to their generality, include the responsibility of the Island as a component part of the British Empire, and all matters pertaining to the appointment, salary, and other conditions of service of any public officer or officers) that any bill introduced, or any motion, resolution or vote proposed for decision, in the Council should have effect, then, if the Council fail to pass such bill, motion, resolution or vote within such time as the Governor may think reasonable and expedient, the Governor at any time within his discretion may notwithstanding any provisions of this Order or of any Standing Orders of the Council, declare that such bill, motion, resolution or vote shall have effect

and thereupon the same shall have effect, as if it had been passed by the Council, and in the case of any such bill the provisions of this Order as to assent to bills and disallowance of Ordinances shall apply accordingly.[17]

40 It shall be lawful for His Majesty to disallow any law to which the Governor has assented and to signify such disallowance through a Secretary of State. Every law so disallowed shall cease to have effect from the time when the signification of such disallowance shall be published by the Governor in the Official Gazette.[18]

41 When a Bill passed by the Legislative Council is presented to the Governor for his assent he shall, according to his discretion, but subject to any Instructions addressed to him under His Majesty's Sign Manual and Signet or through a Secretary of State, declare that he assents thereto, or refuses his assent to the same, or that he reserves the same for the signification of His Majesty's pleasure. If he assents thereto, he shall sign the Bill in token of such assent.[19]

42 A Bill reserved for the signification of His Majesty's pleasure shall take effect as soon as His Majesty shall have given His assent to the same by Order in Council, or through a Secretary of State, and the Governor shall have signified such assent by proclamation published in the Gazette:

Provided that no such proclamation shall be issued after two years from the date on which the Bill was presented to the Governor for his assent.[20]

43 Subject to the provision of this Order the Governor and the Council shall, in the transaction of business and passing of laws, conform as nearly as may be to the directions in that behalf from time to time conveyed to the Governor in Instructions under His Majesty's Sign Manual and Signet . . .

53 His Majesty doth hereby reserve to Himself, His heirs and successors, full power and authority from time to time to revoke alter or amend this Order as to Him or them shall seem fit; and nothing herein contained shall affect His or their undoubted right, by and with the advice of His or their Privy Council, to make from time to time all such laws as may to Him or them appear necessary for the peace, order, and good government of Grenada.

17 The Governor's reserve power of certification is formed in colonial constitutions when the official majority gives way to an unofficial majority. The power is gradually withdrawn as the colony advances to full internal self-government and independence.
18 Certain powers of reservation and disallowance remain as part of all colonial constitutions, disappearing only when the country becomes independent.
19 The Governor's absolute discretion to grant and withhold assent to legislation remains until the colony gets a large measure of responsibility.
20 See footnote 18.

(iv) Extracts from the Dominica Order in Council, 1939. *(S.I. 1896/1939.)*

1 This Order may be cited as the Dominica Order in Council, 1939.

2 The appointed day shall be the first day of January, nineteen hundred and forty, and as from that day the following provisions of this Order shall have effect.

3 Dominica shall be governed and administered as a Colony comprised in the Windward Islands[21] . . .

6 (1) There shall be in and for Dominica a Legislative Council, to be called the Legislative Council of Dominica, constituted as provided in this Order.

(2) The Council shall be composed of the Governor, three *ex officio* members, three nominated members and five elected members . . .

9 No person shall be capable of being elected a member of the Council, or, having been elected, shall sit or vote in the Council, who at the time of election –[22]

(1) is not a British subject; or
(2) is the holder of any public office; or
(3) is a minister of religion; or
(4) is a returning officer of the district for which the election is held; or
(5) is not entitled to vote at the election of a member of the Council for some electoral district; or
(6) does not
  (a) possess a clear income of £200 per annum; or
  (b) own real property in Dominica of the value of at least £500 above all charges and encumbrances affecting the same; or
  (c) occupy land in Dominica as tenant to another, of rental value of at least fifty pounds per annum.

21 The Dominica Act, 1938, provided for the separation of Dominica from the Colony of the Leeward Islands. That separation was not effected until this Order in Council linked Dominica with the Windward Islands group.

22 In most respects this Order in Council is the same as those for the other Windward Islands made in 1936. However, note the slight difference in members qualification in this Order and in the Grenada (Legislative Council) Order in Council, 1936. (Chapter V, Part II, doc. B (iii).)

C. The Jamaican Constitution of 1944 and documents leading to its adoption.[23]

(i) Extracts from the Report of the Select Committee of the Legislative Council appointed to prepare and draft a political constitution for Jamaica. (Legislative Council Minutes, 1939. Appendix no. XXXII.)

PROPOSED AMENDED CONSTITUTION

1 There shall be in and for Jamaica a Legislature constituted of House of Assembly and a Legislative Council.

2 The House of Assembly shall consist of 14 members, one to be elected by each of the 14 parishes for a term of five years. Provided that before the expiration of the said first term the question of number of members shall be reconsidered.

3 The Legislative Council shall be a nominated Council and shall consist of ten members nominated by the Governor from officials in the Colony and other gentlemen who possess the like qualifications as are required of members of the House of Assembly, other than residential qualification. This qualification shall not be required of members who are officials . . .

9 The qualifications and disqualifications for members of the House of Assembly shall be as at present including the residential . . . [The major property and income qualifications were: (a) ownership of lands producing £150 per annum; or (b) if income derived partly from ownership of land and partly business then £200 per annum; or (c) other income £300 per annum.]

13 Qualification of Electors to remain as at present, and subject to the consideration of the representation made by the present Council to the Secretary of State for the Colonies . . . [The major property and income qualifications in Jamaica were: (a) payment of rates on property amounting to 10s. per annum if a male, or £2 per annum if a female; or (b) payment of taxes amounting to £1.10s. per annum if a male, or £2 per annum if a female, in respect of personal property; or (c) a salary of £50 per annum; or (d) an income of £50 per annum with occupation of premises rented at not less than £10 per annum.

23 In 1944 Jamaica moved further ahead of other territories in the development of its constitution. Although documents D(i)-(v) of Part II of this Chapter show developments in constitutions which were not as advanced as that of Jamaica in 1944, this section is inserted before them since, to a larger extent, Jamaica's development was a spur to and a model for the other territories.

However, the representation made to the Secretary of State arose from a resolution of the Council, passed in December 1938, recommending the introduction of universal adult suffrage.]

15 The House of Assembly shall appoint a Speaker for the House who may or may not be a member of the House at a salary of £600 per annum. The Speaker shall have a casting vote only. He shall be appointed at the beginning of each term and for the term only . . .

17 The Legislative Council shall appoint at the beginning of each term a President who may or may not be a member of the Council. The President shall have a casting vote only . . .

21 The Legislative Council shall be entitled to initiate general legislation, but it shall not be entitled to introduce any bill, vote or resolution, imposing any tax or disposing of or charging any part of the public revenue . . .

24 After a bill has passed the third reading in the House of Assembly it shall be transmitted to the Legislative Council for passing or rejection provided that nothing shall prevent both Houses from conferring as to any matter in the bill so sent to the Legislative Council with the view of determining whether the bill shall be rejected or passed.

25 If the House of Assembly shall pass a bill and that bill is rejected by the Legislative Council, the House of Assembly shall be entitled to reintroduce the bill at the next session, and if the bill again passes the House of Assembly and is again rejected by the Legislative Council such second rejection shall have no effect and the bill shall be deemed to have passed the said Council, and on the Governor or Sovereign assenting thereto it shall become law.

26 Any bill which has passed the third reading in the Legislative Council shall be transmitted to the House of Assembly for consideration and rejection or approval, and in the case of approval by the House of Assembly the bill shall then be ready for the assent of the Governor or the Sovereign as the case may be . . .

29 The Governor shall dissolve the House of Assembly and the Legislative Council at the expiration of five years from the date of the return of the first Writs at the last preceding general election, if it shall not have been sooner dissolved . . .

31 It shall be lawful for the Governor with the advice and consent of the House of Assembly and Legislative Council to make laws for the peace, order and government of the Island . . .[24]

24 It was recommended that the Governor should have discretionary powers to assent to legislation, to reserve legislation for His Majesty's approval, and

35 The House of Assembly shall not pass nor shall the Governor assent to any Law, vote or Resolution, imposing any tax or disposing of or charging any part of the public revenue, unless such Law, vote or Resolution shall have been proposed by or by the direction of or shall have the express approval of the Executive Committee.

36 The Speaker of the House of Assembly or the President of the Legislative Council if present or in the absence of the Speaker or the President any member respectively appointed by them in writing or in default of such appointment the Member present who stands first in order of precedence shall preside at every Meeting of the House of Assembly and Legislative Council respectively.

37 All questions proposed for decision in the House of Assembly and Legislative Council shall be determined by a majority of the votes of the members present. The Speaker or other presiding member and the President or other presiding member shall not have an original vote on any question but shall have a casting vote if the votes shall be equally divided. The votes of the Elected Members and the Members of the Legislative Council who are members of the Executive Committee shall be taken last.

(ii) Extracts from the Minority Report of the Select Committee of the Legislative Council appointed to prepare and draft a political constitution for Jamaica.
(Jamaica Legislative Council Minutes, 1939. Appendix no. XXXIII.)

1 After the fullest consideration we recommend that there should be only one Legislative Chamber to be known as the Legislative Council[25] . . .

4 The Legislative Council shall have the power to initiate and conclude trade treaties with countries within the Empire without the sanction of the Imperial Government. Trade treaties with foreign countries shall be initiated and concluded by the Imperial Government.

5 With these reservations we are in agreement with the rest of the report of the majority except where it may conflict with our submissions and regret that we are unable to subscribe to all the proposals set out in the Majority Report of your Committee.

that the Imperial Government should have the power of disallowance. However, it was not recommended that the Governor should have over-riding powers of certification.
25 The Minority Report, signed by three M.L.Cs, recommended a mixed Legislative Council with an elected majority but retaining *ex officio* and nominated members.

(iii) Extracts from the Despatch from the Secretary of State for the Colonies to the Governor of Jamaica, dated 7th March 1941.[26]

Sir, – I have the honour to address you on the subject of the constitution of Jamaica.

3 I set out below the changes in the Island constitution which appear to me desirable and which I trust may prove acceptable. In some respects immediate action can be taken: in others, for reasons I shall outline, it can not. Nevertheless, in the last-named cases, I shall suggest measures which, though intended as temporary, are in line with the recommendations of the West India Royal Commission, and should go some way to smooth the working of the constitution in the immediate future.

4 The Royal Commission recommended that universal adult suffrage should be the object of policy but did not agree as to speed at which this change should be applied. In the case of Jamaica, the Legislative Council resolved in December, 1938:-

> 'that in the opinion of this Council voters list should be amended so as to provide for universal suffrage.'

I am prepared to agree that Jamaica should be granted universal adult suffrage, and I see no reason why this should not be embodied as an integral part of immediate changes which I shall propose.

5 It appears to be generally agreed that the Legislative Council should be enlarged and remodelled. I am prepared to give favourable consideration to a new model which would comprise approximately double the present number of Elected Members and also Nominated Members, together with a reduced number of Ex-Officio Members (on the lines recommended by the West India Royal Commission) making a total of not less than forty. Any Member of the Legislative Council would have power to initiate legislation except on financial matters.

6 For the reasons outlined above,[27] the reconstitution of the Legislative Council proposed above must await the reform of local government, the census, and the holding of elections on the new franchise, if that is accepted.

7 But, as I have indicated above, there are other changes which could be made forthwith. The Royal Commission have recommended (28 (c)) that official representation in Legislative Councils should be confined to the Colonial Secretary, the Treasurer and the Attorney General. This change has already been made in certain other Legislative Councils in the West Indies, and

26 The Secretary of State at this time was Lord Moyne.
27 Weak local government and poor population statistics.

I am prepared to agree that a similar change should be introduced in Jamaica. It is understood that the resulting vacancies will be filled by nominations in which care is taken to ensure that all important sections and interests of the community receive adequate representation. It is also understood that Nominated Members will vote freely, according to their own convictions.

I have noted above that in certain other Legislative assemblies in the West Indies official representation has been similarly reduced. Concurrently, however, extended powers have been given to the Governor. In the present constitution of Jamaica there are certain peculiarities existing in no other Colony. On the one hand the Governor has the power of "paramount importance" provided in Clauses 43 and 44 of the Order-in-Council of 1884 as amended by Order-in-Council of 1895; on the other the Elected Members have the powers laid down in the same clauses, notably the "power of the nine". Both of these powers have formed the subject of criticism and controversy. In the immediate changes at present contemplated I do not propose that the powers vested in the Elected Members should be in any way altered: but I regard it as essential that concurrently, with the reduction of official membership of the Legislative Council the powers of the Governor should be more clearly defined, and in some degree enlarged.

[The definition which follows in this despatch is exactly the same as that given in clause 39 of the Grenada (Legislative Council) Order in Council, 1936. See Chapter IV, Part II, document B (iii).]

If these proposals are accepted, I am prepared to recommend that the Governor should withdraw from the Presidency of the Legislative Council and that in his place there should be a Speaker. In the first instance I propose that the Speaker should be appointed by the Governor, but I am prepared at a later stage to consider his election by the Council, subject to the usual provision for his presentation to the Governor for approval. The question of payment of a salary to the Speaker is one which I should wish you to discuss with the Elected and Nominated Members.

I propose that officials, other than Ex-Officio Members, should be permitted to be present at meetings of the Council, when necessary, and to address the Council, but not to be regarded as Members for the purpose of voting.

I am also prepared to approve of the payment to Members of the Council, both Elected and Nominated, of a fixed consolidated travelling allowance in place of the present variable travelling allowance.[28]

28 This despatch is not in response to the Select Committee's Report. See the next document.

(d) Extracts from the Despatch of the Secretary of State for the Colonies to the Governor of Jamaica, dated 5th January 1942.[29]

2 The proposals contained in my despatch No. 42 of the 7th March, 1941, were based on a sincere desire to provide Jamaica with a more liberal Constitution containing the possibility and the prospect of further advance, and the adverse vote of the elected members on the occasion of the debate of last August has caused me great disappointment. Perusal of the record of the debate and of the petitions and other communications which have been received from various quarters leads me to think that serious misapprehensions exist both as to the nature of the officially sponsored proposals and as to the limits within which I feel bound at the present stage to confine any scheme of constitutional reform. It is also clear that public opinion in Jamaica is at present far from united on the question of the form and direction which constitutional development should assume.

3 I propose first to comment on the main features of the official proposals.

(a) UNIVERSAL ADULT SUFFRAGE

I regard the introduction of universal adult suffrage as the essential foundation of any scheme of constitutional reform in Jamaica.

(b) LEGISLATIVE COUNCIL

I am unable to entertain any proposals which would have the effect of obscuring the vital distinction between responsible and representative Government: the supreme executive authority of the Governor must therefore be preserved, and it is essential that he should have the necessary powers of "certification" and of "veto". I am, however, anxious that by means of enlarged representation in the Legislative Council the people of Jamaica should be given a fuller voice in the management of their affairs, and the proposals contained in my despatch of the 7th March, 1941, were directed to that end. The proposed Legislative Council of approximately 40 members would facilitate the development of work in committees on an advisory footing as recommended by the Royal Commission, thus associating elected members with the day to day business of administration and providing them with experience to fit them for higher responsibilities. I regret to learn that the value of this sytem, which is indeed not precluded even in the present Council of smaller size, appears to be not yet fully appreciated by some of the elected members.

The recommendation of the elected members for the creation of a bicameral legislature has received consideration, but I regret that I am unable to

29 This despatch was also from Lord Moyne. (See previous document.)

accept it. The introduction of adult suffrage which is now proposed may involve in the initial years the election of a considerable number of inexperienced members to the Legislative Council, and it seems clear that in the early stages at least there will be a better opportunity for experience to be gained and the working of the new constitution will be facilitated, if the elected representatives are concentrated in a single chamber, with ex-officio members and nominated members. Moreover, I cannot overlook the fact that previous experience of the bi-cameral system in Jamaica between 1854 and 1865 was not altogether fortunate.

It follows from these observations that I should find it impossible to entertain the proposals of the People's National Party for the conversion of elected members into Ministers with executive powers and for the limitation of the Governor's powers in respect of legislation . . .

(d) GOVERNOR'S POWER OF CERTIFICATION

The official proposals under this head appear to have been seriously misapprehended by the elected members, the People's National Party and others. It seems to have been assumed that the intention is to confer on the Governor some power which he does not already possess. Under the proposals in my despatch of the 7th March, 1941, a substantial majority of elected members in the Legislative Council would be provided for; and it is necessary to make definite provision for the exercise by the Governor of his power of certification whenever he considers it expedient in the public interest. The opportunity has been taken to draft a revised definition of the power of certification. I know of no ground for the suspicion which appears to be prevalent in certain quarters that under the new constitution the power of certification will be abused. I wish to make it clear that I am not prepared to deprive the constitution of this essential safeguard or to agree to any considerable departure from the revised definition of the Governor's reserve power, which has been framed in accordance with the latest precedents.

4 In the situation which has arisen from the rejection of the proposals put before the Legislative Council, it might be suggested that action should be suspended indefinitely. But that is not a conclusion which His Majesty's Government can accept, and I must make it clear that it is their definite policy to proceed with the institution of a more liberal constitution based upon the grant of universal adult suffrage . . .

(v) Extracts from the Proposais for a new Constitution of Jamaica 20th July 1944.[30]
(Kingston, Jamaica, 1944.)

My Lord, . . .

2 By a despatch dated March 7th, 1941, your Lordship authorised the presentation to the Legislative Council of proposals for changes in the Island Constitution . . .

3 The proposals were rejected by the unanimous vote of the Elected Members of the Legislative Council in August, 1941.

4 The situation thus created was dealt with in a despatch from your Lordship dated the 5th of January, 1942, presented to the Legislative Council in March, 1942 . . .

7 The despatch gave rise to an apprehension in some quarters that the constitutional proposals which were placed before the Legislative Council in 1941, and rejected, would shortly be imposed on the country regardless of the wishes of the people.

8 If the despatch is rightly interpreted as affording ground for this fear it is necessary to point out that to force such a Constitution on Jamaica would be a breach of assurance given by His Excellency the Governor on behalf of His Majesty's Government that under no circumstances would any form of constitution be thrust upon Jamaica if it was not desired by the people.

9 We do not believe that it is intended to compel the people of Jamaica to accept a constitution which does not meet with general approval.

10 It is believed that His Majesty's Government will be willing to reconsider the whole subject, and it is hoped that some means may be devised to facilitate an exchange of views thereon. Opportunity for such exchange is wholly denied by the inadequacy of the existing machinery for such communication and the manner in which it has been used.

11 In the faith of these beliefs the Elected Members of the Legislative Council of Jamaica, the Representatives of the People's National Party and the

30 These proposals were published in 1944 but they were submitted to Government in 1942 and were included in the Governor of Jamaica's despatch to the Secretary of State for the Colonies, dated 5th November 1942.

The most radical demands expressed in this document had to do with grants of responsible government and are included in Part III of this chapter. The elapse of time from 1939 had allowed the crystalization of demands for a more representative and more powerful Executive Council.

Representatives of the Federation of Citizens' Association, being the three public bodies which have made proposals in regard to a new Constitution have conferred together and have, by a spontaneous desire to remove the reproach of disunity and by a sincere effort to reconcile conflicting views, achieved complete and unreserved unanimity on all matters pertaining to the immediate proposals for constitutional reforms[31] . . .

14 The proposals for a bi-cameral Legislature originally put forward in 1939 (referred to in paragraph 1 hereof) have been re-examined in the light of the history of this Colony, and its social and economic structure and the conclusion unanimously reached is that with modification designed to render it a better instrument for the evolution and effective maintenance of a planned policy and for the ultimate achievement of Responsible Government, it is a form well suited in every respect to the conditions that locally prevail.[32]

(vi) Extracts from the Despatch of the Secretary of State for the Colonies to the Governor of Jamaica, dated 10th February 1943.[33]

Sir,

I have the honour to refer to your despatch No. 309 of the 5th of November, 1942, transmitting a memorandum signed by the fourteen Elected Members of the Legislative Council, three representatives of the People's National Party and three representatives of the Federation of Citizens Associations, dealing with the constitutional proposals for Jamaica. Copies of this Memorandum and of the Majority Report of the Select Committee of the Legislative Council appointed in 1939 to prepare a draft political constitution for Jamaica are attached for easy reference. You will observe that the proposals contained in the memorandum are in the main, based on the proposals contained in the Majority Report of the Select Committee.

31 This Memorandum was in basic agreement with the proposals of the Select Committee, 1939 Chapter IV, Part II, doc. C (i). And with regard to the over-riding powers of the Governor stated (paragraph 13):-

"a) That the veto power ought not to be in the hands of the Governor at all, or if in his hands ought to be limited and controlled both by explicit provisions in the Constitution and by provision for an appeal to His Majesty in Council.

b) That any and every power of certification is obnoxious and contrary to the principles of Representative as well as Responsible Government."

32 This Memorandum was signed by the fourteen elected Members of the Legislative Council, by three representatives on behalf of the People's National Party, and three on behalf of the Federation of Citizens' Associations.

33 The Secretary of State was now Oliver Stanley.

2 I have given the matter careful and renewed consideration, and have had the advantage of personal discussion with you. I should be glad if you would convey to the Elected Members of the Legislative Council and to the other signatories the conclusions which I have reached.

3 In the light of the large measure of agreement concerning the form of the constitution desired by the people of Jamaica, I am prepared to accept the proposals for a bicameral legislature, consisting of a House of Assembly elected on a basis of universal adult suffrage and a nominated Legislative Council. There are, however, three respects in which I consider that the proposals should be varied. First, the present proposal is that the House of Assembly should consist of fourteen members, one to be elected by each of the fourteen parishes for a term of five years. In my view, the imminent introduction of adult suffrage will make it necessary to enlarge the House of Assembly beyond this number. If the electoral divisions are, as in the past, to follow parochial boundaries the large variations of population between the parishes will make it undesirable to initiate a new constitution on so uneven a basis of representation. It will be necessary, therefore, either to allot more than one member to certain parishes or to adopt electoral divisions more nearly proportioned to the voting population. The precise number might be left undecided until the results of the recent Census enable the situation to be more clearly seen, but I feel that a House of Assembly could not work successfully under the new conditions which are envisaged with less than twenty-four members.

Secondly with regard to the Legislative Council, which it is proposed should consist of ten members nominated from officials and unofficials, I consider that the Council should consist of fifteen members in order that the opportunities of public service may be spread more widely throughout the community. The majority of Council should consist of unofficial members . . .

6 I am prepared to accept the proposal that there should be a Speaker of the House of Assembly, and a President of the Legislative Council elected by those bodies . . .

8 I will deal finally with the question of the Governor's special powers. The memorandum referred to above deprecates any power of certification, by which I assume is meant authority vested in the Governor to give the force of law to a bill, resolution, motion or vote which he considers necessary in the interest of good government but which is rejected by the Legislature or passed by them with amendments of which is unable to approve. I appreciate the strength of the opposition in principle to the vesting of such powers in the hands of the Governor, however rarely the occasion for their use may arise. None the less, I feel that at this stage some reserve power must be provided to meet the rare and unpredictable occasions when the public interest demands

action which the Legislature may be unwilling to take. I propose, therefore that this reserve power should be exercised by the Governor in accordance with the advice of the Executive Committee; that its exercise should be considered only on the written request of the Governor; that any decision to exercise it should be reported immediately to the Secretary of State; and that, except in cases of urgency, it should not be exercised without the Secretary of State's prior approval.

The memorandum also suggests that the power of veto, that is to say, the power to refuse assent to a Bill, ought not to be in the hands of the Governor, or if in his hands, should be subject to restriction prescribed in the Constitution. I feel that in this matter there may be some misunderstanding. Under every Colonial constitution, without exception, when a Bill is presented to the Governor for his assent on behalf of His Majesty the Governor has a discretion to assent, to withhold his assent or to reserve the Bill for His Majesty's pleasure. Any fetter expressly imposed by constitutional instruments upon this discretion would be without precedent in the Colonies. Indeed, the legal position is the same in the self-governing Dominions, though, in their case, the practice is, of course, dependent upon principles of constitutional usage. I should see no objection to an understanding that, on the rare occasions upon which the Governor is not prepared to assent to a Bill, he should in practice either reserve it for His Majesty's pleasure or before refusing assent, consult the Executive Committee and, if they do not agree, the Secretary of State. I could not, however, agree to such a departure in Jamaica from established and universal constitutional law as would be involved in subjecting this power, exercisable by the Governor on behalf of His Majesty to statutory restrictions.

(vii) Extracts from the Jamaica (Constitution) Order in Council, 1944. (S.R. & O. 1215/1944) [34]

PART IV

LEGISLATIVE COUNCIL

22 The Legislative Council shall consist of three *ex officio* Members, not more than two Official Members and not less than ten Unofficial Members.

34 The clauses of this order in council which are included in this section relate specifically to changes in the constitution and powers of the legislature The reader should again note that there were significant changes with regard to the executive which are to be found in the next part of this chapter.

23 The *ex officio* Members shall be the Colonial Secretary, the Attorney General, and the Financial Secretary and Treasurer.

24 The Official Members shall be persons holding office of emolument under the Crown in Jamaica, and shall be appointed by Instructions or Warrant under His Majesty's Sign Manual and Signet, or by the Governor by an Instrument under the Broad Seal in Pursuance of His Majesty's Instructions through a Secretary of State.

25 The Unofficial Members shall be persons not holding any office of emolument under the Crown in Jamaica, and shall be appointed by Instructions through a Secretary of State.

26 Subject to the Provisions of Section 27 of this Order, any person who -

(a) is a British subject of the age of 21 years or upwards; and

(b) is qualified to be registered as a voter for the election of Members of the House of Representatives for some constituency,

shall be qualified to be appointed as an Unofficial Member of the Legislative Council and no other person shall be qualified to be an appointed, or having been so appointed, shall sit or vote in the Council.

27 No person shall be capable of being appointed a Member of the Legislative Council, or, having been appointed, shall sit or vote in the Legislative Council, who at the time of appointment -

(1) is an undischarged bankrupt; or

(2) has, in any part of His Majesty's dominions or in any territory under His Majesty's protection, been sentenced to death or penal servitude or to imprisonment for a term exceeding twelve months and has not either suffered the punishment to which he was sentenced or such other punishment as may by competent authority have been substituted therefor or received a free pardon; or

(3) shall be a party to any subsisting contract with the Government of Jamaica for or on account of the public service and shall not have disclosed to the Governor the nature of such contract and his interest therein; or

(4) is a person found or declared insane under any law in force in Jamaica.

28(1) Subject to the provisions of this Order, every Official or Unofficial Member of the Legislative Council shall hold his seat in the Legislative Council during his Majesty's pleasure and shall in any case cease to be a Member at the next dissolution of the Legislative Council after his appointment, or previously thereto if his seat shall become vacant under the provisions of this Order ... .

31(1) An Unofficial Member of the Legislative Council, not being a Member of the Executive Council, shall be elected by the Legislative Council to be President thereof.

(2) Such election shall take place before the despatch of any other business at the first meeting of the Legislative Council after the appointed day and thereafter at the first meeting after every dissolution, and at the first or second meeting after the occurrence of a vacancy in the office of President arising from any other cause.

(3) The person so elected shall hold office as President until the next dissolution of the Legislative Council.

PART V

HOUSE OF REPRESENTATIVES

34 The House of Representatives shall consist of thirty-two Members to be elected in accordance with the provisions of this Order.

35(1) For the purpose of the election of Members of the House of Representatives . . .

(2) Each constituency shall return one Member.

(3) The boundaries of each constituency shall be defined, for the first election to the House of Representatives, by Resolution of the Legislative Council constituted under the existing Orders, and for each subsequent election to the House of Representatives in such manner as may be provided by law . . .

36(1) Subject to the provisions of subsection (2) of this Section and of Section 37 of this Order, any person who -

(a) is a British subject of the age of 21 years or upwards; and

(b) is qualified to be registered as a voter for the election of Members of the House of Representatives for some constituency

shall be qualified to be elected as a Member of the House, and no other person shall be qualified to be so elected or, having been so elected, shall sit or vote in the House of Representatives.

(2) No person shall be qualified to be elected as a Member of the House for any constituency or having been elected shall sit or vote in the House unless for twelve months immediately preceding the day of election he has been ordinarily resident in the parish in which that constituency is comprised.

37 No person shall be capable of being elected a Member of the House of Representatives, or, having been elected, shall sit or vote in the House of Representatives, who at the time of election -

(1) is the holder of any office of emolument under the Crown in Jamaica; or

(2) is a returning officer of the constituency for which the election is held; or

(3) is an undischarged bankrupt; or

(4) has, in any part of His Majesty's dominions or in any territory under His Majesty's protection, been sentenced to death or penal servitude or to imprisonment for a term exceeding twelve months and has not either suffered the punishment to which he was sentenced or such other punishment as may by competent authority have been substituted therefor or received a free pardon; or

(5) shall be a party to any subsisting contract with the Government of Jamaica for or on account of the public service and shall not have published, within one month before the day of election, in the Gazette or in some newspaper circulating in the constituency for which he is a candidate, a notice setting out the nature of such contract and his interest therein; or

(6) is a person found or declared insane under any law in force in Jamaica; or

(7) is disqualified for election under any law for the time being in force in Jamaica relating to offences connected with the election of Members.

38(1) Subject to the provisions of this Order and of any Proclamation made under Section 5 of this Order, the election of Members of the House of Representatives shall be held, and the qualification and registration of voters for the election of such Members shall be determined and effected, in accordance with the provisions of the Legislative Council Elections Law (Chap. 8 of the Laws of Jamaica, Revised Edition, 1938) as amended . . . or in accordance with any Law amending or replacing those Laws either before or after the appointed day; and subject as aforesaid, all the provisions of the said Laws shall apply in relation to such election and registration.

(2) The Legislature constituted under the existing Orders shall have power, by laws made under those Orders, to make such provision for the purposes mentioned in the preceding subsection as they think fit, notwithstanding that such provision may be repugnant to, or inconsistent with, any provisions of the existing Orders, and it shall not be necessary for any such law to be reserved for the signification of His Majesty's pleasure. This subsection shall come into operation forthwith . . .

40 All questions which may arise as to the right of any person to be or remain a Member of the House shall be referred to and decided by the Supreme Court in accordance with the provision of any law for the time being in force in Jamaica.

41(1) A Member of the House of Representatives, not being a Member of the Executive Council, shall be elected by the House of Representatives to be Speaker thereof.

(2) Such election shall take place before the despatch of any other business at the first meeting of the House after the appointed day and thereafter at the first meeting after every dissolution, and at the first or second meeting after the occurrence of a vacancy in the office of Speaker arising from any other cause.

(3) The person so elected shall hold office as Speaker until the next dissolution of the House:

Provided that if he shall, before such dissolution, otherwise vacate his seat in the House of Representatives, or become a Member of the Executive Council, or by writing under his hand addressed to the Governor, resign the office of Speaker, he shall thereupon vacate that office.

(4) The Speaker, if present, shall preside at the meetings of the House. In his absence, or if the office of Speaker is vacant, that Member shall preside who is first in order of precedence among the Members present who are not Members of the Executive Council . . .

PART VI

LEGISLATION AND PROCEDURE OF LEGISLATURE

44 Subject to the provisions of this Order, it shall be lawful for the Governor, with the advice and consent of the Legislative Council and of the House of Representatives, to make laws for the peace, order and good government of Jamaica.

45(1) If any Bill is passed by the House of Representatives in two successive Sessions and having been passed to the Legislative Council at least one month before the end of the Session, is rejected by the Legislative Council in each of those Sessions, that Bill shall, on its rejection for the second time by the Legislative Council, unless the House of Representatives otherwise resolve, be presented to the Governor for his assent and, if the Governor shall assent thereto, or if he shall reserve the Bill for His Majesty's pleasure and his Majesty shall assent thereto, the Bill shall thereupon become law notwithstanding that the Legislative Council have not consented to the Bill:

Provided that this provision shall not have effect unless one year has elapsed between the date of the second reading in the first of those Sessions of the Bill in the House and the date on which it passes the House in the second of those Sessions . . .

46 Save as otherwise provided in this Order, all questions in the Legislative Council or in the House of Representatives shall be determined by a majority of the votes of Members present:

Provided that the President or other presiding Member of the Legislative Council and the Speaker or other presiding Member of the House of Representatives shall not vote unless the votes of the other members shall be equally divided, in which case he shall give a casting vote.

47(1) Subject to the provisions of subsection (2) of this Section, if the Governor shall consider that it is expedient in the interest of public order, public faith or good government (which expressions shall, without prejudice to their generality, include the responsibility of Jamaica as a component part of the British Empire, and all matters pertaining to the creation or abolition of any public office or to the salary or other conditions of service of any public officer or officers) that any Bill introduced, or any motion, resolution or vote proposed for decision in either Chamber should have effect, then if the Chamber fail to pass such Bill, motion, resolution or vote within such time and in such form as the Governor may think reasonable and expedient, the Governor, at any time in his discretion, may, notwithstanding any provisions of this Order or of any Standing Orders of the Chamber, declare that such Bill, motion, resolution or vote shall have effect as if it had been passed by that Chamber, either in the form in which it was so introduced or proposed or with such amendments as the Governor shall think fit which have been moved or proposed in the Chamber or in any Committee thereof; and thereupon, the said Bill, motion, resolution or vote shall be deemed to have been so passed and further proceedings may be taken thereon, and, in the case of any such Bill, the provisions of this Order relating to assent to Bills and disallowance of laws shall apply, accordingly.

(2) The Governor shall not make any declaration under this Section unless –

(a) The question whether the declaration should be made shall have been submitted in writing by the Governor to the Executive Council and the Executive Council shall have resolved that the declaration be made; and

(b) a Secretary of State shall have approved of such declaration or the Governor shall, at the time of making the declaration, certify in writing that urgent necessity requires that the declaration be made without obtaining such approval.

(3) Whenever the Governor shall make a declaration under this Section without the approval of a Secretary of State, he shall forthwith

report to a Secretary of State the making of, and the reasons for, the declaration and the grounds of urgency.

(4) If any Member of either Chamber objects to any declaration made under this Section, he may, within seven days of the making thereof, submit to the Governor a statement in writing of his reasons for so objecting, and a copy of such statement shall, if furnished by such Member, be forwarded by the Governor as soon as practicable to a Secretary of State.

(5) Any such declaration, other than a declaration relating to a Bill, may be revoked by a Secretary of State, and the Governor shall notify such revocation in the Gazette; and from the date of such notification any motion, resolution or vote which shall have had effect by virtue of the declaration revoked shall cease to have effect, but without prejudice to anything lawfully done thereunder.[35]

51 Subject to the provisions of this Order, the Governor, the Legislative Council and the House of Representatives shall, in the transaction of business and the passing of laws, conform as nearly as may be to the directions contained in any Instructions under His Majesty's Sign Manual and Signet which may from time to time be addressed to the Governor in that behalf.

52 It shall be lawful for the Legislature by law made under this Order to define the privileges, immunities, and powers to be held, enjoyed and exercised by the Legislative Council and House of Representatives and the Members thereof respectively:

Provided that no such privileges, immunities, or powers shall exceed those for the time being held, enjoyed and exercised by the Commons' House of Parliament of the United Kingdom of Great Britain and Northern Ireland, or the Members thereof.

53(1) Subject to the provisions of this Order and of any Instructions under His Majesty's Sign Manual and Signet, the Legislative Council and the House of Representatives may from time to time, make, amend and revoke Standing Orders, including joint Standing Orders, for the regulation

35 Section 48 of this Order in Council gave the Governor discretionary power to assent to legislation, to refuse his assent, or to reserve legislation for His Majesty's pleasure, except that the Governor was obliged to reserve legislation which appeared to be repugnant to or inconsistent with this Order in Council, or which defined or affected the privileges, powers and immunities of both chambers of the legislature or their members.

Section 50 stated the power of disallowance vested in the Imperial Government.

and orderly conduct of their proceeding and the despatch of business, and for the order and manner in which the said Council and House shall confer, correspond, and communicate with each other, and for the passing, intituling, and numbering of Bills, and for the presentation of the same to the Governor for assent. The first Standing Orders shall be made by each Chamber in their first Session.

(2) Until other provision is made under this Section, the Standing Orders of the Legislative Council constituted at the date of this Order, as in force immediately before the appointed day, shall with the necessary modifications and adaptations, be the Standing Orders of the Legislative Council and House of Representatives established under this Order; and the said Standing Orders may be amended or revoked by Standing Orders made under the preceding subsection . . .

55(1) Subject to the provisions of this Order and of the Standing Orders of the Chambers, any Member may propose any question for debate in the Legislative Council or the House, as the case may be, and such question, if seconded by any other Member, shall be debated and disposed of according to the Standing Orders:

Provided that –

(a) no Bill shall be introduced and no motion, resolution or vote shall be proposed, without the approval of the Executive Council if the Speaker shall have certified in writing that it is a money measure;

(b) a Bill so certified shall be first introduced in the House of Representatives; and

(c) no Bill intended to implement the policy of the Government shall be introduced without the approval of the Executive Council.

(2) If the Executive Council so resolve, the Governor –

(a) may send by message to the Speaker the draft of any Bill, motion, resolution or vote which it appears to the Governor should be introduced or moved in the House of Representatives; and

(b) may in the same or a later message require that the Bill, motion, resolution or vote shall be introduced or moved not later than a date specified in such message;

and if such requirement is not complied with, the Bill, motion, resolution or vote shall be deemed for all purposes to have been introduced in the House on the date so specified.

57(1) The Governor may at any time, by Proclamation, prorogue or dissolve the Chambers.

(2) The Governor shall dissolve the Chambers at the expiration of five years from the date of the return of the first writ at the last preceding general election, if they shall not have been sooner dissolved.

58 A general election of Members of the House of Representatives shall be held at such time within four months after the appointed day and within three months after every dissolution of the House of Representatives, as the Governor shall by Proclamation appoint . . .

PART VII

MISCELLANEOUS

62 His Majesty hereby reserves to Himself, His Heirs and Successors, power, with the advice of His or Their Privy Council, to revoke, add to or amend this Order as to Him or Them shall seem fit.[36]

D. The coming of universal adult suffrage and elected majorities in the legislatures of territories other than Jamaica.[37]

(i) Extracts from the Report of the Committee to to examine the extension of the franchise, 1944. (Trinidad and Tobago Council Paper, no.35 of 1944)[38]

RECOMMENDATIONS

(a) LEGISLATIVE COUNCIL

(1) Members' Qualifications. *(Clause XVIII/Royal Order in Council)*

8 No person shall be qualified to be elected a member of the Council or, having been elected to sit or vote in the Council unless he or she

36 This formula, or a very similar one, appears in all Orders in Council and is a statement of royal prerogative, although the sovereign's power to legislate in Council is normally defined by statute.

37 *Note on the franchise of the Bahamas Islands.* The Bahamas, politically dominated by a white merchant elite until the 1960s, did not follow the pattern of the rest of the West Indies in the 1940s and 1950s. The secret ballot was not introduced until 1946; adult males were given the vote in 1959 but with an additional company vote; female suffrage introduced in 1961 brought universal adult suffrage, but the principle of one man one vote was not adhered to until, in 1967, the company vote was abolished by Mr Pindling's government.

38 As mentioned above (note 16, p. 119) Trinidad and Tobago was granted an elected majority in the Legislative Council in 1941.

(a) is entitled to be and is in fact registered as a voter;
(b) is able to read and write English; and
(c) possesses in his or her own right one or more of the following qualifications namely:-
(i) Real estate of the value of at least $5,000 above all charges and encumbrances affecting the same, or from which he or she draws a clear annual income of not less than $480, or

(ii) a clear annual income of over $960 arising from any source. Provided that a person shall not be entitled to be elected or to be a member of the Council if he or she is the holder of any office of emolument under the Crown or under the Government of the Colony or is a Minister of Religion within the meaning of the term as defined in Proviso (2) to Clause XVIII of the Royal Order in Council.

The suggested alterations to the existing relevant provisions of the Royal Order in Council as indicated here as elsewhere, by the words underlined. Further, proviso (1) to Clause XVIII, which requires candidates for election in respect of any electoral district to be qualified by 12 months residence or the ownership of property of a value of £5,000 in that district has been omitted on the unanimous recommendation of the Committee.

9 With regard to the property and income qualifications at (c) above, certain members of the Committee feel very strongly that anyone qualified to be registered as a voter should *ipso facto* be qualified to be elected a Member of the Council. [39]

(2) Voters' qualifications. *(Clause XXII of the Royal Order in Council.)*

10 Every person shall be entitled to be registered as a voter in any one electoral district and when registered, to vote at the election of a member of the Council for such district, who is qualified as follows:-
(a) has attained the age of 21 years (irrespective of sex);
(b) is under no legal incapacity;
(c) has resided in the Colony for at least two years prior to the date of such registration or is domiciled in the Colony and is resident therein at the date of such registration and has resided in the electoral district in which he or she claims to be registered for at least six months prior to the date of such registration.

39 Note that in 1944 in Jamaica qualifications for membership of the legislature were based upon the qualifications for voting.

(d) is a British subject;
(e) is able to satisfy the registering officer that he or she can understand the English language when spoken.

Certain members consider that the age limit under (a) above should be reduced to 18 years.

11 There was considerable debate and sharp cleavage of opinion on the question as to what if any, property and/or income qualifications should be required of voters. A majority of the Committee is of the opinion that there is no good reason for continuing to regard the possession of property or the earning of a certain income as indispensable qualifications for the exercise of the vote and it consequently recommends that no property or income qualifications whatsoever should be required of voters and that any person who is qualified under conditions (a)–(e) above and not debarred by any of the disqualifications recommended at (3) below, should *ipso facto* be qualified to be a voter.

A considerable minority of the Committee, while in agreement that universal adult suffrage should be the ultimate goal, considers that as a first step towards the goal of universal adult suffrage the existing basis on which the franchise is granted should be reduced now by 50 per cent . . . [40]

(3) Voters' Disqualifications *(Clause XXIII of the Royal Order in Council)*

12 No person shall be entitled to be registered as a voter if –
(a) he or she has been sentenced by any Court in any part of His Majesty's Dominions or in any territory under His Majesty's protection to death or penal servitude to imprisonment for any term exceeding 12 months and has not either suffered the punishment to which he or she was sentenced or such other punishment as by competent authority was substituted for the same or received a free pardon from his Majesty;
(b) he or she has been adjudged by a competent Court to be of unsound mind.

40 The minority felt that their recommendations would virtually enfranchise the same number of people as universal adult suffrage. Their stated intention was to exclude those whom they referred to as "nomads", people of no fixed abode. However, it is questionable, and was questioned by Mr Albert Gomes in a rider to this report, whether their reduced property and income qualifications would in any way approximate to universal adult suffrage.

13 With the exception of one member, the Committee recommends the abolition of Clause XXIII (a) of the Royal Order in Council which denies the franchise to persons who within six months immediately preceding the date of registration received poor relief from public funds.

MINORITY REPORT

. . . LEGISLATIVE COUNCIL

2 Clause 10(e) recommends that to be entitled to be registered as a Voter a person must be "able to satisfy the registering officer that he or she can understand the English language when spoken."

3 This in my view is a most impractical and undesirable recommendation. The registering officer will be expected to prepare a Register of Voters from the Rate books or Assessment books of the Rating Authority, together with such enquiries from the Colony's Registration Officer as may be necessary. The Rate books do not indicate whether the owners or occupiers of a house can understand the English language when spoken, nor does the questionnaire which was filled up for registration purposes. If it is considered desirable that this should be one of the qualifications to entitle a person to vote, it is a function which can be more properly exercised by the Returning Officers.

4 To insist that a Voter should understand the English language when spoken, would lead to the irresistable conclusion that this qualification has been introduced to deprive a large portion of the Indian community of the right to vote. This is quite naturally resented as an unfair discrimination against an important section of the population, which has made a valuable contribution to the prosperity of the Colony. The fact that so many of them still cannot understand the English language when spoken is partly due to the absence of compulsory education in our rural areas, and partly to the fact that large numbers of them were working in Agriculture at an age when they ought to have been at school.

5 Indian Soldiers unable to understand the English language have won glories for the Empire in Africa and in other theatres of war, in the struggle for freedom and democracy, and it would seem to be ironical to deprive their Countrymen here of the right to vote merely because they cannot understand the English language when spoken. Large numbers of them, who suffer from this disability can read and write in Hindi and some in Sanscrit, Urdu and Arabic. To deprive those who can read and appreciate Oriental Literature, of the vote because they cannot understand the English language when spoken, and at the same time to grant illiterate persons the

vote merely because they can understand the English language when spoken would seem to be most unfair. Moreover, it should be borne in mind that Indians in this Colony own extensive vested interests and on the whole with their cultural background can exercise the vote quite intelligently.

6 If this discrimination is persisted in, Trinidad Indians would be justified in appealing to the Secretary of State for the Colonies for the protection of their rights as a Minority Community and to ask for safe-guards to ensure that they are given adequate representation as their population and interest would justify on all Elective and Representative Bodies. [41]

(ii) Extracts from a statement made in the House of Commons by the Secretary of State for the Colonies on British Guiana (Franchise), 4th October 1944. (Parliamentary Debates (Commons) vol. 403 1943–44, cc. 925–926.)

A minority of the British Guiana Franchise Commission recommended universal adult suffrage.

It will be recognised that the majority report of the Commission provides for a substantial extension of the franchise, though one still falling short of universal adult suffrage. The matter has been fully debated in the British Guiana Legislative Council, a substantial majority of whom stated that they approved the majority report of the Commission; that report was also accepted unanimously by the unofficial members of the Executive Council. On the other hand representations have been received from numerous bodies in the Colony such as those from the East Indian Association in favour of universal adult suffrage. At a recent Conference of Chairmen of the Village Councils however, 150 delegates passed a resolution strongly supporting the majority report. The matter is clearly one in which there is a considerable division of opinion in the Colony and where a large majority of the Commission, which was fully representative and responsible, and was appointed in exactly the same manner as the Trinidad Franchise Committee, has reported in favour of an extension of the franchise falling short of universal adult suffrage, and as this report has met with the approval of the majority of the Legislative Council, I feel that I should accept it.

41 This minority report was signed by Mr Adrian Rienzi. The question of literacy in, or capacity to understand, spoken English was raised in most territories as a possible voter-qualification. However, it was of particular importance in British Guiana, Trinidad and Tobago, and British Honduras where substantial numbers of people were not English speaking (although in fact by the mid-1940s it was a rapidly declining minority in both British Guiana and Trinidad and Tobago). See also the despatch from the Secretary of State for the Colonies to the Governor of British Honduras, dated 17th January, 1953. Published as British Honduras Council Paper No. 5 of 1953.

It is true that in Trinidad and Jamaica the principle of universal adult suffrage has been accepted but in Trinidad this was recommended by the majority of a Committee which as I have said was appointed in the same manner as the British Guiana Commission, while in Jamaica universal adult suffrage was unanimously recommended by responsible local bodies including the Legislative Council. Moreover conditions in British Guiana are not in all respects parallel to those in Jamaica and Trinidad and I feel that it would not be reasonable that a Colony with differing conditions should be held bound to follow measures adopted in others.

I desire, however, to make it plain that, as envisaged by the Commission, the aim of policy in British Guiana will be the adoption of universal adult suffrage at a later date . . . [42]

Paragraph 19 The majority of the Commission recommended that every elector should be required to pass a literacy test in English. A minority of the Commission recommended that the existing literacy test should be abolished.

As I have already explained, the British Guiana Legislative Council will not be invited to approve the introduction of adult suffrage. There is, therefore, less reason than there was in the case of Trinidad to invite the Council to accept the abolition of all literacy or language tests. But, just as in Trinidad, I saw objection to the recommendation that ability to understand spoken English should be a qualification for the franchise, so I do not feel able to accept the majority recommendation in British Guiana for a literacy test confined to English. I have therefore approved in British Güiana the retention of the existing test of literacy in any language. I have, however, accepted the recommendation of the Commission for a literacy test in English for membership of the Legislative Council on grounds of practical convenience since otherwise members would be unable to carry out their duties. Moreover, the necessity for such a qualification has been expressly submitted in writing to the Franchise Commission by the British Guiana East Indian Association and the Islamic Association, among other organisations . . .

(iii) Constitutional Reform. Windward and Leeward Islands. (Government Notice. Leeward Islands Gazette, 1949, p.87.)

The Secretary of State has recently had under consideration the question of Constitutional Reform in the Windward Islands and Leeward Islands.

He agrees that adult suffrage should be introduced at the next election to Legislative Councils of the two groups. He considers that the right to vote should be subject to a simple literacy test. He also agrees to the removal of

42 Universal adult suffrage was not introduced in British Guiana until 1953.

property qualifications for candidates subject to further examination of the present arrangement for deposits which candidates are required to make.

He has indicated, however, that as yet he has been unable to give consideration to the establishment of wholly elected legislatures in the Windward Islands and Leeward Islands and for the present this must be deferred.

In the Leeward Islands, it is proposed to establish a Committee to examine and report upon the changes required in the law, to meet the desired form of adult suffrage and literacy test and of property qualifications and deposit. As it will take some time for this Committee to report and for the necessary amendments to be made in the law and subsequently for a new voters' list to be compiled, it is proposed that the life of the Legislative Councils of Antigua, St Kitts-Nevis and Montserrat should be extended for one year so that the General Elections due to be held in those Presidencies in October of this year would be postponed until 1950.

(iv) Extracts from the Report of a Committee appointed to consider constitutional reform held at Government Office on Monday 8th August 1949.
(Minutes of the Legislative Council of St Vincent for the half year ended 31st December 1949, pp.24–25.)

The Chairman reminded members that the meeting was called as a result of a resolution moved by the Honourable Acting Crown Attorney at the meeting of the Legislative Council on 26th May, 1949, in the following terms:

> "Whereas the Secretary of State has recently announced that the next election in the Windward and Leeward Islands will be held on a basis of adult suffrage subject to a simple literacy test
>
> "And Whereas the Secretary of State has agreed to the removal of the property qualification for a candidate subject to further examination of the present arrangements for deposits which candidates are required to make
>
> "And Whereas this Council is of the opinion that the introduction of adult suffrage might appropriately be accompanied by an increase in the number of Elected Members
>
> "BE IT THEREFORE RESOLVED that a Committee of this Council be appointed to examine and report on the following:-
>
> (a) the nature of the literacy test and the manner in which it shall be conducted; and any other matters relevant thereto;
>
> (b) the present arrangements for deposits by candidates for election;
>
> (c) an appropriate increase in the number of elected members consequent upon the increase in the number of voters which is antici-

pated upon the introduction of adult suffrage (subject, however to the Secretary of State's statement as to wholly elected legislatures in the Windward and Leeward Islands),

(d) the delimitation and representation of constituencies in the light of (c) above.

The question of the Literacy Test was first considered. The Chairman said that the simplest form of literacy test he could suggest was one which obtains in the case of one of the Canadian Provinces. The voter, before balloting is required to show his name on a list presented. On his doing this he is given a ballot paper and told to sign his name opposite that of the candidate for whom he wishes to vote.

The majority of members agreed that a Literacy Test was desirable, but Mr. McIntosh was strongly opposed to any form of Literacy Test . . .

The meeting finally recommended, by a majority vote, on motion by Mr. Hughes and seconded by Mr. De Freitas, that "No person shall be registered as a voter unless he shall with his own hand have subscribed his name to his claim to be registered and written thereon the date of such subscription in the presence of a person appointed by the Governor-in-Council for the purpose, or of the officer charged with the duty of registering voters; or, if he is incapacitated by blindness or other physical cause from so doing, such subscription and writing shall be performed on his behalf by the officer charged with the duty of registering voters." . . .

Qualifications and Arrangements for Deposits by Candidates for Election:

. . ., all (but two of) the members disagreed with the entire abolition of the income and property qualifications. The majority . . . recommended that both income and property qualifications should be reduced by fifty per cent, and that the amount of deposit should remain as at present . . .

Increase of Elected Members:

There was unanimity on this question. The meeting recommended an increase of three in the present number of elected members, . . .[43]

43 This increase would give a majority of elected members in the Council, a recommendation which was accepted. The new constitutions of the Windward and Leeward Islands in 1951 were more liberal than these recommendations (see following document).

(v) Extracts from the Antigua Constitution and Elections Ordinance, 1951. (Ordinance no. 10. of 1951.)[44]

PART II

CONSTITUTION AND POWERS OF COUNCIL ETC

4 The Council shall consist of the Administrator, two *ex-officio* members, three nominated members and eight elected members.

5 The *ex-officio* members of the Council shall be the Crown Attorney and the Treasurer of the Presidency . . .[45]

7 The elected members of the Council shall be persons qualified for election in accordance with the provisions of, and elected in the manner provided by, this Ordinance . . .

10 Subject to the provisions of section 11 of this Ordinance, any person who –

(a) is a British subject of the age of twenty-one years or upwards; and

(b) has resided in the Presidency for a period of twelve months immediately preceding the date of his nomination for election, or is domiciled in the Presidency and is resident therein at the date aforesaid, shall be qualified to be elected as an elected member of the Council, and no other person shall be qualified to be so elected or, having been so elected, shall sit or vote in the Council . . .[4

20 The Administrator, if present, shall preside at meetings of the Council, and in his absence the Deputy President or, in the absence of the Deputy President or if there be no Deputy President, the *ex-officio* member present who stands first in order of precedence shall preside.[47]

21 The Governor shall have the right of addressing the Council at any time when he shall think fit . . .

24 Subject to the provisions of this Ordinance all questions proposed for decision in the Council shall be determined by a majority of votes of those

44 The constitutions given in 1951 to St. Kitts/Nevis/Anguilla, Dominica, Grenada, St. Lucia and St. Vincent did not differ materially from this Ordinance.

45 Under section 9 of this Ordinance the Administrator retained the power to summon officials to the Council when he felt that this was desirable. However, as under earlier constitutions such officials, who were not members of the legislative, could participate in the proceedings but could not vote.

46 Section 11 of the Ordinance laid down the usual disqualifications for membership.

47 Note the absence of a Speaker. However, the Deputy President was to be elected from among the unofficial member of the Legislative Council (i.e., nominated and elected members).

present and voting. The Administrator or other member presiding shall not have an original vote on any question, but shall have a casting vote if the votes shall be equally divided.

25 (1) The Govenor may at any time, by proclamation, summon, prorogue or dissolve the Council.

(2) The Govenor shall dissolve the Council at the expiration of three years from the date of the return of the first writ at the last preceding general election, if it shall not have been sooner dissolved . . .

27 Subject to the provisions of this Ordinance and the Standing Orders of the Council, any member may introduce any Bill or propose any motion for debate in, or may present any petition to, the Council and the same shall be debated and disposed of according to the Standing Orders:

Provided that, except with the recommendation or consent of the Administrator signified thereto, the Council shall not proceed upon any Bill, amendment, motion or petition which, in the opinion of the Administrator or other presiding member, would –

(a) dispose of or charge any public revenue or public funds of the Presidency or revoke or alter any disposition thereof or charge thereon, or impose, alter or repeal any rate, tax or duty; or

(b) suspend the Standing Orders of the Council or any of them.

28 Subject to the provisions of this Ordinance, it shall be lawful for the Govenor, with the advice of the Council, to make laws for the peace, order and good government of the Presidency . . .

31 (1) If the Govenor shall consider that it is expedient –[48]

(a) in the interests of public order, public faith or of good government (which expressions shall, without prejudice to their generality, include the responsibility of the Presidency as a territory within the British Commonwealth of Nations and all matters pertaining to the creation or abolition of any public office or to the appointment, salary or other conditions of service of any public officer); or

(b) in order to secure detailed control of the finances of the Presidency during such time as, by virtue of the receipt of financial assistance by the Presidency from His Majesty's Exchequer for the purpose of balancing the annual budget or otherwise, such control rests with His Majesty's Government,[49] that any Bill introduced, or

48 This Ordinance was amended in 1956 to include a proviso which stated that the Governor should normally only exercise his power of certification on the advice of the Executive Council. However, either the consent of the Secretary of State or "urgent necessity" allowed him to ignore the advice of the Executive Council.

49 Note the introduction of this sub-paragraph to ensure supervision of the finances of grant-in-aid territories.

any motion proposed, in the Council should have effect, then, if the Council should fail to pass such Bill or motion within such time and in such form as the Governor may think reasonable and expedient, the Governor, at any time in his discretion, may, notwithstanding any provisions of this Ordinance, or of any other law in force in the Presidency or of any Standing Orders of the Council, declare that such Bill or motion shall have effect as if it had been passed by the Council, either in the form in which it was so introduced or proposed or with such amendments as the Governor shall think fit which have been moved or proposed in the Council or any Committee thereof; and thereupon the said Bill or motion shall have effect as if it had been so passed, and in the case of any such Bill, the provisions of this Ordinance relating to assent to Bills and disallowance of laws shall have effect accordingly . . .[50]

PART III

. . . ELECTORAL DISTRICTS AND REGISTRATION OF VOTERS

42 (1) Subject to the provisions of sub-section (2) of this section, every person who –

(a) has attained the age of twenty-one years; and

(b) is not a lunatic so found under any law in force in the Presidency; and

(c) is a British subject; and

(d) has resided in the Presidency for twelve months immediately preceding the date of registration as a voter or is domiciled in the Presidency and is resident therein at the date of such registration and;

(e) is not disqualified under the provisions of this Ordinance from being registered as a voter,

shall be entitled to be registered as a voter and, when registered, to vote at an election.

(2) No person shall be registered as a voter or be entitled to vote at an election who has been sentenced by any court in His Majesty's dominions or in any territory under His Majesty's protection to death, penal servitude, or imprisonment for a term exceeding twelve months, and has not either suffered the punishment to which he was sentenced or such other punishment as by competent authority may have been substituted for the same or received a free pardon from His Majesty.

50 In other respects the powers of the Governor and of the Imperial Government over legislation embodied in this Ordinance are not significantly different from those already illustrated.

E Further increases in the number of elected members of the legislature and the development of bi-cameralism. Also related developments in the office of Speaker and reductions of the Governor's powers.

(i) Extracts from the Despatch from the Secretary of State for the Colonies to the Governor of Trinidad and Tobago, dated 7th January 1949, (Published in The New Constitution, Port of Spain, Trinidad, 1949.)

Sir, . . .

3 I will begin by recalling briefly the recent course of events. The existing constitution, which is based upon universal adult suffrage, has been in operation only since July, 1946. In December, 1946, however, a resolution of the Legislative Council led to the setting up in February, 1947, of a Committee, with the following terms of reference: –

"To consider the reform of the constitution and to submit proposals to be forwarded to His Majesty's Government for a new constitution having regard to the fact that
(a) within recent years certain Colonies have been granted constitutions which place them ahead of Trinidad, and
(b) it is necessary that, in keeping with the spirit of the times, the people of Trinidad and Tobago should be more fully associated in the management of their own affairs".

4 This Committee produced in March, 1948, a report signed by the Chairman, Sir Lennox O'Reilly and sixteen members. A minority report was submitted by Dr. P. V. J. Solomon, one of the elected members of the Legislative Council. Three other reports, dissenting from the main report on minor points were submitted by other members of the committee.

5 [The majority report recommended that:]

The Legislative Council would be composed of three *ex-officio*, six nominated and eighteen elected members. A Speaker would be appointed by the Governor from outside the Council and would have a casting vote only. The exercise of the Governor's legislative powers would, as in the case of Jamaica, be subject to resolution of the Executive Council and the approval of the Secretary of State . . .[51]

7 The recommendations in the two reports were considered by the Legislative Council, which by a majority vote agreed broadly with the recommendations of the majority report, . . .[52]

14 It is an important part of His Majesty's Government's colonial policy that, so soon as it can be brought about by orderly process, in the particular circumstances of each territory, the legislatures to which the control of public affairs is entrusted should become fully elective. There is indeed no conclusive

51 Dr Solomon recommended that the legislature should be an entirely elected unicameral body of twenty-five members.

52 The only change with respect to the Legislative Council was that the appointed Speaker should have neither an original nor a casting vote.

answer to the argument that a system of nomination is contrary to accepted democratic principle, and can be defended only where special considerations obtain. I have therefore considerable sympathy with the views on this subject which are expressed in the minority report; nevertheless I am not prepared to say that at this stage in the development of Trinidad and Tobago, the nominated element could be wholly eliminated without seriously disturbing confidence in the economic and financial stability of the Colony, on which the prosperity and therefore the welfare and standard of living of the people depend. I would add, however, that nominated members should only be introduced to strengthen the experience and knowledge of the Councils in dealing with the complex issues of Government and that they should not be nominated to represent "interest" but should be appointed to serve the broad and best interests of the Colony as a whole.

15 I do not believe, however, that for this purpose it is necessary to retain nominated members to the full number recommended in the majority report, and I consider that a start can be made now in applying the policy of progressive reduction. I propose therefore that, as a first step, the numbers of nominated members in the Legislative Council should be reduced from six to five . . .

18 There is one further proposal of the majority report which requires modification. I refer to paragraph 24 of the report, which recommends that the proviso to clause 47 (2) (a) and (b) of the Jamaica (Constitution) Order in Council, 1944[53], should be applied in Trinidad and Tobago. The proposal of the present Legislative Council, with which I fully agree, that the elected members of Executive Council should be in a majority of one, creates a situation quite different from that envisaged in the Jamaica Order in Council; and the above-mentioned proviso would not be appropriate. It will be necessary to provide in Trinidad and Tobago that should the Executive Council in any instance refuse to authorise the Governor by resolution to use his reserve powers, he may nevertheless do so if (except where urgency makes this impracticable) the Secretary of State's consent is first obtained.

19 To sum up, my conclusion is that the new constitution should provide for:

- (a) a Legislative Council of three *ex-officio*, five nominated and eighteen elected members presided over by a Speaker appointed by the Governor from outside the Council. The Speaker will have neither an original nor a casting vote,
- (b) reserve legislative powers, to be used only when a question of public order, public faith, or good government is involved, similar to those provided for in the Jamaica constitution, but subject to the remarks in paragraph 18 of this despatch.

53 See above, Chapter IV, Part II, doc. C(vii).

(*ii*) *Extracts from the Trinidad and Tobago (Constitution) Order in Council, 1950. (SI 510/1950.)*[54]

PART IV

LEGISLATIVE COUNCIL

29 There shall be a Legislative Council in and for the Colony which shall consist of a Speaker, three *ex-officio Members,* five Nominated Members and eighteen Elected Members.

30 (1) The Speaker shall be a person who is not an *ex-officio,* Nominated, or Elected Member of the Legislative Council and who does not hold any office of emolument under the Crown, and shall be appointed by the Governor, acting in his discretion, by Instrument under the Public Seal.

(2) The Speaker shall hold office during His Majesty's pleasure and, subject thereto, for such period as may be specified in the instrument by which he is appointed, and shall not vacate his office by reason of a dissolution of the Legislative Council:

Provided that the Speaker may, by writing under his hand addressed to the Governor, resign his office; and upon receipt of such resignation by the Governor the office of Speaker shall be come vacant . . .[55]

33 The *ex-offico* Members of the Legislative Council shall be the Colonial Secretary, the Attorney General and the Financial Secretary.

34 (1) Subject to the provisions of section 37 of this Order, the Nominated Members of the Legislative Council shall be British subjects of the age of twenty-one years or upwards and shall be appointed by the Governor, acting in his discretion, by Instrument under the Public Seal.[56]

(2) The Governor shall forthwith report to His Majesty through a Secretary of State every appointment of any person to be a Nominated Member of the Legislative Council.

35 The Elected Members of the Legislative Council shall be persons qualified for election in accordance with the provisions of this Order and

54 A very similar constitution was introduced in British Honduras in 1954.

55 Note that this is a slight advance on the position in the Leewards and Windwards in 1951 where the Administrators still presided over meetings of the Legislative Council. This Order in Council also makes provision for the election of a deputy speaker from among its own members (but not a member who was also on the Executive Council).

56 Note the curious situation where the qualifications for elected membership were more restrictive than those for nominated membership of the Legislative Council.

elected in the manner provided by, or in pursuance of, any law enacted under this order.

36 (1) Subject to the provisions of section 37 of this Order, any person who–

- (a) is a British subject of the age of twenty-one years or upwards; and
- (b) has resided in the Colony for a period of at least two years immediately before the date of his nomination for election or is domiciled in the Colony and is resident there at the date aforesaid; and
- (c) is able to speak and, unless incapicatated by blindness or other physical cause, to read the English language with a degree of proficiency sufficient to enable him to take an active part in the proceedings of the Legislative Council; and
- (d) (i) is in receipt of a clear income in his own right of not less than nine hundred and sixty dollars per annum; or
  - (ii) is the owner in his own right of real estate (which for the purpose of this sub-paragraph includes a leasehold interest) of the value of not less than five thousand dollars over and above all charges and encumbrances in respect thereof, or is in receipt of a clear income in his own right of not less than four hundred and eighty dollars per annum derived from real estate;

shall be qualified to be elected as an Elected Member of the Legislative Council, and no other person shall be qualified to be so elected or, having been so elected, shall sit or vote in the Legislative Council.[57]

PART V

LEGISLATION AND PROCEDURE IN LEGISLATIVE COUNCIL

48 Subject to the provisions of this Order, it shall be lawful for the Governor, with the advice and consent of the Legislative Council, to make laws for the peace order and good government of the Colony.[58]

57 See footnote 56

58 By this Order in Council the Governor retained the discretionary powers of assent, of reservation and of certification, the last-named power to be normally exercised on the advice of the Executive Council, such advice only being over-ridden with the consent of the Secretary of State or where urgency demanded.

The imperial Government retained the power of disallowance.

(iii) Extract from the Trinidad and Tobago (Constitution) (Amendment) Order in Council, 1956. (S.I. 835/1956.)[59]

AMENDMENT OF THE PRINCIPAL ORDER, PARTS IV, V.

23 Section 29 of the Principal Order is hereby revoked and the following section substituted therefor: –

"Legislative Council" 29 There shall be a Legislative Council in and for the Colony which shall consist of thirty-one Members, namely, two *ex-officio* Members, five Nominated Members and twenty-four Elected Members:

Provided that if any person elected to be Speaker of the Legislative Council shall not at the time of his election be a Member of the Legislative Council in addition to the aforesaid thirty-one Members, and in such event the Legislative Council shall consist of thirty-two Members."

24 Section 30 of the Principal Order is hereby revoked and the following section substituted therefor: –

"The Speaker 30 (1) There shall be a Speaker, who shall be a person who is not an *ex-officio* or Nominated Member of the Legislative Council or a Member of the Executive Council, or a person who holds any office of emolument under the Crown, who shall be elected by the Legislative Council.

(2) The election of the Speaker shall take place before the despatch of any other business at the first sitting of the Legislative Council after the 26th day of May, 1956, and thereafter at the first sitting after every dissolution of the Legislative Council.

(3) A person holding office as Speaker may, by writing under his hand addressed to the Governor, resign his office, and upon receipt of such resignation by the Governor the office of Speaker shall become vacant.

(4) Subject to the provisions of subsection (5) of this section, a person holding office as Speaker shall, unless he earlier resigns his office, vacate his office: –

(a) if, being an Elected Member of the Legislative Council, he shall vacate his seat as such Member; or

(b) if, not being an Elected Member of the Legislative Council, he shall do or suffer anything which would, if he were an Elected Member, cause him to vacate his seat as such member

59 Similar amendments were made to the constitution of British Honduras in 1960.

(5) A person holding office as Speaker shall not vacate his office by reason of the dissolution of the Legislative Council but shall, subject to the provisions of this section, continue to hold office until such time as the Legislative Council shall after such dissolution elect a person to be Speaker in pursuance of sub-section (2) of this section . . .

26 Section 33 of the Principal Order is hereby revoked and the following section substituted therefor:-

"*Ex-officio* Members 33 The *ex-officio* Members of the Legislative Council shall be the Colonial Secretary and the Attorney General."

(iv) Extracts from the Report of the Leeward and Windward Islands Constitutional Conference, 1959.
(Cmnd. 804/1959.)[60]

IV ADMINISTRATORS

POWERS OF THE ADMINISTRATORS

10 *Legislative Powers.* The Conference agreed that the existing power of the Governors to secure the enactment of a Bill rejected by the Legislative Council should be abolished. The Conference also agreed that the Administrator should be required to reserve for Her Majesty's pleasure Bills which fall into any of the following categories:-

(a) Bills which appear to him to be inconsistent with Her Majesty's Government's international obligations;
(b) Bills which appear to him likely to prejudice the Royal Prerogative;
(c) Bills which are inconsistent with the Constitutional Instruments (including in the case of Antigua, Montserrat and St. Kitts-Nevis-Anguilla, Bills amending or repealing the Constitution Ordinance of the Territory);
(d) Bills which appear to him to prejudice the efficiency of the Public Service, the Police, the Judiciary or the Audit Service.

The Conference also agreed that in deciding whether a Bill falls into one of these categories the Administrator should act in his discretion.[61] . . .

60 The changes in the constitutions of the Leewards and Windwards recommended by this Report were implemented in 1959.
61 Paragraph 13 of this Report stated that the Conference agreed to retain unchanged Her Majesty's power of disallowance.

V THE LEGISLATIVE COUNCIL

14 *Number of Elected Members.* The Trinidad Conference had proposed that the Legislative Council of each Territory should include not less than nine Elected Members, except in Montserrat where there should be seven. This would involve a minimum increase of two seats in each Territory. It was stated that this proposal was desirable for the reason, *inter alia,* that with an Executive Council composed of five Unofficial Members the Legislature tended to be unduly dominated by the Executive Council. In respect of Dominica, the special point was made that because of the area of the Island and the peculiar difficulties of communication it was desirable in any case to increase the number of constituencies. Thus the numbers would be seven Elected Members each for Montserrat, nine Elected Members for St. Vincent, ten Elected Members each for Antigua, Grenada, St. Kitts-Nevis-Anguilla and St. Lucia and eleven Elected Members for Dominica.

15 *Number of Nominated Members.* The Trinidad Conference had proposed that the number of Nominated Members should be reduced from three to two in all Territories except Montserrat where they should be reduced from two to one. The Conference agreed that each of the Territories should in future have two Nominated Members in their Legislative Council, except Montserrat which should have one Nominated Member.

16 *Method of appointing Nominated Members . . .* It was agreed that the Nominated Members should be appointed by the Administrator in his discretion after consultation with the Chief Minister and with such other persons as he saw fit to consult. It was also agreed, following the precedent adopted in Trinidad, that if it was necessary in order to provide the majority party with a reasonable working majority in the Legislative Council one out of the two Nominated Members would be appointed in such a way as to secure this. This provision would be embodied in a despatch to the Administrators.

17 *Official Members.* The Trinidad Conference had recommended that in future the only Official Member of the Legislative Council should be the Law Officer, except in Montserrat where the Financial Secretary should also be a member. The Conference endorsed the recommendation.

18 *Presiding in the Legislative Council . . .* The Conference agreed that the Legislative Council of each of the Territories except Montserrat should in future be presided over by a Speaker elected by all the members of the Council from either within or without the Council and that the provisions governing the qualifications and tenure of office of a Speaker elected from outside the Council should be similar to those contained in the Federal Constitution. The Conference also agreed, in accordance with the wishes of the

Montserrat Delegation that the Legislative Council in Montserrat should continue for the time being to be presided over by the Administrator rather than by an elected Speaker. The Conference also agreed that the Deputy Speaker should be elected in the same way as the Speaker, though he should be elected from among the members of the Legislative Council. The Conference agreed that the Speaker and anyone for the time being presiding in his place should have only a casting vote . . .

(v) Extracts from the Report of the British Guiana Constitutional Commission, 1950-51. (Col. no. 280/1951.)[62]

29 The decision [of 1928] to abrogate the old constitution and to replace it by an advanced form of the Crown Colony government aroused opposition among those who, while they admitted the shortcomings of the old, felt that the new represented a needless abatement of their constitutional privileges; . . . Criticism fastened upon the composition of the legislature, where the introduction of nominated members would enable them, in combination with the officials, to out-number the elected members, since this provision was additional to the grant of reserved power to the governor. The British Guiana Commission had indeed recommended that the power to govern be given through either of these media – not both. But, if the freedom of action of the nominated unofficial members was to be entirely unfettered, their presence could not ensure to the government the power to govern, and it was properly felt that it was indefensible and intolerable that a man should be constrained to vote against the dictates of his conscience. In Jamaica, alone of the Caribbean territories, the Governor had, until 1922, possessed this power to demand the support of the nominated members, and this requirement had had the effect of deterring many from accepting an offer of nomination.

30 But the important feature of the changes of 1928 was that they held out to British Guiana the promise of advance where none existed before. Under the old constitution, the colony was in a "cul-de-sac", from which there was no outlet for either political or economic development. In 1943, British Guiana moved forward again, when the unofficial members were placed in a clear majority in the Executive Council, and in the Legislative Council the elected members alone outnumbered their nominated and official colleagues by 14 to 10. In 1943, too, advisory committees of the legislature were established, and, two years later, the franchise was further extended. These events, and the appointment of our present commission, have

62 This is frequently referred to as the Waddington Commission Report, after the Chairman Sir E.V. Waddington, G.B.E., K.C.M.G., K.C.V.O.

demonstrated the truth of the words which Sir Cecil Rodwell used in November, 1927, when he said: "The short cut is often the longest way round, and it will be much better . . . to back out on to the main road which leads from the plain and elementary form of Crown Colony government through the various stages of increasing popular representation to the ultimate goal of autonomy within the Empire . . ."

52 Lack of participation by a part of a community in political life cannot make for healthy democracy, and, in addition to those in the country districts whom central politics pass by, we must mention also those who stand consciously aloof. We appreciate that all may not feel the same impulse to choose political life as their form of public service, but we have no sympathy with those who refrain for fastidious reasons. The position and attitude of the European community are particularly important in this context, for, although small in numbers, the Europeans still provide much of the commercial and industrial enterprise and wield a great degree of economic power, and their withdrawal would have disproportionate effect for harm upon political life. Sheer weight of numbers made it certain that, following emancipation, the non-European communities would eventually predominate, but, owing largely to the oligarchical nature of the old constitution, the European community was for a considerable time able to retain a substantial majority in the legislature.

53 Today, the European community finds itself in somewhat of a quandary. Its identification with management impairs, so it feels, its chances of achieving the favour of a predominantly labouring electorate. We were glad, however, to see among the European community a readiness to take a greater part in political life. Indeed, under an advanced constitution, the true interests of the country can only be assured by the active participation of all upon equal terms in its government, for only so can all be brought to a recognition of their dependence each upon the other.

54 In an unhappy choice of phrase, the British Guiana Commission of 1927 described the Colony as being "politically precocious". If this be taken to mean that there is a wide interest in political discussion we would agree, and we would argue, too, that when this is so, a system of semi-representative government places a premium upon demagogy and depresses the standards of public life by confining politicians largely to the role of tacticians rather than enabling them to become statesmen. Absorption in politics is clearly to be seen in the Trade Union Movement, where this aspect of labour organisation has sometimes been stressed at the expense of the industrial. We need survey the Trade Union Movement only briefly, for its place in Guianese life is not our concern. Trade Unions have a valued and essential part to play in a

modern society, and we recognise the excellent work of those who came forward to found them in British Guiana. The true reward of these pioneers lies not only in the improvements that have been won, but in the knowledge "that the need for . . . guidance . . . has now largely disappeared", and that "what they have toiled for has come to pass and that the workers themselves . . . are ready to stand on their own feet and speak for themselves".[63] It is therefore a positive disservice to the Trade Union Movement that the power and prestige given by the presidency of a union should prove so sore a temptation to personal ambition that individuals should seek to found unions "with an eye more to political gain and cheap publicity than to the real benefit of the worker".[64]

55 Trade Unions are at present also subject to external stresses from the widely held expectation of constitutional advance. Nascent political parties see in the adhesion of this or that union an accession to their strength. Since it so happens that in most of the important unions there are officers who incline to different parties, a tug-of-war is at present being waged, and strenuous efforts made to undermine the influence of unions which are potentially the supporters of a rival political party. Too often, these stresses coincide with the personal ambitions of the union's officers, or, in rival unions are exacerbated by personal animosities. This feature, unhealthy as it is, is perhaps unavoidable in the conditions of the moment, when widespread expectation of a grant of adult suffrage faces politicians with imponderable electoral chances. Nor is it entirely to be wondered at that this political ferment should invade the Trade Union Movement, for, under a system of semi-representative government, Trade Unionism, rather than parliamentary pressure, can come to be regarded as the more effective instrument for controlling government. Nevertheless, it is in the best interests of the country that this jockeying should speedily subside, and the proper channels of political campaigning be established.

56 We have set out in this brief survey some of the economic tendencies which must give the legislator pause, and certain other political manifestations which call for comment. The present system of government has been honourably administered, but, disregarding the psychological sense of grievance over the abolition of the old constitution in 1928, it is clear to us that the present system is outworn and no longer satisfies the wishes of the people. Although we have been impressed by the attention that is now being given to economic and social problems by political leaders in British Guiana, we recognise that

63 Report of a Commission of Enquiry into the Sugar Industry of British Guiana, Col. No. 249, 1949, p. 92, paragraph 159. (Report's footnote.)
64 Ibid., paragraph 157. (Report's footnote.)

for some time yet to come the appeal of personalities may be the determinant with the electorate, until the now emerging political parties establish themselves, and build up stable and energetic constituency organisations which are the hallmark of a mature party system. But, when all that has been said, we are of the opinion that the people of British Guiana can well sustain a further measure of constitutional advance. In fact, many, though not all, of the present unwholesome tendencies have been fostered by a sense of inferiority springing from inadequate opportunities for responsible political expression.

57 We have indeed been conscious throughout of the need to recommend the greatest, and not the least, degree of self-government that can be sustained. Proposals which do not match the stature of the community can be as harmful as those which place an unreasonable load upon untried legislators. Nor, indeed, can a grudging attitude find any encouragement in the declared policy of His Majesty's Government to advance all colonial peoples to the goal of self-government as speedily as their political development and economic viability will allow . . .

CHAPTER IV: THE FRANCHISE

59 The attainment of universal adult suffrage was set as one of the more immediate goals for the people of the West Indies by the report of the Royal West India Commission [sic]. It has long been regarded as a privilege of citizenship that distinguishes a politically mature people. It is, moreover, a demand which, when made by the generality of the people, is as difficult to resist as the alternatives to it are to defend. The demand for the grant of universal adult suffrage is often premature and may be advanced in a spirit of competition, rather than upon an impartial assessment of political maturity; but it is inevitable that, when once a breach has been made in the walls of a restrictive franchise, little time can elapse before the grant of an unfettered suffrage. Neither a property qualification nor a simple literary test – or any other "fancy" franchise – can be sufficient or logical criteria of an individual's native sagacity and fitness to be an elector. This was the experience in England after the First Reform Bill, and we therefore take as the starting point of our enquiry the knowledge that the grant of universal adult suffrage cannot long be stayed. Our task must be to determine whether it should be granted now to British Guiana.[65]

65 Under present regulations, a voter is required to pass a literacy test in any language, and to own, occupy or be the tenant of three acres of land, or to own land to the value of $150, or to occupy or be the tenant of property of a rental of $45 a year or to possess an income of $120 a year. (Report's footnote.)

60 Since the report of the Royal West India Commission [sic] was presented universal adult suffrage has been in the minds of the majority of the population of the British Caribbean territories and it has indeed been introduced into many. In British Guiana, therefore, where the standards of intelligence and of articulation are in no way below those obtaining in these other territories, an indefinite deferment of its introduction would cause dissatisfaction; and the arguments which could justify its being now withheld must be cogent and based upon conditions which are not to be found elsewhere.

61 The chief remaining restriction on the suffrage in British Guiana is the literacy test. Many witnesses spoke to us of the dangers which would attend its abolition, and of these we are fully aware. The accession of a large number of illiterate persons to a voter's register will in all likelihood increase political irresponsibility, and place a premium upon demagogy. Elections upon this broader basis will probably encourage the return to the legislature of a number of members who may not be best qualified to exercise legislative functions. Yet, if the basis of the franchise is more restricted, we are doubtful whether, under a system of representative government such as we recommend, the needs and aspirations of the poorer people will meet with adequate recognition. Unless peculiar local circumstances are found to present overwhelming objections, we can find no satisfying justification for denying "humble people the political status of their more fortunate fellows",[66] the more so since this "leap in the dark" has been, almost without exception, taken elsewhere. Indeed, many of the persons who now exercise the franchise are only semi-literate; and these, who can do little more than sign their names, and who may have set themselves to acquire this ability solely in order to exercise the franchise, are as little qualified as their illiterate brethren to distinguish from written evidence the competing merits of rival candidates. Moreover, illiterate persons have been entitled to the vote in local government elections for some years now, and we were informed that they had exercised this privilege with discretion. On the other hand, a thoroughgoing literacy test, however desirable it may be, is, as things now are, impracticable and would be cumbersome to the point of inoperation . . .

63 In our study of the special and local circumstances that might be adduced for the retention of a literacy test, we have paid careful regard to the report of the local Franchise Commission, which was appointed in 1941 to consider this subject in the light of the recommendations of the Royal West India Commission [sic]. After prolonged consideration, the Franchise Commission issued a report, in which, while a minority supported the principle of

66 Report of the Special Commission on the Ceylon Constitution (Donoughmore Report), Cmnd. 3131, 1928, p. 86. (Report's footnote.)

universal adult suffrage, the many proposed the retention of a literacy test, and only minor modifications in the property qualification. In the ensuing discussions, both in the Legislative Council and in the country at large, it became clear that a substantial body of opinion supported the majority recommendations, and no material change in the franchise was effected.

64 We found the position much changed since 1944. A number of witnesses, indeed, still opposed the abolition of the test, but a large and representative body of opinion was strongly in favour of universal adult suffrage. While it would be unreal to suggest the introduction of universal adult suffrage in the absence of a general demand for it, we had to consider whether the arguments which determined the Franchise Commission in 1944 possessed any continuing validity, which could support the retention of literacy test. The crux of the Commission's argument is contained in the sentence in paragraph 40, which reads:

> "We are ready and willing to concede that this very large section ('for the most part . . . persons of East Indian descent . . . (who) labour on the sugar estates and in the villages of the colony') have in their midst a considerable number of persons of both sexes who, though handicapped by lack of education of any kind, are possessed of more than an average amount of intelligence: but we cannot admit the claim that these persons are capable of exercising their votes with the same judgment and unbiased decision that the educated classes of the population may be expected to employ in their support of suitable candidates for election to the Legislative Council; nor are we satisfied that they can be depended upon to exercise the franchise freely and independently."

65 The Commission go on to express the fear that the preponderance of illiterate voters would secure the return of representatives to the Legislative Council chosen exclusively upon racial considerations, rather than upon careful judgment of opposing policies. There may have been present, too, in many minds the fear that the hitherto voteless East Indians would by sheer weight of numbers cause a serious and permanent disturbance in the balance of political power in favour of that community; for, in the absence of any recent census return, the impression was current that the East Indian community was preponderant in most of the constituencies, other than those of Georgetown and New Amsterdam. A cleavage of opinion then developed, which placed the East Indian community and the rest of the population in opposing camps.

66 Since that time, the census figures of 1946 have been published, and disclose that the distribution of population in the constituencies, as they now stand, does not present the preponderance of East Indians that had been expected, and it may be that this was one of the reasons why we received a

widespread demand for universal adult suffrage. Certainly we found that a considerable section of the African community, who at the time of the Franchise Commission had opposed its introduction, had now changed its view.

67 While on grounds other than those of sectional advantage, the arguments adduced by the Franchise Commission have considerable force, it is to our minds repugnant that the retention of a literacy test should operate to the disfranchisement of a large section of one particular community, unless that disfranchisement were justified upon grounds of the patent incapacity of the illiterate. Observation in British Guiana itself, and comparison with neighbouring territories, give no support to this proposition. Illiterates may, indeed, tend to vote upon racial lines more than will the educated classes, but, as has been said, many who now fall within the ambit of the electoral laws can scarcely be described as "educated". Moreover, retention of a literacy test would inevitably be regarded by the East Indian community as evidence of sectional discrimination, and would intensify racial antagonism. The present cleavage would then harden, so that when the great mass of the East Indian community become literate, and so be entitled to the franchise – a time which is reliably estimated to be not far distant – the virus of racialism, which it is at present possible to expel, will have become irremediably established in the body politic.

68 It is, therefore, for a variety of considerations – public demand and expectation, the example of adjoining territories, and disbelief in the efficacy of a literacy test infallibly to segregate the politically responsible from the irresponsible – that we have come to the conclusion that we should recommend its abolition.

69 There were few witnesses who were not in favour of the abolition of property and income qualifications, and this matter gave us less food for thought . . .

CHAPTER V: THE LEGISLATURE

77 The most convenient division of the components of government is threefold – the Legislature, the Executive, and the Judiciary – and we shall discuss each in turn. These are not, of course, watertight compartments, for the Governor has a part to play in each. His assent to bills is the last stage of the legislative process, but for our present purpose it will be sufficient if we confine ourselves to the character of the other elements that go to make up the Legislature.

78 Democratic governments derive "their just powers from the consent of the governed". This doctrine of consent is distinctive of democracy and

fundamental to it. It means, for one thing, that a government elected by a majority of the population should always consult the interests of all. For this reason, and to enable the will of the community to be more perfectly discovered, checks and balances are an integral feature of democratic government as western civilisation understands it . . .

79 We subscribe wholeheartedly to the belief that the preponderant voice in any deliberative assembly should be that of the elected representatives of the people, but we are convinced that a community in which these checks do not exist or are of illusory power is not truly democratic, and we dismiss at once from our consideration all proposals for a legislature which does not in some way or other embody these safeguards. Having said this, there is little need to elaborate the point that the reserved powers of the Governor acting upon the deliberations of a wholly elected single chamber do not accord with democratic experience, and do not offer a practicable alternative to a system of checks and balances embedded in the structure of the legislature itself. The Governor's powers of suspension, veto, and certification, are intended to be exercised only on rare occasions of grave public consequence, and to ensure that "public faith, public order, and other essentials of good government" are preserved. Their frequent use would bring the Governor right into the political arena, where his position as the representative of the Crown would rapidly become intolerable both to the legislature and to himself, and would place a premium upon irresponsibility by encouraging the belief that real power was being withheld.

80 The constitutional checks which have been welded into colonial constitutions are of two sorts; the system of nomination, whereby some portion of an otherwise elected unicameral legislature is reserved for persons nominated by the Governor; or the bicameral system, whereby an upper or revisionary chamber serves as a check upon the legislative acts of the elective chamber. We have given anxious thought to what checks and balances would be most beneficial to British Guiana at the present stage of her constitutional development, and have debated carefully the alternative types of legislature which embody them. We regret that we have not been able to reach identity of outlook in this particular. The unicameral structure appeals to one of our number, but the others of us prefer the operation of a bicameral legislature. This apart, the area of agreement between us is great, and our proposals for the composition and functions of the Executive remain unchanged under both a bicameral and a unicameral system, although the manner of election of the unofficial members will vary slightly[67] . . .

67 In the event a bi-cameral form was decided upon as set out in the British Guiana (Constitution) Order in Council, 1953. (See following document.)

83 Whether the structure be unicameral or bicameral, and excluding always the official members, we recommend that the qualifications for membership of the elective chamber should be those of age, citizenship, and residence, that we propose for an elector, together with the requirements of mental and civic capacity usual for a legislator. To this we should add the further requirement that all should be literate in English. We are conscious that the election of an illiterate person is a remote contingency, but a fluency, both written and spoken, in the language in which the business of government is conducted – and which is also the official language of British Guiana – is nevertheless so essential a part of a legislator's equipment that we feel it should be made mandatory upon him.

84 We have given careful thought to two other proposals that were made to us from time to time: that candidates for the legislature should reside in the constituency for which they seek election; and that a member should be bound under pain of suspension to attend a specified minimum number of meetings of the Legislature and of its committees. We have examined these proposals with sympathy . . . but we are not convinced that they are practicable or indeed more efficacious than the simple power, which resides in the electorate, of dismissing at the next election any candidate who has been remiss or inattentive in the discharge of his duties.

87 The present legislature in British Guiana has a life of five years, and many witnesses urged upon us that this should be retained, since it would enable ministers to familiarise themselves with their tasks, and would afford them a reasonable space of time in which to carry through their programme. It can be argued, too, that if a government requires five years in which to demonstrate its mettle, the electorate cannot, in any shorter time, obtain a clear appreciation of its achievement; and, finally, more frequent elections mean increased expenditure. These arguments have force in that they are clearly based upon the analogy of British practice, but the analogy is not entirely appropriate in the circumstances of British Guiana, where the introduction of an intermediate form of responsible government makes a more frequent reference to the electorate desirable. On the one hand, it will encourage the electorate to appreciate the reality of the grant of universal adult suffrage, and the privileges and duties it confers; on the other, legislators and ministers will be rendered more sensitive to opinion in the constituencies. For these reasons, and because we are confident that ministers will find in a shorter term than five years adequate opportunity to develop their policies, we recommend that the legislature should have a life of three years. Within this term, a session of the legislature should be held at least once a year, while the Governor should possess a discretionary power of prorogation and dissolution.

88 As the elected representatives come increasingly to assume the responsibilities of government, it is proper that the Governor, as His Majesty's representative, should be withdrawn more and more from the political arena. One of the forms in which his political influence is most ponderable arises from his presence in the debates of the Legislature as its president often with an original or a casting vote (or, as in the old Court of Policy, with both), and we welcome the progress that has already been made in British Guiana by the occasional withdrawal of the Governor from the Legislative Council, when his place is taken by a Deputy President, who is an elected member of the Council.[68] The presence of the Governor at the debates of the Legislative Council as its president becomes increasingly anomalous in the circumstances of ministerial government, and we therefore recommend that a Speaker shall be appointed, who shall also be the Chairman of any committee of the whole house.

89 We do not recommend that British practices, by which the Speaker is appointed by the House from among its own members, should be followed in British Guiana. The removal of one member from the arena of dispute on the floor of the house to the impartial office of Speaker deprives that member's constituency of its normal representation, and this feature is open to greater criticism in a chamber where the electives will number only 18 or 24 than in one in which they are over 600. Leaving aside for a moment the possible repercussions which, in a narrowly divided house, the election of one of its members to the Speaker's chair may have upon a party's majority, we have also to remember that the demands of the Executive for men of ability will have first call upon the relatively small membership of the Legislature. The office of Speaker demands a capacity for judicious and impartial supervision of debate which may not commend its owner for a further extension of electoral favour, and we cannot deprecate too earnestly the mischief which frequent changes in the occupancy of the Speaker's chair can cause by depriving the house of the knowledge of constitutional practice and of the humours of men which comes to any Speaker over a period of years. We, therefore, recommend that the Governor be empowered to appoint at his discretion an independent person to be Speaker, who shall not be a member of the Legislature, and who is not the holder of any office of emolument under the Crown. The Speaker shall hold his office during pleasure, although it shall be permissive for him at any time to resign.

68 Where similar arrangements existed in the rest of the West Indies it was a frequent occurrence for the Deputy President to preside at meetings of the Legislative Council in place of the Governor.

90 We recommend that a Deputy Speaker, who is not to be a member of the legislative body, shall be appointed by the members of the elective house from among their own number . . .

CHAPTER VI: THE EXECUTIVE

117 The devolution of real responsibility upon elected members, by vesting them with ministerial functions and by establishing the Court of Policy as the principal instrument of policy, involves a diminution of the day-to-day executive activities of the Governor. He will now move to a position close to that occupied by the Sovereign in the United Kingdom, and will be bound customarily to act in accordance with the advice tendered to him in the Court of Policy. Nevertheless, in any colony where a grant of responsible government has been made, it is an established principle, with which we are in complete agreement, that, until the goal of autonomy within the Commonwealth has been attained, the Governor should retain the discretionary powers of dissent, reservation[69] and declaration, to enable him, rather as an umpire, to safeguard the interests of public order, public faith, and other essentials of good government. These powers are by their nature instruments of last resort to be used only in matters of grave public consequence.

118 Under the old order, the participation of the Governor in the hurly-burly of politics is the rule; under the new it must be the exception . . .

(vi) Extracts from the British Guiana (Constitution) Order in Council, 1953. (S.I. 586/1953.)[70]

PART IV

STATE COUNCIL

31 There shall be a State Council in and for the Colony which shall consist of nine Members qualified and appointed in accordance with the provisions of this Part of this Order.[71]

69 The Governor may in his discretion reserve any bill for the signification of His Majesty's pleasure, and there are also certain categories of bills to which he may not assent unless they contain a clause suspending their operation until His Majesty's pleasure has been made known. We recommend, for the reasons set out in paragraph 147, that this requirement be applied to any bill affecting the interests of the Amerindian peoples. (Report's footnote.)

70 See Appendix A, for the documents dealing with the suspension of this constitution, related and subsequent events.

71 This Order in Council made provision for an appointed President of the State Council.

32(1) Of the nine Members –

(a) two shall be appointed by the Governor in accordance with the recommendation of the six Ministers elected by the House of Assembly; the making of a recommendation to the Governor shall be the first duty of such Ministers after their election;
Provided that if the Ministers fail (whether after their election or after the occurrence of a vacancy in respect of the seat of a Member of the State Council appointed under this paragraph) within such time as the Governor, acting in his discretion, considers reasonable, to recommend a person or persons for appointment, the Governor may, acting in his discretion, after consultation with the Ministers, make an appointment or appointments, as the case may require;

(b) one shall be appointed by the Governor, acting in his discretion, after consultation with such Elected Members or groups of Elected Members or with both such Members and groups as, in his opinion, constitute the minority in the House of Assembly;

(c) thereafter, six shall be appointed by the Governor, acting in his discretion:
Provided that the Governor shall not appoint, under this paragraph, any person who has unsuccessfully sought election to the House of Assembly at or since the immediately preceding general election of Elected Members to that Chamber.[72]

33 Subject to the provisions of section 34 of this Order, any person who –

(a) is a British subject of the age of thirty-five years or upwards; and

(b) has resided in the Colony for a period of at least two years immediately before the date of his appointment or is domiciled in the Colony and is resident therein at the date aforesaid; and

(c) is able to speak and, unless incapacitated by blindness or other physical cause, to read the English language with a degree of proficiency sufficient to enable him to take an active part in the proceedings of the State Council,

shall be qualified to be appointed a Member of the State Council, and no other person shall be qualified to be so appointed or, having been so appointed, shall sit or vote in the Council[73] . . .

72 A frequent criticism of the Senate appointments in independent Jamaica has been that some of these appointments have been made from such unsuccessful candidates.
73 Section 34 of this Order in Council gives the usual disqualifications from membership.

PART V

HOUSE OF ASSEMBLY

43 There shall be a House of Assembly in and for the Colony which shall consist of a Speaker,[74] three *ex officio* Members and twenty-four Elected Members.

PART VI

LEGISLATION AND PROCEDURE IN LEGISLATURE

59 Subject to the provisions of this Order, it shall be lawful for the Governor, with the advice and consent of the State Council and of the House of Assembly, to make laws for the peace, order and good government of the Colony.[75]

60 Subject to the provisions of this Order, the Governor and the Chambers shall, in the transaction of business and the making of laws, conform as nearly as may be to the directions contained in any Instructions under Her Majesty's Sign Manual and Signet which may from time to time be addressed to the Governor in that behalf . . .

67(1) Save as is provided in subsection (2) of this section and in section 63 of this Order and subject to the Standing Orders of the Chambers, any Member of either Chamber may introduce any Bill, or propose any motion for debate in, or may present any petition to, the Chamber of which he is a Member, and the same shall be debated and disposed of according to the Standing Orders of that Chamber.

(2) Except with the recommendation or consent of the Governor signified thereto, neither Chamber shall proceed upon any Bill, motion or petition which, in the opinion of the person presiding in the Chamber, would dispose of or charge any public revenue or public funds of the Colony, or revoke or alter any disposition thereof or charge thereon, or impose, alter or repeal any rate, tax or duty.

68(1) A Money Bill shall be first introduced in the House of Assembly.

(2) In this section and in sections 69 and 70 of this Order, "Money Bill" means a Bill which, in the opinion of the Speaker, contains only provisions

74 The Order makes provision for an appointed Speaker and an elected Deputy Speaker.

75 The powers of the Governor and the Imperial Government over legislation are the same as those set out in the Trinidad and Tobago (Constitution) Order in Council, 1950. (Chapter IV, Part II, doc. E(ii).)

dealing with all or any of the following subjects, namely, the imposition, repeal, remission, alteration, or regulation of taxation; the imposition, for the payment of debt or other financial purposes, of charges on public money or the variation or repeal of any such charges; the grant of money to the Crown or to any authority or person, or the variation or revocation or any such grant; the appropriation, receipt, custody, investment, issue or audit of accounts of public money; the raising or guarantee of any loan or the repayment thereof; or subordinate matters incidental to those subjects or any of them. In this definition the expressions "taxation", "public money" and "loan", respectively, do not include any taxation, money or loan raised by local authorities or bodies for local purposes.

69(1) Subject to the provisions of this Order, if a Money Bill, having been passed by the House of Assembly and sent to the State Council at least three months before the end of the session, is rejected by the State Council within three months after it is sent to that Chamber, the Bill, with any amendments which are certified by the Speaker to have been made by the State Council and agreed to by the House of Assembly, shall, if the House of Assembly so resolve, be presented to the Governor for assent; and, if the Governor shall assent thereto, or if he shall reserve the Bill for the signification of Her Majesty's pleasure and Her Majesty shall assent thereto, the Bill shall become a law notwithstanding that the State Council have not consented to the Bill.[76]

(2) There shall be endorsed on every Money Bill when it is sent to the State Council the certificate of the Speaker signed by him that it is a Money Bill and, when it is presented to the Governor for assent in pursuance of the provisions of this section, a further certificate of the Speaker signed by him that the provisions of this section have been duly compiled with.

70(1) Subject to the provisions of this Order, if any Government Bill other than a Money Bill is passed by the House of Assembly in two successive sessions (whether or not the Chambers are dissolved between those sessions), and, having been sent to the State Council at least three months before the end of the session, is rejected by the State Council in each of those sessions within three months after it is so sent, that Bill shall, after it is rejected for the second time by the State Council, if the House of Assembly so resolve, be presented to the Governor for assent and, if the Governor shall assent thereto, or, if he shall reserve the Bill for the signification of Her Majesty's pleasure and Her Majesty shall assent thereto, the Bill shall become a law notwithstanding that the State Council have not consented to the Bill:

76 Note the greater restrictions on the powers of the State Council as outlined in this Order in Council than those of the Jamaican Legislative Council established by Order in Council in 1944 (Chapter IV, Part II, doc. C(vii)).

Provided that this provision shall not have effect unless one year has elapsed between the date of the termination of the first debate on the Bill in the House of Assembly in the first of those sessions and the date on which it passes the House in the second of those sessions.

(2) When a Bill is presented to the Governor for assent in pursuance of the provisions of this section there shall be endorsed on the Bill the certificate of the Speaker signed by him that the provisions of this section have been duly complied with . . .

(vii) Extracts from the Report of the Committee of Unofficial Members of the Legislative Council on proposals for constitutional reforms, 1957. (Jamaica. Government Printers, Kingston, 1957.)

4 (1) . . .

(2) The reasons in favour of a revisionary house are fundamental but few and may be simply summarised. They originate in the first place, historically; in the second place, for revisionary purposes or, in the third place, in order to enfranchise, as it were, important classifications of the body politic which might otherwise have no voice in the direction of the affairs of their country:

(i) . . .

(ii) The second reason for a bicameral legislature is the fundamental one, that is to say, its revisionary function. Human experience is overwhelmingly in favour of "the second look" and it is the recognition of this simple fact that accounts for the existence of a second chamber wherever (with minor exceptions) democracy is understood and practiced . . . Furthermore the public seldom becomes fully aware of the implications of important legislation until it has completed its passage through the primary house . . . particularly when second reading is completed at one sitting. It is then, if at all, that the voice of public opinion is raised – but all too late if there is no second chamber. There is also the pedestrian necessity to revise and check in the ordinary sense of those words . . . Finally, it should surely be understood and always borne in mind that the procedure now accepted wherever bi-cameral legislature exists, is not that the second chamber can reject any measure for all time but merely that it can insist that the primary house itself review its original decision in the light of considerations put before it by the revisionary house. If the primary house does not accept the recommendations of the second chamber it has the power to force its will upon the State. A revisionary house does not make laws; it only makes suggestions.

(iii) The third reason for a bi-cameral legislature originates in the advisability of ensuring that all sections of the state are

> represented in the legislature – to a lesser extent, of guarding against freak results at the polls. The sheer weight of numbers involved in adult franchise bearing down on principles of democracy which had their origin when citizens were few, may also be said to have disenfranchised some important elements in the community . . . Experience is not to be confused with ability nor is ability a substitute for experience and it is in this context that it is idle to pretend that those who could not face the hustings are therefore incapable of helping to bear the burden of public administration for the common weal.

6 After due consideration of the May, 1954, report of its predecessors. . . which recommended a gradual development from an all-nominated to an all-elected second chamber and after reviewing other methods of selection, the committee has come to the unanimous conclusion that the second chamber should be entirely nominated by the Governor after consultation with the leaders of the Parliamentary majority and minority respectively. The reasons for making this recommendation are as follows:

(1) The present Parliamentary majority and minority are understood to be unalterably opposed to any second chamber based on the elective principle. It is not for this committee to speculate as to their reasons for this opposition but it must be said that the great majority of this Committee are of the same view. A small minority still feels that election on the basis of very broad constituencies – not more than three or four for the whole island – might well provide the type of representation which is sought to be assured in a second chamber while at the same time giving it the added influence of being election-based.

(2) The abandonment of the elective principle leaves few practicable alternatives. Indirect election whether by a college of electors or by the primary chamber is open to the same objections, though in a more limited form, as are advanced against straight election. Election or nomination by groups of the state such as agricultural, commercial, industrial and other divisions presents technical difficulties of great complexity and tends to encourage a limited and partisan view which is most to be avoided in a second chamber . . .

(3) . . .

(4) . . .

7 . . . Again one falls back on appointment by an impartial and independent authority – the Governor.

8 It is an important part of the committee's recommendation that prior to making his appointments to the Second Chamber the Governor must consult

with the leaders of the Parliamentary majority and minority respectively . . . In the opinion of the committee there is an important distinction between the Chief Minister himself appointing any of the members of the second chamber on the one hand and the Governor doing so on the other, after consultation with the Chief Minister.

(viii) Extracts from the Report of the Select Committee of the House of Representatives on proposals for constitutional reform, 1958. (Jamaica Minutes of the House of Representatives, 1958. Appendix XII.)

JAMAICA, 1958 REPORT

5 This report is presented on the back-ground of the Constitution as it now exists and deals with the major points remaining over to be considered after the immediate changes which were effected last year took effect . . . [77]

6 The major points which fell to be dealt with are as follows:-

(a) *Legislature*

(i) whether the Legislature should consist of two Chambers or of the House of Representatives only;

(ii) assuming that the Legislative Council was retained, what its numbers should be and how the members should be appointed;

(iii) what should be the number of the members of the House of Representatives and how the number of seats should be distributed among the parishes.

(b) *Legislative Powers*

The extent to which the Legislative Council, if retained, should have the right to delay the enactment of money bills and other bills.

(c) *Reserve Powers*

What should happen to the reserve powers properly so called and to the existing provisions requiring bills to be reserved for the special assent of Her Majesty in Council as set out in the existing Constitution.

9 Your Committee proposes that a new Constitution be made for Jamaica using the existing Constitution as a basis and incorporating the following provisions:

77 Most of the changes referred to had to do with additional grants of responsible government. The only significant change in the legislature was that all officials were removed from the Legislative Council save the Attorney-General. (Jamaica (Constitution) Order in Council, 1957. Section 4 (1)(a).)

Legislature

(i) The Legislature shall consist of 2 Chambers to be known respectively as the Legislative Council and the House of Representatives.

(ii) The Legislative Council shall consist of persons appointed by the Governor after consultation with the political leaders of the Parties represented in the House of Representatives.

(iii) The Chief Minister, who may be designated Premier, shall have the right to recommend the appointment of not more than 3 persons to be members of the Legislative Council.

(iv) The Legislative Council shall consist of 21 members.

(v) No official shall be a member of the Legislative Council.

(vi) The Legislative Council will elect a President and a Deputy President.

(vii) The House of Representatives shall consist of 45 members . . .

(viii) The House of Representatives shall elect a Speaker and a Deputy Speaker.

(ix) . . .

(x) . . .

Legislative Powers

(The Committee recommend that the Legislative Council have powers similar to those of the House of Lords in the British Parliament.)

Reservation of Bills

(xvii) No bill shall be reserved for the Special assent of Her Majesty in Council except a bill purporting to affect Defence or international relations or appearing to be inconsistent with the Constitution itself.

(xviii) The Governor's veto power in respect of legislation should be exercised in accordance with constitutional procedures which should require him to act on the advice of the Cabinet.

Reserve Powers

(xix) All the reserve powers, that is to say the powers contained in section 47 of the Jamaica (Constitution) Order in Council 1944 whereby the Governor may declare that any Bill, Motion, Resolution or Vote shall have effect notwithstanding that it may not have been approved by the Legislature, and the power to reject the advice of the Council of Ministers in the interest of public order, public faith or good Government, shall be removed from the Constitution.

(ix) Extracts from the Jamaica (Constitution) Order in Council, 1959. (S.I. 862/1959.)[78]

PART III – THE LEGISLATURE

Composition

14 There shall be a Legislature in and for Jamaica which shall consist of Her Majesty, a Legislative Council and a House of Representatives.

15(1) The Legislative Council shall consist of persons who, being qualified for appointment as members in accordance with the provisions of this Order, have been so appointed in accordance with the provisions of this section.

(2) Not more than three nor less than two (as the Governor, acting in accordance with the advice of the Premier, may from time to time decide) of the members of the Legislative Council shall be persons who have been appointed by the Governor, acting as aforesaid, by instrument under the Broad Seal.

(3) The remaining members of the Legislative Council shall consist of eighteen persons who have been appointed by the Governor, by instrument under the Broad Seal, after consultation with such persons as, in his discretion, he considers can speak for the differing political points of view of groups represented in the House of Representatives.

16(1) The House of Representatives shall consist of persons who, being qualified for election as members in accordance with the provisions of this Order, have been so elected in the manner provided by or under any law for the time being in force in Jamaica.

(2) There shall be one member of the House of Representatives for each constituency constituted in accordance with the provisions of section 45 or section 106 of this Order.

17 Subject to the provisions of the following section, any person who, at the date of his appointment or nomination for election –

(a) is a British subject of the age of twenty-one years or upwards; and

78 This Order in Council brought full internal self-government to Jamaica. Though varying in many details, especially in the composition of the Senate, very similar legislatures (with the same restrictions on the power of the second chamber) were established on the achievement of full internal self-government in Trinidad and Tobago, 1960, and in Barbados, 1964, and on the achievement of a large measure of internal self-government in the Bahama Islands, 1963 and in British Honduras, 1964. British Guiana reverted to a unicameral legislature (see Chapter IV, Part II, doc. F(iii)) and the constitution of the Associated States are dealt with in the next chapter.

(b) has been ordinarily resident in Jamaica for the immediately preceding twelve months,

shall be qualified to be appointed as a member of the Legislative Council or elected as a member of the House of Representatives and no other person shall be so qualified . . .

Powers and Procedure

26 Subject to the provisions of the West Indies (Federation) Order in Council, 1957 (a), and of this Order, the Legislature shall have power to make laws for the peace, order and good government of Jamaica.[79]

27 Subject to the provisions of this Order, each chamber of the Legislature may from time to time make, amend or revoke Standing Orders for the regulation and orderly conduct of its own proceedings and the despatch of business . . .

37(1) A Bill shall not become law until –

(a) the Governor has assented thereto in Her Majesty's name and on Her Majesty's behalf and has signed it in token of such assent, or

(b) Her Majesty has given her assent thereto through a Secretary of State and the Governor has signified such assent by Proclamation published in the *Gazette*.

(2) A Bill shall be presented to the Governor for assent if, and (subject to the provisions of sections 33 and 34 of this Order) shall not be so presented unless, it has been approved by both chambers of the Legislature either without amendment or with such amendments only as are agreed to by both chambers.

(3) When a Bill is presented to the Governor for assent he shall declare that he assents or refuses assent thereto or that he reserves the Bill for the signification of Her Majesty's pleasure:

Provided that, unless he has been authorised by a Secretary of State to assent thereto, the Governor shall reserve for the signification of Her Majesty's pleasure any Bill –

(a) which appears to him acting in his discretion –

(i) to be inconsistent with any obligation imposed on Her Majesty by any treaty, convention or agreement or arrangement relating to any country or international or similar organisation outside Jamaica; or

(ii) to be likely to prejudice the Royal prerogative; or

79 The Jamaican Legislative Council as established by this Order in Council could not originate a money bill, could only delay a money bill for one month, and could only delay ordinary legislation and statutory instruments for seven months.

(b) which is in any way repugnant to or inconsistent with the provisions of this Order . . .

39(1) Any law of the Legislature which has been assented to by the Governor and which appears to Her Majesty's Government in the United Kingdom –

(a) to alter, to the injury of the stockholders, any of the provisions relating to any Jamaican Government stock, being securities in which a trustee may invest by virtue of section 2 of the Colonial Stock Act, 1900 (a); or

(b) to involve a departure from the original contract in respect of any such stock,

may be disallowed by Her Majesty through a Secretary of State.

(2) Whenever any such law has been disallowed by Her Majesty, the Governor shall cause notice of such disallowance to be published in the *Gazette.*

(3) Every law so disallowed shall cease to have effect as soon as notice of such disallowance is published as aforesaid and thereupon any enactment repealed or amended by or in pursuance of the law disallowed shall have effect as if such law had not been made. Subject to the foregoing provisions of this subsection, the provisions of subsection (2) of section 38 of the Interpretation Act, 1889 (b), shall apply in relation to such disallowance as they apply in relation to the repeal of an Act of Parliament.

(4) In this section "Jamaican Government stock" means stock forming the whole or part of the public debt of Jamaica[80] . . .

42(1) The Governor may at any time, by Proclamation published in the *Gazette*, prorogue the Legislature.

(2) The Governor, acting in his discretion, may at any time, by Proclamation published in the *Gazette*, dissolve the Legislature.[81]

(3) The Governor shall dissolve the Legislature at the expiration of five years from the date when the House of Representatives first meets after any general election unless it has been sooner dissolved.

(4) If, between a dissolution of the Legislature and the next ensuing general election of members to the House of Representatives, an emergency arises of such a nature that, in the opinion of the Premier, it is necessary for the two chambers of the Legislature to be summoned before that general election can

80 Note the considerable reduction in the Governor's powers: the power of certification having been removed; the discretionary power of reservation being reduced and the power of assent (except where a Bill should be reserved) being exercisable only on the advice of the Cabinet. Furthermore the power of disallowance of the Imperial Government is reduced to laws relating to Government stock.

81 Note that the power to dissolve the legislature is still not exercised on the advice of the Premier.

be held, the Governor, acting in accordance with the advice of the Premier, may, by Proclamation published in the *Gazette,* summon the two chambers of the preceding Legislature and that Legislature shall thereupon be deemed (except for the purposes of the following section) not to have been dissolved but shall be deemed (except as aforesaid) to be dissolved on the date on which the next ensuing general election is held.

43(1) A general election of members of the House of Representatives shall be held at such time within three months after every dissolution of the Legislature as the Governor shall appoint by Proclamation published in the *Gazette.*

(2) As soon as may be after every general election, the Governor shall proceed under section 15 of this Order to the appointment of members of the Legislative Council.

44 The Legislature may by law determine and regulate the privileges, immunities and powers of the two chambers of the Legislature and the members thereof, but no such privileges, immunities or powers shall exceed those of the Commons' House of Parliament of the United Kingdom or of the members thereof.

PART IV – DELIMITATION OF CONSTITUENCIES

45(1) Subject to the provisions of section 106 of this Order, Jamaica shall, for the purpose of the election of members to the House of Representatives, be divided into such number of constituencies, being not less than 45 nor more than 60, as may from time to time be provided by Order made by the Governor under this section.

(2) The House of Representatives shall, as soon as practicable after it first meets following any general election, appoint a Standing Committee, of which the Speaker shall be Chairman, for the purpose of the continuous review of –

(a) the number of constituencies into which Jamaica is to be divided and

(b) the boundaries of such constituencies.

(3) Subject to the provisions of this section, the constitution and procedure of the Standing Committee shall be determined by the Standing Orders of the House of Representatives.

(4) The Standing Committee shall, . . . submit to the House of Representatives reports [82] . . .

82 The Committee, in making any recommendation to change boundaries, should give effect to the rules set out in the Third Schedule to this Order:

(5) Reports under the preceding subsection shall be submitted by the Standing Committee –

- (a) in the case of its first report after the appointed day, not less than three nor more than seven years from that day; and
- (b) in the case of any subsequent report, not less than three nor more than seven years from the date of the submission of its last report; Provided that a report made under paragraph (b) of the preceding subsection shall not be submitted less than six years from the appointed day or from the date of the submission of the last report of the Committee.

(6) Where the Standing Committee intends to consider making a report, it shall, by notice in writing, inform the Minister responsible for the conduct of elections (hereafter in this section called "the Minister") accordingly, and a copy of that notice shall be published in the *Gazette*.

(7) As soon as may be after the Standing Committee has submitted a report to the House of Representatives under paragraph (a) of subsection (4) of this section, the Minister shall lay before the House of Representatives for its approval the draft of an Order by the Governor for giving effect, whether with or without modifications, to the recommendations contained in the report, and that draft may make provision for any matters which appear to the Minister to be incidental to or consequential upon the other provisions of the draft.

THIRD SCHEDULE

NUMBER AND BOUNDARIES OF CONSTITUENCIES

1 The number of constituencies shall be such as will most conveniently permit the application of the following paragraph.

2 The electorate shall, so far as is practicable, be equal in all constituencies.

3 The Standing Committee may depart from the strict application of the preceding paragraph if it considers it desirable so to do having regard to –

- (a) the varying physical features and transportation facilities within Jamaica;
- (b) the difference between urban and rural areas in respect of density of population.

4 For the purposes of this Schedule –

- (a) the electorate of a constituency means the number of persons whose names appear on the official lists of electors for the area comprised in that constituency in force on the enumeration date under the law for the time being regulating the conduct of elections;
- (b) the enumeration date means, in relation to any report of the Standing Committee, the date on which the notice with respect of that report is published in accordance with subsection (6) of section 45 of this Order.

(8) Where any draft made under this section gives effect to any such recommendations with modifications, the Minister shall lay before the House of Representatives together with the draft a statement of the reasons for the modifications.

(9) If the motion for the approval of any draft made under this section is rejected by the House of Representatives, or is withdrawn by leave of that chamber, the Minister shall amend the draft and lay the amended draft before the House of Representatives.

(10) If any draft made under this section is approved by resolution of the House of Representatives, the Minister shall submit it to the Governor who shall make an Order (which shall be published in the *Gazette*) in terms of the draft; and that Order shall come into force on such day as may be specified therein and, until revoked by a further Order made by the Governor in accordance with the provisions of this section, shall have the force of law in Jamaica:

Provided that the coming into force of any such Order shall not affect any election to the House of Representatives until a proclamation is made by the Governor appointing the date for the holding of a general election of members to the House of Representatives or affect the constitution of the House of Representatives until the dissolution of the Legislature then in being.

(11) The question of the validity of any Order by the Governor purporting to be made under this section and reciting that a draft thereof has been approved by resolution of the House of Representatives shall not be enquired into in any court.

F. Unicameralism and proportional representation in British Guiana.

(i) Extracts from the Report of the British Guiana Constitutional Conference, 1960. (Cmnd. 998/1960.)[83]

INTRODUCTION

1 This Conference was convened by the Secretary of State for the Colonies at the request of the British Guiana Legislature to consider what measures of constitutional advances should take place in British Guiana.

83 After this report the British Guiana (Constitution) Order in Council, 1961 established: (1) a bicameral legislature; (2) election to the Legislative Assembly by the first-past-the-post system from single member constituencies; (3) the Governor's power of certification of legislation dealing with defence or international affairs to be exercised in his discretion; (4) the Governor's power

11 The Conference proceeded to discuss the matters on the agenda. On many points it transpired that the Secretary of State's proposals fell far short of the desires of members of the British Guiana Delegation. Differences of view were frankly stated and discussed and, save in respect of the interim changes, a compromise was reached. The conclusions of the Conference so reached are summarised in the following paragraphs.

LEGISLATURE

14 The new Constitution would provide for a bicameral Legislature which would consist of an elected chamber to be called the "Legislative Assembly" and a nominated chamber to be called the "Senate".[84]

LEGISLATIVE POWERS

23 The Governor would assent or refuse to assent to Bills in accordance with the advice of Ministers. However, unless he were authorised by the Secretary of State to assent thereto, the Governor would be required to reserve for the signification of Her Majesty's pleasure any Bill which, in his opinion, affected defence, external affairs or the Royal Prerogative or was inconsistent with the Constitution. This provision would also apply to Bills affecting the maintenance of law and order until responsibility for these subjects had passed to a Minister. Similarly, the above provision would also apply to Bills affecting the terms and conditions of service, including pensions, of public officers until the time when the Public, Police and Judicial Service Commissions became executive.

24 The Governor would have a reserved legislative power which would be restricted to Bills and motions which, in his opinion, were necessary or expedient for the purpose of defence or external affairs or, until responsibility for law and order had passed to a Minister, or the Service Commissions had become executive, as the case may be, for maintaining law and order or securing satisfactory terms and conditions of service of public officers. To make this power fully effective, the Governor would have to be able to secure that a

of reservation, again exercised in his discretion, where the Bill appears to him to affect defence, international affairs, the Royal Prerogative, or to be repugnant to or inconsistent with the provisions of the Constitution; and (5) H.M.'s Government's power of disallowance only in matters relating to Government Stock.

84 The suggestion was that the second chamber should have the same limitations on its powers that the Jamaican second chamber had.

Bill or motion for any of the above purposes was introduced or proposed in either chamber of the Legislature.[85]

25 The powers of Her Majesty to legislate for British Guiana by Order in Council under the British Guiana Act, 1928, would be retained in the next constitutional stage. The Secretary of State in consideration of the special circumstances of British Guiana gave an assurance that it was his intention not to advise that these powers be exercised except for the purpose of enacting constitutional instruments or to deal with grave emergency.

26 Her Majesty's power to disallow a law of the British Guiana Legislature would be retained only in the case of laws affecting British Guiana Government stock . . .

ELECTORAL SYSTEM

39 It was accepted that election to the Legislative Assembly should be by the "first past the post" system in single-member constituencies. A Boundary Commission would be appointed without delay with the object of delimiting new constituency boundaries if possible before the end of 1960.

40 The Commission would consist of a single Commissioner selected by the Lord Chancellor. The Commissioner should be a member or retired member of the Superior Judiciary; he would be assisted by expert advisers, including experts with local knowledge . . .

42 For the purpose of general elections under the new Constitution, there would continue to be universal adult suffrage.

(ii) Extracts from the Report of the British Guiana Independence Conference, 1963. (Cmnd. 2203/1963.)

1 At the British Guiana Constitutional Conference in 1960, a constitution providing for full internal self-government was agreed and the principle of independence for British Guiana was accepted.

2 In August, 1961, the new constitution was brought into effect and a general election was held. The People's Progressive Party (led by Dr. Cheddi Jagan) gained 42.6 per cent of the votes cast and 20 seats in the Legislative Assembly; the People's National Congress (led by Mr. Forbes Burnham) obtained 41 per cent of the votes and 11 seats; and the United Force (led by Mr. Peter d'Aguiar) secured 16.4 per cent of the votes and 4 seats. (Of the 35

85 Note that these paragraphs indicate that the Secretary of State was withholding the grant of full internal self-government.

seats, the People's Progressive Party did not contest six and the United Force did not contest one.)

3 In November, 1961, the Legislature of British Guiana passed a Resolution calling on Her Majesty's Government in the United Kingdom to grant independence to British Guiana. On receipt of this Resolution, the Secretary of State for the Colonies informed Dr. Jagan of his willingness to hold a Conference for the purpose of settling the form of the Constitution and of fixing a date for independence.

4 The Conference met in London at Lancaster House on 23rd October, 1962, under the chairmanship of the Secretary of State for the Colonies, Mr. Duncan Sandys. It was attended by delegates from three political parties represented in the Legislative Assembly of British Guiana . . .

6 Eighteen sessions of the Conference were held. A number of constitutional points were settled. But it was found that no substantial progress could be made until decisions were reached on three major questions:

- (a) Should elections be fought on the basis of single-member constituencies as at present or on the basis of proportional representation?
- (b) Should the right to vote be accorded at the age of 21 as at present or at the age of 18?
- (c) Should fresh elections be held before Independence?

7 The People's Progressive Party advocated single-member constituencies, voting at 18, and no elections before Independence. The People's National Congress and the United Force asked for proportional representation, voting at 21, and fresh elections.

8 These issues were exhaustively discussed, but no agreement could be reached.

9 These talks having proved fruitless, the three leaders decided to ask the Secretary of State to settle the outstanding issues on the authority of the British Government. The request was embodied in a letter to him, dated 25th October 1963, in the following terms:-

> *"At your request we have made further efforts to resolve the differences between us on the constitutional issues which require to be settled before British Guiana secures independence, in particular, the electoral system, the voting age, and the question whether fresh elections should be held before independence.*
>
> *We regret to have to report to you that we have not succeeded in reaching agreement; and we have reluctantly come to the conclusion that there is no prospect of an agreed solution. Another adjournment o[f] the Conference for further discussions between ourselves would therefo[re]*

serve no useful purpose and would result only in further delaying British Guiana's independence and in continued uncertainty in the country.

In these circumstances we are agreed to ask the British Government to settle on their authority all outstanding constitutional issues, and we undertake to accept their decisions.

Signed:
CHEDDI JAGAN.
L.F.S. BURNHAM.
P.S. D'AGUIAR."

10 After further meetings with the leaders of the three delegations, the Secretary of State announced his decisions at a final plenary session on 31st October 1963. In his statement (Annex A), Mr. Sandys said that he was satisfied that the root cause of British Guiana's troubles was the development of party politics along racial lines. He had therefore decided that the system of proportional representation should be introduced, since this would tend to encourage coalitions between parties and would make it easier for new political groupings to form on a multi-racial basis. Preparations for elections under this system would be put in hand without delay, after which the British Government would convene a conference to fix a date for independence.

11 Disappointment was expressed that the Secretary of State's decisions did not include a firm date for independence. However, Mr. Sandys emphasized that the British Government had no wish to delay British Guiana's independence any longer than was absolutely necessary to enable power to be transferred in conditions of peace and stability.

ANNEX A

STATEMENT BY THE SECRETARY OF STATE FOR THE COLONIES ANNOUNCING HIS DECISIONS

I had hoped that after a year's adjournment the political leaders of British Guiana could have succeeded in reaching agreement. But since that had proved impossible there was clearly no advantage in the further postponement of decisions. Therefore, although it was for me an unenviable task, I am sure that in all the circumstances you were right to ask the British Government to settle on your behalf your unresolved differences.

British Guiana faces many difficulties, but all that you have told me at this Conference, and all that I saw during my visit to your country last July, have convinced me that there is one problem which transcends all others, namely the growth of racialism. That is the curse of British Guiana today.

The whole life of the country is poisoned and weakened by mutual suspicion and fear between the two predominant racial groups, the Indians and the Africans. This state of tension has become acute in the last few years, and has led to racial murder, arson and violence. Last summer it reached the point where law and order could not be maintained without the assistance of two battalions of British soldiers. In fact the Premier told me that, if the British troops were withdrawn, the situation would get completely out of control.

Before British Guiana can safely assume the responsibilities of sovereign independence, it is clear that by one means or another harmony and confidence must be restored.

This need not necessarily take long. There is no deep-rooted or historical enmity between the races; nor is there any basic clash of interests between them; nor is there animosity between the religious groups, Christian, Hindu and Muslim.

The root of the trouble lies almost entirely in the development of party politics along racial lines. In its present acute form this can be traced to the split in the country's main political party in 1955. It was then that the People's Progressive Party, which had previously drawn its support from both the main races, broke into two bitterly opposed political groups, the one predominantly Indian, led by Dr. Jagan, and the other predominantly African, led by Mr. Burnham. Both parties have, for their political ends, fanned the racial emotions of their followers, with the result that each has come to be regarded as the champion of one race and the enemy of the other.

In this atmosphere of mutual suspicion, objectivity has entirely disappeared. Every political act is, or is alleged to be, dictated by racial prejudice. The Africans accuse the Government party of governing in the interests only of the Indians, and demand a share in political decisions. On the other side, the Indians accuse the Police, which is mainly African, of partiality towards the Africans and demand the creation of a separate defence force, recruited more extensively from the Indian community, to counterbalance the Police.

This state of general distrust has had a profoundly demoralising effect throughout the country. It has not only undermined political stability, but gravely threatens economic progress. It has led to such financial difficulties that the Government is unable, despite severe economies, to balance its budget, and will be obliged to seek outside assistance.

British Guiana is thus faced with an acute crisis of confidence. While this manifests itself primarily in a racial form, the cause is basically political. It is therefore a political solution which must be sought.

The aim of any such solution must be to create a reasonable degree of mutual trust and co-operation between the races. In the grave situation which has developed, no single remedy will be sufficient. The problem must be tackled from all possible angles.

In the first place, the Constitution must provide the strongest safeguards to protect minorities to preserve basic human rights, to ensure the impartiality of the Police, and to insulate the Judiciary and the Public Service from party political influences. On constitutional issues there should be a right of Appeal to the Judicial Committee of the Privy Council. The Constitutions of a number of new Commonwealth countries contain provisions designed to achieve these objectives, and, with necessary adaptations, I propose to apply them to British Guiana.

In view of the racial character of the problem I consider that there should, in addition, be some special provisions to penalise those who seek to promote antagonism between the races.

At the same time, every possible step must be taken to improve the relationship between the Government and the Opposition, of whatever political complexions they may be. Under a democratic system minorities must accept the decisions of the majority. But there are limits beyond which it is neither right nor safe for a Government to disregard the feelings and wishes of large sections of the people. In a country with a small population and slender resources, it is more than ever important that the Government should endeavour to rule with the general consent of the population. Bi-partisan policies may not be possible, but the political temperature can be greatly reduced by sincere and effective consultation. Of this there has been all too little in British Guiana, due to the intransigent and uncompromising attitude of both sides. The need for improvement in the methods and practice of consultation is recognised in all quarters, and all three political leaders have put forward a variety of proposals to this end. These will be studied and will, where appropriate, be adopted.

It is also necessary to strengthen the forces available to maintain law and order. A Country should only in the most rare and exceptional circumstances have to call upon troops to assist the civil power; and after independence it would, of course, be most undesirable for British Guiana to have to rely upon the army of another country to preserve internal security. It is arguable whether the additional forces required for this purpose should be regarded as an army or as an extension of the police. But whatever may be decided on this point, these should be constituted before independence by the Governor, who would endeavour to ensure that recruits were not drawn predominantly from any one racial group.

The measures I have indicated should to some extent help to reduce the present tensions and fears. But, if confidence and co-operation are to be restored, more positive steps must be taken to encourage the healthy development of political life along non-racial lines. The opposition parties have insisted that, in order to achieve this, a change in the electoral system is essential. On the other hand, this view has been strongly contended by the Government delegation.

I have listened carefully to the arguments advanced in favour of single member constituencies ("first past the post"), and those advanced in favour of various types of proportional representation. I must, however, say that I got the impression that the advocates of the different solutions, while propounding impeccable principles, were more concerned with their own electoral prospects than with the furtherance of racial harmony in British Guiana.

After taking into account all that has been said, I have tried to examine this problem with complete objectivity and with one aim only, namely to assess what electoral system would be most likely to give to your country peace and good government.

A powerful case was made for the retention of the system of "first past the post". It was pointed out that this is the standard practice in almost every country where the British Parliamentary system has been introduced; that it tends to produce clear Parliamentary majorities, thereby helping the winning party to provide effective government; and that it gives constituents direct contact with a member of Parliament who has a special responsibility for looking after their interests.

The main arguments advanced in favour of proportional representation are, first, that it is absolutely fair, in that the proportion of seats exactly reflects the proportion of votes cast for each party; and, secondly, that it would be likely to compel the formation of coalitions between parties and races which, in the circumstances of British Guiana, would be most desirable.

In addition, I considered a variety of electoral devices, specially designed to encourage cross-voting between races and parties. These included a proposal that votes cast by one race which were matched with votes by other races should be given increased value, thereby rewarding parties which secured a multi-racial following. Although this scheme was at first sight attractive, I felt obliged to reject it, since it involved registering voters on separate racial rolls, which might in practice have the effect of accentuating rather than diminishing racial consciousness.

I also examined a proposal that electors should be required to cast first and second preference votes, the latter counting a half or a quarter. The object was to encourage middle-of-the-road parties, acceptable to the two main races. However, I discarded this idea on the grounds that it might give a very unfair advantage to the opposition parties if they were to make an electoral pact, and that it could be frustrated by the formation of dummy parties.

I considered a number of other ingenious proposals, but in every case I found that the disadvantages outweighed the advantages. I was thus forced to the conclusion that the choice lay between the existing system of "first past the post" or some straightforward form of proportional representation. In deciding between these two alternatives, I felt it right not only to weigh the theoretical arguments for and against each system, but above all to take into account the actual conditions and practical problems in British Guiana.

The system of "first past the post" has undoubtedly fulfilled the principal claim of its supporters, in that it has in successive elections given to the winning party a substantial parliamentary majority. In 1953 the P.P.P., with 51 per cent. of the votes, obtained 75 per cent. of the seats. In 1957, with 47 per cent. of the votes, it secured 64 per cent. of the seats. In 1961 the P.P.P. polled 43 per cent. of the votes and obtained 57 per cent. of the seats, as compared with the P.N.C. party, which polled only 2 per cent. fewer votes but obtained only 31 per cent. of the seats.

The wide disparity between votes and seats which this system has consistently produced in British Guiana has not unnaturally engendered a sense of frustration and grievance among the opposition parties, which together polled a majority of the votes at the last two elections. On the other hand, it is argued that a certain measure of over-representation should be accepted as the price of strong government.

Unfortunately, in British Guiana this electoral system, while providing clear parliamentary majorities, has not provided strong government. The fact is that the administration of the country has been largely paralysed, the Government is insolvent, and law and order can be maintained only with the help of outside troops. Without attempting to apportion blame, the reason for this state of affairs is that the ruling party has alienated the confidence of the non-Indian communities, while they on their side have obstructed and resisted the Government at every turn.

Against this background, I have had to consider whether the situation would be improved by the introduction of proportional representation. The supporters of this system claim that, since no one race constitutes a majority of the electorate, all parties will have to appeal for support to all races. In practice I doubt whether either the Indian or the African party could, under its present leadership, hope to increase appreciably its following among the other racial groups. On the other hand, I am satisfied that there is validity in the argument that in present circumstances, where no party commands an overall majority of votes, proportional representation would be likely to result in the formation of a coalition government of parties supported by different races, and that this would go some way towards reducing the present tension.

But the creation of temporary alliances in Parliament between the representatives of rival groups, though a step in the right direction, is not enough. Normal conditions will not be restored until the present racial alignments are replaced by genuinely political alignments based upon a common belief in political and economic objectives.

So long as the whole political field is occupied by three parties, each identified with a different racial group, it is hard to see how non-racial politics can develop. It would seem, therefore, that the best hope of altering the present rigid pattern may well lie in the formation of new parties which are not handicapped by past animosities. It must, however, be recognised that, under a system based upon single-member constituencies, new parties would have little hope of winning any seats and would probably never be formed.

In the light of these various considerations, I concluded that it must be our deliberate aim to stimulate a radical change in the present pattern of racial alignments. It was therefore my duty to choose the electoral system which would be most likely to encourage inter-party coalitions and multi-racial groupings and which would make it easy for new parties to form. Having thus defined the objective, the answer was clear. British Guiana must change over to a system of proportional representation.

It remained for me to consider which form of proportional representation should be adopted. Of the various systems which have been advocated at this conference, I am satisfied that the simplest and fairest is that under which the whole country forms a single constituency and seats are allocated in proportion to the votes cast for each party. I am furthermore convinced that this is the system best suited to the present circumstances of British Guiana.

It remains to be decided whether, in order to obtain seats, a party should be required to poll a qualifying minimum percentage of the total national vote. During our discussions the figures of two, five and ten per cent. were mentioned. In normal circumstances, it would be desirable to discourage splinter parties. But, in view of the overriding importance of reshaping the political pattern, there would be no advantage at present in restricting the creation of new parties, which at first will inevitably be small.

However, once these new parties, some of which may still have racial connections, have been brought into being, it is to be hoped that some may amalgamate into larger multi-racial groupings and contest subsequent elections together. To encourage this process of fusion, it may well be desirable, after the first election, to introduce a minimum qualifying percentage. The level at which this should be fixed need not be determined now.

No case has been made to show that a lowering of the voting age would help to solve the problems which face British Guiana. I do not therefore propose to make any change.

In order to prevent personation and other forms of cheating, about which complaints have been made, there should be a fresh registration of electors, who should be issued with reliable identity cards. The work of registration, and the responsibility, for preparing and conducting the first elections under the new system should be entrusted to a special commissioner appointed by the British Government from outside British Guiana. Subsequent elections should be conducted by an independent commission to be set up under the constitution.

Another question I was asked to decide was whether there should be fresh elections before independence. If it were proposed to retain the existing electoral system, there would be no justification for holding further elections. However, since the system is to be changed, it is clearly right that fresh elections under the new system should be held before independence. Preparations for them should be put in hand as soon as practicable.

After the elections are over, the British Government will convene a conference to settle any remaining constitutional issues, and to fix a date for independence.

(iii) Extracts from the British Guiana (Constitution) Order in Council, 1961. (S.I. 921/1964.)

SCHEDULE 1
PART IV – THE LEGISLATURE
THE HOUSE OF ASSEMBLY

46 There shall be, for British Guiana, a House of Assembly.[86]

47(1) Subject to paragraph (2) of this article, the House of Assembly shall consist of fifty-three members.

(2) For the purpose of returning the said fifty-three members to the House of Assembly British Guiana shall form a single electoral area and the said members shall be elected in accordance with such system of proportional representation, and otherwise in such manner, as may be provided by regulations made by the Governor.[87]

(3) Any regulations made under this article may charge upon the revenues or public funds of British Guiana any expenditure incurred for the purposes of any such regulation and the Governor may, by warrant under his hand, authorise the withdrawal from the public funds of British Guiana of any sum of money certified by such warrant to be required for the purpose of meeting any expenditure so charged.

(4) If any person who is not a member of the House of Assembly is elected to be Speaker of the House he shall, by virtue of holding the office of Speaker, be a member of the House in addition to the fifty-three members aforesaid.

86 The powers of the Governor and the Imperial Government were unchanged by this Order.

87 Elections under the new system of P.R. were held in 1964. The People's Progressive Party with 45.8% of the votes won 24 seats; the People's National Congress with 40.5% of the votes won 22 seats; and the United Force with 12.4% of the votes won 7 seats. A coalition government was formed by the P.N.C. and the U.F.

(5) The powers of the Governor under this article shall be exercised by him in his discretion.

48(1) Subject to the provisions of paragraph (2) of this article a person shall be qualified to be registered as an elector for election to the House of Assembly if, and shall not be so qualified unless, on the qualifying date, he –

- (a) is a British subject of the age of twenty-one years or upwards;
- (b) is resident in British Guiana and either has been so resident for a period of two years immediately before the qualifying date or is domiciled in British Guiana.[88]

PART III
THE DEVELOPMENT OF RESPONSIBLE GOVERNMENT

A. Introduction

(i) The nature of responsible government: extract from the Report of the British Caribbean Standing Closer Association Committee, 1948-49. (Col. No. 255/1950.)

82 ... We next consider the nature of the Government – that is to say, the agency through which the powers of the State, formally and constitutionally concentrated in the Governor-General, are actually exercised. At this point we should like to emphasise the practical importance of the distinction between Government and Legislature. It is the duty of the Government to govern, and the actual responsibility for its specific executive actions cannot be shared with any other agency, e.g. the Legislature, except at the risk of confusion and delay and consequent prejudice to the public interest. The ultimate control of Government by the electorate is, according to British practice and experience, best preserved by the device of ensuring that the Legislature in effect chooses, and can change, by withholding support from, a preponderant element in the Executive itself. In Great Britain, the Executive is His Majesty's Government, consisting of the King's Ministers, who derive their executive authority from His Majesty as Head of the State and not from the Legislature. But the Legislature can and does exercise control over the policy of the Government by virtue of its power to pass or refuse to pass bills to carry out

88 Qualifications for a member of the House included that of literacy in English as well as the qualifications for a voter (Section 49 of this Order).

that policy, and particularly by its power to vote or withhold financial supplies. By the use of these powers, the Legislature can ensure that the policy and practice of the Government is under its own general control, without however itself assuming direct responsibility for more than the nature and composition of the Government. This does not mean that the Legislature may not question and discuss the detailed acts of Government. Such questionings constitute a large proportion of the work of the Parliament of Great Britain, and Governments in practice show themselves most sensitive to the views of the Legislature in such matters, in view of their dependence on the Legislature for their continued existence. In brief, the Legislature can throw out the Government, whereupon another emerges which can count upon the support of the Legislature or, if that proves impossible, fresh elections can be held at any time to obtain a clear expression of the views of the electorate on current major issues.

(ii) The demand for responsible government: extract from a speech by Mr (later Sir) Alexander Bustamante from the Report of the Conference on the Closer Association of the British West Indian Colonies, Montego Bay, Jamaica, 11th-19th September 1947. Part 11, Proceedings. (Col. No. 218/1948.)

. . . It makes me angry, and really angry, that after 200 years of British rule England still wants to have us here as subjects instead of giving us our freedom, instead of giving us self-government. Why does England want to keep us? Is it to keep us in the same filth, mud, squalor? No, we revolt against that condition. You have given us an improved constitution. You have handed us what you term an improved constitution on the one hand and then on the other hand you say to us: "You are not fit and proper persons to govern yourselves and so we shall have the English side with the majority of votes in the Executive Council and make it nil" – that is what the constitution means today. Even though I bear all the blame of His Excellency the Governor, even though I bear all the blame for a lot of people, I do not care about blame. This is one thing that has been done, you have given us this constitution – it is an advanced constitution – to prove to the world and to prove to us that we Jamaicans are fit and proper persons to govern ourselves, and in the same voice you say here: "I am putting the martingale on you – we will curb you – you will have no authority under that improved constitution".

What am I asking for the present? I have already said we as Jamaicans are adults, we are quite ready to throw our burden on our shoulders and face the danger of independence. What I want is this, for this country. The constitution which you have given us you say is a five-year trial, it is a poor five-year trial, we cannot prove our ability if His Excellency the Governor has all the power and is inclined to accept the recommendation of the Secretary of State for the Colonies as to what is to be done. What we want, therefore, is this – that the constitution be changed before any five years' time and that the elected side be given the majority on the Executive Council so that we will bear the blame, for we will have the responsibility.

The next thing we desire is this – to have the Legislative Council abolished. This is what the Imperial Government did, Sir – they created a Legislative Council nominated by His Excellency the Governor, and the Governor has nominated every man who does not sympathise with the smaller man. We are revolting against the fact that the English side of the Executive Council has the great majority of votes, and after that we want our freedom. I would rather go step by step. After that, steps should be taken to see that we have the majority of votes in the Executive Council, to which my friend here belongs and which will be a thing of the past soon, be abolished. The next thing we want is real self-government, where we shall elect our own Governor and not that the Imperial Government should elect someone from abroad with no knowledge of Jamaica or knowledge of conditions in the country or knowledge of the psychology of the people and their understanding. It is all good and well to sit at such a Conference as this and give a few jokes and utter a few words of diplomacy. That does not help. Perhaps I am not a diplomat. I am an outspoken Jamaican who has come from the gutter. I want to repeat that the thing we are asking for immediately, and I know almost the entire country will back me up with the exception of that little section called the "petty section", is the majority on Executive Council, and however much we work I say that I get the blame for His Excellency, and I am tired of bearing the blame of any man.

(iii) The rules which govern ministerial conduct: Despatch from the Secretary of State for the Colonies to the Governor of British Guiana, dated 2nd May 1953.

Sir,

The occasion of the institution of a new Executive Council under the Constitutional Instruments for British Guiana provides a suitable opportunity for me to address you on certain matters, a proper appreciation of which I regard as being of fundamental importance at this particular time to the people of the Colony.

2 In contrast to the present practice, the unofficial members of the new Executive Council will be directly responsible for the direction and control of a large proportion of Government business. The constitution provides, amongst other things, that unofficial members of the Executive Council,

while so charged with the administration of any Departments or subjects, will be styled "Ministers". In the course of their ministerial duties members will be called upon, both individually and collectively, to deal with and to take decisions upon a wide variety of subjects touching almost all aspects of the life of the community; and situations will no doubt arise from time to time where they may find that their public duties affect or even conflict with their personal and private interests. Situations of this nature could arise in a number of ways and I need mention here only the more obvious contributory factors such as the nature and extent of a member's private business activities, his financial interest in particular companies or schemes, or his activities and interests as an official of a trade union.

3 Under the new British Guiana Constitution, provision is made for the disqualification for elected membership of the House of Assembly (subject to stated exemptions) of a director or manager of a company which is a party to any subsisting contract with the Government for or on account of the Public Service. There is a similar provision in respect of membership of the State Council. These provisions do not apply to persons who are merely shareholders in any company. It is however to be expected that when a member of the House of Assembly or the State Council becomes a member of the Executive Council he should, on assumption of office, disclose to the Governor in confidence a full list of his holdings of stocks or shares in all companies whether they are or are not at the same time parties to Government contracts; and, in addition, that he should use the strictest discretion in deciding, in circumstances where his private interest and his public duty conflict, whether he can properly continue to hold such stocks or shares. The question also arises where, in the case of unofficial members of Executive Council, those members should at the time of their appointment or election to Executive Council, divest themselves for the period of their membership of that body of any other outside interests which might conflict with their public responsibilities. Since the unofficial members are to receive salaries from public funds in respect of their functions as Ministers, that can reasonably be expected of them. I believe that this matter is one which is best left to the sanction of public opinion and to the development of custom and usage under the Constitution. The subject is, nevertheless, one of cardinal importance in the development of a healthy system of government, and is therefore, to be borne carefully in mind by all those whose task it will be to work for development along these lines.

4 While there are certain practical difficulties in attempting to formulate a complete code of behaviour for persons who are appointed to important public offices and who are charged, in varying degrees, with the direction and conduct of the affairs of Government, some definite rules have been laid down in the United Kingdom which may be of assistance in the

working of the new Constitution in British Guiana. In the United Kingdom, certain easily identifiable forms of misconduct, e.g., disclosure of official secrets and corruption generally, are the subject of legislation (the Official Secrets Acts and the Prevention of Corruption Acts). In addition, there is a code of ethics prescribed by rules which have been laid down by successive Governments over a long period. These rules are based on custom and usage of the Constitution, and any serious infringement of them, even though not punishable by law, would incur the drastic penalty of dismissal from office. It may be appropriate, at this juncture in the Colony's progress towards self-government, for me to give the following summary of the rules which govern Ministerial conduct in the United Kingdom:-

(a) All directorships held by Ministers must be resigned except honorary directorships, directorships in connection with philanthropic undertakings and directorships in private companies which deal wholly or mainly with family affairs or interests and are not primarily engaged in trading. A similar rule applies in the case of Ministers who hold official positions in trade unions.

(b) Ministers ought not to enter into any transactions whereby their private pecuniary interest might, even conceivably, come into conflict with their public duty.

(c) No Minister is justified in any circumstances, in using official information that comes to him as a Minister, for his own private profit or for that of his friends.

(d) No Minister ought to put himself, or allow himself to be put, in a position to be tempted to use his official influence in support of any scheme or in furtherance of any contact in regard to which he has an undisclosed private interest.

(e) No Minister ought to accept any kind of favour from persons who are in negotiation with, or seeking to enter into contractual or proprietary or pecuniary relations with the Government.

(f) Ministers should scrupulously avoid speculative investments in securities as to which, from their position and their special means of early or confidential information they have, or may have, an advantage over other people in anticipating market changes.

(g) Ministers should not practice journalism while holding office. This prohibition does not, however, extend to writings of a literary, historical, scientific, philosophical or romantic character.

5 The above rules are by no means exhaustive, but they serve to illustrate the manner in which, in the United Kingdom, the holders of high public office in the service of the Crown are expected and required to conduct themselves; and they may be regarded as "rules of obligation". There are, in addition, certain "rules of prudence" which have never been formulated and

which it would be very difficult to formulate in precise or universal terms. One of these rules, however, is that Ministers should carefully avoid all transactions such as the acceptance of gifts of substantial value from members of the public which can give colour or countenance to the belief that they are doing anything which the "rules of obligation" forbid.

B. The nominated Executive Council with only a limited right to be consulted by the Governor.[89]

(i) Extracts from the Leeward Islands Letters Patent, dated 17th November 1936. (S.R. & O./1936.)

LETTERS PATENT passed under the Great Seal of the Realm constituting the Office of Governor and Commander-in-Chief of the Leeward Islands.[90]

Edward the Eighth, by the Grace of God of Great Britain, Ireland, and the British Dominions beyond the seas King, Defender of the Faith, Emperor of India;

To all to whom these Presents shall come, Greeting!

Whereas under and by virtue of "The Leeward Islands Act, 1871" as amended by certain Acts of the Governor and General Legislative Council of the Leeward Islands, Our Leeward Islands form one Colony consisting of five Presidencies, namely, Antigua, Saint Christopher and Nevis, Montserrat, and Dominica, with their respective Dependencies, and the Virgin Islands (hereinafter referred to as "the Presidencies") . . .

And whereas we are minded to make further provision for the Government of the Leeward Islands;

Now know ye that We do by these Our Letters Patent revoke and determine the said recited Letters Patent of the Ninth day of June, 1898, the Second day of October, 1902, and the First day of January, 1912, but without prejudice to anything lawfully done thereunder, and We do declare Our Will and pleasure as follows:-

89 Nominated Executive Councils, with nominations being at the discretion of the Governor, existed in Jamaica until 1944, in Trinidad until 1950, in the Windward Islands until 1951, in British Guiana until 1953, in British Honduras and the Leeward Islands until 1954 and in the Bahama Islands until 1963. In Barbados the Governor continued to nominate but after 1946 by convention he would nominate on the advice of the man best able to command a majority in the House of Assembly.

90 Similar Letters Patent were introduced for the Windward Islands in 1936.

1 There shall be a Governor and Commander-in-Chief in and over Our Colony of the Leeward Islands, and appointments to the said office shall be made by Commission under Our Sign Manual and Signet.

2 We do hereby empower and command the said Governor and Commander-in-Chief (hereinafter called the Governor) to do all things that belong to his said office in accordance with these Our Letters Patent, and such Commission as may be issued to him under Our Sign Manual and Signet, and such Instructions as may from time to time be addressed to him under Our Sign Manual and Signet or through one of Our Principal Secretaries of State, and in accordance with such Orders in Our Privy Council and other laws as may from time to time be in force within the Leeward Islands . . .

6 There shall be in each of the Presidencies of Antigua, Saint Christopher and Nevis and Dominica an Administrator and in each of the Presidencies of Montserrat and the Virgin Islands a Commissioner, appointed by Us under Our Sign Manual and Signet or, in default of such appointment, appointed by the Governor by an Instrument under the Public Seal of the Leeward Islands, who shall administer the Government of the Presidency in question except when the Governor shall be there present . . .

7 The said Administrators and Commissioners shall, in discharge of their respective offices, conform to and observe all such lawful instructions as the Governor shall address to them for their guidance; subject, nevertheless, to all such rules and regulations in that behalf as are contained in any Instructions under Our Sign Manual and Signet . . .

9 In accordance with The Leeward Islands Act, 1871, as amended, We do hereby delegate to the Governor, but subject always to the provisions of the said Act, and to any Instructions addressed to him under Our Sign Manual and Signet, or through one of Our Principal Secretaries of State, the power of appointing from time to time Members of the Executive Council of the Leeward Islands, and such officers of the General Government as he may think requisite for the conduct of the Government of the Leeward Islands.

Every Member of the said Executive Council so appointed shall hold his office during Our pleasure and, subject thereto, for such period and upon such conditions as may be provided in any such Instructions.

10 There shall be an Executive Council for each of the Presidencies, and the said Councils shall, respectively, consist of such persons as We shall direct by any Instructions under Our Sign Manual and Signet. All such persons shall hold their places in the said Councils during Our pleasure and, subject thereto, for such period and upon such conditions as may be specified in any such Instructions.

11 All public moneys raised, or which shall be raised, by authority of any law within any of the Presidencies, shall be issued by Warrant under the hand of the Governor, and be disposed of for the support of the Government

of such Presidency, or for such other purposes as shall be particularly appointed by such law and not otherwise.

12 The Governor, in Our name and on Our behalf, may make and execute, under the Public Seal of any of the Presidencies, grants and dispositions of any lands within such Presidency which may be lawfully granted or disposed of by Us: Provided that every such grant or disposition be made in conformity either with some law or regulation in force in the Presidency in which such land is situate, or with some Instructions addressed to the Governor under Our Sign Manual and Signet, or through one of Our Principal Secretaries of State.

13 The Governor may constitute and appoint all such Judges and other necessary Officers in any of the Presidencies as may be lawfully constituted or appointed by Us, all of whom, unless otherwise provided by law, shall hold their offices during Our pleasure.

14 The Governor may, subject to such instructions as may from time to time be given to him by Us through one of Our Principal Secretaries of State, upon sufficient cause to him appearing, dismiss or suspend from the exercise of his office any person holding any public office within any of the said Islands, or subject as aforesaid, may take such other disciplinary action as may seem to him desirable.

15 When any crime has been committed for which the offender may be tried within the Leeward Islands, the Governor may, as he shall see occasion, in Our name and on Our behalf, grant a pardon to any accomplice in such crime who shall give such information as shall lead to the conviction of the principal offender, or of any one of such offenders if more than one; and further may grant to any offender convicted in any Court within the Leeward Islands a pardon, either free or subject to lawful conditions, or any remission of the sentence passed on such offender, or any respite of the execution of sentence for such period as the Governor thinks fit; and may remit any fines, penalties, or forfeitures due or accrued to Us. Provided always, that the Governor shall in no case, except where the offence has been of a political nature unaccompanied by any other grave crime, make it a condition of any pardon or remission of sentence that the offender shall be banished from or shall absent himself or be removed from the Leeward Islands, or from any of the said Presidencies.

16 The Governor may exercise, within the Leeward Islands, all powers lawfully exercisable by Us in respect of the issue of marriage licences, the probate of wills or the custody and management of the persons or estates of idiots and lunatics.

17 And We do hereby require and command all officers, civil and military, and all others the inhabitants of the Leeward Islands to be obedient, aiding and assisting unto the Governor, and to the said several Administrators

and Commissioners, in execution of these Our Letters Patent, and of the powers and authorities herein contained . . .

19 And We do hereby reserve to Ourselves, Our heirs and successors, full power and authority from time to time to revoke, alter, or amend these Our Letters Patent as to Us or them shall seem fit . . .

(ii) Extracts from Royal Instructions to the Governor of the Leeward Islands, dated 17th November 1936.[91] *(S.R. & O./1936.)*

2 The Governor shall reside in the Presidency of Antigua or such other Presidency as may from time to time be appointed by one of Our Principal Secretaries of State, except when the interests of Our Service appear to him to require his presence in any other of the Presidencies.

3 Once at least in each year, at such time of the year as shall be found most convenient, the Governor shall visit in person each of the Presidencies, remaining there during such a period as he may consider necessary in the interests of Our service.

4 During the absence of the Governor from any of the Presidencies these Our Instructions shall be deemed to be addressed to and shall be observed by the Administrator or Commissioner of such Presidency, in so far as they relate to such powers and authorities of the Governor as are for the time being exerciseable by such Administrator or Commissioner.

5 The Administrators and Commissioners of the Presidencies shall correspond with the Governor on all subjects connected with their respective offices, and, unless they be directed by the Governor, in cases of urgency or for other reasons, to correspond on particular questions directly with the Secretary of State, shall transmit to the Governor all official reports and information touching the same, and shall apply to the Governor for all such instructions as they may require for their guidance, and shall conform to and obey all such lawful instructions as the Governor shall address to them respecting the discharge of their respective offices.

6 The Governor shall transmit to Us, through one of Our Principal Secretaries of State by the first convenient opportunity, copies of all important despatches, reports, and communications received by him from the Administrators or Commissioners of any of the Presidencies, and of all important instructions or communications addressed by him to any such Officers.

91 Similar Instructions were given to the Governor of the Windward Islands in 1936.

7 There shall be a Federal Secretary, an Attorney-General, and an Auditor for the General Government of the Leeward Islands. The office of Federal Secretary shall be held by the Administrator of Antigua and the functions of that office shall be performed by any acting Administrator of Antigua.

8 The Executive Council of the Leeward Islands shall consist of the persons for the time being lawfully discharging the functions of Administrator of Antigua, Administrator of Saint Christopher and Nevis, Administrator of Dominica, and Attorney General of the Leeward Islands, who shall be called *ex-officio* members, and such other persons as We may from time to time appoint by any Instructions or Warrants under Our Sign Manual and Signet or as the Governor may appoint by an Instrument under the Public Seal of the Leeward Islands, in pursuance of any instructions from Us through one of Our Principal Secretaries of State, or under the power delegated to him by Our said Letters Patent.

Every such Member not being an *ex-officio* member shall vacate his seat in the Council at the end of three years from the date of the Instrument by or in pursuance of which he is appointed, or at such earlier date as may be provided by that Instrument, but any such Member may be reappointed.

If any Member of the Council, other than an *ex-officio* member, holding office in the Public Service of the Leeward Islands or of any Presidency shall cease so to hold office his seat in the Council shall thereupon become vacant.

Whenever, upon any special occasion, the Governor desires to obtain the advice of any person within the Leeward Islands relating to affairs therein, he may, in such manner as he shall think fit, appoint such person as an Extraordinary Member of the Council for such special occasion . . .

10 The Executive Councils of the Presidencies shall consist of the persons for the time being lawfully discharging the functions of Administrator or Commissioner of the Presidency (when the Governor is present), and of Federal Secretary and of Attorney General of the Leeward Islands,[92] who shall be called *ex-officio* Members, and of such persons as We may from time to time appoint by any Instructions or Warrants under Our Sign Manual and Signet or as the Governor may appoint by an Instrument under the Public Seal of the Leeward Islands in pursuance of any instructions from Us through one of Our Principal Secretaries of State.

Every such Member of any of the said Councils not being an *ex-officio* Member shall vacate his seat in the Council at the end of three years from the date of the Instrument by or in pursuance of which he is appointed, or at such earlier date as may be provided by that Instrument, but any such Member may be reappointed.

92 This was changed by the Instructions of 30th December 1950 to the Crown Attorney and the Treasurer of the Presidency.

If any Member of the Council of any of the Presidencies, other than an *ex-officio* Member, holding office in the Public Service of the Leeward Islands or of any Presidency shall cease so to hold office, his seat in the Council shall thereupon become vacant.

Whenever, upon any special occasion, the Governor, Administrator or Commissioner desires to obtain the advice of any person within any of the Presidencies relating to affairs therein, he may summon for such special occasion any such person as an Extraordinary Member of the Executive Council of the Presidency. . .

16 The said Executive Councils shall not proceed to the despatch of business unless duly summoned by authority of the Governor or of the Administrator or Commissioner, nor unless two Members at the least (exclusive of the Governor, the Administrator or Commissioner or the Member presiding) be present and assisting throughout the whole of the meetings at which any such business shall be despatched . . .

23 In the execution of the powers and authorities granted to the Governor by Our said Letters Patent or otherwise, he shall in all cases not relating exclusively to any one Presidency consult with the Executive Council of the Leeward Islands and in all cases relating exclusively to any Presidency the Governor or Administrator or Commissioner shall consult with the Executive Council of the Presidency, excepting only in cases which may be of such a nature that, in his judgement, Our service would sustain material prejudice by consulting the said respective Councils thereupon, or when the matters to be decided shall be too unimportant to require their advice, or too urgent to admit of their advice being given by the time within which it may be necessary for him to act in respect of any such matters. In all such urgent cases the Governor or Administrator or Commissioner shall, at the earliest practicable period, communicate to the Executive Council of the Leeward Islands or of the Presidency as the case may be the measures which he may so have adopted, with the reasons thereof.

24 The Governor, or, in the case of the Executive Council of a Presidency, the Administrator, or Commissioner, shall alone be entitled to submit questions to the said Executive Councils for their advice or decision; but if the Governor, Administrator, or Commissioner, decline to submit any question to an Executive Council when requested in writing by any Member so to do, it shall be competent to such Member to require that there be recorded upon the Minutes his written application, together with the answer returned by the Governor, Administrator, or Commissioner, to the same.

25 The Governor, or Administrator, or Commissioner, may act in opposition to the advice given to him by the Members of any Executive Council, if

he shall in any case deem it right to do so, but in any such case the Governor shall fully report the matter to Us, and when an Administrator or Commissioner so acts, he shall fully report the matter to the Governor by the first convenient opportunity, with the grounds and reason of his action. In every such case it shall be competent to any Member of the Council to require that there be recorded at length on the Minutes the grounds of any advice or opinion he may give upon the question . . .

31 Twice in each year the Governor shall transmit to Us, through one of Our Principal Secretaries of State, fair copies of the Minutes of the proceedings of the General Legislative Council and of the Legislative Councils of Antigua, Saint Christopher and Nevis, Dominica and Montserrat.

32 Every appointment made by the Governor under the powers delegated to him in Our said Letters Patent shall be reported to Us through one of Our Principal Secretaries of State.

33 All commissions to be granted by the Governor to any person or persons for exercising any office or employment shall, unless otherwise provided by law, be granted during pleasure only.

34 Before disposing of any vacant or other lands to Us belonging in the Leeward Islands, the Governor shall cause the same to be publicly advertised, and to be surveyed, and such reservations to be made thereout as he may think necessary for roads or other public purposes. No Governor, Administrator, Commissioner, or any other Public Officer for the time being holding office in the Leeward Islands shall, directly or indirectly, purchase for himself any of such lands without Our special permission given to him in that behalf through one of Our Principal Secretaries of State.

C. The introduction of elected members to the Executive Council, but with no change in its powers or functions.

(i) Extracts from Royal Instructions to the Governor of the Windward Islands, dated 10th August 1951.[93]
(Instruments not statutory instruments, appendix to S.I./1951.)

9(1) The Executive Council,[94] of each of the Islands shall consist of the following:-

93 See next document for the Leeward Islands.
94 The actual powers and functions of the Executive Councils and the relationship between them and the Governor and the Administrators were not changed by these Instructions.

(i) Two, or, if the Governor is present in the Executive Council, three, *ex-officio* Members;

(ii) One Member, being a person holding a public office in the Island, appointed as provided in Clause 11 of these Instructions, who shall be styled the Official Member;

(iii) One Member, being a Nominated Member of the Legislative Council of the Island, appointed as provided in Clause 11 of these Instructions, who shall be styled the Nominated Member; and

(iv) Three Members, being Elected Members of the Legislative Council of the Island, elected as provided in Clause 12 of these Instructions, who shall be styled Elected Members.[95]

10 The *ex-officio* Members shall be:-

(i) the Administrator, if the Governor is present in the Executive Council; and

(ii) in the case of Grenada, the Attorney-General, and, in the case of Saint Vincent, Saint Lucia and Dominica, the Crown Attorney; and

(iii) in the case of Grenada, Saint Vincent and Saint Lucia, the Treasurer, and, in the case of Dominica, the Financial Secretary.

11(1) The Official Members and the Nominated Members shall be appointed by the Governor by Instrument under the Public Seal of the Island concerned.

(2) The Governor shall forthwith report to Us through a Secretary of State every appointment made under paragraph (1) of this Clause.

12(1) At the first meeting of the Legislative Council of an Island after the commencement of the Legislative Council Order in Council constituting that Council, and thereafter at the first meeting after every dissolution thereof or as soon as convenient after such meeting, the Legislative Council shall elect from among its Elected Members, three Members to serve as Elected Members of the Executive Council of that Island.

(2) Whenever the seat of an Elected Member of an Executive Council becomes vacant from any cause other than the dissolution of the Legislative Council of that Island, the Legislative Council shall, as soon as convenient, in like manner elect a Member to fill the vacancy . . .

17 Whenever upon any special occasion the Governor or an Administrator desires to obtain the advice of any person in an Island touching Our affairs therein he may, in writing, summon such person to the Executive Council of that Island for such special occasion . . .

95 The Elected Members could have their appointment revoked by a two-thirds majority in the Legislative Council.

19(1) The Executive Councils shall not be summoned except by the authority of the Governor or of the Administrator . . .

20(1) The Governor shall, so far as he considers it to be necessary for the exercise of his powers and the performance of his duties, attend the meetings of the Executive Council of the Island in which he is, from time to time, present; and, whenever he shall so attend, he shall preside.

(2) Every Administrator shall, so far as is practicable, attend at all meetings of the Executive Council of the Island of which he is Administrator; and, whenever he shall so attend in the absence of the Governor, he shall preside.

(3) In the absence of both the Governor and the Administrator, such Member as the Governor may appoint, or, in default of such appointment or in the absence of any Member so appointed, the senior Member of the Executive Council actually present shall preside.

(ii) Extracts from the Address by the Governor to the General Legislative Council of the Leeward Islands, 15th October 1951.
(Leeward Islands Gazette, Supplement to the Gazette of 18th October 1951.)

It is now ten months since I announced that the Secretary of State had agreed to the introduction of constitutional reform on the lines of the constitutional reform granted in the Windward Islands. The draft legislation and constitutional instruments to give effect to these changes were sent to London in January, and at that time I hoped that we could have the elections in August so that the new Councils would be able to consider the Estimates for 1952. Alas – all our hopes and plans have come to nothing owing to the delay in finalising the draft legislation. I would not attempt to excuse the delay; it should not have occurred; but in fairness to the legal experts who had to handle this work in London I should say that the Leeward Islands have one of the most complicated constitutions in the world. It has been necessary to prepare not only three Constitution and Elections Ordinances for the three Presidencies concerned, but also a new Leeward Islands Act, and new Letters Patent and Royal Instructions. One verbal change in one of these drafts may affect all the others, and I know that the draftsmen have been faced with a task of extreme complexity . . .

This is not the place to refer to opposition in some places to certain aspects of the constitutional proposals; the proposals must first be considered by the Legislatures concerned. But this is the place to make my own position clear, and also the position of the Government Service as a whole.

As I said in my address last year, no administration, however benevolent and efficient, can make lasting progress unless it has the force of public opinion behind it. In this Colony perhaps more than in most, there is a desperate need to associate the public with the Government. Constitutional reform is vital to the further development of this Colony, whatever anyone may say to the contrary. But there is a danger – one very obvious danger – which we must face. A constitution which merely gives power to the elected members without at the same time giving them some responsibility for their actions can lead to disaster. It has been said – by myself among others – that the constitutional proposals for the Leeward Islands grant power to the Legislature without giving it responsibility as well; the Legislature can oppose and block any financial provision or any legislation, but its representatives in the Executive Council, being in the minority, can plead an alibi and say that they have no responsibility for the actions of the Government. That is perfectly true; but I believe that we can make these new constitutions work provided that we all sincerely try to do so. For my part I intend to see that as much responsibility as possible is placed upon the elected members within the framework which may be approved by His Majesty's Government; and I pledge myself and the Government Service to do all in our power to see that the new constitutions are operated in this way. I know that there are Jeremiahs who say that the economy of the Colony will be ruined or that the efficiency of the Civil Service will be undermined. I refuse to believe that the people of the Leeward Islands are any less sensible than those in other parts of the world who are already enjoying greater power and responsibility in managing their own affairs. But let there be no misunderstanding on this score. The Government Service and I can – as the saying goes – "fall over backwards" in trying to make the new constitutions work; but our somersaults will be of no avail unless we can enter this adventure with the co-operation of the elected members.

D. The committee-system experiment.[96]

(i) Extracts from the Address by the Governor to the General Legislative Council, 6th January 1953. (Leeward Islands Gazette, 22nd January 1953.)

The past year . . . has seen the introduction of new constitutions in Antigua, in St. Kitts-Nevis and Anguilla, in Montserrat, and in the Federal Government. Even more important, it has seen the introduction of means whereby the elected members in all the four Presidencies can exercise a far greater influence on Government policies and can keep a far closer watch on the execution of

96 See the Report of the West India Royal Commission, Chapter XXII, paragraphs 4-6.

those policies; it has seen the first step taken towards the introduction of a full ministerial system of government . . .

I have mentioned the constitutional changes first because I believe that these changes have contributed more than anything else to such progress as has been made during the past year. The impact made by the elected members as Chairman of Committees[97] in Antigua, Montserrat and the Virgin Islands has been considerable. And I have no doubt that the "Members" in St. Kitts will produce the same result when they have had as much time in office as those in the other three Presidencies. Although many of us complain that the pace is still too slow, and that many problems still remain unsolved, there can be no doubt that the ideas and driving force provided by the elected members has encouraged the initiation of new projects, and has given a faster tempo to every form of development.

(ii) Announcement made by the Acting Administrator of Grenada as President of the Legislative Council, 20th December 1954. (Grenada Legislative Council Minutes, 1954, pp. 19-21.)

There is yet another announcement of great importance that I have to make today. It concerns one of the items on the Order Paper – the Committee System. On the threshold of West Indian Federation which we hope will materialise within our lifetime, and with the possibility of Constitutional Advance as a result of the potential of Federation within this region, it is proposed that, in Grenada, an opportunity should be furnished to members of the Legislative Council to have more than a mere nodding acquaintance with the machinery and operation of Government correspondence and business, and a greater working knowledge than they now have through their contact with the Administrative machine in Finance Committee and in Executive Council. No provision exists in the Constitution for a Committee System, but it was suggested and recommended by the Royal Commission who came to these parts in 1938-39 that some such system might, with profit, be introduced in these Islands.

97 Together with the formal changes embodied in Instructions, informal changes were initiated in the Windward Islands and Leeward Islands whereby committees of the Legislative Councils were established to consider subject areas of government policy. These committees were neither legislative nor executive in function, but were deliberative. The idea, as with the rather different committees established in Ceylon under the Donoughmore Constitution, was to introduce colonial politicians under a non-responsible constitution, to the business of government. (See the following document.)

I cannot speak with absolute certainty, but I have some recollection that it was the idea of the Royal Commission that people other than members of the Executive and Legislative Councils who had expert and technical knowledge in particular fields might be asked to serve on these Committees together with members of the Legislature.

In the Leeward Islands and in St. Vincent, over the last two to four years, a similar system to that which it is now proposed to introduce here, has been operating. In the Leeward Islands it has advanced to the point where the Chairmen of these Committees have been provided with desks in the central Secretariat so that they could be on the spot to see the normal day to day operation of Government correspondence and business.

In St. Vincent that step has only recently been taken. They have been operating their Committees for the past two years. I had the honour of introducing the system in St. Vincent.

Before going into any details of the system, I might say that it has at least, this benefit: because of the greater acquaintanceship of members of the Legislature with Government correspondence and Government business through this system, St. Vincent who formerly took as much as three weeks in 1951 to get through their Finance Committee Budget Sessions, were able recently to get through their Budget Sessions of Finance Committee in 1½ days. That can be attributed, I think to the system, and it has been stated with certainty by the Administrator of St. Vincent that the Committee System has been mainly responsible for the expeditious handling of such matters.

So far as the bones of this Committee System are concerned, the Unofficial Members of the Legislative Council will be divided into three Committees. The Committees will be as follows:

1 Trade and Production Committee . . .

2 Communications and Works Committee . . .

3 Education and Social Services . . .

Each Committee will be briefed with the responsibility for discussing the subjects which come within its purview. These Committees will be purely advisory to the Administration, Finance Committee and Executive Council.

Each Committee will comprise four members, one of whom will be a Nominated Member. Because the total membership of the Unofficial of this Council is 11, it will have to be arranged for one Member of the Legislative Council to sit on two Committees.

At a later stage in this meeting, Honourable Members will be invited to go into the question of the allocation of the membership of this Council among these proposed Committees. At their inaugural meetings, each Committee will elect its own Chairman.

In so far as the operation of the Committee System vis-a-vis the Secretariat is concerned, routine subjects which come to the Administrator and

Government Office for attention will be dealt with as at present. For instance, suppose there is a question of expenditure by some Department on some specific service for which provision already exists in the Estimates, and the Head of the Department is probably merely seeking the Administrator's advice or authority as to how the money relating to some small item should be spent, that would hardly be a matter for top-level discussions by a Committee. Purely routine matters, therefore, will continue to be dealt with as at present even though some of them might be matters coming within the scope of a Committee's business . . .

There are one or two points that I would like to make about the operation of the Committee System for the information of Honourable Members, pending my circulation of an explanatory memorandum to them on the subject. Each Committee will have its own Secretary who will have to be a responsible officer because he will have to prepare memoranda for circulation to Members of the Committee and will have to be its Executive Officer. Therefore a reasonably senior, responsible and qualified Civil Servant will have to be made the Secretary of each Committee.

The subjects which would be put to the various Committees by the Administrator would be subjects which would normally have to be dealt with finally by the Executive Council or Finance Committee. If a Committee needed information from some outside source, the secretary to the Committee has forwarded its recommendations to the Administrator, the Secretariat will take up the subject from that point: the Administration may either make a decision on the basis of the Committee's recommendation, or it may be sent on for further advice from either Executive Council or Finance Committee. If some financial matter is involved the Administrator will send it to Finance Committee, but if it is a question of policy he will send it to Executive Council.

If a Committee feels that it needs more information on a subject, or that it would like to quiz the Head of Department concerned, the Head of the Department would be invited to attend a meeting of the Committee to furnish his views and the answers to such reasonable and pertinent questions as the Committee may ask. Either the Secretary or the Chairman of a Committee will forward the Committee's recommendations to the Administrator.

All advice and recommendations from the Committee or Chairman will be recorded in writing and signed by the Chairman or by the Secretaries on behalf of the Committees. The Secretaries will furnish the Chairman with all available information within their knowledge of the subjects coming within the sphere of the Committee's business. I may point out that the Chairman and Members of a Committee are not entitled to issue orders to Government Officers. But they are entitled to make suggestions regarding the Government Departments coming within their sphere of influence, provided that those suggestions are made in writing and addressed to the Administrator and not to the Head of the Department concerned.

The Chairmen of Committees may invite Heads of Departments to attend meetings. They can ask Heads of Departments to discuss matters with them at a meeting of the Committee or outside of the Committee. They can ask Heads of Departments to accompany them when visiting institutions and so on. In the event of a difference of opinion between the Head of a Department and the Chairman of a Committee the matter will be decided by the Administrator.

It will be possible for Finance Committee and Executive Council to have the benefit of the prior knowledge of members of the Committee of a particular subject, and discussions in Executive Council and Finance Committee could thereby be facilitated. Apart from the Officials who will be present there will be four Unofficial Members who had already discussed and become acquainted with the subject in the Committee concerned.

The recommendations made by a Committee will require ratification either by Executive Council who is the policy-making body or by Legislative Council who makes laws and votes funds. It must be remembered that the Committee System to be introduced in Grenada is not a Ministerial System because the Committees are purely advisory and executive authority still remains in the hands of the Administrator with the advice of Executive Council.

By the introduction of these Committees, however, it is hoped that the Administrator will obtain from Unofficial Members more practical assistance.

Provision will be made for a desk and an office for each Chairman of a Committee in the premises of Government Office so that the Chairman will be in close touch with his Secretary and with the files of Government Office which will have to be referred to from time to time. Arrangements are also being made for a larger office attached to the Chairman's Office which will accommodate the Secretary of the Committee and another clerk attached to that particular Committee. The larger office will also be utilised for Committee meetings. The Committees will decide whether they will have regular meetings or *ad hoc* meetings as and when there is a sufficiency of subjects for discussion. The Chairman will be the person who will indicate to the Secretary whenever he desires to hold a meeting of the Committee. Accommodation arrangements are now in progress and it is hoped that the Committee System will be brought into operation as early as practicable in the coming year.

I have attempted to give you a rough outline of this Committee System which it is proposed to introduce. I have not the slightest doubt that this will represent a considerable advance, of benefit not only to all members of the Legislative Council who, as I have stated before, will thereby get an opportunity of learning more of what goes on in so far as the Administrative machine is concerned. On the other hand, the Administration will benefit from the advice of the Committees who will go into the subjects with which they deal in greater detail than it has been possible for members of the Legislature to do in the past.

It is hoped that there will be less friction between the Administration and the Legislative Council which, at times in the past has assumed the role of a kind of opposition party – Government officials and the Administration being regarded as the Government – . . .

E. The development of the Executive Council as the chief instrument of policy, and the quasi-ministerial system

(i) Extracts from the Report of the Select Committee of the Legislative Council appointed to draft a political constitution for Jamaica, 1939. (Jamaica Legislative Council Minutes, 1939. Appendix XXXII.)

18 There shall be an Executive Committee to consist of ten members with the Governor as Chairman with a casting vote only. Five of these members to be selected by the House of Assembly, three to be officials and two non-officials who must be members of the Legislative Council and appointed by the Governor. Six members to form a quorum.

19 Whenever any member of the Executive Committee shall become incapable of exercising his functions as such member or is temporarily absent from Jamaica, the House of Assembly or the Legislative Council shall respectively by resolution select some other member of the House or Council to be provisionally a member of the Executive Committee in place of the member who is so incapable or is temporarily absent from Jamaica. Every person so provisionally selected shall be to all intents and purposes a member of the Executive Committee until the member whose place he has been selected to fill is capable of exercising the functions of a member of the Executive Committee or shall have returned to Jamaica.

20 The duties of the Executive Committee are as follows:-

The members of the Executive Committee who are in the House of Assembly and in the Legislative Council shall be the official organ of inter-communication between the Governor and such House and Council respectively, and for the authoritative disclosure of the policy of the Government on all questions political, financial and administrative. The Executive Committee shall also assist the Governor in preparing the Estimates, in levying and disbursing public moneys, and in the general administration and affairs of this

Island, and when required by a Minute under the hand of the Governor, shall give their opinion in writing on all matters submitted to them, and shall also when required in writing, advise on, prepare and perfect all Estimates, ways and means, papers, messages, answers, bills and other proceedings which the Governor deems advisable to be submitted or communicated to either branch of the Legislature, or to any person, etc.

(ii) Extracts from the Proposals for a New Constitution, published 1944. (Kingston, 1944.)

12 This Memorandum[98] represents the conclusions reached after the most careful deliberations. While the conclusions are not intended to be submitted to His Majesty's Government in England as a final statement of what will be acceptable to the people but rather as proposals for discussion, none the less the proposals themselves indicate that four matters are regarded as of overriding importance.

13 The four matters are:-

(a) That the veto power ought not to be in the hands of the Governor at all, or if in his hands ought to be limited and controlled both by explicit provisions in the Constitution and by provision for an appeal to His Majesty in Council.

(b) That any and every power of certification is obnoxious and contrary to the principles of Representative as well as Responsible Government.

(c) That a progressively increasing responsibility for the conduct of executive affairs ought to be provided for so that a measure of Responsible Government should be provided from the moment the new Constitution comes into force, and the Constitution itself should envisage and provide for the progressive devolution of executive authority and control from the Civil Service to the constitutional and democratic elements of the Government of the Colony.

(d) That consistent with the above the Civil Service ought to be reconstituted with reference to the creation in Jamaica of machinery for its provision and governance subject to safeguarding rights of appeal to the Secretary of State for the Colonies as hereafter set out . . .

15 Treating these proposals then as the basic document, the following modifications and additions are proposed:-

98 The Memorandum was signed by the fourteen Members of the Legislative Council, three representatives of the People's National Party, and three representatives of the Federation of Citizens' Associations.

(a) That the form, powers and duties of the Executive Committee be re-defined so as to provide:-

(i) That the Executive Committee shall consist in the first instance of 10 Members of whom 7 to be elected by the House of Assembly from among its Members and 3 to be officials nominated by the Governor.

(ii) That the Executive Committee shall be the principal instrument of policy and shall have power to initiate all Laws – financial and otherwise.

(iii) That the Executive Committee shall have the duty of preparing the Annual Budget and all supplementary budgetary provisions.

(iv) That upon the complete development of the ministerial system proposed in paragraph (b) hereunder the Executive Committee shall become a Council of Ministers and shall have plenary powers in local affairs as the Executive centre of the Constitution of the Colony.

(b) (i) That a system be instituted whereby members of the House of Assembly be appointed as Ministers in charge of Departments of Administration such system to commence on a limited basis and to provide for progressive expansion.

(ii) Such Ministers [sic] shall be Members of the Executive Committee.

(iii) The particular method of initiating and the details concerning the gradual and progressive establishment of such a system are reserved for discussion and elaboration if the general principle is found acceptable.

(c) That the local Civil Service be appointed and controlled by a local Civil Service Commission constituted by Law for that purpose until such time as a West Indian Civil Service may be established and that pending the creation of such West Indian Service there be a right of appeal to the Secretary of State for the Colonies in all serious matters concerning discipline and punishment, pension rights and the like.

This proposal regards a West Indian Federation as a logical West Indian development and envisages the creation of a West Indian Civil Service as being closely involved in that development.

(iii) Extracts from the Despatch from the Secretary of State for the Colonies to the Governor of Jamaica, dated 5th January 1942 (Reproduced in the Proceedings of the Jamaica Legislative Council of 10th February 1942.)

(c) PRIVY COUNCIL

The proposals which were made in my despatch of the 7th March, 1941, contemplated no change in the constitution of the Privy Council. I am, however, prepared to consider reconstitution of Privy Council so as to admit a certain number of elected members and steps in this direction have already been made. But I shall be obliged if you will explain to the Legislative Council that it is an essential feature of the constitutions of non-self-governing Colonies that the Executive Council (in Jamaica, the Privy Council) is purely advisory to the Governor; that matters which come before the Governor in Council are not settled by vote, and that the Governor is not bound to accept the Council's advice. In the case of Jamaica the necessary provision is contained in Clauses IX to XI of the Royal Instructions, and I should not feel able at this stage to advise His Majesty to vary the terms of those Instructions. I am accordingly unable to accept the proposals of the elected members or of the People's National Party in the matter of the constitution and powers of the Privy Council.

(iv) Extracts from the Despatch from the Secretary of State for the Colonies to the Governor of Jamaica, dated 10th February 1943. (Cmnd. 6427/1943.)[99]

4 I now turn to the proposals contained in the memorandum regarding the establishment of an Executive Committee. These are (a) that the Executive Committee should consist of ten members, of whom seven should be elected by the House of Assembly from amongst its members and three should be officials nominated by the Governor; (b) the Executive Committee should be the principal instrument of policy and should have power to initiate all laws, financial and otherwise; (c) it should have the duty of preparing the Budget and all supplementary budgetary provisions. I accept the proposals at (b) and (c) above. The Executive Committee would therefore absorb all the present functions (except matters of Royal Prerogative) of the Privy Council which would disappear from the constitution. All financial measures, whether by bill or otherwise, and all other bills, would need the approval of the majority of

99 Oliver Stanley had replaced Lord Moyne at the Colonial Office in the period between the sending of the despatch quoted in the last section and this despatch.

the Executive Committee before being susceptible of proposal and discussion in either the House of Assembly or the Legislative Council. I regret, however, that I am unable to agree with (a), and I am sure that on mature reflection the signatories of the memorandum will not wish to press for so radical and immediate a change. The introduction of universal suffrage and the very considerable advance towards Responsible Government now proposed are bound to place new and increased stresses on the machinery of Government at the very time when the Island is facing a critical period in its history and will have to meet post-war problems of the utmost complexity. For these reasons I consider that the proposals contained in the Majority Report of the Select Committee should stand, viz. that the Executive Committee should consist of five elected members, three officials and two unofficials nominated by the Governor. These unofficials should be Members of Legislative Council. The Governor would be Chairman of this Committee and would have a casting, but not an original vote. I further consider that a period of five years, i.e., a full electoral period – should elapse in order to test the working of the new system. At the end of five years, the Constitution would be reviewed in the light of its working and the justification for further advance.

5 The signatories of the memorandum have suggested that the Executive Committee should develop into a Council of Ministers and recommend that a system be instituted wherein members of the House of Assembly should be appointed as Ministers in charge of the departments of administration (such system to begin on a limited basis and to provide for progressive expansion) that such Ministers should be members of the Executive Committee and that the particular method of establishing such a system should be reserved for further discussion. The House of Assembly will be entitled to select five members of the Executive Committee and a simple method of doing so would be to form five small committees of the Assembly to concentrate respectively on (a) general purposes; (b) agriculture and lands; (c) education; (d) social welfare and (e) communications. The five chairmen of these committees might be appointed to the Executive Committee and that system, if successful, would in fact provide an embryo ministerial system whose limited application would await the next stage when the first review would take place. I commend this suggestion for consideration. I would add that no provision in the constitution is needed to prescribe this procedure nor indeed would it be desirable to introduce such rigidity into the arrangement.

7 The signatories of the memorandum have asked that the local Civil Service should be appointed and controlled by a local Civil Service Commission until such time as a West Indian Civil Service may be established. I regret that I am unable to accept this suggestion, as I am not satisfied that it would be possible by this means to secure proper independent service.

(v) Extract from a Message to the Legislative Council from the Governor of Jamaica, 20th September 1944.
(Jamaica Legislative Council Minutes, 20th September 1944, p. 253.)

HONOURABLE GENTLEMEN,

At the conferences which I held with you on the 28th of July and the 3rd of August, 1944, when the proposals for the new Constitution of Jamaica, published under date of the 20th of July, 1944, were reviewed, it was agreed that certain representations for the further amendment of those proposals should be made to the Secretary of State for the Colonies. I now have the honour to lay before you the comments of the Secretary of State concerning those representations.

1 I am prepared to agree to reference being made to the Executive Council as an Instrument of Policy . . . I suggest that the first line of that Clause should read "The Executive Council shall be the principal instrument of policy and shall perform such functions, etc." . . .

4 There shall be a Captain-General and Governor-in-Chief in and over Jamaica, and appointments to the said Office shall be made by Commission under Our Sign Manual and Signet.

5 We do hereby authorize, empower and command the Governor to do all things belonging to his Office in accordance with these Letters Patent, and such Commission as aforesaid, and such Instructions as may from time to time be given to him by Us under Our Sign Manual and Signet or through a Secretary of State, and in accordance with such Orders in Our Privy Council and other laws as may from time to time be in force in Jamaica . . .

9 The Governor may, in Our name and on Our behalf, make and execute, under the Broad Seal, grants and dispositions of any lands or other immovable property within Jamaica which may be lawfully granted or disposed of by Us.

10 The Governor may constitute and appoint in Our name and on Our behalf all such Judges and other Officers as may lawfully be constituted or appointed by Us, all of whom, unless otherwise provided by law, shall hold their offices during Our pleasure.

11 The Governor may, subject to the provisions of any law for the time being in force in Jamaica and to such instructions as may from time to time be given to him by Us through a Secretary of State, upon sufficient cause to him appearing, dismiss or suspend from the exercise of his office any person holding any public office in Jamaica, or, subject as aforesaid, may take such other disciplinary action as may seem to him desirable.

12 When any offence has been committed for which the offender may be

tried in Jamaica, the Governor may, as he shall see occasion, in Our name and on Our behalf, grant a pardon to any accomplice in such offence who shall give such information as shall lead to the conviction of the principal offender, or of any one of such offenders if more than one; and further may grant to any offender convicted of any such offence in any Court within Jamaica, a pardon, either free or subject to lawful conditions, or any respite, either indefinite or for such period as the Governor may think fit, of the execution of any sentence passed on such offender, and may remit the whole or any part of any such sentence or of any penalties or forfeitures otherwise due to Us.

13 The Governor shall keep and use the Broad Seal for sealing all things whatsoever that shall pass the said Seal.

14 We do hereby require and command all Our Officers, Civil and Military, and all other the inhabitants of Jamaica to be obedient, aiding and assisting unto the Governor.

15 We do hereby reserve to Ourselves, Our Heirs and Successors full power and authority to revoke, add to, or amend these Letters Patent as to Us or Them shall seem fit.

(vi) Extracts from the Jamaica (Constitution) Order in Council, 1944. (S.R. & O. 1215/1944.)

PART II

PRIVY COUNCIL

6(1) There shall be a Privy Council in and for Jamaica, and the said Council shall consist of such persons, appointed in such manner, as His Majesty may direct by Instructions under His Sign Manual and Signet.

(2) The Members of the Privy Council shall hold their places in the Council during His Majesty's pleasure and, subject thereto, for such period and upon such conditions as may be specified in any Instructions as aforesaid.

7(1) It shall be the duty of the Privy Council to advise the Governor in relation to the exercise of any powers, and the performance of any duties, conferred or imposed upon him by any Letters Patent passed under the Great Seal, in accordance with, and subject to, the provisions of any such Letters Patent or any Instructions given to the Governor by His Majesty under the Royal Sign Manual and Signet or through a Secretary of State.

(2) The Privy Council shall also perform such other functions as may be prescribed by any other enactment or instrument having the force of law in Jamaica.

PART III

EXECUTIVE COUNCIL

8 There shall be an Executive Council in and for Jamaica, constituted in accordance with the provisions of this Order.

9(1) The Executive Council shall be the principal instrument of policy and shall perform such functions and exercise such powers and duties as may from time to time be prescribed by or under this Order, any other Orders of His Majesty in Council, any Instructions under His Majesty's Sign Manual and Signet or any Law or other instrument having the force of law in Jamaica.[100]

100 Handbook of Jamaica, 1946. Government Printing Office, Kingston, 1946 (not an official publication) p. 29: "In the formulation of policy and in the execution of all other authorities and powers conferred upon him, except those conferred by Articles 10, 11 and 12 of the Letters Patent, the Governor shall consult with the Executive Council, (save in certain circumstances specified in Clause 13 of the Instructions) and shall act in accordance with the Council's advice. He may, however, act against the advice of the Council with the prior approval of the Secretary of State, or, if in his judgement urgent necessity so requires, without such prior approval. (Clause 13 of the Instructions.)

"(The exceptions to the Governor's prior consultation laid down by Articles 10, 11 and 12 of the Letters Patent are where His Majesty's service would sustain material injury by consultation, where the matters are trivial, and where the matters are too urgent for prior consultation. The exceptional cases when the Governor can reject the advice of the Executive Council, defined by Article 12 of the Letters Patent and Clause 13 of the Instructions, are the same as those excusing the Governor from prior consultation, except that the Governor can reject advice: "if in any case it shall in his judgement be right so to do . . ." The Governor, however, must report to the Council with his reasons when he fails to consult, and he must report to the Secretary of State if he rejects advice. Such a report could always include other advice and opinions expressed by any Member of the Council.)

"Although not provided for in the Constitution, it has been arranged, with the approval of the House or Representatives, that the various subjects which form the work of several Government Departments, shall be divided into 5 main groups as indicated below and that each of the five Elected Members of the Executive Council, who are now designated Ministers, shall be assigned one of these groups and that he shall be responsible in the House for matters affecting the Government Departments which deal with the subjects assigned to him:-

1 Finance and General Purposes
2 Communications
3 Agriculture, Lands and Commerce
4 Education
5 Social Welfare".

(2) It shall be the duty of the Executive Council to prepare the Annual Estimates of Revenue and Expenditure and all Supplementary Estimates of Expenditure.

10 The Executive Council shall consist of the Governor as Chairman, three Official Members, two persons not holding office of emolument under the Crown in Jamaica who (save as otherwise expressly provided in this Order) are Members of the Legislative Council, who shall be styled Nominated Members, and five persons who (save as aforesaid) are Members of the House of Representatives, who shall be styled Elected Members.

11 The Official Members shall be the Colonial Secretary, the Attorney-General, and the Financial Secretary and Treasurer.

12 The Nominated Members shall be appointed by Instructions or Warrant under His Majesty's Sign Manual and Signet, or by the Governor by Instrument under the Broad Seal in pursuance of His Majesty's instructions through a Secretary of State.

13(1) At the first meeting of the House of Representatives and thereafter at the first meeting after every general election, or as soon as convenient after such meeting, the House shall elect from among its Members five Members to serve as Elected Members of the Executive Council.[101]

(2) Whenever the seat of an Elected Member becomes vacant from any cause other than the dissolution of the House of Representatives, the House shall, as soon as convenient, in like manner elect a Member to fill the vacancy.

14(1) Subject to the provisions of this Order, every Nominated Member of the Executive Council shall hold his seat in the Council during His Majesty's pleasure.

(2) The House of Representatives may, by resolution, in favour of which there are cast the votes of not less than two-thirds of all the Members of the House, revoke the election to the Executive Council of any Elected Member thereof, and, upon the passing of such resolution, the seat of the Member in the Executive Council shall become vacant.

(3) The seat of a Member of the Executive Council (other than an Official Member) shall become vacant –

(a) if he shall cease to be a Member of the House or the Legislative Council, as the case may be, from any cause other than the dissolution thereof; or

101 Note the election of Members of the Executive Council – this Order in Council did not introduce the British convention of the Head of State calling on the man best able to command a majority in the legislature and asking him to choose his colleagues.

(b) if he shall by writing under his hand addressed to the Governor, resign his seat in the Executive Council; or

(c) if he shall be absent from Jamaica without written permission from the Governor.

(4) A Nominated or Elected Member shall not vacate his seat in the Executive Council on the dissolution of the Chamber of which he is a Member, but shall vacate such seat at the first meeting of that Chamber held thereafter.

(5) Any person vacating a seat as a Nominated or Elected Member may, if qualified, be again appointed or elected from time to time.

(6) If a Nominated Member shall be appointed temporarily to any office of emolument under the Crown in Jamaica or to act in any such office, he shall not sit as a Nominated Member of the Executive Council so long as he continues to hold or act in that office . . .

18(1) The Executive Council shall not be summoned except by the authority of the Governor, but shall be so summoned on the written request of at least five Members of the Executive Council.

(2) The Executive Council shall not be disqualified for the transaction of business by reason of any vacancy among the Members; but no business except that of adjournment shall be transacted if objection is taken by any Member present that there are less than four Members present besides the Governor or other Member presiding.

19 The Governor shall, so far as is practicable, attend and preside at all meetings of the Executive Council, and in his absence such Member as the Governor may appoint or, in the absence of such Member or if no Member be so appointed, the senior Member of the Council actually present shall preside.

20 Where any matter is dependent upon the decision of the Executive Council, any decision shall be regarded as the decision of the Executive Council if a majority of the votes cast are in favour thereof. The Governor shall not have an original vote, but, if upon any question the votes shall be equally divided, he shall have a casting vote. In the absence of the Governor, the Member presiding shall have an original vote and also, if upon any question the votes shall be equally divided, a casting vote . . .

(vii) Extracts from the Despatch of the Secretary of State for the Colonies to the Governor of Trinidad and Tobago, dated 7th January 1949. (Published in Trinidad in The New Constitution, *Government Printing Office, Port of Spain, 1949.)*

5 In the majority report it was recommended that the Executive Council should be "the chief instrument of policy" and responsible to the Legislative Council, and that it should be composed of three *ex officio* members (Colonial

Secretary, Attorney General, and Financial Secretary), and three nominated and six elected members from the Legislative Council. The Governor would preside and have a casting vote. It was also proposed that the unofficial members of the Executive Council should be actively associated in the work of administration of Government Departments . . .

8 The publication of the Reports and the subsequent discussion in the Legislative Council have further stimulated public interest in the question of constitutional progress. I have received many resolutions and petitions from representative bodies in the Colony. I have also had the opportunity of personal discussion with representatives of a number of important sections of opinion, and also with yourself. It is clear from the various representations which have been made to me that there is unanimity in the view that the present constitution, which gives representation without executive responsibility, is unsatisfactory, and that the time has come to take a definite step forward.

9 I agree that the stage has been reached when the people of Trinidad and Tobago must be enabled to assume greater responsibility for the control of their own affairs. As I stated in my opening speech at the Conference on Closer Association held at Montego Bay in 1947, it is one of the tasks of His Majesty's Government to see that such responsibility is passed increasingly from London to the peoples of the territories themselves, and I am anxious, whenever possible, to increase the measure of responsibility for government borne by Colonial Legislatures. The question which is now clearly posed by the reports of the Constitution Committee is whether responsible government should be reached in Trinidad and Tobago at one step, or through a further transitional stage.

10 The proposals in the majority report are based on a feeling that such a transitional stage is desirable.[102] The supporters of these proposals hold the view that a nominated element should be retained for the present in both the Executive and Legislative Councils. In their opinion the experience and knowledge of nominated members are vitally necessary to the welfare of the Colony during its present stage of development; and the presence of persons with such experience and knowledge gives strength to both Councils in their deliberations on problems concerning the well being and development of the Colony. Further, they consider it desirable that before full responsibility is assumed by the elected representatives of the people, there should be a period during which the members of the Legislature, who under the constitution

102 That is a transitional stage between no responsible government and full responsibility.

envisaged in the majority report would be associated with the work of Government Departments, should have an opportunity of gaining direct experience and training in the conduct of public business.

11 I am satisfied that the aim of policy for Trinidad and Tobago must be the early attainment of a constitution under which the Government will be directly responsible to the people whose affairs it controls; and I am fully aware of the earnest desire of many sections of opinion that this aim should be achieved now. At the same time, a substantial body of opinion is in favour of a further intermediate stage, and this view, as reflected in the majority report, is shared by the majority of the members of the present Legislative Council.

There is a further point of some importance. In the minority report it is recommended that the members of the Executive Council should have full ministerial responsibility and be collectively responsible to the Legislature. Experience has shown, however, that the success of Parliamentary government depends largely on the existence of responsible political parties with coherent and definite programmes. It cannot be said, however, that in Trinidad this condition is as yet fulfilled. No doubt the limitations of the existing constitution in part account for this failure. It is clear, however, that until there has been a further opportunity under more favourable circumstances for political parties to develop and work out definite programmes, the grant of responsible government would be unlikely to succeed.

12 In these circumstances it is pertinent to consider how far the majority proposals themselves as amended by the Legislative Council go to place the elected representatives in a position of responsibility. Those proposals contemplate a definite elected majority in the Executive Council, which is designed to be the chief instrument of Government policy. As I see it, this would afford the elected element full opportunity to assume responsibility forthwith for all internal affairs, subject only to provision for the use by the Governor of reserve powers in certain defined circumstances and under limitations similar to those provided in the constitution of Jamaica. (Provision for reserve powers is envisaged in both the majority and minority reports.) The majority proposals, as amended in Legislative Council, go in fact beyond the existing provision in Jamaica, which was at the time of its introduction in 1944 widely regarded as a striking advance towards responsibility. At the same time they would retain for the time being certain features which would constitute some reassurance for those who would view with hesitation the immediate grant of responsible government. I shall make some observations later upon certain of the elements by which that reassurance is provided, and particularly upon the retention of nominated members. Subject to these, and to certain modifications which, as indicated below, I propose to make, I consider that the

amended majority proposals, far reaching as they are, afford a basis upon which all parties should be able to co-operate sincerely and effectively. At the same time, those proposals, if carried into effect, would provide the unofficial members of the Legislature with full opportunities of gaining the necessary experience in the administrative conduct of affairs, a feature for which the existing arrangements have not provided but which, as mentioned above, experience elsewhere has shown to be essential to the successful launching of self-government.

13 After most carefully reviewing these various considerations I have reached the conclusion that, looking to the ultimate political future of Trinidad and Tobago, the wisest course will be to accept, for a period, a constitution based generally on the proposals in the majority report, as amended by the Legislative Council. In saying this, however, I wish to emphasise the intention, so far as His Majesty's Government are concerned, that any such arrangement should be of a transitional nature, and should be designed to bring about the circumstances which would enable responsibility to be assumed without the misgivings which are now felt by many of those who would be directly concerned. At the same time, I wish to draw attention to certain respects in which, in my view, the amended majority proposals themselves require modification. One of these, as already indicated above, relates to the provision for nominated members . . .

15 In the Executive Council there should be one nominated member only, and the elected members should, as proposed, be in a majority of one over the *ex-officio* and nominated members combined. This result should be obtained by reducing the number of elected members from seven to five. This would also have the advantage of making the Executive Council a more compact body.

16 There is some support for the view that the elected members of the Executive Council should be chosen by vote of the elected side only of the legislature. I believe it to be of particular importance, however, to encourage the view that the members of the Executive Council should be responsible to the Legislative Council as a whole, rather than to a section of that body only. I consider, therefore, that all members of the Legislative Council should have a vote in the selection of the elected members of the Executive Council. The single nominated member of the Executive Council should be nominated by the Governor because it is obviously anomalous to give an elective character in the Executive Council to a member who owes his position in the Legislative Council to nomination. He should hold office as an Executive Councillor at pleasure.

17 As regards the removal of elected members of the Executive Council. I

consider that this should be subject to a two-thirds majority of the Legislative Council.

19 To sum up, my conclusion is that the new constitution should provide for: . . .

(ii) an Executive Council of three *ex-officio* members, one nominated member (appointed by His Majesty on the recommendation of the Governor), and five elected members to be elected by the Legislative Council; . . .

In addition, arrangements should be made for the unofficial members of the Executive Council to be actively associated in the work of administration of Government departments. I propose to give further consideration, in consultation with you, to the question how this can best be effected.

Finally, a Public Services Commission should be set up. I shall address you separately on the constitution and functions of such a commission, and I note that you will wish to inform me of the views of the Civil Service Association in this matter before final conclusions are reached.[103]

(viii) Extracts from Government Notice No. 94, Trinidad and Tobago Gazette, 1950: Association of members of Executive Council with the work of Administration of Government Departments.[104]

1 There will be, under the Chairmanship of the Governor, NINE members of Executive Council, namely Colonial Secretary, Attorney General, Financial Secretary, five elected members and one nominated member of the Legislative Council.

2 DEPARTMENTS OF GOVERNMENT

Subject to financial provision being made, the power to determine and define from time to time what departments of Government there shall be will be vested in the Governor in Executive Council, i.e. the Governor acting after consultation with the Executive Council and (save in the exceptional circumstances prescribed in the Royal Instructions) in accordance with the advice of the Executive Council.

103 The changes introduced in 1950 by Order in Council, Letters Patent and Royal Instructions embodied these recommendations of the Secretary of State. The powers of the Executive Council and its relationship with the Governor were substantially those introduced in Jamaica in 1944.

104 A quasi-ministerial system similar to that in Jamaica was introduced into British Guiana in 1953, into British Honduras in 1954, into the Windward Islands in 1955 and into Antigua and St. Kitts/Nevis/Anguilla in 1956.

3 ASSIGNMENT OF DEPARTMENTS TO MEMBERS OF EXECUTIVE COUNCIL

The administration of departments of Government will be assigned to members of Executive Council as follows:-

(a) *Ex-officio* members. The Governor will have power in his discretion to assign from time to time to each of the *ex-officio* members of Executive Council the administration of such departments and such subjects as he thinks fit.

(b) *Other members*

(i) The Governor will have power in his discretion to prescribe from time to time which departments and subjects may be assigned to members of Executive Council other than *ex-officio* members.

(ii) The Governor in Executive Council will have power from time to time to assign to any member of Executive Council, other than an *ex-officio* member, any department or subject for the time being prescribed by the Governor under (i) above, but will not be required to assign a department or subject to every such member and may assign more than one department to any such member.

4 NOMINATED MEMBER OF EXECUTIVE COUNCIL

Although the constitution will make no distinction between the elected members and the nominated member as regards their right to have departments or subjects assigned to them, it is not anticipated that the nominated member will, in normal circumstances, in fact have a department or subject assigned to him.

5 MINISTERS

A member of Executive Council (other than an *ex-officio* member) to whom any department or subject is assigned will, while charged with the administration of any department or subject, be styled a Minister.

6 SPECIAL OFFICES

The Economic Adviser and the Statistician will not be under the control of any particular minister but will be controlled by the Governor in Executive Council. Their advice will be available to all ministers.

7 The Sub-Intendant will be responsible for Crown lands direct to the Governor as Intendant.

8 The relationship of the Director of Audit and his department to

the Secretary of State, the Governor and the local administration will not be altered.

9 SALARIES

(a) (i) A minister will receive an annual salary in respect of his office as minister.
(ii) A member of Executive Council (other than an *ex-officio* member) who is not a minister will receive an annual salary in respect of his membership of Executive Council . . .

10 MINISTERIAL FUNCTIONS OF MEMBERS OF EXECUTIVE COUNCIL

Members of Executive Council to whom departments are assigned will be responsible for their subjects and departments both in Executive Council and in Legislative Council. They will also be responsible for the carrying out of policy approved by Executive Council and for the day to day administration of their departments.

11 In this transitional stage the central secretariat will remain and the five ministers will be accommodated either in the same building or nearby. The Secretariat will remain organised into branches very much as at present with an Assistant Secretary at the head of each branch, but the Assistant Secretaries will submit files and papers to the minister concerned instead of to the Under Secretary and the Colonial Secretary. Ministers will have access to all files of their own departments except personnel files. They will not have access to the files of any other departments except with the permission of the member of Executive Council concerned. The Colonial Secretary, Attorney General and Financial Secretary, in view of the nature of their duties, will be allowed access to all files and papers.

12 DISAGREEMENT BETWEEN HEADS OF DEPARTMENTS AND MINISTERS

If there is disagreement between the minister in charge of any department and the officer who is for the time being head of that department, the latter may submit to the minister, in writing, a statement of his reasons for disagreeing with the minister and of his own recommendations on the question at issue. The minister will then be required to forward to the Clerk of Executive Council a copy of the statement together with any written statement which he may himself wish to make. The Governor in Council will consider the statement or statements and decide the question at issue.

13 PERSONNEL MATTERS

In all matters relating to personnel and conditions of service, heads of departments will deal direct with the Colonial Secretary and the Governor, who will seek the advice and assistance of the Public Service Commission in appropriate cases . . .

15 FINANCE COMMITTEE

Apart from the Finance Committee which will presumably be composed as at present of all unofficial members of the Legislative Council under the chairmanship of the Financial Secretary, it is considered that standing committees of Legislative Council should not be necessary on any matter for which any member of Executive Council is responsible.[105] It is also considered that in present circumstances there should be no deputy ministers or parliamentary secretaries and no provision has, therefore, been made for such officers.

(ix) Extracts from the Report of the British Guiana Constitutional Commission, 1950-51. (Col. No. 280/1951.)

Chapter VI

THE EXECUTIVE

92 We now have to consider the second of the three branches of the constitution – the Executive. In the progress of a colonial territory towards self-government, there is a difficult stage during which the elected representatives of the people are in a substantial majority in the legislature, and yet the ultimate responsibility for the conduct of public affairs remains in the hands of appointed officials. This situation – which may be called semi-representative government – was described more than a century ago by Charles Buller in the famous metaphor that "We have made the fire, but have stopped the chimney".[106]

93 Irresponsibility is bred if responsibility is too long withheld. We are entirely convinced that the time has now come in British Guiana when semi-representative institutions should give place to a form of ministerially responsible government. We are no less convinced that the responsibility to be placed upon the shoulders of ministers must be real. If this is not so, they will

105 Note the explicit rejection of a committee system.
106 Essay on Responsible Government, ed. Hume Wrong (Oxford, 1926), p. 94. (Footnote in the original.)

enjoy power, but can evade responsibility. Where ministers are not vested with effective control over their departments, or can claim that the decisions taken in Executive Council are at variance with the wishes of the elective element, they tend to concern themselves only with the outward and visible signs of office, and to avoid the labour necessary to an effective supervision of departmental activity. On the other hand, in territories where departmental responsibility has been squarely transferred to ministers, their assiduity and devotion to duty is impressive.

94 The traditions of colonial institutions make it more than ever desirable that this transfer of responsibility, when made, should be manifest. The functions of government have in the past been entrusted in varying degree to permanent officials, who could act independently of the advice of popular representatives. Necessary as this may have been in the more primitive conditions of past time,[107] it has encouraged and tends to perpetuate the unwholesome tradition that "government" has been and will always remain something divorced from the community. As a result, the essential difference between the Executive and the Legislature is often not fully appreciated. It is the duty of the Executive to govern, and this responsibility cannot be divided or abdicated without confusion or inefficiency. The Executive in the United Kingdom and in other democratic countries is responsible to the Legislature, and the Legislature is associated with the policy of the government since it alone can authorise those bills – and particularly finance bills – in which the policy of the Executive is expressed. But, while the members of the government derive support for their policies from the Legislature, expressed in favourable majorities, they are vested with their executive power by the King as the Head of the State. There is thus no inconsistency between the responsibility which a member of the Executive owes to the Head of the State (in a colony, to the Governor as His Majesty's representative) and that which he owes to the Legislature of which he is a member: these two loyalties are in face complementary.

95 This situation is not always perfectly understood. Even when a grant of responsible government has been made by the distribution of ministerial portfolios to elected members, the tradition may still linger that government remains something aloof and separated from the popular will. There is thus developed a tendency to escape from responsibility and to maintain an attitude of mind of an opposition even after becoming a member of government.

96 The essential feature of any constitution which involves the grant of a form of responsible government is that the Executive Council becomes the "principal instrument of policy" and that the advice tendered to the

107 See paragraphs 20-23. (Footnote in the original.)

Governor by the Executive Council must possess the ultimate sanction of the Legislature. This can only be done – and the principle is therefore fundamental – by ensuring that the Executive Council shall comprise a majority of elected ministers;[108] for, since these ministers are to be exposed to the constant criticism of the Legislature and of the broader public beyond, it is only just to them that their policies should not be outvoted in the Executive Council by a majority combination of officials and unrepresentative nominated members. Furthermore, if a coherent party system should develop, it would be more than ever desirable that ministers should find no impediment in the way of bringing their programme before the Legislature. Any other arrangement would foster suspicion that there were men "behind the scenes" who were manipulating the government against the will of the Legislature.

97 We must now consider the method whereby members of the Legislature shall be appointed to the Executive Council. Ministerial responsibility in England is collective, and predicates the existence of a fully-fledged party system. This does not yet apply in British Guiana. Political groups are indeed coming into existence with distinctive programmes, based upon differing social and economic concepts, and there are signs that some of these may be able to maintain stable and effective party organisations, not only at the centre but also in the constituencies, and to inspire a reasoned loyalty transcending racial and personal allegiance. It would be unrealistic, however, to recommend constitutional arrangements based upon fully developed party organisations which do not as yet exist. We accordingly propose that ministers should be individually responsible for the portfolios allotted to them. A vote of censure on one minister carried in the Legislature by a simple majority would thus bring about his dismissal, but it would not necessarily entail that consequential resignation of his colleagues which is implicit in collective responsibility. It is to be expected that, when a group of ministers are associated in the day-to-day operations of government, they will develop a team-spirit, even when they are not bound together by a closely defined party allegiance; and the experience of co-operation, involving, as it does, constant give-and-take in reaching policy decisions, can be a potent force in fostering cohesion and community of purpose, not only among the ministers themselves but also among the groups supporting them in the Legislature. By this,

108 We consequently dismiss, as being inconsistent with this principle, the position which obtained in the old Court of Policy, where the votes of the elected representatives were exactly balanced with those of the official and nominated members, and the responsibility for executive decision was thus thrown back on the Governor as Chairman. (Footnote in the original.)

[It should be noted that this was precisely the kind of balanced Executive Council given to Jamaica in 1944.]

the political climate necessary for the successful operation of "cabinet" government can gradually develop.

98 When a system of individual ministerial responsibility is adopted, elections to ministerial office are usually effected by the vote of the entire Legislature. This is at variance with the procedure under a system of collective ministerial responsibility, under which the Head of the State invites the member whom he believes to possess a majority in the elective chamber to form a government – a procedure tantamount to the election by the Legislature of one man acceptable to itself to the post of Prime Minister. It is commonly held that this practice does not lend itself to adoption in the absence of a party system, but it is sometimes argued that party differentiations are the product, and not the antecedent, of a system of collective responsibility. Those who take this view further contend that a sense of common loyalty is a tender plant, which needs favourable conditions in which to flourish – conditions which the practice of individual ministerial responsibility does not satisfy – and they maintain that, despite the absence of a party system, the action of the Legislature should be confined to the choice of one of its number to be a Prime Minister, who shall himself select his several unofficial colleagues. But this means, they argue, the other ministers will be bound more closely to him as the fount of their office, and a sense of common loyalty and, perhaps more important, of discipline will be achieved, leading to the more speedy emergence of party differentiations.

99 We have submitted this argument to careful examination, for it has much to commend it. We have nevertheless rejected it, since it does not possess the flexibility which is a feature of the alternative system. Collective responsibility carries with it the necessity of collective resignation in the face of an adverse vote, and this, which might not be an infrequent phenomenon in a house of emergent party groups, would not make for stable or confident government. Furthermore, the corollary of a discipline imposed upon the members of the Executive Council must be a discipline upon the members of the Legislature through party whips. Without this, the Prime Minister would have no sanction for his authority, and his position would be rendered unreal and anomalous. We, therefore, recommend that the selection of the unofficial ministers be determined by the ballot of the Legislature (or in a bicameral system of the elective house), with the modification, however, that the ministers so chosen should elect one of their number to be "*primus inter pares*" among them, with the designation of "Leader of the House". By this means, flexibility will be maintained, a sense of common purpose fostered, but not imposed, and the way made smooth for the emergence, as circumstances may dictate, of the office of a Prime Minister and of the practice of collective ministerial responsibility . . .

101 We propose that the Court of Policy[109] shall consist of the Governor, who shall preside and possess a casting vote only, and ten other members. Of these, the chief officials – the Colonial (or, as we propose he should now be called, the Chief) Secretary, the Financial Secretary and the Attorney-General – shall be three, and seven shall be unofficial members of the Legislature who shall be designated ministers. Six of these ministers shall be elected members of the Legislature. In a unicameral type of legislature, they will be chosen by the ballot of all the members of that house; in a bicameral system, by that of the elected members of the House of Assembly. The seventh minister will, in a unicameral legislature, be appointed by the Governor from the members of the legislature, while, in a bicameral system, he will be chosen by the members of the revisionary chamber from among their own number. In either event, the elected members will possess the majority, and the fundamental principle we have earlier propounded is thereby satisfied.

102 We should perhaps indicate the reasons which have led us, while stressing the importance of this principle of an elected majority, to recommend the retention of the three official members. First, they will be needed to handle certain portfolios – Law and Order, Finance – which cannot yet be transferred with confidence to elected ministers. We say this with no reflection upon the integrity of prospective ministers, but from an appreciation of the degree of specialised knowledge required to direct the work of these departments. There can be no guarantee that the small population of British Guiana will be able regularly to throw up persons possessed of this wealth of knowledge and experience. Moreover, there can be no certainty that, were such persons available, they would be successful candidates at an election, or, even if they were, that they would be chosen to be members of the Court of Policy. Secondly, we must not lose sight of the fact that the elected representatives of the people of British Guiana have not hitherto been given the opportunities to become experienced in affairs of state. The officials will be invaluable members of the Court of Policy for the guidance which their expert knowledge can give to its discussions. The legal and financial implications of measures of policy demand skilled examination, and the counsel which the official members can afford is not something with which ministers new to responsibility can with wisdom dispense. Moreover, the three official members will, we are confident, share a sense of common responsibility with their elected colleagues.[110] They will be bound by the decision of the majority of the Court of Policy and this stipulation will lay any fears, however unjustified, that they may seek to act against the will of the majority.

109 In paragraph 100 the Commission recommended the adoption of the old name: the Court of Policy.
110 See Appendix A for how far, in the event they did feel a sense of common responsibility.

103 We have considered what functions should fall under this system of government to the Chief Secretary. There were, indeed, those among our witnesses who went so far as to suggest the abolition of the post of Chief Secretary. It is certainly true that, when members of the public have direct access to the various ministries, and the ministers themselves are in a position to defend and explain the policies of their departments before the Court of Policy, the burden on the Chief Secretary will be greatly diminished. Nevertheless, there will remain many important subjects which will not attach to other ministers and will best depend upon him for resolution. Among these, although this citation is not exhaustive and can be reserved for local decision, we would instance the conduct of foreign and commonwealth affairs, defence, which should include the police force,[111] and information matters. As head of the civil service, another wide range of duties will fall to him. There will further be the delicate task, which he can best perform, of assisting the operation of the new system, of encouraging the efficient execution of business, and of promoting understanding between elected minister and permanent official. It is possible that, in the fullness of time, the popular representatives will have gained such familiarity with the business of government that his position, together, indeed, with that of the other official members, can with advantage be reviewed, but that time is not yet.

104 In providing for the presence in the Court of Policy of a seventh unofficial member, who shall either be nominated by the Governor or elected by and from the members of the revisionary chamber, we wish to secure the participation in the work of government of one member who can supply experience which elected representatives may lack. He would bring to the deliberations of the Court of Policy a further measure of knowledge – and that from the unofficial angle – and, should his views at any time incline him away from the side of the elected ministers, they will still be in the majority. We favour his being a minister without portfolio, but expect that he would devote himself to a variety of non-controversial subjects, which cannot easily be allocated to other ministers . . .

105 Since the members of the Court of Policy owe responsibility as members of the government to the Head of the Executive, who is the Governor, it is in the order of things that, while the elected unofficial ministers should be chosen by the vote of the elective house, the distribution of the portfolios of government among them should be made by the Governor, in

111 That the police should be free from all political pressure and their impartiality strenuously preserved is, of course, a truism. The Governor's control and his power to call out the force to maintain the peace in an emergency must be completely unimpaired. This power is fully safeguarded by our recommendations here and in paragraph 117. (Footnote in the original.)

consultation with the ministers themselves . . . The following grouping has, however, commended itself to us as being both comprehensive and logical: Labour, Industry and Commerce; Agriculture, Forestry and Mines; Public Works and Communications; Health; Education; Local Government and Social Welfare.

106 We have given earnest thought to the desirability of providing a portfolio for economic affairs. In sustained economic development lies the key to British Guiana's future, and we felt that much advantage would derive from its care being made the special concern of one minister. At the same time, we appreciate that such a minister, if he is to be more than a figurehead or mere co-ordinating agent, would, in the nature of things, trespass upon and detract from the authority of the other departmental ministers, particularly that of the Ministers of Labour, Industry and Commerce, Agriculture, Forestry and Mines, Public Works and Communications and of the Financial Secretary. We propose, therefore, upon the analogy of the cabinet committees of the United Kingdom, that there should be established a special economic committee of the Court of Policy, which should consist of these four members. The chairmanship should be held by one of the three unofficial members who should be its inspiration and driving force. We make this recommendation because diffusion of responsibility may induce timidity and inaction, and it is a matter of paramount importance that the responsibility for initiative should be squarely placed upon the shoulders of one man. As with cabinet committees in this country, this committee should not be made statutory.

107 The burden of office is likely to be considerable, and while it would be unfortunate if too great a proportion of the members of the Legislature were vested with executive office, we would urge the appointment of a small number of junior ministers – to be known as Under-Secretaries – to afford ministers support in debate, and to assist them in the despatch of their departmental business. One junior ministry which we feel to be of particular importance is the Financial Under-Secretaryship. Apart from the obvious argument that, if elected members are eventually to assume responsibility for the Ministry of Finance, the sooner they are associated with its work the better, we trust that the appointment of this junior minister, and his participation in debate, will afford the elected members a greater confidence that they are fully associated with all aspects of policy. We would also urge that consideration be given to the appointment of a junior minister to the Ministry of Labour, Industry and Commerce, since the burden of this office is likely to be exceptionally heavy.

108 Ministers are entitled to a loyal and willing co-operation from the permanent officials of their departments, and we see every reason to expect that this co-operation will be given, and that they will work in harmonious association. Nevertheless, a minister and the permanent head of his

department may, upon occasion, differ upon a matter of principle, and, where this happens, the disagreement should be resolved, after discussion in the Court of Policy, as the Governor may direct. To enable this to be done, the permanent official should submit a written statement of his own standpoint to his minister, who will forward it to the Court of Policy together with any observations he may wish to make . . .

110 The Court of Policy shall be summoned only upon the authority of the Governor, but shall be summoned by him upon the written request of at least five members. No business shall be transacted in it if objection be made by any member that there are less than five members present other than the Chairman . . .

112 The division between the Executive and Legislature is not, as we have said, clearcut, and a further example of an overlap between the two is to be found in the existence of advisory committees of the Legislative Council. The present advisory committees of the Legislative Council were instituted in 1943 with the purpose of associating members of the Legislature more intimately with the work of departmental administration. They were expressly withheld from any executive functions, but it was hoped that the members of the advisory committees "as delegates of the whole council (would) be in a peculiarly advantageous position to lead and advise their colleagues on the particular matters which come within the purview of the department for which they can speak". In so doing, they would promote harmonious relations between the Executive and the Legislature, and, to this end, it was intended that the chairmen of the advisory committees should be members of the Executive Council, where they would be in touch with the other activities of government, and where they would gain that experience of public administration which clearly fore-shadowed the development of a ministerial system.[112]

113 We have carefully examined the working of this innovation, but we regret that the full expectations with which its introduction was greeted have not been fulfilled. There are many reasons for this. First, the chairman of two of the committees are not elected, but nominated, members, so that those persons who might have been considered to be potential ministers have not been afforded the necessary experience. Secondly, the association between the Executive and the Legislature has not been maintained, for of two committees only do the Chairmen serve on the Executive Council. There is little purpose in investigating the reasons for these developments; rather we would point to their results in fostering amongst the members of the advisory committees a feeling of their impotence to affect the course of government, since

112 Letter of 1st November, 1943, from H.E. The Governor as directive to chairmen of Advisory Committees. (Footnote in the original.)

decisions have rested with an executive council on which their views are not represented. Nevertheless, it is still our view that the advisory committees have afforded the members of the Legislature a useful insight into the business of government, and have been a valuable forum in which policy could be examined and proposals ventilated. If the deviations from the original model had been remedied, the committees would have been capable of contributing even more.

114 The question arises, however, whether their usefulness would not come to an end with the institution of a ministerial system. We are satisfied that this would be so. Nothing should be allowed to confuse or undermine the cardinal principle that a minister must assume real responsibility for the department in his charge, and we fear that on two counts the association with him of a committee of the Legislature would have this effect. First, if he accepts the advice of his committee, he can plausibly maintain that the responsibility for the decision is not wholly his but is shared by members of the committee; and, secondly, if he acts counter to that advice, his position will be embarrassing when the matter comes to be debated in the Legislature. For these reasons we recommend that advisory committees of the Legislature should no longer be appointed.

F. Collective responsibility and the Chief Minister.[113]

(i) Extracts from the Governor's Speech to the Barbados Parliament, 1st October 1946.
(Minutes of the Barbados House of Assembly, 1946, pp. 405-6.
("The Bushe Experiment."))

29 Let me turn from this picture of frustration to consider the cause of the trouble. It is to be found, I think, in the Barbados constitution which as it works at present appears to be incapable of coping with modern conditions. The defect of the constitution lies in the imperfect distribution of

113 Changes introducing collective responsibility and the office of Chief Minister but with official membership still retained, and with discretionary powers still vested in the Governor, were implemented in Barbados in 1946, in Jamaica and British Guiana in 1953, in Trinidad and Tobago in 1956, in the Leeward Islands (apart from Montserrat and the Virgin Islands) and the Windward Islands in 1959, and in British Honduras in 1960. In the Bahama Islands a rather more advanced form of responsible government was introduced in 1963, but prior to that date the Executive Council was an entirely nominated body consulted by the Governor but not binding him by its advice and having no executive function in itself.

Power and Responsibility. The Governor has the whole responsibility of Government but he is given no power. The House of Assembly possesses the power but has no responsibility.

30 Throughout the history of British Parliamentary institutions, it has been realised that the great evil which must be avoided is Power without Responsibility, and, in order to avoid it, it has been the custom to entrust the executive power to a Cabinet and not a Chamber, that is, to a small body of persons upon whom responsibility can be fixed and not a large body of persons who can avoid a personal responsibility. But although Cabinets wield large executive power, they must not be without control. That is where Parliament comes into the picture. As the "Grand Inquest" of the nation, its members can ask the Government questions and insist upon being answered; they can bring their points to the test of argument on the floor of the House. If not satisfied, they can vote against the Government. They can, indeed, defeat the Government though the immediate consequence of that would normally be a dissolution when members would have to shoulder their responsibility, and justify their action to the electorate.

31 In Barbados for decades, every imaginary device has been employed to deprive the Governor or the Government of any effective power and to concentrate it in the House of Assembly. The unique financial system which is crippling to speedy and efficient Government; the numerous Statutory Boards independent of Government though utilising public funds; the control by Acts of the Legislature of a vast field of action which should be administrative, and the various safeguards and restrictions on prompt administrative action may all have been suitable for the time when policy consisted in inaction, but are wholly unsuitable to a time when policy should consist in progress and reform.

32 On the other hand, the House of Assembly, I have no doubt, feels that while it can "oppose" it cannot effectively "propose" and that the Government is not sufficiently representative of Parliament; and its reluctance to accept what it regards as government by the Governor and his officials, while showing a misapprehension of the system as it works to-day, is historically understandable.

33 As a result, the position of the Government at the present time is an impossible one. It has no certain expectation of support in the House of Assembly, and it has no assurance that any decision involving legislative or financial action will be made effective. Its policy, therefore, becomes an unknown quantity and it cannot make long term plans at all. Under such conditions progress is impossible and if they were to continue there would be no reasonable prospect of meeting and dealing with the difficulties of a rapidly changing world.

34 It seems to me, therefore, essential that the Executive should be

based more clearly upon representation from the House of Assembly and thus linked more firmly with the Legislature.

35 On the assembling of the new House, therefore, the Officer Administering the Government will send for the person who appears to him to be best able to command a majority in the House of Assembly and will ask him to submit to him names from the House for membership of the Executive Committee, and Members of the Executive Committee will be asked respectively to take charge of the general policy relating to particular departments of Government for the purpose of dealing with the affairs of those Departments in Executive Committee and in the House of Assembly.

36 The Executive Committee will then in practice cease to be merely a collection of individuals nominated by the Governor for the purpose of advising him, and will become an effective organ of government accepting collective responsibility for policy, though the Governor must under the constitution as at present existing retain ultimate responsibility.

37 Such an alteration in constitutional procedure will also bring, I trust, a new sense of responsibility to the House of Assembly. At present the House can reject Government measures, refuse supply, and confound Government policy in the calm assurance that the Government will carry on notwithstanding. That is what I call irresponsibility. The duty and responsibility of Parliament is to support, if not one Government, then another, or to face a dissolution with all its consequences.

38 As a corollary to that, there must be a relationship of responsibility by the nominated members of the Executive Committee to the House of Assembly, and they must be prepared to resign if they lose the confidence of the House.

39 My design, which clearly must depend upon the general assent and co-operation of the new Assembly, will, I hope, create gradually these mutual responsibilities. It involves no legal alteration of the constitution. It is tentative and experimental, and upon its success or failure must depend the progression or the retrogression of a Parliamentary system of Government in Barbados[114] . . .

114 Two things are here worthy of note: first, that Barbados, unlike the Crown Colonies, was able to make the change to responsible government without changing the law of the constitution; and secondly, that in fact the changes in the practice of the Barbados Constitution introduced by the "Bushe Experiment" of 1946 were well in advance of the other Territories.

(ii) Extracts from the Governor's Speech to the Jamaican Legislature, 1952. (Proceedings of the House of Representatives, 1952, Vol. 1, pp. 145-7.)

It was felt by all those whom I consulted that the practical and sensible course would be to see where experience since the 1944 constitution was introduced showed that weaknesses and shortcomings existed, and then to undertake reforms designed to eradicate those weaknesses and shortcomings, rather than to throw the whole of our constitutional system back into the melting pot.

The next issue on which there seemed to be general agreement was that although the changes might later be shown to be necessary in the Legislature, it was in the Executive that reforms were most urgently required . . .

. . . In regard to the Executive, I found that it was fully agreed by all those whom I consulted that the system which we have operated since 1944 had certain basic weaknesses.

I entirely share that view, and my own experience when I was in Jamaica six or seven years ago together with my experience in the past year confirm the conclusion that the system of executive government which we operate, while it has served a useful purpose, has grave disadvantages. There is full agreement that an overhaul is overdue . . .

All are agreed that the first weakness in our existing system is the over-concentration of administrative authority in the Executive Council.

The Executive Council was originally declared to be the principal instrument of policy. So it should be: but it is also under our present systems, the principal instrument of administration.

Under the existing constitution, practically every question which needs a Government decision has to be referred to the Executive Council. The result is that the Council is so over-burdened with administrative matters that it has inadequate time to consider questions of major policy. Moreover grave delays are caused in administrative action.

Another result is that an almost intolerable burden is placed on the official members of the Council who are responsible for seeing that all the decisions of the Council are carried out.

Yet another result of the concentration of administrative functions in the Executive Council is that the leading officials outside the Council have insufficient opportunity for exercising the initiative and responsibility which their seniority and experience would justify. No one of the groups whom I consulted had any doubt that this system requires radical change . . .

It was agreed that separate Ministries, each under the direction of a Minister and each manned by the best material we can provide from the Government service, must be given responsibility first for initiation of proposals on policy for consideration by the Executive Council and then for the execution of the policy decided upon by the Council.

The Executive Council must and should remain the principal instrument of policy: it should no longer be the principal instrument of administration.

In addition to agreement on that vital matter, it seemed to me that general agreement existed on another very important issue. There has in the past been a good deal of public misunderstanding about the working of Executive Council. We do not attempt to dispose of our business in the Council by working in competing blocs and forcing each issue to a vote. In fact it is rare for us to take a vote at all. Rather we approach the many and varied and complicated problems which come before us in a spirit of co-operation with all of us seeking the best solution and each member freely expressing his view. Moreover, nominated members of the Executive Council are not only free to speak and vote in the Council in accordance with their own opinions: they are under a clear obligation to do so.

Nevertheless the system we now operate in the Executive Council may be called a system of balance in that if the elected members were to vote one way and then non-elected members were to vote another the matter would have to be decided by my casting vote. In fact the casting vote is very seldom used but any system of balance has grave disadvantages. It encourages irresponsibility.

It is a cardinal principle of the British Cabinet System that, whatever differences of view have appeared in the discussions in the Cabinet, when once a decision of the Cabinet is reached every member of the Cabinet must either resign or support the decision.

He must also use his best endeavour, where action in the Legislature is required, to secure acceptance of the decision in the Legislature.

We do not hear so much these days about the "official government" and the "elected government" and I should not fail to pay tribute to the loyal way in which Ministers have increasingly respected this principle. But if we are to achieve greater responsibility in the Government of Jamaica it must be clear to everyone where responsibility lies – and under our present system responsibility is divided. No one can tell whether a Bill or a money measure or an administrative decision conforms with the views and the wishes of elected Ministers or not.

I have long maintained that we should seek to make our system of government not less representative and less responsible but more representative and more responsible and I believe that there is wide agreement that the time has come to end the system of balance, and to increase the number of elected ministers and thus to establish an elected majority in the Executive Council.

There is one other important reform on which I find that agreement exists. The present system whereby a Minister who is in complete disagreement with other Ministers must be retained unless a two-thirds majority of the House of Representatives in favour of his removal can be secured is not recognised as unsound.

It means that the Opposition could, it wished, [sic] keep a Minister in office even when he had forfeited the confidence both of his fellow Ministers and his party. It is, I think, fully agreed that a new system should be worked out under which both appointment and removal of elected Ministers should be on the recommendation of the Leader of the Majority Party. . . .[115]

Before going on to discuss what our next steps should be following this statement from the Secretary of State, I should like to make one comment about the Governor's powers. You know very well that the reserve powers have been very seldom exercised and I am glad that I have never had to resort to their use. I hope that I shall not have to use them in future, but you will appreciate that to make the exercise of reserve powers subject to the approval of a Council in which there were an elected majority would, in effect, mean that the Governor had no reserve powers at all.

You will see from the Secretary of State's statement that if the proposals for an elected majority in Executive Council is put into effect the necessary changes will be made in the constitutional instruments to retain the Governor's reserve power, subject only to the approval of the Secretary of State.

At the same time, I should emphasize the vital change which the constitutional proposals, which I have explained, will have in regard to the Governor's powers.

In the past, the Governor, if supported on any issue by both nominated and official members, has been in a position, by the exercising of a casting vote in Executive Council, to pursue a course contrary to that supported by elected Ministers. That he has scarcely ever exercised his casting vote in Executive Council is beside the point. The fact is that at present the Governor, in the circumstances I have described, has the power to override the views of the elected Ministers.

The difference in future, if the proposals which I have explained are accepted, will be that if occasion ever arose in which the Governor wished to exercise reserve powers in regard to legislation or finance contrary to the advice of the elected members he would not be able to do so by resort to a casting vote in the Council in secret.

He would have to do so by exercise of his reserve powers in public. He would have to take public responsibility for his action.

I think that Ministers have a right to say, in effect: "If our advice is not to be followed, then the responsibility should be clearly fixed by the Governor acting not in secret but in public." I myself fully agree that if ever I feel bound to act in contrary to the advice of a majority in the Executive Council I should take full responsibility for so doing.

115 The Governor went on to state that the Secretary of State had communicated his agreement to all these points. The changes were implemented in 1953.

(iii) Extracts from the Interim Report of the Select Committee of the Jamaica House of Representatives appointed by the House to prepare a constitution providing for self-government to be submitted for approval to the Rt. Hon. Secretary of State for the Colonies. (Minutes of the Jamaica House of Representatives, 1954, Appendix XCIX.)

On the 22nd of July, 1952, by Resolution of the House of Representatives, a Select Committee . . . was appointed to prepare a constitution providing for Self-Government for Jamaica to be submitted for approval to the Secretary of State for the Colonies . . .

4 Your Committee commenced its deliberations by accepting the following basic propositions and guiding itself by them and by what they imply:-

(a) Jamaica's experience in the working of Parliamentary institutions justifies the view that our immediate long-term aim must be the achievement of Dominion Status within as short a time as possible after further experience has been gained in the working of the present Constitution as amended in terms of the proposals embodied in this Report.

(b) That amendments should be made to the existing Constitution to take effect immediately or as near thereto as may be reasonably possible after the general elections of 1954.

(c) That the proposed amendments should secure to Jamaica immediate full Self-Government in internal affairs.

(d) That in view of the recommendation for full Self-Government in internal affairs the power of the Secretary of State for the Colonies to appoint or control the appointment of the higher levels of the Civil Service in Jamaica requires to be dealt with – Our aim should be to establish a position in this vital matter consistent with Self-Government and to prepare now for the time when we will, through our own independent Civil Service Commission have complete responsibility for providing for our own Civil Service.

(e) That decision as to the future of the Legislative Council and as to the number of Constituencies which ought to be provided should await the formulation of the Constitution providing for Dominion Status for Jamaica or for a further advance beyond the present Constitution as same may be amended by virtue of these recommendations.

5 Your Committee therefore has the honour to recommend that the following amendments be made to the existing Constitution of Jamaica as soon as possible after the General Elections to be held in the year 1954:-

EXECUTIVE COUNCIL

(a) That the Constitution of the Executive Council be amended by removing therefrom the three Official Members.

(b) That His Excellency the Governor should cease to be an *ex-officio* member and to preside and that the Chief Minister or his deputy should preside at all meetings of the Executive Council. It should be provided however that the Governor shall have the right to summon a special meeting of the Executive Council and that at such special meeting he shall preside but shall not have a vote.

(c) That there should be ten Ministers instead of eight in the Executive Council to allow for the establishment of a Ministry of Justice and a Ministry of Home Affairs.

(d) The Ministry of Justice to have the following functions:-
- (i) The Administration of Justice
- (ii) The drafting of legislation
- (iii) The functions of the Public Trustee.

(e) The Ministry of Home Affairs to have the following functions:-
- (i) The administration of Local Government in regard to the responsibility of Central Government therein.
- (ii) The maintenance of order to include the direction of the Police Force.[116]
- (iii) Security, Immigration and Emigration.[116]

(f) That the Nominated Members should be appointed by the Governor on the nomination of the Chief Minister.

ATTORNEY GENERAL

In order to secure that the Attorney General shall be completely free from Political control in regard to the prosecution of offences and other matters wherein he acts with such freedom under the British Constitution there shall be written into the Constitution of Jamaica a provision as follows:-

> That the Attorney General shall in Jamaica act at his sole discretion in all matters wherein by Constitutional usage in England he acts at such discretion.

JUDICIAL SERVICE

That there should be a Judicial Services Commission to advise the Governor in the exercise of his powers of appointments, promotions, transfers, termination of appointment, dismissals and disciplinary control of all members of the Judicial Service.

116 These powers are usually the last granted before independence.

THE PUBLIC SERVICE

The appointment, transfer, dismissal and disciplinary control of public officers should be vested in the Governor acting on the recommendation of the Public Service Commission provided that appointments and transfers to certain specified offices, such as that of Attorney General, should be made by the Governor acting in his discretion.

(iv) Statement by the Secretary of State for the Colonies on Constitutional Changes in Trinidad and Tobago, 3rd November 1958. (Parliamentary Debates (Commons) Vol. 594, 1958, c.c. 18-22.)

I have had discussions with Dr. P.V. Solomon, the Minister of Education and Culture, representing the Government of Trinidad and Tobago, about constitutional proposals based on the two Motions passed by the Legislative Council in September, 1957, and June, 1958. The Governor, Sir Edward Beetham, and the Attorney-General, Mr. Ellis Clarke, were present throughout the talks, and Mr. W.J. Alexander, a Nominated Member of the Legislative Council, attended the initial meetings. I also had discussions with representatives of the Democratic Labour Party, the main opposition party in Trinidad, at which the Governor was present.

In putting forward the views of his Government, Dr. Solomon confirmed their decision, earlier communicated to me, not to seek the removal of Her Majesty's powers to legislate by Order in Council and to disallow Ordinances. On the other hand, the Government wished three changes not included in either of the Motions to be made: that the Governor should consult the Premier regarding the appointment of Nominated Members before making such appointments acting in his discretion; that the Governor should dissolve and prorogue the Legislative Council on the advice of the Premier and that a Judicial Service Commission should be set up. Dr. Solomon explained that the purpose in proposing that the Governor should consult the Premier before appointing Nominated Members in his discretion was to ensure that, if the necessity arose, the direction given by me in 1956 that the Governor should consult the leader of the majority party regarding the appointment of suitable Nominated Members so as to permit him to have a reasonable working majority should continue to apply. I confirmed that this would be the case and in the light of this assurance Dr. Solomon on behalf of his Government withdrew this proposed amendment. On the question of the dissolution and prorogation of the Legislative Council, it was not the intention of the Trinidad Government that any amendment should go beyond the conventions in force in the United Kingdom. Dr. Solomon explained that the proposals in respect of the Judicial Service Commission were a logical development following the establishment of the Public Service Commission and the Police Service Commission.

I took note of the views of the Trinidad Government, expressed by Dr. Solomon, that the retention of the Governor's power to refuse to assent to Bills was unnecessary inasmuch as Bills could be reserved for the signification of Her Majesty's pleasure. It was recognised, however, that future constitutional changes would involve the transfer from Her Majesty to Her representative in the territory of the Sovereign's discretion to assent to Bills. In the circumstances Dr. Solomon agreed that the appropriate course would be to leave the present provisions in the Constitution unaltered, and instructions to be given to the Governor not to exercise the power to refuse to assent unless so directed by Her Majesty.

Subject to the points which are explained in this statement, I agreed that the changes now sought by the Government of Trinidad and Tobago were appropriate at this stage of constitutional development in the territory and undertook to recommend them to Her Majesty in Council. These changes may be summarised as follows:

(a) the Governor will call upon the leader of the majority party in the Legislative Council to form a government; if no party has a clear majority of elected seats, the Governor will call upon the person most likely to command a majority;

(b) the Chief Minister will be empowered to select and remove Ministers and Parliamentary Secretaries;

(c) the Chief Minister and not the Governor will preside at Executive Council meetings. The Governor, however, in his discretion may summon a special meeting of the Executive Council at which he will preside. The name "Executive Council" will be changed to "Cabinet" and that of "Chief Minister" to "Premier";

(d) the Colonial Secretary (to be redesignated "Chief Secretary") and the Attorney-General will retain their seats in the Cabinet and Legislative Council but will no longer be entitled to vote in the former;

(e) the Public Service Commission and the Police Service Commission will be remodelled as independent bodies with full-time chairmen, and the Governor will be bound to accept their advice except with regard to discipline and a few senior appointments;

(f) provisions dealing with the salaries of Ministers, Parliamentary Secretaries, the Speaker and Deputy Speaker, will be deleted from the Constitution but provision will be made preventing the reduction of the salaries of the Speaker and the Deputy Speaker during their continuance of office;

(g) the Premier will not be obliged to recommend the appointment of the full number (four) of Parliamentary Secretaries;

(h) if the Speaker is elected from outside the Legislative Council he will not have a casting vote;

(i) so long as it appears to the Governor that the Premier commands the support of the majority of the elected members of the Legislative Council the Governor will act in accordance with his advice in the dissolution and prorogation of the Legislative Council;

(j) the establishment of a Judicial and Legal Service Commission with executive functions except in regard to judges, in which case the Commission will be advisory to the Governor;

(k) the provision for the appointment of a ninth Minister.

In explaining the Trinidad Government's desire for the appointment of a ninth Minister, Dr. Solomon drew attention to the fact that under the present Constitution the Governor had discretion to declare which Departments and subjects may be assigned to Ministers and that no amendment to the Constitution was therefore necessary before responsibility for the Police could be transferred to a Minister. The transfer of Police to a Minister was regarded by the Trinidad Government as a logical next step and appropriate at this stage since the Minister of Finance was already responsible for pay, etc., and establishment matters, and the independence and responsibility of the Attorney-General for the initiation, conduct and discontinuance of criminal proceedings would remain unaffected. Furthermore, there would shortly be established an independent Police Service Commission with executive authority. The ninth Minister would fill a twofold need: firstly, an additional Minister would in any event be necessary when Police was transferred to a Minister; and, secondly, quite apart from the question of the transfer of the Police, an additional Minister was necessary now if present Government business was to continue to be effectively discharged. In view of the position explained at the beginning of this paragraph, it was agreed that the transfer of the Police to a Minister could be considered as an issue quite separate from the constitutional changes now under discussion. In order not to delay these changes, which had been agreed in principle and which the Trinidad Government wished to see effected as soon as the necessary amending Instruments could be made, it was decided that the transfer of the Police to a Minister should be the subject of further consultation with me. Meanwhile I agreed to a provision for a ninth Minister as such.

While conscious of the reasons which led the Government to request the removal of the Governor's reserved Legislative powers, I was unable to reach a decision since there are considerable difficulties of a legal and constitutional character which have to be resolved. I am, however, hopeful that it will be possible to reach a decision before the agreed changes are submitted to Her Majesty in Council.

I welcomed the intention of the Government of Trinidad and Tobago to seek the appointment of a Select Committee of the Legislative Council to consider changes in the Constitution of a more fundamental nature than those which had been under discussion. The time is most opportune to consider further changes of this nature – changes which will lead the territory to a constitutional position which will be more appropriate in view of the approach of The West Indies to full independence within the British Commonwealth. The prospect of full independence within the Commonwealth for the Federation means that in Trinidad it is desirable to prepare the ground now for the changes which will be necessary by that time.

Meanwhile, the changes listed at paragraph 4 above, will be submitted to Her Majesty in Council as soon as the necessary Instruments can be prepared.

(v) Extracts from the Report of the Select Committee on a new Constitution for Trinidad and Tobago, 1959. (Trinidad and Tobago Council Paper No. 11 of 1959.)

The Select Committee appointed, in pursuance of a resolution of the Legislative Council passed on the 21st November, 1958, to make recommendations for a New Constitution for Trinidad and Tobago, have agreed to the following Report:-

PRELIMINARY

1 The resolution of the Legislative Council was in the following terms: "That a Select Committee of this Honourable Council under the Chairmanship of the Speaker be appointed immediately to make recommendations for a New Constitution for Trinidad and Tobago."

2 The Speaker appointed eleven Members of the Legislative Council, as hereunder, to be Members of the Select Committee.[117]

THE SOVEREIGN

28(1) By a majority vote it was agreed, and we recommend, that the Sovereign shall be represented by a Governor appointed on the advice of the Cabinet of Trinidad and Tobago, that the Governor shall hold office at the Sovereign's pleasure and shall have only those powers exercised by the Sovereign in the United Kingdom . . .

THE EXECUTIVE

31 By a majority of votes, it was agreed, and we recommend –

(a) that the Executive Authority shall be vested in a Cabinet which shall be the principal instrument of policy and the Governor shall be obligated to act on its advice in all internal affairs; and

117 The Select Committee consisted of 6 People's National Movement members, 4 Democratic Labour Party members (Opposition) and 1 Butler Party member (Opposition).

(b) that the Cabinet shall consist of a Premier, the Attorney General, and such other members (not exceeding 10) of the Legislature as the Premier thinks fit. Not more than two members shall be from the Senate: provided that where the Attorney General is a Senator, not more than three members shall be from the Senate. Members of the Cabinet shall have full ministerial responsibility for departments and subjects assigned to them by the Premier.

(2) Mr. S. Capildeo voted against. He stated (a) that the Attorney General should be appointed from among the practising barristers of the Territory, (b) that his post should be a non-political one, and (c) that he should be the chief civil servant in a Ministry to be called the Ministry of Justice, the Minister in charge of which could be an Elected Member of the House of Representatives. Mr. Butler expressed the view that the Attorney General should not be a civil servant, that in his capacity as such he should be removed from the House of Representatives, that the Attorney General must face the polls as an Elected Member, and that he should go out of office as Attorney General if and when his Government falls.

THE PREMIER

32 It was agreed, and we recommend –

(a) that the Premier shall be chosen in accordance with the conventions and practice which obtain in the United Kingdom and shall preside over the Cabinet;

(b) that the Premier shall appoint a Deputy Premier and may determine the order of precedence of the other Ministers;

(c) that the Premier may also appoint such number of Parliamentary Secretaries as he may think fit and charge them with specific duties. Their authority and responsibility shall stem from such appointments.

THE ATTORNEY GENERAL

33(1) In the People's National Movement Memorandum it is stated as follows:-

"We consider that the time has come when the Attorney Generalship should be a political appointment, and the holder should go out of office with the Government. He may be appointed from amongst the members of the Legislature or from outside."

(2) By a majority vote, it was agreed, and we recommend, that the Attorney General should not be a civil servant, and that he shall be a Member of the House of Representatives or a Senator . . .

(vi) Extracts from the Trinidad and Tobago (Constitution) (Amendment) Order in Council, 1959. (S.I. 1044/1959.)

"PART II

Cabinet

4 (1) There shall be a Cabinet in and for the Territory which shall, subject to section 11 of this Order, consist of nine Ministers, who shall be Elected Members, and two *ex-officio* Members.[118]

(2) Of the Ministers one, who shall be styled the Premier shall be appointed in accordance with subsection (1) of section 6 of this Order and the others shall be appointed in accordance with subsection (3) of that section.

(3) The *ex-officio* Members of the Cabinet shall be the Chief Secretary and the Attorney-General.

5 (1) The Cabinet shall be the principal instrument of policy and shall perform such functions and duties, and exercise such powers, as from time to time may be prescribed . . .

(2) The Governor shall, save as otherwise provided by any Instructions under Her Majesty's Sign Manual and Signet –

(a) consult with the Cabinet in the exercise of all powers conferred upon him by this Order other than powers which he is by this Order directed or empowered to exercise in his discretion or after consultation with or on the advice or recommendation of any person or authority other than the Cabinet; and

(b) act in accordance with the advice of:-

(i) the Cabinet in any matter on which he is by this subsection obliged to consult with the Cabinet;

(ii) any person or authority other than the Cabinet in exercise of any power which he is directed or empowered by this Order to exercise on the advice or recommendation of such person or authority.

6 (1) Wherever there shall be occasion for the appointment of a Premier, the Governor, acting in his discretion, shall by Instrument under the Public Seal appoint to be Premier –

(a) the Elected Member who is the leader in the Legislative Council of the Party which commands the support of the majority of the Elected Members, or

118 Note the continuing presence of two *ex-officio* Members.

(b) if it appears to him that such party does not have an undisputed leader in the Legislative Council or that no party commands the support of such a majority, the Elected Member who in his judgement is most likely to command the support of the Elected Members, and who is willing to accept the office of Premier . . .

(3) Whenever the office of a Minister other than the Premier is vacant the Governor shall, on the advice of the Premier, by Instrument under the Public Seal, appoint to that office a person who is an Elected Member.

7 (1) The Premier shall vacate his office –

(a) if he ceases to be an Elected Member otherwise than by a dissolution of the Legislative Council;

(b) if he resigns his office by writing under his hand addressed to the Governor, upon receipt of such resignation by the Governor; or

(c) if between the date of a dissolution of the Legislative Council and the date of the first appointment of a Premier thereafter any circumstances arise which, if he were an Elected Member, would cause him to vacate his seat in the Legislative Council.

(2) The Premier shall also be deemed to have vacated his office immediately prior to the appointment by the Governor of a person to be Premier under subsection (1) of section 6 of this Order, following the holding of a general election.

(3) The Governor, acting in his discretion, may declare the office of Premier vacant if the Premier is absent from the Territory without having given the Governor prior notice of such absence; and upon the Governor making a declaration under this subsection the Premier shall vacate his office.

(4) Whenever it appears to the Governor that the Premier has ceased to command the support of the majority of the Elected Members the Governor may, in his discretion, by Instrument under the Public Seal, revoke the appointment of the Premier and the Premier shall unless he sooner vacates his office be deemed to have vacated this office in pursuance of subsection (2) of this section:

Provided that before so revoking the Premier's appointment, the Governor shall consult with the Premier and, if the Premier so requests, the Governor, acting in his discretion, may dissolve the Legislative Council instead of revoking the appointment.

8 (1) A Minister other than the Premier shall vacate his office –

(a) when the Governor appoints a person to be Premier under subsection (1) of section 6 of this Order;

(b) if he ceases to be an Elected Member for any reason other than the dissolution of the Legislative Council;

(c) if he resigns his office by writing under his hand addressed to the

Governor, upon receipt of such resignation by the Governor; or

(d) if between the date of a dissolution of the Legislative Council and the date of the first appointment of a Premier thereafter any circumstances arise which, if he were an Elected Member, would cause him to vacate his seat in the Legislative Council.

(2) The Governor, acting on the advice of the Premier, may declare the office of a Minister other than the Premier vacant if the Minister is absent from the Territory without the permission of the Governor, acting on the advice of the Premier; and upon the Governor making a declaration under this subsection the Minister shall vacate his office.

(3) The Premier may recommend to the Governor the revocation of the appointment of any other Minister and upon receiving such a recommendation the Governor shall, by Instrument under the Public Seal, revoke the appointment of the Minister to whom it relates and that Minister shall thereupon vacate his office . . .

13 The Governor shall, for the due exercise of his functions, be entitled to all papers which are available to the Cabinet and to any other information concerning the government of the Territory which is so available.

14 Any question whether any person is a Minister shall be referred to, and determined by, the Governor, acting in his discretion.

15 Meetings of the Cabinet shall be summoned by the Premier:

Provided that the Governor, acting in his discretion, may summon a special meeting of the Cabinet whenever he thinks fit and may attend and preside at such a meeting.[119]

16(1) Subject to the provisions of section 15 of this Order, there shall preside at any meeting of the Cabinet –

(a) the Premier; or

(b) in the absence of the Premier, such other Minister as the Premier may appoint; or

(c) if no Minister so appointed is present, such other Minister as the Ministers present may elect . . .

17(1) The Governor, acting in his discretion, may by directions in writing –

(a) charge any *ex-officio* Member of the Cabinet with the administration of any department or subject not being the subject of finance;

(b) declare what other departments or subjects, not including the subject of finance, may be assigned to a Minister; and

(c) revoke or vary any directions given under this subsection.

119 Note the continuing power of the Governor to summon the Cabinet.

(2) The subject of finance shall be assigned to a Minister.

(3) The Governor, on the advice of the Premier, may by directions in writing –

(a) charge any Minister with the administration of the subject of finance, and, during such time as it shall be declared, under paragraph (b) of subsection (1) of this section, to be a department or subject which may be assigned to a Minister, with the administration of any other department or subject; and

(b) revoke or vary any direction given under this subsection"

Amendment of principal Order

4 Section 26a of the principal Order is revoked and the following sections are inserted immediately after section 17 of the principal Order as amended by this Order.

"Parliamentary Secretaries

18(1) Whenever a Premier has been appointed by the Governor . . . the Premier may recommend to the Governor for appointment from among the Elected Members not more than four persons, not being Ministers or the Speaker or the Deputy Speaker, to be Parliamentary Secretaries, and upon receiving such a recommendation the Governor shall, by Instrument under the Public Seal, appoint such persons to be Parliamentary Secretaries . . .

19 The Governor, on the advice of the Premier, may by directions in writing charge a Parliamentary Secretary with assisting a Minister in the exercise of his Ministerial duties and may likewise at any time revoke or vary any such directions.

20 Any question whether any person is a Parliamentary Secretary shall be referred to, and determined by, the Governor, acting in his discretion . . . "

(vii) Extracts from Additional Instructions to the Governor of Trinidad and Tobago, dated 15th June 1959.
(Instruments not statutory instruments, appendix to S.I./1959.)

Amendment of the Instructions of 1950

3 Clause 4 of the Instructions is revoked and the following clause is substituted therefor:-

"4 (1) Nothing in this clause shall be construed as applying to any power conferred upon the Governor by the Order in Council or to matters for which provision is made by clause 15 of these Instructions.

(2) The Governor shall, subject to the provisions of clause 5 of these Instructions, consult with the Cabinet in the formulation of policy and in the exercise of all other powers conferred upon him except –

(a) the powers conferred upon the Governor by Articles 8, 9, 10, 11 and 12 of the Letters Patent and clause 1 of these Instructions;[120]

(b) any other power conferred upon the Governor in respect of which it is provided by law, either expressly or by implication, that he shall not be obliged to consult with the Cabinet in the exercise thereof:

(c) any other power conferred upon the Governor by any law where he is directed or empowered to exercise that power in his discretion or after consultation with or on the advice of any person or authority, other than the Cabinet, or where in pursuance of any law such power has been delegated by him to some other person or authority.

(3) The Governor shall, subject to the provisions of clause 5 of these Instructions, act in accordance with the advice of the Cabinet in any matter on which he is by this clause obliged to consult with the Cabinet . . .[121]

(viii) Extracts from the Bahama Islands (Constitution) Order in Council, 1963. (S.I. 2084/1963.)

Allocation of portfolios to Ministers

73(1) Subject to the provisions of this Constitution, the Governor, acting in accordance with the advice of the Premier, may by directions in writing charge any Minister with responsibility for any matter or any department of government and designate the style by which any Minister so charged shall be known.

(2) In pursuance of the powers conferred by subsection (1) of this section, the Governor may direct that a Minister shall be assisted in the exercise of his responsibilities for any matter or department of government by a Board consisting of such persons as the Governor, acting in accordance with the advice of the Premier, may appoint.

120 These powers are the power to (1) appoint a Deputy Governor, (2) dispose of Crown Lands, (3) appoint judges, (4) make regulations for the discipline of the public service, (5) grant pardon in criminal cases.
121 This still allows the Governor not to consult the Cabinet where there would be material prejudice to the Imperial service, and where matters are either trivial or too urgent for consultation.

(3) Any such Board as is referred to in subsection (2) of this section shall have such consultative and administrative functions as may be assigned to it by a law of the Legislature or by directions of the Minister concerned but, in exercising any functions so assigned to it, the Board shall be subject to the directions of the Minister, who shall remain responsible to the Cabinet and the Legislature for all the business of the Board.

(4) Nothing in this section shall empower the Governor to confer on any Minister authority to exercise any power or discharge any duty that is conferred or imposed by this Constitution or any other law on the Governor or any person or authority other than a Minister.

(5) Without prejudice to the generality of subsection (4) of this section, except for the purpose of submitting questions relating to such matters to the Cabinet and conducting government business relating to such matters in either chamber of the Legislature and subject to the provisions of section 74 of this Constitution a Minister shall not be charged with responsibility for –

(a) the discharge by the courts of the Bahama Islands of their judicial functions;

(b) the initiation, conduct and discontinuance of criminal proceedings;

(c) the audit of the accounts of the Bahama Islands;

(d) the making of appointments (including appointments on promotion, appointments on transfer and the confirmation of appointments) to offices in the public service, the removal or disciplinary control (including the withholding of increments of salary) of persons holding or acting in such offices and the grant of any benefits in relation to pensions and gratuities in pursuance of section 109 of this Constitution; or

(e) the exercise of the Prerogative of Mercy.

(6) For the purposes of subsection (5) (d) of this section, the office of a judge of the Supreme Court or a member of the personal staff of the Governor shall be deemed to be an office in the public service.

(7) Subject to the provisions of this Constitution, where any Minister has been charged with the responsibility for a matter or department of government in pursuance of this section, he shall exercise general direction and control over the work relating to that matter and over that department and, subject to such direction and control by the Minister, the work and the department shall be under the supervision of a public officer appointed for the purpose:

Provided that for the purposes of this subsection a public officer may be appointed to supervise the work relating to several matters and departments.

74(1) The Governor, acting in his discretion, shall be responsible for the following matters:-

(a) external affairs, that is to say, such matters relating to external affairs as may be specified in any Instructions given to him by Her Majesty under Her Majesty's Sign Manual and Signet or through a Secretary of State;

(b) defence, including the armed forces;

(c) internal security; and

(d) all matters relating to the Police Force;

Provided that the Governor shall keep the Cabinet informed of any matters relating to external affairs or defence which may involve the economic or financial interests of the Bahama Islands or the enactment of laws by the Legislature of the Bahama Islands.

(2) The Governor, acting in his discretion, may from time to time –

(a) designate a Minister with whom he may consult on matters relating to the Police Force; or

(b) delegate, with the prior approval of a Secretary of State, to a Minister designated by him after consultation with the Premier such responsibility for matters relating to internal security and the Police Force as the Governor may think fit upon such conditions as he may impose.

75 The Governor shall, for the due exercise of his functions, be entitled to all papers which are available to the Cabinet and to any other information concerning the government of the Bahama Islands which is so available.

(ix) Extracts from the British Honduras Letters Patent, dated 1st January 1964.
(Instruments not statutory instruments, appendix to S.I./1964.)

15 The Governor, acting in his discretion, shall be responsible for the following matters –

(a) external affairs;

(b) defence (including the armed forces);

(c) internal security; and

(d) the terms and conditions of service (including leave and passages) of public officers.

16(1) In the exercise of his functions under these Our Letters or any other law the Governor shall obtain, and act in accordance with, the advice of the Cabinet or a Minister acting under the general authority of the Cabinet.

(2) The provisions of paragraph (1) of this Article shall not apply in relation to the exercise by the Governor of –

(a) any function conferred upon him by these Our Letters or any other law that is expressed to be exercisable by him in his discretion or in accordance with the advice of or after consultation with any person or authority other than the Cabinet; or

(b) any function conferred on him by these Our Letters or any other law with respect to any matter specified in Article 15 of these Our Letters (which relates to matters for which the Governor has special responsibilitics); or

(c) any function conferred upon him by any law other than these Our Letters that he is authorized by such law to exercise without obtaining the advice of the Cabinet.

(3) Where the Governor is directed by these Our Letters or any other law to exercise any function after consultation with any person or authority other than the Cabinet, he shall not be obliged to exercise that function in accordance with the advice of that person or authority.

(4) Where the Governor has obtained the advice of the Cabinet or a Minister in pursuance of paragraph (1) of this Article, he may act otherwise than in accordance with that advice if in his judgement it is necessary or expedient so to act for the purposes of a matter for which the Governor is responsible under Article 15 of these Our Letters.

(5) Where any function is vested by any law other than these Our Letters in any person or authority other than the Governor (not being a court of law), the Governor may exercise that function in such circumstances and to such extent as he may consider necessary or expedient for the purposes of any matter that is specified in Article 15 of these Our Letters.

(6) Where the Governor is required by these Our Letters or any other law to act in accordance with the advice of or after consultation with any person or authority the question whether he has in any matter so acted shall not be called in question in any court of law . . .

24(1) There shall be an External Affairs Committee which shall consist of –

(a) the Governor as Chairman;

(b) the Premier; and

(c) such other Ministers as the Governor, acting in accordance with the advice of the Premier, may from time to time appoint.

(2) Any appointment made under sub-paragraph (c) of the last foregoing paragraph may be revoked by the Governor acting in accordance with the advice of the Premier.

(3) The Committee shall be a consultative Committee on external affairs, and the Governor may consult the Committee on any matter relating to external affairs, but he shall not be obliged to act in accordance with the advice of the Committee.

(4) The Governor may summon a meeting of the Council whenever he considers it desirable to do so or whenever the Premier requests that a meeting shall be held.

(5) The Council may act notwithstanding any vacancy in its membership and its proceedings shall not be invalidated by the presence or participation of any person not entitled to be present at or to participate in those proceedings.

(6) Subject to the provisions of this Article the Council may regulate its own procedure.

25(1) There shall be a Security Council which shall consist of the Governor and such other members as the Governor, acting in his discretion, may from time to time appoint.

(2) The Governor, acting in his discretion, may revoke any appointment made under the last foregoing paragraph.

(3) The function of the Security Council shall be to advise the Governor, at his request, on the discharge of his responsibilities for internal security under Article 15 of these Our Letters.

(4) The Council shall not be summoned except by the authority of the Governor who shall as far as practicable attend and preside at all meetings of the Council.

(5) The Governor may summon a meeting of the Council whenever he considers it desirable to do so or whenever the Premier requests that a meeting shall be held.

(6) The Governor may consult the Council on any matter if he considers such consultation will assist him in the discharge of his responsibilities for internal security under Article 15 of these Our Letters, but he shall not be obliged to consult the Council before discharging his responsibilities as aforesaid, and when he does consult the Council he shall not be obliged to act in accordance with its advice.

(7) The Council may act notwithstanding any vacancy in its membership and its proceedings shall not be invalidated by the presence or participation of any person not entitled to be present at or to participate in those proceedings.

(8) Subject to the provisions of this Article the Council may regulate its own procedure . . .

G. Full internal self-government.

(i) Extracts from the Report of the Select Committee appointed by the House of Representatives on the 31st of October 1956, to prepare proposals for a constitution providing for complete self-government in all internal affairs to be submitted for approval to the Rt. Hon. Secretary of State for the Colonies. (Minutes of the Jamaica House of Representatives, 1957. Appendix No. XLI.)

On the 31st day of October, 1956 by Resolution of the House of Representatives, a Select Committee . . . was appointed to prepare proposals for a Constitution providing for complete self-Government in all internal affairs and to report to the House in order that their proposals as accepted by the House may be referred to the Right Honourable the Secretary of State for the Colonies.

2 On the 14th day of March, 1957, His Excellency the Governor in his address to the Legislature on the opening of the Spring Session of 1957 made certain proposals for immediate constitutional changes . . .

The actual proposals made are as set out in Annexure I to this report.

3 On the 25th day of April, 1957, the House of Representatives unanimously approved of a Resolution welcoming these proposals and pursuant to this resolution, the proposals were brought before the Committee which had been established in accordance with the resolution mentioned in paragraph 1 . . .

5 The Committee at the commencement of its deliberations decided to consider the Governor's proposals under two main heads:-

(a) the implications of the proposals themselves; and

(b) the proposals in relation to the Interim Report of the Select Committee of the Jamaica House of Representatives appointed by Resolution of the House of Representatives on the 22nd July, 1952, which was presented to the House, debated and approved in September, 1954. This Interim Report is attached as Annexure II.

6 The examination of the Interim Report of 1954 and a comparison of that Report with the Governor's proposals disclosed the following points which were dealt with as is hereinafter set out:-

(a) The Committee noted that the proposals made by the Governor did not deal with the establishment of a Ministry of Justice, the establishment of a Judicial Service Commission and the Public Service generally, all these being matters dealt with in the Report of 1954.

(b) It was agreed in regard to the establishment of a Ministry of Justice, that this was not necessary at this stage. It was agreed, however, that the subject "The Administration of Justice" should be assigned to some appropriate Minister, probably the Minister of Home Affairs, together with all the Departments and matters arising thereunder. It was noted that the drafting of legislation a matter referred to in the 1954 report, was now being dealt with by an established Drafting Department and that there was a special Legislation Committee of Executive Council with particular duties in regard to this matter.

(c) In regard to the Judicial Service, the Committee was advised that there were proposals for the early passing of a Law to provide for the creation of a Judicial Services Commission.

(d) As to the Public Service generally, it was agreed that the existing arrangements should not at present be altered in any way.

7 All the other matters dealt with in the 1954 report were accepted as covered directly, or by necessary implication, by the Governor's proposals and the following conclusions were reached:-

(a) That there should be a Council of Ministers to take the place of the existing Executive Council and that the Council of Ministers should ordinarily be presided over by the Chief Minister but that the Governor should have the right to summon special meetings of the Council, on which occasions he would preside.

(b) That the Council would consist of 10 Ministers and two Members of the Legislative Council[122] to be appointed by the Governor on the recommendation of the Chief Minister.

(c) That there should be a Minister of Home Affairs and that the Ministry of Home Affairs should, in addition to such other subjects as may be assigned, have general responsibility for the maintenance of order, the Police Force, Security, Immigration and Emigration.

(d) That all officials should be removed from the Legislative Council save the Attorney General.

(e) That the title of the Colonial Secretary should be changed to that of Chief Secretary.

(f) That the Members of the Legislative Council who are Members of the Council of Ministers should have the style and rank of Ministers without portfolio and should be responsible in the Legislative Council for presentation of Government business in that Council.

(g) That the new constitutional proposals should include a special provision in relation to the Attorney General as follows:-

122 Note that this was the name of the second chamber of the Jamaican legislature at the time.

"That the Attorney General shall in Jamaica act at his sole discretion in all matters wherein by Constitutional usage in England he acts at such discretion."

8 At the meeting on the 4th of June the Unofficial Members of the Honourable Legislative Council . . . agreed with all the proposals as set out in the said paragraph.

9 As to the provision in paragraph 7 (g), it was noted that in addition to the Constitutional right which the Attorney General had to act at his discretion in regard to the initiation and conduct of criminal proceedings he had also a constitutional right to act at his discretion in regard to permitting his name to be used in proceedings brought against statutory bodies or public officers at the relation of private individuals.

It was considered that it might be sufficient to include in the Constitution a provision that responsibility for the initiation and conduct of criminal proceedings should not be assigned to a Minister but should vest in the Attorney General.

10 Your Committee has the honour to recommend that the existing Constitution of Jamaica be amended in accordance with the provisions of paragraph 7 hereof.[123]

11 The representatives of the Parliamentary Minority to wit –
Sir Alexander Bustamante, Mr. D.B. Sangster and Mr. E.L. Allen accept this report subject to the reservation set out below –

RESERVATION

The representatives of the Parliamentary Minority . . . are of opinion that the name "Executive Council" should remain unchanged and that the Members of the Legislative Council who are members of the reconstituted Executive Council should not have the style and rank of Ministers without portfolio.

ANNEXURE I
EXTRACT FROM GOVERNOR'S ADDRESS TO LEGISLATURE

And now I have a practical suggestion to make: It will take some time to review and revise all the provisions of the existing constitution, and to do the complete job of which I spoke last year. Moreover I think that we are all agreed that when the new constitution is introduced there should be a larger House of Representatives and that therefore the bringing into effect of a complete new constitution must await the next Jamaican General Election.

123 The recommendations were accepted and introduced into the Constitution of Jamaica in 1957.

Although the introduction of the complete new constitution must wait till then the practical proposal which I wish to put forward, about which I have already spoken to the Chief Minister and the Leader of the Opposition, is this: I propose that in advance of the full constitutional changes we should during this session of the Legislature and during this year take another important step in the development of our system of representative government. I propose that that step should be fully in accordance with the constitutional purposes which both parties have publicly supported.

My suggestion is that this year the Executive Council should be reconstituted as a Council of Ministers, and that apart from the Chief Minister, the Council should have eleven members. Of that number eight or nine would be Members of the House of Representatives appointed by the Governor on the recommendation of the Chief Minister, and not less than two or more than three would be Members of the Legislative Council also appointed by the Governor on the recommendation of the Chief Minister. That would give a Council of twelve in all to replace the existing Council of fifteen. Moreover I propose that the Chief Minister should normally call meetings of the new Council and that he should normally preside over it.

These proposals would involve the withdrawal of the Governor and the Colonial Secretary and the Financial Secretary and the Attorney General from the Executive Council, and I also propose that the Colonial Secretary and the Financial Secretary should withdraw from the Legislative Council though I think that it would be well for the Attorney General to remain a Member of the Legislative Council. Two unofficial Members would be added to the Legislative Council to replace the Colonial Secretary and the Financial Secretary.

Although the Chief Minister would normally call meetings of the Executive Council and preside over it, I propose that the Governor should have the right to call a meeting of the Council at his discretion and that when the Governor is present in the Council he should preside. I further propose that the title of the Colonial Secretary should be changed at the same time to that of Chief Secretary.

(ii) Extracts from the Report of the Select Committee of the House of Representatives on proposals for constitutional reform, 1958. (Minutes of the Jamaica House of Representatives, 1958. Appendix XII.)

6 The major points which fell to be dealt with are as follows:-

(d) *The Civil Service Commission and the Privy Council*

The extent to which the Civil Service Commission should be responsible for the appointment and promotion of Civil Servants and the Governor's power in relation thereto, and questions relating to the

Privy Council and its responsibility in regard to disciplinary matters affecting the Civil Service . . .

9 Your Committee proposes that a new Constitution be made for Jamaica using the existing Constitution as a basis and incorporating the following provisions:-

Executive

(xi) The Council of Ministers shall be known as the Cabinet. The number of Ministers shall not exceed 15, of whom not more than 12 shall be members of the House of Representatives . . .

The Civil Service

(xxii) The Civil Service Commission shall be responsible for the appointment and promotion of Civil Servants, the Governor acting on the recommendation of the Commission but having the right to refer a recommendation once only for further consideration.

The Privy Council

(xxiii) The Privy Council shall be retained and in addition to its duties of being advisory to the Governor in matters relating to the exercise of the Royal Prerogative, shall continue to be responsible for disciplinary matters relating to the Civil Service.

(iii) Extracts from the Jamaica (Constitution) Order in Council, 1959.[124] *(S.I. 862/1959.)*

PART III – THE GOVERNOR

9 (1) The Governor shall consult with the Cabinet (or a Minister acting under the general authority of the Cabinet) in the exercise of all his functions other than –

(a) any function which is expressed (in whatever terms) to be exercisable by him on or in accordance with the recommendation or advice of, or with the concurrence of, or after consultation with, any person or authority other than the Cabinet; and

(b) any function which is expressed (in whatever terms) to be exercisable by him in his discretion.

124 Full internal self-government was granted to Barbados, British Guiana, Trinidad and Tobago in 1961, and to the Bahama Islands in 1969. British Honduras was granted a large measure of internal self-government in 1964 but certain powers over finance and security were retained by the Governor.

Chapter 6 deals with the peculiar constitutional arrangements of associate statehood given to Antigua, St Kitts/Nevis/Anguilla, Grenada, Dominica, and St Lucia in 1968, and St Vincent in 1969.

(2) The Governor shall act in accordance with the advice of the Cabinet (or of the said Minister) in the exercise of any function in the exercise of which he is obliged by this section to consult with the Cabinet (or the said Minister).

(3) Where the Governor is directed by this Order to exercise any function on the recommendation of any person or authority, he shall exercise that function in accordance with such recommendation:

Provided that –

(a) before he acts in accordance therewith, he may, in his discretion, once refer that recommendation back for reconsideration by the person or authority concerned; and

(b) if that person or authority, having reconsidered the original recommendation under the preceding paragraph, substitutes therefor a different recommendation, the provisions of this subsection shall apply to that different recommendation as they apply to the original recommendation.

(4) Where the Governor is directed by this Order to exercise any function after consultation with any person or authority other than the Cabinet (or a Minister acting under the general authority of the Cabinet), he shall not be obliged to exercise that function in accordance with the advice of that person or authority.

(5) Where the Governor is directed by this Order to exercise any function in accordance with the recommendation or advice of, or with the concurrence of, or after consultation with, any person or authority, the question whether he has so exercised that function shall not be enquired into in any court.

(6) Subject to any instructions which Her Majesty may from time to time see fit to give him, the Governor shall, in the exercise of any function conferred on him by this Order which is expressed (in whatever terms) to be exercisable by him in his discretion, act, so far as may be, in accordance with any constitutional conventions applicable to the exercise of any similar function by Her Majesty in the United Kingdom:

Provided that the question whether he has so exercised that function shall not be enquired into in any court.

10 Subject to the provisions of any law for the time being in force in Jamaica and to any instructions from time to time given to him by Her Majesty, the Governor, in Her Majesty's name and on Her Majesty's behalf, may, under the Broad Seal, make grants and dispositions of land or other immovable property in Jamaica which may lawfully be granted or disposed of by Her Majesty.

11 The Governor may, in the name of and on behalf of Her Majesty, constitute such offices for Jamaica as may lawfully be constituted by Her Majesty, and, subject to the provisions of this Order and of any other law for the time

being in force in Jamaica, the Governor may likewise –

(a) make appointments, to be held during pleasure, to any office so constituted; and

(b) dismiss any person so appointed or take such other disciplinary action in relation to him as the Governor may think fit.

12(1) The Governor may, in Her Majesty's name and on Her Majesty's behalf –

(a) grant to any person concerned in or convicted of any offence to which this section applies a pardon, either free or subject to lawful conditions; or

(b) grant to any person a respite, either indefinite or for a specified period, from the execution of any sentence passed on that person for such an offence; or

(c) substitute a less severe form of punishment for that imposed by any sentence for such an offence; or

(d) remit the whole or any part of any sentence passed for such an offence or any penalty or forfeiture otherwise due to Her Majesty on account of such an offence.

(2) The offences to which this section applies are offences against any law in force in Jamaica other than a law of the Federal Legislature.

(3) In the exercise of the powers conferred on him by this section, the Governor shall act in his discretion.

13 The Governor shall keep and use the Broad Seal for sealing all things whatsoever that shall pass the said Seal.

PART V – THE EXECUTIVE

46(1) The executive authority of Jamaica shall be vested in Her Majesty.

(2) Subject to the provisions of this Order, the executive authority of Jamaica may be exercised on behalf of Her Majesty by the Governor, but nothing in this subsection shall operate so as to prejudice the provisions of any law for the time being in force in Jamaica whereby functions are conferred on persons or authorities other than the Governor.

47(1) There shall be in and for Jamaica a Cabinet which shall consist of the Premier and not less than eleven other Ministers appointed in accordance with the provisions of the following section.[125]

(2) The Cabinet shall be the principal instrument of policy and shall be charged with the general direction and control of the Government of Jamaica

125 The provisions of this Order in Council with regard to the appointment of Ministers, including the Premier, and their tenure of office were those already established in Jamaica and followed the British conventions.

and shall be collectively responsible therefor to the Legislature . . .

53 The Premier shall, so far as is practicable, attend and preside at all meetings of the Cabinet and in his absence such other Minister shall preside as the Premier shall appoint:

Provided that whenever the Governor is present at any meeting of the Cabinet which he has summoned under the provisions of the following section, he shall preside.[126]

54 The Governor, acting in his discretion may summon a special meeting of the Cabinet whenever he thinks fit, but, subject thereto, the Cabinet shall not be summoned except by the authority of the Premier.[126]

55 The Governor shall, for the due exercise of his functions, be entitled to all papers which are available to the Cabinet and to any other information concerning the government of Jamaica which is so available . . .

59(1) Subject to the provisions of subsection (3) of section 56 of this Order, where any Minister has been charged with the responsibility for a subject or department of government, he shall exercise general direction and control over the work relating to that subject and over that department; and, subject as aforesaid and to such direction and control, the aforesaid work and the department shall be under the supervision of a Permanent Secretary appointed in accordance with the provisions of section 78 of this Order.

(2) A person may be a Permanent Secretary in respect of more than one department of government.

(3) The office of Financial Secretary is hereby constituted and, for the purposes of this section, he shall be deemed to be a Permanent Secretary.

60(1) There shall be in and for Jamaica a Privy Council which shall consist of such persons appointed in such manner as Her Majesty may direct by instructions given to the Governor from time to time under Her Sign Manual and Signet or through a Secretary of State . . . [127]

61(1) There shall be in and for Jamaica an Attorney-General who shall be appointed by the Governor, acting in his discretion . . . [128]

126 These provisions illustrate the line of distinction between full internal self-government and independence.

127 The function of the Privy Council was to advise the Governor in the exercise of the prerogative of pardon.

128 On independence the Attorney-General's would become a political office, but so long as it remained an official appointment the officer was protected in his office, his salary being paid from the Consolidated Fund and security of tenure being well protected.

(3) The Attorney-General shall receive such salary and allowances as may from time to time be prescribed by or under any law or by a resolution of the House of Representatives or by the Governor: . . .

CHAPTER 5

FEDERATION AND FEDERAL EXPERIMENTS

PART I

EARLY MOVES TOWARDS UNION 1921-1946

A The West Indian Conference

(i) Extracts from the Despatch from the Secretary of State for the Colonies to the Governors of the West Indian Colonies, dated 14th October 1921. (Leeward Islands Gazette, 1921, p. 269.)

Sir,

I have the honour to transmit to you, for your consideration, the accompanying copy of a letter from Sir Edward Davson regarding proposals for the establishment of a Conference or Council of the West Indian Colonies. . . .

3 If these proposals commend themselves substantially to local public opinion I shall be happy to give every assistance in my power in modifying them to meet any views which the Colonies may express in the matter. . . .

(ii) Letter and Memorandum from Sir Edward Davson, Chairman of the Associated West Indian Chambers of Conference, to the Under-Secretary of State for the Colonies, dated 4th August 1921. (Leeward Islands Gazette, 1921, pp. 269-70.)

On the 22nd September, 1920, I addressed a letter to you with reference to the closer union of the West Indian Colonies and I laid before you certain proposals towards that end . . .

Resolutions

I . . . enclose Regulations passed by the following bodies:–

The Jamaica Imperial Association, The Chambers of Commerce of British Guiana, Trinidad and British Honduras, the Agricultural and Commercial Societies of St. Vincent and Montserrat; other bodies have expressed the view that they did not feel competent to give a detailed expression of opinion of the scheme at the present juncture.

A perusal of the Resolutions and of the Press cuttings will indicate that the principle of the scheme has met with almost general approval; I may add that I have received many private expressions of opinion in this sense . . .

Memorandum Regarding the formation of a
Central West Indian Body.

It will be remembered that my original scheme was based on the fact that conferences held from time to time in the West Indies to consider matters of common interest, had without exception, proved successful: my proposals briefly, were that these conferences should be given a definite status and that over them should be placed a Central Body or Council to consider and deal with Resolutions passed by them. I also proposed that a permanent Secretariat should be established in the West Indies in connection therewith.

While West Indian opinion is apparently in favour of the formation of a Central Body it is also in favour of such a Body including representation of the people rather than being entirely official as was at first proposed. Indeed, it has been suggested that its formation is closely connected with the question of popular representation and that its members should as far as possible be elected representatives. It must be plain, however, that the granting or extension of representative Government in those Colonies which are desirous of it, must be a matter of time and the aim should be so to constitute the Central Body as to give popular representation proportionate to the degree to which any Colony has acquired it while also giving some representation to those others which remain under Crown Colony Government.

I propose therefore that a Central West Indian Council should be formed, to be composed of both official and non-official members representing and appointed by each individual Colony together with a Permanent Secretariat. This Council would meet at fixed intervals to consider and make recommendations on matters of common interest and to deal as far as possible, with resolutions from the Departmental Conferences (which would be systematized into standing committees for matters coming within their scope) thus becoming a body capable of expressing a united West Indian opinion . . .

(iii) Extracts from the Report of the Preliminary West Indian Conference held in London, May-June 1926 (Verbatim Minutes). Crown Agents for the Colonies, London, 1926.)

The Secretary of State: . . .

This is not a Colonial Office Conference, but a West Indian Conference; one in which the initiative has come, not from the Secretary of State, but from the Colonial Legislators themselves, and it is in pursuance of their expressed wishes that the arrangements for this Conference have been made . . . . All the same, as you know, the main reason why this Conference is met in London is not in order to be near the Colonial Office, but because, owing to the present very inadequate state of communications between the West Indian Colonies, London is still the most convenient centre and rendezvous in the West Indies . . .

The problem is now to secure unity of action towards the outside world, and the most effective co-operation for the common good between nations and communities which share a common loyalty, common tradition and common aspirations, but which, at the same time, are widely sundered by the seas, and each one of them keenly jealous of its own individuality and of its constitutional status, and suspicious of anything that may seem to threaten the slightest interference with the free and independent play of its national or local life . . . . Those who first approached the problem, following the natural constitutional logic of the position, and influenced by the success of the confederations of the American Colonies after the Revolution, and of the British North American Colonies when they created the Dominion of Canada, looked at first towards something in the nature of a Federal solution. They found that they were not only up against great practical difficulties, but also against something even stronger, a deep-rooted instinct which refused to consider that particular form of solution . . . We have found in practice an alternative method, the method of free co-operation in close and frequent personal consultation. That system of Imperial Conferences, which began at first as a mere meeting on occasions of ceremony and Imperial rejoicing, has developed into a real, though informal and infinitely flexible organ of co-operation, which has developed many branch organisations, and which is still capable of great development in the future. . . .

Now your history in the West Indies has followed very much the same course. Those who first studied the problem of enabling the West Indies, with their large population, with their great potential wealth, to work together more effectively instead of each living in a small watertight compartment, at first were inclined to think that the problem could be solved by some definite scheme of federation, and many . . . did succeed in bringing before the West Indian Colonies the need for effective closer action. In later years, the West

Indies have come to realise, I think, as we have realised in the wider field of the Empire, that there is an alternative method, and that this alternative method, the method of closer conference, more frequent and regular conference, beginning with *ad hoc* Conferences, Conferences of Chambers of Commerce, Conferences on Customs, Conferences on Education and on Medical affairs, has shown in practice that the method is capable of expansion and development to the great benefit of the West Indies. . . . That movement, I think, may be said to have taken its first definite shape in 1920, and to have received its real impetus towards a successful conclusion when, three years ago, the Legislature of Jamaica definitely recommended that a Standing Conference for the West Indies should be created. . . .

Sir EDWARD DAVSON: . . . This, then is why we are assembled here together, to see whether we cannot create from our experience in the past something permanent which will enable us in the future to foster that spirit of co-operation which we have desired to create in the past. . . . We naturally take as our example the far higher example of the Imperial Conferences because there, by the wit and wisdom of our people we have created a body which is an instrument for the most effective co-operation, and the most effective consultation which at present the Empire is capable of producing; therefore when we consult together upon these matters we shall be bearing in mind our relation, even if it be in a small way, to that greater Imperial Conference. . . .

Mr. H.B.G. AUSTIN (Barbados): . . . Four years ago, when the idea of a Conference such as we are assemblied at to-day, was first suggested in my Colony, the Legislature negatived the idea by a very considerable majority . . . . but as the years went on, and the benefits that accrued from other Conferences, the Conferences at Ottawa, the Conference of the Associated West Indies Chambers of Commerce, the Conference in connection with Customs affairs and with legal matters, came to be realised, the point of view changed somewhat, and the Legislature on this occasion decided that they should have representatives at this Conference. . . .

(iv) Extracts from the Report of the West Indian Conference. (Cmnd. 2672/1926.)

2. *Origin of the Idea of a Standing Conference:–* We think it well, in the first place, to summarise as shortly as possible the history of the proposal which we have been called upon to consider. During the last twenty years the conference system has been steadily growing among us. There have been agricultural, customs, education, medical and quarantine conferences and a conference of Law Officers on the formation of a West Indian Court of Appeal; there have been the Ottawa conferences of 1912, 1920 and 1925; and there have been also the conferences of the Associated West Indian Chambers of Commerce. On the whole these conferences have been most successful.

Among their achievements are the Quarantine Convention, the West Indian Court of Appeal and the three important trade agreements with Canada. Yet it can hardly be denied that they have indicated rather than exhausted the possibilities of consultation and co-operation and that much more might have been accomplished if there had been a central authority responsible for promoting, extending and following up the work of these conferences.

The first step in the direction of the creation of a body of this kind was taken by the Jamaica Imperial Association, which forwarded to the meeting of the Associated Chambers of Commerce of the West Indies held in 1920 at Barbados a resolution advocating the establishment of a consultative body, consisting of representatives of the Government and Legislature of each Colony and of each Chamber of Commerce, to advise upon common affairs. The idea was discussed, but the proposed composition of the body appeared open to objection and the resolution actually passed by the Associated Chambers confined itself to recommending the system of conference with a view to the development of common interests. On the basis of that resolution and of the sentiments expressed at the Barbados meeting, Sir Edward Davson, then President of the Associated Chambers, drew up a scheme for a central council which was widely discussed in the West Indies and subsequently amended by its author in the light of the detailed criticism which it received. This amended scheme, providing for a Central Conference, composed of officials and unofficials, with a permanent secretariat, and meeting at fixed intervals to make recommendations on matters of common interest, was submitted to the Secretary of State, who referred it to the various Governments, intimating that if these proposals commended themselves to local public opinion he would be glad to arrange for a preliminary conference on them to take place. The majority of the replies received were favourable, but there were certain important exceptions, and the scheme, though unanimously approved in 1922 by the Associated Chambers of Commerce, remained in abeyance until it was revived by a resolution passed in 1923 by the Legislature of Jamaica, expressing willingness to consider sympathetically any proposal that could be made for establishing a Standing Conference. This resolution was transmitted to the Governments previously consulted and met with so favourable a reception that you, Sir, in pursuance of the expressed wishes of the majority of the Legislatures, issued an invitation to the various Governments, which was unanimously accepted, to send representatives to a preliminary conference for the purpose specified in the preceding paragraph.

3 *General Principle of the Establishment of a Standing Conference:-* The first question which we have to consider is that of the general principle of the establishment of a Standing Conference, as a purely advisory body, with no executive powers, meeting at regular intervals and performing for its consti-

tuents functions analogous to those with the Imperial Conference performs for the Empire as a whole. From the establishment of such a body it appears to us that nothing but good can ensue. Without in any way impairing the autonomy of its members it would provide them with a flexible, well understood and eminently British piece of political machinery for adjusting their own internal and inter-colonial relations, consulting on their similar domestic problems, and exerting within the councils of the Empire a weight and influence, commensurate with their collective populations, wealth and resources, which as isolated units they do not and cannot hope to command. In spite of the distances that separate us and the diverse conditions that prevail, we do not think that it will be disputed that we have many interests in common; that common interests should lead to concerted policy and action; and that for this purpose we require not merely some more adequate and effective means of co-operation than is provided by the present system of occasional departmental and *ad hoc* conferences, but a body, as has been said, "capable of putting forward a definite West Indian opinion for the information of the Imperial Government (which has till now been lacking to the great loss of these Colonies) and possibly entitling it in due course to a voice in the deliberations of the Imperial Conference, thus at length raising the West Indies to their proper status in the Empire." . . .

5(b) *Selection:* Since the implementing of the recommendations of the Conference will depend on their approval by the Legislatures, it is most important that representatives should be in a position to explain, and if necessary, defend these recommendations before the bodies responsible for deciding whether to carry them into effect. For this reason, though we consider that the selection of representatives is essentially a domestic matter, which should be left to the Government of each Colony, in consultation with the Legislature, we recommend that representatives should be, as far as possible, members of their respective Legislatures or Governments. . . .

7. *Subjects Falling within the Scope of the Conference:* . . . We have prepared the following list of subjects which might be regarded as falling within the scope of the Conference:-

Agriculture, including Veterinary matters and regulations dealing with animal and plant diseases.

Aviation.

Banking, – Currency and note issues.

Civil Service.

Commercial, including Imperial Preferences and Trade Agreements;
Shipping Laws and Regulations;
Port and Harbour Dues and Regulations;
Steamship Services;

Cable and Wireless Services.
Customs, including Tariff questions and Customs Regulations.
Defence.
Education, and the consideration of the establishment of a West Indian University.
Imperial College of Tropical Agriculture
Law, with special reference to uniformity of Laws as far as practicable, and to the operation of the West Indian Court of Appeal.
Marketing of Produce.
Medical, including Administration;
Hygiene;
Sanitation;
Quarantine Laws against human disease.
Police.
Public Utility Services.
Tourist Trade.
Trade Representation.
And All Questions, administrative and other, affecting the interests of the Colonies, and their relations with other parts of the Empire.

As the last words indicate, this list is intended to be illustrative, and not exhaustive. . . .

13 *Relation to Imperial Conference:* . . . If the Standing Conference is successfully established it will represent eight or perhaps more of the oldest Colonies in the Empire, with a total population of over two millions, a total annual trade of nearly forty million pounds, and great undeveloped resources. We do not claim the same status as the self-governing Dominions, but we nevertheless venture to suggest that the West Indies as a whole might be allowed to have separate representation and to speak with their own voice on matters concerning their welfare and their relations with other parts of the Empire at the great imperial prototype, which in our narrower sphere we are endeavouring to imitate, where the home government and the governments of the self-governing Dominions discuss the common affairs of the Empire as a whole.

(v) Extracts from Report of the West Indies Conference held in Barbados, January-February 1929. (Crown Agents for the Colonies, London, 1929.)

The Governor of Barbados: The very existence of this Conference implies contemplation of the ideas of unified action. The time has gone when the conception of community interest or co-ordination of effort in the West Indies brought with it the fear that such things meant necessarily abandonment of our independence and sacrifice of our right to individual management of our own affairs. The wisdom of Providence has separated us from each other by the estranging sea, and this, as well as our diverse conditions of climate, soil and people, present *[sic]* obvious obstacles to abolition or absorption of local systems of administration. But time has brought with it realization of the practical disadvantages of self-centred isolation. The development of communications within the past few years has resulted in what is virtually a shrinkage in the size of the world. Nations and communities hitherto strangers to each other except in name, are now in close contact, and there have followed combinations of interest and competition in trade of a nature and intensity beyond anything in our previous experience. From all sides we are met by the complaint of the difficulty in maintaining profitable trade relations and – what is almost more important – efficient communication.

Our position is a remarkable one – perhaps unique in the world's history. The British West Indies consist of certain large and prosperous communities with a chain of smaller, less developed and less wealthy members. From the fact that all are represented here to-day, it seems fair to assume that the attitude of the larger communities is this: "We can" – they may be taken as saying – "stand, we believe, by ourselves: but apart from our natural desire to support the weaker members of the group to which we belong we believe we can benefit ourselves, as well as you, if we join with you in forming, for marketing purposes, one trade unit." . . .

Sir Edward Davson: There was a time when these Colonies of the West Indies thought that all that was required was that they should concentrate their minds on their own affairs, and to further their own particular interests for the benefit of their own particular communities; and at that time they were apt to regard the affairs of their neighbouring Colonies with a spirit of – shall I say? – indifference. But times changed, and it was gradually realised as a spontaneous growth amongst each of them that there was much benefit to be derived by keeping in close touch with their neighbours, by establishing some form of co-operation; by considering questions of mutual interest together, and, generally, by endeavouring to combine where combination would be effective. And so we find, gradually, a system growing up of conferences on this or that subject, and of delegates meeting together from the different Colonies to consider these questions and reporting to their Governments. That was no scheme imposed from outside. That was not the work of any one man. It was simply an effort of the West Indies by their own wit and wisdom to devise some means of grappling with the problems with which they were gradually being faced. But even that was not sufficient. It was felt that these Conferences in their way were disconnected and haphazard, and that something was needed to regularise them; that something was needed to improve their status.

And so we find the institution of this London Conference to consider what can be done. The London Conference has, I think, rightly decided that the course selected by these people themselves was the right course, and that the system of Conferences should be encouraged and given official status, and they took as their model in this respect the Imperial Conference – that just as the Imperial Conference functions for the whole of the Empire as a consultative body, so it held the idea that the West Indies Conference should be a replica, and it should, on the same lines, function for the West Indies. They should meet together, consult together, and recommend their decisions to their respective Governments. I emphasize that word "recommend", because neither in the greater nor in the lesser Conferences is there, nor can there be, any suggestion for the creation of any superstructure which is going to be put over the free and autonomous Governments. . . .

Mr. W.E.F. Jackson (Trinidad): . . . We are sometimes criticised in these Colonies (we have many critics inside and outside the Colonies), but we are sometimes criticised for a certain insularity of outlook in our separate communities, and even for inter-island jealousies and for a general lack of the spirit of co-operation. I think that criticism is totally undeserved, and springs from the total lack of appreciation of the true position of our islands and of the associated Colonies. We live in a period of amalgamations and confederations. We are quite accustomed in the lifetime of most of us to hear that this or that body of Provinces or States has united into a single entity. But these have been amalgamations or confederations in contiguous territories, and I think Your Excellency has made the suggestion that we should have to go back probably two thousand years to find a case of amalgamation or association in successful form of the islands of an archipelago. There is nobody who has any actual experience of its effects who does not know what a divider the ocean is, and therefore our presence to-day is a remarkable achievement of which I say quite frankly that we in the West Indies have every reason to be proud. If we cannot in a moment learn to produce many tunes on our new instrument that is no reason for discouragement. We have got to learn to play on it, and, naturally, it will take us a little time to do so, but I can think of no more hopeful augury that that we should meet here to-day in this ancient Colony, with its British history, ideals, and traditions, because it makes us feel that we are thoroughly at home.

Mr. T.A. Marryshow (Grenada): . . . Every West Indian should feel proud of the history of this island. It is glorious history, Sir, that at one time Barbados was even more English than the English. The Colony has a record of its own in unbroken attachment to the Throne. Time was when this Colony was determined and plucky enough to refuse recognition of the rule of Cromwell, and remained Royalist without any break or lapse. All down the line Barbados has maintained its great tradition. Now, Sir, to come to the question of the West Indies Conference, . . . a scheme was put before these Colonies which supplied provision for a large measure of unofficial representation. This Conference, therefore, is mainly a people's affair, and I think it points to something very substantial in the future. I feel firmly convinced that all the representatives of the various Colonies around this table are men who are prepared to work for the success of this Conference and the welfare of the West Indies. It is, as has been hinted, in its experimental stage. We are going to see what we can make of it, step by step, the urge being to fashion something that will stand for West Indian unity and West Indian solidarity. We sit around this table this morning as patriotic British people who believe in British institutions and who want to find the way of working for the greater West Indies of the future. Important West Indian history is, without doubt, in the making today. Undoubtedly a nation is rising, and may the wise men, the men of leadership, men of insight who have associated themselves with this Conference, rise to the call of the hour. This Conference must be no mere plaything of politics. It must not be a mechanical creation of official convenience. It must be something to make sense, appeal to those aspirations which we hold dear, and the measure of its inreach as an instrument capable of stirring our internal consciousness, and of helping us to realise our aspirations – the measures of its ability or inability to do those things must be the measure of its success of failure. Those aspirations should be fulfilled in the near future, and they are involved in the claim that these West Indian Colonies should be brought closer and closer together to be recognised as one component part of the Empire, and that the ancient West Indies should take their rightful place among nations of the King's Dominions. We must keep the ideal ever before our minds, for in the measure and in the proportion as we discover and consolidate avenues of approach to that great ideal – the ideal of a West Indian Dominion, to which our history and our resources entitle us – we are either true or false to our fathers of the past and to our children of the future.

B The consideration of some form of closer association – involving the Leeward Islands, the Windward Islands, Trinidad and Tobago, and occasionally Barbados.

(i) Extract from the Report of the Hon. E.F.L. Wood, M.P., on his visit to the West Indies and British Guiana, 1922. (Cmnd. 1679-1922.)

Subject, however, to the governing consideration that any change to work smoothly must be one that carries the willing assent of a great majority of the communities concerned, there is one suggestion, made to me on more than one occasion, that deserves attention. This is a proposal for the association in some form of the Windward Islands with Trinidad. The advocates of this view contend that considerable advantages would be likely to accrue from some such arrangement. It is urged that it would effect considerable financial savings for the smaller islands, and that in such a grouping under a single Governor, with some possible consequent administrative reorganisation, would be found the means of assisting the weaker Colonies to grade up their essential services. It is further maintained that, in the Windward Islands at least, such a change would not be unpopular. The present Windward federation. loose as it is, excites opposition in St. Lucia and St. Vincent, owing to the fact that it is based upon Grenada. The other Colonies see little justification for this distinction in favour of Grenada, which is one of themselves; and therefore the arrangement breeds dissatisfaction. There would, it is said, be less likelihood of similar feeling in the case of Trinidad, which they all regard somewhat in the light of an elder brother, and towards which they are already impelled by economic tendencies.

I do not profess to have adequate means of judging the weight of these arguments. Moreover, even if opinion in the Windward Islands was favourable, a conclusion on the general feasibility of the proposition must clearly depend principally upon the opinion of Trinidad, which would be the predominant partner in the firm. If Trinidad were willing to entertain the idea, it would certainly seem that the association might be of material advantage to the smaller Colonies, and Trinidad, for other reasons, might not be unwilling to assist in this particular contribution to the cause of West Indian unity. . . .

(ii) Extracts from the Address by the Governor of the Windward Islands to the Grenada Legislative Council. (Minutes of the Grenada Legislative Council, 3rd November, 1922 pp. 7-8)

As (Mr. Wood) states a step of this kind would not be taken by the Secretary of State unless he was convinced that it was the wish of the peoples of the Colonies by which such change would be affected, and it is with this object that I bring the matter before the Legislative Council today as I wish Honourable Members to consider the suggestion most carefully. I wish also all the public bodies in this Island to give their most careful consideration to this suggestion, the District Boards, the Agricultural and Commercial Society and the Chamber of Commerce, the Press, the last named whom I wish to express not only their views on the suggestion but also the views and criticisms of their readers . . . . You are all aware in the island of Grenada that there are three parties concerned, one which is opposed to it, another for it, and the third those who are quite indifferent. . . .

There is no doubt that there would be advantages in being associated with so important a colony as Trinidad. We might be able to establish a uniform Tariff, there might be the practicability of a uniform Customs Tariff and free trade between the Islands and . . . improved traffic communication between Trinidad and the Windward Islands Group.

Then again, as regards Administration, undoubtedly there would be advantages, the Windward Islands Group can hardly afford to pay for a thoroughly qualified Public Works Expert, one who can undertake large works in the islands. Each island can afford a man who can undertake maintenance works but if larger works were required and we were connected with Trinidad we could draw on them for the services of a properly qualified man. Then again, there was the amalgamation of the Medical Department, which is being urged from many quarters, then, also, the amalgamation of the Police Department and this I do consider would be very advantageous. The men for the Police Force would have the advantage of Training [sic] in Trinidad and this would ensure a better maintenance of discipline and in every respect we would have a more efficient Force than we possess at present. Then again the whole Defence Scheme of the islands should be worked from Trinidad. Eventually there might be the amalgamation of the Judiciary Department.

I consider that any question of general legislative union would be impracticable at present. . . . my own opinion is that both St. Lucia and St. Vincent are not so keen on Confederation as they are on 'Defederation'. A case of 'the little cock to crow on its own heap unmolested'. As regards Defederation under no circumstances would the Secretary of State for the Colonies consider the question as it would be entirely contrary to his policy. He is quite prepared, if it is the wish of the peoples of these Islands, to give serious consideration of the association or confederation of the Windward Islands and the larger Colony of Trinidad. . . . The Secretary of State has directed me to proceed to Trinidad to confer with the Governor of that Colony on the subject. . . . After the idea has been publicly criticised and examined I think the arguments in its favour as a stepping stone towards a possible greater measure of unity among the Islands of the Caribbean Sea in the future, may be considered to carry weight. . . .

I have already stated that any general legislative union may be dismissed at present. It is quite beyond the range of practical politics, but I must say that I would be wanting in straightforwardness if I did not point out that such a step as confederation with Trinidad would be a step towards a great Federal Council. It may not come in our time but if the scheme were adopted it would be the first step in that direction. . . .

(iii) Extracts from the Despatch from Governor, Windward Islands, to the Secretary of State for Colonies, dated 2nd April, 1923. (Correspondence referring to the proposed Association of the Windward Islands with Trinidad. Trinidad and Tobago Council Paper No. 103 of 1923.)

. . . the idea of association as suggested is admirable in theory, and would be the first step towards the larger scheme of confederation of the different groups of the West Indian Colonies. Owing to present conditions it is practically impossible to introduce within the next five to seven years the system of association as indicated by Mr. Wood on page 32 of his report. . . . The present financial condition of the different Colonies will not permit at present of the proposed scheme being successful; if forced I fear it will mean failure to the scheme and be a retrograde step towards confederation. At the same time I am of the opinion that now the idea has been launched, it would be an error not to make some attempt, small as it may be, to associate the Windward Islands with Trinidad, and each year in succession to develop the scheme more and more by further association, so that when the period of my successor's time expires the present idea of merging the Governorship of Trinidad with that of the Windward Islands may be a far easier task than it would be at the present time.

At present no scheme is possible that would not mean extra expenditure to Trinidad or the Windward Islands.

From my conversations with leading men in Trinidad I regretted to find that local sentiment was by no means enthusiastic towards the association.

The Governor of Trinidad is also of opinion that there would be opposition to his absence from Trinidad and that Colony would expect a larger contribution to his salary and expenses than the Windward Islands would be prepared to give.

The present financial position of the three Islands of the Windward Island Group would prevent them from joining any association which involved greater expenditure on administration than is disbursed at present. Without in any way providing for improved communication between Trinidad and the Windward Islands, which Trinidad would naturally expect the Windward Islands to contribute towards. . . .

During our consultation on this subject both Sir Samuel Wilson[1] and myself agreed that there were three ways to bring about the proposed association. I will deal with them categorically, adding my remarks under each head.

(a) The abolition of the Windward Islands Governorship and the placing of Grenada, St. Lucia, and St. Vincent directly under

[1] The then Governor of Trinidad and Tobago.

> the Governor of Trinidad, and at the same time the unification of the Civil Services, or at any rate such as the Constabulary, Medical and Public Works. . . .

At present the difficulties in carrying out the scheme in its entirety are insurmountable. . . . In view of the large questions at present engaging the attention of the Governor of Trinidad, and the present financial condition of that Colony, the pressure of work is so great that it would be impossible for the Governor of that Colony to absent himself from the seat of his Government for even six weeks each year, or to assume any additional responsibilities. . . .

(b) The abolition of the Governorship of the Windward Islands and the placing of Grenada, St. Lucia and St. Vincent under the general control of the Governor of Trinidad, but the system of administration to be so decentralised as to provide for the Administrators of Grenada, St. Lucia and St. Vincent dealing direct with the Secretary of State on all matters of purely local interest and only communicating through the Governor of Trinidad on questions affecting all the Islands. . . . .

It is a hybrid of the policy that should be aimed at. . . . It leans towards defederation and in the end will strangle any change of confederation, and will cause general dissatisfaction. The great handicap to successful administration in these Islands has been the want of centralisation. Unfortunately the seed sown many years ago has been allowed to germinate and the roots are now so strongly embedded that the process of uprooting will have to be undertaken very carefully and gradually. If the Administrators are given greater powers than they possess at present and if the Governor of Trinidad is recognised as purely a nominal head, it would not be very long before an agitation were set on foot for each island to have its own Governor and be freed from the profuseness of an absentee Governor – in other words defederation. . . .

(c) No radical change to be made in the existing arrangement, but an inter-colonial conference with possibly a permanent Secretariat to meet every year to discuss questions of general interest to all the Islands.

To work towards attaining (a) I think conferences would be useful. In late years this has taken place, for example, those on Customs, Medical, and Educational matters. I am strongly in favour of such conferences being encouraged, but can see no necessity for setting up a special office for the purpose. . . .

(iv) Extracts from the Despatch from the Secretary of State for the Colonies to the Governor of Trinidad and Tobago, dated 4th March 1931. (Trinidad and Tobago Council Paper No. 32 of 1931.)

. . . I have recently been giving careful consideration to the question of the possibility of bringing about some form of closer union between Trinidad, the Windward Islands and the Leeward Islands, and to the many issues which such an administrative change would involve. . . .

In paragraph 474 of the Report of the West Indies Sugar Commission (Part IV), the Commissioners express the following views:-

> "It appears to us not only that the simplification of the system of government of the Leeward Islands and St. Lucia is necessary, unless the existing system is to be maintained continuously at the cost of the Imperial Exchequer, but an administrative association of all these Islands with St. Vincent and Grenada would be more conducive to their agricultural progress and prosperity and to the maintenance of a continuous, instead of an intermittent, policy of land settlement and improvement of peasant agriculture and co-operation. We think that a conjunction of all these islands could not fail to be advantageous, and we strongly recommend the consideration of these possibilities to your Lordship."

The question has also been engaging your attention and was referred to in a recent debate in the Legislative Council.

The present crisis in the sugar industry has brought about an economic situation, particularly in the Leeward Islands and St. Lucia, which makes it important to explore every possible avenue to the increase of economy and efficiency in the administration, while the improvement of sea communications and the rapid development of aerial navigation have materially diminished the obstacles formerly existing to closer union, and have emphasised the possibilities of co-operation in many of the activities of government. Moreover, as you will be aware from the grave statement recently made in the House of Commons by the Chancellor of the Exchequer, the financial situation of the Imperial Exchequer itself is now such that His Majesty's Ministers on their side are bound to ask that every possible means should be explored which may lead to a reduction of the burden which the necessity of affording relief to distressed Colonies during the present depression imposes on the home taxpayer. I have accordingly given the subject considerable attention, and have now come to the conclusion that the time is ripe for enquiry to be held into the possibilities of closer union and co-operation between Trinidad, the Windward and the Leeward Islands, or some of them. I may add that it appears to me that, at least at the present time, there is little likelihood that such an enquiry could usefully be extended to other Colonies.

(v) Extracts from the Address by the Governor to the General Legislative Council of the Leeward Islands on 28th April 1931. (Supplement to the Leeward Islands Gazette, 30th April 1931.)

Nevertheless, the necessity for the grants-in-aid, unfortunately coming at a time when the mother-country was also severely feeling the general depression, caused suggestions to be made by certain members of the House of Commons that since the Colony of the Leeward Islands appeared not to be able to pay its way it was time to consider the question of its absorption, together with the Windward Islands, into a combination governed from Trinidad. The Under Secretary of State for the Colonies replied that he did not know whether there was a great saving to be effected in that way, that it certainly looked promising, but that distances between the islands were considerable, and that it would be always necessary to have Agents of Government in the islands. With regard to the distances, or what has the same effect, the lack of communication, we have an object lesson here at this Council today. I originally fixed the opening of the Council week for April 20th, partly because that date fitted in best with the members from the Virgin Islands, which are always the most difficult islands for passenger communication. It also happened to suit St. Kitts slightly better than the following week. I at once received an urgent telegram from Dominica pointing out that such a date would entail an absence from home of the Dominion members for 23 days, and the Montserrat members for 27 days! The best compromise I could effect to suit all parties was the present one, which means about 12 days for those from the Virgin Islands, 10 days from St. Kitts, and 9 days each for Dominica and Montserrat, some by cargo boats. But even the 10 days for St. Kitts have now proved too long for the unofficial members of that Presidency, and I am not surprised, as they are both busy men. The result is that they have had to sail here in a small and risky sloop. So that you will see the problem of communications is even now not so easy as it looks; and it might be very much worse if the headquarters were elsewhere. . . . The Under Secretary went on to state that the matter of the further combination of these colonies was under consideration, and the result is that . . . a Commission is coming out here to report upon the desirability or otherwise of such a step. . . . It is a serious matter to have to advise whether or not this Colony should cease to exist, and its islands possibly be reduced to the status of dependencies of Trinidad. . . . They may be able to show that a real economy would be effected which would be sufficient to outweigh any other disadvantages. Even if things do not develop as far as this, I personally believe that great economies, possibly the greatest of all, might be effected by a unification of certain of the more important services among all these West Indian islands, such as Medical, Agriculture, Police, Educational, etc. . . . As to the political aspect of it, I have already stated that it is not in my opinion to discuss this. My personal view is that a general federation of the West Indies, with the people having a larger voice in the management of their own affairs, is bound to come some day, and I for one am certainly not opposed to it, as I think it is a natural path of progress. The principal questions are the stages by which it is to be effected, and when the time for such a complete federation will be ripe. The possibility of a preliminary federation of some of the colonies is a matter for this proposed Commission to report upon, and I will therefore say no more on this subject, except that I am in favour of anything that will tend to reduce the overhead cost of administration and simplify the form of government.

(vi) Extracts from the reply by Members of the General Legislative Council to the Address by the Governor of the Leeward Islands, 28th April 1931. (Supplement to the Leeward Island Gazette, 7th May 1931.)

We take this opportunity of reminding Your Excellency of your promise to reduce the high cost of administering the Government, and we have the keenest interest in the appointment of a Commission to inquire into the question of West Indian Federation, believing that such a Federation will lead to economy in Government administration.

We wish, however, to put on record our view that although we have no objection to Trinidad being the seat of Government of a West Indian Federation, yet we have no desire to become dependencies of that Colony. . . .

(vii) Extracts from the Report of the West Indies Closer Union Commission, 1933. (Cmnd. 4383/1933.)

* **INTRODUCTORY**

* The task entrusted to us was:-

> "To examine on the spot the possibilities of closer union between Trinidad, the Windward Islands, and the Leeward Islands, or some of them. . . ."

Our enquiries, therefore, have been directed to discovering . . . whether local opinion throughout these scattered islands is in favour of some form of closer union between the groups, and, if so, what form of union would be acceptable to them. Our terms of reference . . . deliberately excluded . . . Barbados. The main reason for this exclusion is no doubt the difference of constitution which marks Barbados from its neighbours. . . . The three Colonies, however, with which we are concerned also differ widely from one another in the forms of constitution under which they are governed and these differences happen in themselves to illustrate three distinct forms of union. . . .

(1) A loose Federation with local autonomy of its several units.
(2) An association of three Colonies under one Governor but otherwise independent of one another.
(3) The complete amalgamation of two units with a common purse and one Legislature.

It is not, however, merely in the form of Government that the three Colonies differ: deep-seated differences exist, not only between the Colonies themselves, but between the islands in each Colony. . . . Each cherishes its own individuality, the product of its history and traditions. Islands originally colonized by the French retain the religion and to a great extent the language of the early colonists. One, St Lucia, has its own code of laws, of French origin. In some islands the large compact estate predominates: in others, owing to the lack of internal communications or some other cause, the land is owned chiefly by small peasant proprietors. Some are almost entirely dependent on the sugar industry, others on cacao or fruit, whilst in Trinidad of recent years the oil industry has reached important dimensions. The first difficulty that obtrudes itself, upon my attempt to find a bond of closer union between these scattered islands is the number of divergencies which meet one at every turn. To discover a common denominator is a baffling problem. With these differences in view it is a small wonder that each community is interested solely in its own affairs and pays scant attention to those of its neighbours.

Herein lies the root of the difficulty which we have encountered throughout the whole of our investigations. Most of the islands – indeed we may say all – pay lip-service to the general idea of federation, but the corporations and individuals who appeared before us made it clear that to make any federation or closer union acceptable it must achieve economy in administration combined with other distinct advantages and must in no case entail the absorption of their island by some larger unit or the destruction of its own individuality. . . .

The Leeward Islands

Antigua and St. Kitts are mainly dependent on sugar, an industry usually carried out on large estates, on which the land-owners employ a considerable number of labourers. Political consciousness is hardly awake, and . . . it is only natural that in Antigua and St. Kitts, we found the inhabitants little interested in the question of closer union but greatly disturbed by the state of their finances, and anxious to discover some means of attaining equilibrium by curtailing expenditure on administration. . . . We were impressed, however, by the weight of opinion in favour of a greater and more effective control of finance by the local community, and by the feeling that local opinions were sometimes perhaps unnecessarily over-ridden or set aside by the permanent officials. . . .

Dominica

Dominica differs entirely from the other islands of the Leewards Federation. . . . Fruit-growing is the main industry and is carred out to a great extent by peasant proprietors on somewhat primitive principles. Dominica has always been politically-minded, and is the only island of the Leewards Federation in which the electoral principle was introduced after, and as a result of, Lord Irwin's visit in 1922. It has recently passed through a political crisis, and a Conference attended by representatives from the other Caribbean islands had met there a few weeks before our arrival and drawn up a Report, including a proposal for a federated West Indies. On our arrival, therefore, we found the island in a state of political excitement which seemed hardly favourable for a calm discussion of the problem entrusted to us. During the fortnight we spent there, however, we found all those who gave evidence before us, including the leaders of the political movement, ready to discuss matters in a spirit of earnest reasonableness which impressed us very favourably. As was to be expected, the most vocal clamoured for an immediate federation of the British West Indies accompanied by practical self-government, . . . but even the most ardent advocates were prepared, we found, to admit that the far-reaching changes which they envisaged could only be attained by stages, and by the mutual consent of all concerned. Other witnesses expressed themselves strongly opposed to any form of self-government, though in favour of increased control in local affairs. It is worth recording that many of the witnesses in this and other islands most strongly opposed to any form of self-government at this stage were coloured or of direct African descent.

The Windward Islands

St. Lucia, St. Vincent and Grenada are far more politically conscious than the Leeward Islands, Dominica excepted; but here again we found little enthusiasm for any scheme of closer union, and much anxiety over their own financial situation and prospects. . . . All, as in the Leewards, were inclined to blame the administration for the financial situation in which they found themselves, and, ignoring the world-wide fall in prices which has had so disastrous an effect on the finances of all countries, to imagine that if they had had greater control over their own affairs, their economic difficulties would not have occurred, or would at least have been less grave. . . . But here again we found even the most scathing critics of the present form of government ready to discuss matters frankly and reasonably, whilst other witnesses expressed themselves as generally satisfied with the existing state of affairs, though they made various suggestions whereby they thought the position might be improved.

Trinidad and Tobago

The conditions in this Colony are entirely dissimilar from those in the small islands to the north. Whereas for the past five years the average annual revenue of the richest of the northern islands has amounted to little over £150,000, this Colony enjoys an annual revenue of close on a million and three-quarters sterling, whilst its population according to the latest census is 386,158 against a total for the whole of the Windward and Leeward Islands combined of 290,085. . . .

Trinidad is thus a thriving Colony with hitherto ample funds at its disposal for its own development, though the recent world crisis has by no means left it unaffected, . . . and is not in the mood for taking on new responsibilities until it has weathered the economic blizzard through which the world is passing. Tobago has always been a financial burden to Trinidad since the amalgamation of the two, whatever the advantages of the union may have been, and Trinidad is strongly averse from embarking on more experiments in the direction of closer union with other islands. In the curious amalgam of races which comprises its population, of which East Indians form a third, it has its own problems, and requires time to settle down into a co-ordinate community. . . . It was clear to us that no proposal of closer political union with any of the northern islands would receive support at the present juncture, and that it would be useless to discuss the matter further. . . .

SUMMARY

RECOMMENDATIONS

Unification of Leeward and Windward Islands

The islands at present forming the Colonies of the Leeward Islands and the Windward Islands should be united into one Colony under a Governor, with Headquarters at St. Lucia.

The present federation of the Leeward Islands should be dissolved and each Presidency should be given in general the same independence as is at present possessed by the three islands of the Windward group, each retaining as now its own Executive and Legislative Council under the Presidency of the Administrator or Commissioner, enacting its own laws, and regulating in general its own finance and local affairs.

The three islands of the Windwards group should similarly remain autonomous as now. We recommend no unification of services at the present stage except in the case of the Police Force and of Agriculture, for which latter a detailed scheme is put forward. . . .

We are aware that the mere association of these scattered islands including as it does the local autonomy of each, appears to be a retrograde rather than a progressive step in the direction of closer union. We have already referred, however, to the psychological effect of uniting under one guiding and controlling hand these two groups of islands hitherto separated politically and administratively, and we consider that this is a factor of which the importance can hardly be over-estimated.

We desire to make it clear that our proposals do not pretend to be more than a first step – and that a tentative one – towards a real federation not only of the islands with which we are dealing but of other units in the West Indies which may eventually be found willing to join. We hope that, partly as a result of the Annual Conferences between the several islands of the group under the chairmanship of the Governor, the early institution of which we regard as of the utmost importance, the islands may themselves evolve a much closer union than the very loose one we are now suggesting. Obviously the next step should be the establishment of Federal Executive and Legislative Councils, dealing with matters of common interest to all the islands, as distinguished from those of purely local concern. In this connection we should like to refer to the West Indies Conference inaugurated in 1926, at which delegates from all the islands meet periodically to discuss the matters of common interest. Meetings of this Conference at regular intervals will, we trust, be continued, and by this means the idea of a wider West Indian Federation will be kept in sight, and, it is to be hoped in course of time, be attained.

(viii) Extracts from the Report of the Dominica Conference, held at Roseau, 1932. Appendix B to the Report of the West Indies Closer Union Commission, 1933. (Cmnd. 4383/1933.)

RECOMMENDATIONS

Federation of the British West Indies

Proposal for the Federation and General Government of the British West Indies were considered, and the following recommendations were adopted:-

Constituent Sections of the Federation – The Federation shall consist of the Colonies of Trinidad, Barbados, Grenada, St. Vincent, St. Lucia and the Leeward Islands.

Provision for bringing other Islands within the Federation – It shall be lawful for His Majesty, by Order in Council, from time to time, on address from the Legislative Body of any of the West Indian Colonies not included in any Federation, or of the Colony of British Guiana, and from the Federal

Legislature, to bring such Colony within the Federation on such terms and conditions in each case as are in the addresses expressed.

Constitution of Federal Legislature – There shall be a single Chamber Legislature to be styled "The Federal House of Assembly" composed of 27 elected and six official members.

A West Indian Judiciary

The Conference recommends that a High Court of Justice, with jurisdiction throughout the Federation, be established; and that for the convenience of litigants, and for the purpose of distributing and regulating sittings of the Court, the Federation be divided into three Circuits, namely –

(a) The Trinidad Circuit;
(b) The Barbados Circuit; and
(c) The Windward and Leeward Islands Circuit.

The Court shall consist of the Chief Justice of the West Indies, who shall also be President of the West Indian Court of Appeal and of the full complement of Judges now required for the due administration of Justice in Trinidad and Barbados, with three Puisne Judges to serve in the Windward-Leeward Circuit.

Customs

The Conference recommends that a Customs Convention be set up with a view to securing the greatest possible measure of uniformity in island tariffs, and of lowering or removing inter-insular tariff barriers, wherever practicable.

Reconstitution of Island Legislature

It is necessary and desirable that in each island the nominated and unofficial element should disappear and be replaced by elected members; and that the number of elected members should be increased so as to provide for a clear elected majority, in case of conflict between the Island Government and the Island Legislature in any matter of paramount importance the issue to be referred to the Governor-General.

Qualification for Membership of Island Legislatures – No person shall be capable of being elected a member of the island Legislature unless he or she (a) possesses a clear annual income of two hundred pounds, or (b) owns real property in the island of the value of at least five hundred pounds above all charges and incumbrances affecting the same, or (c) is in occupation of lands in the island of an annual rental value of at least fifty pounds, and is (a) a British subject and (b) a registered voter.

Qualifications of Voters – For the time being the question of voters' qualifications shall be left to the local Legislatures, it being understood that no adult who pays any direct tax shall be deprived of a vote, and that any property or income qualification that may be imposed shall be sufficiently low to provide for the free expression of opinion of all classes, and that adult franchise is the ultimate aim of the Federation: the qualifications of voters to be reviewed triennially in each unit with a view to bringing adult suffrage gradually into general operation.

Effective Control of Public Money – A Finance Committee shall be appointed by each Island Legislature to assist the Officer Administering the Government to prepare and submit estimates and supplementary votes, provided that all aids and supplies to the Executive shall be the sole gift of the Legislature, and that no public expenditure shall be incurred without the sanction of the Legislature having previously been obtained. . . .

Closer Union Commission, Reception of

It was agreed that provided the terms of reference of the Closer Union Commission were extended so as to include a constitutional advance towards self-government, a delegation representative of the Conference should meet the Commission at each island to urge that the recommendations of the Conference be implemented, but that, unless the terms of reference be widened to include this subject, no Conference Delegation should meet the Commission.

Political Organisation

It was decided that a political organisation be formed to carry on the work of the Conference, to defend the liberties and promote the political interests of the people of the British West Indies, and to secure common political action in matters of common interest. This organisation, to be called the "West Indian National League", will have its headquarters at Grenada, and will seek to work in association with existing progressive political institution throughout the West Indies.

(ix) Statement by the Secretary of State for the Colonies on Closer Union proposals for the West Indies, 31st October 1934. (Parliamentary Debates (Commons), Vol. 293, 1933-34, cc. 192-93.)

Sir P. Cunliffe-Lister: A motion for the adoption, as they stand, of the proposals of the Closer Union Commission has been debated in the legislatures of the Windward and Leeward Islands. Having regard to the divergence of opinion expressed, more especially in view of the additional expense involved as indicated in estimates placed before the legislatures, I have reached the conclusion that it is not practicable to proceed with a scheme of closer union at present.

(x) Extract from Report of the West India Royal Commission, 1938-39. (Cmnd. 6607/1945.) Chapter XVIII.

Amalgamation of Leeward Islands and Windward Islands

12 A practical test, on a small scale, of what appear to us to be the advantages of federation could most easily be made by combining all the Leeward and Windward Islands in one federation on the lines of that now existing in the former group. If local opinion is prepared to accept the principle of federation it need not, in our view, be long delayed after inter-island communication has been substantially improved. . . . We recommend, therefore, that subject to the two considerations mentioned above, the advisability of amalgamating the Leeward Islands and the Windward Islands should be borne carefully in mind as a desirable political end to be adopted at the earliest opportunity, both for the benefits which it may be expected to bring to those groups of islands, and as a means of demonstrating the advantages of closer co-operation. . . the Federal Legislature should be entrusted with wide powers and only questions of local application should be left to the control of the Commissioners in the several islands acting on the advice of Local Councils. . . .

(xi) Extract from the Reply by the Unofficial Members to the Address by the Governor, at the Opening of the General Legislative Council of the Leeward Islands, 29th November 1939. (Supplement to the Leeward Islands Gazette, 14th December 1939.)

2 We note with satisfaction that this meeting will conclude the long period of negotiations which have been necessary to bring about the transfer of Dominica to the Colony of the Windward Islands, and we are glad to observe from the Estimates before us that the cost of the Federal Government to the remaining partners of the Federation will not be increased thereby. We express the hope that the transfer of Dominica to the Windward Islands will result in the improvement of the economic conditions in that island and will make for closer collaboration between the West Indian Colonies as a whole.

3 We believe that the unification of the Judiciary marks a real advance in co-operation between these islands and we feel certain that Your Excellency will do all in your power to ensure that the salaries paid to the holders of the judicial offices are such as to attract men of experience and ability.

4 We appreciate that the time is not opportune to give effect to the proposals for the unification of the Police Services of the Windward and Leeward Islands, but we trust that, when times are more settled, this unification

will be brought about, since we are convinced that it will result in a much needed improvement of the Police Forces in the Colonies concerned.

(xii) Despatch from the Secretary of State for the Colonies to the Governors of the Leeward Islands and Windward Islands, dated 14th March 1946. (Supplement to Leeward Islands Gazette, 4th April 1946.)

2 I received a report of the Conference of Delegates from the Windward Islands Legislatures which was held at Grenada on the 17th and 18th January, 1945. This Conference, I have been informed, had met to consider the Royal Commission's recommendations under the general head "Constitutional and Closer Union" published in Cmnd. 6174 and not specifically to deal with the question of federation. Nevertheless the views expressed on federation and matters connected therewith have provided me with valuable information as to the trend of opinion in the Windward Islands.

3 It is evident that the conference was inclined to rate the importance of constitutional reform higher than that of federation, and I gather that local opinion in the Windward Islands will expect that constitutional reform should be granted before consideration is given to the possibilities of federation. I should say at once that I am not in favour of immediate constitutional reform before the question of federation is discussed, for this might result in the necessity of preparing and putting into force two sets of instruments effecting constitutional changes within a comparatively short period and so lead to misunderstanding and confusion. Agreement on an arrangement for the unification of the Leeward and Windward Islands would not however, prejudice the grant of constitutional reform, and it would naturally be convenient if the two matters were discussed side by side. . . .

4 Quite apart from the strong local sentiment which exists among the constituents of the two groups, there are two main difficulties which have hitherto prevented the taking of any practical steps towards federation, namely communications and finance. With the end of the war, however, a considerable improvement in air transport and other forms of inter-island communications may be expected and the time may now be approaching when the steps advocated by the Royal Commission can become a practical possibility, provided that the financial difficulties could be overcome. . . .

5 Although the Royal Commission's proposals, as published, advocated federation on the lines of that existing in the Leeward Islands, it is clear that they had fully in mind the disadvantages of the existing system in that group, where the Islands are only loosely federated: and it was their view that in any arrangement for federation there should be a Federal Legislature entrusted with wide powers and that "only questions of local application should be left

to the control of the Commissioners (or Administrators) in the several islands acting on the advice of Local Councils". . . . In this way it was hoped that the Islands forming the two groups would become more closely knit and that expenditure could be more efficiently applied and better controlled under central direction. The Islands of the group would moreover also be better able to take their proper part in general British West Indian affairs. The delegates at the Windward Islands conference made it clear that they desire that plenary powers of legislation should still be vested in the local legislatures. In my view, a federation of this nature would have all the disadvantages of the Leeward Islands federation, and by the retention of all the existing legislatures with plenary powers, would do nothing to remove the handicap to progress at present involved by the large number of legislatures or to bring about a spirit of co-operation for common ends. I have therefore come to the conclusion that it will serve no useful purpose to pursue the idea of a federation of the two groups on such a basis.

6 I am not willing, however, to adopt a negative attitude towards the Royal Commission's recommendation. Indeed, having regard to the prospects of rapid improvement in communications and of their much greater development in the near future, I am inclined to think that the object to be aimed at is the complete amalgamation of the two groups into one Colony, and I desire to commend this to your earnest consideration. Given adequate communications between the Islands, it should be possible for the two groups to be administered by one Governor and one Executive and one Legislative Council, the present Island legislature as such being abolished and being replaced in each Island by a local Council which would deal with matters of purely local concern. As regards finance I am prepared to recommend that His Majesty's Government should furnish assistance of the nature and to the extent indicated in paragraph 8 below. This assistance would not involve Treasury control of the Colony's finances.

7 Having regard to the above I have therefore formed the view that the union of the two groups might be carried out on the following lines:

(a) A strong central government should be set up with wide powers over all matters of general administration.

(b) The Government should consist of a Governor, a minority of central officials and a majority of nominated and elected members drawn equally from the two groups on a central Legislative Council. The Governor's reserve powers would be based on the existing models. The elected members at the present stage would represent the various Colonies and Presidencies as constituencies, and it would be a matter for consideration whether they should be elected directly or indirectly.

(c) The Colonial and Presidential Councils would become local

Councils dealing with purely local matters. These might be termed District or Island Councils – the exact designation would no doubt be a matter for decision according to local sentiment in the two groups. It would however be essential, in the light of the considerations advanced in paragraph 5 of this despatch that the authority of such Councils should be subordinate to that of the central Legislative Council.

(d) While the Island Treasurers would continue to collect certain kinds of revenue on a local basis (and if, as is likely, those proved insufficient, they would have to be supplemented by the Federal Government), there must be a single common purse. It would be for consideration whether Federal Revenue should include receipts from all sources save those ear-marked as purely local or alternatively, receipts from a common Customs Tariff and a common Income Tax only.

(xiii) Resolution of the General Legislative Council of the Leeward Islands. (Government Notice. Leeward Islands Gazette, 4th April 1946.)

The General Legislative Council of the Leewards Islands,

Having studied with interest and attention the despatch, dated March 14th, 1946, from the Right Honourable the Secretary of State for the Colonies on the subject of the Closer Union of the Leeward and Windwards Islands;

1 Records its satisfaction that the proposals set out in the despatch provide:-

(a) that the Central Legislative Council for the combined Colonies should contain a majority of unofficial members,

(b) that the unofficial members should be drawn equally from the two groups,

(c) that the financial arrangements should be such as to prevent the weaker units from becoming a burden on the stronger,

(d) that the assistance provided by H.M. Treasury for this purpose should not entail direct Treasury control,

(e) that, although Grenada would probably become the administrative centre for the combined Colonies, the Central Legislative Council could meet from time to time in an Island of the Leeward group,

2 Recognises that the improvement of inter-island communication (both by air, sea and radio-telephony) must be a condition precedent to the successful operation of the new constitutional framework proposed;

3 Expresses its acceptance, in principal, of the Secretary of State's proposals as the basis for entering into further discussions; but reserves its views on many important questions of detail until such further discussions shall have taken place.

C The consideration of federation for the West Indies

(i) Extracts from the Report of the Hon. E.F.L. Wood, M.P., on his visit to the West Indies and British Guiana, 1922 (Cmnd. 1979/1922.)

WEST INDIAN FEDERATION

Various schemes for some form of federation of the British West Indies have been put forward from time to time during recent years by public men in England. . . .

At the back of all these schemes lies the feeling that under the pressure of modern economic and political conditions, the future development of the West Indies and their right to be heard in the council of the Empire necessitate a greater unity of direction and policy. . . .

I think there can be no doubt that the comparative isolation of the British West Indies, and their inability to carry their due weight in the affairs of the Empire, are partly the consequence of lacking any definite and single organisation able to speak for the West Indian Colonies as a whole. . . . Separation also appears to involve government in excessive overhead charges, by requiring the full paraphernalia of administrative machinery for communities numerically so small. . . .

. . . were such a proposition practicable, public opinion in the Imperial Parliament would welcome the formation of a West Indian federation. But, seen through West Indian spectacles, the perspective of the matter is very different, and I am quite satisfied that, however much it would be to the evident advantage of these Colonies to secure machinery for greater unity and co-operation, there are practical and political objections which, for the present at any rate, make this impossible. . . .

Even when the separation is only a matter of a couple of miles, as between Nevis, and St. Kitts, it is enough to effect a barrier between the social, political and economic life of the two communities. Sentiment and development do not flow naturally over the sea from one island to another. Among the West Indian islands is found an astonishing diversity of physical feature, climate, language, religion and historical tradition. It is not surprising that, when there is so much to distinguish, the centrifugal tendency should be deep-rooted. Further it must be borne in mind that the greatest importance is attached under the form of government prevailing in the West Indies to a close personal contact of all classes of people in the various islands with the Governor or responsible head of the administration, and his ready accessibility to them when difficulties arise. A High Commissioner for the West Indies would not be able effectively to establish such personal contact, and experience of the working of the existing federations in the Leeward and Windward Islands emphasises the significance of this consideration from the point of view of the feelings and interests of the islands, where the Governor does not reside for any length of time. The political instinct against federation is complex in its origin and composition, but this particular aspect of it is of fundamental importance in estimating its justification and persistence. Moreover, the enjoyment of difference political history and institutions even in neighbouring islands tends to bar the way to co-operative effort. Barbados is less than a hundred miles from either St. Vincent or St. Lucia; yet it is impossible to imagine a contrast more marked than that between Barbados and its two neighbours. Barbados has enjoyed since the 17th century an uninterrupted and unchanged constitution, of which the inhabitants are extremely proud, based upon a House of Assembly elected entirely by a small electorate with high franchise qualifications. Although, in theory, the Secretary of State through the Governor is still responsible for the Government of Barbados, it is in fact in the hands of the House of Assembly that political power lies, since, without their consent, the Governor is powerless to carry either votes of money or legislation. Historically, socially, and politically, Barbados is poles asunder from St. Vincent and St. Lucia, which are Crown Colonies where the constitution provides for an official majority responsible to the Secretary of State. In these Windward Islands there is a considerable coloured and negro peasant proprietary, such as does not exist in Barbados, where the land and industry are almost exclusively in the hands of European large proprietors.

In any possible scheme of federation of British Colonies situated on the eastern side of the Caribbean Sea, I have no doubt that Barbados would put forward a demand to be excluded. . . . But enough has been said to make it clear that the establishment of West Indian political unity is likely to be a plant of slow and tender growth. If any advance in this direction is to be achieved, it can only be as the result of a deliberate demand of local opinion, springing from the realisation of the advantages of co-operation under modern world conditions. Such development is likely only to be prejudiced, if ground were ever given for the fear that it was being imposed upon reluctant communities from without.

(ii) Extract from a speech by the Under-Secretary of State for the Colonies. (Parliamentary Debates (Commons), Vol. 167, 1923. c. 492.)

With regard to the ever fresh question of the possibility of anything in the nature of federation in the West Indies, it is perfectly clear that the tentative proposals made by my right hon. Friend met with considerable local difficulties, and anything in the direction of progress in that much desired direction must be a plant of slow growth. Though it is most desirable that the public services – the medical service, the police service, and such like – if it can be brought about, should be uniform, that can only be done if we can get the various islands, and especially the islands which can actually see one another across the Straits, to come together and to agree to some tentative form of federation.

(iii) Extracts from the Report of the West India Royal Commission, 1938-39. (Cmnd. 6607/1945.) Chapter XVIII.

Evidence of present local opinion

Although the question of closer union has remained officially in abeyance since [1933], there is evidence that a lively and growing interest has continued to be taken in it in many political circles in the West Indies, some of which now advocate, as part of their programmes, wide measures of federation to cover all the British Colonies in the Caribbean area. For example, the Guianese and West Indies Labour Congress put before us definite proposals – in the form of a Bill to provide for a federal constitution for the British West Indies – for the appointment of a Governor-General for the Colony of the Bahamas, as well as the seven Colonies falling within our terms of reference, and for the creation of a Federal Executive Council with an official majority, and a Federal Legislative Council elected in and from the eight Colonies composing the federation. It is true that the meeting of the Congress convened for the purpose of preparing the memorandum submitted to us was attended by representatives from only three Colonies (Barbados, British Guiana and Trinidad), but it is evident that throughout the British West Indies contact is being maintained between those in each Colony who are most interested in securing rapid political progress, and constitutional developments, such as the widening of the franchise, in any area may be found to reinforce the strength of the movement for federation of the whole group. . . .

9 Our general impression, from the evidence which we heard, is that while local opinion has made a considerable advance in the direction of political unity since 1932, it is doubtful whether the time is yet ripe for the introduction of any large scheme of federation. Local pride is a most important

factor and recent experience has shown that efforts to secure co-operation for the common good from all the West Indian Colonies are still at times frustrated by an insularity which is illustrated by the scepticism felt by even well informed people who freely express the view that nothing beneficial to their Colony could result from institutions established elsewhere in the West Indies. There is room, therfore, for doubting the readiness of West Indian opinion to accept federation in principle. Even if the doubt could be removed, the practical difficulties appear still to be insuperable. . . . Nevertheless, a combination into one political entity of all the British possessions in the Caribbean area is the ideal to which, in our opinion, policy should be directed. With that in view an attempt should be made to overcome local prejudice against federation, both by the exposition of its theoretical advantages and by testing these in practice, as soon as a suitable opportunity presents itself, through the amalgamation of some of the smaller units. . . .

Advantages of Federation

10 The Commission of 1932-33 recorded that the witnesses before them made it clear that for any federation or closer union to be acceptable it must achieve economy in administration. That is, no doubt, a desirable end in itself, but it would be shortsighted policy to reject the principle of amalgamation because in its initial stages it would not secure savings on salaries or other administrative expenses. On any long view it appears unquestionable that monies available for social services can be better and more wisely controlled if those services in a large number of islands are made to work to a uniform plan under common direction. The savings thus obtained should soon outweigh any immediate additional expense. In particular, if Your Majesty's Government are to make more financial provision for the needs of the West Indies, it appears to us to be more important that those monies should be well and wisely spent than that small economies in administration should be obtained. Any measure of closer union, however small, should help in this direction. Moreover through the payment of higher salaries, which could no doubt be made available from the funds of any amalgamated group of Colonies, the services of officers with better qualifications and greater experience should be obtainable and considerable benefits might be expected to result.

11 Other advantages which could be secured by any amalgamation of West Indian Colonies are that the unification of local services, to which we refer later in this Chapter, would be facilitated, and that free trade would be possible, and should in fact be the rule, within any federated group.

PART II

THE WEST INDIAN FEDERATION

A Memorandum on the Closer Association of the British West Indian Colonies, 1946-47

(i) Extracts from the Despatch from the Secretary of State for the Colonies to the Governors of the West Indian Colonies, dated 14th March 1945. (Appendix I of Cmnd. 7120/1947.)

I have recently been considering the question of constitutional policy in relation to the Colonies of the Caribbean area considered as a whole. The declared aim of British policy is to quicken the progress of all Colonial peoples towards the ultimate goal of self-government and I take this opportunity of re-affirming that basic aim in relation to the Caribbean area. I feel, however, that the time has come to amplify this general statement of the purpose of His Majesty's Government by indicating the considerations which in their view should be borne in mind in the development of self-governing institutions in the British Colonies in the Caribbean.

2 It will, I think, be generally agreed that under modern conditions it has become more difficult for very small units, whatever their outward political form may be, to maintain full and complete independence in all aspects of Government. Nor do existing tendencies make it appear any more likely that such independence would be easier for these small communities in the future. Indeed the trend of post-war development, under the stimulus of greatly improved air communications, may well show a marked impulse towards a closer political and other association of those smaller territorial units which, through proximity or a common language, have mutual interests. I consider it important, therefore, that the more immediate purpose of developing self-governing institutions in the individual British Caribbean Colonies should keep in view the larger project of their political federation, as being the end to which, in the view of the Royal Commission, policy should be directed.

3 The question of West Indian federation has a long history which it is unnecessary for me to recapitulate here. I recognise that the existing differences . . . would make it impracticable to set up immediately a federal organisation. Moreover, in spite of the desire which has been expressed in certain quarters for a West Indian federation it may be that public opinion generally would not be ready to accept a federal constitution and His Majesty's Government would not wish to enforce such a constitution against the wishes of any large section of the community . . . . However, . . . I consider that the aim of British policy should be the development of federation in the Caribbean at such time as the balance of opinion in the various Colonies is in favour of a

change, and when the development of communications makes it administratively practicable. The ultimate aim of any federation which may be established would be full internal self-government within the British Commonwealth. But it will no doubt be generally appreciated that financial stability (which is of course very different from economic self-sufficiency) is an essential accompaniment of full self-government and that the latter cannot be a reality without the former. One important responsibility of any federation would, therefore, be to show that federal administration can be carried on without requiring recurrent financial assistance from outside. Another general consideration is that it may eventually be found that two federations, one of the eastern and one of the western groups, may prove to be preferable to a single federation, while the Bahama Islands may prefer to remain outside federation, at any rate for some time. These however, are questions which I feel should not be prejudged. Further, any federation must naturally take account of the relationship of individual Colonies with their non-British neighbours.

4 In the light of these circumstances I regard it as desirable that a lead should be given by His Majesty's Government in favour of the aim of federation, and that British policy should aim at the fostering of a sense of West Indian unity and of the removal of the present obstacles in the way of federation. In particular, the fullest possible use should be made of every unifying influence, as circumstances permit, by the development of joint West Indian services, joint conferences, and through the organisation established under the Comptroller for Development and Welfare. It will be recognised that in recent years, and particularly during the war, there has been an increase in the matters which have been dealt with on a West Indian as opposed to a purely Colony basis, and that a yet wider field where such unified action could advantageously be taken is now open, e.g. in such matters as the establishment of a West Indian meteorological service, the adoption of the same quarantine code, the development of broadcasting and so forth. Further it is important that in considering the question of federation, attention should not be focused solely on political matters. There is scope for the development of unified action in the administrative and economic fields. Clearly the economic interests of the British West Indian Colonies would be furthered by common action in many fields. Here I would invite attention to the proposals in my published despatch of the 9th October, 1944, on the question of a West Indian customs union. His Majesty's Government trust that these and other ways of promoting regional activities will engage the interest and attention of many members of all Colonial Legislatures in the area and other persons in a position to influence public opinion and that they will be willing to lend their full and whole-hearted co-operation in the question of federation, particularly by their encouragement of all efforts towards common endeavour for the public good.

5 In stating that the aim of British policy should be the fostering of a

sense of West Indian unity, and the establishment of federation at the appropriate time, I wish to make it clear that I should not regard the wide question of federation of the area as a whole as debarring in any way closer association between the existing groups. Such developments as the possible federation of the Leeward and Windward Islands, as recommended by the West Indian Royal Commission, should not be regarded as in any way alternative to the wider federation. Rather I should regard them as not only desirable in themselves, but also as an important step towards the wider projects.

6 With the aim of federation in view it is desirable that political developments in each colony should be definitely related to the wider policy I have enunciated and should, as far as possible, follow similar lines. I recognise, however, that existing differences would make any uniformity of political development impossible at the present time and that constitutional advance in each Colony must depend upon its circumstances and needs. At the same time, all such advances should be based on the general policy of fostering the growth of citizenship and a sense of responsibility. Much could be done in that direction by the development of institutions of local government which, even in the form they would have to take among the less advanced sections of any community, should give valuable experience in committee work and so forth, and might be expected, therefore, to lead in time to more participation by the people in the work of the central government. I recognise that the history of local government organisations in the West Indies has been a mixed one and that there has been serious criticism of the work of some. Others, however, have proved themselves, and I trust that they will develop since local government work is essential to the full participation of the people in the conduct of affairs and to the reality of West Indian citizenship. I attach particular importance to the development of village councils and community work, on the lines already recommended, by the Comptroller and his Social Welfare Adviser, as a step towards the growth of social responsibility.

7 I consider that it is desirable that the policy of His Majesty's Government in this matter should be announced and full opportunity given for public discussion of it. I would propose, if you agree, that this despatch should be published in all the Colonies concerned, and it would, I consider, be an advantage if an early opportunity could thereafter be taken to obtain the opinions of Colonial Legislatures by arranging for each of them to debate the issue of political federation in the West Indies. If all these Legislatures were then to declare themselves in favour of the aim of federation, the next step would be the consideration of the means whereby proposals could be drawn up for such closer association between West Indian Colonies as may prove immediately feasible . . . .

(ii) Extract from the Despatch from the Secretary of State for the Colonies to the Governors of the West Indian Colonies dated 14th February 1947. (Part I of Cmnd. 7120/1947.)

2 [The despatch of the 14th of March, 1945] was subsequently debated in the Legislatures of all the Colonies to which it had been addressed. In the Bahamas both Houses agreed in declining to consider participation in any form of closer association of the British West Indian Colonies. In the other Colonies concerned, however – Barbados, British Guiana, British Honduras, Jamaica, the Leeward Islands, Trinidad and the Windward Islands – the Legislatures have expressed their readiness to enter into a Conference of the kind proposed by Colonel Stanley, while indicating, however, that they are at present prepared to commit themselves no further than to discussion.

3 ...I therefore wish to propose that such a Conference should be convened, at some agreed place in the West Indies, in the latter part, say September, of the year 1947.

8 . . . I am aware that it has been widely assumed since the Royal Commission's report was published that consideration of the question of closer union of all the British West Indian Colonies would be deferred until experience was available of the working of any closer union of the Leeward and Windward Islands. In view, however, of the indications that public opinion in the British West Indies is now ready to undertake consideration of the wider question, I do not consider that it is necessary, or indeed desirable, to postpone the holding of the Conference which I have in mind. The closer union of the Leeward and Windward Islands, now accepted in principle at the St. Kitts Conference, is, in my opinion, most desirable in the interests of those Islands themselves, and not least since it will enable them to take part more effectively in any wider federation. Apart from this, however, the relations between those Islands do not affect the merits of closer association of the British West Indies as a whole. In any case, I hope that by the time the projected Conference is held the Leeward and Windward Island Legislatures will have accepted in principle the resolutions of the St. Kitts Conference and that their delegates will thus be enabled to take part in the forthcoming discussions on the assumption that the Leeward and Windward Islands would enter as one group into any closer West Indian association which may be agreed upon; and which in any event would take some time to bring into practical effect . . . .

9 . . . It has appeared to me, that [the Conference] might usefully be provided as a starting point for its discussions, with a short memorandum setting out the nature of the problem which will be before it. I enclose a memorandum which has been prepared with this object in view. This memorandum is not intended in any way to be exhaustive or to give any lead, but merely as a factual review, in the briefest compass, of the considerations which appear to

arise.

(iii) Extracts from the Memorandum on Closer Association of the British West Indies. (Part II of Cmnd. 7120/1947.)

4 ... It is doubtful if any federal or other arrangements would have much prospect of success which did not entail a substantial transfer, although to a body fully representative of the British West Indian peoples, of powers and jurisdiction at present enjoyed by responsible Colonial Legislatures, and equally which did not rest upon a satisfactory financial basis. ...

5 ... Subject to this, the Conference would have complete freedom in its approach to the problem. Nevertheless, it would seem that the first approach must be to take note of the basic factors of the present situation in their bearing upon the question of closer association, and to indicate the advantages and disadvantages inherent in closer association. Among the basic factors there must not be overlooked certain ethnographic and historical differences between the various Colonies. ...

6 ... The difficulty of communication between the Colonies is an important factor which has hitherto operated to keep the several territories in isolation from one another. ...

7 ... Even more fundamental, perhaps, is the great disparity between the individual Colonies in respect of constitutional development and of natural wealth and public revenue. ... In spite of these differencies, however, the Colonies are alike in that, apart from the powers reserved in varying forms to the Governor as representative of His Majesty, and from the necessity of balancing their budgets and providing funds for development, the Legislatures control their local affairs. This independence is strongly cherished, and the extent, if any, to which the several Legislatures are prepared to modify or transfer certain of their present or evolving powers in favour of a central authority resting on the British West Indian Colonies as a whole, is a cardinal factor in considering any proposals for a change.

8 ... there are considerable inequalities of natural wealth and financial resources between the Colonies. Such inequalities are by no means uncommon in the case of federated territories, but their significance in the present connexion is that to the wealthier Colonies any proposal for closer union may present itself as bringing upon them part of the burdens of the smaller units. ... Another point which need not now be elaborated, for it will be mentioned later, is that any central institutions which may become necessary for the purpose of closer association must involve expenditure. Not all of this can be expected to be met in the first few years by the economies and increased efficiency resulting from the unification of existing territorial services or the adjustment of Government establishments in the several Colonies.

9 ... Nevertheless, there are weighty considerations which point to the need for closer association of the individual Colonies and for the development of some central organ of government. If any considerable and sustained advance in the political and social fields is to be achieved, it would seem essential that the separate units, especially the smaller ones, should take a wider view of the problems which confront them all. Economically and administratively, also, it is important that men and women (who should wherever possible be British West Indians) with the highest professional and technical qualifications should be available to administer the various Government services, but in most cases it is not economic that the activities of persons so qualified should be restricted to comparatively small units of administration. . . .

11 Possibly the most important reason of all for the view that closer association is necessary lies in the fact that it is clearly impossible in the modern world for the present separate communities, small and isolated as most of them are, to achieve and maintain full self-government on their own. It is not, for example, practical politics to suppose that communities of two hundred thousand souls, or in some cases even less, should play an independent part in international discussions. On the other hand, a community of well over two million people in the Caribbean area, with much that is homogeneous in their culture, could reasonably hope to achieve real self-government, and to be strong enough to stand against economic and cultural pressure and to formulate and carry through a policy and way of life of its own.

12 It may be argued that, if the building up of such a community is the aim, the logical course would be to unite all the Colonies under one government with a single legislature and a single administrative machine. There can be no doubt that, so far as the material interests of the Colonies are concerned, this would have many advantages. The economies and increased efficiency to be secured by tackling the administrative, social and economic problems of the area with larger services under unified direction would be considerable. These results, would however, be secured only by the disappearance of the existing Legislatures with their individual traditions and close contacts with the peoples, and it is very doubtful if British West Indian opinion is yet ready for such a solution. Nor can it be said with any confidence that the development of communications between the Colonies is likely, in the immediate future, to reach the stage at which a unitary government would be easily workable in practice.

13 At the other extreme, another course could be urged – instead of setting up a central organisation, to let things continue on the present lines but encourage the development of central institutions such as the office of the Comptroller for Development and Welfare. Other new central institutions of a functional character, could perhaps be created and, as opportunity offered,

administrative, legal, medical, police and similar services could be promoted. Concurrently with such gradual steps towards community of policy and administration there might be extended the practice of holding *ad hoc* conferences for the consideration of special problems, and the encouragement of participation in the Caribbean Commission and its ancillary organs by the British West Indian Colonies as an organic whole, instead of as single units.

14 This latter course might appeal to certain sections of opinion, as involving no immediate modification of the existing political and administrative arrangements in the several Colonies, and in particular no sacrifice of the jurisdiction and power of the Legislature in each. It would involve no immediate financial burden for the maintenance of an additional administrative machine and would leave the door open for any more formal constitutional integration which might become acceptable in the course of time. It would, however, in effect represent no more than a policy of waiting upon events, it would delay the creation of a central authority for the British West Indies and it could not be considered as likely, within any period which it is possible to foresee, to create the conditions indicated in paragraph 11 above as essential to the successful maintenance of full self-government in the British West Indies as a whole.

15 It would no doubt be possible, while still avoiding the creation of any central constitutional authority, to adapt one or other of the systems of which trial has been made in other parts of the British Colonial Empire with the aim of providing for joint consideration and administration of matters of common concern to neighbouring territories. The East African Governors' Conference and the West African Council are examples of such experiments, but these bodies have hitherto been in the main composed of Governors and their officials and advisers. Institutions of this kind, with no basis in popular representation, could not well be fitted into the British West Indian political framework, and would in any case be unacceptable to public opinion. A British West Indian Council, however, composed of duly elected representatives from each of the Colonies concerned, would not be open to the same objection.

16 Such a Council might be composed of territorial representatives drawn from the Colonies in agreed proportions – for example, on a population basis – subject to the need for keeping the size of the Council within reasonable limits. Members of the Council might be chosen from the members of the Colonial Legislatures. The Council would not have legislative powers, but would be at liberty to debate and pass resolutions upon any matter of general interest to the British West Indian Colonies; and, if so desired, it might exercise executive powers, ascribed or delegated to it by the Colonial Legislatures, for the administration of certain common services. Assuming that the Chairman of such a Council was, in the initial stages, appointed by the Secretary of State, consideration might perhaps be given to the possiblity of his disposing

on the spot of many matters at present referred by Colonial Governors to London. Any such devolution would, however, almost certainly involve the appointment as Chairman of a Member of Parliament holding Ministerial rank, and it would clearly be impracticable for such a person to reside permanently in the British West Indies.

17 A British West Indian Council of this type would, without committing the separate territories to the expense of maintaining a federal government, offer a regular means of contact and consultation, informed by technical advisers, between political representatives of each Colony, upon whom in turn would fall the duty of recommending the Council's views to the Legislatures in their Colonies in order to secure common decisions and joint action. It would also, with the agreement of the Colonies concerned, provide machinery for the control of common services. Further, it would offer a means whereby constitutional and other developments could be continuously discussed. It might possibly, in course of time, be converted into a legislative body for the British West Indies as a whole.

18 It cannot by any means be assumed, however, that this simple evolutionary progress would ensue from the setting up of a British West Indian Council. In the absence of legislative powers, that is to say, unless something in the nature of a federal government were created, it would be impossible to ensure the acceptance of resolutions of the Council by the Colonial Legislatures; and in the absence of any real responsibility the debates in the Council might tend to be conducted in an atmosphere of unreality. Moreover, in the light of experience in the British West Indies, it also seems improbable that any authority would be in a position to operate joint services smoothly and efficiently if it had no power to raise its own revenue for the purpose and was dependent upon financial contributions from a number of Governments. On the whole, therefore, it may be thought that the expedient of a British West Indian Council should not receive consideration so long as the possibility remains of securing agreement upon a federal constitution in some form.

19 It is clear from the language used in previous discussions of the possibility of closer association between the British West Indian Councils that the method contemplated has been some form of the federal system.

B Extracts from Proceedings of the Conference on the Closer Association of the British West Indian Colonies, Montego Bay, Jamaica, 11th-19th September 1947. (Col. No. 218/1948.)

The Governor of Jamaica:

. . . a distinct trend developed in the direction of greater co-operation, and during the past eight or nine years we have seen many organisations set up which cover the British West Indies and British Guiana generally. I have in mind the Incorporated Chambers of Commerce (which, I think, was one of the earliest), the West Indies Sugar Association, the Federation of Civil Service Associations in the Caribbean Area, the British West Indian Lime Oil Sales Company, the West Indian Conference which is held under the auspices of the Caribbean Commission, and the Caribbean Labour Congress, to mention only a few. In the last year or two, during which air communications have improved and world economic conditions have deteriorated, force of circumstances has resulted in the calling of many West Indian conferences. Indeed, it is becoming the practice now to call such conferences on a very wide range of subjects. I might mention the recent Conference held regarding the supply of oils and fats to the Caribbean area and the Conference held in Barbados recently to discuss the questions of shipping affecting the West Indies. . . .

The Secretary of State for the Colonies:

. . . We have moved as a nation from a conception of Colonies as provinces for material exploitation for the benefit of alien interest to a conception of Commonwealth in which that Commonwealth shall include free nations living out their own lives and all co-operating for the good, the stability, the peace and the happiness of the world. It is our task as a British Government to create, so far as we can, the conditions which are essential for good nationhood in all the territories under our control, and we have therefore, latterly, at a very great pace, been trying to apply these liberal principles in all the territories inside the Empire. It is not only the problem of political change, but also of creating conditions of social and economic development in order that sound foundations for the function of democracy shall be laid. It is not only to make modifications so that representative government shall be achieved, but also to see that responsibility shall pass increasingly from London to the peoples of the territories themselves. That is demanded of the modern world, if we delay, then disaster overtakes us. We have therefore, in our planning ahead as a Government in London, to take what the more cautious amongst us call risks, but I am aware, and I have had this experience as I have looked on conditions throughout Jamaica, that it is not only necessary that when people ask for bread you give them bread, but also essential that, if they are to get the fullness of living, they should have a value in the political life which can only come from representation and a voice in the affairs of their Government. Our conception of all the constitutions in the Colonial Empire today is that these constitutions have been sought and have been given, and if they are of a static kind, we must devise organisations which can be adjusted to the changing needs and development of the people until they fill the bill of requirements of the people. We cannot stand in the way, nor would we if we could, of a people which is stretching out for responsibility and control of its own affairs, but while we are trying to meet the needs of the separate territories, we are conscious that we cannot bring them realisation of their hopes unless there is development of association between these separate territories, collaboration and co-operation in some kind of political organisation through which, by a pooling of knowledge and resources, you can help raise standards of living and help give the people the more adequate living that they are demanding, so that there must be simultaneous development of responsible Government in the separate Colonies alongside of political organisation for the completion of the hopes of the people. . . .

. . . In the light of modern conditions, whatever be those difficulties, if we are to go forward at this speed and meet the social pressures of our people, if we are to satisfy their legitimate clamour for change, for reform, for material needs, then some conception of federation must be realised at the present time. I know, of course, that there is a wide recognition of the economies in the Colonies, and the efficiency, which can be gained as a result of closer association. And I am not unmindful, too, of the facts which His Excellency Sir John Huggins has directed your attention to this morning, of the movements already taking place for greater co-operation between the territories in this region of the world. The discussions by those engaged in the departments of labour, the conferences by those engaged in the medical services, the conferences of those engaged in commerce and trade, all indicate the need for closer collaboration. There is the emphasis which has been shown by the Caribbean Commission on research and the common requirements of all the West Indies in order to help social progress along. It is generally recognised that there ought to be throughout the territories great expert and technical knowledge available for tackling some of the difficulties, some of the problems, that we find, particularly in the smaller territories which cannot afford to make available such technical advice or such knowledge. There has been, too, the Comptroller's organisation, which has brought to the Colonies a certain amount of expert and technical knowledge and which has furnished us with reports of the greatest value , ... Soon steps are to be taken for the establishing of a university of the West Indies as a whole, and the beginning of work, to which I attach very great importance, for the building up of resistance to the economic and social problems of the region to which we belong.

Now, His Majesty's Government is anxious that results shall follow from this Conference because experience has taught us, as I have already said, that many of your problems can only be tackled effectively if some wider association becomes possible. It is our experience, it is the experience of the Comptroller and his staff, and I am sure that it has been the experience of you who are representatives of the people, that you cannot hope within the limits of your own economic resources, within the narrow boundaries of your own Colonies, to stand up effectively to the social pressures which your own people are applying. Their wants in the field of education, of housing, of health, of community life cannot possibly be met on the narrow basis of the individual Colonies. If you, as representatives, are to face the responsibility of office for the building up of the standards of living of the people you represent, then there must be some new fundamental conception born if satisfaction is to come to your work. Now I do not want for a moment by the slightest suspicion to convey the idea that His Majesty's Government is urging closer union in order to unload its own responsibility on to the West Indian territories. What we would seek to do is to create the conditions whereby the transfer of responsibility can be made effective by giving the territories the tools to tackle properly the problems which confront them. There is no suggestion that His Majesty's Government should withdraw its aid, that it should cease to make available the central services which at the moment it is busily creating under the 1945 Colonial Development and Welfare Act since March, 1946, apart from the monies spent under the 1940 Act up to March, 1946. . . .

Federation, as I see it, need not interfere with the identity and individuality of the separate Colonies. It need not be derogatory of the autonomy, the legitimate autonomy, essential for domestic responsiblity in the individual territories. Nor need federation subject any single territory, . . . to the domination of any other territory. But some surrender of ultimate authority in certain major issues does become necessary if the small units of the West Indies are in the future to maintain any true measure of responsibility and independence in all aspects of their government; for the continuance of small autonomous units, is becoming rapidly an anachronism in the modern world, and the only effective way of preventing domination and obtaining security is, together with local autonomy within the individual territories, establishing federation and full internal self-government within the British Commonwealth.

Now this must be the aim of our Conference. How can we provide authority and responsibility in the individual territories consistent with full responsibility and government by a federation which can go forward to full self-governing status inside the Commonwealth? I do not think that Britain would hesitate – once federation is realised and a machine which is responsive to popular needs and demands throughout all the territories is created – to concede this measure of full responsible government inside the Commonwealth.

This Conference will make no final decisions, of course. The peoples must be fully consulted after this.

Mr. Alexander Bustamante (Jamaica):

. . . I am sorry to say that the opinion that I have formed is that [the Secretary of State] has come here with his mind absolutely made up to push something down our throats, and I will give my reason if the Chairman will allow me to continue. . . . He said that unless we accept federation for the Colonies, there will be calamity and disaster. I do not share the Chairman's prophecy. . . . All of us have come here, I believe, with one intention and one desire, to endeavour to find a solution for greater unity and greater co-operation, greater and greater friendship and collaboration with all the British West Indies, and I do not like to feel that you intended to intimidate us. . . .

I personally can see no reason why one day, whether that day is tomorrow or next year or another year, there should not be federation of the British West Indies, but I must say frankly that I am more than suspicious of the motive behind this federation, and I will tell you why. Most of the British West Indian Colonies have been asking for greater self-determination. As far as Jamaica is concerned we have left the stage of infancy and we have grown up into manhood where we can manage our own affairs, and I believe there are other West Indian islands almost in the same position. The reason why I have become suspicious about the motive relative to the formation of this federation is that, whilst most of us West Indians have been asking for self-government, we are told that self-government for the time being is really not good for us and the thing we deserve is federation. That is not good enough for me nor for Jamaica and I speak for the great majority of the people in this country. . . .

I want to ask you as Chairman of this Conference why is it that instead of offering us that which we are entitled to, that which is our heritage and right – freedom – you strongly suggest, not alone suggest, but recommend, federation, with almost a threat that unless we accept it there will be calamity and disaster in the Colonies. We feel, and I feel, speaking on behalf of Jamaica, and almost in its entirety now, that the time has come not just for federation but for self-government, for I have never seen during my short stay in this country anyone who has been sent from abroad who knows anything more about the science of government than we do. I have never seen anyone from abroad who knows as much as we do in running our own Government. . . .

We come to federation – I can see federation one day, but now you have said in your speech today, if I understand and remember rightly, that the first step must be federation, and then after that we may work up ourselves to self-government. . . .

Jamaica can walk, Trinidad is creeping, Barbados and Demerara are right behind Trinidad or almost the same. St. Kitts and St. Vincent are attempting to creep and only attempting, Antigua is creeping, and of all the other small islands, some can barely creep on the palm of their hands, and others on hands and feet, and others not at all, yet you say to us, "We want you to federate". How can the walking and the creeping and the babe who has not begun to creep yet, how can they walk in the same avenue? It cannot be done.

All of us have a different constitution so if all of us were to join together in a federation, instead of Jamaica (and) Trinidad . . . progressing, we would have to make a retrograde step and try to help on all these countries who cannot creep. . . . Federation can come, but I cannot see the advisability of federation without self-government or greater self-determination for each and every island. . . . The people in this country have no idea or knowledge of the true meaning of federation, and when you say that by federating the British West Indies will become prosperous, you do not have the mind to deceive the people, but, I can tell you, it is deception. It is deception of the worst type. If you know that most of the British West Indies are almost bankrupt and pauperised, how is this prosperity to come overnight? It is not going to come in a hundred years. . . .

I am not against federation. One day federation will come, but I cannot see the possibility of walking with a group of creeping and non-creeping persons. I cannot see the possibility of prosperity through federation with twenty or forty or fifty pauperised countries. What have these little islands, or my little island, to trade with each other? . . . I would like it to be explained to me how there will be prosperity if we federate. Yes, there are some things we could have unification of – currency, the civil service – and we can try to trade with each other, but what is preventing us now? The reply is transportation. Is federation bringing us transportation? If you can give us transportation with federation why cannot you give us transportation amongst themselves?

Mr. A. Gomes (Trinidad):

Now, Sir, there is a way in which self-government can become the enemy of federation. If we permit the present method of development in the West Indies, and by that I mean the system of graduating single isolated units in varying stages towards self-government, we tend to encourage the centrifugal movement, and we tend rather to create conditions whereby the territories move further away one from the other. When you proceed, for example, to give Jamaica a slightly better constitution than Trinidad, and then you proceed as part of the policy to give Barbados a slightly better constitution than either Jamaica or Trinidad, you merely extend these distinctions, and perhaps you tend more and more to keep the regions apart and to emphasise the methods of insulation and the competitive spirit and jealousies. That is why it is essential that as soon as possible an attempt should be made within the federal crucible to establish constitutional uniformity among the constituent territories.

You see, Sir, my whole case is predicated on the inevitability of federation in the British West Indies. . . . Need we argue as to the necessity of federation of the British West Indies? After all, the necessity for federation exists in the West Indies today, and further than that, a federal structure exists in the West Indies today. How else can we regard the functions of Colonial Development and Welfare than as those of a rudimentary federal structure?

C Extracts from Report of the Conference on the Closer Association of the British West Indian Colonies, Montego Bay, Jamaica, 11th-19th September 1947. (Cmnd. 7291/1948.)

IV THE RESOLUTIONS OF THE CONFERENCE

15 The Resolutions were:–

RESOLUTION 1

RESOLVED:

That this Conference, recognising the desirability of a political federation of the British Caribbean territories, accepts the principles of a federation in which each constituent unit retains complete control over all matters except those specifically assigned to the federal government.

RESOLUTION 2

RESOLVED:

That this Conference believes that an increasing measure of responsibility should be extended to the several units of the British Caribbean territories, whose political development must be pursued as an aim in itself, without prejudice and in no way subordinate to progress towards federation. . . .

RESOLUTION 6

RESOLVED:

That this Conference recommends:-

(1) the immediate constitution of a Standing Closer Association Committe composed of delegates appointed by the Legislatures of each unit in the British Caribbean area . . . and of a Chairman and Secretary appointed by the Secretary of State;

(2) that the terms of reference of the above Committee be to consider and make recommendations in relation to:–

(i) the fiscal, customs and tariff policy of the British territories in the Caribbean area, so, however, that the Committee shall have regard to any recommendations in relation to these matters which may previously have been made by any Commission constituted for this purpose subsequent to the nineteenth day of September 1947; and

(ii) the legislation of such territories;

(b) the unification of the currency of such territories;

(c) the unification so far as may be practicable, of the public services of such territories, so, however, that the Committee shall have regard to any recommendations in relation to such unification which may previously have been made by any Commission constituted for that purpose subsequent to the nineteenth day of September, 1947, and to which effect may not previously have been given;

(d) the form of a federal constitution and federal judiciary most likely to give effect to the aspirations of the people of such territories; and

(e) the means of financing the operation of all federal services, regard being had to all proposals in relation to this subject made to the Conference on Closer Association of the British West Indian Colonies held at Montego Bay, Jamaica in September 1947.

(3) that the headquarters of the above Committee be in Barbados; and

(4) that the Committee above referred to be requested to report to the Governments of the British Caribbean territories not later than the 30th June, 1949. . . .

RESOLUTION 7

RESOLVED:

That this Conference recommends the appointment by the Secretary of State of a Commission to examine, in consultation with the Governments of the territories in the British Caribbean area, the question of the establishment of a Customs Union. . . .

Report of the Fiscal Sub-Committee

4 . . . In the absence of any precise assessment of the degree to which it is proposed to endow the federal government with the powers and functions which are at present exercised by individual Governments in the British Caribbean region, we have thought it desirable to make our recommendations in terms of two sets of conditions:-

(a) that after preliminary examination of constitutional and financial matters, some form of federal government will be established in, say, two or three years' time, even if this involves legislative powers over no more than a very few specified subjects and represents relatively restricted delegation of powers at present exercised by the Governments of the participating territories; or

(b) that, pending agreement as to the form which should be taken by such an experimental measure of political and constitutional federation, support would be forthcoming, in view of its obvious advantages, for the establishment at a very early date of a full customs union. (This concept of a full customs union would imply that the Governments of the participating territories would, for the time being, limit their delegation of powers solely to the central control and administration of all matters relating to customs). . . .

5 We wish to record our view, which is supported by the long history of federal finance in other regions, that it would be unsound financially to attempt to finance a federal government, even in its early stages, by the method of annual contributions from participating Governments, however calculated, after the expenditure had been incurred by the federal government. We therefore recommend:–

(1) That from the outset any form of federal government should be financed from at least one independent and major source of revenue, in the collection of which it should have complete legislative and administrative control.

It is recognised that at least in the early years the yield of such revenue would probably be in excess of that required to meet the limited needs of the central government, and in that case the additional revenue would be re-allocated by grants to the participating Governments upon some agreed basis, probably in the proportion in which the original revenue had been derived.

6 The selection of the field of taxation which should initially be reserved to the federal government presents no difficulties. We recommend:–

(2) That the yield of customs duties should provide the primary source of revenue for the federal government and that this should remain the sole source of federal finance until such time as the increasing functions of the central government make necessary supplementary sources of income.

(3) That in the event in due course of the federal government being endowed with increased functions, such as the centralisation and unification of the major government services, the cost of which would exceed in the yield of revenue derived from customs duties, the yield of income tax should be allocated as the second source of federal income. . . .

10 In order to facilitate a readier acceptance of the practicability of a growth towards a federal organisation or of a full customs union, we recommend: . . .

(6) That the Secretary of State for the Colonies should be invited to examine the possibilities of effecting changes in the methods of Treasury control of grant-aided Colonies.

(7) That the Secretary of State for the Colonies be further invited to consider as an experimental measure the advantages of substituting

a block grant for three years to aid such territories and freeing them from direct year-to-year budgetary control during the three-year period covered by such grant.

In explanation of the above recommendations, we record the view that we contemplate that, should a federal government be established, it would receive such grants in the first instance and in consultation with the Government requiring aid would agree upon the proportion of the grant to be expended in any one year.

CUSTOMS

11 We are of the opinion that, even if for practical and other reasons the realisation of a form of federal government took some years to achieve, it would still be desirable to take early steps towards the establishment of a full customs union for the British Caribbean territories. We are inclined to this view both on the measure and as a basis for economic co-operation which, although it might be initiated independently of a constitutional and political federation, would contribute towards the fulfilment of the major aim. We recommend:–

(8) that the Committee should declare itself unreservedly in favour of a full customs union of the British Caribbean territories. . . .

13 We are of the opinion that full co-operation in customs and tariff matters presents such obvious advantages to the British Caribbean territories that it should not be delayed for any longer period than is necessary to undertake the investigations upon which a customs union may be soundly based. We recommend:–

(9) That the Committee make provision for the establishment of a customs union by adopting one of the following alternatives: either

(a) if a federal government were to be set up at an early date, even with powers restricted to a very few subjects, it would naturally provide the legislative authority for the customs union which would then operate in the normal manner of a customs department of a unitary government; or

(b) if it appeared that the establishment of such a nucleus of federal government were likely to be delayed, the Governments of the individual territories should agree by contract to establish a full customs union by surrendering their present powers over such matters and by endowing a duly constituted Board, upon which they were represented, with full powers to frame regulations for the administration of customs matters and for the determination of tariff rates. The Board should also be the authority for the negotiation of external trade agreements. It is implied that the acts of this Board should be accepted unreservedly by the participating Governments, and that its acts when gazetted in the constituent units would be accorded the status of law.

D Extracts from the Report of the Standing Closer Association Committee, 1948-49. (Col. No. 255/1950.)

8 In this Chapter, we discuss certain of the underlying principles which have guided us in framing our more detailed proposals. Certain principles were provided in our terms of reference, notably that a Federal constitution should follow the Australian pattern, with residual powers remaining with the constituent units, and we have naturally been much influenced by the records of the discussions at Montego Bay. . . .

9 We start from the assumption that the main underlying purpose of our task is to seek the shortest path towards a real political independence for the British peoples of the region, within the framework of the British Commonwealth – what is meant in fact by "Dominion Status". We assume further that we have been charged with this task because there is general agreement that this object cannot be obtained without some form of federal association between the territories concerned, but that with Federation its attainment becomes practicable. We are aware that in some circles there is a demand for full independence, or for self-government, either in advance of or simultaneously with Federation, on the basis of existing political units. While we reaffirm the view expressed at the Montego Bay Conference that the political development of the units must be pursued as an aim in itself, we are satisfied that the sheer force of circumstances of the modern world makes independence on a unit basis a mirage. Independence or self-government as a Federation is however a practical possibility, and we have framed our proposals with this specific objective in view. . . .

10 . . . Our reasons for this view lie in the fields of economics, public finance and administration, but particularly economics, the basis of all the rest.

11 It is now a truism to say that political independence is unreal unless it is based on financial stability which, in turn, must rest on a solid foundation of economic productivity – i.e. on an adequate "national income". It is true that there are many states in the world today which are legally sovereign and independent; but it can be asserted that of these only those which can pay their way can really be said to enjoy full independence. From this point of view it does not matter what form is taken by outside financial support.

Grants from United Kingdom public funds are familiar to this region, whether in the form of grant-aid with its concomitant of Treasury control of estimates, or of grants under the Colonial Development and Welfare Act, which do not involve Treasury control of estimates. Other states, though nominally independent, have been assisted in other ways e.g. by private banks or firms, and their history shows that their real, though not perhaps their apparent independence, is no less curbed by this form of assistance than it is by the overt and acknowledged receipt of assistance as from one Government to another. . . .

13 . . . it is the case that, over the region as a whole, broadly speaking, public revenues cover public expenditures at the present time. . . . But on closer examination the picture is not so reassuring. In the first place, several territories are at present in receipt of grant-aid and are likely to continue to require it. Some others may at any time come to require it. Secondly, there is scarcely a territory, even among the largest, whose finances do not give some cause for concern, and which might not, as a result of some by no means unprecedented misfortune or disaster, be brought to insolvency. Thirdly, there is a basic instability about even the present apparently satisfactory state of the public finances. . . .

15 . . . the not-too-abundant resources of the region will require to be freely fertilised with brains, skill and hard work. This can undoubtedly be done, provided always that the political and administrative arrangements of the region are such as to enable modern knowledge to be particularly and confidently applied where it is most needed, and to ensure that value is received for value created.

16 . . . We are satisfied the region will not achieve economic stability while it consists of a large number of quite separate political units, and consequently that the hopes of such units of achieving real political independence, as such, are slight.

17 This said, we may place on record our considered and emphatic view that Federation, and only Federation, affords a reasonable prospect of achieving economic stability and through it that political independence which is our constant object. We have chosen these words with care. We do not claim that Federation will immediately and automatically solve the economic and fiscal problems of the region, or that it cannot fail. We do claim that it will put in the hands of men responsible to the region as a whole, powers and opportunities, particularly in respect to the place of the region in world trade, which do not exist at present, and which these men according to their abilities and inclinations can use for the betterment of the region. Federation as such will not solve our problems, but will provide the conditions in which they can be dealt with.

18 We desire here to emphasise this point. There is in some quarters a dis-

position to imagine that immediately a Federation is established certain difficulties will cease to exist. Conversely, others appear to hold that, because the establishment of a Federation will of itself only mean another legislature and administration, and consequent expense, in addition to those already existing (which is true so far as it goes) it will not help the region. Both views are false, because problems are never solved automatically by new constitutions but only by the efforts of men to whom new constitutions may give appropriate powers and responsibilities which did not exist before. These two apparently contradictory views are thus closely akin, in that they rest on the fallacy that results are or should be achieved by adjustments of political and administrative machinery, instead of by the efforts of men who may be helped or hindered by the machinery but who cannot thereby be absolved from effort. Federation will not absolve the region from the necessity for physical and mental and moral effort – it may, if successful, help that effort to issue in greater productivity, more security and higher standards of living, than can the same effort exercised within the present political framework.

19 Briefly, the services that Federation can render, and which can be adequately rendered in no other way, can be summarised as prompt, effective action in the economic field on behalf of the region as a whole. . . .

20 . . . In summary, we believe that the attainment of independence within the British Commonwealth is the legitimate political objective of the region. Since a state has a real as distinct from a purely formal independence only to the extent of its independence of external financial assistance, it is clear that the economic stability of the region must be improved as rapidly as possible.It is our considered judgement that this can only be done by setting up a federal government and entrusting to it important powers and responsibilities particularly, though not exclusively in the economic field.

RELATIONS BETWEEN THE FEDERATION AND THE CONSTITUENT TERRITORIES: THE DIVISION OF POWERS

21 . . . Federal Government should have only such powers as are specifically made over to it, and that all others – the "residual powers" – should remain where they are, with the territorial Governments. . . . Geography alone suggests the wisdom of not attempting too close or all-bracing a Federation for this widely scattered region. . . . More important reasons, at this stage, for adhering to the Australian pattern, and to a relatively limited list of "Federal" functions, are the social and economic diversity of the region, and the strength of local political and other traditions. . . . these local traditions are not lightly to be cast aside. They form a valuable bond among the peoples who hold to them, and in many respects uniformity is not an unqualified good. The region has not so many human resources that we can afford unnecessarily to weaken

traditions which hold people together in local pride and self-respect. One is by no means the worse West Indian for being a good Vincentian.

22 . . . Under Federation, except in respect of the powers which are explicitly assigned to it, the Federal Government is in no sense "over" the territorial Governments and their actions are not subject to Federal sanction or review. The territories will keep all their powers except in so far as they specifically surrender them. Conversely, the Federal Government, in the exercise of the Federal powers conferred upon it, is not obliged to seek the approval of confirmation of territorial Governments.

23 We recommend . . . that the subjects on which Federation may legislate should be divided into two classes – those on which only the Federation may legislate (the "exclusive" list), and those on which both the Federation and the Constituent territories may legislate, but where Federal law will automatically prevail (the "concurrent" list). The former will be short, and include only those subjects on which, under Federation, there can be no room for variation, and which are essential to the existence of the Federation as such.

24 . . . It will be seen that the main emphasis is on external relations, of all kinds, and matters connected therewith – e.g. the power to implement such agreements. We propose also that the Federation should be empowered to deal with communications (of all kinds) between the territories as well as externally, but that it should be concerned with purely internal communications matters only in so far as federal commitments in respect of external or inter-territorial communications make this necessary. . . .

38 To summarise the argument and proposals in this Chapter, we endorse the principle that the Federation should have its own source of revenue in its sole control; that this should in the first instance consist of Customs revenues; that not less than 75% of the net receipts from Customs revenues should be returned automatically to the territories in proportion to the units of final consumption of the goods on which the import duties were levied; that, as soon as the Federal Government assumes control of postal services and revenues, grants in lieu of postal profits should for a period of five years be made to those territories which apply for them; that the unit Governments should be free to float loans within the region; but that external loans should be floated only by the Federal Government, whether on its own behalf or on behalf of Unit Governments; that for an initial period His Majesty's Government should make to the Federal Government an annual grant in lieu of grant-aid to Unit Governments, this grant to be employed solely for re-issue to such Governments and to be supplemented as required from Federal funds; that provision be made for financial agreements between the Federation and Unit Governments; and that Federal finances and financial relations with Unit Governments should be subject to review after five years.

FINANCIAL RELATIONS WITH HIS MAJESTY'S GOVERNMENT IN THE UNITED KINGDOM

40 Until the economic situation of the region materially improves, so long will His Majesty's Government, in fact, though perhaps not in law, have to stand behind the region and be ready to render financial assistance when required. So long as His Majesty's Government is in the position of ultimate guarantor it follows inescapably that His Majesty's Government will expect to exercise control in some form over general economic and financial policy. While that is the case, the region cannot claim to have attained full political independence. It is of the first importance that the peoples of the region should realise that, if they are to be free to control their destiny without political supervision on the part of His Majesty's Government, they must be prepared to conduct their economic and financial affairs in such a way as to reduce to a minimum the necessity for applying to His Majesty's Government for financial aid. . . .

45 To sum up the argument of this Chapter, the position of His Majesty's Government as ultimate and formal guarantor is recognised; that in relation to grant-aid certain controls are inevitable; that in relation to loans safeguards may be imposed; that, nevertheless, there must be no direct and general control of the economic and financial affairs of the Federation.

THE FEDERAL LEGISLATURE AND THE LEGISLATIVE PROCESS

47 We start with the assumption, that the preponderant voice in the Legislature should be that of persons elected by the people on as wide a franchise as possible. . . .

49 First, whether the representatives should be directly elected or chosen by territorial legislatures. . . . We have no doubt whatsoever but that the principle of direct election should be followed. The world is not without experience of other procedures, and it is safe to say that an assembly consisting of the nominees of other legislatures cannot but remain subordinate to those legislatures, which strikes at the root of the federal principle. . . .

50 Secondly, franchise. Here again we have no difficulty nor doubt. We consider that elections should be by universal, adult suffrage. . . .

53 We are thus led to the third of the fundamental points. . . . whether the Federal Legislature should consist of one Chamber or two. . . .

54 It is of the essence of a Federation that there shall be a balance, throughout its organisation, between unity and diversity; that the territories, merged for some purposes, should retain their identities for others. Now a

single chamber, with numbers proportioned to populations, would adequately represent the Federation as a single unit but it would not reflect the fact that the constituent territories enter upon Federation as equals. Moreover, it is not apparent how this could be done while retaining the unicameral principle. . . . We reject the idea of adding nominated members to the elective Chamber, since the expedient of mixing nominated and elected members in a single legislative body is not viewed with favour and is on the whole on the way out. Whatever may be the reasons for adhering to it where it already exists, we see no reasons for introducing it into an entirely new Constitution. We were led therefore to the conclusion that, as in other Federations, there is no option but to set up a separate Second Chamber if only that these may be adequately reflected and represent the equality of the constituent units. . . .

56 . . . in a bicameral legislature the "originative" and dominant chamber – which we may henceforth call the House of Assembly – should be directly elected. . . . It is therefore necessary to consider on what basis the members of the second or revisionary chamber – which we suggest be styled the Senate – should be appointed. . . .

57 If the Senate were also to be elected by popular vote, and there should be a divergence of view between the Assembly and the Senate, each could claim equally that it spoke with popular sanction. However it would be difficult, in such a situation, to place the Senate, as we shall propose, in a position of definite constitutional subordination to the Assembly, since the primacy accorded to the one, on grounds of popular election, could hardly be denied to the other if it were also to be elected. Nor do we consider it desirable that the two Houses should be constitutionally equal, on the ground that they derive their authority from the same popular source. It is important that the two Houses of a bicameral legislature should have somewhat different functions and powers if they are not to be a mere duplication of each other. If each is to play its proper part in the legislative process, each should have its clearly recognised place in the constitutional pattern, and there should be no doubt, on any ground, which is the dominant partner. For these reasons, which we believe to be of general application, we have come to the conclusion that, in recognition of its subordinate though nonetheless important role in the legislature, the Senate should be nominated and not elected. . . .

63 Taking first the House of Assembly, we had great difficulty in devising a system of distribution of seats which at the same time adequately reflects the relative populations of the respective territories, is not too large and does not overweight a small number of the territories in relation to the rest. To take the last point first, it is obvious that to allot seats strictly in accordance with population would involve giving one territory, Jamaica, half of the entire membership, and thus open up the possibility that the representatives

of that one territory, with the co-operation of only one or two other representatives, could dominate the Assembly. We are confident that in practice this danger is unreal, in that it is improbable that the representatives of any single territory will in fact be sufficiently of one mind invariably to act and vote as a single block. We consider it more probable that party divisions will emerge which will cut across territorial divisions. Nevertheless, even the appearance of such a possibility is to be avoided, and we agreed therefore that the larger units, while rightly receiving greater representation than the smaller, should not do so in strict proportion to their populations, but in a diminishing proportion. Turning to the other end of the scale, we came to the conclusion that the minimum number of elected representatives from each territory should be two, subject to the proviso that where a territory had a population of less than 15,000 the number should be one. The greatest difficulty was experienced in deciding upon a suitable representation for the intermediate territories, and in fixing numbers, we found it necessary to take into account not numbers only, but such matters as economic development and productivity, financial stability and so on while at the same time recognising that these features might change from time to time. The result is that our proposed allocation of seats defies reduction to even the most complicated mathematical formula relating it to population figures. We cannot pretend that the allocation is wholly satisfactory. . . . Our proposed allocation is as follows:

Barbados	...	4
British Guiana	...	6
British Honduras	...	2
Jamaica	...	16
Leeward Islands	...	
Antigua	...	2
St. Kitts	...	2
Montserrat	...	1
Trinidad	...	9
Windward Islands	...	
Grenada	...	2
St. Vincent	...	2
St. Lucia	...	2
Dominica	...	2
Total	...	50

68 Turning to the Senate, we found that the question of the distribution of seats presented little difficulty, since one of the functions of a Second Chamber in a federal constitution is to reflect the position of the territories as equal partners, population differences being reflected in the other House. The only question therefore was whether there should in respect of each territory

be two Senators or one. In order to guard against unavoidable absences, we decided to recommend that the number should be two, subject only to the qualification that no territory should be represented by more Senators than it has members of the House Assembly. . . .

74 We now come to the important question of the respective powers of the Assembly and the Senate in relation to legislation. The normal practice is that all legislation shall require the assent of both Chambers before submission to the Head of the State. But to ensure the primacy of the House of Assembly, and in accordance with current British constitutional practice, we consider that the constitution should provide:

(a) that Money Bills (that is, shortly, Bills containing only clauses dealing with taxation or the expenditure of public money) may only originate in the House of Assembly, on the motion of the Government;

(b) that the Senate's powers in relation to Money Bills should be very strictly limited;

(c) that the certification that a Bill is a Money Bill (in accordance with a definition to be included in the Constitution) shall be a matter for the Speaker of the House of Assembly, after consultation with a Law Officer;

(d) that in the case of Bills other than Money Bills, the Senate shall have a delaying power of twelve months only.

Except as otherwise provided, it should be permissible for any measure, whether private or Governmentally-sponsored, to be introduced for the first time in either Chamber as convenience may dictate. . . .

75 The last stage in the legislative process is the granting of assent on behalf of His Majesty to Bills passed by both Chambers, or otherwise constitutionally appropriate for each assent. This will be the duty of the Head of the State, in accordance with common practice; and we recommend that he should in his discretion be empowered to assent or to withhold assent from any Bill, but that in respect only of defined categories of Bills he should have discretion to reserve such Bills for the significance of His Majesty's pleasure. . . .

76 Having regard to the inescapable responsibilities of His Majesty's Government arising out of problems of defence, international relations and ultimate financial stability of the Federation in its external relationships, it has been thought necessary to provide that, in certain carefully defined circumstances related to the foregoing, His Majesty in Council should have certain overriding powers of legislation sufficient to enable those responsibilities to be discharged. These powers . . . relate to defence, the regulation of the relations between the Federation and foreign countries, securing and maintaining financial stability and, in certain emergencies, securing and maintaining

public order and supplies and services.

77 We do not recommend that any power of disallowance be reserved to His Majesty once a measure has received the assent of the Governor-General except in the single instance of certain laws affecting Federal Government stock which the Federal Government desires the United Kingdom Treasury to list as trustee securities in the United Kingdom. This provision is one which is necessitated by Treasury regulations in exchange for the advantages to be gained by having the stock so listed.

78 We make no recommendations for any special procedure for constitutional amendment. That is to say, the Constitution, which we anticipate will be embodied in an Order in Council, should be amendable by His Majesty in Council. We recommend however that it be provided that no amendment diminishing the proportionate representation of any Unit in either Chamber of the Federal Legislature, or the number of representatives of a Unit in the House of Assembly, or increasing, diminishing or otherwise altering the limits of a Unit, should have effect unless a majority of the electors voting in any Unit concerned approve such an amendment.

E Extracts from the Report of the Conference on the West Indian Federation held in London in April 1953. (Cmnd. 8837/1953.)

MODIFICATIONS OF S.C.A.C. FEDERATION PLAN

6 We have agreed that some changes should be made in the Consolidated Recommendations of the Standing Closer Association Committee. These Consolidated Recommendations, the S.C.A.C. Report stressed, were "not intended to be a final draft of a constitutional instrument, but to be clear and unambiguous drafting instructions to the experts on whom . . . will fall the onerous task of preparing the actual instrument itself". This is equally true of the additions and alterations we have made. The Consolidated Recommendations are being reprinted to show the changes to which we have agreed, and the reprint will be published shortly. These changes are described in the following paragraphs.

(The references in italics at the beginning of the paragraphs below are to paragraphs of the Consolidated Recommendations of the S.C.A.C. Report).

The Preamble

7 There should be added to the S.C.A.C. plan a preamble to the Constitution setting out the objects of federation and declaring our common intention

that there should be the greatest possible freedom of movement for persons and goods within the Federation (see also paragraph 10(c) below).

Chapter I. The Federation

8 *(Paragraphs 1, 2 and 3)* References to British Guiana and British Honduras should be omitted from the paragraphs dealing with the establishment and the member units of the Federation as these territories have not agreed to come into the Federation. . . .

Chapter II. The Federal Legislature

9 *(Paragraph 4)* The designation of the "House of Assembly"should be altered to "House of Representatives".

10 *(Paragraphs 6 and 7)* The following changes should be made in the Exclusive and Concurrent Legislative Lists:

(a) "Raising loans outside the Federation" should be transferred from the Exclusive to the Concurrent List. We think that loans for unit purposes should continue for the present to be raised by the unit Governments.

(b) "Immigration, emigration and deportation" should be transferred from the Concurrent to the Exclusive List.

(c) Item (xxiv) should be deleted from the Concurrent List, and the following two items inserted in the Exclusive List:
   (i) Movement of persons other than aliens between units,
   (ii) Movement of aliens between units.

   The former item should be qualified by a proviso that the power to legislate for the movement of persons other than aliens between units shall not be exercised to restrict such movement on economic or any other grounds.

(d) The footnote to *paragraph 7* should be deleted and a proviso added to item (xxiii) that Federal legislation on divorce, and so far as may be found necessary, on other matrimonial matters should not come into force in a unit without the consent of the Legislature of that unit.

(e) Item (xxxii) on the Concurrent List relating to scientific survey should be widened to read as follows:

   "Surveys, investigations and research on any matter connected with the economic and social development of the area".

(f) "Agricultural education and advisory services" should be added to the Concurrent List.

(g) The power to levy income tax should be added to the Concurrent List, but we recommend that the financial agreements between the units and the Federal Government, to which we refer later should provide that the Federal Government should not levy an income tax within the first five years and that the position should then be reviewed. This would not preclude federal legislation unifying the income tax law, as distinct from the rates of taxation throughout the area. Our intention in making this recommendation is that the Federal Government should not levy an income tax until it begins to assume, with the approval of unit Government, additional functions necessitating a fresh addition to its revenue. . . .

13 *(Paragraph 10 (2))* During the first five years of the Federation a member of a unit Legislature or Executive should not be disqualified for appointment as a Senator (see also paragraphs 17 and 22 below): . . .

15 *(Paragraphs 17 and 18)* The decisions of British Guiana and British Honduras reduce the number of members of the House of Representatives from 50 to 42. We have, however, agreed to add one extra seat each for Barbados, Jamaica and Trinidad, so making the total number of seats 45, to be allocated as follows:

Barbados	...	5
Jamaica	...	17
Antigua	...	2
St. Kitts, Nevis and Anguilla	...	2
Montserrat	...	1
Trinidad and Tobago	...	10
Grenada	...	2
St. Vincent	...	2
St. Lucia	...	2
Dominica	...	2
		45

Montserrat, having only one seat, should be allowed when electing its member to elect at the same time an alternate who should be entitled to sit when the substantive member is absent through illness or with the leave of the Federal Legislature. . . .

Chapter V. Finance

25 *(Paragraph 60)* The Consolidated Recommendations provided that at the outset the revenues of the Federation should be obtained by the retention by the Federal Government of "25 per cent of the produce of the customs duties levied on imports into the territory comprised in the Federation." We have substituted for this figure a percentage to be independently determined within a maximum of 15 per cent. Our intention is that this percentage

should be sufficient to meet the estimated annual costs of the Federal Government, plus half as much again for approved Federal purposes including the establishment and maintenance of a Federal reserve. These estimated annual costs should be established by independent enquiry on the eve of federation; the resulting figure, increased by 50 per cent, would be translated into a percentage of the estimated customs revenue of the area. This percentage would be fixed for the first five years. Fresh negotiations should take place towards the end of that period in respect of the subsequent period, but there should be no annual re-assessment of costs.

26 The independent enquiry we have in mind would be conducted by a financial expert chosen by the Secretary of State who would consult the responsible authorities in all the territories concerned. We naturally do not wish to prejudice the estimate which such an enquiry may establish but we feel that West Indian Legislatures should know in advance the maximum contribution which could be required of them. We have therefore provided that this should in no case be more than 15 per cent of the customs revenue, a figure which should in our view be sufficient to cover the requirements of the Federal Government calculated on the proposed basis. If the results of the independent enquiry indicate a smaller percentage, however, the amount retained by the Federal Government for the first five years will be reduced accordingly. . . .

28 *(Paragraph 66)* This paragraph, which deals with public loans, should be amended in consequence of the transference of the power of raising loans outside the Federation from the Exclusive to the Concurrent List (see paragraph 10(a) above). . . .

Chapter VIII. Miscellaneous

31 In paragraph 78 of the main body of the S.C.A.C. Report it was recommended that no provision should be made in the Constitution itself for its amendment. We consider, however, that it would be better to lay down a definite procedure for constitutional amendment and have agreed upon the insertion of the following provisions:

> "A (1) Subject to paragraph (B), the provisions of the Constitution will be subject to amendment by Federal law: Provided that a Bill for the amendment of the Constitution (in this paragraph referred to as a "constitutional Bill") shall be enacted by the Federal Legislature and
>
> (a) will require to be passed in the House of Representatives by an affirmative vote of two-thirds of the total membership thereof;
>
> (b) will require to be assented to by resolutions passed by the Legislature in each of six or more units,
>
> (c) will not be assented to by the Governor-General but will be reserved by him for the significance of Her Majesty's pleasure.

(2) Resolutions by unit Legislatures assenting to constitutional Bills shall

(a) where the unit Legislature consists of two Chambers be required to be passed by two-thirds of the membership of the lower House and assented to by the upper House, and

(b) where the unit Legislature consists of one Chamber, be required to be passed by two-thirds of the membership of that Chamber.

B Notwithstanding anything in paragraph (A) no Bill to amend the Constitution by amending the Legislative Lists, this paragraph or paragraph (C) of this Scheme will be introduced into the Federal Legislature until after the expiry of five years from the date of the coming into force of the Constitution unless a draft of that Bill has been laid before the Legislature of each of the units and each of those Legislatures, and where the Legislature consists of two Chambers, each Chamber thereof, has passed a resolution that it does not object to the introduction of that Bill into the Federal Legislature.

C During the fifth year from the date of the coming into force of the Constitution, there will be convened a conference consisting of delegations from the Federation, from each of the units and from the United Kingdom, chosen by their respective Governments for the purpose of reviewing the Federal Constitution."

32 We endorse, subject to one proviso, the recommendation in paragraph 78 of the main body of the S.C.A.C. Report that no amendment diminishing the proportionate representation of any unit in either Chamber of the Federal Legislature, or the number of representatives of a unit in the House of Representatives, or increasing, diminishing or otherwise altering the limits of a unit, should have effect unless a majority of the electors voting in any unit concerned approve such an amendment. The proviso is that a unit Legislature should have power to decide on any such occasion that the decision of the unit concerned should be ascertained in other ways than by special reference to the electorate. . . .

43 We considered the proposal in the S.C.A.C. Report that the seat of government of the Federation should be in Trinidad. After full discussion, we reached agreement that it should be in Grenada.

F Extracts from the Report of the Conference on the British Caribbean Federation, 1956. (Cmnd. 9733/1956.)

III CONSTITUTIONAL MATTERS

10 We agree that the Plan for a British Caribbean Federation put forward by the London Conference in April, 1953, and subsequently endorsed by the Legislatures of all the territories concerned, shall be the basis for the Federal Constitution, subject to the variations set out below.

11 The preamble to the Constitution shall include a recital to the effect that all persons in the Federation shall continue to enjoy the free exercises of their respective modes of religious worship. The preamble shall also contain a recital in respect of customs union which is set out in full in Chapter IV.

12 We agree that the following item shall be inserted in the Exclusive Legislature List:

> "The establishment, maintenance and regulation of Federal agencies for the purpose of advising or otherwise assisting any Government, person or authority."

(It will be understood that the advice or assistance of these agencies will only be made available at the request of any Government, person or authority concerned.)

13 We agree that the proposals for amending the Federal Constitution in the 1953 Plan shall be varied in the following manner:

(a) The Constitution shall be amendable by Order in Council as proposed in paragraph 78 of the S.C.A.C. Report, subject to the deletion of the provision in that paragraph for a referendum to the substitution therefor of the provisions in paragraph 92 (3) of the 1953 Plan. The guarantee included in the 1953 Plan with regard to the numerical representation of Units in the Federal Legislature will not, therefore, be altered in any way.

(b) A special clause shall be added to the Constitutional instruments to provide for the entry of other territories to the Federation. This is to provide in particular for the possible accession at a later date of British Guiana and British Honduras. . . .

17 We agree that the provision of the S.C.A.C. Report (Clauses 10 (2) and 22 (2) of the Consolidated Recommendations) with regard to membership of the Legislative or Executive bodies of the Units and the Federal Legislature shall be restored – i.e. the ban on duality of membership shall be reinstated. . . .

18 The Fiscal Commissioner assumed in paragraph 12 of his Report that in the initial phase no substantial executive services would be transferred from Units to the Federation. Under the 1953 Plan, however, certain non-revenue

producing services relating to defence matters, imigration, emigration and deportation were included in the Exclusive Legislative List and would have to be transferred to the Federation immediately. As this may not be practicable, we agree that the Constitution shall provide that where, immediately before the coming into force of the Constitution, the legislature of any Unit has power to make laws relating to a matter included in the Exclusive Legislative List, that power shall not cease until a notification is published by the Governor-General in the Official Gazette of the Unit concerned. Until that date, such a matter shall be deemed to be included in the Concurrent Legislative List.

19 We consider that the following common or joint services are among those which are likely to need to be co-ordinated by the Federal authorities rather than through a continuance of separate contributions from Unit governments:–

- (i) University College of the West Indies
- (ii) Student services in the United Kingdom, United States of America and Canada
- (iii) Intra-regional shipping
- (iv) Miscellaneous contributions.

We regard the University College of the West Indies as a matter for the Exclusive Legislative List, though higher education in general, including professional and technological training, will be included in the Concurrent Legislative List.

20 We also agree that the Legislative List shall be amended to take account of the recommendations of the 1955 Trinidad Conference on Movement of Persons within the Federation.

21 We agree that, as external affairs are on the Exclusive Legislative List, it will be necessary for the Federal Government to assume responsibility for group membership or associate membership of any international organisation in which some or all of the Federated Colonies at present participate.

22 In order to clarify the meaning of the item "External Affairs" in the Exclusive Legislative List, we agree that this item shall be expanded to read as follows:–

> "External affairs, that is to say such external relations (not being relations between the United Kingdom and any unit) as may from time to time be entrusted to the Federation by Her Majesty's Government in the United Kingdom".

We further agree that, though the Federal Legislature shall be able to enact legislation for implementing treaties on any matter, it may be very inconvenient if Unit Legislatures are unable to pass legislation for implementing treaties in regard to concurrent and residual matters. We accordingly agree that a clause shall be inserted in the constitutional instrument enabling this Unit Legislatures to do this. . . .

IV FINANCIAL AND ECONOMIC MATTERS

24 We have discussed the Report of the Fiscal Commissioner (Cmnd. 9618) and reached agreement on the points set out below.

25 There shall be included in the preamble to the Constitution a recital to the effect that it is essential for the economic strength of the area that there should be an integrated trade policy for the Federation, and that there should be introduced, as far and as quickly as practicable, a Customs Union, including internal free trade.

26. There shall be set up as soon as possible, and in any case during 1956, a Commission on Trade and Tariffs to examine and report to the Federal Government on the economic, fiscal and other technical problems involved in the establishment of a Customs Union for the Federal area, bearing in mind the possible accession of British Guiana and British Honduras, and to work out a scheme for a Customs Union, to be implemented if necessary by stages. The Commission shall be directed to make its report not later than two years after the setting up of the Federal Government.

27 There shall be provision in the Constitution that the Federal Government shall, during the first five years, obtain its revenue from:–

(a) the profits on the currency issue (i.e. income from commissions and interest on investments held as backing for the currency after deducting expenses of issue and statutory additons to the reserve funds), and

(b) a mandatory levy on the Unit Governments, calculated on the percentage incidence of the Federal duties as determined from the figures in Column (2) of Table 8 of the Report of the Fiscal Commissioner and amounting in total to not more than the maximum estimated tax yield as set out in Column (3) of Table 7 of that Report.

28 There shall also be provision in the Constitution for the Federal Government to have concurrent legislative power to raise revenue by means of excise and customs duties, in the manner and subject to the restrictions set out in the recommendations of the Fiscal Commissioner: provided that any revenue so raised in any year during the first five years of Federation shall reduce *pro tanto* the amount in that year of the mandatory levy referred to in paragraph 27 (b) above.

29 There shall be added to paragraph 94 of the 1953 Plan the following sentence:–

> "The Conference should, *inter alia,* review, in the light of progress made towards establishing a Customs Union within the Federation and other relevant factors, the powers conferred by the Constitution on the Federal Government to impose taxes on income".

30 In connection with 27(a) above we agree that, as the Federal Government will receive the net profits on the currency issue, it will also assume liability for the losses and deficiencies on the currency issue which are at present the liability of the Unit Governments.
31 In view of the increased estimated cost as set out in paragraph 22 of the Report of the Fiscal Commissioner, Her Majesty's Government undertake to increase their contribution to the cost of the Federal capital from £500,000 to such sum as may be required up to a maximum of £1m. . . .

34 We also discussed two more general matters, not specifically dealt with in the Report of the Fiscal Commissioner:

(i) We agree in principle to the establishment of a Loans Council, with the task of co-ordinating borrowing by the Units and the Federation, to be set up by administrative action, subject to whatever legislative sanction may be required by Unit legislatures and with terms of reference to be worked out between the Unit Governments and the Federal Government. We also agree that the Federation shall have the power to guarantee a loan raised by a Unit Government.

(ii) We discussed proposals put forward by the West Indian delegations in regard to outside assistance towards the economic and social development of the Caribbean area. Her Majesty's Government welcome the initiative taken by the West Indian delegations in raising this matter and undertake to consider the next step to be taken on it, and to consult further with the West Indian Governments concerned, as soon as possible after the conclusion of the Conference. . . .

G Statement by the Secretary of State for the Colonies on the Conference on the British Caribbean Federation. (Parliamentary Debates (Commons), Vol. 549, 1955-56, cc. 1183-84.)

The delegates from the British Caribbean who were fully authorised to speak for their territories, agreed unanimously that their respective countries should be bound together in federation and solemnly declared their earnest wish that leave should be sought to introduce a Bill into the United Kingdom Parliament accordingly. They agreed that Federal Elections should take place in the first quarter of 1958.

The Conference reached decisions on a small number of constitutional variations in the 1953 Federal Plan, including some changes in the Federal Legislative List, an alteration in the composition of the Federal Executive, and a simplification of the method of revising the Constitution, especially in relation to the possible later admission to the Federation of British Guiana and British Honduras. The Conference agreed on the method to be adopted initially for securing Federal revenue. This presents a compromise between the recommendations of the Fiscal Commissioner and the method envisaged in the 1953 Federal Plan. It also agreed to set up a Commission to report to the Federal Government on a customs union which was considered to be highly desirable in principle. It agreed on the setting up of a Federal Supreme Court but deferred the question of the site of the Federal capital, until this had been reported on by an impartial fact-finding commision.

Much constitutional and administrative work still remains to be done. To undertake this work it was agreed that the Conference should continue as a standing body in the West Indies, under the name of the Standing Federation Committee and under the Chairmanship of the Comptroller for Development and Welfare in the West Indies. British Caribbean Governments will be represented on this Committee in the same proportions as for the meetings held in London, and British Guiana and British Honduras will continue to be represented by observers. It is envisaged that, when the Governor-General has been appointed, the Committee will operate as an advisory body to him until such time as the first Federal Elections have taken place. Arrangements for these elections, together with a decision on the site of the capital as a result of the recommendations of the fact-finding commission will be among the important tasks facing the Committee.

Her Majesty's Government have promised assistance to the Federation in a number of ways, including:

(i) Subject to the approval of Parliament, an increase in Her Majesty's Government's contribution to the cost of the Federal capital from £500,000 to such sums as may be required up to a maximum of £1m.,

(ii) facilitation of access by the Federal Government to the London market for the raising of loans when the need arises;

(iii) the provision of funds to the Federal Government to enable that Government to continue for the present assistance in the form of grants-in-aid of administration to a number of the smaller territories joining the Federation;

(iv) a continuation of assistance under the Colonial Development and Welfare Acts.

Now that these years of slow but persistent progress towards federation have resulted in this measure of agreement between West Indian Governments, it is the intention of my right hon. Friend to seek leave to introduce into Parliament an enabling Bill. This will pave the way for an Order in Council embodying the constitution. I hope that Parliament may be willing to pass the Bill through all stages in both Houses before the Summer Recess.

H Extracts from the British Caribbean Federation Act, 1956. c. 63. (U.K. Public General Acts.)

An Act to provide for the federation of certain West Indian colonies and for the transfer, to a court established for the purposes of the federation, of the jurisdiction of the Court of Appeal established by the West Indian Court of Appeal Act, 1919, and the dissolution of that Court; to provide for conferring on the first-mentioned court jurisdiction to hear and determine the appeals from the courts which are not for the time being included in the federation and to repeal the British Honduras (Court of Appeal) Act, 1881; and for purposes connected with the matters aforesaid.

(2nd August, 1956).

1 (1) Her Majesty may, by an Order in Council, –

(a) provide for the federation of the colonies specified in the Schedule to this Act (with their respective dependencies, if any) and, in that connection, –

(i) provide for the establishment of a Federal Government, a Federal Legislature, a Federal Supreme Court and such other Federal authorities as may appear to Her Majesty to be necessary or expedient;

(ii) confer, or provide for conferring, on the said Government, Legislature, Court and authorities, and on any other Governments, Legislatures, Courts and authorities (whether within those colonies or elsewhere) such powers and duties as may be specified by or under the Order, including (in the case of any Legislature) power to make laws having extra-territorial operation;

(b) amend, in such manner as may appear to Her Majesty to be necessary or expedient, having regard to the federation, the enactments, Letters Patent, Orders in Council or other instruments relating to the government of those colonies respectively and their dependencies; . . .

3 The Secretary of State may make to the Government of the federa-

tion established by Order in Council under section one of this Act (in this section referred to as "the Federal Government") –

(a) grants, of amounts not exceeding in the aggregate one million pounds, towards defraying the cost of establishing the seat of the Federal Government;

(b) in respect of the period of twelve months beginning with the first day of January next after the establishment of the said federation and of each of the nine next succeeding periods of twelve months beginning with the anniversary of that day, a grant of such amount as he may, with the approval of the Treasury, determine, for the purpose of enabling the Federal Government to make grants to the governments or colonies for the time being included in the said federation whose resources are, in the opinion of the Federal Government, insufficient to enable them to defray their administrative expenses.

4 The expenses incurred by the Secretary of State under the last foregoing section shall be defrayed out of moneys provided by Parliament, and any increase attributable to an Order in Council made under or by virtue of section one of this Act in sums payable under any other enactment out of moneys so provided or out of the Consolidated Fund of the United Kingdom, shall be paid out of moneys so provided or out of that Fund, as the case may be. . . .

SCHEDULE

Colonies Included in the Federation.

Barbados
Jamaica
Antigua
Montserrat
Saint Christopher, Nevis and Anguilla
Trinidad and Tobago
Dominica
Grenada
Saint Lucia
Saint Vincent.

I Extracts from the West Indies (Federation) Order in Council, 1957. (S.I. 1364/1957.)

ANNEX
THE CONSTITUTION OF THE WEST INDIES

Whereas the peoples of The West Indies consider it essential to their future well-being that the Colonies of Antigua, Barbados, Dominica, Grenada, Jamaica, Montserrat, Saint Christopher Nevis and Anguilla, Saint Lucia, Saint Vincent and Trinidad and Tobago should be associated in a Federation;

And Whereas all inhabitants of these Colonies should continue, under such a Federation, to enjoy the free exercise of their respective modes of religious worship;

And Whereas there should be the greatest possible freedom of movement for persons and goods within such a Federation;

And Whereas it is essential for the economic strength of the area that there should be an integrated trade policy for the Federation and that there should be introduced in the Federation, as far and as quickly as practicable, a customs union, including internal free trade;

Now, therefore, the said Colonies shall be associated in a Federation in accordance with the following provisions: . . . .

Chapter I
THE FEDERATION

2(2) The Governor-General may, by order, declare that any land in the island of Trinidad is an area used or to be used as, or in conjunction with, the seat of the Federal Government:

Provided that the Governor-General shall not, without the consent of the Governor of the Colony of Trinidad and Tobago, make any such declaration with respect to land that is not vested in Her Majesty for the purposes of the Federation or in any person or authority on behalf of the Federation.

(3) The Federal Legislature may make laws for any such area with respect to any matter, whether or not that matter is included in the Exclusive Legislative List or the Concurrent Legislation List, and the Legislature of the Colony of Trinidad and Tobago may make laws for any such area with respect to any matter that is not included in the Exclusive Legislative List.

Chapter II
THE FEDERAL LEGISLATURE

General

7 The legislative power of the Federation shall be vested in a Federal Legislature consisting of Her Majesty, a Senate and a House of Representatives.

The Senate

8(1) Subject to article 13 of this Constitution, the Senate shall consist of nineteen members (in this Constitution referred to as "Senators") who shall be appointed by the Governor-General by instrument under the public seal in accordance with this article.

(2) Two Senators shall be appointed for each Territory except Montserrat and one Senator shall be appointed for Montserrat.

(3) In the exercise of the power conferred upon him by this article to appoint a person as a Senator for any Territory the Governor-General shall, subject to the two next following articles, act in his discretion after consultation with the Governor of that Territory. . . .

11 If at the time of his appointment as a Senator a person is a member of the Legislature or of the Executive Council of any Territory –

(a) he shall not take part in the proceedings of the Senate until he has ceased to be a member of that Legislature or Executive Council; and

(b) if he has not ceased to be such a member at the expiration of a period of twenty-one days after the date of his appointment as a Senator he shall thereupon vacate his seat in the Senate. . . .

The House of Representatives

15(1) Subject to paragraph (2) of this article and to the next following article, the House of Representatives shall consist of forty-five members of whom five shall be elected in Barbados, seventeen in Jamaica, ten in Trinidad and Tobago, one in Montserrat and two in each of the other Territories. . . .

16(1) In addition to the member to be elected in Montserrat under the last foregoing article (in this Constitution referred to as "the member of Montserrat") there shall be elected in Montserrat a further member of the House of Representatives (in this Constitution referred to as "the alternate member for Montserrat"). . . .

22 If at the time of his election as a member of the House of Represen-

tatives a person is a member of the Legislature or of the Executive Council of any Territory –

(a) he shall not take part in the proceedings of the House until he has ceased to be a member of that Legislature or Executive Council; and

(b) if he has not ceased to be such a member at the expiration of a period of twenty-one days after the date of his election as a member of the House he shall thereupon vacate his seat in the House. . . .

Chapter III
LEGISLATIVE POWERS WITHIN THE FEDERATION

Powers of Legislatures of the Federation and the Territories

43(1) Subject to the provisions of this Constitution, the Federal Legislature shall have power to make laws for the peace, order and good government of the Federation with respect to any matter that is included in the Exclusive Legislative List or the Concurrent Legislative List and with respect to any matter incidental to any matter so included or incidental to any power conferred by or under this Constitution on the Governor-General, the Federal Judicature or any department, officer or other authority of the Federal Government.

(2) Subject to the provisions of this Constitution, the Legislature of a Territory shall not have power to make laws with respect to any matter that is included in the Exclusive Legislative List:

Provided that, where immediately before the coming into force of this article the Legislature of any Territory had power to make laws with respect to any matter included in the Exclusive Legislative List, that power shall not cease with respect to that matter until such date as the Governor-General may, by proclamation published in the Gazette, appoint, and until that date that matter shall in relation to that Territory be deemed to be included in the Concurrent Legislative List.

(3) Subject to the provisions of this Constitution and of the constitution of the Territory, the Legislature of any Territory (as well as the Federal Legislature) shall have power to make laws for that Territory with respect to any matter included in the Government Legislative List. . . .

44(1) The Federal Legislature may by law confer on the Legislature of a Territory authority to make laws for that Territory with respect to any matter included in the Exclusive Legislative List.

(2) The Legislature of a Territory may by law confer upon the Federal

Legislature authority to make laws for that Territory with respect to any matter that is not included in that Exclusive Legislative List or the Concurrent Legislative List and is within the legislative competence of the Legislature of that Territory.

(3) Any authority conferred upon the Federal Legislature or the Legislature of a Territory under this article may be general or may be granted for such period or subject to such conditions or restrictions as may be specified in the law by which it is conferred, and while such authority remains in force the matter to which it extends shall in relation to the Territory concerned and to the extent of the authority conferred, be deemed to be included in the Concurrent Legislative List.

(4) Any such authority, whether granted generally or for a specified period, may be revoked at any time by a subsequent law of the Legislature by which it was conferred:

Provided that no such law shall come into force earlier than the expiration of six months from the date of the making thereof.

45(1) If any law of the Legislature of a Territory is inconsistent with any law of the Federal Legislature which the Federal Legislature was competent to enact, whether the Federal law was made before or after the Territorial law, then the Federal law shall, to the extent of the inconsistency, prevail over the Territorial law; and a law of the Federal Legislature with respect to any matter for the time being within the legislative competence of that Legislature may amend or repeal, or provide for the amendment or repeal of, any law of the Legislature of a Territory with respect to that matter. . . .

46 Nothing in this Constitution shall be construed as precluding the Federal Legislature or the Legislature of a Territory from making provision by law for the appropriation of the public funds of the Federation or of that Territory, as the case may be, for a purpose for which that Legislature has no other power to make laws.

47(1) A law of the Federal Legislature may make provision for the implementation in relation to the Federation or any one or more of the Territories of agreements with and other obligations towards or arrangements relating to countries outside the Federation or inter-national organisations with respect to any matter, whether or not that matter is included in the Exclusive Legislative List or the Concurrent Legislative List.

(2) A law of the Legislature of a Territory may make provision for the implementation in relation to that Territory of agreements with and other obligations towards or arrangements relating to countries outside the Federation or international organisations with respect to any matter that is not included in the Exclusive Legislative Lists.

48(1) A federal emergency law may make provision with respect to matters not included in the Exclusive Legislative List or the Concurrent Legislative List and a territorial emergency law may make provision with respect to matters included in the Exclusive Legislative List [but shall have effect only during a period of emergency] . . . .

Special provisions regarding the Territorial laws that provide for controlling the movement of persons

50(1) As soon as is practicable after the end of a period of five years beginning with thc date when this Constitution comes into force the Governor of each Territory shall cause to be laid before each chamber of the Federal Legislature a copy of every law enacted by the Legislature of that Territory (whether before or after the date aforesaid) which is in force at the end of the aforesaid period of five years and is a law to which this article applies; and it shall be the duty of each of those chambers to review any law of which a copy is so laid before it.

(2) If each chamber of the Federal Legislature has not within ninety days after the end of the aforesaid period of five years resolved that it does not object to a law of the Legislature of a Territory of which a copy is required to be laid before it under paragraph (1) of this article, then (unless the law sooner expires or is repealed and whether or not copies thereof have been laid as aforesaid) the law shall be deemed to be repealed at the end of the said sixty days to the extent that it makes provision for controlling the movement of persons between that Territory and any other Territory for any reason other than a reason that is specified in the law, or in some other law amended by law, and is connected with the maintenance of public health or the maintenance of public security.

(1) If at any time after the end of a period of five years beginning with the date when this Constitution comes into force the Legislature of a Territory enacts any law to which this article applies, the Governor of that Territory shall, as soon as is practicable after the enactment of such law, cause a copy thereof to be laid before each chamber of the Federal Legislature; and it shall be the duty of each of those chambers to review any law of which a copy is so laid before it.

(2) A law of the Legislature of a Territory of which a copy is required to be laid before each chamber of the Federal Legislature under paragraph (1) of this article shall not come into operation before the end of a period of sixty days after the date of its enactment; and if each of those chambers has not within that period resolved that it does not object to the law, then (whether

or not copies of the law have been laid as aforesaid) the law shall be deemed to be repealed at the end of the said sixty days to the extent that it makes provision for controlling the movement of persons between the Territory and any other Territory for any reason other than a reason that is specified in the law, or in some other law amended by the law, and is connected with the maintenance of public health or the maintenance of public security.

Chapter V
JURISDICTION OF THE FEDERAL SUPREME COURT

80(1) The Federal Supreme Court shall, to the exclusion of any other court, have original jurisdiction –

(a) in proceedings between the Federation and a Territory or between one Territory and another Territory;

(b) in any proceedings in which a writ or order or mandamus or prohibition or an injunction is sought by the Federation against an officer or authority of a Territory or by a Territory against an officer or authority of the Federation; and

(c) in any suit for a penalty under article 113 of this Constitution.

(2) In this article references to the Federation or a Territory include references to a person suing or being sued on behalf of the Federation or a Territory, as the case may be.

81(1) The Federal Supreme Court shall, to the exclusion of any other court, have original jurisdiction to determine any question as to the interpretation of this Constitution which is referred to it under the following paragraphs of this article.

(2) If any question as to the interpretation of this Constitution arises in any proceedings in a superior court of a Territory, that court may, if it sees fit, refer that question to the Federal Supreme Court.

(3) If any question as to the interpretation of this Constitution arises in any proceedings in any other court of a Territory, the person presiding in that court may apply to a superior court of that Territory for an order of that court referring that question to the Federal Supreme Court, and the superior court may, as it sees fit, either make the order or refuse it.

(4) If any party to the proceedings referred to in paragraph (3) of this article requires that the person presiding in the court shall make such an application as is so referred to, then, unless in his opinion the request is frivolous or vexatious, the person shall do so. . . .

Chapter VI
FINANCE

93(1) The Governments of the Territories shall, in respect of each of the first five financial years, together pay to the Federal Government for the purposes of that Government such sum or sums as the Governor-General may demand from the Territories in respect of that year:

Provided that –

(i) the total amount demanded from the Territories in respect of any year shall not exceed nine million one hundred and twenty thousand dollars; . . .

94(1) If, in respect of any of the first five financial years, any revenues (in this article referred to as "customs and excise revenues") accrue to the Federal Government from customs and excise duties levied under any law of the Federal Legislature on scheduled commodities and the amount of those customs and excise revenues, taken together with the amount (if any) paid to the Federal Government in respect of that year under the last foregoing article, exceeds the sum of nine million one hundred and twenty thousand dollars, then the Federal Government shall pay to the Governments of the Territories a sum equal to the amount of that excess so that the Government of each Territory shall receive a share of the said sum proportionate to the amount of those customs and excise revenues that was derived from that Territory. . . .

95(1) If in any of the first five financial years any customs or excise duty is levied under any law of the Federal Legislature on any scheduled commodity at a rate higher than the scheduled rate, the Federal Government shall pay to the Governments of the Territories a sum equal to the amount of the proceeds of the duty for that year that is attributable to the fact that the duty was levied at a rate higher than the scheduled rate so that the Government of each Territory shall receive a share of the said sum proportionate to the amount of the proceeds of the duty for that year that was derived from that Territory.

(2) If in any financial year any customs or excise duty is levied under any law of the Federal Legislature on any commodity other than a scheduled commodity, the Federal Government shall pay to the Governments of the Territories a sum equal to the amount of the proceeds of the duty for that year so that the Government of each Territory shall receive a share of the said sum equal to the amount of the proceeds of the duty for that year that was derived from that Territory.

96(1) If, under any law made in pursuance of paragraph (1) of article 53 of this Constitution, any revenues (in this article referred to as "special revenues" are raised in respect of any of the first five financial years for a purpose referred to in sub-paragraph (c) of that paragraph and the amount of those special revenues, taken together with the amount of the federal revenues for that year, exceeds the sum of nine million one hundred and twenty thousand dollars, then there shall be paid to the Governments of the Territories from the proceeds of those special revenues a sum equal to the amount of that excess so that the Government of each Territory shall receive a share of the said sum proportionate to the amount of those special revenues that was derived from that Territory. . . .

97 If, by virtue of any law of the Federal Legislature, the Federal Government becomes entitled for the first time to the revenues arising in any Territory from postal services then, during a period of five years beginning with the date when the Federal Government becomes entitled to those revenues, the Federal Government shall (so long as it continues to be so entitled) pay in each year to the Government of that Territory, if that Government so requires, a sum equal in amount to the average annual profits that accrued to that Government from postal services during the period of five years immediately preceding the date aforesaid. . . .

Chapter VII
MISCELLANEOUS

117(1) Her Majesty in Council may by Order amend or revoke any of the provisions of this Constitution including this article and may by such an Order amend this Constitution for the purpose of including within the Federation other colonies (with their dependencies, if any).

(2) No draft of an Order proposed to be made under paragraph (1) of this article that –

(a) reduces the number of seats in the House of Representatives to be held by members of the House of Representatives elected in any Territory, or

(b) reduces the proportion of the total number of seats in the Senate or the House of Representatives to be held by Senators appointed for, or members of the House of Representatives elected in, any Territory,

shall be submitted to Her Majesty in Council unless the legislative chamber of that Territory, or, in the case of a Territory having two legislative chambers, each of those chambers, has by resolution signified that such reduction is acceptable to that chamber:

Provided that the foregoing provisions of this paragraph shall not apply in relation to any provision made under paragraph (1) of this article for creating, in connection with the accession to the Federation of the Colony of British Guiana or the Colony of British Honduras, additional seats in the Senate or the House of Representatives to be held by Senators appointed for, or members of the House of Representatives elected in, the Colony of British Guiana or the Colony of British Honduras, as the case may be . . . .

(4)No draft of an Order proposed to be made under paragraph (1) of this article that amends any of the provisions of this article shall be submitted to Her Majesty in Council unless the legislative chamber of each Territory or, in the case of a Territory having two legislative chambers, each of those chambers, has by resolution signified that the alteration effected by the amendment is acceptable to it.

118 Not later than the fifth anniversary of the date on which this Constitution comes into force there shall be convened a conference consisting of delegates from the Federation, from each of the Colonies referred to in paragraph (1) of article 1 of this Constitution and from the United Kingdom, chosen by their respective Governments, for the purpose of reviewing this Constitution; and that conference shall, among other things, review, in the light of progress made towards establishing a customs union within the Federation and other relevant factors, the powers conferred by this Constitution on the Federal Legislature to make provision for the levying of taxes on income and profits.

J Extracts from the Review of the Federal Constitution: Summary of Matters and Recommendations for consideration by the Inter-Govermental Conference on 2nd May 1961. (Government of the West Indies, Printed at Federal House, Port of Spain, Trinidad.)

On June 26th 1958, a Resolution was passed unanimously by the House of Representatives, urging that 'the Conference envisaged by Section 118 of the Constitution be convened not later than June 1959 in order to achieve the goal of self-government and Dominion Status within the Commonwealth at the earliest possible moment'.

The Federal and Unit Governments subsequently agreed that . . . the Conference . . . should be preceded by a preliminary Conference at which representatives of West Indian Governments would consider matters arising from the working of the existing Constitution and would formulate a pattern of proposals to be submitted to H.M.G. at the Conference under Article 118. .

The Conference found difficulty in reaching agreement on the main issues discussed and decided that joint detailed research and study of a wide range of subjects was essential before effective agreement could be achieved. The Conference therefore set up two Inter-Governmental Committees comprising Ministers of the Federal and Unit Governments, to examine and report on the detailed implications of Independence for the West Indies:

Committee I –

To examine and report on Constitutional Political matters, including the basis of representation in the Federal Legislature and the structure of Federation with regard to financial, economic, defence, overseas representation, freedom of movement of persons within the Federation and other matters; it should also present a study of possible frameworks.

Committee II –

To consider and advise on the most effective means of achieving a Customs Union, including internal free trade, in accordance with the aim expressed in the preamble to the Constitution. This would include Federal taxation policy and concessions, and incentives to industry.

These two Ministerial Committees, in dealing with their field of subjects at various stages, in turn set up Working Parties; Committee I set up a Ministerial Working Party to examine the question of representation in the Federal Legislature, and a Working Party of Officials (ALPHA) to examine and report on all other subjects assigned to that Committee. Committee II set up a Working Party of Officials (ORION) to examine and report on Customs Union and related matters. . . .

Inter-Governmental Conference and
the London Conference

In recent months the Federal and Unit Governments and H.M.G. in considering the timing and arrangements for resumption of the Inter-Governmental Conference and convening the London Conference envisaged in Article 118 and other necessary steps towards independence, have all expressed their firm resolve that independence be achieved with the least possible delay. . . .

APPENDIX

Summary of Matters and Recommendations on Constitutional and Political Issues which the Inter-Governmental Conference beginning on 2nd May will consider.

(i) Essential Attributes of Sovereignty

The 'Minimum criteria' which were defined by H.M.G. and endorsed by Committee I as orthodox and reasonable. They have been regarded as necessary to sustain sovereignty, and necessarily existing in the Federation before H.M.G. could sponsor it for independent membership of the Commonwealth:

(a) the possession of a defence force, capable of keeping the peace within the Federation's boundaries and posing at least a deterrent to any minor incursion by an outside aggressor;

(b) a diplomatic organisation, capable of maintaining the external relations of the Federation with the United Nations and the more important friendly neighbourly countries, especially of course the Commonwealth;

(c) an effective central administration capable of executing the policy of the Federal Government within the field of activity given it by the constitution;

(d) adequate financial resources, based on independent taxing and loan-raising powers sufficient to enable it to finance its own recurrent expenditure and obligations as those develop;

(e) the start of a workable programme for a Customs Union;

(f) central control of the currency;

(g) freedom of movement of peoples within its boundaries;

(h) the constitutional right and ability to negotiate and implement international treaties and agreements in the principal fields in which sovereign states normally negotiate with one another. . . .

(ii) Parity of Constitutional Powers

That prior to or at Independence all Unit Territories should enjoy full internal-government.

(iii) Accession of new Units

That provision should be made in the Constitution for the accession to the Federation of new Units. . . .

(iv) Unit powers over matters on Exclusive List

That the Constitution should provide, as in the present Article 43(2), for Territorial Legislatures to legislate on matters on the Exclusive Legislative List until the Governor-General, by proclamation, declares otherwise.

(v) Reserve List

The proposal agreed on by Committee I of the Inter-Governmental Conference, that the Federal Constitution should provide for a Reserve List, in addition to the Exclusive and Concurrent Legislative Lists, on which the subjects of Income Tax and Development of Industries would be placed for a period to be agreed.

It was agreed that while Income Tax and Industrial Development were fields in which the Federal Government should have a direct interest it was not at present proposed that the Federal Government should enter these fields, in view of the possibility that the economy of one or more Territories might be hampered or endangered should these subjects be brought under Federal control during the early years of Independence.

The procedure for transferring items from the Reserve List was referred to ALPHA, and the proposals submitted are as follows:

(a) If there is a prohibition against any such transfer for 10 years then at the end of that period the proposed amending law must be passed by each House of the Federal Legislature by an absolute majority and must then be approved by absolute majorities in a majority of the representatives, Houses of the Legislatures of the Territories representing a majority of the electors in the Federation qualified to vote as electors at Federal elections.

(b) If there is no prohibition for any given period, the proposed amending law must be passed by each House of the Federal Legislature by a two-thirds majority and must then be approved by absolute majorities in a majority of the representative Houses of the Territorial Legislatures representing not less than two-thirds of the population of the Federation.

(vi) Residual Powers

That the power to legislate on matters which are not included in either the Exclusive or Concurrent Lists should, as at present, remain with Unit Governments. . . .

(x) Machinery for formal consultation between the Federal and Unit Governments.

The recommendation of Committee I that:

(i) Provision should be made in the Constitution for a Regional Council of Ministers as a consultative body consisting of Unit Premiers and Chief Ministers, with the Prime Minister as Chairman;

(ii) The Council should be required to meet at least once per year but meetings could be summoned at the request of any of the members who would have the right to request also that any item be placed on the agenda.

(iii) Whenever the Federal Government proposed to assume responsibility in whole or in part for any subject or service on the Concurrent Legislative List which had hitherto been within the jurisdiction of a Unit or Units, the matter must first be discussed in the Regional Council of Ministers;

(iv) The Council could by regulation provide for the setting up of standing and other ad hoc Committees.

(xi) Representation in the Federal Legislature

The recommendation of Committee I of

(a) A Formula for Representation, embodying:

(i) the principle of representation by population;

(ii) provision of a basic seat for each of the ten Units, thus ensuring that each Territory is represented regardless of size or population;

(iii) provision for an additional seat for every complete population unit of 55,000 in each Territory making up a total House of 64, based on 1958 estimated population figures;

(iv) provision for each Unit to retain its present number of seats, except Jamaica (to be increased to 31) and Trinidad (to be increased to 15) whose percentages of the total seats would still be less than their respective percentages of the total population of the Federating Territories.

(b) Ceiling on Total Seats in Lower House:

There should be a ceiling on the total number of seats in the Lower House, and this should be written into the Federal Constitution. The number should not exceed a total of 70 for the 10 Territories now constituting The West Indies;

(c) Quinquennial Review:

There should be a Standing Committee of the Federal House of Representatives to undertake a quinquennial review of the unit of population per Representative in the light of Population Changes;

(d) Territorial Equality in Senate:

In order to preserve the principle of Territorial equality among the Units of the Federation, Montserrat should also have two Senators.

(xii) Common Citizenship and Freedom of Movement

The recommendation of Committee I that the principle of common citizenship and freedom of movement of citizens of the Federation within its borders should be written into the Constitution. . . .

After study of the matter, ALPHA has presented to the Inter-Governmental Conference, conclusions summarised as follows:

(a) That the problems of inter-territorial migration are not confined to Trinidad and Tobago. Barbados and to a less extent Antigua are also receivers of immigration.

(b) That this migration induces and sustains deepseated short and longterm effects which are harmful and hampers materially the development of the exporting Territories and the Federation generally.

(c) Trinidad and Tobago is however by far the largest receiver of immigration and the volume . . . imposes a specially intensive burden on that Territory.

The Working Party considered that correctives to the migration problem lay in economic and social measures . . . . ALPHA accordingly presented it as reasonable that a period for intense planning and adjustment should be allowed to ensure that the economic and social problems relating to an increased inflow of migrants to Trinidad (and perhaps other receiving Territories) following complete removal of restrictions, could be resolved.

Based upon the above conclusions, ALPHA has submitted to the Inter-Governmental Conference for consideration the following formula of proposals for constitutional arrangements relating to freedom of movement within the Federation upon Independence:

(a) The item 'control of movement of persons between the Territories' would be included on the Exclusive Legislative List at Independence (as recommended by Committee 1, para. 58 of its report of November 1960).

(b) However, until 31st December 1966, the Territorial Legislatures would retain a concurrent power to legislate with respect to this subject and thus those Territories that wished to do so could impose restrictions upon the entry of persons from other Territories. Those powers should subsist during the period, by non-action by the Governor-General by Proclamation to declare the subject exclusive. Present Article 44 which is to be retained would give the necessary Territorial power to legislate until 31st December 1966.

(c) Those Units who wished to legislate to establish, by arrangement, freedom of movement with other Territories, would be entitled to do so.

(d) On the 1st January, 1967, the power to legislate with respect to this matter would automatically become exclusively federal. . . .

K Extracts from the Report of the West Indies Constitutional Conference, 1961. (Cmnd. 1417/1961.)

CHAPTER II

THE INTER-GOVERNMENTAL AND LANCASTER HOUSE CONFERENCES

6 The Inter-Governmental Conference was finally reconvened on 2nd May, 1961. Once again Her Majesty's Government was represented by Colonial Office observers. The conference concluded on 16th May, 1961 having reached agreement (on some questions on a majority basis) on a wide range of questions, but leaving certain important issues outstanding, including a review of the details of the existing Federal Constitution. . . .

CHAPTER III

THE PROPOSED FEDERAL CONSTITUTION

The House of Representatives

11 The first House of Representatives will consist of 64 members of whom five will be elected in Barbados, 30 in Jamaica, 16 in Trinidad and Tobago, one in Montserrat and two in each of the other Territories. This is the result, based on the 1960 estimated population figures, of the formula contained in the Inter-Governmental Conference Decision No. 10, . . .

Development of Industries: Taxes on Income and Profits

20 Any proposal that the Federal Government should assume powers to legislate on the subjects "Development of Industries" and "Taxes on Income and Profits" will not come into force until the proposal has been approved by a majority of each House of the Federal Legislature and by an absolute majority of the Representative House of each Unit Legislature. There will be a review of this arrangement at the end of nine years at which, if no earlier decision has been taken to allow the Federal Legislature to exercise its powers in this matter, the Federal and Unit Governments will consider together whether any change should be made in these arrangements; provided that in the absence of agreement by all Governments there arrangements will continue. Further reviews will take place under arrangements to be agreed.

Freedom of Movement

21 Amendment of the provisions of the Federal Constitution dealing with this matter will be subject to special arrangements. It is accepted that the aim of the Federation should be to move, as quickly as possible, to a position whereby all inhabitants of the Federation will be able to move freely from Territory to Territory subject to no controls or impediments, other than those required in the general public interest (e.g. by public health requirements). Bearing in mind, however, that an immediate withdrawal of all existing migration controls throughout the Federation would cause serious social and economic stresses to certain Territories, the following arrangements have been agreed:–

- (i) the Federal Constitution will contain a declaration of intention that freedom of movement is to be the ultimate objective;
- (ii) this declaration will not invalidate laws reasonably necessary in the public interest of the Federation or of any Unit;
- (iii) control of the movement of persons will appear on the Exclusive Legislative List;
- (iv) during a period of nine years after Independence the exclusive powers of the Federal Government will not be exercised except

with the concurrence of the Unit Governments;

(v) the question of shortening this period will be reviewed at the end of the fourth year by the Federal Government in conjunction with all Territorial Governments;

(vi) during this period, no Unit Territory will legislate to increase or expand any restrictions upon migration now obtaining without the consent of the Federal Government; and

(vii) after the expiration of this period, each Territorial Government will have the right to determine, with the concurrence of the Federal Government, the appropriate remedial measures required to deal with any economic disruption that results in a Territory from inter-Territorial migration. . . .

Customs Union

26 The Customs Union Plan provides for the phased introduction of internal free trade and the adoption of a common external tariff to be completed within a maximum period of nine years. The supervision of the Plan will be carried out by a special Inter-Governmental Committee of Ministers, under the chairmanship of the Federal Minister of Trade and Industry. . . .

Federal Revenues

27 The mandatory levy will be abolished, and the Federal Government will be given an independent taxing power sufficient to enable it to finance its developing obligations. This taxing power will be governed by the following arrangements:

(a) The Federal Government's principal source of revenue will be the import duties of customs on all the items in List 1 in the Customs Union Plan excluding petroleum products. . . .

L Extract from the Report of the East Caribbean Federation Conference, 1962. (Cmnd. 1746/1962.)

Chapter I

INTRODUCTION

1 Between 1947 and 1956 several Conferences were held in London and in the West Indies to discuss the possibility of forming a federation of the British territories in the Caribbean area. At a Conference in London in February, 1956[1] the representatives of the Governments of Jamaica, Trinidad

1 Report published as Cmnd. 9733.

and Tobago, Barbados, the Leeward Islands, (other than the British Virgin Islands) and the Windward Islands decided upon federation between their ten territories. The Federation of The West Indies came into being in 1958 under an Order in Council[2] made under the British Caribbean Federation Act, 1956.

2 At a Conference held in London in May and June, 1961[3] attended by representatives of the Governments of the Federation of The West Indies and the Unit territories, agreement was reached on a revision of the Federal and Unit constitutions appropriate to independence which it was agreed should come about on 31st May, 1962. The conclusions of the Conference were agreed "subject to such decisions as may be obtained by each delegation from their respective legislatures and peoples".

3 The Government of Jamaica had already announced in May, 1960, that the electorate of the territory would be afforded an opportunity to determine by referendum whether Jamaica should remain a member of the Federation. This referendum was held on 19th September, 1961, when a majority of the electorate voted against Jamaica remaining in the Federation of the West Indies. In October, 1961, it was announced that the United Kingdom Government accepted the result of the referendum as a final indication of Jamaica's wishes and were prepared to introduce legislation to provide for Jamaica's withdrawal from the Federation.

4 On 13th January, 1962, the Secretary of State for the Colonies arrived in the West Indies for consultation with the Governments of the Federation and of the Units (other than Jamaica). On 14th January, 1962, the General Council of the governing party in Trinidad and Tobago unanimously approved a resolution which stated that the territory's participation in any new federation of the Eastern Caribbean should be rejected and that Trinidad and Tobago should proceed forthwith to independence. This policy was later adopted by a special convention of the party and the Premier of Trinidad and Tobago subsequently notified the Secretary of State that his Government had endorsed it. On 19th January, 1962 the Premier of Barbados and the Chief Ministers of the Leeward and Windward Islands held a meeting with the Secretary of State, at which they presented proposals for a federation between their eight territories.

2 Statutory Instrument No. 1364 of 1957

3 Report published as Cmnd. 1417.

M Extracts from the West Indies Act, 1962. c. 19. (U.K. Public General Acts.)

THE WEST INDIES ACT, 1962

An Act to enable provision to be made for the cessation of the inclusion of colonies in the federation established under the British Caribbean Federation Act, 1956, and for the dissolution of that federation and for matters consequential on the happening of either of those events; to enable provision to be made for the establishment of common courts and other authorities for, and fresh provision to be made for the government of, certain West Indian colonies; to enable provision to be made for the establishment of new forms of governments for combinations of such colonies; and for purposes connected with the matters aforesaid.

(18th April, 1962)

Be it enacted by the Queen's most Excellent Majesty, by and with the advice and consent of the Lords Spiritual and Temporal, and Commons, in this present Parliament assembled, and by the authority of the same, as follows:–

1 Her Majesty may –

(a) By Order in Council provide for a colony's ceasing to be included in the Federation established by virtue of section one of the British Caribbean Federation Act, 1956, by the name of the West Indies (in this Act referred to as "the Federation");

(b) by Order in Council dissolve the Federation and, with it, the authorities established by virtue of sub-paragraph (i) of paragraph (a) of subsection (1) of that section (in this Act referred to as the "Federal authorities"). . . .

PART III
THE EAST CARIBBEAN

A Extracts from the Report on the East Caribbean Federation, 1962 (Cmnd. 1746/1962.)

CHAPTER 1

INTRODUCTION

5 . . . the Secretary of State announced in the House of Commons on 6th February, 1962, that the United Kingdom Government had decided to introduce legislation under which the Federation of the West Indies could be dissolved. This legislation passed into law as The West Indies Act, 1962, which received the Royal Assent on 18th April, 1962; and an Order in Council was made on 23rd May, 1962, providing for the dissolution of the Federation on 31st May, 1962.

6 Between 26th February and 3rd March, 1962, representatives of the Governments of Barbados, the Leeward Islands and the Windward Islands held a Conference in Barbados to consider further the question of setting up a federation of their territories. At this Conference they confirmed their desire that such a federation should be established, and submitted detailed proposals to the Secretary of State. On 16th April, 1962, the Secretary of State informed the House of Commons that the United Kingdom Government had reached the conclusion that a federation of Barbados and the Leeward and Windward Islands appeared to offer the best solution to the problems of the area, provided that the federal constitution was such as to provide adequate powers to the central government and to offer a reasonable prospect of economic and financial stability.

7 A Conference of representatives of the eight Governments to consider this proposal opened in . . . London on 9th May, 1962. . . .

CHAPTER II

THE FEDERATION

8 The Conference agreed to recommend that there should be a federation of the eight territories. . . .

9 The West Indian Governments represented at the Conference expressed the desire that on the attainment of independence the new Federation should seek membership of the Commonwealth, and the constitutional proposals below reflect this desire. . . .

11 The Conference recommended that the Federation should be called "The West Indies Federation" and that the Federal capital should be in Barbados.

CHAPTER III

THE GOVERNOR-GENERAL

12 There would be a Governor-General for the Federation. Before independence he would be appointed by the Queen on the advice of the Secretary of State for the Colonies and his powers would be those appropriate to a constitution conferring internal self-government in the Federal sphere. In the period between the setting up of the Federation and its attainment of independence there would continue to be Queen's Representatives in the Units, and the method of their appointment would remain as at present.

CHAPTER IV

STRUCTURE OF THE FEDERAL GOVERNMENT

The Federal Legislature

13 The legislative power of the Federation would be vested in the Federal Legislature, which would consist of Her Majesty, a Senate and a House of Representatives. The respective powers of the Senate and the House of Representatives would be defined in the Federal constitution. Dual membership of the Legislatures of a Unit and of the Federation would not be permitted.

The Senate

14 Each Unit would be represented in the Senate by one Senator. There would be provision for an alternate representative in respect of each Unit. The Senators would be appointed by the Governor-General on the advice of the leading ministers of the Units which they represented. The members of the Senate would not be paid salaries.

The House of Representatives

15 The House of Representatives would be elected in accordance with the following formula –

(a) The number of members of the House of Representatives to be elected in a territory will be one member plus an additional member for each complete unit of population in that territory; and

(b) the unit of population will be 50,000.

There would be provision for an alternate member for any territory which did not qualify for any members in additon to the basic member.

The Federal Executive

16 The Federal Cabinet would consist of a Prime Minister and such number of other Ministers as the Prime Minister might decide: by convention this number would not exceed five. The Governor-General would assign portfolios to Ministers on the advice of the Prime Minister.

B Statement by the Secretary of State for the Colonies on His Visit to the West Indies, 22nd January 1963. (Parliamentary Debates (Commons), Vol. 670, 1962-63, cc. 13-14.)

The Secretary of State for the Colonies, Mr. Duncan Sandys, held a meeting in Barbados with Ministers of the territories concerned on 28th and 29th December to consider the next steps to be taken to implement the agreed conclusions of the London Conference of May, 1962, regarding the establishment of a "West Indies Federation".

In view of the current discussions between the Government of Grenada and the Government of Trinidad and Tobago regarding a possible union between the two countries, the Government of Grenada was not represented at the meeting. The Secretary of State explained that when the Government of Grenada had sought his permission to examine this matter with the Government of Trinidad and Tobago he had replied that he would not wish to raise any objection, on the understanding that these initial discussions would be purely exploratory and without commitment either to the British Government or the Government of Grenada.

The Ministers of the seven other territories re-affirmed their conviction that federation offers the best prospect for the economic and political progress of their territories. They emphasised that the uncertainty about Grenada's attitude did not in any way affect the determination of their governments to proceed with this plan; and they welcomed the assurance by Mr. Sandys of the British Government's continued readiness to support this project, irrespective of whether Grenada decided to participate.

It was noted that the legislatures of Montserrat, St. Kitts-Nevis-Anguilla and St Vincent had already passed resolutions expressing general approval of the recommendations of the London Conference, as set out in the White Paper (No. 1746). The Ministers of Antigua, Barbados, Dominica and St. Lucia stated that it was their intention likewise to seek decisions from their legislatures during the course of January.

It was also noted that the expert inquiries on fiscal matters, civil service organisation, economic development and the proposed customs union, which had been set in train at the London Conference, were well advanced and that reports were expected within the next three months.

In the light of this, it was decided to aim at convening a conference in London next June to reach final decisions about the form of the Federation.

C Extract from a Statement by the Secretary of State for the Colonies on the East Caribbean, 2nd July 1963. (Parliamentary Debates (Commons), Vol. 680, 1962-63, cc. 27-28.)

. . . the Parliamentary Under Secretary of State for the Colonies, Mr. Nigel Fisher, had discussions in Barbados with the Chief Ministers of the seven territories on 24th to 31st May. These discussions revealed a significant divergence of opinion between the governments concerned. Some of the differences arose from further reflection upon the original proposals, while others arose from consideration of recent expert studies of the administrative, fiscal and economic aspects of the problem.

At the final session of the conference on 31st May, the Chief Ministers presented to Mr. Fisher a statement suggesting a new procedure for establishing the federation. This statement had been agreed between the seven Ministers, subject to the reservations by three of them.

Since the suggestions in this statement involved radical changes in the proposals previously considered, and since time would clearly be required to study them, it was agreed that the Constitutional Conference in London would have to be postponed until later in the year.

D Extracts from the Circular Despatch from the Secretary of State for the Colonies to the Officers responsible for the administration of the East Caribbean Colonies dated 9th August, 1963.

9 As I understand the proposals of the Regional Council of Ministers, it is their wish that the Federation should become independent the moment the first Federal Government takes office, following the first elections. This is of course a highly unusual procedure. I am, however, prepared to consider it, but I must point out to you some of the consequences.

10 The proposed procedure would give the new Federal Government no opportunity to settle down before launched into independence. There are a number of matters related to the status of independence upon which decisions would be necessary almost immediately after the new Federal Government was established: These include the appointment of representatives of the Federation abroad, the acceptance of international rights and obligations inherited from the British Government, the negotiation of aid agreements with other independent countries, and the application for membership of the Common-

wealth which would have to be considered by all the then existing members. It would also be necessary to enact citizenship legislation. An interim authority established in connection with the setting up of the Federation . . . would not be in a position to reach final decisions on such matters, particularly when it came to entering into obligations with other Governments which those Governments could consider binding. In addition to the foregoing matters, the Ministers in the Federal Government would, in the initial period of the Federation's existence, have to undertake the formulation of detailed policy in the domestic field and the running in of an untried Government machine. To throw burdens of this magnitude on a newly-formed Government in a Federation which has only just been created without allowing time for consolidation could, I consider, lead to serious difficulties.

11 Most of these difficulties could be avoided if the date of independence were so fixed as to allow for a period to elapse after the first Federal Government had taken office, following the first elections. This period would not need to be long but should be sufficient to allow the new Government formally to request membership of the Commonwealth after reference to its legislature and for the other Commonwealth Governments to consider the request and to allow for proper arrangements to be made about the inheritance of international rights and obligations, representation abroad and similar matters.

12 I now turn to matters affecting the Federal Scheme itself on which divergencies of view were revealed at the Barbados discussions. . . .

13 First, I should like to have confirmation from all Governments that, apart from the important procedural matters dealt with above, the type of constitution to be discussed at the next conference will be as proposed in Cmnd. 1746. This will not mean that it will not be open to Governments to suggest amendments to it, particularly in the light of the expert surveys; but it does mean that it will not be open to the next conference to try to devise some radically different scheme.

14 The second question which gave rise to difficulty during the Barbados discussions was that of the executive powers of the Federation. I should like confirmation that it is now accepted by all Governments that the Federal Government should not be precluded by the constitution from having executive power over all matters in the legislative lists . . . . I should be prepared to discuss with you further special arrangements for a limited period such as the Regional Council of Ministers requested in their statement of 31st May to Mr. Fisher in respect of Income Tax, Postal Services and Police; but, with the possible exception of the Police Services, I am strongly of the opinion that a Unit Government should not have the right in perpetuity to withhold from the Federal Government the exercise of its proper powers in these fields.

15 Thirdly, I was pleased to note . . . that the principle of a unified public service for administrative, professional and technical staff is now accepted.

16 Next, I wish to turn to the question of the Federal Judiciary . . . . I am advised that the proposals presented by the Legal Committee of the Barbados Conference should be broadly acceptable, subject to further examination at the next conference. I would, however, suggest that they should be made known to Bar Associations and other interested bodies so that they can make known their views upon them.

17 Fifthly, there is the question of internal self-government in the Units. If the Federation is to be independent at its inception, consideration will also have to be given at the next conference to the form of unit constitutions at independence and to the stages by which the Units will advance through self-government to independence within the Federation.

18 Finally, I come to a number of financial matters. The first of these concerns the proposals for a Loan Council. . . . This was a matter which was examined with great care at the Marlborough House Conference in May 1962. It was, I understand, reopened during the discussions in Barbados. . . . As we are all agreed that one of the main purposes of setting up the Federation would be to make the area more viable economically, I could not accept any changes. . . . which would have the effect of weakening the loan raising powers of the Federation.

19 The second financial point to which I wish to refer concerns the sources of Federal revenue. I think it is generally agreed that the Federation must have sources of revenue under its own control which will be adequate for its needs. It will be most important to provide, under the constitution, that the sources of Federal revenue are sufficiently flexible for the Federal Government to be able to increase its revenues as its responsibilities grow. The exact formula for achieving this end will have to be worked out in detail at the next conference; but I wish to be sure at this stage that the principle is accepted. . . .

20 The third financial matter to which I wish to refer is . . . the question of H.M.G.'s assistance to the Federation after it is established. As stated in paragraph 32 of Cmnd. 1746, Her Majesty's Government recognise that a Federation would stand in need of external assistance for a period after it was established, both on capital and budgetary account. This is a matter which I should be prepared to discuss further with you at the next conference. I should also be prepared to discuss the general terms on which such aid might be made available after the establishment of the Federation. I see no possibility, however, of considering at the next conference the levels of aid for as long a period as ten years ahead.

21 Before the next conference can take place, a great deal of preparatory work requires to be done. As you have no adequate permanent machinery in the West Indies for undertaking this work yourselves, I would suggest that there should be a meeting of officials in the West Indies, to consider and advise on the instructions to legal draftsmen and on the civil service and fiscal

aspects of the proposed Federation. If this were agreed, I should be prepared to send out officials from the Colonial Office to help you in this work.

22 I should be grateful to have the comments of your Government on this despatch by the 15th September. They should be copied to all the other Governments concerned. If they show a sufficient measure of agreement on the points outstanding, then I will consult you about the timing of the next steps, which I should like to see follow as quickly as possible thereafter.

23 This despatch is being addressed to the Governor of Barbados and the Administrators of Antigua, St. Kitts, Montserrat, Dominica, St. Lucia and St. Vincent. It is being copied to the Chairman of the Regional Council of Ministers and, for information, to the Administrator of Grenada.

E Extracts from the Despatch from the Chairman of the Regional Council for Ministers (East Caribbean) to the Secretary of State for the Colonies, dated 14th September 1963.

I have the honour to refer to your circular despatch No. 405/63 of the 9th August . . . on the subject of a Federation for the Eastern Caribbean and to inform you that, on the suggestion of the Premier of Barbados, a meeting of the Regional Council of Ministers was convened in Antigua on 9th September to consider and submit to you agreed recommendations on the contents of the despatch. . . .

3 The majority of the delegates welcomed your statement in paragraph 5 of the despatch that the next Conference would take place on the basis that it would settle the terms of a constitution for an independent Federation.

Resolutions agreeing that the Conference be held on this basis have already been passed by both Houses of the Legislature in Barbados (unanimously in the Legislative Council).

The Barbados Government has pointed out that . . . the Barbados Government in successive conferences held since January 1962 has never deviated from the original and unanimous declaration of all the Governments concerned in favour of independence at its inception.

4 The Antigua, Dominica, St. Lucia, St. Vincent and St. Kitts Governments are prepared to seek authority from their legislatures to discuss at a London Conference an independent federation but all the Governments insist that a firm indication of Her Majesty's Government's intention to make the necessary capital and budgetary provision should first be obtained and that there should be a clear understanding of the financial and international obligations involved before independence is achieved. All delegates stressed the view before the conference of the measure of financial assistance which can be expected from Her Majesty's Government.

5 The Chief Minister of Montserrat is not at present in favour of submitting a resolution in the terms proposed to his legislature, but his attitude to the procedure for setting up the Federation is set out in the last sentence of paragraph 6 below and he is prepared to seek the approval of his legislature for proceeding on that basis.

6 Turning to the procedure for setting up the Federation . . . most delegates feel unable to be bound by the dates mentioned. . . . The Chief Minister of St. Kitts would wish to discuss the procedure proposed at the London Conference without committing himself to any definite dates. . . . He also feels that the life of the Federal Council of Ministers should, within reason, be as short as possible and he doubts whether it is necessary for a Governor-General to be appointed until very shortly before the Federation is launched, as he feels that the duties of that post might appropriately be performed until then by the Chairman Regional Council of Ministers. . . .

The Chief Minister of St. Lucia feels that the following should be the steps by which independence should be achieved:-

(a) The enactment of legislation to establish the Federation – February, 1964.
(b) Appointment of Governor-General.
(c) Federal elections – about August, 1964.
(d) Inauguration of Federal Parliament with full internal self-government – October 1964.
(e) Proclamation of Independence – July 4th, 1965.
(f) In the period between (a) and (b) the establishment of the Regional Council of Ministers as a body corporate to advise the Governor-General with powers to legislate on all matters necessary for the establishment of the Federation.
(g) Full internal self-government to be given to all units, on the inauguration of the Federation.
(h) An interim Public Service Commission to be appointed by Governor-General as soon as possible after his appointment, with subsequent appointment of essential pre-Federal Staff.

The Chief Minister of Montserrat would be prepared to support a similar procedure.

7 . . . with respect, the difficulties outlined in paragraphs 9-11 of the despatch are not considered insurmountable. Most Ministers feel that it is unnecessary for any lengthy period to be prescribed within which the new Federal Government could settle down and point out that there has been no insistence on such a period in the case of several other territories which have recently achieved independence; similar standards, in their view, should be applied to all territories approaching independence. Moreover they feel that an independent state will be far more capable of tackling the problems of a Fed-

eration effectively than a Government of inferior status. There already exist Commissions for the Eastern Caribbean in London and Montreal and there should be no long delay in obtaining approval of the appointment of Heads of these Commissions or any other similar Commissions which might be established abroad. They also feel that an arrangement could be made whereby existing international rights and obligations assumed by the British Government and applicable to the territories comprising the Federation could be continued for a period as has been done in the case of Trinidad and Tobago until the Federal Government had reached decisions on them.

It is also felt that aid agreements with other independent countries could be more effectively and expeditiously negotiated without the restrictions which Her Majesty's Government at present exercises. The need to refer the question of Commonwealth Membership to the Federal legislature is not appreciated since no such requirement, so far as is known, has been insisted upon in the case of other territories (e.g. Trinidad and Tobago) which have been granted independence in this area. It is considered that provisions relating to citizenship should appropriately be included and set out in the constitution itself in the same way as the Bill of Rights.

Finally no great difficulty is foreseen in Ministers of the Federal Government speedily reaching policy decisions in the domestic field as these would have been broadly settled before the Ministers offered themselves for election. Experienced civil servants will, it is expected, be recruited into the service of the Federal Government and there seems no reason to believe that they could not constitute a reliable machine for carrying out the policy of Federal Ministers.

The Chief Minister of Dominica felt that it was impossible to ignore the desirability of some period being prescribed in which the new Federation could settle down and expressed the fear that if inexperienced politicians were to be elected to the new Federal Government they would be faced with a very formidable task.

The Chief Minister of St. Lucia felt that he would need convincing that the difficulties outlined in paragraphs 9-11 of your despatch under reference did not exist.

The Chief Minister of St. Kitts felt that he would like to confront representatives of Her Majesty's Government about the difficulties envisaged and assess whether in fact the difficulties were insurmountable.

If he was convinced that they were insurmountable he would be prepared to agree to fixing the date of independence at the earliest and most suitable date by which all the necessary formalities and obligations of the new Federaation could be discharged. That date in his view should be fixed by the Constitution as an optimum date leaving the Federal Government free to declare itself independent earlier if the circumstances made this possible.

8 With regard to paragraph 12 of your despatch, it was agreed that a constitution of the type set out in Cmnd. 1746 would provide a suitable framework for the Federal constitution provided that suitable amendments and safeguards were made in the constitution to reflect the various adjustments which would be necessary in the light of the expert surveys and the agreement set out in this despatch.

9 With regard to paragraph 14 of your despatch, the Conference gave earnest and prolonged consideration to the question of the definition of the executive powers of the Federation. As a result, it was agreed that paragraph 24 of the White Paper Cmnd. 1746 should be amended so as to provide that the following services at present provided by unit Governments would be transferred to the Federal Government:

(i) Audit.
(ii) Customs and Excise.
(iii) Federal Judiciary, Supreme Courts and the Federal Legal and Judicial Commission which would be responsible for the appointment, promotion, transfer and discipline of Magistrates.
(iv) Prisons.
(v) Telecommunications (other than Broadcasting, Television and Unit Telephone Services).
(vi) Civil Aviation.
(vii) Meteorology.
(viii) Exchange Control.
(ix) External and Internal Movement of persons and Passport Services (subject to paragraph 30 of Cmnd. 1746).
(x) Weights and Measures.
(xi) The Service and execution in any Unit of the Civil and Criminal processes, judgements, decrees, orders and decisions of the Courts in any other Unit and the attendance of persons from any Unit at the Courts in any other Unit.

In respect of the transfer of the administration of Postal Services, Police and Income Tax from the unit Governments to the Federal Government, the St. Kitts, St. Lucia, St. Vincent and Antigua delegations were in favour of a five year period being prescribed within which the administration of these departments would remain with the Units, and that subsequently transfer to the Federal Government could only be carried out in accordance with the entrenched provisions of the Federal Constitution as outlined in paragraph 43 of the White Paper.

The Barbados delegation felt that the entrenched provisions of paragraph 43 of the White Paper should be applied from the establishment of the Federation without waiting for a period of five years.

The Chief Minister of Dominica, having regard to the deletion of the item (v) (Police) from paragraph 24 of the White Paper and the inclusion of a number of items from the concurrent legislative list, was unable to agree to either proposal. He felt that Income Tax, Magistrates' Courts and Postal Services should be administered by the Federal Government.

The Chief Minister of Montserrat said that he was unable to depart from his position as set out below.

10 It will be observed that Item (iii) of paragraph 24 of the White Paper "Income Tax" has been removed from the control of the Federal Government and established as a unit responsibility. The Federal Government, however, save in the case of Montserrat, would exercise legislative power with respect to the rates of tax on company incomes and the types of allowance on which relief from personal income tax could be claimed. The unit Governments would legislate with respect to the rates of personal income tax and allowances. The Federal Government would exercise supervision through an Inspector General of Inland Revenue.

11 With regard to Police it was agreed that the Federal Government should be responsible for the Police Training School and for the creation of a nucleus police force specially trained for security duties. The Police Forces in each unit, would, however, remain under the control of the unit Governments and gazetted officers in respect of appointment, promotion, transfer or discipline would be under the control of the Federal Police Commission. The Federal Government would have power to take control of all police forces in case of emergency. . . .

14 As regards federal sources of revenue all delegations agreed that the sources of revenue of the Federation had been agreed after lengthy discussion at the Sixth Meeting of the Regional Council of Ministers held in Barbados in May, 1963, and that flexibility could be achieved by adjusting the amount of revenue to be returned to unit Governments.

15 With regard to the question of Her Majesty's Government's assistance to the Federation after its establishment (paragraph 20 of your despatch) the Conference was impressed by the arguments advanced by Dr. O'Loughlin at the conference in support of assistance for a ten year period. In her view it would be unrealistic to attempt to settle financial aid for a lesser period as to do so would threaten the achievement of full financial independence by the Unit Governments. During a ten year period the Federation could be enabled to stand on its feet financially and, in her assessment, if financial aid of the order suggested in her Report was forthcoming, all unit Governments should be able to escape from grant-in-aid and become economically viable at the end of a ten year period with the possible exception of Montserrat. Moreover there would be serious organisational difficulties to absorbing a capital programme of the size necessary to secure viability in any shorter period, although it would not be impossible.

Ministers strongly felt that the statement contained in paragraph 20 of your despatch that no possibility was seen at the next conference of considering the levels of aid for a period as long as ten years could only cause the greatest concern and could jeopardise the success of the Federation as a whole. The Conference unanimously endorsed a request that financial assistance on the scale envisaged in Dr. O'Loughlin's Economic Survey be made available and that no conference to settle the details of a constitution for an independent Federation be held until satisfactory assurances about the quantum and duration of assistance from Her Majesty's Government had been obtained.

F Extracts from the Report of the Civil Service Commissioner on Federation of the East Caribbean Territories, 1963. (Cmnd. 1992/1963.)

21 The history of attempts to establish some sort of Federation in the West Indies is not an appropriate subject to outline and discuss in this Report. However, a brief reference to the collapse of the Federation set up in 1958 must be made, if only because it is still so fresh in people's minds, not least in the minds of civil servants. The break up of that Federation, after the Parliamentary and administrative machine had been built up and had actually operated for four years, inevitably led to a great many difficult problems. One of these concerned the future of public servants who in good faith had joined the Federal service only to see it disintegrate under their very eyes. . . . The main point we wish to emphasise is that in view of this recent history it would not be surprising if the prospect of employment by a new Federal Government were looked upon with a degree of doubt by some of the members of the existing unit public services. For this reason it would be essential that the plans for the new Federal Services should be prepared with the utmost care and explained in full detail before any appointments were actually made. . . .

22 While speaking of the collapse of the 1958 Federation it may not be inappropriate to mention an incident of nearly 100 years ago that is now seldom referred to but which gave rise to a phrase that is still heard now and again. We understand that at the time of the Governorship of Mr. (later Sir John) Pope Hennessey (1875-1876) an effort was made to introduce a Federation and this was strenuously resisted in some quarters. In Barbados the resistance developed from heated arguments to fights and disturbances. We were credibly informed that as a result of that incident any brawl or free fight in some of the country areas in the island is even now apt to be described by the local people as "a regular federation". If this light-hearted interjection has any relevance it must tend to underline the need for a conscious and determined effort to win support for Federation in advance of its coming, and the need

to plan the new organisation carefully and wisely so as to gain confidence for it before it is established. . . .

Federal Services

24 . . . the following services at present provided by Unit Governments would be transferred to the Federal Government:–

Audit
Customs and Excise
Income Tax
Judiciary, including not only Judges but also Magistrates and the administration of the Courts
Police
Postal Services
Prisons
Telecommunications (other than broadcasting, television and unit telephone services). . . .

We have extended the above list by including Civil Aviation (Air Traffic Control). This subject . . . seems to us to be ideally a subject for the Federal Government and we notice that it is in fact incorporated in the exclusive legislative list.

Unification

25 . . . the London Conference Report . . . accepts in principle the idea of a Unified Public Service for both Federal and Unit Governments, covering the senior administrative, professional and technical grades; and leads up to our appointment to enquire into practical problems involved.

26 The principle of unification has been under discussion for a very long time and has been endorsed by several Commissions over the years. . . . At the same time we must add that in talking with officials they more often than not enlarged on the practical difficulties involved and the obstacles in the way of movement from unit to unit. Frequently such movement was described as "going abroad". And that was by no means the only evidence we found of an insular outlook that must be broken down as quickly as possible if a Unified Public Service – if not Federation itself – is to take root and prosper.

27 On the other hand it was encouraging to meet some of the younger, well qualified and progressive types, mostly but not entirely in the professional and technical groups, who were enthusiastic about unification and inclined to minimise the difficulties. They could hardly wait to get to grips with the challenges ahead of them. This is the spirit to foster and we feel sure it can be fostered and will grow sturdily if the initial planning of unification is sound and if too much is not expected too soon. . . .

G Extracts from the Circular Despatch from the Secretary of State for the Colonies to the Officers Responsible for the Administration of the East Caribbean Colonies, dated 22nd March 1965.

4 In my view, the first requirement if the federation is to endure is that the Federal Government should have the power to deal with all matters of major concern to the region as a whole. This is particularly important in relation to matters concerning the economic development of the region. The Eastern Caribbean will remain dependent for some years to come on external aid for its economic development; and the Federal Government must be strong enough not only to ensure that this aid is used to the best advantage but also to inspire the donors of such aid, and private investors, with confidence in its capacity to ensure political stability and promote the welfare and development of the region.

5 At the same time I recognise that the system of government we are considering is a federal system and that under such a system the Unit Governments must be left clearly responsible for the matters which are of purely Unit concern. I also recognise that in many areas of government it is not possible in the constitution to draw a sharp distinction between matters of Unit concern and matters which affect the region as a whole. The exact division of powers between the Federal and the Unit Governments is still open for negotiations; . . . It would, however, in my view be essential to provide that in general the executive authority of the Federation should extend to those matters with which the Federal Legislature has for the time being power to make laws. . . .

6 I turn next to the question of Federal finances. The exact method by which public revenue is divided between the Federal and Unit Governments is one which always gives rise to difficulty in any Federal Constitution. It is clearly a matter to which all the Governments concerned in the present negotiations have already given a great deal of thought, and it is also one on which . . . the Governments concerned are still not entirely agreed among themselves. It would be essential in my view that the Federal Government should have its own sources of finance and that these should be adequate to permit it, when it so decides, to carry out all the functions which under the constitution it is empowered to undertake. The exact way in which this is to be achieved will be for further negotiation; but I should like some further consideration to be given to the possiblity that from the outset the Federal Government might derive some of its revenue from income tax.

7 A further matter to which I attach importance concerns the powers of the Federation in relation to any matter tending to undermine financial stability or good government in any part of the Federation. Paragraph 19 of

the draft Federal Scheme proposes that control over external borrowing should be on the Exclusive List and that the Federal Government would be empowered to raise loans on the joint security of the revenues of the Federal and Unit Governments. Under these circumstances, it seems to me that serious misgovernment or financial maladministration in one part of the Federation could damage the credit-worthiness of the whole. Paragraph 20 of the draft Federal Scheme gives the Federal Government the power to set up Commissions of Enquiry in such circumstances but does not provide the Federal Government with any powers to deal with the situation after the Commission of Enquiry has reported. This in my view is a serious defect in the proposals, and I should wish to consider with you in any further negotiations how this might be remedied. . . .

H Extracts from the White Paper on Federal Negotiations 1962-65. (Government Printing Office, Bridgetown, Barbados, 1965.)

8 . . . early in January, 1962, the Chief Ministers of the Windward and Leeward Islands, and the Premier of Barbados unanimously rejected the proposal contained in a resolution passed by the ruling Party in Trinidad and Tobago that the eight territories were welcome to have unitary statehood with Trinidad and Tobago. Instead, they took advantage of the then Secretary of State's visit to Trinidad, to assemble and to present a joint memorandum to Mr. Maudling with whom they held discussions on January 19th, 1962. Thus did discussion on a new Federation begin.

9 At this meeting with Mr. Maudling, the Premier of Barbados *emphasised that considerable economic and financial assistance was required for regional development, and that the new Federation must be an independent state within the Commonwealth simultaneously with the dissolution of the then Federation.* In this he was fully supported by the other Ministers who stressed the urgency of the matter, and insisted that the recommendations of the Economic Aid Mission which was sent to the Windward and Leeward Islands after the Lancaster House Conference, should be implemented.

10 On the question of Independence, Mr. Maudling said that this required careful examination since the question of viability was important. This the Premier and Chief Ministers effectively answered with evidence showing the National Incomes of several countries which, on that basis alone, were less entitled to the enjoyment of sovereignty than the proposed Federation.

11 After the departure of the Secretary of State, the Chief Ministers of the Windward and Leeward Islands and the Premier of Barbados held a Conference in Bridgetown from February 26th to March 3rd, 1962 and continued

more detailed examination of the proposed Federal Constitution. A despatch, No. 130, was forwarded to the Secretary of State on 14th March. The Secretary of State, replied on 30th April, 1962 urging a stronger central Government than proposed; that Income Tax should be an exclusively Federal matter, as well as Higher Education and External Loans. The Secretary of State also queried the necessity for a full ministerial system in the unit territories and rejected the idea that the decisions arrived at the Windward and Leeward Islands Constitutional Conference held in June, 1961, for internal self-government in those territories, would be appropriate in the new Federation.

12 As for the conclusion that the proposed Federation would be in need of a considerable amount of financial assistance, the Secretary of State stated: *"I should make it plain at once that the British Government, in view of their many heavy commitments in other areas of the world where needs are in many cases even greater, are unlikely to be able to assist the West Indies on a greater scale than has so far been envisaged. It will therefore be necessary to attract to it aid from elsewhere."*

13 In May, 1962, a Conference was held in London between the United Kingdom Government and the representatives of the eight remaining territories. The recommendations of the Conference were published in June in Cmnd. Paper 1746. This Report was laid on the table of the Legislature and its proposals were debated from June 20th, 1962, and concluded on February 19th, 1963. The resolution that "this House approve in principle the Report of the Eastern Caribbean Federation Conference, 1962," . . . was passed. . . .

19 On the 19th January, 1962, the Premier of Barbados, in presenting the proposals drawn up by the representatives of the eight Governments, informed the Secretary of State:–

"(1) they felt strongly that the new association must be an independent state within the Commonwealth immediately on its establishment, simultaneously with the dissolution of the present Federation;

(2) for the survival of the new Federation it would be imperative to have a large measure of financial assistance over a period. . . at the same time considerable assistance for economic development was needed" – . . . .

28 . . . far from a crystallisation of proposals for positive assistance to the Eastern Caribbean, the attitude of the British is becoming vaguer and more nebulous as time goes on. Indeed when the Premier of Barbados enquired from the Secretary of State in December, 1963, how soon a positive statement could be expected on the quantum of financial assistance that would be forthcoming, . . . the Secretary of State's reply was that the British Government was not *"buying a Federation"*, and that the islands should want a Federation

for a Federation's sake. The Premier's reply was that the people of Barbados had no Federation to sell, and were looking not for colonies, but partners.

29 The Ninth Meeting of the Regional Council of Ministers was held in Barbados in October, 1964, when the Draft Federal Scheme was discussed. The newly elected Government of St. Lucia attended the Regional Council of Ministers for the first time. The Scheme was accepted with reservations by the Government of Antigua on Income Tax, Agriculture, Police and Postal Services; by the Government of St. Kitts on Customs Union; by the Government of St. Vincent on Police; and by the Governments of Dominica and St. Lucia on the utilisation of Federal Revenues. On 31st October, the meeting was adjourned until 7th December, 1964, in order to give the respective Governments time to consider these reservations, and to arrive at a decision on the publication of the draft Federal Scheme as was being urged by the Secretary of State, and by various sections of the Press both at home and abroad. At this meeting it was decided that no publication of the Scheme would be made until outstanding matters had been settled, and the views of the Government of Antigua on the points reserved had been communicated to each Government.

30 As a result of a decision taken at the Ninth Meeting of the Regional Council of Ministers, the Draft Federal Scheme was published on 10th February, 1965. . . .

The scheme included procedural steps for establishing the Federation and the reservations of the Governments of Antigua, St. Lucia and Dominica. . .

35 Between the receipt of the despatch (dated 22nd March, 1965) and the convening of the Tenth Meeting of the Regional Council of Ministers, April 26th, the Government of Antigua indicated that it would not be in the best interests of the people of that territory to enter into a Federation on the terms laid down by the Secretary of State and the Draft Federal Scheme.

36 During the month of March, the Draft Federal Scheme was debated in the Legislative Council of St. Lucia and, on the invitation of the Government Ministers, the Scheme was rejected.

37 . . . The withdrawal of the Government of Antigua and the rejection of the Draft Federal Scheme by the Legislature of St. Lucia, suddenly created a new situation for the Governments, and an atmosphere of pessimism shortly before the Tenth Meeting of the Regional Council of Ministers which had been fixed for the last week of April, 1965.

38 . . . The Barbados Cabinet decided –

(i) that on the general principle of the desirability of an East Caribbean Federation, there was no change in this Government's position as expressed some three years ago;

(ii) that one of the contributing factors to the state of disagreement and indecision among the seven territories was the continued failure of the United Kingdom Government to state in unequivocal terms the quantum of capital finance which it was prepared to make available to the Federation for the long overdue development of the constituent territories;

(iii) that any further discussions on proposals for the establishment of an East Caribbean Federation would be dependent on the willingness of the United Kingdom to state its intentions with regard to (ii) above.

39 Discussion of the proposed Federation began on the morning of April 27th, 1965. . . . The Chief Ministers of Dominica, St. Vincent and St. Kitts-Nevis-Anguilla expressed their willingness to proceed with proposals for the establishment of a Federation of six territories. The Chief Minister of Montserrat said that, with the withdrawal of Antigua, his Government would be very reluctant to enter into a Federation. The Chief Minister of St. Lucia, after much delay, stated that the St. Lucia Delegation was "prepared to recommend to the St. Lucia Government that they should continue their discussion with such other territories as wish to establish some form of association in the Easter Caribbean". The particular form of association he could not, however, state because "a number of things had changed since they had been summoned to the meeting". (*e.g.* Antigua's withdrawal and Montserrat's reluctance to continue).

40 The Premier of Barbados submitted to the meeting the decision of the Barbados Cabinet of 24th April, 1965, and further informed the Conference that, in view of the withdrawal of Antigua from the Federal exercise, and the uncertainty of the Governments of St. Lucia and Montserrat as regards the form of association required, whether unitary or federal, he felt that publicity ought to be given to the new situation that had arisen, and that after consultation with the political parties and discussion in the Legislature, the Government of Barbados would be in a position to make their views known and at such time they might be willing to resume discussions.

41 After one of the St. Lucia delegates had challenged the *bona fides* of the Barbados Cabinet decision in rather offensive terms, the Premier of Barbados felt himself constrained to withdraw from the meeting which was adjourned to the following day.

42 On the resumption the St. Lucia Ministers did not attend and the Chief Minister of Dominica withdrew from the meeting since no other leader of a delegation was present. After dealing with certain minor items on the agenda and the estimates of the overseas Commissions the Tenth Meeting of the Regional Council of Ministers adjourned *sine die* on Thursday, 29th April, 1965.

43 An examination of the efforts of the Regional Council of Ministers to

arrive at some consensus on the shape and form of a federal structure, reveals several changes of attitude from time to time which on the surface expose the Governments to possible charges of inconsistency and of being unable to make firm decisions.

(i) At the meeting with the Secretary of State in Trinidad early in 1962, the Governments requested that an Independent Federation should be established on the same date as the dissolution of the former West Indies Federation.

At the Conference in London in 1962, the Governments appear to have accepted a dilatory proposal that the date of Independence would be a matter to be discussed some indeterminable time after the establishment of the Federation. At a later date the Governments reverted to their former demand for Independence for the Federation from its inauguration.

(ii) The division of legislative powers between the federal government and the territorial governments was set out in the Report of that Conference and was accepted by the Governments as a basis for a Federal Constitution. Subsequently, several Governments expressed their disagreement with the allocation of subjects as they appeared in the Exclusive and Concurrent lists.

(iii) The question of the location of the Federal Capital was settled by the Governments of the Windward and Leeward Islands even before the arrival of the Barbados Delegation in Trinidad in January, 1962. The Government of St. Lucia has challenged the wisdom of that decision and, along with the Government of Montserrat, has attempted to reopen the question. . . .

THE CASE FOR BARBADOS INDEPENDENCE

95 "In trying to assess the characteristics of the people, it must be realised that they do constitute a nation. In the first place they feel themselves to be one".

(Bruce Hamilton writing on "Barbados and the Confederation Question 1871-1885" published by the Crown Agents 1956).

99 At any time since 1962 the Government of Barbados could have concluded the constitutional arrangements for Independence, if it had been prepared to dissociate this territory from attempts to establish an Eastern Caribbean Federation.

100 The main misgivings about separate Independence for Barbados appear to be –

(a) *that by so doing it would make the establishment of a Federation more difficult,*

(b) *that it would be too costly,*

(c) *that the country cannot defend itself, and*

(d) *that the country could not be economically viable on its own. . . .*

106 . . . *The core of the problem is that, whether there is a Federation or not, the Government of the United Kingdom, as Sir Ellis Clarke was at pains to point out, has a binding political, economic, legal and moral obligation to its territories in the Eastern Caribbean other than Barbados.*

108 . . . we do not want to have [federation] . . . without the assurance that the people of this island will not become the holders in due course of a dishonoured promissory note. To sum up, the justification for economic aid to the Windward and Leeward Islands does not arise from the establishment of a Federation. Therefore its establishment could not be rendered more difficult by Barbados' Independence unless it was intended that Barbados should assume the responsiblity which so clearly lies at other people's doors. . . .

116 The fact that they cannot afford to maintain an Army, Navy or Air Force cannot in any way weaken a people's resolve to manage their own affairs. Freed from the temptations to posture and to strike attitudes, they can bring to international affairs a sanity which larger, and therefore deeply committed, nations cannot do. They have no 'a priori' enemies, because they have only friendship to give and fair treatment to receive. The test of sovereignty in the middle Twentieth Century is not therefore a country's ability to defend itself against attack since no country on earth could so qualify in the age of nuclear warfare.

117 The issue of economic viability is soon disposed of. We pay our way now and we intend to continue to do so. We will strengthen the economy by trade and will not cringe for aid. The United Kingdom Government has invariably furnished considerable financial assistance to the emergent countries of the Commonwealth as they move into Independence. . . .

118 It is difficult to understand the reluctance of the United Kingdom to make reparations to the Eastern Caribbean.

119 This territory has long possessed all the adjuncts of a nation approaching sovereignty. It has never since its settlement in the early seventeenth century, received any grant in support of its administration. Three hundred years of representative institutions in a parliamentary system have been crowned with the reality of full internal self government. It possesses an infrastructure superior to that enjoyed by many independent states admitted to membership of the United Nations Organisation, both at its inception and in the recent past. Its rate of economic growth, particularly since 1961, indicates that, in this field, the burdens of Indpendence can be adequately sustained and that these burdens need not be unduly onerous.

120 In any case, the arguments for Independence do not rest on the mere rebuttal of weak arguments against it. The real and final test of people's fitness for sovereignty is their willingness to discharge the obligations arising out of Independence.

121 In the history of the Commonwealth, no former British territory has moved into Independence with a longer tradition of Parliamentary Government than Barbados. No country has endured a longer period of tutelage. In recent years, of all the British Colonies to achieve Independence, Jamaica alone possessed a representative assembly going back, though not without interruption, to 1664. Important countries like Ceylon, Ghana, Nigeria, Cyprus and Malta, and even Trinidad and Tobago, enjoyed responsible Government only for a few years immediately preceding their attainment of Independence.
122 The Government has made no formal arrangement with the United of this territory will not meet the full responsibility which the challenge of Independence will provide. On the contrary, it is convinced their sense of pride and their industry, are more than adequate to support the dignity of Nationhood. Moreover, it is further convinced that the people of this island will so meet their obligations in the new setting that their fellow citizens in the Eastern Caribbean will reap the benefits of our exertion and example.
123 The Government has made nor formal arrangement with the United Kingdom Government for Independence, although recent official pronouncements have indicated that the Government of the United Kingdom would willingly entertain the proposal.

CHAPTER 6

THE ASSOCIATED STATES

A Proposals for a new constitutional status for the "six".

(i) Extracts from Constitutional Proposals for Antigua, St. Kitts/Nevis/Anguilla, Dominica, St. Lucia, St. Vincent and Grenada. (Cmnd. 2865/1965.)

Since the Federation of the West Indies was dissolved in 1962, the possibility of forming federation between Barbados, Antigua, Montserrat, St. Kitts/Nevis/Anguilla, Dominica, St. Lucia, St. Vincent and Grenada has been the subject of extensive but inconclusive discussion. Grenada withdrew from the talks in 1962 and Antigua in 1965; and in August 1965, the Government of Barbados proposed to its Legislature that Barbados should proceed to separate independence before considering federation further.

2 The British Government still believe that closer association between the territories offers the best future prospect for the area but they recognise that this is a matter for local decision. In the meantime, some of the Governments concerned have asked for early constitutional changes giving them greater control over their own affairs. The British Government have great sympathy with the object of these requests, but they feel that the time has come to replace the existing colonial relationship by a new form of association. Accordingly they have made new and comprehensive constitutional proposals to each of the Governments of Antigua, St. Kitts/Nevis/Anguilla, Dominica, St. Lucia, St. Vincent and Grenada which, if they are acceptable to the territories and to Parliament, will, they believe, achieve these two objectives. (The British Government intend to discuss constitutional changes for the smaller territory of Montserrat separately with that Government at a later date.)

3 The proposals[1] offer each territory arrangements under which it would become a state in association with Britain, with control of its internal affairs and with the right to amend its own constitution, including the power to end the association with Britain and to declare itself independent. . . .

4 So long as the territories remained states in association with Britain, the British Government would accept responsiblity for their external affairs and defence and the British Parliament and Her Majesty in Council would have legislative powers for the discharge of this responsibility. Apart from these powers and responsibilities, and powers concerned with the application in the territories of the British Nationality Acts, the British Parliament would have no powers to legislate for the territories without their consent and the British Government would have no responsibility for the conduct of their affairs.

5 A salient feature of the arrangements proposed by the British Government would be the entrenchment of safeguards in the constitution of the territories for the maintenance of the constitutions, for the preservation of democratic forms of government and for the protection of fundamental rights. The British Government propose that a Superior Court for the region should be established as a means of securing the observances of these safeguards.[2] The Court would have jurisdiction to determine whether any law or any executive act was inconsistent with the constitutions and also to settle all questions on the interpretation of the constitutions; and it would have power to issue and to enforce orders or directions to ensure compliance with the constitutions. The President of the Court would be appointed by the Lord Chancellor.

6 The territories would continue to be eligible to receive aid from Britain under the British Government's aid programme. The British Government recognise that some of them will continue to need budgetary aid, and under the new arrangements it will be possible for such aid to be provided in much the same way as it is to certain independent Commonwealth countries. . .

8 Once the constitutional future of these territories is settled, the British Government hope that their Governments will have discussions among themselves about future regional co-operation.

1 See Memorandum in Appendix I below, This was sent to all the Administrators of the territories under cover of despatches from the Secretary of State for the Colonies.

2 See Document C(ii) below in this chapter.

Appendix I

MEMORANDUM

OUTLINE CONSTITUTION FOR . . . .

THE QUEEN'S REPRESENTATIVE

The Queen's Representative will be appointed by Her Majesty.[3] In relation to such appointments it will be understood, although not expressed as law, that the Secretary of State will be guided by the advice of the Chief Minister of the territory when submitting advice to Her Majesty; there will be consultation between the British Government and the Chief Minister before the Chief Minister makes any recommendation to the Secretary of State. The Queen's Representative will be required, as a matter of practice, to be a British subject, but there will be no restriction as to the territory from which he is drawn. . . .

5 The Queen's Representative will act in all matters on the advice of his Ministers except –

(a) in the exercise of any functions conferred on him relating to the appointment of the Chief Minister or a leader of opposition or the revocation of such an appointment;

(b) in the exercise of any functions which the Constitution or any other law requires him to exercise on the advice of other persons or authorities (e.g. the Service Commissions);

(c) that he may, if advised by Ministers to dissolve the legislature, refuse to act in accordance with that advice if he considers it in the interests of the territory to do so.[4]

THE BRITISH GOVERNMENT REPRESENTATIVE

6 There will be a representative of the British Government in the area who will conduct the relations of the British Government with the territories which enter into association arrangements on the lines proposed in this memorandum.

THE LEGISLATIVE CHAMBERS[5]

8 The legislature of the territory will have powers of legislation in respect of all matters; the present powers to reserve bills or disallow laws pass-

3 And would normally hold office for five years.
4 In the Independence Constitutions of the West Indies this discretion is den-

5 The Memorandum allows for either unicameral or bicameral legislatures.

ed by the territorial legislature will be discontinued.

9 Subject to the enactment of the necessary legislation by the British Parliament –

(a) the legislature of the territory will have power to alter the Constitution in accordance with the procedures described in paragraphs 10 to 12 below;

(b) section 2 of the Colonial Laws Validity Act 1865 will not apply to laws enacted by the legislature of the territory after the new Constitution comes into force;[6]

(c) Acts of the British Parliament passed after the commencement of the new Constitution (other than Acts passed in pursuance of the powers referred to in paragraph 24 below or Acts relating to citizenship referred to in paragraph 27 below) will not extend to the territory except at the request and with the consent of the territory signified by resolution of the chamber or chambers of the legislature of the territory.

ALTERATIONS TO CONSTITUTION

10 The Constitution will initially be established by Order of Her Majesty in Council. Thereafter there will be two methods by which the Constitution may be altered as follows:–

(a) by the legislature of the territory in accordance with the procedures described in paragraphs 11 and 12 below – this will be the normal method;

(b) by the British Parliament or Her Majesty in Council; subject to what is said in paragraph 13 about alteration of the relationship between Britain and the territory, alterations of the Constitution will only be made by the British Parliament or Her Majesty in Council at the request and with the consent of the territory, signified by resolution of the chamber or chambers of the legislature of the territory passed by simple majority. It will be understood that there will be no obligation on the British Parliament or Her Majesty in Council to comply with a request from the territory to alter its Constitution.

11 Following practices commonly adopted in independent countries which have autonomy in matters of constitutional alteration, there will be special procedures for amendment of the Constitution; for this purpose certain basic clauses will be distinguished as enshrining the arrangements for

6 Section 2 of the Colonial Laws Validity, Act 1865 states that Colonial Laws are null and void only to the extent to which they are repugnant to any law of the United Kingdom which extends to the Colony.

democratic government and for the relationship between Britain and the territory and the procedure for alteration of these clauses will involve approval of the electorate. With the exception of the basic clauses, the legislature of the territory will be empowered to amend any provision of the Constitution by a majority of not less than two-thirds of all the members of the elected chamber and, if there are two chambers by a majority of all the members of the upper chamber.

12 The legislature of the territory will be empowered to alter the basic clauses referred to above by a law passed in accordance with the procedure set out above (i.e. by a majority of not less than two-thirds of all the members of the elected chamber and, if there are two chambers, by a majority of all the members of the upper chamber) but this law will have to be approved in a referendum by not less than two-thirds of the votes cast; the persons entitled to vote in the referendum will be the electorate for the purpose of elections to the elected chamber. There will be a period of three months' delay between the introduction of a bill to amend any of the basic clauses and the first debate on the bill is the legislative chambers. The basic clause to which this procedure will apply will include the provisions of the Constitution relating to –

(a) the position of Her Majesty and Her Representatives;
(b) the establishment of the legislature, its duration, sessions and dissolution
(c) the franchise, the arrangements in the Constitution relating to the delimitation of constituencies and the holding and supervision of elections to the elected chamber of the legislature;
(d) the fundamental rights and freedoms (see paragraph 14 below);
(e) the establishment, jurisdiction and powers of the superior courts, the appointment and removal of judges and other judicial officers and any rights of appeal guaranteed by the Constitution (see paragraphs 17 to 19 below);
(f) the provisions for the protection of the public service;
(g) control by the legislature over expenditure;
(h) the responsibility and powers of the British authorities (see paragraphs 10, 23 to 25 and 27);
(i) the procedure for alteration of the Constitution by the legislature of the territory.

13 Both the territory and Britain will be able to terminate the association unilaterally; the legislature of the territory will have power to do so by revoking the constitutional provisions relating to the responsibilities and powers of and British authorities as a whole in accordance with the procedures set out above the revocation of these provisions may also be effected by the British Parliament or Her Majesty in Council by a law which will not require

the request and consent of the territory. Apart from making constitutional alterations to terminate the association, neither Britain nor the territory will be able to change the relationship (e.g. by modifying the responsibilities or powers of Britain) without the consent of the other party; arrangements will be made for this purpose and to this extent the powers of constitutional alteration of the legislature of the territory set out above will be limited.

FUNDAMENTAL RIGHTS AND FREEDOMS

14 The Constitution will include a Chapter which will prescribe the fundamental rights and freedoms to be enjoyed by the people of the territory. These rights and freedoms will include the following:–

(a) the right of life;
(b) the right of personal liberty;
(c) protection from slavery and forced labour;
(d) protection from inhuman treatment;
(e) protection from deprivation of property;
(f) protection against arbitrary search or entry upon property;
(g) the right to a fair trial in criminal and civil proceedings;
(h) freedom of conscience;
(i) freedom of expression;
(j) freedom of assembly;
(k) freedom of association;
(l) freedom of movement;
(m) protection from discrimination on grounds of race, political opinions, colour or creed.

15 The superior court for the region referred to in paragraphs 17 to 19 below will have special jurisdiction to enforce the Chapter of the Constitution relating to fundamental rights and freedoms. The Chapter will in general follow the pattern of similar provisions made in independent countries in the Commonwealth.

THE EXECUTIVE

16 The Constitution will make provision for a Cabinet, the appointment and tenure of office of Ministers and the assignment of responsibility to Ministers on the usual lines. The title of "Premier" would in the British Government's view be an appropriate title for the Chief Minister.

THE JUDICIARY

17 There will be a superior court for the region which will have special jurisdiction and powers to safeguard the Constitution and will also be the appeal court for the associated territories; the court will have by virtue of the Constitution, jurisdiction to determine whether any law or any executive

act is inconsistent with the Constitution and also in all other questions on the interpretation of the Constitution; the court will have power to issue to any person or authority any orders or directions which it considers necessary to ensure that the Constitution is compiled with and to enforce these orders and directions. The representative of the British Government (in addition to any other person entitled to do so) will have the right to initiate proceedings in the court to determine whether any law or any executive act is inconsistent with the Constitution. An appeal will lie as of right from final decisions of the court to the Privy Council; constitutional questions arising in other courts in the territory will be referred to the court for a decision.

18 The superior court will consist of a President and not less than two other judges. The President will be appointed by the Lord Chancellor of England; the other judges will be appointed by a Special Commission, consisting of the President as Chairman and two other members one of whom will be a retired judge.

19 There will also be a single Supreme Court for the territories entering into association arrangements and a single Service Commission responsible for the appointment of judges, magistrates and officials of the courts. The British Government hope that it will also be possible for legal officers to continue to be appointed by the same Commission. The tenure of office of judges of the superior court and the Supreme Court will be protected. The territory will contribute a proportion of the cost of the superior court and Supreme Court, the amount of which will be a charge on the revenue of the territory and will not be subject to appropriation by the legislature.

THE CIVIL SERVICE

20 The constitutional provisions for this purpose will be consistent with the general aim that the civil service of the territory should be competent and politically neutral. The appointment, promotion, discipline and removal from office of public servants will be the responsibility of a Service Commission or Commissions; these Commissions will be independent of the executive Government in carrying out their functions in relation to individual cases. There will be provision for each department of Government placed under a Minister to be supervised by a Permanent Secretary who will be a public officer; the Chief Minister will have a voice in any appointments to the office of Permanent Secretary. The pension rights of public officers will be protected against unfavourable alteration, and the approval of the appropriate Service Commission will be required for the withholding or reduction of the pension of a public officer.

THE POLICE

21 The arrangements for the appointment, promotion discipline and removal from office of members of the Police Force will be in accordance with the principles outlined in paragraph 20. . . .

FINANCIAL PROCEDURE AND AUDIT

22 The Constitution will contain provision to secure that there is no expenditure from public funds except when there is statutory authority for such expenditure and unless a prescribed procedure has been complied with which secures full Parliamentary scrutiny. It will include provisions relating to the procedure for the approval of the annual budget, the authorisation of supplementary expenditure during a financial year and the provision of funds to meet contingent expenditure in advance of legislative approval. The Constitution will also contain provision establishing the office of Director of Audit with responsibility for auditing the public accounts and reporting on them to the legislature so that the legislature may satisfy itself that no expenditure has in fact taken place without proper authority.

THE RESPONSIBILITY RETAINED BY THE BRITISH GOVERNMENT

23 Except as stated below the British authorities will have no powers of intervention in, and no responsibility for, the government of the territory.

24 Responsibility for external affairs and defence will lie with the British Government and for the discharge of this responsibility (which will include the fulfilment and protection of Britain's Commonwealth and international obligations and interests) the British Government will have the necessary executive authority in the territory. Parliament and Her Majesty in Council will have legislative powers in the interests of Britain's defence and external affairs responsibilities. These legislative powers will extend to the making of any provision (including provision relating to any matter in the field of internal government) which appear to Parliament or Her Majesty in Council necessary to prevent circumstances arising or continuing in the territory that may prejudice the discharge of Britain's responsibilities. Such legislation will prevail over any law in force in the territory, with the exception of the Constitution, and may confer functions on any officers or authorities of the Government of the territory as well as upon other persons or authorities. The power to enact such legislation will not be invoked unless the Government of the territory has been requested to take the appropriate action within a time to be specified in each case and has not done so.

25 In order to enable the British Government and their representative to carry out their functions in relation to defence and external affairs it will be necessary for the representative of the British Government to be kept fully informed on matters relating to or affecting these responsibilities of the British Government.

CONTROL OF CRIMINAL PROSECUTIONS: THE POWER OF PARDON

26 Arrangements will have to be negotiated which ensure that the powers of the public prosecutor and the authority responsible for pardons

may be exercised in accordance with principles which are generally accepted as appropriate to the exercise of such functions and that they are free from political bias.

CITIZENSHIP

27 Citizenship will continue to be governed by the British Nationality Acts unless a territory establishes a separate citizenship; since these Acts provide for a common nationality not only for the territory but also for other countries including Britain, it will be necessary for the British Parliament to retain powers of legislation in respect of them. As regards the establishment of a separate citizenship by a territory the procedures for amendment of the basic clauses of the Constitutions (see paragraph 12 above) will, unless the territory becomes independent, apply to legislation of the territory to establish or alter citizenshp of the territory. It has been the practice for the British Government to negotiate with any territory proceeding to independence the arrangements for its separate citizenship; in view of the fact that the territory will have the right to proceed unilaterally to independence at any time it is the intention of the British Government that an agreement should be negotiated between the British Government and the Government of the territory prior to the introduction of the new Constitution, as to the principal classes of persons who will be entitled to citizenship of the territory in the event of separate citizenship being established.

(ii) Extracts from the Report of the Antigua Constitutional Conference, 1966. (Cmnd. 2963/1966.)[7]

The purpose of this Conference was to settle in detail arrangements by which Antigua would move to self-government in a new relationship of association with Britain. This would take the place of the existing colonial relationship . . . .

NATURE OF THE ASSOCIATION

5 The prime characteristic of the new association between the United Kingdom and Antigua is that it will be a free and voluntary one and will be terminable by either country at any time.

6 Because the colonial relationship between Antigua and the United Kingdom is to be terminated in favour of a free relationship of a different and novel character, provision for the association will require the authority of an Act of the Parliament of the United Kingdom.

7 Very similar conferences were held for the Windward Islands and for St. Kitts/Nevis/Anguilla. Reports were published in Cmnd. 3021/1966 and Cmnd. 3031/1966.

THE CONSTITUTION OF ANTIGUA

7 The United Kingdom legislation establishing the association between the United Kingdom and Antigua should provide for the grant of a new Constitution for Antigua under which Antigua would be fully self-governing in all its internal affairs, and which would come into force at the commencement of the association.[8] . . .

RESPONSIBILITIES AND POWERS OF THE UNITED KINGDOM

9 It was agreed that the United Kingdom will be responsible for defence and external relations. In discharging this responsibility the United Kingdom will act in close consultation with Antigua in matters which affect the territory. It was accordingly agreed that during the continuence of the association the relations between the United Kingdom and Antigua should be governed by the arrangements described in paragraphs 10 to 19.

10 The United Kingdom legislation establishing the association between the United Kingdom and Antigua would provide that the Government of the United Kingdom are to be responsible for the defence and external relations of Antigua and confer on the Government of the United Kingdom executive authority for this purpose.

11 The United Kingdom legislation should also provide that the United Kingdom could confer a general or specific authority upon the Government of Antigua, subject to any exceptions, limitations or conditions that may be appropriate, to deal on their behalf with specified matters in the field of external relation

12 The United Kingdom legislation should contain provisions to the effect that no Act of Parliament of the United Kingdom passed after the commencement of the association would extend to Antigua as part of its law unless it is expressly declared in the Act that Antigua has requested and consented to the enactment of the Act.

13 Similarly, the United Kingdom legislation providing for the Constitution of Antigua should reserve to Her Majesty a general power to make laws by order in Council but no such Order in Council should have effect as part of the law of Antigua unless it is expressly declared in the Order in Council that Antigua has requested and consented to the making of the Order in Council.

14 For the purposes of the two preceding paragraphs the request and consent of Antigua should be signified by resolutions of both Houses of the Parliament of Antigua.

15 The legislative provisions described in paragraphs 12 and 13 above should be subject to an exception under which an Act of Parliament of the United Kingdom or an Order of Her Majesty in Council would have effect as part of the law of Antigua if it is expressly declared in the Act or Order in Council that in the opinion of the Parliament or Government of the United Kin dom the Act or Order in Council is required to have effect in Antigua in the

8 The main outlines were those suggested in the Memorandum, reproduced in part in the previous document.

in the interests and responsibilities of the Government of the United Kingdom for defence and external relations. It would not be possible, by means of an Act of Parliament or Order in Council having effect by virtue of the exception, to amend, suspend or revoke the Constitution of Antigua (nor of course would it be possible for the Parliament of Antigua to amend the Constitution of Antigua by the insertion of provisions inconsistent with the United Kingdom legislation described in the preceding four paragraphs) while the association exists.

16 An Agreement should be entered into by the Government of the United Kingdom and the Government of Antigua before the commencement of the association between the United Kingdom and Antigua referring to the provisions of the United Kingdom Legislation described in paragraphs 10, 12 and 13 above having effect so long as the association continues.[9] . . .

17 The Government of the United Kingdom, in pursuance of the provisions of the United Kingdom legislation referred to at paragraph 11 above should at the commencement of the association entrust the Government of Antigua with authority in the field of external relations by means of a despatch drawn up on the basis of Annex D.

18 It is the firm intention of both Governments that the arrangements with respect to defence and external relations described in the preceding eight paragraphs should be operated in a spirit of co-operation and mutual confidence. The spirit is reflected in the Heads of Agreement at Annex C, which provide for the fullest possible consultation at all stages, and in the outline of a despatch at Annex D under which there will be a substantial degree of entrustment to the Government of Antigua in the field of external relations from the outset of the association. The Government of Antigua recognise that the Government of the United Kingdom, so long as they are responsible for the defence and external relations of Antigua, may legitimately take account, not only of the specific interest of Antigua but also of the general interests of the United Kingdom itself and its associated states and territories, while expressing the view that there should be no occasion for the use of powers of legislation by the United Kingdom at any time during the continuance of the association, which could be terminated by Antigua at any time.

19 The Government of the United Kingdom for their part acknowledge that, as the association is a voluntary one terminable by either country, every possible endeavour should be made to resolve any difference of view between the two Governments by means of a free negotiation and to maintain the spirit of co-operation and mutual confidence that now exists and that makes a voluntary association possible. The Government of the United Kingdom regard the legislative powers of the Parliament of the United Kingdom and Her Majesty in Council over Antigua in respect of defence and external relations

9 See Document B(ii) of this chapter.

as an ultimate safeguard of the legitimate interests of the United Kingdom, necessary because it would not be reasonable to expect the United Kingdom to bear a responsibility without having the means of discharging it whatever course events might take, but unlikely to be invoked except as a last resort in circumstances that in practice seem unlikely to arise.

TERMINATION OF THE ASSOCIATION

20 Either country should be free to terminate the association at any time. The procedure for the termination of the association by Antigua will be by Act of the Parliament of Antigua passed by the same procedure as is desdribed in paragraphs 13 to 15 of Annex B for amendment of the "basic clauses" of the Constitution. These include the requirement of a two-thirds majority in the House of Representatives and a two-thirds majority in a referendum; provided that no referendum will be required where the association is terminated for the purpose of giving constitutional effect to arrangements under which Antigua (either by itself or together with other territories) joins with an independent Commonwealth country in the Caribbean, whether by uniting or federating with that country or in some other form of constitutional association with that country, under which that country would be responsible for the defence and external relations of Antigua.[10]

CITIZENSHIP

21 During the existence of the association Antigua will continue to share a common citizenship with the United Kingdom and Colonies.[11] Accordingly the legislative provisions described in paragraphs 12 and 13 above will be subject to the exception that United Kingdom legislation on nationality will not require the request and consent of Antigua in order to extend to Antigua as part of its law.

THE CIVIL SERVICE

22 The Government of Antigua and the United Kingdom Government will, prior to the coming into force of these arrangements, enter into a Public Officers' Agreement of the kind usual when constitutional arrangements are being introduced which involve the Public Service and Police Service Commissions becoming executive. The agreement will secure the salaries, pensions and other conditions of service of officers originally appointed by, or with the approval of, the Secretary of State. Other arrangements relating to

10 Although not mentioned here the procedure for termination of the association by the United Kingdom would be the Order in Council. The inequality of the relationship is clearly illustrated by the lack of any requirement for even ordinary legislative action on the part of the United Kingdom.
11 A point raised recently in some of the Associated States is that the common citizenship does not confer the right of entry into the United Kingdom.

the Civil Service usual when the Public Service and Police Service Commissions are made executive will also apply.

FINANCE AND ECONOMIC

23 Assurances were given by the United Kingdom delegation that after the new constitutional arrangements came into force, Antigua would continue to be eligible to receive aid from Britain under the British Government's aid programme. On development aid the delegation confirmed that the United Kingdom would carry out in full the undertakings already given to Antigua in connection with the Overseas Development and Services Act 1965.

COMMON SERVICES

24 The Conference considered the question of future regional co-operation between Antigua and other territories in the area, to which reference had been made in paragraph 8 of Cmnd. 2865 and took note of a paper on common services put forward by the Antigua delegation. The Antigua government would be willing to discuss this matter with other Governments in the area later this year. . . .

(iii) Extracts from the Report of the Windward Islands Constitutional Conference, 1966 (Cmnd. 3021/1966.)

8 At the opening of the Conference all delegations from the Windward Islands expressed the view that the proposals in Cmnd. 2865, dealing as they did with fundamental constitutional matters, ought consequently to have involved arrangements for aid and trade. They asked for assurances that the proposed constitutional changes would not place them in a less favourable position as regards trade, aid and immigration. Indeed they considered that the opportunity should be taken of these new constitutional arrangements to bring the territories into a more favourable and closer relationship with the United Kingdom in these matters than they enjoy at the moment. They considered that this would give the association stability and provide a satisfactory framework for raising the living standards of the people of the associated territories. In reply the British delegation stated that the constitutional changes proposed would be irrelevant in the context of development aid, trade and immigration. In view of their many commitments the British Government could not contemplate any increase in aid for these territories above the allocations already made, though they would undertake various measures to ensure that their aid was spent more effectively. They pointed out that during the last financial year British aid to these four islands had been increased compared with previous allocations and, at £2.15m., represented roughly £6 for every man, woman and child in the islands. The British Government were well

aware of the importance of the United Kingdom market as an outlet for their main export crops but said that the proposed constitutional changes would not of themselves alter present trading arrangements. Equally the British Government would not feel able to offer the inhabitants of these countries specially favourable treatment as compared with other Commonwealth immigrants into the United Kingdom. The British Government however fully appreciated the economic difficulties of these territories and the special nature of their economic problems. This was one of the reasons why the British Development Division had recently been established in the Caribbean so that the United Kingdom department responsible for aid could be more closely and directly associated with the territorial Governments in their efforts to deal with their economic problems. The British Government also undertook to examine other suggestions for promoting the economic prosperity of these territories which were discussed at the Conference. (The question of budgetary aid and development aid to these territories under the new constitutional arrangements is discussed further below in paragraph 25.)

THE ALTERNATIVE TO THESE PROPOSALS

9 During the Conference the Secretary of State was asked to say whether he would be prepared to consider full internal self-government for these territories on the normal colonial pattern as an alternative to the present proposals. The Secretary of State replied by pointing out that when full internal self-government was granted to a territory which remained a colony, the United Kingdom retained the ultimate power to legislate for all aspects of that territory's affairs, including its constitution, and the United Kingdom Government was answerable to Parliament accordingly. This was a situation which had been found acceptable in the case of territories on the road to independence within a reasonably short period and within a foreseeable future. but was likely to create difficulties for both sides if unduly prolonged. The British Government were held internationally responsible for matters which they had no effective means of controlling. At the same time the British Government were constantly urged to try to interfere in matters which the local Government regarded as their sole responsibility. This, therefore, was not an arrangement which the British Government wanted to enter into with territories which, because of their size and because of the vulnerability of their economies and other factors, were not contemplating early independence. The scheme in Cmnd. 2865 was designed to grant to such territories full internal self-government while avoiding the difficulties which arose if the United Kingdom Government continued to have the ultimate authority to legislate for all aspects of their constitutions and was answerable to Parliament for all their affairs. The scheme in Cmnd. 2865 is designed to show where Britain's responsibility begins and ends and it is hoped it would be

more satisfactory to both sides.

CONCLUSIONS OF THE CONFERENCE

10 It was agreed that subject to the approval of the Legislatures concerned each of the four territories would enter into an association with Britain.[12] . . .

B The nature of associate statehood

(i) Extracts from the West Indies Act, 1967 c.4.
(U.K. Public General Acts.)

An Act to confer on certain West Indian territories a new status of association with the United Kingdom, and to enable that status to be terminated at any time; to make provision for other matters in connection with, or consequential upon, the creation or termination of that status or other constitutional changes which may occur in relation to any of these territories; to make further provision as to grants under the Overseas Aid Act 1966; and for purposes connected with the matters aforesaid.

(16th February 1967)

1(1) On the appointed day each of the territories to which this section applies shall assume, and (subject to the provisions of this Act) shall thereafter maintain, a status of association with the United Kingdom in accordance with the following provisions of this Act.

(2) The territories to which this section applies are these which, immediately before the appointed day, constitute respectively the Colonies of –

(a) Antigua;
(b) Dominica;
(c) Grenada;
(d) Saint Christopher, Nevis and Anguilla;
(e) Saint Lucia; and
(f) Saint Vincent.[13]

(3) A territory to which this section applies shall, on and after the appointed day and so long as its status of association with the United Kingdom has not been terminated, be known as an associated state.

12 The terms of the association agreed to and the form of the internal constitutions followed the lines laid down in Cmnd. 2865/1965. Document A(i) of this chapter.
13 Owing to internal political problems St. Vincent did not become an associated state until 1969.

2(1) Subject to the following subsection, on and after the appointed day Her Majesty's Government in the United Kingdom shall have no responsibility for the government of any associated state except in respect of –

(a) any matter which in the opinion of Her Majesty's Government in the United Kingdom is a matter relating to defence (whether of an associated state or of the United Kingdom or of any other territory for whose government Her Majesty's Government in the United Kingdom are wholly or partly responsible) or to external affairs;

(b) any matter relating to nationality or citizenship; and

(c) any matter relating to the Succession to the Throne or the Royal Style and Titles

(2) The preceding subsection shall not affect any responsibility of Her Majesty's Government in the United Kingdom in relation to the exercise of –

(a) any power conferred on Her Majesty by this Act, or

(b) any other power exercisable by Her Majesty under the law of any associated state.

3(1) Except as provided by subsections (2) to (4) of this section, no Act of the Parliament of the United Kingdom passed on or after the appointed day shall extend, or be deemed to extend, to an associated state as part of its law, unless it is expressly declared in that Act that the state has requested and consented to its being enacted.

(2) Where any Act of the Parliament of the United Kingdom contains a provision expressly declaring –

(a) that that Act, or an enactment contained in it which is specified in that provision, extends to all associated states, or to such one or more associated states as may be so specified, and

(b) that it is required so to extend in the interests of the responsibilities of Her Majesty's Government in the United Kingdom relating to defence and external affairs,

that Act or that enactment, as the case may be, shall extend in accordance with that provision notwithstanding anything in the preceding subsection.

(3) Where any Act of the Parliament of the United Kingdom amends the law relating to nationality or citizenship, and contains a provision expressly declaring that the Act, or (where the Act relates also to other matters) an enactment contained in it which amends the law relating to nationality or citizenship and is specified in that provision, extends to all associated states, or to such one or more associated states as may be so specified, the Act, or that enactment, as the case may be, shall extend in accordance with that provision notwithstanding anything in subsection (1) of this section.

(4) Subsection (1) of this section shall not apply to any Act of the Parliament of the United Kingdom, or to any enactment contained in such an Act,

in so far as it relates to the Succession to the Throne or the Royal Style and Titles.

(5) Notwithstanding anything in the Interpretation Act 1889, the expression "colony" in any Act of the Parliament of the United Kingdom passed on or after the appointed day shall not include an associated state.

4(1) On and after the appointed day the provisions of Schedule 1 to this Act shall have effect with respect to the legislative powers of an associated state.

(2) The executive authority of the Government of an associated state shall not include any power or duty which the legislature of that state could not lawfully confer or impose on that Government in accordance with Schedule 1 to this Act.

5(1) In relation to any territory to which section 1 of this Act applies, Her Majesty may by Order in Council (in this Act referred to as a "Constitution Order") made before the appointed day provide for it a new constitution which (subject to the following provisions of this section) is to come into effect on that day.

(2) The constitution provided by a Constitution Order for a territory to which section 1 of this Act applies may include provision as to the extent to which, and the manner in which, the legislature of the territory may alter –

(a) that constitution, or any part of that constitution specified in that provision, or

(b) any other law of a description so specified, in so far as the law has effect as part of the law of that territory.

(3) The constitution provided by a Constitution Order for any such territory may include provision for separate citizenship of that territory which is not to have effect until, on or after the termination of the status of association of that territory with the United Kingdom, it is brought into force in such manner as may be specified in the constitution.

(4) Where the constitution of an associated state provided by a Constitution Order has come into effect, Her Majesty may at any time, by Order in Council made at the request and with the consent of that state, alter that constitution or any part of that constitution, or alter any law which alters that constitution or any part of it.

(5) The last preceding subsection shall have effect without prejudice to any power exercisable by the legislature of an associated state as mentioned in subsection (2) of this section. . . .

6(1) Her Majesty may by Order in Council made before the appointed day provide for the establishment of one or more courts which; . . . shall be courts constituted in common for the territories to which section 1 of this Act applies, and may by that Order provide that any such court shall, in relation to any of these territories, have such jurisdiction and powers as may be so specified or determined.

(2) An Order in Council under this section may include provision whereby, in relation to Montserrat or the Virgin Islands, any court established under the Order shall have such jurisdiction and powers, and there shall be imposed or conferred on judges and officers of any such court such duties and powers, as may be specified in, or determined in accordance with, the Order.

(3) An Order in Council under this section may include provision –

(a) for the establishment. . . of a commission having such duties and powers in relation to any court established under the Order, and to judges and officers of any such court, and in relation to other persons and related matters, as may be specified in, or determined in accordance with, the Order; . . . .

7(1) Without prejudice to the provisions of section 5(4) of this Act, Her Majesty may by Order in Council made at the request and with the consent of any associated state make, as part of the law of that state, any provision which appears to Her Majesty to be necessary or expedient for the peace, order or good government of that state.

(2) Where it appears to Her Majesty that in the interests of the responsibilities of Her Majesty's Government in the United Kingdom relating to defence and external affairs a change should be made in the law of an associated state, Her Majesty may by Order in Council expressly stating that fact make, as part of the law of that state, such provision as appears to Her Majesty to be appropriate, including (if by reason of war or other emergency it appears to Her Majesty to be necessary and that fact is expresssly stated in the Order) provision derogating from the provisions of the constitution of that state relating to fundamental rights and freedoms. . . .

9(1) Subject to the provisions of this section, Her Majesty may by Order in Council –

(a) federate or otherwise unite two or more associated states with each other, or federate or otherwise unite one or more associated states with one or more other territories which are not associated states;

(b) divide an associated state into two or more separate territories;

(c) transfer part of the territory of an associated state to another territory (whether an associated state or not) or incorporate part of another territory (whether an associated state or not) in an associated state.

(2) No order in Council shall be made under this section –

(a) so as to affect an associated state unless it is made at the request and with the consent of that state, or

(b) so as to affect any territory other than an associated state unless it is a territory in relation to which the Order, in so far as it affects that terrritory, could be made apart from this Act. . . .

10(1) The legislature of any associated state may at any time, by a law made in accordance with the provisions of Schedule 2 to this Act, terminate the status of association ot that state with the United Kingdom as from such date as may be specified in that law.

(2) Her Majesty may at any time, by Order in Council made in respect of any associated state, terminate the status of association of that state with the United Kingdom as from such date as may be specified in the Order.[14]

(3) Any law made by virtue of subsection (1) of this section, and any Order in Council made under the last preceding subsection, may provide that, on the date specified in that law or that Order, the associated state in question shall cease to form part of Her Majesty's dominions.[15] . . .

12(1) In relation to an associated state the British Nationality Acts 1948 to 1965 shall have effect subject to the provisions of Schedule 3 to this Act.

(2) A citizen of the United Kingdom and Colonies may, if on the grounds of his connection with an associated state he so desires, be known as a citizen of the United Kingdom, Associated States and Colonies. . . .

16(1) Subsection (4) of section 1 of the Overseas Aid Act 1966 (which relates to grants under that Act to certain Governments) shall have effect as if the Governments specified in that subsection included the Governments of associated states.[16]

(2) There shall be paid out of moneys provided by Parliament any increase attributable to this section in the sums payable out of moneys so provided under that Act.

(3) For the purposes of the making of grants under section 8 of the West Indies Act 1962, a territory to which section 1 of this Act applies shall, on and after the appointed day, be treated as not being a colony within the meaning of that Act.[17]

14 The effect of termination would be to establish independence.

15 That is either to opt out of, or to be removed from, the Commonwealth, or to be established as a republic within the Commonwealth.

16 the Overseas Aid Act, 1966 c. 21 Section 1 Subsection 4 gives power to the Minister of Overseas Development to make grants to a certain Governments who are unable to meet administrative expenses.

17 Under the West Indies Act, 1962 c. 19 the power to make grants for the purpose of defraying administrative expenses in the colonies which were to become associated states under this Act, was vested in the Secretary of State for the Colonies.

SCHEDULE 1

LEGISLATIVE POWERS OF ASSOCIATED STATES

1 Subject to the following provisions of the Schedule –

(a) the Colonial Laws Validity Act 1865 shall not apply to any law made on or after the appointed day by the legislature of an associated state, and

(b) no law and no provision of any law made on or after the appointed day by any such legislature shall be void or inoperative on the ground that it is repugnant to the law of England, or to the provisions of any Act of the Parliament of the United Kingdom, or to any order, rule or regulation made under any such Act.[18]

and accordingly the powers of the legislature of an associated state shall include the power to repeal or to amend any such Act, order, rule or regulation in so far as it has effect as part of the law of that state.

2 The legislature of an associated state shall have full power to make laws having extra-territorial operation. . . .

4(1) The following provisions of this paragraph shall have effect notwithstanding anything in the preceding provisions of this Schedule, but without prejudice to the exercise of any power conferred by section 10 of this Act.

(2) The legislature of an associated state shall not have power (whether in pursuance of any provision contained in a Constitution Order in accordance with section 5 (2) of this Act or otherwise) to repeal or amend, or make any law repugnant to –

(a) this Act;

(b) any Act, or enactment contained in an Act, of the Parliament of the United Kingdom in so far as it relates to nationality or citizenship;

(c) any Act or enactment contained in an Act, of the Parliament of the United Kingdom in so far as it relates to the Succession to the Throne or the Royal Style and Titles;

(d) an Act, or enactment contained in an Act, of the Parliament of the United Kingdom which extends to that state in accordance with section 3 (2) of this Act; or

(e) any Order in Council made by virtue of section 7 (2) of this Act in so far as it has effect as part of the law of that state.

18 Section 3 of this Schedule refers specifically to sections 735 and 736 of the Merchant Shipping Act, 1894 c.60 and section 4 of the Colonial Courts of Admiralty Act, 1890 c.27 as no longer extending to the associated states.

(3) Without prejudice to the last preceding sub-paragraph, the legislature of an associated state shall not have power (whether in pursuance of any provision contained in a Constitution Order in accordance with section 5 (2) of this Act or otherwise) to make any law whereby –

(a) the Government of that state would be authorised or required to conduct any external affairs, except in so far as, by arrangements made in accordance with the next following sub-paragraph, that Government may be authorised to conduct any external affairs on behalf of Her Majesty's Government in the United Kingdom, or

(b) the Government of that state would be authorised or required to restrict or otherwise interfere with the conduct by Her Majesty's Government in the United Kingdom of defence or of external affairs.

(4) The arrangements referred to in sub-paragraph (3)(a) of this paragraph are any arrangements which may be made between Her Majesty's Government in the United Kingdom and the Government of an associated state authorising the latter Government on behalf of the former Government to conduct external affairs in respect of such matters or classes of matters, and subject to any such exceptions, limitations and conditions, as may be specified in the arrangements,

(5) Sub-paragraphs (a) and (b) of paragraph 1 of this Schedule shall not have effect in relation to any law which, in accordance with the preceding provisions of this paragraph, the legislature of an associated state has no power to make.

SCHEDULE 2

PROCEDURE FOR TERMINATING STATUS OF ASSOCIATION

2 Subject to the following provisions of this Schedule –

(a) there must be an interval of not less than ninety days between the introduction of the Bill[19] and the beginning of the proceedings in the legislature on second reading of the Bill;

(b) on the third reading of the Bill in the legislature, the Bill must be supported by the votes of not less than two-thirds of all the elected members of the legislature;

(c) if approved on third reading in the legislature, the Bill must be submitted to a referendum and must not be submitted to the Governor of the State for his assent unless not less than two-thirds of the votes validly cast on that referendum are cast in support of the Bill.

19 That is the Bill making provision for termination of association.

3(1) If the legislature consists of two Houses (by whatever name called) the following provisions of this paragraph shall have effect instead of the provisions of paragraph 2 of this Schedule.

(2) There must be an interval of not less than ninety days between the introduction of the Bill in the lower House and the beginning of the proceedings on second reading of the Bill in that House.

(3) On the third reading of the Bill in that House, the Bill must be supported by the votes of not less than two-thirds of all the elected members of that House.

(4) If the Bill is passed by the upper House with amendments, any agreement of the lower House to these amendments must be supported by the votes of not less than two-thirds of all the elected members of the lower House.

(5) If the Bill having been passed by the lower House, is passed by the upper House in the same Session either without amendment or with amendments which are agreed to by the lower House in accordance with the last preceding sub-paragraph, the Bill must be submitted to a referendum, and must not be submitted to the Governor of the state for his assent unless not less than two-thirds of the votes validly cast on that referendum are cast in support of the Bill.

(6) If in one Session the Bill is passed by the lower House in accordance with sub-paragraphs (2) and (3) of this paragraph, and either it is not passed by the upper House or it is passed by the upper House with amendments which are not agreed to by the lower House in accordance with sub-paragraph (4) of this paragraph, and in the next Session the Bill is again passed by the lower House in accordance with sub-paragraphs (2) and (3) of this paragraph, there must be an interval of not less than six months between the passage of the Bill by the lower House in the first of these Sessions and its passage by the lower House in the second of them.

(7) If, in the circumstances specified in the preceding sub-paragraph, the Bill in the second of the two Sessions is sent to the upper House without amendment, but with suggestions for amending it, these suggested amendments must be supported by the votes of not less than two-thirds of all the elected members of the lower House.

(8) Sub-paragraph (5) of this paragraph shall have effect in relation to the passage of the Bill in the second of these Sessions as it has effect in relation to the passage of the Bill in the Session in which it is first introduced.

(9) If in the second of these Sessions the Bill either is not passed by the upper House or is passed by the upper House with amendments which are neither amendments suggested by the lower House in accordance with sub-paragraph (7) of this paragraph nor amendments which are agreed to by the

lower House in accordance with sub-paragraph (4) of this paragraph, the Bill must be submitted to a referendum, and must not be submitted to the Governor of the State for his assent unless not less than two-thirds of the votes validly cast on that referendum are cast in support of the Bill.

(10) Except in the circumstances specified in the last preceding sub-paragraph, the Bill must not be submitted to a referendum or submitted to the Governor of the state for his assent unless it has been passed by both Houses of the legislature in accordance with the preceding provisions of this paragraph.

4(1) The provisions of this paragraph shall have effect where, before the introduction of the Bill, arrangements have been made between the Government of the state and the Government of a territory to which this paragraph applies whereby, immediately after the termination of the status of association of the state with the United Kingdom, –

(a) the state will enter into a federation or union or some other form of association with that territory (with or without other territories), and

(b) the Government resulting from that federation, union or other form of association, or the Government of that territory, will be responsible for the defence and external affairs of the state,

and the Bill refers to these arrangements and makes provision for giving effect to them on the part of the state.

(2) This paragraph applies to any territory which –

(a) lies between the equator and the 20th parallel of north latitude and between longitude 50 degrees west and longitude 90 degrees west, and

(b) at the time when the arrangements in question are made is a territory within the Commonwealth for whose government Her Majesty's Government in the United Kingdom have no responsibility.

(3) In the circumstances specified in sub-paragraph (1) of this paragraph, the Bill may be submitted to the Governor for his assent without a referendum and accordingly paragraph 2 (c) or (as the case may be) sub-paragraphs (5) of paragraph 3 of this Schedule shall not apply.

(ii) Extracts from the Antigua Agreement, 1967.[20]

This Agreement is made the 16th day of February 1967 between the Right Honourable Herbert Dewden, C.B.E., Secretary of State for Commonwealth Affairs, on behalf of Her Majesty's Government in the United Kingdom of the one part and the Honourable Vere Cornwall Bird, Chief Minister of Antigua, on behalf of the Government of Antigua of the other part . . . .

20 Similar agreements were made with all associated states.

1(1) This Agreement may be cited as the Antigua Agreement 1967. . . .
2 The Government of Antigua shall take all steps (including where necessary, steps to secure the enactment of legislation by the legislature of Antigua or by other competent authority in Antigua) to provide or permit the establishment of such facilities as may be required in Antigua by Her Majesty's Government in the United Kingdom in the interest of their responsibilities relating to the defence of Antigua or of any other territory having a status of association with the United Kingdom or of the United Kingdom or of any other territory for whose government Her Majesty's Government in the United Kingdom are wholly or partly responsible or of any other part of the Commonwealth or of any of the allies of the United Kingdom.
3 The Government of Antigua shall not, without the consent of Her Majesty's Government in the United Kingdom, grant access to any part of Antigua or its territorial waters to the armed forces or agents of any other Government or allow them the use of any airfields, communications or harbour or other military facilities in Antigua. . . .
5 Any armed forces of the United Kingdom sent to Antigua for defence purposes shall not be used in aid of the civil power in Antigua or for any purposes other than defence purposes except with the consent of Her Majesty's Government in the United Kingdom and at the request of the Government of Antigua:

Provided that the request of the Government of Antigua shall not be necessary if at any time they are unable, through circumstances beyond their control, to make a request.
6 Her Majesty's Government in the United Kingdom shall consult with the Government of Antigua before entering into international obligations with respect to Antigua.
7 The extent to which the Government of Antigua will be authorised to conduct external affairs shall be defined from time to time by despatch addressed to the Government of Antigua by Her Majesty's Government in the United Kingdom.[21]
8 The Government of Antigua shall take all steps (including where necessary, steps to secure the enactment of legislation by the legislature of Antigua or by other competent authority in Antigua) that, after full consultation between Her Majesty's Government in the United Kingdom and the Government of Antigua, are required by Her Majesty's Government in the United Kingdom:–

(a) to secure the discharge of the responsibilities of Her Majesty's Government in the United Kingdom relating to external affairs; or
(b) otherwise in the interests of good relations between Antigua or

[21] See the following document.

the United Kingdom and any other country or territory.

9 The Government of Antigua shall not take steps to secure, or support proposals for, the enactment of any legislation having effect in Antigua that might attack the discharge of the responsibilities of Her Majesty's Government in the United Kingdom relating to external affairs or the maintenance of good relations between Antigua or the United Kingdom and any other country or territory without prior consultation with Her Majesty's Government in the United Kingdom; and the Government of Antigua shall not proceed with, or support any proposals for, the enactment of legislation as aforesaid if they are informed by Her Majesty's Government in the United Kingdom that its enactment would be detrimental to the discharge of these responsibilities or the maintenance of such good relations.

10(1) Where in the opinion of Her Majesty's Government in the United Kingdom the enactment of legislation having effect in Antigua is required in the interests of the responsibilities of Her Majesty's Government in the United Kingdom relating to defence (whether of Antigua or of any other territory having a status of association with the United Kingdom or of the United Kingdom or of any other territory for whose government Her Majesty's Government in the United Kingdom are wholly or partly responsible) or external affairs, Her Majesty's Government in the United Kingdom shall request the Government of Antigua either:–

(a) to signify their agreement to the enactment of the legislation by the Parliament of the United Kingdom or by Her Majesty in Council; or

(b) to take steps to secure the enactment of the legislation by the legislature of Antigua or by other competent authority in Antigua.

(2) If the agreement of the Government of Antigua to the enactment of the legislation is signified under paragraph 1 (a) of this article, Her Majesty's Government in the United Kingdom may take steps to secure the enactment of the legislation accordingly.

(3) If the Government of Antigua see difficulty in acceding to a request made by Her Majesty's Government in the United Kingdom under paragraph (1) of this article, then the fullest consultation that is practicable in the circumstances of the case shall take place between Her Majesty's Government in the United Kingdom and the Government of Antigua with a view of resolving the difficulty.

(4) Where after consultation under paragraph (3) of this article there is a failure to reach agreement concerning the enactment of legislation, and Her Majesty's Government in the United Kingdom remain of the opinion that it is nevertheless necessary for legislation to be enacted in the interests of the responsibilities of Her Majesty's Government in the United Kingdom referred to in paragraph (1) of this article, Her Majesty's Government in the United King-

dom shall give as much notice as possible of their intention to secure the enactment of the legislation by the Parliament of the United Kingdom or by Her Majesty in Council; and before taking such steps shall so far as is practicable afford the Government of Antigua the opportunity of considering whether, in all the circumstances, the Government of Antigua would wish to take steps to terminate the status of association of Antigua with the United Kingdom:

Provided that Her Majesty's Government in the United Kingdom shall not take steps to secure the enactment of the legislation if its effect would be to amend, suspend or revoke the Constitution of Antigua (otherwise than by way of derogation from the provisions of the Constitution relating to fundamental rights and freedoms by reason of war of other emergency), or to amend, suspend or revoke any provision of the West Indies Act 1967 in so far as it forms part of the law of Antigua, unless the Government of Antigua gives its consent to the enactment of the legislation.

(5) The provisions of this article shall be without prejudice to the provisions of articles 2 and 8 of this Agreement.

11 In order to enable Her Majesty's Government in the United Kingdom to discharge their responsibilities relating to defence and external affairs, the Government of Antigua shall keep Her Majesty's Government in the United Kingdom fully informed on all matters affecting these responsibilties.

(iii) Extracts from the Despatch from the Secretary of State for the Colonies to the Administrator of Antigua, dated 16th February, 1967 on the delegation of authority in external affairs.[22]

2 Her Majesty's Government in the United Kingdom wish it to be formally recorded that in carrying out their general responsibility for the external affairs of Antigua they will seek the fullest consultation with the Government of Antigua and will at all times have special regard to the interests of the Government of Antigua and of the association between the two Governments.

3 Subject to paragraph 5 of this despatch Her Majesty's Government in the United Kingdom hereby delegate executive authority to the Government of Antigua to conduct on behalf of Her Majesty's Government external affairs as follows –

(a) authority to apply for full or associate membership, as may be provided for in the Constitution of the organisation concerned, of those United Nations Specialised Agencies or similar international organisations of which the United Kingdom is itself a member and for membership of which Antigua is eligible;

22 Similar despatches were sent to the other associated states.

(b) authority to arrange or permit visits by representatives of or persons in the employ of any organisation under sub-paragraph (a) above of which Antigua is a full or associate member;

(c) authority to negotiate and conclude trade agreements with other countries, whether bilateral or multilateral, relating solely to the treatment of goods. (Agreements relating to establishment matters i.e., those affecting the rights of persons and companies of the contracting parties, will continue to be dealt with in commercial treaties negotiated by Her Majesty's Government. Her Majesty's Government will, however, be prepared, in appropriate circumstances to delegate to the Government of Antigua *ad hoc* authority to conclude individual trade agreements in which establishment matters are included. Agreements affecting Antigua relating to civil aviation and shipping will continue to be dealt with in accordance with present practice whereby Her Majesty's Government engage in the fullest consultation with the Government of Antigua and invite their participation in such negotiations as are necessary);

(d) authority to arrange or permit visits of up to thirty days for trade or commercial purposes by representatives or residents of Antigua to any other country, and by representatives or residents of any other country to Antigua (though questions relating to the establishment of permanent or temporary representation of other countries in Antigua or of Antigua in other countries will continue to be determined by Her Majesty's Government after consultation with the Government of Antigua);

(e) authority to negotiate and conclude agreements of purely local concern with any independent member of the Commonwealth in the Caribbean area or any other Associated State or any British colony in the Caribbean area or with such authorities in other neighbouring islands as the Government of Antigua may request and Her Majesty's Government approve;

(f) authority to negotiate and conclude agreements for financial and technical assistance or of a cultural or scientific nature with –
   (i) any independent member of the Commonwealth;
   (ii) the United States of America or such other countries as the Government of Antigua may request and Her Majesty's Government may approve; or
   (iii) any international organisation of which the United Kingdom is a member;

(g) authority to negotiate and conclude agreements with other countries, whether multilateral or bilateral, relating to emigration from Antigua to these countries and to emigrant labour schemes.

4 In addition Her Majesty's Government will give sympathetic consideration to any request by the Government of Antigua for authority to take action on individual questions of external affairs not covered by paragraph 3 of this despatch.

5 In view of the general responsibility of Her Majesty's Government for external affairs under the terms of the association agreed between Her Majesty's Government and the Government of Antigua, Her Majesty's Government's delegation of executive authority to the Government of Antigua to conduct the external affairs referred to in paragraph 3 (c), (e), and (g) of this despatch is made subject to the understanding that the Government of Antigua will inform Her Majesty's Government in advance of any proposal for the exercise of the delegated executive authority and will keep Her Majesty's Government fully informed of the progress and conduct of any negotiations relating to these external affairs. Any subsequent delegation under paragraph 4 will be subject to the same understanding.

6 Her Majesty's Government will inform the Government of Antigua if it shall appear that the actions or proposals of the Government of Antigua in the field of external affairs conflict with the international commitments, responsibility or policies of Her Majesty's Government or if they are likely to lead to such conflict. The Government of Antigua have agreed that after consultation they will accept the decision of Her Majesty's Government in such matters.

7 In the furtherance of the interests of Antigua and of the association between the United Kingdom and Antigua, Her Majesty's Government will –

(a) endeavour to assist in the training of officials from Antigua who will be required to deal with matters connected with the conduct of external affairs and defence;

(b) consider the inclusion of a representative of the Government of Antigua or of the Governments of the Associated States, either as an adviser or observer or in a similar capacity, in any United Kingdom delegation whenever a subject materially affecting the interests of Antigua or of the Associated States is being discussed in an international body of which the United Kingdom is a member; and

(c) consider the appointment of a person nominated by the Government of Antigua to advise a diplomatic mission in the exercise of consular functions in respect of persons belonging to Antigua in a place abroad if such an appointment were at any time felt to be necessary.

8 The arrangements contained in this despatch become effective when Antigua assumes the status of association with the United Kingdom in accordance with the West Indies Act 1967, subject to the acceptance by your

Government of the stipulations set out in paragraph 5.

C. The establishment of an Associated State Supreme Court

(i) Extracts from the West Indies Associated States Supreme Court Agreement, 1967.

3 The arrangements for which provision has been made by the West Indies Associated States Supreme Court Order 1967 shall have the force of law in each State for so long as this Agreement continues in force as respects that State.

4(1) The headquarters of the Supreme Court and of the Legal and Judicial Services Commission shall be situate in Grenada. . . .

5(1) The Government of each State shall take steps to secure the appointment in accordance with the Constitution of the State of a registrar of the High Court for that State and such other officers of the High Court (all of whom shall be officers in the public service of that State) as may be required to enable the High Court to exercise its jurisdiction and powers in relation to that State.

(2) Any registrars and other officers appointed for a State in pursuance of paragraph (1) of this article shall reside in that State and shall be responsible to the Chief Justice for the due discharge of their respective functions and (without prejudice to the powers of any court, of the Judicial and Legal Services Commission, or of the Administrator or the Public Service Commission of the State) shall not, in the performance of their duties as such, be subject to the discretion or control of any officer or authority other than the Chief Justice or such judge or officer of the Supreme Court as may be authorised in that behalf by the Chief Justice. . . .

7(1) The Government of Grenada shall bear the capital cost involved in providing and maintaining in Grenada the accommodation specified in article 4 (2)[23] of this Agreement.

(2) Subject to the provisions of this article, the Government of each State shall bear the cost of the administration of the Court of Appeal and the High Court in relation to the exercise of their respective jurisdiction and powers as respects that State and the cost of providing officers of the High Court for that State in pursuance of article 5 of this Agreement.

(3) The following expenses of the Court of Appeal and the High Court shall

23 Provision of accommodation for the headquarters of the Supreme Court, Judicial and Legal Services Commission, Chief Justice, Justices of Appeal, the Chief Registrar and other officers appointed for all the States.

(except in so far as they are met by contributions paid by the Government of Montserrat and the Virgin Islands in pursuance of any agreement on that behalf between Her Majesty's Government in the United Kingdom and the Government of the States) be borne by the Governments of all the States in equal shares, that is to say:–

(a) the cost of administering the headquarters of the Supreme Court and of the Judicial and Legal Services Commission;

(b) the salaries and allowances of the judges of the Supreme Court, the members of the Judicial and Legal Services Commission, the Chief Registrar, any other officers of the Supreme Court appointed for all the States and the employees of the Judicial and Legal Services Commission, the cost of any pension, gratuity or other like benefit payable to or in respect of any of them and any other expenses payable to or in respect of any of them from public funds, in accordance with their respective terms and conditions of service; and

(c) the cost involved in providing and maintaining any accommodation provided in pursuance of article 6 (2) of this Agreement.[24]

(4) The Government of a State shall be entitled to receive and retain all court fees and other revenues of the Court of Appeal and the High Court relating to their respective jurisidiction and powers in relation to that state.

(5) The proceeds of the income tax paid by the Chief Justice and Justices of Appeal to the Government of Grenada and by any such Puisne Judge as is referred to in article 6 (2) of this Agreement to the Government of the State in which he resides on their respective salaries as such shall be shared in equal proportions with the other States.

8 All accounts of the Court of Appeal and the High Court maintained in any State shall be audited annually by the Director of Audit of that State, who shall certify in respect of the period of twelve months ending on the last day of December in each year what respective sums are payable for that period in respect of those accounts by the Governments of the States in accordance with the provisions of this Agreement.

9 The administration of all courts in each State subordinate to the Court of Appeal or the High Court (other than courts-martial) shall be subject to inspection by the Chief Justice or any judge or officer of the Supreme Court authorised by him in that behalf, each of whom shall be entitled to make such enquiries and to be furnished with such information as he may require for that purpose; and the Chief Justice may from time to time make recommendations thereon to the Government of any State concerned.

24 Accommodation for Puisne Judges residing in any State on the direction of the Chief Justice.

10 The Governments of the States shall take such steps as may be reasonably practicable, having regard to the circumstances of each State, to promote uniformity in the laws of the State conferring jurisdiction and powers on the Court of Appeal and the High Court and regulating the practice and procedure of these courts, the execution and enforcement of the process of those courts, the right of practising before those courts and the representation of persons in any proceedings before these courts.

11 This Agreement may be varied by further Agreement between the Governments of all the States in respect of which it is for the time being in force:

Provided that –

(a) if any of these Governments wishes to propose any variation they shall give the remainder of those Governments at least six months' notice in writing of the proposed variation and the Governments of all those States shall consult together before the expiration of the notice to consider the desirability of adopting the proposal, with or without modification;

(b) no variation of any arrangement that is required under this Agreement to have the force of law in any State shall have effect unless and until the law of all the States has been duly amended to such extent as may be necessary to give effect to the variation.

(ii) Extracts from the West Indies Associated States Supreme Court Order, 1967. (S.I. 223/1967.)

PART II – THE SUPREME COURT

4(1) There shall be a Supreme Court for the States which shall be styled the West Indies Associated States Supreme Court and shall be a superior court of record.

(2) The Supreme Court shall consist of a Court of Appeal and a High Court of Justice . . . .

5(1) The Chief Justice shall be appointed by Her Majesty by Letters Patent and the Justices of Appeal and the Puisne Judges shall be appointed on behalf of Her Majesty by the Judicial and Legal Services Commission.

(2) A person shall not qualified to be appointed –

(a) as Chief Justice or a Justice of Appeal unless –

(i) he has been for a period or period amounting in the aggregate to not less than five years a judge of a court of unlimited jurisdiction in civil and criminal matters in some part of the Commonwealth or a court having jurisdiction in appeals from such a court; or

(ii) he is qualified to practise as an advocate in such a court, and has so practised for a period of or periods amounting in the aggregate to, not less than fifteen years;

(b) as a Puisne Judge unless –

(i) he is or has been a judge of a court of unlimited jurisdiction in civil and criminal matters in some part of the Commonwealth or a court having jurisdiction in appeals from such a court; or

(ii) he is qualified to practise as an advocate in such a court, and has so practised, for a period of or periods amounting in the aggregate to not less than ten years . . . .

8(1) Subject to the following provisions of this section, a judge of the Court of Appeal shall hold office until he attains the age of sixty-five and a Puisne Judge shall hold office until he attains the age of sixty-two years:

Provided that the Judicial and Legal Services Commission acting with the concurrence of the Premiers of all the States may permit a judge to continue in his office after attaining the age prescribed in this subsection for a period or periods not exceeding in the aggregate three years . . . .

(3) A judge may be removed from office only for inability to discharge the functions of his office (whether arising from infirmity of body or mind or any other cause) or for misbehaviour, and shall not be so removed except in accordance with the following provisions of this section.

(4) The Chief Justice may be removed from office by order of Her Majesty and other judges of the Supreme Court shall be removed from office by order of the Judicial and Legal Services Commission if the question of the removal from office has, in pursuance of the next following subsection, be referred to the Judicial Committee of Her Majesty's Privy Council under any enactment enabling Her Majesty in that behalf and the Judicial Committee has advised Her Majesty that the Chief Justice or the judge, as the case may be, ought to be removed from office for inability as aforesaid or misbehaviour.

(5) If, in the case of the Chief Justice, the Premier of one of the States to which this Order applies represents to the Lord High Chancellor of Great Britain or if, in the case of any other judge of the Supreme Court, the Judicial and Legal Services Commission represents to the Chief Justice that the question of removing the Chief Justice or other judge, as the case may be, for inability as aforesaid or for misbehaviour ought to be investigated then –

(a) the Lord Chancellor or the Chief Justice, as the case may be, shall appoint a tribunal which shall consist of a Chairman and not less than two other members selected by the Lord Chancellor or the Chief Justice, as the case may be, from among persons who hold or have held office as a judge of a court of unlimited jurisdiction in criminal and civil matters in some part of the Commonwealth or as a judge of a court having jurisdiction in appeals from any such court; and

(b) that tribunal shall enquire into the matter and report on the facts thereof to the Lord Chancellor or the Chief Justice, as the case may be, and recommend whether the question of the removal of the Chief Justice or other judge, as the case may be, should be referred by Her Majesty to the Judicial Committee.

(6) The provisions set out in schedule 2 to this Order shall apply in relation to tribunals appointed under the last foregoing subsection or to the members thereof.

(7) If the question of removing the Chief Justice or other judge of the Supreme Court has been referred to a tribunal under subsection (5) of this section the Lord Chancellor, in the case of the Chief Justice, or the Judicial and Legal Services Commission, in the case of any other judge of the court, may suspend the Chief Justice, or other judge, as the case may be, from performing the functions of his office.

(8) Any such suspension may at any time be revoked by the Lord Chancellor or the Judicial and Legal Services Commission, as the case may be, and shall in any case cease to have effect –

(a) if the tribunal recommends that the question of the removal of the judge from office should not be referred by Her Majesty to the Judicial Committee; or

(b) if the Judicial Committee advises that the judge ought not to be removed from office.

(9) Any expenses, in connection with proceedings under this section, authorised by the Lord Chancellor or the Chief Justice, as the case may be, shall be regarded as part of the expenses of the Supreme Court.

9(1) The High Court shall have, in relation to a State, such jurisdiction and powers as may be conferred on it by the Constitution or any other law of the State.

(2) The Court of Appeal shall have, in relation to a State, such jurisdiction to hear and determine appeals and to exercise such powers as may be conferred upon it by the Constitution or any other law of the State.

(3) The process of the Supreme Court shall run throughout the States and any judgment of the Court shall have full force and effect and may be executed and enforced in any of the States.

(4) The provisions of subsection (3) of this section shall be without prejudice to the provisions of the constitution of each State relating to fundamental rights and freedoms.

10 The High Court and Court of Appeal may exercise such jurisdiction and powers, and any judge or Chief Registrar of the Supreme Court may exercise such functions, as may be conferred upon them respectively in relation to Montserrat or the Virgin Islands by or under any law in force in Montserrat or the Virgin Islands, as the case may be.

PART III – GENERAL

11(1) The Chief Justice, the Justices of Appeal and the Puisne Judges shall be paid the salaries specified in schedule 3 to this Order, and shall be entitled to such allowances and shall have such terms and conditions of office as may from time to time be determined by the Judicial and Legal Services Commission with the concurrence of the Premiers of all the States.

Provided that –

(a) the salaries specified in schedule 3 to this Order may be altered by order made by the Judicial and Legal Services Commission with the concurrence of the Premiers of all the States;

(b) the salary and allowances (other than allowances which are not taken into account in the computation of pensions) of a judge shall not be reduced and the terms and conditions of office applicable to a judge upon his appointment shall not be made less favourable to him during the currency of that appointment.

(2) Where a judge is entitled to exercise an option in relation to his salary or the other matters referred to in proviso (b) to subsection (1) of this section, the option as exercised by him shall be deemed for the purposes of that proviso to be in his favour.

12 There shall be, for all the States, an office of Chief Registrar and such other offices of the Supreme Court as the Chief Justice may from time to time prescribe by order made with the concurrence of the Premiers of all the States; and the holders of such offices shall be paid such salaries and allowances and shall have such terms and conditions of office as may from time to time be determined by the Chief Justice with the concurrence of the Premiers of all the States.

(2) Power to make appointments to the office of Chief Registrar and to the other offices prescribed under this section and to exercise disciplinary control over persons holding or acting in such offices shall vest in the Judicial and Legal Services Commission . . . .

16 The Chief Justice shall assign a Puisne Judge to each State who shall reside in the State to which he is assigned . . . .

PART IV – JUDICIAL AND LEGAL COMMISSION

18(1) There shall be a Judicial and Legal Services Commission (hereinafter referred to as the "Commission") for the States which shall consist of the following persons, that is to say –

(a) the Chief Justice, who shall be the Chairman;

(b) such Justice of Appeal or Puisne Judge as may from time to time be designated in that behalf by the Chief Justice;

(c) a person, appointed by the Chief Justice with the concurrence of the Premiers of not less than four of the States, who has been a judge of a court of unlimited jurisdiction in civil and criminal matters in some part of the Commonwealth or a court having jurisdiction in appeals from any such court, not being a person who is practising as an advocate before the Supreme Court; and

(d) two members selected in accordance with the provisions of subsection (2) of this section.

(2) The persons for the time discharging the functions of Chairman of the Public Service Commissions of two States, being States for the time being designated in that behalf by the Chief Justice, shall be ex-officio members of the Commission:

Provided that –

(a) except as otherwise provided in any agreement between the Governments of all the States, the Chief Justice shall designate States in such manner that the Chairman of the Public Service Commissions of the States sit as members of the Commission in rotation for periods of three years, the order of rotation among the States to be as follows:–

(i) Antigua and Dominica;

(ii) Grenada and Saint Christopher, Nevis and Anguilla;

(iii) Saint Lucia and Saint Vincent; and

(b) where the Chairman of the Public Service Commission of any designated State is in practice as an advocate before the Supreme Court, that Public Service Commission shall nominate another of its members, not being a person so in practice, to sit on the Commission in his stead.

(3) The office of the appointed member of the Commission shall become vacant –

(a) at the expiration of three years from the date of his appointment;

(b) if he practices as an advocate before the Supreme Court; or

(c) if the question of his ceasing to be a member of the Commission has been referred by the Chief Justice, acting on the recommendation of the Premiers of not less than four of the States, to a tribunal consisting of a Chairman and two other persons appointed by the Chief Justice, and that tribunal has recommended that such person should cease to be a member of the Commission.

(4) The Commission shall not be disqualified for the transaction of business by reason of any vacancy amongst its members.

19(1) The Commission shall perform such functions as are conferred on it by this Order or any other law for the time being in force in any State . . . .

D Note on the internal constitutions of the West Indies Associated States.

The internal constitutions of the associated states follow the lines suggested in the Constitutional Proposals published in command paper 2865 of 1965, included in this collection of documents as document A (ii) of this chapter. Furthermore, these constitutions are sufficiently similar to the independence constitutions of Jamaica, Trinidad and Tobago, Guyana and Barbados not to be included as separate documents in this work.

However, certain points of interest can be mentioned here.[25]

1 Legislatures

The associated states have taken advantage of the suggestion that their legislatures could be either unicameral or bicameral. Dominica, St. Kitts/Nevis/Anguilla, and St. Lucia have unicameral legislatures of mixed membership, that is containing a small nominated element in addition to the elected members. However, the Constitution Order of St. Lucia contains provisions which allow for the establishment of a bicameral legislature by simple resolution of the House of Assembly. The Senate so established would consist of seven members appointed on the advice of the Premier,[26] two on the advice of the Leader of the Opposition, and two on the advice of the Premier after he has consulted with religious, economic or social bodies or associations. On the establishment of a Senate the House of Assembly of St. Lucia would become wholly elected.

The remaining states, Grenada and Antigua have bicameral legislatures with wholly elected Houses of Assembly, but the Senates differ in composition. The Senate of Grenada follows the lines outlined above for St. Lucia but the respective numbers are 5 : 2 : 2. However, in Antigua the composition of the Senate is seven Senators appointed on the advice of the

25 This note does not contain any reference to the constitution of St. Vincent.
26 The head of government of these states has the title of Premier, not Prime Minister, a distinction signifying their less than independent status.

Premier, and three being appointed by the Governor but after he has consulted with the Premier. The wording suggests that the Governor would not be legally bound by any suggestions made by the Premier in this instance. However, with the development of responsible government it must be acknowledged that it becomes increasingly difficult for the Head of State to reject any advice given by the Head of Government, even where he is not legally bound by that advice.

2 *Supervision of elections*

There is considerable variation of practice established by the different constitutions of the associated states with respect to the supervision of elections.

(i) Antigua has no provision at all in its constitution. The public officer with responsibility for elections would therefore be subject to ministerial control, would be appointed in the usual manner, and would be protected in office no more than any other public servant.

(ii) Dominica gives the responsibility for the administration and conduct of elections to the Governor who "shall act in his own deliberate judgment".

(iii) St. Kitts/Nevis/Anguilla and St. Lucia have an independent public officer called the Supervisor of Elections, appointed on the advice of the Public Service Commission after consultation with the Premier, and not subject to the direction or supervision of anyone else in the performance of his duties.

(iv) Grenada has establishment for a similar officer, except that he is appointed by the Governor acting in his discretion.

3 *Delimitation of boundaries*

Again there is variation in the constitutional arrangements made for the delimitation of constituency boundaries except that in all the associated states the validity of any Order made by the Governor under the authority of the relevant sections of the constitutions cannot be enquired into in any court of law.

(i) Antigua's constitution makes provision for boundary delimitation to be examined by a Commission appointed on the advice of the Premier, consisting of a Chairman and from two to four other members. Members of the Commission can also be dismissed on the advice of the Premier.

(ii) St. Kitts/Nevis/Anguilla has a Boundaries Commission made up of the Speaker of the House as Chairman, with two members of the House of Assembly appointed on the advice of the Premier, and two members of the House of Assembly appointed on the advice of the Leader of the Opposition.

(iii) St. Lucia uses a Standing Committee of the House of Assembly leaving its composition to the rules of procedure of the House.

(iv) Grenada and Dominica have established under their constitutions independent Commissions: The Speaker of the House as Chairman, two members appointed on the advice of the Premier, two members appointed on the advice of the Leader of the Opposition, and none of the ordinary members may be members of the legislature or public officers. The ordinary members of the Commission are specially protected in their tenure of office, only being dismissable on grounds of inability to perform the functions of the office or misbehaviour, and only after the question of dismissal has been referred to an independent tribunal appointed by the Chief Justice. In Grenada theCommissioners are further protected by their salaries being charged to the Consolidated Fund, so that salaries cannot be reduced during any individual's tenure of office.

4 *Attorney General*

Although differing in detail all the constitutions of the associated states make provision allowing for an official or an elected Attorney General, and stipulate that when elected he shall cease to perform the functions of a Director of Public Prosecutions. On the Attorney General's office being held by an elected member of the House, the office of Director of Public Prosecutions shall be filled by an independent official who shall be protected in his tenure of office and in his receipt of salary.

5 *Public Service Commission*

In all the associated states the method of dismissal of members of the Public Service Commissions is the same, and is that already outlined in the section dealing with the Boundary Delimitation Commission in Grenada. The composition and method of appointment varies, but for the most part puts power firmly in the hands of the Premiers of the States.

(i) Antigua and St. Lucia give an unrestricted power of appointment to their Premiers – all members being appointed on the advice of the Premier.

(ii) In Dominica and St. Kitts/Nevis/Anguilla much the same thing obtains except that in the case of one member the Premier must select from among nominees of the appropriate representative body (the Civil Service Association).

(iii) In Grenada the Chairman and two other members are appointed on the advice of the Premier, and the remaining two members are appointed on the advice of the Civil Service Association.

6 *Public Service Appeals Board*

All the associated states have constitutional provision for Public Service Appeals Boards whose function will be to hear and determine appeals from decisions of the Public Service Commissions in disciplinary cases. These Boards differ in composition.

CHAPTER 7
THE INDE DENCE CONSTITUTIONS: 1
THE STABLISHMENT OF THE STATE AND THE SEP RATION OF POWERS

A The adoption of the constitution.

(i) The preamble to the Constitution of Guyana, the Guyana Independence Order, 1966. (S.I. 575/1966.)

THE CONSTITUTION OF GUYANA

Whereas the People of Guyana[1] –

(a) acknowledge that reverence for the Diety and respect for the inherent dignity and the equal and inalienable rights of all men are the foundation of freedom, justice and peace in society;

(b) affirm the entitlement of all men to the fundamental rights and freedoms of the individual;

(c) recognise that the said rights and freedoms are best established and secured in a democratic society, founded on the rule of law:

Now, therefore, the following articles, which make provision for the government of Guyana as such a democratic society, shall have effect as the Constitution of Guyana.

(ii) Extracts from the Barbados Independence Order, 1966. (S.I. 1455/1966.)

At the Court at Buckingham Palace, the 22nd day of November 1966
Present,
The Queen's Most Excellent Majesty in Council

Her Majesty, by virtue and in exercise of the powers vested in Her by section 5 of the Barbados Independence Act 1966 and of all other powers enabling Her in that behalf, is pleased, by and with the advice of Her Privy Council, to

1 Note that it is Guyana alone which invokes the authority of the people.

order, and it is hereby ordered, as follows:–

1(1) This Order may be cited as the Barbados Independence Order 1966.

(2) This Order shall come into operation on 30th November 1966 (in this Order referred to as "the appointed day"):

Provided that the Governor may at any time after 22nd November 1966 exercise any of the powers conferred upon the Governor-General . . . to such extent as may, in his opinion, be necessary or expedient to enable the Constitution to function as from the appointed day.

(3) For the purposes of the exercise by the Governor . . . of the powers conferred the references . . . to the Prime Minister and the Leader of the Opposition shall be construed as if they were references respectively to the Premier and to the Leader of the Opposition as defined for the purposes of Schedule 2 to the Barbados (Letters Patent Consolidation) Order 1964; and the other powers referred to in that proviso shall be exercised by the Governor acting in accordance with the advice of the Premier . . . .

2(1) The Barbados (Letters Patent Consolidation) Order 1964 (in this Order referred to as "the existing Order") is revoked; but the revocation of the existing Order shall not affect the operation on and after the appointed day of any law made or having effect as if made in pursuance of the existing Order and having effect as part of the law of Barbados immediately before the appointed day (including any law made before the appointed day and coming into operation on or after that day) . . . .

3 Subject to the provisions of this Order, the Constitution shall come into effect on the appointed day.

4(1) Subject to the provisions of this section, the existing laws shall be construed with such modifications, adaptations, qualifications and exceptions as may be necessary to bring them into conformity with the Barbados Independence Act 1966 and this Order.

(2) Where any matter that fails to be prescribed or otherwise provided for under the Constitution by Parliament or by any other authority or person is prescribed or provided for by or under an existing law (including any amendment to any such law made under this section) or is otherwise prescribed or provided for immediately before the appointed day by or under the existing Order, that prescription or provision shall, as from that day, have effect (with such modifications, adaptations, qualifications and exceptions as may be necessary to bring it into conformity with the Barbados Independence Act 1966 and this Order) as if it had been made under the Constitution by Parliament or, as the case may require, by the other authority or person.

(3) The Governor-General may by order made at any time before 30th November 1967 make such amendments to any existing law as may appear to

him to be necessary or expedient for bringing that law into conformity with the provisions of the Barbados Independence Act 1966 and this Order or otherwise for giving effect to or enabling effect to be given to those provisions . . . .

(6) In this section "existing law" means any law having effect as part of the law of Barbados immediately before the appointed day (including any law made before the appointed day and coming into operation on or after that day).

5(1) The persons who immediately before the appointed day are members of the Senate established by the existing Order . . . shall as from the appointed day be members of the Senate established by the Constitution as if they had been appointed as such under . . . the Constitution and shall hold their seats as Senators in accordance with the provisions of the Constitution.

(2) The persons who immediately before the appointed day are President and Deputy President of the existing Senate shall as from the appointed day be President and Deputy President respectively of the Senate established by the Constitution as if they had been elected as such under section 40 of the Constitution and shall hold office in accordance with the provisions of that section.

(3) The persons who immediately before the appointed day are members of the House of Assembly then established for Barbados (in this section referred to as "the existing Assembly") shall as from the appointed day be members of the House of Assembly established by the Constitution as if elected as such in pursuance of section 41 (2) of the Constitution and shall hold their seats in that House in accordance with the provisions of the Constitution.

(4) The persons who immediately before the appointed day are Speaker and Deputy Speaker of the existing Assembly shall as from the appointed day be Speaker and Deputy Speaker respectively of the House of Assembly established by the Constitution as if elected as such by that House in pursuance of any provisions in that behalf . . . .

(6) The Standing Orders of the existing Senate and the existing Assembly as in force immediately before the appointed day shall, except as may be otherwise provided in pursuance of section 50 (1) of the Constitution, be the Standing Orders respectively of the Senate and the House of Assembly established by the Constitution but they shall be construed with such modifications, adaptations, qualifications and exceptions as may be necessary to bring them into conformity with the Constitution.

(7) Notwithstanding anything contained in section 61 (3) of the Constitution (but subject to the provisions of subsections (4) and (5) of that section) Parliament shall, unless sooner dissolved, stand dissolved on the expiration of five years from the first sitting of the existing Assembly after

the general election of members of the Assembly last preceding the appointed day.

6(1) The person who immediately before the appointed day holds the office of Premier under the existing Order shall, as from the appointed day, hold office as Prime Minister as if he had been appointed thereto under section 65 (1) of the Constitution.

(2) The persons (other than the Premier) who immediately before the appointed day hold office as Ministers under the existing Order shall, as from the appointed day, hold the like offices as if they had been appointed thereto under section 65 (2) of the Constitution.

(3) Any person holding the office of Prime Minister or other Minister by virtue of subsection (1) or (2) who immediately before the appointed day was charged with responsibility for any subject or department of government shall, as from the appointed day, be deemed to have been assigned responsibility for the corresponding business or department of the Government under section 72 of the Constitution.

(4) The persons who immediately before the appointed day hold office as Parliamentary Secretaries under the existing Order shall, as from the appointed day, hold the like offices as if they had been appointed thereto under section 73 (1) of the Constitution . . . .

7 The person who immediately before the appointed day is the Leader of the Opposition (as defined for the purposes of Schedule 2 to the existing Order) shall, as from the appointed day, hold office as Leader of the Opposition as if he had been appointed thereto under section 74 of the Constitution.

8 The persons who immediately before the appointed day are members of the Privy Council established by the existing Order, having been appointed as such under clause 3 of the Barbados Royal Instructions 1964, shall, as from the appointed day, hold office as members of the Privy Council established by the Constitution as if they had been appointed thereto under section 76 (1) of the Constitution:

Provided that for the purposes of subsection (3) of that section the date of appointment of any such person shall be the date on which the period of his last appointment under the said clause 3 commenced or was deemed to have commenced for the purposes of that clause.

9(1) Every person who immediately before the appointed day holds or is acting in a public office shall, as from the appointed day, hold or act in that office or the corresponding office established by the Constitution as if he had been appointed to do so in accordance with the provisions of the Constitution:

Provided that any person who under any existing law would have been required to vacate his office on the attainment of any age or on the expiration of any period shall vacate his office on the attainment of that age or at the expiration of that period.

(2) The Provisions of subsection (1) shall apply in relation to the office of a Judge as if that office were a public office . . . .

12(1) Parliament may alter any of the provisions of this Order in the same manner as it may alter any of the provisions of the Constitution:

Provided that section 3, section 5 (1) and (7), section 9 of this section may be altered by Parliament only in the same manner as the provisions specified in section 49 (2) of the Constitution.

B The supremacy of the constitution – extract from the Jamaica (Constitution) Order in Council, 1962, (S.I. 1550/1962.)

2 – Subject to the provisions of sections 49 and 50 of this Constitution, if any other law is inconsistent with this Constitution, this Constitution shall prevail and the other law shall, to the extent of the inconsistency, be void.

C Citizenship: extracts from the Jamaica (Constitution) Order in Council, 1962. (S.I. 1550/1962.)

CHAPTER II
CITIZENSHIP

3(1) Every person who, having been born in the former Colony of Jamaica, is on the fifth day of August 1962 a citizen of the United Kingdom and Colonies shall become a citizen of Jamaica on the sixth day of August 1962.

(2) Every person who, having been born outside of the former Colony of Jamaica, is on the fifth day of August 1962 a citizen of the United Kingdom and Colonies, shall if his father becomes or would but for his death have become a citizen of Jamaica in accordance with the provisions of subsection (1) of this section, become a citizen of Jamaica on the sixth day of August 1962.

4(1) Any woman who, on the fifth day of August 1962 is or had been married to a person –

(a) who becomes a citizen of Jamaica by virtue of section 3 of this Constitution; or

(b) who, having died before the sixth day of August 1962 would, but for his death, have become a citizen of Jamaica by virtue of that section,

shall be entitled, upon making application in such manner as may be prescribed and, if she is a British protected person or an alien, upon taking the oath of allegiance, to be registered as a citizen of Jamaica.

(2) Any person who, on the fifth day of August 1962 is a citizen of the United Kingdom and Colonies –

(a) having become such a citizen under the British Nationality Act, 1948 (a) by virtue of his having been naturalised in the former Colony of Jamaica as a British subject, before that Act came into force; or

(b) having become such a citizen by virtue of his having been naturalised or registered in the former Colony of Jamaica under that Act,

shall be entitled, upon making application before the sixth day of August 1964, in such manner as may be prescribed, to be registered as a citizen of Jamaica:

Provided that a person who has not attained the age of twenty-one years (other than a woman who is or has been married) may not make an application under this subsection himself but an application may be made on his behalf by his parent or guardian.

(3) Any woman who on the fifth day of August 1962 is or has been married to a person who subsequently becomes a citizen of Jamaica by registration under subsection (2) of this section shall be entitled, upon making application in such manner as may be prescribed and, if she is a British protected person or an alien, upon taking the oath of allegiance to be registered as a citizen of Jamaica.

5 Every person born in Jamaica after the fifth day of August 1962 shall become a citizen of Jamaica at the date of his birth:

Provided that a person shall not become a citizen of Jamaica by virtue of this section if at the time of his birth –

(a) his father possesses such immunity from suit and legal process as is accorded to an envoy of a foreign sovereign power accredited to Her Majesty in right of Her Government in Jamaica and neither of his parents is a citizen of Jamaica; or

(b) his father is an enemy alien and the birth occurs in a place then under occupation by the enemy.

6 A person born outside Jamaica after the fifth day of August 1962 shall become a citizen of Jamaica at the date of his birth if at that date his father is a citizen of Jamaica otherwise than by virtue of this section or subsection (2) of section 3 of this Constitution.

7 Any woman who, after the fifth day of August 1962 married a person who is or becomes a citizen of Jamaica shall be entitled upon making application in such manner as may be prescribed and, if she is a British protected person or an alien, upon taking the oath of allegiance, to be registered as a citizen of Jamaica.

8(1) If the Governor-General is satisfied that any citizen of Jamaica has at any time after the fifth day of August 1962 acquired by registration, naturalisation or other voluntary and formal act (other than marriage) the citizenship of any country other than Jamaica, the Governor-General may by order deprive that person of his citizenship.

(2) If the Governor-General is satisfied that any citizen of Jamaica has at any time after the fifth day of August 1962 voluntarily claimed and exercised in a country other than Jamaica any rights available to him under the law of that country, being rights accorded exclusively to its citizens, the Governor-General may by order deprive that person of his citizenship.

9(1) Every person who under this Constitution or any Act of Parliament is a citizen of Jamaica or under any enactment for the time being in force in any country to which this section applies is a citizen of that country shall, by virtue of that citizenship, have the status of a Commonwealth citizen.

(2) Every person who is a British subject without citizenship under the British Nationality Act, 1948, or who continues to be a British subject under section 2 of that Act shall by virtue of that status have the status of a Commonwealth citizen.

(3) Save as may be otherwise provided by Parliament, the countries to which this section applies are the United Kingdom and Colonies, Canada, Australia, New Zealand, India, Pakistan, Ceylon, Ghana, the Federation of Malaya, the Federation of Nigeria, the Republic of Cyprus, Sierra Leone, Tanganyika, the Federation of Rhodesia and Nyasaland and the State of Singapore . . . .

11 Parliament may make provision –

(a) for the acquisition of citizenship of Jamaica by persons who do not become citizens of Jamaica by virtue of the provisions of this Chapter;

(b) for depriving of his citizenship of Jamaica any person who is a citizen of Jamaica otherwise than by virtue of section 3 or section 5 or section 6 of this Constitution; or

(c) for the renunciation by any person of his citizenship of Jamaica . . . .

D Fundamental rights and freedoms[2]

(i) Extracts from the Jamaica (Constitution) Order in Council, 1962. (S.I. 1550/1962.)

CHAPTER III
FUNDAMENTAL RIGHTS AND FREEDOMS

13 Whereas every person in Jamaica is entitled to the fundamental rights and freedoms of the individual, that is to say, has the right, whatever his race, place of origin, political opinions, colour, creed or sex, but subject to respect for the rights and freedoms of others and for the public interest, to each and all of the following, namely –

(a) life, liberty, security of the person, the enjoyment of property and the protection of the law;

(b) freedom of conscience, of expression and peaceful assembly and association; and

(c) respect for his private and family life,

the subsequent provisions of this Chapter shall have effect for the purpose of affording protection to the aforesaid rights and freedoms, subject to such limitations of that protection as are contained in those provisions being limitations designed to ensure that the enjoyment of the said rights and freedoms by any individual does not prejudice the rights and freedoms of others or the public interest.

14(1) No person shall intentionally be deprived of his life save in execution of the sentence of a court in respect of a criminal offence of which he has been convicted.

(2) Without prejudice to any liability for a contravention of any other law with respect to the use of force in such cases as are hereinafter mentioned, a

2 While differing in detail and occasionally in substance the independence constitutions of the Commonwealth Caribbean follow the same broad pattern of granting rights but with considerable limitations and without curbing the government's capacity to legally reduce those rights in the public interest.

person shall not be regarded as having been deprived of his life in contravention of this section if he dies as the result of the use of force to such extent as is reasonably justifiable in the circumstances of the case –

(a) for the defence of any person from violence or for the defence of property;
(b) in order to effect a lawful arrest or to prevent the escape of a person lawfully detained;
(c) for the purpose of suppressing a riot, insurrection or mutiny; or
(d) in order lawfully to prevent the commission by that person of a criminal offence,

or if he dies as the result of lawful act of war.

15(1) No person shall be deprived of his personal liberty save as may in any of the following cases be authorised by law –

(a) in consequence of his unfitness to plead to a criminal charge; or
(b) in execution of the sentence or order of a court, whether in Jamaica or elsewhere, in respect of a criminal offence of which he has been convicted; or
(c) in execution of an order of the Supreme Court or of the Court of Appeal or such other court as may be prescribed by Parliament on the grounds of his contempt of any such court or of another court or tribunal; or
(d) in execution of the order of a court made in order to secure the fulfilment of any obligation imposed on him by law; or
(e) for the purpose of bringing him before a court in execution of the order of a court; or
(f) upon reasonable suspicion of his having committed or of being about to commit a criminal offence; or
(g) in the case of a person who has not attained the age of twenty-one years, for the purpose of his education or welfare; or
(h) for the purpose of preventing the spread of an infectious or contagious disease; or
(i) in the case of a person who is, or is reasonably suspected to be, of unsound mind, addicted to drugs or alcohol, or a vagrant, for the purpose of his care of treatment or the protection of the community; or
(j) for the purpose of preventing the unlawful entry of that person into Jamaica, or for the purpose of effecting the expulsion, extradition or other lawful removal of that person from Jamaica or the taking of proceedings relating thereto; or
(k) to such extent as may be necessary in the execution of a lawful order requiring that person to remain within a specified area

within Jamaica or prohibiting him from being within such an area, or to such extent as may be reasonably justifiable for restraining that person during any visit that he is permitted to make to any part of Jamaica in which, in consequence of any such order, his presence would otherwise be unlawful.

(2) Any person who is arrested or detained shall be informed as soon as reasonably practicable, in a language which he understands, of the reasons for his arrest or detention.

(3) Any person who is arrested or detained –

(a) for the purpose of bringing him before a court in execution of the order of a court; or

(b) upon reasonable suspicion of his having committed or being about to commit a criminal offence,

and who is not released, shall be brought without delay before a court; and if any person arrested or detained upon reasonable suspicion of his having committed or being about to commit a criminal offence is not tried within a reasonable time, then, without prejudice to any further proceedings which may be brought against him, he shall be released either unconditionally or upon reasonable conditions, including in particular such conditions as are reasonably necessary to ensure that he appears at a later date for trial or for proceedings preliminary to trial.

(4) Any person who is unlawfully arrested or detained by any other person shall be entitled to compensation therefor from that person.

(5) Nothing contained in or done under the authority of any law shall be held to be inconsistent with or in contravention of this section to the extent that the law in question authorises the taking during a period of public emergency of measures that are reasonably justifiable for the purpose of dealing with the situation that exists during that period of public emergency.

(6) If any person who is lawfully detained by virtue only of such a law as is referred to in subsection (5) of this section so requests at any time during the period of that detention not earlier than six months after he last made such a request during that period, his case shall be reviewed by an independent and impartial tribunal established by law and presided over by a person appointed by the Chief Justice of Jamaica from among the persons entitled to practise or to be admitted to practise in Jamaica as barristers or solicitors.

(7) On any review by a tribunal in pursuance of subsection (6) of this section of the case of any detained person, the tribunal may make recommendations concerning the necessity or expediency of continuing his detention to the authority by whom it was ordered but, unless it is otherwise provided by law, that authority shall not be obliged to act in accordance with any such recommendations.

16(1) No person shall be deprived of his freedom of movement, and for the purposes of this section the said freedom means the right to move freely throughout Jamaica, the right to reside in any part of Jamaica, the right to enter Jamaica and immunity from expulsion from Jamaica.

(2) Any restriction on a person's freedom of movement which is involved in his lawful detention shall not be held to be inconsistent with or in contravention of this section.

(3) Nothing contained in or done under the authority of any law shall be held to be inconsistent with or in contravention of this section to the extent that the law in question makes provision –

- (a) which is reasonably required in the interests of defence, public safety, public order, public morality or public health; or
- (b) for the imposition of restrictions on the movement or residence within Jamaica of any person who is not a citizen thereof or the exclusion or expulsion from Jamaica of any such person; or
- (c) for the imposition of restrictions on the acquisition or use by any person of land or other property in Jamaica; or
- (d) for the imposition of restrictions upon the movement or residence within Jamaica of public officers, police officers or members of a defence force; or
- (e) for the removal of a person from Jamaica to be tried outside Jamaica for a criminal offence or to undergo imprisonment outside Jamaica for a criminal offence or to undergo imprisonment outside Jamaica in execution of the sentence of a court in respect of a criminal offence of which he has been convicted.

(4) If any person whose freedom of movement has been restricted by virtue only of such a provision as is referred to in paragraph (a) of subsection (5) of this section so requests at any time during the period of that restriction not earlier than six months after he last made such a request during that period, his case shall be reviewed by an independent and impartial tribunal established by law and presided over by a person appointed by the Chief Justice of Jamaica from among the persons entitled to practise or to be admitted to practise in Jamaica as barristers or solicitors.

(5) On any review by a tribunal in pursuance of subsection (4) of this section of the case of any person whose freedom of movement has been restricted, the tribunal may make recommendations concerning the necessity or expediency of continuing that restriction to the authority by whom it was ordered but, unless it is otherwise provided by law, that authority shall not be obliged to act in accordance with any such recommendations.

17(1) No person shall be subjected to torture or to inhuman or degrading punishment or other treatment.

(2) Nothing contained in or done under the authority of any law shall be held to be inconsistent with or in contravention of this section to the extent that the law in question authorises the infliction of any description of punishment which was lawful in Jamaica immediately before the appointed day.

18(1) No property of any description shall be compulsorily taken possession of and no interest in or right over property of any description shall be compulsorily acquired except by or under the provisions of a law that –

(a) prescribes the principles on which and the manner in which compensation therefor is to be determined and given; and

(b) secures to any person claiming an interest in or right over such property a right of access to a court for the purpose of –

(i) establishing such interest or right (if any)

(ii) determining the amount of such compensation (if any) to which he is entitled; and

(iii) enforcing his right to any such compensation.

(2) Nothing in this section shall be construed as affecting the making or operation of any law so far as it provides for the taking or possession or acquisition of property –

(a) in satisfaction of any tax, rate or due;

(b) by way of penalty for breach of the law, whether under civil process or after conviction of a criminal offence;

(c) upon the attempted removal of the property in question out of or into Jamaica in contravention of any law;

(d) by way of the taking of a sample for the purposes of any law;

(e) where the property consists of an animal upon its being found trespassing or straying;

(f) as an incident of a lease, tenancy, licence, mortgage, charge, bill of sale, pledge or contract;

(g) by way of the vesting or administration of trust property, enemy property, or the property of persons adjudged or otherwise declared bankrupt or insolvent, persons of unsound mind, deceased persons, or bodies corporate or unincorporate in the course of being wound up;

(h) in the execution of judgments or orders of courts;

(i) by reason of its being in a dangerous state or injurious to the health of human beings, animals or plants;

(j) in consequence of any law with respect to the limitation of actions;

(k) for so long only as may be necessary for the purposes of any examination, investigation, trial or inquiry or, in the case of land, the carrying out thereon –
   (i) of work of soil conservation or the conservation of other natural resources; or
   (ii) of agricultural development or improvement which the owner or occupier of the land has been required, and has without reasonable and lawful excuse refused or failed, to carry out.

(3) Nothing in this section shall be construed as affecting the making or operation of any law so far as it provides for the orderly marketing or production or growth or extraction of any agricultural product or mineral or any article or thing prepared for market or manufactured therefor or for the reasonable restriction of the use of any property in the interests of safeguarding the interests of others or the protection of tenants, licenses or others having rights in or over such property.

(4) Nothing in this section shall be construed as affecting the making or operation of any law for the compulsory taking of possession in the public interest of any property, or the compulsory acquisition in the public interest of any interest in or right over property, where that property, interest or right is held by a body corporate which is established for public purposes by any law and in which no monies have been invested other than monies provided by Parliament or by the Legislature of the former Colony of Jamaica.

(5) In this section "compensation" means the consideration to be given to a person for any interest or right which he may have in or over property which has been compulsorily taken possession of or compulsorily acquired as prescribed and determined in accordance with the provisions of the law by or under which the property has been compulsorily taken possession of or compulsorily acquired.

19(1) Except with his own consent, no person shall be subjected to the search of his person or his property or the entry by others on his premises.

(2) Nothing contained in or done under the authority of any law shall be held to be inconsistent with or in contravention of this section to the extent that the law in question makes provision which is reasonably required –

(a) in the interests of defence, public safety, public order, public morality, public health, public revenue, town and country planning or the development and utilisation of any property in such a manner as to promote the public benefit; or

(b) for the purpose of preventing or detecting crime; or

(c) for the purpose of protecting the rights or freedom of other persons.

20(1) Whenever any person is charged with a criminal offence he shall, unless the charge is withdrawn, be afforded a fair hearing within a reasonable time by an independent and impartial court established by law.

(2) Any court or other authority prescribed by law for the determination of the existence or the extent of civil rights or obligations shall be independent and impartial; and where proceedings for such a determination are instituted by any person before such a court or other authority, the case shall be given a fair hearing within a reasonable time.

(3) All proceedings of every court and proceedings relating to the determination of the existence or the extent of a person's civil rights or obligations before any court or other authority, including the announcement of the decision of the court or other authority, shall be held in public.

(4) Nothing in subsection (3) of this section shall prevent any court or any authority such as is mentioned in that subsection from excluding from the proceedings persons other than the parties thereto and their legal representatives –

- (a) in interlocutory civil proceedings; or
- (b) in appeal proceedings under any law relating to income tax; or
- (c) to such extent as the court or other authority –
  - (i) may consider necessary or expedient in circumstances where publicity would prejudice the interests of justice; or
  - (ii) may be empowered or required by law to do so in the interests of defence, public safety, public order, public morality, the welfare of persons under the age of twenty-one years or the protection of the private lives of persons concerned in the proceedings.

(5) Every person who is charged with a criminal offence shall be presumed to be innocent until he is proved or has pleaded guilty:

Provided that nothing contained in or done under the authority of any law shall be held to be inconsistent with or in contravention of this subsection to the extent that the law in question imposes upon any person charged as aforesaid the burden of proving particular facts.

(6) Every person who is charged with a criminal offence –

- (a) shall be informed as soon as reasonably practicable, in a language which he understands, of the nature of the offence charged;
- (b) shall be given adequate time and facilities for the preparation of his defence;
- (c) shall be permitted to defend himself in person or by a legal representative of his own choice;
- (d) shall be afforded facilities to examine in person or by his legal representative the witnesses called by the prosecution before any court and to obtain the attendance of witnesses, subject to the

payment of their reasonable expenses, and carry out the examination of such witnesses to testify on his behalf before the court on the same conditions as those applying to witnesses called by the prosecution; and

(e) shall be permitted to have without payment the assistance of an interpreter if he cannot understand the English language.

(7) No person shall be held to be guilty of a criminal offence on account of any act or omission which did not, at the time it took place, constitute such an offence, and no penalty shall be imposed for any criminal offence which is severer in degree or description than the maximum penalty which might have been imposed for that offence at the time when it was committed.

(8) No person who shows that he has been tried by any competent court for a criminal offence and either convicted or acquitted shall again be tried for that offence or for any other criminal offence of which he could have been convicted at the trial for that offence save upon the order of a superior court made in the course of appeal proceedings relating to the conviction or acquittal; and no person shall be tried for a criminal offence if he shows that he has been pardoned for that offence:

Provided that nothing in any law shall be held to be inconsistent with or in contravention of this subsection by reason only that it authorises any court to try a member of a defence force for a criminal offence notwithstanding any trial and conviction or acquittal of that member under service law; but any court so trying such a member and convicting him shall in sentencing him to any punishment take into account any punishment awarded him under service law.

(9) Nothing contained in or done under the authority of any law shall be held to be inconsistent with or in contravention of any provision of this section other than subsection (7) thereof to the extent that the law in question authorises the taking during a period of public emergency of measures that are reasonably justifiable for the purpose of dealing with the situation that exists during that period of public emergency.

(10) In paragraph (c) and (d) of subsection (6) of this section "legal representative" means a barrister entitled to practise as such in Jamaica or, except in relation to proceedings before a court in which a solicitor has no right of audience, a solicitor who is so entitled.

21(1) Except with his own consent, no person shall be hindered in the enjoyment of his freedom of conscience, and for the purposes of this section the said freedom includes freedom of thought and of religion, freedom to change his religion or belief, and freedom, either alone or in community with others, and both in public and in private, to manifest and propagate his religion or belief in worship, teaching, practice and observance.

(2) Except with his own consent (or, if he is a minor, the consent of his parent or guardian), no person attending any place of education shall be required to receive religious instruction or to take part in or attend any religious ceremony or observance if that instruction, ceremony or observance relates to a religion or a religious body or denomination other than his own.

(3) The constitution of a religious body or denomination shall not be altered except with the consent of the governing authority of that body or denomination.

(4) No religious body or denomination shall be prevented from providing religious instruction for persons of that body or denomination in the course of any education provided by that body or denomination whether or not that body or denomination is in receipt of any government subsidy, grant or other form of financial assistance designed to meet, in whole or in part, the cost of such course of education.

(5) No person shall be compelled to take any oath which is contrary to his religion or belief or to take any oath in a manner which is contrary to his religion or belief.

(6) Nothing contained in or done under the authority of any law shall be held to be inconsistent with or in contravention of this section to the extent that the law in question makes provision which is reasonably required –

- (a) in the interests of defence, public safety, public order, public morality or public health; or
- (b) for the purpose of protecting the rights and freedoms of other persons, including the right to observe and practise any religion without the unsolicited intervention of members of any other religion . . .[3]

25(1) Subject to the provisions of subsection (4) of this section, if any person alleges that any of the provisions of sections 14 to 24 (inclusive) of this Constitution has been, is being or is likely to be contravened in relation to him, then without prejudice to any other action with respect to the same matter which is lawfully available, that person may apply to the Supreme Court for redress.

(2) The Supreme Court shall have original jurisdiction to hear and determine any application made by any person in pursuance of subsection (1) of this section and may make such orders, issue such writs and give such direction as it may consider appropriate for the purpose of enforcing, or securing the enforcement of, any of the provisions of the said sections 14 to 24 (inclusive) to the protection of which the person concerned is entitled:

3 Similar provisions, with similar qualifications concern protection of freedom of expression, freedom of assembly, and freedom from discrimination.
discrimination.

Provided that the Supreme Court shall not exercise its powers under this subsection if it is satisfied that adequate means of redress for the contravention alleged are or have been available to the person concerned under any other law.

(3) Any person aggrieved by any determination of the Supreme Court under this section may appeal therefrom to the Court of Appeal.

(4) Parliament may make provision, or may authorise the making of provision, with respect to the practice and procedure of any court for the purpose of this section and may confer upon that court such powers, or may authorise the conferment thereon of such powers, in addition to those conferred by this section as may appear to be necessary or desirable for the purpose of enabling that court more effectively to exercise the jurisdiction conferred upon it by this section.

(ii) Extracts from the Barbados Constitution, the Barbados Independence Order, 1966. (S.I. 1455/1966.)

20(1) Except with his own consent, no person shall be hindered in the enjoyment of his freedom of expression, and for the purposes of this section the said freedom includes the freedom to hold opinions without interference, freedom to receive ideas and information without interference, freedom to communicate ideas and information without interference and freedom from interference with his correspondence or other means of communication.

(2) Nothing contained in or done under the authority of any law shall be held to be inconsistent with or in contravention of this section to the extent that the law in question makes provision –

(a) that is reasonably required in the interests of defence, public safety, public order, public morality or public health; or

(b) that is reasonably required for the purpose of protecting the reputations, rights and freedoms of other persons or the private lives of persons, concerned in legal proceedings, preventing the disclosure of information received in confidence, maintaining the authority and independence of the courts or regulating the administration of technical operation of telephony, telegraphy, posts, wireless broadcasting, television or other means of communication or regulating public exhibitions or public entertainments; or

(c) that imposes restrictions upon public officers or members of a disciplined force.

21(1) Except with his own consent, no person shall be hindered in the enjoyment of his freedom of assembly and association, that is to say, his right to assemble freely and associate with other persons and in particular to form or belong to political parties or to form or belong to trade unions or other associations for the protection of his interests.

(2) Nothing contained in or done under the authority of any law shall be held to be inconsistent with or in contravention of this section to the extent that the law in question makes provision –

(a) that is reasonably required in the interests of defence public safety, public order, public morality or public health; or

(b) that is reasonably required for the purpose of protecting the rights or freedom of other persons; or

(c) that imposes restrictions upon public officers or members of a disciplined force.

22(1) No person shall be deprived of his freedom of movement that is to say, the right to move freely throughout Barbados, the right to reside in any part of Barbados, the right to enter Barbados, the right to leave Barbados and immunity from expulsion from Barbados.

(2) Any restriction on a person's freedom of movement that is involved in his lawful detention shall not be held to be inconsistent with or in contravention of this section.

(3) Nothing contained in or done under the authority of any law shall be held to be inconsistent with or in contravention of this section to the extent that the law in question makes provisions –

(a) for the imposition of restrictions on the movement or residence within Barbados of any person or on any person's right to leave Barbados that are reasonably required in the interests of defence, public safety or public order;

(b) for the imposition of restrictions on the movement or residence within Barbados or on the right to leave Barbados of persons generally or any class of persons that are reasonably required in the interests of defence, public safety, public order, public morality or public health;

(c) for the imposition of restrictions on the movement or residence within Barbados of any person who is not a citizen thereof or the exclusion or expulsion from Barbados of any such person;

(d) for the imposition of restrictions on the acquisition or use of land or other property in Barbados;

(e) for the imposition of restrictions, by order of a court, on the movement or residence within Barbados of any person or on any person's right to leave Barbados either in consequence of his having been found guilty of a criminal offence under the law of Barbados or for the purpose of ensuring that he appears before a court at a later date for trial for such a criminal offence or for proceedings preliminary to trial or for proceedings relating to his extradition or lawful removal from Barbados;

(f) for the imposition of restrictions upon the movement or residence within Barbados or on the right to leave Barbados of public officers or members of a disciplined force;

(g) for the removal of persons from Barbados –

(i) to be tried or punished in some other country for a criminal offence under the law of that country;

(ii) to undergo imprisonment in some other country in execution of the sentence of a court in respect of a criminal offence under the law of Barbados of which he has been convicted;

(iii) to be detained in an institution in some other country for the purpose of giving effect to the order of a court made in pursuance of a law of Barbados relating to the treatment of offenders under a specified age; or

(iv) to be detained for care or treatment in a hospital or other institution in pursuance of a law of Barbados relating to persons suffering from defect or disease of the mind; or

(h) for the imposition of restrictions on the right of any person to leave Barbados that are reasonably required in order to secure the fulfilment of any obligations imposed on that person by law.

(4) Where a person's freedom of movement is restricted by virtue of such a provision as is referred to in subsection (3) (a), the following provisions shall apply –

(a) he shall, as soon as reasonably practicable and in any case not more than five days after the commencement of the restriction, be furnished with a statement in writing, in a language that he understands, of the grounds upon which the restriction has been imposed;

(b) not more than fourteen days after the commencement of the restriction, a notification shall be published in the Gazette stating that his freedom of movement has been restricted and giving particulars of the provision of law under which the restriction is authorised;

(c) he may from time to time request that his case be reviewed under paragraph (d) but, where he has made such a request, no subsequent request shall be made before the expiration of three months from the making of the previous request;

(d) where a request is made under paragraph (c), the case shall, within one month of the making of the request, be reviewed by an independent and impartial tribunal established by law and presided over by a person appointed by the Chief Justice from among persons entitled to practise in Barbados as barristers or solicitors and

(e) he shall be afforded reasonable facilities to consult and instruct, at his own expense, a legal adviser of his own choice, being a person entitled to practise as aforesaid, and he and any such legal adviser shall be permitted to make written or oral representations or both to the tribunal appointed for the review of his case.

(5) On any review by a tribunal in pursuance of subsection (4) of the case of any person whose freedom of movement has been restricted, the tribunal may make recommendations concerning the necessity or expediency of continuing that restriction to the authority by whom it was ordered, but unless it is otherwise provided by law, that authority shall not be obliged to act in accordance with any such recommendations.

E The Head of State

(i) Extract from the Trinidad and Tobago (Constitution) Order in Council, 1962. (S.I. 1875/1962.)

CHAPTER III
THE GOVERNOR-GENERAL

19 There shall be a Governor-General and Commander-in-Chief of Trinidad and Tobago, who shall be appointed by Her Majesty and shall hold office during Her Majesty's pleasure and who shall be Her Majesty's representative in Trinidad and Tobago.

(ii) Extract from the Jamaica (Constitution) Order in Council, 1962. (S.I. 1550/1962.)

32(1) The Governor-General shall act in accordance with the advice of the Cabinet or a Minister acting under the general authority of the Cabinet in the exercise of his functions other than –

(a) any function which is expressed (in whatever terms) to be exercisable by him on or in accordance with the recommendation or advice of, or with the concurrence of, or after consultation with, any person or authority other than the Cabinet; and

(b) any function which is expressed (in whatever terms) to be exercisable by him in his discretion.

(2) Where the Governor-General is directed to exercise any function on the recommendation of any person or authority, he shall exercise that function in accordance with such recommendation:

Provided that –

(a) before he acts in accordance therewith, he may, in his discretion, once refer that recommendation back for reconsideration by the person or authority concerned; and

(b) if that person or authority, having reconsidered the original recommendation under the preceding paragraph, substitutes therefor a different recommendation, the provisions of this subsection shall apply to that different recommendation as they apply to the original recommendation.

(3) Where the Governor-General is directed to exercise any function after consultation with any person or authority he shall not be obliged to exercise that function in accordance with the advice of that person or authority.

(4) Where the Governor-General is directed to exercise any function in accordance with the recommendation or advice of, or with the concurrence of, or after consultation with, or on the representation of, any person or authority, the question whether he has so exercised that function shall not be enquired into in any court.

(5) Where the Governor-General is directed to exercise any function on the recommendation of the Prime Minister after consultation with the Leader of the Opposition the following steps shall be taken:–[4]

(a) the Prime Minister shall first consult the Leader of the Opposition and thereafter tender his recommendation to the Governor-General;

(b) the Governor-General shall then inform the Leader of the Opposition of this recommendation and if the Leader of the Opposition concurs therein the Governor-General shall act in accordance with such recommendation;

4 Consultation between Government and Opposition in Trinidad and Tobago is largely governed by convention, as was stated in the Report of the Conference on Trinidad and Tobago Independence, 1962 (Cmnd. 1757/1962). "59 . . . the Conference agreed that it was a matter of great importance to honour the convention whereby the Prime Minister consults the Leader of the Opposition on all appropriate occasions, in particular on all matters of national concern, including appointments to suitable offices of a national character – for example the chairmanship of the Election and Boundary Commissions."

(c) if the Leader of the Opposition does not concur in the recommendation the Governor-General shall so inform the Prime Minister and refer the recommendation back to him;

(d) the Prime Minister shall then advise the Governor-General and the Governor-General shall act in accordance with that advice.

(6) Any reference in this Constitution to the functions of the Governor-General shall be construed as a reference to his powers and duties in the exercise of the executive authority of Jamaica and to any other powers and duties conferred or imposed on him as Governor-General by or under this Constitution or any other law.

(iii) Extracts from the Guyana Constitution, the Guyana Independence Order, 1966. (S.I. 575/1966.)

PART 3
POWERS AND PROCEDURE OF PARLIAMENT

73(5) If the National Assembly, upon a motion introduced by the Prime Minister and supported by the votes of a majority of all the members of the National Assembly, resolves that, on such day after the passing of the resolution as may be specified therein, Guyana shall become a Republic[5] and accordingly cease to be a part of Her Majesty's dominions and that for that purpose the alterations to this Constitution set out in the second Schedule to this Constitution shall have effect . . . :

Provided that –

(a) notice of a motion under this paragraph shall be given not less than three months before the National Assembly proceeds upon the motion; and

(b) notice of such a motion shall not be given before 1st January 1969.

Second Schedule

Alterations to the Constitution to have effect if a Resolution is passed in accordance with Article 73(5).

5 Guyana became a republic in 1970.

PART II

CHAPTER IV – THE PRESIDENT

30(1) There shall be a President of Guyana, who shall be the Head of State and Commander-in-Chief of the armed forces of Guyana.

(2) The President shall be elected by the National Assembly in accordance with this article.

(3) A person shall not be eligible for election as President unless he is a citizen of Guyana of the age of forty years or upwards, and a person shall be disqualified for election as President if he is disqualified for election as a member of the Assembly by virtue of any provision of article 60 of this Constitution other than paragraph (1) or of any law enacted in pursuance thereof other than a law enacted in pursuance of paragraph 2 (a) or (c) thereof.

(4) The President shall be elected by secret ballot at a meeting of the Assembly held for the purpose of electing the President (in this article referred to as an "election meeting"); and each elected member of the Assembly shall be entitled to a single vote in each ballot for the election of the President taken at such a meeting (in this article referred to as a "Presidential ballot").

(5) An election meeting shall commence on such date (in this article referred to as "the Presidential election date") and at such time as the President shall determine by order published in the Gazette at least twenty-one days before the election date.

(6) A person shall not be a candidate for election as President at an election meeting unless he is nominated for election or re-election as the President by a nominated paper which –

(a) is signed by him and by three more elected members of the Assembly; and

(b) is delivered to the Speaker at least fourteen days before the Presidential election date.

(8) A candidate in a Presidential ballot shall be declared to be elected if, and shall not be declared to be elected unless, he receives the votes of more than half of all the elected members of the Assembly.

(9) If in a Presidential ballot –

(a) there are three or more condidates; and

(b) none of the candidates is elected; and

(c) one of the candidates receives a smaller number of votes than eac of the others,

that one of the candidates shall not be a candidate in any subsequent Presidential ballot at the same election meeting.

(10) If in a Presidential ballot –

(a) the conditions specified in sub-paragraphs (a) and (b) of the preceding paragraph are satisfied but the condition specified in sub-paragraph (c) of that paragraph is not; and

(b) two of the candidates each receives the same number of votes and that number is smaller than the number of votes received by the other candidate or each of the other candidates, as the case may be,

a ballot shall forthwith be held for the purpose of determining which of the two shall be treated for the purpose of the preceding paragraph as the candidate mentioned in sub-paragraph (c) thereof; and the candidate who receives the smaller number of the votes cast in that ballot shall be so treated and that paragraph shall apply accordingly.

(11) Where in a ballot taken in pursuance of the preceding paragraph each candidate receives the same number of votes, one of them, as determined by lot, shall be deemed to have received the smaller number of votes.

(12) If in a Presidential ballot no candidate is declared elected, a further Presidential ballot shall be taken at the same election meeting; and an election meeting shall continue until a candidate is declared elected in a Presidential ballot taken at that meeting but may be adjourned from time to time for not more than two days exclusive of the days on which and to which it is adjourned.

(13) The Court of Appeal shall have exclusive jurisdiction to hear and determine any question as to the validity of an election of a President in so far as that question depends upon the qualification of any person for election or the interpretation of this Constitution; and any decision of that Court under this paragraph shall be final . . . .

31(1) Subject to the provisions of the next following paragraph, a person holding the Office of President shall vacate that office at the expiration of the period of six years beginning with the day on which he was last elected as President.

(2) The Office of President shall become vacant before the expiration of the said period –

(a) if the person holding that office resigns it by writing under his hand addressed to the Speaker; or

(b) if, in pursuance of the preceding article, he or another person is elected as President.

(3) A person elected as President shall be disqualified for any other office, employment or appointment to which this paragraph applies and accordingly on entering upon the duties of the Office of President shall vacate any such other office, employment or appointment held by him.

(4) The preceding paragraph applies to the offices of Minister, Attorney-General, Speaker, member, Clerk or Deputy Clerk of the National Assembly, any Judge of the Supreme Court of Judicature, member of the Elections Commission, the Judicial Service Commission, the Public Service Commission or the Police Service Commission, any public office, employment in any armed force of Guyana and any paid appointment as a member or employee of a body coporate established by law of Guyana for public purposes . . . .[6]

F The Legislature

(i) Extracts from the Trinidad and Tobago (Constitution) Order in Council, 1962. (S.I. 1875/1962.)

CHAPTER IV: PARLIAMENT

PART I
COMPOSITION OF PARLIAMENT

22 There shall be a Parliament of Trinidad and Tobago which shall consist of Her Majesty, a Senate and a House of Representatives.

The Senate[7]

23(1) The Senate shall consist of twenty-four members (in this Constitution referred to as "Senators") who shall be appointed by the Governor-General in accordance with this section.

6 Upon the introduction of a republican constitution, Guyana did not acquire an executive head of state. The functions of the President are essentially the same as the functions of the Governors-General of the other independent Commonwealth Caribbean countries.

7 Of the four independent territories of the Commonwealth Caribbean all but Guyana have adopted a bicameral form of legislature and follow the Westminster pattern of a weak, revisionary second chamber. These Senates do not differ significantly in the powers which they can exercise. However, they do differ in composition from the Senate of Trinidad and Tobago which is used here for illustration. Jamaica's Senate is composed of thirteen Senators appointed on the advice of the Prime Minister and eight Senators appointed on the advice of the Leader of the Opposition. Unlike the Senators of Trinidad and Tobago they cannot be dismissed during their tenure of office. The Senate of Barbados is more like that of Trinidad and Tobago. It consists of twelve Senators appointed on the advice of the Prime Minister, two appointed on the advice of the Leader of the Opposition, and seven at the discretion of the Governor-General, after he has consulted with "such persons

(2) Of the twenty-four Senators –

(a) thirteen shall be appointed by the Governor-General acting in accordance with the advice of the Prime Minister;

(b) four shall be appointed by the Governor-General acting in accordance with the advice of the Leader of the Opposition; and

(c) seven shall be appointed by the Governor-General acting in accordance with the advice of the Prime Minister after the Prime Minister has consulted those religious, economic or social bodies or associations from which the Prime Minister considers that such Senators should be selected . . . .

25(1) No person shall be qualified to be appointed as a Senator who –

(a) is a citizen of a country other than Trinidad and Tobago having become such a citizen voluntarily or is under a declaration of allegiance to such a country;

(b) is a member of the House of Representatives;

(c) is an undischarged bankrupt having been adjudged or otherwise declared bankrupt under any law in force in Trinidad and Tobago;

(d) is a person certified to be insane or otherwise adjudged to be of unsound mind under any law in force in Trinidad and Tobago;

(e) is under sentence of death imposed on him by a court or is serving a sentence of imprisonment (by whatever name called) exceeding twelve months imposed on him by a court or substituted by competent authority for some other sentence imposed on him by a court, or is under such a sentence of imprisonment the execution of which has been suspended;

(f) is disqualified for membership of the House of Representatives by virtue of any law in force in Trinidad and Tobago by reason of his having been convicted of any offence relating to elections; or

(g) is not qualified to be registered as an elector at a Parliamentary election under any law in force in Trinidad and Tobago.

7 (cont.)
as, in his discretion, he considers can speak for those interests (religious, economic or social) and ought to be represented". The Barbadian Senators can be dismissed in the same way as those of Trinidad and Tobago, except that the Governor-General cannot dismiss those Senators which he appoints at his discretion, although their seats can be declared vacant if they become disqualified, or at the next dissolution of Parliament or upon nomination as candidates for the House of Assembly.

26(1) Every Senator shall vacate his seat in the Senate at the next dissolution of Parliament after his appointment.

(2) A Senator shall also vacate his seat in the Senate –

(a) if he is absent from the sittings of the Senate for such period and in such circumstances as may be prescribed in the rules of the procedure of the Senate;

(b) if, with his consent, he is nominated as a candidate for election to the House of Representatives, or if he is elected to be a member of the House of Representatives;

(c) if he ceases to be a citizen of Trinidad and Tobago;

(d) . . . if any circumstances arise that, if he were not a Senator, would cause him to be disqualified for appointment as such . . . .

(e) if the Governor-General, acting in accordance with the advice of the Prime Minister in the case of a Senator appointed in accordance with that advice, or in accordance with the advice of the Leader of the Opposition in the case of a Senator appointed in accordance with that advice, declares the seat of that Senator to be vacant.

35(1) Any question whether –

(a) any person has been validly appointed as a Senator or validly elected as a member of the House of Representatives;

(b) any Senator or member of the House of Representatives has vacated his seat or is required, under the provisions of subsection (3) of section 26 or subsection (3) of section 32 of this Constitution to cease to exercise any of his functions as a Senator or as a member of the House of Representatives; or

(c) any person has been validly elected as Speaker of the House of Representatives from among persons who are not Senators or members of the House of Representatives,

shall be determined by the High Court in accordance with the provisions of any law in force in Trinidad and Tobago.

PART 2
POWERS AND PROCEDURES OF PARLIAMENT

36 Subject to the provisions of this Constitution, Parliament may make laws for the peace, order and good government of Trinidad and Tobago.

37 No civil or criminal proceedings may be instituted against any member of either House for words spoken before, or written in a report to, the House

of which he is a member or a committee thereof or any joint committee of the Senate and the House of Representatives or by reason of any matter or thing brought by him therein by petition, bill, resolution, motion, or otherwise.

38(1) Subject to the provisions of this section, Parliament may alter any of the provisions of this Constitution or (in so far as it forms part of the law of Trinidad and Tobago) any of the provisions of the Trinidad and Tobago Independence Act, 1962.[8]

(2) In so far as it alters –

(a) sections 1 to 8 (inclusive), sections 84, 90, 91, 92, 93, 94, 96, 97, 98, 99, 100 or 101; or

(b) section 105 in its application to any of the provisions specified in paragraph (a) of this subsection,

8 The procedure for alteration of the other independence constitutions is as follows:–

Jamaica: (1) ordinarily entrenched clauses can be altered by a Bill supported by two-thirds majorities in both Houses of Parliament, except that if it is rejected by the Senate it would have to be referred to the electorate and approved by a three-fifths majority of all electors voting;

(2) specially entrenched clauses can be altered by a Bill supported by two-thirds majorities in both Houses of Parliament and by a simple majority of the electorate voting in the referendum, except that if the Bill is rejected by the Senate the majority in the referendum would have to be two-thirds;

(3) for both ordinarily and specially entrenched clauses the constitution imposes elapses of time between the various stages of introducing the Bill, the debating of it etc.;

(4) it should finally be noted that in Jamaica a special Act of Parliament, supported by two-thirds majorities in both Houses, can over-ride all provisions of the Jamaican Constitution relating to fundamental rights and freedoms.

Barbados: (1) ordinarily entrenched clauses can be altered by a Bill supported by simple majorities in both Houses of Parliament;

(2) specially entrenched clauses can be amended by two-thirds majorities in both Houses of Parliament.

Guyana: (1) only has in its Constitution specially entrenched clauses and those clauses which can be amended by a simple Act of Parliament;

(2) those clauses which are entrenched require, for alteration, a two-thirds majority in the National Assembly and a simple majority of all electors voting in a referendum;

(3) note in Document E (iii) of this chapter the simpler procedure for changing the Guyanese constitution to a republican form.

a bill for an Act of Parliament under this section shall not be passed by Parliament unless at the final voting thereon in each House it is supported by the votes of not less than two-thirds of all the members of each House.[9]

(3) In so far as it alters –

(a) this section;

(b) sections 19, 22, 23, 29, 34, 37, subsection (2) of section 49, subsections (2), (3) and (4) of section 50, sections 51, 53, 54, 55, 73, 74, 75, 76, 78, 79, 80, 82, 83 or 89 or the Second Schedule;

(c) section 105 in its application to any of the provisions specified in paragraph (a) or (b) of this subsection; or

(d) any of the provisions of the Trinidad and Tobago Independence Act, 1962,

a bill for an Act of Parliament under this section shall not be passed by Parliament unless it is supported at the final voting thereon

(i) in the House of Representatives by the votes of not less than three-fourths of all the members of the House; and

(ii) in the Senate by the votes of not less than two-thirds of all the members of the Senate.[10]

(5) The provisions of this Constitution or (in so far as it forms part of the law of Trinidad and Tobago) the Trinidad and Tobago Independence Act, 1962 shall not be altered except in accordance with the provisions of this section.[9]

9 This is ordinary entrenchment.

10 This is special entrenchment. See Appendix B to the Report of the Conference on Trinidad and Tobago Independence, 1962. (Cmnd. 1757/1962).

Ordinarily entrenched

Provisions relating to human rights and fundamental freedom. Prorogation of Parliament. Appointment, dismissal and disciplinary control of judicial officers. Establishment of office and functions of Auditor-General. Public Debt. Public Service Commission. Appointment, dismissal and disciplinary control of public officers. Appointment and removal of principal representatives of Trinidad and Tobago abroad. Auditor-General. Tenure of office of Auditor-General. Police Service Commission. Appointment, dismissal and disciplinary control of police officers. Protection of pension rights. Powers of Commissions in relation to grant of pensions, etc.

Specially entrenched

Office of Governor-General. Establishment of Parliament. Composition of Senate. Composition of House of Representatives. Amendment of Constitution. Annual meetings of Parliament. Dissolution of Parliament. General Elections and appointment of Senators. Boundaries Commission. Procedure for Review of Constituency boundaries. Establishment of Supreme

39(1) Subject to the provisions of this Constitution, each House may regulate its own procedure . . . .

44(1) Subject to the provisions of this Constitution, the power of Parliament to make laws shall be exercised by bills passed by the Senate and the House of Representatives and assented to by the Governor-General on behalf of Her Majesty.

(2) When a Bill is presented to the Governor-General for assent, he shall signify that he assents or that he withholds assent.[11]

(3) A Bill shall not become law unless it has been duly passed and assented to in accordance with this Constitution.

45(1) A Bill other than a Money Bill may be introduced in either House; a Money Bill shall not be introduced in the Senate.

(2) Except on the recommendation or with the consent of the Cabinet neither House shall –

- (a) proceed upon any Bill (including any amendment to a Bill) which, in the opinion of the person presiding, makes provision for any of the following purposes –
  - (i) for imposing or increasing any tax;
  - (ii) for imposing or increasing any charge on the revenues or other funds of Trinidad and Tobago or for altering any such charge otherwise than by reducing it; or
  - (iii) for compounding or remitting any debt due to Trinidad and Tobago;

10 (cont.)
Court. Constitution of High Court. Appointment of Puisne Judges. Tenure of office of Puisne Judges. Constitution of Court of Appeal. Appointment of Judges of Court of Appeal. Tenure of office of Judges of Court of Appeal. Appeals from Court of Appeal to Her Majesty in Council. Judicial and Legal Service Commission. Remuneration of Governor-General and certain other officers. Elections Commissions. Universal adult franchise subject to the qualifications laid down by Parliament. Freedom of Speech in Parliament. Interpretation (so far as it relates to the foregoing). The Trinidad and Tobago Independence Act, 1962.

11 It should be remembered that the Governor-General (or the President of Guyana) would only exercise this power on advice. Only where the constitution specifically grants a discretionary power would the Head of State act without advice.

(b) proceed upon any motion (including any amendment to a motion) the effect of which, in the opinion of the person presiding, would be to make provision for any of the purposes aforesaid; or

(c) receive any petition which, in the opinion of the person presiding, requests that provision be made for any of the purposes aforesaid.

46(1) If a Money Bill, having been passed by the House of Representatives and sent to the Senate at least one month before the end of the session, is not passed by the Senate without amendment within one month after it is sent to the Senate, the Bill shall, unless the House of Representatives otherwise resolves, be presented to the Governor-General for assent notwithstanding that the Senate has not consented to the Bill.

(2) There shall be endorsed on every Money Bill when it is sent to the Senate the certificate of the Speaker signed by him that it is a Money Bill; and there shall be endorsed on any Money Bill that is presented to the Governor-General for assent in pursuance of subsection (1) of this section, the certificate of the Speaker signed by him that it is a Money Bill and that the provisions of that subsection have been complied with.

47(1) If any Bill other than a Money Bill is passed by the House of Representatives in two successive sessions (whether or not Parliament is dissolved between these sessions) and, having been sent to the Senate in each of those sessions at least one month before the end of the session, is rejected by the Senate in each of those sessions, that Bill, shall, on its rejection for the second time by the Senate, unless the House of Representatives otherwise resolves, be presented to the Governor-General for assent notwithstanding that the Senate has not consented to the Bill:

Provided that the foregoing provisions of this subsection shall not have effect unless at least six months have elapsed between the date on which the Bill is passed by the House of Representatives in the first session and the date on which it is passed by that House in the second session.

(3) The House of Representatives may, if it thinks fit, on the passage through that House of a Bill that is deemed to be the same Bill as a former Bill sent to the Senate in the preceding session, suggest any amendments without inserting the amendments in the Bill, and any such amendments shall be considered by the Senate, and if agreed to by the Senate, shall be treated as amendments made by the Senate and agreed to by the House of Representatives; but the exercise of this power by the House of Representatives shall not affect the operation of this section in the event of the rejection of the Bill in the Senate.

(6) The provisions of this section shall not apply to a Bill for an Act of Parliament which is required by section 5 or section 38 of this Constitution to be supported at the final voting thereon in the Senate by the votes of not less than three-fifths or two-thirds respectively of all the members of the Senate.

48(1) In sections 45, 46 and 47 of this Constitution, "Money Bill" means a public Bill which, in the opinion of the Speaker, contains only provisions dealing with all or any of the following matters, namely the imposition, repeal, remission, alteration or regulation of taxation; the imposition, for the payment of debt or other financial purposes, of charges on public money or the variation of repeal of any such charges; the grant of money to the Crown or to any authority or person, or the variation or revocation of any such grant; the appropriation, receipt, custody, investment, issue or audit of accounts of public money; the raising or guarantee of any loan or the repayment thereof, or the establishment, alteration, administration or abolition of any sinking fund provided in connection with any such loan; or subordinate matters incidental to any of the matters aforesaid; and in this subsection the expressions "taxation", "debt", "public money" and "loan" do not include any taxation imposed, debt incurred or money provided or loan raised by any local authority or body for local purposes.

(2) For the purposes of section 47 of this Constitution, a Bill shall be deemed to be rejected by the Senate if –

(a) it is not passed by the Senate without amendment; or

(b) it is passed by the Senate with any amendment which is not agreed to by the House of Representatives.

(4) A certificate of the Speaker or the Deputy Speaker under section 46 or 47 of this Constitution shall be conclusive for all purposes and shall not be questioned in any court.

(5) Before giving any certificate under section 46 or 47 of this Constitution the Speaker or the Deputy Speaker, as the case may be, shall consult the Attorney-General or, if the Attorney-General is absent from the seat of government, such member of the Attorney-General's staff as the Attorney-General may designate for that purpose.

PART 3

Summoning, Prorogation and Dissolution

49(1) Each session of Parliament shall be held at such place within Trinidad and Tobago and shall commence at such time as the Governor-General may by Proclamation appoint.

(2) There shall be a session of each House once at least in every year, so

that a period of six months shall not intervene between the last sitting of Parliament in one session and the first sitting thereof in the next session.

50(1) The Governor-General, acting in accordance with the advice of the Prime Minister, may at any time prorogue or dissolve Parliament.

(2) Subject to the provisions of subsection (3) of this section, Parliament, unless sooner dissolved, shall continue for five years from the date of its first sitting after any dissolution and shall then stand dissolved.

(3) At any time when Trinidad and Tobago is at war, Parliament may extend the period of five years specified in subsection (2) of this section for not more than twelve months at a time:

Provided that the life of Parliament shall not be extended under this subsection for more than five years.

(4) If, between a dissolution of Parliament and the next ensuing general election of members to the House of Representatives, an emergency arises of such a nature that, in the opinion of the Prime Minister, it is necessary for the two Houses to be summoned before that general election can be held, the Governor-General, acting in accordance with the advice of the Prime Minister, may summon the two Houses of the preceding Parliament and that Parliament shall thereupon be deemed (except for the purposes of section 51 of this Constitution) not to have been dissolved but shall be deemed (except as aforesaid) to be dissolved on the date on which the next ensuing general election is held.

51(1) A general election of members of the House of Representatives shall be held at such time within three months after every dissolution of Parliament as the Governor-General, acting in accordance with the advice of the Prime Minister, shall appoint.

(2) As soon as practicable after every general election, the Governor-General shall proceed under section 23 of this Constitution to the appointment of Senators.

(ii) Extracts from the Jamaica (Constitution) Order in Council, 1962. (S.I. 1550/1962.)

CHAPTER V: PARLIAMENT

Part I
Composition of Parliament

34 There shall be a Parliament of Jamaica which shall consist of Her Majesty, a Senate and a House of Representatives.

36 The House of Representatives shall consist of persons who, being qualified for election as members in accordance with the provisions of this Constitution, have been so elected in the manner provided by or under any law for the time being in force in Jamaica and who shall be known as "Members of Parliament".

37(1) Subject to the provisions of subsection (2) of this section a person shall be qualified to be registered as an elector for elections to the House of Representatives if, and shall not be so qualified unless he is –

(a) a citizen of Jamaica resident in Jamaica at the date of registration, or

(b) a Commonwealth citizen (other than a citizen of Jamaica) who is resident in Jamaica at the time of registration and who has been so resident for at least twelve months immediately preceding that date,

and has attained the prescribed age.

(2) No person shall be qualified, to be registered as an elector for elections to the House of Representatives who –

(a) is under sentence of death imposed on him by a court in any part of the Commonwealth, or is serving a sentence of imprisonment (by whatever name called) of or exceeding six months imposed on him by such a court or substituted by competent authority for some other sentence imposed on him by such a court or is under such a sentence of imprisonment the execution of which is suspended; or

(b) is disqualified for such registration by or under any law for the time being in force in Jamaica because he has been convicted of any offence connected with the election of members of the House of Representatives or of any local authority or body for local purposes; or

(c) is, under any law for the time being in force in Jamaica, certified to be insane or otherwise adjudged to be of unsound mind or detained as a criminal lunatic; or

(d) is disqualified for such registration by any law for the time being in force in Jamaica by reason of his holding, or acting in, any office the functions of which involve responsibility for, or in connection with the election in the constituency in which such person would otherwise be entitled to vote.

(3) In this section – "the prescribed age" means –

(a) the age of twenty-one years, or

(b) such other age being less than the age of twenty-one years but not less than the age of eighteen years that may from time to time be prescribed by a special Act; and "a special Act" means an Act of Parliament the Bill for which has been passed by both Houses and at the final vote thereon in each House has been supported by the votes of a majority of all the members of that House.[12]

(4) A special Act may be repealed or amended by another special Act and in no other manner.

38(1) Any law for the time being provided for the election of members of the House of Representatives shall –

(a) contain provisions designed to ensure that so far as is practicable any person entitled to vote at an election of members of the House of Representatives shall have a reasonable opportunity of so voting; and

(b) contain provisions relating to the conduct of elections of members of the House of Representatives, including provisions relating to the identification of electors, designed to ensure that as far as is practicable no person shall vote at an election of a member of the House of Representatives –

(i) who is not entitled to vote; or

(ii) when he is not entitled to vote; or

(iii) where he is not entitled to vote:

Provided that this paragraph shall not come into operation until the first day of January 1964.

(2) No election of a member of the House of Representatives shall be called in question on the ground that the law under which that election was conducted was inconsistent with this section.

39 Subject to the provisions of section 40 of this Constitution, any person who at the date of his appointment or nomination for election –

(a) is a Commonwealth citizen of the age of twenty-one years or upwards; and

(b) has been ordinarily resident in Jamaica for the immediately preceding twelve months,

shall be qualified to be appointed as a Senator or elected as a member of the House of Representatives and no other person shall be so qualified.

51(1) Subject to the provisions of this Constitution, each House may regulate its own procedure and for this purpose may make Standing Orders.

52(1) The President or, in his absence, the Deputy President or, if they are both absent, a member of the Senate (not being a Minister or a Parliamentary Secretary) elected by the Senate for that sitting shall preside at each sitting of the Senate.

12 Such a "special Act" was passed in 1972, thereby reducing the voting age to eighteen.

(2) The Speaker or, in his absence, the Deputy Speaker or, if they are both absent, a member of the House of Representatives (not being a Minister or a Parliamentary Secretary) elected by the House of Representatives for that sitting shall preside at each sitting of the House of Representatives.

(3) References in this section to circumstances in which the President, Deputy President, Speaker or Deputy Speaker is absent include references to circumstances in which the office of President, Deputy President, Speaker or Deputy Speaker is vacant.

53(1) If at any time during a sitting of either House objection is taken by a member that there is not a quorum present and, after such interval as may be prescribed in the Standing Orders of that House, the person presiding ascertains that there is still not a quorum present, he shall thereupon adjourn the House.

(iii) Extract from the Guyana Constitution, the Guyana Independence Order, 1966. (S.I. 575/1966.)

57 There shall be a Parliament of Guyana, which shall consist of Her Majesty,[13] and a National Assembly.

Part II – Elections

66(1) The election of members of the National Assembly shall be conducted by secret ballot in accordance with the system of proportional representation prescribed by this article.

(2) Subject to the provisions of the next following paragraph –

(a) votes shall be cast throughout Guyana in favour of lists of candidates;

(b) each elector shall have one vote and may cast it in favour of any of the lists; and

(c) the seats of elected members in the Assembly shall be allocated between the lists in such a manner that the proportion that the number of such seats allocated to each list bears to the number of votes cast in favour of the list is as nearly as may be the same for each list.

(3) Parliament may make provision for the division of Guyana into such number of electoral areas, not being more than half the number of elected members of the Assembly, as Parliament may prescribe and for the election in

13 This would become the President.

each such area of one member of the Assembly, each elector having for this purpose one vote in addition to the vote which he may cast in favour of a list of candidates, but, if Parliament makes provision as aforesaid, then –

(a) a person may stand as a candidate for election in any such electoral area only if, in such manner as Parliament may prescribe, he has declared that he supports, or has otherwise identified himself with one of the lists; and

(b) those seats in the Assembly for which members are not elected in electoral areas as aforesaid shall be allocated between the lists in accordance with the results of the voting throughout Guyana in favour of lists in such manner that the proportion that the number of seats allocated to each list, when added to the number of members identified with that list elected in electoral areas, bears to the number of votes cast in favour of that list is as nearly as may be the same for each list.

(4) Subject to the provisions of this Constitution Parliament may make provision for –

(a) the registration of electors;

(b) the manner in which lists of candidates shall be prepared and entered for an election;

(c) the manner in which the number of seats to be allocated to each list shall be calculated in order to give effect to the provisions of paragraph (2) or paragraph (3), as the case may be, of this article;

(d) for the combination of lists of candidates for the purpose of the allocation of seats (but not for the purpose of voting);

(e) for the extraction from the lists and the declaration of names of the candidates who have been elected; and

(f) generally for the conduct of elections and for the giving effect to the provisions of this article.

G Executive Powers

(i) Extracts from the Jamaica (Constitution) Order in Council, 1962. (S.I. 1550/1962.)[14]

Chapter VI
Executive Powers

68(1) The executive authority of Jamaica is vested in Her Majesty.

(2) Subject to the provisions of this Constitution, the executive authority of Jamaica may be exercised on behalf of Her Majesty by the Governor-General either directly or through officers subordinate to him.

(3) Nothing in this section shall prevent Parliament from conferring functions on persons or authorities other than the Governor-General.

69(1) There shall be in and for Jamaica a Cabinet which shall consist of the Prime Minister and not less than eleven other Ministers appointed in accordance with the provisions of section 70 of this Constitution.

(2) The Cabinet shall be the principal instrument of policy and shall be charged with the general direction and control of the Government of Jamaica and shall be collectively responsible therefor to Parliament.

70(1) Whenever the Governor-General has occasion to appoint a Prime Minister he, acting in his discretion, shall appoint the member of the House of Representatives who, in his judgment, is best able to command the confidence of a majority of the members of that House and shall, acting in accordance with the advice of the Prime Minister, appoint the other Ministers from among the members of the two Houses.

(2) Not less than two nor more than three of the Ministers shall be persons who are members of the Senate.

(3) If occasion arises for making an appointment while Parliament is dissolved, a person who was a member of the House of Representatives immediately before the dissolution may be appointed Prime Minister and a person who was a member of either House immediately before the dissolution may, subject to the provisions of subsection (2) of this section, be appointed as any other Minister as if, in each case, such person were still a member of the House in question, but any person so appointed shall vacate office at the beginning of the next session of that House if he is not then a member thereof.

14 The provisions of the Constitution of Jamaica with respect to the executive can be taken as typical for the Commonwealth Caribbean, except that the Head of State in Guyana is a President.

71(1) The office of Prime Minister shall become vacant –

(a) if he resigns his office;

(b) if he ceases to be a member of the House of Representatives otherwise than by a dissolution of Parliament;

(c) if, under the provisions of subsection (3) of subsection (4) of section 41 of this Constitution, he is required to cease to exercise any of his functions as a member of the House of Representatives;

(d) when, after any dissolution of Parliament, the Prime Minister is informed by the Governor-General acting in his discretion, that the Governor-General is about to re-appoint him as Prime Minister or appoint another person as Prime Minister; or

(e) if the Governor-General revokes his appointment in accordance with the provisions of subsection (2) of this section.

(2) If the House of Representatives by a resolution which has received the affirmative vote of a majority of all the members thereof has resolved that the appointment of the Prime Minister ought to be revoked, the Governor-General shall, subject to the provisions of subsection (3) of this section, by instrument under the Broad Seal, revoke his appointment.

(3) If the House of Representatives has passed a resolution as provided by subsection (2) of this section that the appointment of the Prime Minister ought to be revoked, the Governor-General shall consult with the Prime Minister and, if the Prime Minister within three days so requests, the Governor-General shall dissolve Parlaiment instead of revoking the appointment.

(4) The office of a Minister, other than the office of Prime Minister, shall become vacant –

(a) upon the appointment or re-appointment of any person to the office of Prime Minister;

(b) if his appointment to his office is revoked by the Governor-General, acting in accordance with the advise of the Prime Minister, by instrument under the Broad Seal;

(c) if, for any reason other than a dissolution of Parliament, he ceases to be a member of the House of which he was a member at the date of his appointment as a Minister;

(d) if, under the provisions of subsection (3) or subsection (4) of section 41 of this Constitution, he is required to cease to exercise any of his functions as a member of either House; or

(e) if he resigns his office.

78(1) The Governor-General, acting in accordance with the advice of the Prime Minister, may by instrument under the Broad Seal, appoint Parliamentary Secretaries from among the members of the two Houses to assist Ministers in the discharge of their functions.

(2) The number of Parliamentary Secretaries appointed from the members of the Senate shall not at any time exceed three.

79(1) There shall be an Attorney-General who shall be the principal legal adviser to the Government of Jamaica.

(2) Power to appoint a person to hold or act in the office of Attorney-General and to remove from that office a person holding or acting in it shall, subject to subsection (4) of this section, be exercised by the Governor-General acting in accordance with the advice of the Prime Minister.

80(1) There shall be a Leader of the Opposition who shall be appointed by the Governor-General by instrument under the Broad Seal.

(2) Whenever the Governor-General has occasion to appoint a Leader of the Opposition he shall, in his discretion, appoint the member of the House of Representatives who, in his judgment, is best able to command the support of a majority of those members who do not support the Government, or, if there is no such person, the member of that House who, in his judgment, commands the support of the largest single group of such members who are prepared to support one leader.

(3) The Office of Leader of the Opposition shall become vacant –

- (a) if he resigns his office;
- (b) if, after any dissolution of Parliament, he is informed by the Governor-General acting in his discretion that the Governor-General is about to appoint another person as Leader of the Opposition;
- (c) if he ceases to be a member of the House of Representatives otherwise than by reason of a dissolution of Parliament;
- (d) if, under the provisions of subsection (3) and (4) of section 41 of this Constitution, he is required to cease to exercise any of his functions as a member of the House of Representatives; or
- (e) if his appointment is revoked under the provisions of subsection (5) of this section.

(4) If occasion arises for making an appointment while Parliament is dissolved, a person who was a member of the House of Representatives immediately before the dissolution may be appointed Leader of the Opposition as if such person were still a member of that House but the person so appointed shall vacate office at the beginning of the next session of that House if he is not a member thereof.

(5) If, in the judgment of the Governor-General, the Leader of the Opposition no longer is able to command the support of a majority of those members of the House of Representatives who do not support the

Government, or, as the case may be, the support of the largest single group of such members who are prepared to support one leader, the Governor-General, acting in his discretion, shall revoke the appointment of the Leader of the Opposition.

81 During any period in which there is a vacancy in the office of the Leader of the Opposition by reason of the fact that no person is both qualified in accordance with this Constitution for, and willing to accept, appointment to that office, the Governor-General shall act in accordance with the advice of the Prime Minister on any matter in respect of which it is provided in this Constitution either –

(a) that the Governor-General shall act on the advice of the Leader of the Opposition, or

(b) that the Governor-General shall act on the recommendation of the Prime Minister after consultation with the Leader of the Opposition.

82(1) There shall be in and for Jamaica a Privy Council which shall consist of six members appointed by the Governor-General, after consultation with the Prime Minister, by instrument under the Broad Seal.

(2) At least two of the members of the Privy Council shall be persons who hold or have held public office.

(3) The Privy Council shall have such powers and duties as may be conferred or imposed upon it by or under, this Constitution or any other law.

83(1) The seat of a member of the Privy Council shall become vacant –

(a) at the expiration of three years from the date of his appointment or such earlier time as may be specified in the instrument by which he was appointed;

(b) if he resigns his seat; or

(c) if his appointment is revoked by the Governor-General, after consultation with the Prime Minister, by instrument under the Broad Seal.

84 The Governor-General, acting after consultation with the Prime Minister, may, by instrument under the Broad Seal, declare that a member of the Privy Council, is by reason of absence or infirmity of body or mind, temporarily unable to discharge his functions as a member of the Council, and thereupon that member shall not take part in the proceedings of the Council until he is declared in like manner to be again able to discharge those functions.

87 The Governor-General shall, so far as is practicable, attend and preside at all meetings of the Privy Council.

88(1) The Privy Council shall not be summoned except by the authority of the Governor-General acting in his discretion.

(3) Subject to the provisions of this Constitution, the Privy Council may regulate its own procedure.

90(1) The Governor-General may, in Her Majesty's name and Her Majesty's behalf –

- (a) grant to any person convicted of any offence against the law of Jamaica a pardon, either free or subject to lawful conditions;
- (b) grant to any person a respite, either indefinite or for a specified period, from the execution of any punishment imposed on that person for such an offence;
- (c) substitute a less severe form of punishment for that imposed on any person for such an offence; or
- (d) remit the whole or part of any punishment imposed on any person for such an offence or any penalty or forfeiture otherwise due to the Crown on account of such an offence.

(2) In the exercise of the powers conferred on him by this section the Governor-General shall act on the recommendation of the Privy Council.

91(1) Where any person has been sentenced to death for an offence against the law of Jamaica, the Governor-General shall cause a written report of the case from the trial judge, together with such other information derived from the record of the case or elsewhere as the Governor-General may require, to be forwarded to the Privy Council so that the Privy Council may advise him in accordance with the provisions of section 90 of this Constitution.

(2) The power of requiring information conferred on the Governor-General by subsection (1) of this section shall be exercised by him on the recommendation of the Privy Council or, in any case in which in his judgment the matter is too urgent to admit of such recommendation being obtained by the time within which it may be necessary for him to act, in his discretion.[15]

93(1) Where any Minister has been charged with the responsibility for a subject or department of government, he shall exercise general direction and control over the work relating to that subject and over that department; and subject as aforesaid and to such direction and control, the aforesaid work and

15 The prerogative of mercy exists in all the countries of the Commonwealth Caribbean. However, they do not all follow the elaborate provisions of Jamaica for a Privy Council.

the department shall be under the supervision of a Permanent Secretary appointed in accordance with the provisions of section 126 of this Constitution.

H The Judicature

(i) Extracts from the Trinidad and Tobago (Constitution) Order in Council, 1962. (S.I. 1875/1962.)[16]

CHAPTER VI: THE JUDICATURE

Part I
The Supreme Court

73 There shall be a Supreme Court of Judicature for Trinidad and Tobago consisting of a High Court of Justice (hereinafter referred to as "the High Court") and a Court of Appeal with such jurisdiction and powers as are conferred on those Courts respectively by this Constitution or any other law.

The High Court

74(1) (a) The Chief Justice of Trinidad and Tobago shall be *ex-officio*, a Judge of the High Court.

(b) The other Judges of the High Court shall be such number of Puisne Judges as may be prescribed by Parliament.

(2) No office of Judge of the High Court shall be abolished while there is a substantive holder thereof.

(3) The High Court shall be a superior court of record and, save as otherwise provided by a Parliament, shall have all the powers of such a court, including all such powers as are vested in the Supreme Court of Trinidad and Tobago immediately before the commencement of this Constitution.

75(1) The Puisne Judges shall be appointed by the Governor-General, acting in accordance with the advice of the Judicial and Legal Service Commission.

(2) A person shall not be appointed a Puisne Judge unless he has such qualifications for appointment as may be prescribed by Parliament.

(3) If the office of any Puisne Judge is vacant or if any such Judge is for any reason unable to perform the functions of his office or if the state of business in the High Court so requires, the Governor-General, acting in

16 The provisions of the Constitution of Trinidad and Tobago with respect to the Judicature can be taken as typical of the independent Commonwealth Caribbean.

accordance with the advice of the Judicial and Legal Service Commission, may appoint a person qualified for appointment as a Puisne Judge, to be temporarily a Puisne Judge of the High Court:

Provided that a person may be so appointed notwithstanding that he has attained the age of sixty-two years.

(4) Any person appointed under this section to be temporarily a Puisne Judge of the High Court shall hold office until his appointment is revoked by the Governor-General, acting in accordance with the advice of the Judicial and Legal Service Commission.

76(1) Subject to the provisions of this section a person holding the office of a Puisne Judge shall vacate that office on attaining the age of sixty-two years.

(3) A Puisne Judge may be removed from office only for inability to perform the functions of his office (whether arising from infirmity of mind or body or any other cause) or for misbehaviour, and shall not be so removed except in accordance with the provisions of this section.

(4) A Puisne Judge shall be removed from office by the Governor-General if the question of removal of that judge has, at the request of the Governor-General, made in pursuance of subsection (5) of this section, been referred by Her Majesty to the Judicial Committee of Her Majesty's Privy Council[15] under any enactment enabling Her Majesty in that behalf, and the Judicial Committee has advised Her Majesty that the judge ought to be removed from office for inability as aforesaid or for misbehaviour.

(5) If the Judicial and Legal Service Commission represents to the Governor-General that the question of removing a Puisne Judge under this section ought to be investigated, then –

(a) the Governor-General shall appoint a tribunal, which shall consist of a Chairman and not less than two other members, selected by the Governor-General, acting in accordance with the advice of the Prime Minister after consultation with the Judicial and Legal Service Commission, from among persons who hold or have held office as judge of a court having unlimited jurisdiction in civil and criminal matters in some part of the Commonwealth or a court having jurisdiction in appeals from any such court;

(b) the tribunal shall enquire into the matter and report on the facts thereof to the Governor-General and recommand to the Governor-General whether he should request that the question of removal

17 The role of the Judicial Committee of the Privy Council in the judicial process in the West Indies in currently under debate.

of that judge from office should be referred by Her Majesty to the Judicial Committee; and

(c) if the tribunal so recommends, the Governor-General shall request that the question should be referred accordingly.

(6) If the question of removinga Puisne Judge from office has been referred to a tribunal under subsection (5) of this section, the Governor-General, acting in accordance with the advice of the Chief Justice, may suspend the judge from performing the functions of his office, and any such suspension may at any time be revoked by the Governor-General, acting in accordance with the advice of the Chief Justice, and shall in any case cease to have effect –

(a) if the tribunal recommends to the Governor-General that he should not request that the question of removal of the judge from office should be referred by Her Majesty to the Judicial Committee; or

(b) if the Judicial Committee advises Her Majesty that the judge ought not to be removed from office.

(7) The provisions of this section shall be without prejudice to the provisions of subsection (4) of section 75 of this Constitution.

The Court of Appeal

78(1) The Judges of the Court of Appeal shall be the Chief Justice, who shall be President of the Court, and such number of Justices of Appeal as may be prescribed by Parliament.

(2) No office of Judge of the Court of Appeal shall be abolished while there is a substantive holder thereof.

(3) The Court of Appeal shall be a superior court of record and, save as otherwise provided by Parliament, shall have all the powers of such a court.

79(1) The Chief Justice shall be appointed by the Governor-General, acting in accordance with the advice of the Prime Minister.

(2) The Justices of Appeal shall be appointed by the Governor-General, acting in accordance with the advice of the Judicial and Legal Service Commission.

(3) A person shall not be appointed a Judge of the Court of Appeal unless he has such qualifications for appointment as may be prescribed by Parliament.

(4) (a) If the office of Chief Justice is vacant or if the person holding that office is for any reason unable to perform the functions of his office, then, until a person has been appointed to and has assumed the functions of that office or until the person holding that office has resumed those functions, as the case may be, those

functions shall be performed by such one of the Justices of Appeal as may be designated in that behalf by the Governor-General, acting in accordance with the advice of the Prime Minister.

(b) If the office of any Justice of Appeal is vacant or if any such Judge is appointed to act as Chief Justice or is for any reason unable to perform the functions of his office or the state of business in the Court of Appeal so requires, the Governor-General, acting in accordance with the advice of the Judicial and Legal Service Commission, may appoint a person qualified for appointment as a Judge of the Court of Appeal to be temporarily a Justice of Appeal:

Provided that a person may be so appointed notwithstanding that he has attained the age of sixty-five years.

(5) Any person appointed under this section to be temporarily a Justice of Appeal shall hold office until his appointment is revoked by the Governor-General, acting in accordance with the advice of the Judicial and Legal Service Commission.

80(1) Subject to the provisions of this section, a person holding the office of a Judge of the Court of Appeal shall vacate that office on attaining the age of sixty-five years.

(3) A Judge of the Court of Appeal may be removed from office only for inability to perform the functions of his office (whether arising from infirmity of mind or body or any other cause) or for misbehaviour, and shall not be so removed except in accordance with the provisions of this section.

(4) A Judge of the Court of Appeal shall be removed from office by the Governor-General if the question of removal of that Judge has, at the request of the Governor-General, made in pursuance of subsection (5) of this section, been referred by Her Majesty to the Judicial Committee of Her Majesty's Privy Council under any enactment enabling Her Majesty's Privy Council under any enactment enabling Her Majesty in that behalf, and the Judicial Committee has advised Her Majesty that the Judge ought to be removed from office for inability as aforesaid or for misbehaviour.

(5) If the Prime Minister, in the case of the Chief Justice, or the Judicial and Legal Service Commission, in the case of a Justice of Appeal, represents to the Governor-General that the question of removing a Judge under this section ought to be investigated, then –

(a) the Governor-General shall appoint a tribunal, which shall consist of a chairman and not less than two other members, selected by the Governor-General, acting in accordance with the advice of the

Prime Minister in the case of the Chief Justice or the Prime Minister after consultation with the Judicial and Legal Service Commission in the case of a Justice of Appeal, from among persons who hold or have held office as a judge of a court having unlimited jurisdiction in civil and criminal matters in some part of the Commonwealth or a court having jurisdiction in appeals from any such court;

(b) the tribunal shall enquire into the matter and report on the facts thereof to the Governor-General and recommend to the Governor-General whether he should request that the question of removal of that Judge from office should be referred by Her Majesty to the Judicial Committee; and

(c) if the tribunal so recommends, the Governor-General shall request that the question should be referred accordingly.

(6) If the question of removing a Judge from office has been referred to a tribunal under subsection (5) of this section, the Governor-General, acting in accordance with the advice of the Prime Minister in the case of the Chief Justice or the Chief Justice in the case of a Justice of Appeal, may suspend the Judge from performing the functions of his office, and any such suspension may at any time be revoked by the Governor-General, acting in accordance with the advice of the Prime Minister in the case of the Chief Justice or the Chief Justice in the case of a Justice of Appeal, and shall in any case cease to have effect –

(a) if the tribunal recommends to the Governor-General that he should not request that the question of removal of the Judge from office should be referred by Her Majesty to the Judicial Committee; or

(b) if the Judicial Committee advises Her Majesty that the Judge ought not to be removed from office.

(7) The provisions of this section shall be without prejudice to the provisions of subsection (5) of section 79 of this constitution.

Part 2
Appeals to Her Majesty in Council

82(1) An appeal shall lie from decisions of the Court of Appeal to Her Majesty in Council as of right in the following cases –

(a) where the matter in dispute on the appeal to Her Majesty in Council is of the value of fifteen hundred dollars or upwards or where the appeal involves directly or indirectly a claim to or a question respecting property or a right of the value of fifteen hundred dollars or upwards, final decisions in any civil proceedings;

(b) final decisions in proceedings for dissolution or nullity of marriage;

(c) final decisions in any civil, criminal or other proceedings which involve a question as to the interpretation of this Constitution; and

(d) such other cases as may be prescribed by Parliament.

(3) Nothing in this section shall affect any right of Her Majesty to grant special leave to appeal from decisions of the Court of Appeal to Her Majesty in Council in any civil, criminal or other matter.

(4) The foregoing provisions of this section shall be subject to the provisions of subsection (4) of section 35 of this Constitution.

CHAPTER 8

THE INDEPENDENCE CONSTITUTIONS II: OTHER CHECKS AND BALANCES

A The delimitation of constituencies [1]

(i) Extracts from the Trinidad and Tobago (Constitution) Order in Council, 1962. (S.I. 187/1962.)

Part 4
Delimitation of Constituencies

52 (1) Trinidad and Tobago shall be divided into thirty constituencies or such other number as may be provided for by an Order made by the Governor-General in accordance with the provisions of this Part and each such constituency shall return one member to the House of Representatives.

(2) Not less than two such constituencies shall be in the island of Tobago.

53 (1) There shall be a Boundaries Commission for Trinidad and Tobago (in this Part referred to as "the Commission").

(2) The members of the Commission shall be a Chairman and not less than two nor more than four other members.

(3) The members of the Commission shall be appointed by the Governor-General, acting in accordance with the advice of the Prime Minister.

1 In this section extracts from the Jamaican and Trinidad and Tobago constitutions are used for comparison. Barbados makes no special provision for boundary delimitation in its constitution and Guyana, operating its system of proportional representation is not comparable (see document E (iii) of Chapter VII p. 435).

(4) A person shall not be qualified to hold the office of a member of the Commission if he is a Minister, a Parliamentary Secretary, a Senator, a temporary member of the Senate, a member of the House of Representatives or a public officer.

(5) Subject to the provisions of this section, a member of the Commission shall vacate his office –

(a) at the expiration of five years from the date of his appointment; or

(b) if any circumstances arise that, if he were not a member of the Commission, would cause him to be disqualified for appointment as such.

(6) A member of the Commission may be removed from office by the Governor-General, acting in accordance with the advice of the Prime Minister, for inability to discharge the functions of his office (whether arising from infirmity of mind or body or any other cause) or for misbehaviour.

(7) A member of the Commission shall not be removed from office except in accordance with the provisions of this section.

(8) The Commission may regulate its own procedure, and, with the consent of the Prime Minister or a Minister designated by the Prime Minister for the purpose, confer powers and impose duties on any public officer or on any authority of the Government of Trinidad and Tobago for the purpose of the discharge of its functions; and at any meeting of the Commission a quorum shall be constituted if three members are present; and, if a quorum is present, the Commission shall not be disqualified for the transaction of business by reason of any vacancy among its members, and any proceeding of the Commission shall be valid notwithstanding that some person who was not entitled so to do took part therein.

(9) In the exercise of its functions under this Constitution, save as otherwise provided in subsection (8) of this section, the Commission shall not be subject to the control or direction of any other person or authority.

54 (1) The Commission shall, in accordance with the provisions of this section, review the number and boundaries of the constituencies into which Trinidad and Tobago is divided and submit to the Speaker reports either –

(a) showing the constituencies into which it recommends that Trinidad and Tobago should be divided in order to give effect to the rules set out in the Second Schedule to this Constitution; or

(b) stating that, in the opinion of the Commission, no alteration is required to the existing number or boundaries of constituencies in order to give effect to the said rules.

(2) Reports under subsection (1) of this section shall be submitted by the Commission –

(a) in the case of its first report after the day on which the Constitution comes into force not less than one, not more than five years from that day; and

(b) in the case of any subsequent report, not less than two nor more than five years from the date of the submission of its last report.

(3) As soon as may be after the Commission has submitted a report under paragraph (a) of subsection (1) of this section, the Minister designated by the Prime Minister for this purpose (in this section called "the Minister") shall lay before the House of Representatives for its approval the draft of an Order by the Governor-General for giving effect, whether with or without modifications, to the recommendations contained in the report, and that draft may make provisions for any matters which appear to the Minister to be incidental to or consequential upon the other provisions of the draft.

(4) Where any draft made under this section gives effect to any such recommendations with modifications, the Minister shall lay before the House of Representatives together with the draft a statement of the reasons for the modifications.

(5) If the motion for the approval of any draft made under this section is rejected by the House of Representatives, or is withdrawn by leave of that House, the Minister shall amend the draft and lay the amended draft before the House of Representatives.

(6) If any draft made under this section is approved by resolution of the House of Representatives, the Minister shall submit it to the Governor-General who shall make the Order in terms of the draft; and that Order shall come into force on such day as may be specified therein and, until revoked by a further Order made by the Governor-General in accordance with the provisions of this section, shall have the force of law.

(7) The question of the validity of any Order by the Governor-General purporting to be made under this section and reciting that a draft thereof has been approved by resolution of the House of Representatives shall not be enquired into in any court.

(ii) Extracts from Jamaica (Constitution) Order in Council, 1962. (S.I. 1550/1962.)

Part 4
Delimitation of Constituencies

66 (1) Until otherwise provided by an Order made by the Governor-General under section 67 of this Constitution, Jamaica shall for the purpose of electing the members of the House of Representatives, be divided into the forty-five constituencies prescribed by the Constituencies (Boundaries) Order, 1959

made by the Governor of the former Colony of Jamaica and published in the *Gazette* of the 28th day of May, 1959.

(2) Every constituency established under this section or under section 67 of this Constitution shall return one member to the House of Representatives.

67 (1) Subject to the provisions of section 66 of this Constitution, Jamaica shall, for the purpose of election of members to the House of Representatives, be divided into such number of constituencies, being not less than forty-five nor more than sixty, as may from time to time be provided by Order made by the Governor-General under this section.

(2) As soon as practicable after the House of Representatives first meets after the appointed day or following any general election there shall be established a Standing Committee of the House consisting of –

- (a) the Speaker, as Chairman;
- (b) three members of the House appointed by the Prime Minister; and
- (c) three members of the House appointed by the Leader of the Opposition.

(3) It shall be the function of the Standing Committee to keep under continuous review –

- (a) the number of constituencies into which Jamaica is to be divided; and
- (b) the boundaries of such constituencies.

(5) The Standing Committee shall, in accordance with the provisions of the following subsection, submit to the House of Representatives reports either –

- (a) showing the constituencies into which it recommends that Jamaica should be divided in order to give effect to the rules set out in the Second Schedule to this Constitution; or
- (b) stating that, in the opinion of the Committee, no alteration is required in the existing number or boundaries of constituencies in order to give effect to the said rules.

(6) Reports under subsection (5) of this section shall be submitted by the Standing Committee –

- (a) in the case of its first report after the appointed day, not less than four nor more than six years from that day; and
- (b) in the case of any subsequent report, not less than four nor more than six years from the date of the submission of its last report.

(7) Where the Standing Committee intends to consider making a report, it shall, by notice in writing, inform the Minister responsible for the conduct

of elections (hereafter in this section called "the Minister") accordingly, and a copy of that notice shall be published in the *Gazette.*

(8) As soon as may be after the Standing Committee has submitted a report to the House under paragraph (a) of subsection (5) of this section, the Minister shall lay before the House for its approval the draft of an Order by the Governor-General for giving effect to the recommendations contained in the report and that draft may make provision for any matters which appear to the Minister to be incidental to or consequential upon the other provisions of the draft.

(9) Where any draft made under this section gives effect to any such recommendations with modifications, the Minister shall lay before the House together with the draft a statement of the reasons for the modifications.

(10) If the motion for the approval of any draft made under this section is rejected by the House of Representatives, or is withdrawn by leave of that House, the Minister shall amend the draft and lay the amended draft before the House of Representatives.

(11) If any draft made under this section is approved by resolution of the House, the Minister shall submit it to the Governor-General who shall make an Order (which shall be published in the *Gazette*) in terms of the draft; and that Order shall come into force on such day as may be specified therein and, until revoked by a further Order made by the Governor-General in accordance with the provisions of this section, shall have the force of law:

Provided that the coming into force of any such Order shall not affect any election to the House of Representatives until a proclamation is made by the Governor-General appointing the date for the holding of a general election of members to the House of Representatives or affect the constitution of the House of Representatives until the dissolution of the Parliament then in being.

(12) An Act of Parliament may provide for the institution of proceedings in the Supreme Court for the purpose of determining whether or not any report made under subsection (5) of this section gives effect to the provisions of this section and empower the Supreme Court, subject to an appeal to the Court of Appeal, to make whatever orders are necessary in order to ensure that effect is given to those provisions and to make orders relating to the costs of these proceedings.

(13) Subject to the provisions of any Act to which subsection (12) of this section refers, the question of the validity of any Order by the Governor-General purporting to be made under this section and reciting that a draft thereof has been approved by resolution of the House of Representatives shall not be enquired into in any court.[2]

2 The Second Schedule to this Order in Council which lays down the rules governing boundary delimitation specifies: (a) that constituency boundaries

B Elections Commission [3]

(i) Extracts from the Trinidad and Tobago (Constitution) Order in Council, 1962. (S.I. 1875/1962.)

Part 5
Elections Commission

55 (1) There shall be an Elections Commission for Trinidad and Tobago.

(2) The members of the Elections Commission shall be a Chairman and not less than two nor more than four other members.

(3) The members of the Elections Commission shall be appointed by the Governor-General, acting in accordance with the advice of the Prime Minister.

(4) A person shall not be qualified to hold the office of a member of the Elections Commission if he is a Minister, a Parliamentary Secretary, a Senator, a temporary member of the Senate, a member of the House of Representatives or a public officer.

(5) Subject to the provisions of this section, a member of the Elections Commission shall vacate his office –

(a) at the expiration of five years from the date of his appointment; or

(b) if any circumstances arise that, if he were not a member of the Commission, would cause him to be disqualified for appointment as such.

(6) A member of the Elections Commission may be removed from office only for inability to discharge the functions thereof (whether arising from infirmity of mind or body or any other cause) or for misbehaviour, and shall not be so removed except in accordance with the provisions of this section.

shall not cross parish boundaries; (b) that each parish should have at least two constituencies; (c) that the constituencies should have electorates as near as possible in number to the electorate quota (obtained by dividing the total of the electorate of the country by the number of constituencies); (d) that the electorate of a constituency can deviate from the quota in order to take into account physical features, transportation facilities, and the differences in population density between urban and rural areas; but (e) that the deviation cannot be more than 50 per cent in excess of the quota nor less than $66\frac{2}{3}$ per cent of the quota.

3 In this section the constitutions of Guyana and Trinidad and Tobago are used for comparison. Neither Jamaica nor Barbados have special constitutional provision for an Elections Commission.

(7) A member of the Elections Commission shall be removed from office by the Governor-General if the question of his removal from office has been referred to a tribunal appointed under subsection (8) of this section and the tribunal has recommended to the Governor-General that he ought to be removed from office for inability as aforesaid or for misbehaviour.

(8) If the Prime Minister represents to the Governor-General that the question of removal of a member of the Elections Commission from office for inability as aforesaid or for misbehaviour ought to be investigated, then –

(a) the Governor-General shall appoint a tribunal, which shall consist of a Chairman and not less than two other members, selected by the Governor-General, acting in accordance with the advice of the Judicial and Legal Service Commission, from among persons who hold or have held office as a judge of a court having unlimited jurisdiction in civil and criminal matters in some part of the Commonwealth or a court having jurisdiction in appeals from any such court; and

(b) the tribunal shall enquire into the matter and report on the facts thereof to the Governor-General and recommend to the Governor-General whether the member of the Elections Commission ought to be removed from office for inability as aforesaid or for misbehaviour.

(9) The Elections Commission may regulate its own procedure, and, with the consent of the Prime Minister or a Minister designated by the Prime Minister for the purpose, confer powers and impose duties on any public officer or on any authority of the Government of Trinidad and Tobago for the purpose of the discharge of its functions; and at any meeting of the Commission a quorum shall be constituted if three members are present; and, if a quorum is present, the Commission shall not be disqualified for the transaction of business by reason of any vacancy among its members, and any proceeding of the Commission shall be valid notwithstanding that some person who was not entitled so to do took part therein.

(10) The registration of voters and the conduct of elections in every constituency shall be subject to the direction and supervision of the Elections Commission.

(11) In the exercise of its functions under subsection (9), save as otherwise therein provided, and subsection (1) of this section the Elections Commission shall not be subject to the direction or control of any other person or authority.

(ii) Extracts from the Guyana Constitution, the Guyana Independence Order, 1966. (S.I. 575/1966.)

Chapter V
Parliament
Part II – Elections

68 (1) There shall be an Elections Commission for Guyana consisting of a Chairman and such other members as may be appointed in accordance with the provisions of this article.

(2) Subject to the provisions of paragraph (6) of this article, the Chairman of the Elections Commission shall be appointed by the Governor-General, acting in accordance with the advice of the Prime Minister, from among persons who hold or have held office as a judge of a court having unlimited jurisdiction in civil and criminal matters in some part of the Commonwealth or a court having jurisdiction in appeals from any other court.

(3) In addition to the Chairman, there shall be one member of the Commission (hereinafter referred to as a "representative member") in respect of every list of candidates which at the election next preceding the appointment of such member obtained not less than five seats in the Assembly:

Provided that no appointment shall be made under this paragraph during the period of three months immediately following the date of an election.

(5) Subject to the provisions of paragraph (6) of this article, a representative member shall be appointed by the Governor-General, acting in accordance with the advice of the member of the Assembly whose name appears first on the list in respect of which the member is appointed or, if a majority of the members of the Assembly who belong to that list notify the Governor-General that he should act in accordance with the advice of some other member of the Assembly who belongs to that list, in accordance with the advice of that member:

Provided that if occasion arises for making an appointment while Parliament stands dissolved this subsection shall have effect as if Parliament had not been dissolved.

(6) A person shall be disqualified for appointment as a member of the Commission if he is a public officer or an alien.

(7) A member of the Elections Commission shall vacate his office –

(a) at the expiration of three months from the date of the election next following this appointment; or

(b) if any circumstances arise that, if he were not a member of the

Commission, would cause him to be disqualified for appointment as such

(8) The provision of article 118 of this Constitution (which relates to removal from office)[4] shall apply to the office of member of the Elections Commission, and, for the purposes of paragraphs (4) and (6) of that article, the prescribed authority, shall be the Prime Minister:

Provided that, before tendering any advice to the Governor-General under paragraph (4) of the said article in relation to the representative member appointed in respect of a list other than that to which the Prime Minister belongs, the Prime Minister shall consult the person on whose advice, if the office of that member were vacant, the Governor-General would act under paragraph (5) of this article in appointing a person to fill the vacancy.

. . .

69 (1) The Elections Commission shall have such functions connected with or relating to the registration of electors or the conduct of elections as are conferred upon it by or under this Constitution or, subject thereto, any Act of Parliament; and subject to the provisions of this Constitution, the Commission –

(a) shall exercise general direction and supervision over the registration of electors and the administrative conduct of elections; and

(b) shall issue such instructions and take such action as appear to it necessary or expedient to ensure impartiality, fairness and compliance with the provisions of this Constitution or of any Act of Parliament on the part of persons exercising powers or performing duties connected with or relating to the matters aforesaid.

C Service Commissions

(i) Judicial and Legal Service Commission.
(a) Extract from Trinidad and Tobago (Constitution) Order in Council, 1962.
(S.I. 1875/1962.)

Part 3

JUDICIAL AND LEGAL SERVICE COMMISSION

83 (1) There shall be a Judicial and Legal Service Commission for Trinidad and Tobago.

4 See Document G of this chapter, footnote 24, page 488.

(2) The members of the Judicial and Legal Service Commission shall be[5]

(a) the Chief Justice who shall be Chairman;

(b) such other Judge of the Court of Appeal or the High Court as may be designated by the Governor-General acting in accordance with the advice of the Prime Minister;

(c) the Chairman of the Public Service Commission; and

(d) two other members who shall be appointed by the Governor-General, acting in accordance with the advice of the Prime Minister.

(3) The following provisions shall apply in relation to the members of the Judicial and Legal Service Commission to be appointed under paragraph (d) of subsection (2) of this section –

5 The composition of this Commission in the other independent West Indian countries is as follows:

(a) Jamaica: the Chief Justice, the President of the Court of Appeal, the Chairman of the Public Service Commission, and three members appointed by the Governor-General on the advice of the Prime Minister, after the Prime Minister has consulted with the Leader of the Opposition. Such appointed members must be – one from among men who are or have been judges; one from a list of three persons, not in active practice as barristers or solicitors, submitted by the Bar Council; and one from a list of three persons, not in active practice as barristers or solicitors, submitted by the Council of the Law Society. Furthermore such appointed members should not hold public office other than office as a member of the Public Service Commission or the Police Service Commission.

(b) Guyana: the Chancellor (the President of the Court of Appeal) as Chairman, the Chief Justice, the Chairman of the Public Service Commission, and members appointed by the Governor-General on the advice of the Prime Minister in the following way – one from among men who are or have been judges, and not less than one nor more than two others from among persons not in active practice as advocates or solicitors, after the Prime Minister has consulted such bodies as appear to him to represent advocates and solicitors respectively in Guyana – provided that the person(s) is not a public officer.

(c) Barbados: the Chief Justice as Chairman, the Chairman of the Public Service Commission (or his nominee from the Public Service Commission) and three other appointed members. Here the appointed members are appointed on the advice of the Prime Minister after he has consulted with the Leader of the Opposition from among persons who are or have been judges. In the event that no such person is available or willing to serve, the Governor-General may, in the same way, appoint someone who has been entitled to practise in Barbados as a barrister for ten years but is not in active practice.

(a) one such person shall not be qualified for appointment as such unless he is or has been a judge of a court having unlimited jurisdiction in civil and criminal matters in some part of the Commonwealth or a court having jurisdiction in appeals from any such court;

(b) before tendering any advice to the Governor-General with respect to the other such person the Prime Minister shall consult with appropriate bodies and organisations;

(c) a person appointed as such may be removed from office by the Governor-General, acting in accordance with the advice of the Prime Minister, for inability to discharge the functions of his office (whether arising from infirmity of mind or body or any other cause) or for misbehaviour:
Provided that if such person is a judge of the Court of Appeal or a Judge of the High Court, he shall not be so removed unless, in accordance with the provisions of section 80 or section 76, as the case may be, of this Constitution, he is removed from his office as a Judge;

(d) a person appointed as such shall not be removed from office except in accordance with the provisions of this subsection;[6] and

(e) subject to the provisions of this subsection, a person appointed as such shall vacate his office at the expiration of three years from the date of his appointment.

(b) Extract from the Jamaica (Constitution) Order in Council, 1962. (S.I. 1550/1962.)

112 (1) Power to make appointments to the offices to which this section applies and, subject to the provisions of subsections (3) and (4) of this section, to remove and to exercise disciplinary control over persons holding or acting in such offices is hereby vested in the Governor-General acting on the advice of the Judicial Service Commission.

6 The procedure for removal from office of appointed members is basically the same in Jamaica as in Trinidad and Tobago except that the Prime Minister would give his advice after having consulted with the Leader of the Opposition. Guyana and Barbados both have more elaborate safeguards. In Guyana the procedure is that laid down by Article 118 of the Constitution (see document G of this chapter, footnote 23(1), page 486, with the Prime Minister advising that the question of removal from office be investigated, and the Chancellor advising on suspension from duties during the enquiry. The procedure in Barbados is the same as that of Guyana except that the tribunal of enquiry is appointed on the advice of the Chief Justice, and the Chief Justice would also advise on suspension from duties.

(2) This section applies to the offices of Resident Magistrate, Judge of the Traffic Court, Registrar of the Supreme Court, Registrar of the Court of Appeal and to such other offices connected with the courts of Jamaica as, subject to the provisions of this Constitution, may be prescribed by Parliament.

(3) Before the Governor-General acts in accordance with the advice of the Judicial Service Commission that any officer holding or acting in any office to which this section applies should be removed or that any penalty should be imposed on him by way of disciplinary control he shall inform the officer of that advice and, if the officer then applies for the case to be referred to the Privy Council, the Governor-General shall not act in accordance with the advice but shall refer the case to the Privy Council accordingly:

Provided that the Governor-General, acting on the advice of the Commission, may nevertheless suspend that officer from the exercise of his office pending the determination of the reference to the Privy Council.

(4) Where a reference is made to the Privy Council under the provisions of subsection (3) of this section, the Privy Council shall consider the case and shall advise the Governor-General what action should be taken in respect of the officer and the Governor-General shall then act in accordance with such advice.[7]

113 The Governor-General, acting on the advice of the Judicial Service Commission, may by instrument under the Broad Seal direct that, subject to such conditions as may be specified in that instrument, power to make appointments to such offices, being offices to which section 112 of this Constitution applies, as may be so specified shall (without prejudice to the exercise of such power by the Governor-General acting on the advice of the Judicial Service Commission) be exercisable by such one or more members of the Commission or by such other authority or public officer as may be so specified, but in any case where the person to be appointed under this section holds or is acting in any office power to make appointments to which is vested by this Constitution in the Governor-General acting on the advice of the Public Service Commission or the Police Service Commission, the person or authority specified in the aforesaid instrument shall consult with the Public Service Commission or the Police Service Commission, as the case may be, before making such appointment.

7 In Trinidad and Tobago and Guyana there is no appeal as is provided for in both Jamaica and Barbados to their Privy Councils. A further difference is that in Trinidad and Tobago the Prime Minister does have a negative voice in the appointment of the Solicitor-General, the Chief Legal Draftsman, the Registrar-General and the Crown Solicitor.

(ii) Public Service Commission

(a) Extracts from Trinidad and Tobago (Constitution) Order in Council, 1962. (S.I. 1875/1962.)

Chapter VIII
THE PUBLIC SERVICE
THE PUBLIC SERVICE COMMISSION

92 (1) There shall be a Public Service Commission for Trinidad and Tobago which shall consist of a Chairman, a Deputy Chairman and not less than two or more than four other members.

(2) The members of the Public Service Commission shall be appointed by the Governor-General, acting in accordance with the advice of the Prime Minister.[8]

(3) A person shall not be qualified to be appointed to or to hold the office of a member of the Public Service Commission if he is a Senator or a temporary member of the Senate or a member of the House of Representatives or a Minister or a Parliamentary Secretary or if he holds or is acting in or has held any public office within the period of three years immediately preceding such appointment.

(4) A person who has held office or acted as a member of the Public Service Commission shall not, within a period of three years commencing with the date on which he last so held office or acted, be eligible for appointment to any public office.

(5) The office of a member of the Public Service Commission shall become vacant at the expiration of five years from the date of his appointment or such shorter period, not being less than three years, as may be specified at the time of his appointment.

8 In Jamaica and Barbados the composition of the Public Service Commission is: a Chairman and three to five other members appointed on the recommendation of the Prime Minister after he has consulted with the Leader of the Opposition, except that in Jamaica one of these appointed members must be chosen from a list of qualified persons submitted by the representative body of the public service.

In Guyana the Commission consists of five to six members: three appointed on the recommendation of the Prime Minister after he has consulted with the Leader of the Opposition, two on the advice of the Prime Minister after he has consulted with bodies representing public officers, and if the Prime Minister so advises one other member appointed on his advice.

(6) A member of the Public Service Commission may be removed from office by the Governor-General, acting in accordance with the advice of the Prime Minister, for inability to discharge the functions of his office (whether arising from infirmity of mind or body or any other cause) or for misbehaviour.

(7) A member of the Public Service Commission shall not be removed from office except in accordance with the provisions of this section.[9]

(8) If the office of a member of the Public Service Commission is vacant or a member is for any reason unable to perform the functions of his office, the Governor-General, acting in accordance with the advice of the Prime Minister, may appoint a person who is qualified for appointment as a member of the Commission to act as a member of the Commission, and any person so appointed shall, subject to the provisions of subsection (3) of this section, continue to act until his appointment is revoked by the Governor-General, acting in accordance with the advice of the Prime Minister.

93 (1) Subject to the provisions of this Constitution, power to appoint persons to hold or act in public offices (including power to make appointments on promotion and transfer and to confirm appointments) and to remove and exercise disciplinary control over persons holding or acting in such offices shall vest in the Public Service Commission:

Provided that the Commission may, with the approval of the Prime Minister and subject to such conditions as it may think fit, delegate any of its powers under this section, by directions in writing, to any of its members or to any public officer.

(2) This section shall apply in relation to the office of teacher as defined in section 2 of the School Teachers' Pensions Ordinance[10] and to any person holding or acting in that office, as it applies to public offices and to persons holding or acting in those offices.

(3) No appointment shall be made under this section to any office on the personal staff of the Governor-General unless the Governor-General signifies his approval of the appointment.

(4) Before the Public Service Commission appoints to any public office any person holding or acting in any office power to make appointments to which is vested by this Constitution in the Judicial and Legal Commission, it shall consult with that Commission.

9 The procedures in the different countries for removal from office differ in the same way as is outlined above (document C (i) (a) of this chapter, footnote 1) for the Judicial Service Commissions.

10 Laws of Trinidad and Tobago, 1950, c. 11. No. 4. (Footnote in the original.)

(5) Before the Public Service Commission appoints to any public office any person holding or acting in any office power to make appointments to which is vested by this Constitution in the Police Service Commission, it shall consult with that Commission.

(6) The Public Service Commission shall not remove, or inflict any punishment on, a public officer on the grounds of any act done or omitted to be done by that officer in the exercise of a judicial function, conferred upon him unless the Judicial and Legal Service Commission concurs therein.

(7) (a) Before the Public Service Commission makes any appointment to an office to which this subjection applies it shall consult with the Prime Minister.

(b) A person shall not be appointed to an office to which this subsection applies if the Prime Minister signifies to the Public Service Commission his objection to the appointment of that person to that office.

(c) The offices to which this subsection applies are the office of permanent secretary (except in relation to appointments on transfer from another such office carrying the same salary), the offices of the Director of Personnel Administration, of head of a department of government, of chief professional adviser in a Ministry of government and the office of deputy ~~to~~ any such office.

(8) Power to make appointments to any office of permanent secretary on transfer from another such office carrying the same salary shall vest in the Governor-General, acting in accordance with the advice of the Prime Minister.[11]

. . .

94 (1) Power to appoint persons to hold or act in the offices to which this section applies (including power to make appointments on promotion and transfer and to confirm appointments) and to remove persons so appointed from any such office shall vest in the Governor-General, acting in accordance with the advice of the Prime Minister.

11 Again the powers of the Public Service Commissions are very much the same in all the territories. However, in Jamaica and Barbados the Privy Council acts as an appeals board for disciplinary cases. In neither Jamaica, Guyana nor Barbados does the Prime Minister have a final veto over initial appointments of permanent secretaries: in Guyana and Barbados he has the right to be consulted prior to the Public Service Commission advising the Governor-General, and in Jamaica, upon his objection to a recommendation by the Commission the Governor-General would refer the matter back to the Commission. However, should the Commission abide by its initial recommendation the Governor-General would then accept its advice.

(2) Before tendering any advice for the purposes of this section in relation to any person who holds or acts in any public office other than an office to which this section applies, the Prime Minister shall consult the appropriate Service Commission.

(3) The offices to which this section applies are the offices of any Ambassador, High Commissioner or other principal representative of Trinidad and Tobago in any other country.

95 (1) Power to make appointments on transfer to the offices to which this section applies shall vest in the Prime Minister.

(2) The offices to which this section applies are –

(a) offices, the holders of which are required to reside outside Trinidad and Tobago for the proper discharge of their functions;

(b) such offices in the Ministry for the external affairs of Trinidad and Tobago as may, from time to time be designated by the Prime Minister.

(iii) Police Service Commission

(a) Extract from the Trinidad and Tobago (Constitution) Order in Council, 1962. (S.I. 1875/1962.)

98 (1) There shall be a Police Service Commission for Trinidad and Tobago which shall consist of a Chairman and four other members.

(2) (a) The members of the Police Service Commission shall be appointed by the Governor-General, acting in accordance with the advice of the Prime Minister.[12]

(b) The Chairman of the Police Service Commission shall be either the Chairman or the Deputy Chairman of the Public Service Commission.[13]

(3) A person shall not be qualified to be appointed to or to hold the office of a member of the Police Service Commission if he is a Senator or a temporary member of the Senate or a member of the House of Representatives or a Minister or a Parliamentary Secretary or if he holds or is acting in or has held any public office within the period of three years immediately preceding such appointment.

12 In the three other independent West Indian countries these appointments are made on the recommendation of the Prime Minister, after he has consulted with the Leader of the Opposition.

13 Guyana also specifies that the Chairman of the Police Service Commission shall be the Chairman of the Public Service Commission.

(4) A person who has held office or acted as a member of the Police Service Commission shall not, within a period of three years commencing with the date on which he last so held office or acted, be eligible for appointment to any public office.

(5) The office of a member of the Police Service Commission shall become vacant at the expiration of five years from the date of his appointment or such shorter period, not being less than three years as may be specified at the time of his appointment.

(6) A member of the Police Service Commission may be removed from office by the Governor-General, acting in accordance with the advice of the Prime Minister, for inability to discharge the functions of his office (whether arising from infirmity of mind or body or any other cause) or for misbehaviour.

(7) A member of the Police Service Commission shall not be removed from office except in accordance with the provisions of this section.[14]

(8) If the office of a member of the Police Service Commission is vacant or a member is for any reason unable to perform the functions of his office, the Governor-General, acting in accordance with the advice of the Prime Minister, may appoint a person who is qualified for appointment as a member of the Commission to act as a member of the Commission, and any person so appointed shall, subject to the provisions of subsection (3) of this section, continue to act until his appointment is revoked by the Governor-General, acting in accordance with the advice of the Prime Minister.

99 (1) Power to appoint persons to hold or act in offices in the Police Force (including appointments on promotion and transfer and the confirmation of appointments) and to remove and exercise disciplinary control over persons holding or acting in such offices shall vest in the Police Service Commission:

Provided that the Commission may, with the approval of the Prime Minister and subject to such conditions as it may think fit delegate any of its powers under this section to any of its members or to the Commissioner of Police or any other officer of the Police Force.

(2) Before the Police Service Commission appoints to any office in the Police Force any person holding or acting in any office power to make appointments to which is vested by this Constitution in the Judicial and Legal Service Commission, it shall consult with that Commission.

(3) Before the Police Service Commission appoints to any office in the Police Force any person holding or acting in any office power to make appointments to which is vested by this Constitution in the Public Service Commission, it shall consult with that Commission.

14 See the procedure for dismissal in the other territories as outlined in document C (i) (a) of this chapter, footnote 6, page 472.

(4) The Police Service Commission shall not remove, or inflict any punishment on, the holder of an office in the Police Force on the grounds of any act done or omitted to be done by him in the exercise of a judicial function conferred upon him unless the Judicial and Legal Service Commission concurs therein.

(5) Before the Police Service Commission makes an appointment to the office of Commissioner or Deputy Commissioner of Police it shall consult the Prime Minister, and a person shall not be appointed to such an office if the Prime Minister signifies to the Police Service Commission his objection to the appointment of that person to such an office.[15]

D The Auditor-General

(i) Extracts from the Jamaica (Constitution) Order in Council, 1962. (S.I. 1550/1962.)

120 (1) There shall be in and for Jamaica an Auditor-General who shall be appointed by the Governor-General by instrument under the Broad Seal.

(2) If the office of Auditor-General is vacant or the Auditor-General is for any reason unable to perform the functions of his office, the Governor-General may appoint a person to act as Auditor-General and any person so appointed shall, subject to the provisions of subsection (1) of section 121 of this Constitution, continue to act until the office of Auditor-General is filled or until his appointment is revoked by the Governor-General.

(3) A person who has held the office of Auditor-General shall not be eligible for appointment to any other public office.

(4) The Auditor-General shall receive salary and allowances as may from time to time be prescribed by or under any law or by a resolution of the House of Representatives:

Provided that –

(a) no such resolution may reduce any salary or allowance for the time being prescribed by or under a law; and

15 The powers over appointment, dismissal, promotion etc., are basically the same in all territories and are very similar to the powers of the Public Service Commissions. Again the Privy Council acts as an appeals board in disciplinary cases in Jamaica and Barbados. The Jamaican Constitution makes no special mention of the Commissioner of Police but in Guyana, as in Trinidad, the Prime Minister is given a veto over appointments to the office of Commissioner and Deputy Commissioner, and in Barbados the Prime Minister has to be consulted before the Commission makes a recommendation on the appointment of the Commissioner of Police.

(b) the salary of the Auditor-General shall not be reduced during his continuance in office.

(5) The salary for the time being payable to the Auditor-General under this Constitution shall be charged on and paid out of the Consolidated Fund.

(6) In the exercise of his powers under this section the Governor-General shall act in accordance with the recommendation of the Public Service Commission:

Provided that –

(a) before he acts in accordance therewith he shall inform the Prime Minister of the nature of that recommendation and shall, if the Prime Minister so requires, once refer that recommendation (hereafter in this subsection called the "original recommendation") back to the Public Service Commission for reconsideration; and

(b) if, upon such reconsideration, the Public Service Commission submits a different recommendation, the provisions of this subsection and of subsection (2) of section 32 of this Constitution shall apply to that different recommendation as they apply to the original recommendation.[16]

121 (1) Subject to the provisions of subsection (3) to (6) (inclusive) of this section, the Auditor-General shall hold office until he attains the age of sixty years:

Provided that –

(a) he may at any time resign his office; and

(b) the Governor-General, acting in the manner prescribed by subsection (6) of section 120 of this Constitution, may permit an Auditor-General who has attained the age of sixty years to remain in office until he has reached such later age, not exceeding sixty-five years, as may (before the Auditor-General has reached the age of sixty years) have been agreed between the Governor-General and the Auditor-General.

(2) Nothing done by the Auditor-General shall be invalid by reason only that he has attained the age at which he is required by this section to vacate his office.

(3) The Auditor-General may be removed from office only for inability to discharge the functions thereof (whether arising from infirmity of body or mind or any other cause) or for misbehaviour, and shall not be so removed except in accordance with the provisions of subsection (4) of this section.

16 In Barbados and Guyana the Auditor-General (Director of Audit in Guyana) is appointed on the advice of the Public Service Commission, but in Barbados after the Commission has consulted with the Prime Minister. In Trinidad and Tobago he is appointed on the advice of the Prime Minister.

(4) The Auditor-General shall be removed from office by the Governor-General by instrument under the Broad Seal if the question of his removal from office has been referred to a tribunal appointed under subsection (5) of this section and the tribunal has recommended to the Governor-General that he ought to be removed from office for inability as aforesaid or for misbehaviour.

(5) If the Prime Minister or the Chairman of the Public Service Commission advises the Governor-General that the question of removing the Auditor-General from office for inability as aforesaid or for misbehaviour ought to be investigated, then –

(a) the Governor-General shall appoint a tribunal which shall consist of a Chairman and not less than two other members, selected by the Governor-General, acting on the advice of the Chief Justice, from among persons who hold or have held the office of a judge of a court having unlimited jurisdiction in civil and criminal matters in some part of the Commonwealth or a court having jurisdiction in appeals from any such court; and

(b) that tribunal shall enquire into the matter and report on the facts thereof to the Governor-General and recommend to the Governor-General whether the Auditor-General ought to be removed from office for inability as aforesaid or for misbehaviour.

(6) The provisions of the Commissions of Enquiry Law as in force immediately before the appointed day shall, subject to the provisions of this section and of the Third Schedule to this Constitution, apply as nearly as may be in relation to tribunals appointed under subsection (5) of this section or, as the context may require, to the members thereof as they apply in relation to Commissions or Commissioners appointed under that Law, and for that purpose shall have effect as if they formed part of this Constitution.

(7) If the question of removing the Auditor-General from office has been referred to a tribunal under subsection (5) of this section, the Governor-General acting in the manner prescribed by subsection (6) of section 120 of this Constitution, may suspend the Auditor-General from performing the functions of his office and any such suspension may at any time be revoked by the Governor-General, acting as aforesaid, and shall in any case cease to have effect if the tribunal recommends to the Governor-General that the Auditor-General should not be removed from office.[17]

122 (1) The accounts of the Court of Appeal, the accounts of the Supreme Court, the accounts of the offices of the Clerks to the Senate and the House of Representatives and the accounts of all departments and offices of the

17 The provisions with regard to tenure of office of the Auditor-General are very similar in the other independent countries of the West Indies.

Government of Jamaica (including the offices of the Cabinet, the Judicial Service Commission, the Public Service Commission and the Police Service Commission but excluding the department of the Auditor-General) shall, at least once in every year, be audited and reported on by the Auditor-General who, with his subordinate staff, shall at all times be entitled to have access to all books, records, returns and reports relating to such accounts.

(2) The Auditor-General shall submit his reports made under subsection (1) of this section to the Speaker (or, if the office of Speaker is vacant or the Speaker is for any reason unable to perform the functions of his office, to the Deputy Speaker) who shall cause them to be laid before the House of Representatives.

(3) In the exercise of his functions under the provisions of subsections (1) and (2) of this section, the Auditor-General shall not be subject to the direction or control of any other person or authority.

(4) The accounts of the department of the Auditor-General shall be audited and reported on by the Minister responsible for finance, and the provisions of subsections (1) and (2) of this section shall apply in relation to the exercise by that Minister of those functions as they apply in relation to audits and reports made by the Auditor-General.

(5) Nothing in this section shall prevent the performance by the Auditor-General of –

- (a) such other functions in relation to the accounts of the Government of Jamaica and the accounts of other public authorities and other bodies administering public funds in Jamaica as may be prescribed by or under any law for the time being in force in Jamaica; or
- (b) such other functions in relation to the supervision and control of expenditure from public funds in Jamaica as may be so prescribed
- (c) such other functions in relation to the accounts of any other government as he may be empowered to perform by any authority competent in that behalf.

E The Director of Public Prosecutions

(i) Extracts from the Jamaica (Constitution) Order in Council, 1962. (S.I. 1550/1962.)

94 (1) There shall be a Director of Public Prosecutions, whose office shall be a public office.[18]

18 In Guyana, as in Jamaica, the Director of Public Prosecutions is appointe on the advice of the Public Service Commission, but in Guyana the

(2) A person shall not be qualified to hold or act in the office of Director of Public Prosecutions unless he is qualified for appointment as a Judge of the Supreme Court.

(3) The Director of Public Prosecutions shall have power in any case in which he considers it desirable so to do –

(a) to institute and undertake criminal proceedings against any person before any court other than a court-martial in respect of any offence against the law of Jamaica;

(b) to take over and continue any such criminal proceedings that may have been instituted by any other person or authority; and

(c) to discontinue at any stage before judgement is delivered any such criminal proceedings instituted or undertaken by himself or any other person or authority.

(4) The powers of the Director of Public Prosecutions under subsection (3) of this section may be exercised by him in person or through other persons acting under and in accordance with his general or special instructions.

(5) The powers conferred upon the Director of Public Prosecutions by paragraphs (b) and (c) of subsection (3) of this section shall be vested in him to the exclusion of any other person or authority.

Provided that where any other person or authority has instituted criminal proceedings, nothing in this subsection shall prevent the withdrawal of those proceedings by or at the instance of that person or authority and with the leave of the Court.

(6) In the exercise of the powers conferred upon him by this section the Director of Public Prosecutions shall not be subject to the direction or control of any other person or authority.

95 (1) The Director of Public Prosecutions shall receive such emoluments and be subject to such terms and conditions of service as may from time to time be prescribed by or under law:

Provided that the emoluments and terms and conditions of service of the Director of Public Prosecutions, other than allowances that are not taken into account in computing pensions, shall not be altered to his disadvantage during his continuance in office.

(2) The salary for the time being payable to the Director of Public Prosecutions under this Constitution shall be charged on and paid out of the Consolidated Fund.[19]

Commission must first consult the Prime Minister. In Barbados the appointment is made on the advice of the Judicial and Legal Service Commission. In Trinidad and Tobago there is no such office, the functions being performed by the political appointee: the Attorney-General.

19 Provisions with regard to the tenure of office of the Director of Public Prosecutions are the same as those relating to the Auditor-General.

F The Attorney-General

(i) Extracts from the Guyana Constitution, the Guyana Independence Order, 1966. (S.I. 575/1966.)[20]

Chapter V

42 (1) There shall be an Attorney-General of Guyana who shall be the principal legal adviser to the Government of Guyana and who shall be appointed by the Governor-General.

(2) A person shall not be qualified to be appointed as Attorney-General unless he is qualified to be appointed as a Puisne Judge of the High Court and is a Commonwealth citizen.

(3) If the Attorney General is an elected member of the National Assembly, at the time of his appointment or subsequently becomes such a member, he shall be a Minister by virtue of holding the office of Attorney-General and the provisions of paragraphs (4) and (5) of article 37 of this Constitution shall apply to the Office of Attorney-General.[21]

20 In the other independent territories the Attorney-General is a normal ministerial appointment, the only distinction being that the constitutions specifically refer to his portfolio as legal adviser to the Government.

21 Article 37 (4) The office of any other Minister shall become vacant if the holder of the office –

(a) ceases to be a member of the Assembly for any cause other than a dissolution of Parliament;

(b) is not a member of the Assembly when the Assembly first meets after a dissolution of Parliament; or

(c) is, by virtue of article 61 (3) of this Constitution, required to cease to perform his functions as a member of the Assembly.

(5) The Office of a Minister other than the Prime Minister shall become vacant –

(a) if the Governor-General, acting in accordance with the advice of the Prime Minister, so directs;

(b) if the Prime Minister resigns his office within seven days after the passing of a resolution such as is mentioned in paragraph 1 of this article or the Governor-General revokes the appointment of the Prime Minister under that paragraph; or

(c) on the appointment of any person to the office of Prime Minister.

Article 61 (2) A member of the National Assembly shall also vacate his seat therein –

(d) subject to the following paragraph, if any circumstances arise that, i

(4) If the Attorney-General is not an elected member of the Assembly but is qualified to be elected as such a member, he may be appointed by the Governor-General to be a Minister.

. . .

(5) If an Attorney-General appointed to be a Minister under the preceding paragraph resigns his office as Attorney-General he shall also vacate his office as a Minister.

(6) If the Attorney-General is not a Minister he shall vacate his office if he ceases to be a Commonwealth Citizen or if his appointment is revoked by the Governor-General.

. . .

(8) The powers of the Governor-General under this article shall be exercised by him in accordance with the advice of the Prime Minister.

he were not a member of the Assembly, would cause him to be disqualified for election as a member thereof by virtue of the preceding article or of any law enacted in pursuance thereof.

(3) (a) If circumstances such as are referred to in subparagraph (d) of the preceding paragraph arise in relation to a member of the Assembly by virtue of the fact that he is declared insolvent, adjudged to be of unsound mind, sentenced, or convicted or reported guilty of an offence and it is open to the member to appeal against the decision (either with the leave or other authority or without such leave), he shall forthwith cease to perform his functions as a member of the Assembly but, subject to the next following subparagraph, he shall not vacate his seat until the expiration of thirty days thereafter.

Provided that the Speaker may, at the request of the member, from time to time extend that period for further periods of thirty days to enable the member to pursue an appeal against the decisions, so, however, that extensions of time exceeding in the aggregate one hundred and fifty days shall not be given without the approval of the Assembly.

(b) If, on the determination of any appeal, such circumstances continue to exist and no further appeal is open to the member of the Assembly, or if by reason of the expiration of any period for entering an appeal or notice thereof or the refusal of leave to appeal or for any other reason, it ceases to be open to the member to appeal, he shall forthwith vacate his seat.

(c) If at any time before the member of the Assembly vacate his seat such circumstances as aforesaid cease to exist, his seat shall not become vacant by reason of those circumstances and he may resume the performance of his functions as a member of the Assembly.

G The Ombudsman[22]

(i) Extracts from the Guyana Constitution,
the Guyana Independence Order, 1966.
(S.I. 575/1966.)

Chapter V
Part 2
The Ombudsman

52 (1) For the purpose of conducting investigations in accordance with the provisions of this Part of this Constitution, there shall be an Ombudsman.

(2) The Ombudsman shall be appointed by the Governor-General acting on the recommendation of the Prime Minister after consultation with the Leader of the Opposition.

(3) The Ombudsman shall not perform the functions of any public office and shall not, without the approval of the Prime Minister in each particular case, hold any other office of emolument, other than his office as Ombudsman, or engage in any occupation, for reward outside the duties of his office.

(4) Subject to the provisions of the next following paragraph, a person holding the office of Ombudsman shall vacate that office at the expiration of four years from the date of his appointment.

(5) The provisions of article 118 of this Constitution (which relate to removal from office) shall apply, to the office of Ombudsman, and for the purposes of paragraphs (4) and (6) of that article the prescribed authority shall be the Prime Minister.[23]

22 In the Commonwealth Caribbean this office is peculiar to Guyana.

23 Article 118 (1) Where it is provided in this Constitution that this article shall apply to any office, a person holding such office . . . shall not be removed therefrom or suspended from the exercise of the functions thereof except in accordance with the provisions of this article; and the prescribed authority for the purposes of paragraphs (4) and (6) of this article shall, in relation to any office, be the authority prescribed for that purpose by the provision of this Constitution by which this article is applied to that office.

(2) The officer may be removed from office only for inability to discharge the functions of his office (whether arising from infirmity of body or mind or any other cause whatsoever) or for misbehaviour.

(3) The officer shall be removed from office by the Governor-General if the question of his removal from office has been referred to a tribunal appointed under this article and the tribunal has recommended to the Governor-General that the officer ought to be removed from office for inability as aforesaid or for misbehaviour.

53 (1) Subject to the provisions of this article the Ombudsman may investigate any action taken by any department of Government or by any other authority to which this article applies, or by Ministers, officers or members of such department or authority, being action taken in exercise of the administrative functions of that department or authority on or after 26th May, 1966.

(2) The Ombudsman may investigate any such action as aforesaid in any of the following circumstances, that is to say –

(a) if a complaint in respect of the action is duly made to the Ombudsman by any person or body of persons, whether incorporated or not, alleging that the complainant has sustained injustice in consequence of a fault in administration;

(b) if a Minister or a member of the National Assembly requests the Ombudsman to investigate the action on the ground that a person or body of persons specified in the request has or may have sustained such injustice;

(c) in any other circumstances in which the Ombudsman considers that he ought to investigate the action on the ground that some person or body of persons has or may have sustained such injustice.

(3) The Ombudsman shall not investigate under this Part –

(a) any action in respect of which the complainant has or had –

(i) a remedy by way of proceedings in a court; or

(ii) a right of appeal, reference or review to or before an independent and impartial tribunal other than a court; or

(4) If the prescribed authority advises the Governor-General that the question of removing the officer from office under this article ought to be investigated then –

(a) the Governor-General shall appoint a tribunal which shall consist of a Chairman and not less than two other members, selected by the Prime Minister after consultation with the Judicial Services Commission from among persons who hold or have held office as a judge of a court of unlimited jurisdiction in civil and criminal matters in some part of the Commonwealth or a court having jurisdiction in appeals from any such court or who are qualified to be admitted to practise in Guyana as advocates or solicitors and have been so qualified for such periods as may be prescribed by Parliament . . . and

(b) that tribunal shall enquire into the matter and report on the facts thereof to the Governor-General and recommend to him whether the officer ought to be removed under this article . . .

(b) any such action, or action taken in respect to any such matter as is described in the First Schedule to this Constitution.[24]

Provided that the Ombudsman –

(i) may conduct an investigation notwithstanding that the complainant has or had remedy by way of proceedings in a court if satisfied that in the particular circumstances it is not reasonable to expect him to take or to have taken such proceedings;

(ii) shall not in any case be precluded from conducting an investigation in respect of any matter by reason only that it is open to the complainant to apply to the High Court for redress under article 19 (1) of this Constitution (which relates to redress for contraventions of provisions for the protection of fundamental rights and freedoms).

24 First Schedule.

Action and Matters not Subject to Investigation under Part 2 of Chapter V.

1. Matters certified by a Minister to affect relations or dealings between the Government of Guyana and any other Government or any international organisation.

2. Action taken for the purposes of protecting the security of the State or of investigating crime including action taken with respect to passports for either of these purposes.

3. The commencement or conduct of any civil or criminal proceedings in any court.

4. Action taken in respect of appointment to offices or other employment in the service of the Crown or appointments made by or with the approval of the Governor-General or any Minister, and action taken in relation to any person as the holder or former holder of any such office, employment or appointment.

5. Action taken with respect to orders or directions to any disciplined force or member thereof . . .

6. The exercise of the powers conferred by article 49 of this Constitution (the prerogative of mercy).

7. The grant of honours, awards or privileges within the gift of the Crown.

8. Action taken in matters relating to contractual or other commercial dealings with members of the public other than action by an authority mentioned in subparagraph (a) of article 53 (5) of this Constitution.

9. Any action taken in any country outside Guyana by or on behalf of any officer representing the Government of Guyana or any officer of that Government.

10. Any action which by virtue of any provision of this Constitution may not be inquired into by any Court.

(4) In determining whether to initiate, continue or discontinue an investigation under this Part, the Ombudsman shall, subject to the foregoing provisions of this article, and in accordance with his individual judgment and in particular, and without prejudice to the generality of the foregoing, the Ombudsman may refuse to initiate or may discontinue any investigation if it appears to him that –

(a) the complaint relates to action of which the complainant has had knowledge for more than twelve months before the complaint was received by the Ombudsman;

(b) the subject matter of the complaint is trivial;

(c) the complaint is frivolous or vexatious or is not made in good faith;

(d) the complainant has not a sufficient interest in the subject matter of the complaint.

(5) The authorities other than departments of Government to which this article applies are –

(a) any authority empowered to determine the person with whom any contract or class of contracts shall be entered into by or on behalf of the Government of Guyana; and

(b) such other authorities as may be prescribed by Parliament.

(6) For the purposes of this article the Judicial Service Commission, the Public Service Commission and the Police Service Commission shall not be regarded as departments of Government.

(7) For the purposes of paragraph (2) (a) of this article a complaint may be made by a person aggrieved himself or, if he is dead or for any reason unable to act for himself, by any person duly authorised to represent him.

(8) Any question whether a complaint or a request for an investigation is duly made under this Part or any law enacted in pursuance of article 55 of this Constitution shall be determined by the Ombudsman.

(9) Where a complaint or request for an investigation is duly made as aforesaid and the Ombudsman decides not to investigate the action to which the complaint or request relates or to discontinue an investigation of that action, he shall inform the person or body of persons who made the complaint or request of his decision.

(10) In this article "action" includes failure to act and "action taken" shall be construed accordingly.

54 (1) After conducting an investigation under this Part the Ombudsman shall inform the department or authority concerned of the result of that investigation and if he is of the opinion that any person or body of persons has sustained injustice in consequence of a fault in administration, he shall inform that department or authority of the reasons for that opinion and may

make such recommendations for action by that department or authority as he thinks fit.

(2) After conducting an investigation under this Part in pursuance of a complaint or a request for an investigation made by a Minister or a member of the National Assembly, the Ombudsman shall –

(a) if he is of the opinion that the complainant, or in the case of an investigation conducted in pursuance of such a request, the person or body of persons specified in the request has sustained injustice in consequence of a fault in administration, inform the person or body of persons who made the complaint or request that he is of that opinion and the nature of the injustice that he considers has been sustained;

(b) if he is of the opinion that the complainant or, in the case of an investigation conducted in pursuance of such a request, the person or body of persons specified in the request has not sustained injustice, inform the person or body of persons who made the complaint or request that he is of that opinion and the reasons therefor.

(3) Where the Ombudsman has made recommendation under paragraph (1) of this article and within a reasonable time thereafter no action has been taken which appears to the Ombudsman adequately to remedy the injustice, he may lay before the Assembly a special report on the case.

(4) The Ombudsman shall annually lay before the Assembly a general report on the performance of his functions under this Part.

55 Parliament may make provision for such supplementary and ancillary matters as may appear necessary or expedient in consequence of any of the provisions of this Part . . .

APPENDIX A

THE SUSPENSION OF THE CONSTITUTION OF BRITISH GUIANA 1953

(i) Extracts from the Report on the Suspension of the Constitution ordered on 8th October 1953. (Cmnd. 8980/1953)

I Introduction

1 The new Constitution introduced in British Guiana last April was based on report (Col. No. 280) of an independent Commission.[1] . . . It conferred upon the people for the first time universal adult suffrage and provided for a bi-cameral Legislature . . . The Constitution provided for the appointment of six elected members of the House of Assembly as Ministers with departmental responsibility and gave them a majority of two in the Executive Council, the principal instrument of policy. The Governor was obliged (save in exceptional cases) to consult, and take the advice of, this Council.

2 In the General Election at the end of April for the House of Assembly under the new Constitution the People's Progressive Party (P.P.P.) gained 51 per cent of the votes, and 18 out of 24 seats. With this majority it secured the election of members of the Party to the six Ministerial posts filled from the House of Assembly.[2] . . . Two further members of the P.P.P. were appointed to the State Council on the recommendation of the six Ministers.

3 The People's Progressive Party, therefore, held six out of ten places in the Executive Council. It also had a working majority in the House of

1 See Chapter IV Part II, doc. E (v).

2 The P.P.P. Ministers were Dr C.B. Jagan, Mr L.F.S. Burnham, Mr A. Chase, Mr S. King (now Eusi Kwayana), Dr J.P. Lachmansingh, and Mr J.N. Singh. Dr Jagan became Leader of the House and Mrs Jagan the Deputy Speaker.

Assembly, but not in the State Council. It would also have had a majority if the Governor had decided to call a Joint Session of the two Houses for any purpose.

II Activities of Ministers

4 The conduct of Ministers showed no concern for the true welfare of the Colony and threatened its progress as an orderly state: it had seriously endangered the economic life of the country and had set it on the road to collapse. Examples of this conduct are:-

(i) Fomenting of strikes for political ends (paragraphs 15-18);
(ii) Attempting to oust established trade unions by legislative action paragraph 19;[3]
(iii) Removal of the ban on the entry of West Indian communists (paragraph 8);[4]
(iv) Introduction of a bill to repeal the Undesirable Publications Ordinance and the flooding of the territory with communist literature (paragraph 8);[5]
(v) Misuse of rights of appointment to Boards and Committees (paragraph 13);[6]
(vi) Spreading of racial hatred (paragraph 14);

3 This issue was also dealt with in the Report of the British Guiana Constitutional Commission, 1954. (Cmnd. 9274/1954.) However, much of the evidence brought forward in these two reports would suggest that the established trade union in the sugar fields (the Manpower Citizen's Association) did not have the support of the workers whereas the Guiana Industrial Workers' Union was able to call a successful strike paralysing the industry but was not recognized.

4 Here it might be sufficient to point to the very dubious nature of such bans from a democratic point of view.

5 Again, such an ordinance giving sweeping powers to ban "undesirable publications" is of dubious validity in any democratic country.

6 In the Report of the British Guiana Constitutional Commission, 1954 (Cmnd. 9274/1954), paragraph 47, it was acknowledged that administration was ill-adapted to the needs of the Colony, especially in view of the need for central planning for development. Here it needs to be recognized that many countries, which would be acknowledged as democratic by the British authorities, do make political appointments to the public service and to statutory boards etc. (e.g. the Unites States and that furthermore the Labour Party in 1945 itself speculated about the need to make such appointments given their heavy and radical legislative programme.

(vii) Plan to secularize Church schools and to re-write textbooks to give them a political bias (paragraph 36);[7]
(viii) Neglect of their administrative duties (paragraphs 22-23);
(ix) Undermining of the loyalty of the Police (paragraphs 9-11);
(x) Attempts to gain control of the Public Service (paragraph 12);
(xi) Threats of violence (paragraphs 28-33).[8]

5 Each one of these acts judged separately was serious enough, and the cumulative effect was disastrous. Viewed in the light of the Communist connexions of Ministers, their aim was unmistakeable.

6 In the succeeding paragraphs the events of the period May-September, 1953 are described roughly in chronological order.

The Loyal Address and Withdrawal of Bans on Entry of Communists and Communist Literature

7 At the first business session of the new House of Assembly held on 17th June the Party refused to move a loyal address to the Queen in response to Her Majesty's gracious message at the introduction of the new Constitution (though a loyal address was passed unanimously when moved by the Leader of the Opposition).

8 At the same time and contrary to the general policy of other West Indian Governments; the P.P.P. Ministers insisted on the removal of the ban on the entry of certain well-known West Indian Communists into British Guiana. They introduced a bill to repeal the Undesirable Publications Ordinance, thus removing the power of the Governor in Council to exclude subversive literature. Communist literature brought in by Dr. Jagan in 1951 was seized by customs officials. The proposed bill sought to invalidate this seizure and was thus attempting to make these officials liable to legal proceedings for their official action. It has not yet passed into law, but meanwhile communist literature has been pouring into the country.

Undermining of the Loyalty of the Police

9 Ministers intended to organize a "People's Police". On 3rd May, Dr. Jagan said "Comrades, in the past when we asked for bread we were given

7 In Cmnd. 9274/1954, paragraph 30, it was stated that the present system, with the bulk of Government expenditure on education going to denominational schools, was unlikely to continue much longer.

Leaving aside the rhetoric of the P.P.P. the stated need to re-write the textbooks could be seen as a simple recognition of the urgent need to give education in British Guiana a sound base in the realities of the country and the region.

8 No actual evidence of violence was quoted in this report or in Cmnd. 9274/1954.

bullets and those who fired at workers were honoured by the masters. But when the P.P.P. gets into power the same bullets which were fired on those poor people will be fired on our oppressors. We shall organise a Police Force; it will be known as the People's Police".

10 Ministers in their speeches made clear their dissatisfaction that the existing police force was not under the control of the P.P.P.; they encouraged dissatisfied policemen to take their complaints to party leaders and used the dissidents to spread discontent and disaffection.

11 The Minister of Labour tried to interfere with the control of the police by the Chief Secretary. He informed the Chief Secretary that he proposed to issue a statement for the guidance of the police and requested the Chief Secretary to draw their attention to it . . .

(vi) Action by Her Majesty's Government

42 It became clear by the end of September that British Guiana was facing a rapid deterioration in the efficiency of its administration in its economy and in its security. This deterioration threatened not only public order, but the very livelihood of the people. The Governor's reserve powers were certainly never intended to deal with a situation of this kind, so that effective action could not be taken within the terms of the Constitution to remedy matters. After consultation with the Governor, Her Majesty's Government were driven reluctantly to the conclusion that the only course was to take steps to suspend the Constitution. To have waited until further deterioration in the situation had brought loss of life would have been a betrayal of Her Majesty's Government's responsibilities.

43 Her Majesty's Government realised the gravity of this step. Some Ministers had threatened violence and tension was great. They and other extremists might have used this occasion for stirring up disorder. Her Majesty's Government accordingly decided to transfer to British Guiana the troops which were stationed in Jamaica and British Honduras to support the security forces and to ensure the maintenance of order. In the event the action taken by Her Majesty's Government was greeted with widespread relief in the Colony and there were no incidents beyond the general strike which the P.P.P. Ministers are [sic] attempting to organise. In the West Indies the unofficial members of several Executive Council and Committees have supported Her Majesty's Government's action. Strong criticisms of the P.P.P. by leaders of the two principal political parties in Jamaica have been published in the Press.

44 Pending the making of the Order in Council to suspend the Constitution P.P.P. Ministers were deprived of responsibility for departments and steps were taken to amend the Constitution so that the Governor, in exercising his powers, under the Constitution, was no longer obliged to act on the advice of Executive Council . . .

Appendix A

(ii) Extracts from the Debate in the British House of Commons on the action of Her Majesty's Government in British Guiana, 22nd October 1953. (Parliamentary Debates (Commons), Vol. 518, 1953-54, cc. 2159-2174.)

The Secretary of State for the Colonies (Mr. Oliver Lyttleton):

I beg to move,
"That this House approves the action of Her Majesty's Government in British Guiana."

The proposal to suspend the Constitution is indeed a grave step. Viewed in any light, it is a setback to the principle upon which all political parties in this House are agreed, namely, that our colonial policy should be directed towards giving the peoples in the Colonial Territories an increasing responsibility for the management of their own affairs[9] . . .

We have readily done so in many territories. To look no further than the West Indies, the Constitutions based on universal adult suffrage in Trinidad, Barbados and Jamaica, to quote three examples, show that the risks taken were justified. That sense of responsibility upon which alone these arrangements can take root and grow is becoming evident . . .

. . . Risks are necessary in these matters unless the pace of constitutional advance is to be altogether too pedestrian or is to be too much out of harmony with the aspirations of these people. But if we accept the corollary, which is that when events have proved that the risks were unjustified, when events, as often happens in human affairs, have falsified our predictions and dashed our hopes, we must be prepared to retrace our steps and try something else, always keeping in mind the ultimate goal to which our thoughts and policy should be directed.

. . . the opinions which I have just expressed are widely held in the West Indies by political leaders of parties of different political complexions. I first quote Mr. Grantley Adams, . . .

"Our experience of Jagan and his sympathisers leads us to feel certain that social and economic progress in the British West Indies is much more likely to be harmed by that sort of person than by the most reactionary. However much we must regret suspension of any constitution, we should deplore far more the continuance of a Government that put Communist ideology before the good of the people".

Mr. Bustamante, the Chief Minister in Jamaica, said:

"If British Guiana were fighting for complete self-government within the democratic nations I would have stood beside British Guiana, but British

9 Note than the statement does not mention independence. See below page 496.

Guiana today can get no sympathy from me – can get no sympathy from the free-thinking world.

I am sorry for the people there. I am not sorry for the leaders. They are not leaders at all. They do not know what they are doing."

Mr. Manley's party, the P.N.P. . . .

"It was a betrayal of the cause of colonial peoples the world over, and a reckless and stupid betrayal of those who voted for them."

I think it very significant to notice that the P.P.P. leaders have not yet appealed to public opinion in the West Indies where they are known only too well. Their appeal has been elsewhere.

At this point let me lay out two broad propositions which I hope will have the consent of the House; that among the duties that fall to the Government in this country and to the Secretary of State for the Colonies there are two which are outstanding in the political field. The first I have already touched upon. It is to pursue a policy which gives an increasing share of responsibility for their own affairs to the people of these Colonial Territories. But the second one is no less important. It is that Her Majesty's Government in the United Kingdom and the Secretary of State for the Colonies have responsibility laid upon them by this House, which they cannot set aside without the leave of this House, to see that peace and order, good government and conditions of social and economic advance are promoted . . .

Let me be quite clear. So long as Her Majesty's Government have a responsibility to this House for the affairs of Colonial Territories, that is to say, before those territories gain complete independence – and some may never be in the position to do so –
(*Interruption*) – some of them may never be in a position to do so – (Hon. Members: Why?) – Hon. Members who follow these affairs know that I am referring there to Colonies likely to be permanently grant-aided – there are no means by which they can lay aside their responsibilities for peace and order . . .

Today we must face the sad fact that constitutional advance in British Guiana has failed, for the moment. The evidence of that failure is set before the House in the White Paper. What emerges, I suggest, is a coherent picture of Ministers, no doubt largely dominated by Communist ideas, who gradually reduce government to a farce, who are threatening the order of the Colony, threatening the livelihood of its inhabitants, and undermining not only its present economic stability but also all chances of building it up.

Many of the statements that have been made, and indeed the measures that have been concerted, will appear to us literally incredible, but they are unfortunately all part of the deadly design to turn British Guiana into a totalitarian state dominated by Communist ideas, whose whole political, industrial and social life would be concentrated in the hands and in the power of one party.

Dr. Rita Hinden, a member of the Commission, I would mention to hon. Members opposite, which originally propounded this Constitution, in a thoughtful article no longer ago than 17th October, used these words:

"But one very disturbing thing emerged when our Commission took its public evidence. The People's Progressive Party representatives and also the trade unions connected with them who gave evidence had quite a different conception of democracy from what we had. They interpreted democracy as what I can only describe as 'one-party rule'."

She went on:

"They have acted consistently with the theory they propounded to us. They could now do what they wanted; they could override every obstacle that impeded them; they could use their majority to alter the processes of law to their convenience and thus eliminate all trace of opposition. In other words. democratic institutions were to be given by Britain as the stepping-stone to the totalitarian state."

. . .

Mrs. Barbara Castle (Blackburn, East): Seeing that the right hon. Gentleman is making a quotation from Dr. Rita Hinden, is it not fair to continue and to inform the House that she made it perfectly clear as a member of the Commission that the reserve powers were included in the Constitution for the express purpose of dealing with that situation?

Mr. Lyttelton: . . .

I now turn to the subject of Communism. I do not want to recite again the reasons set out in the White Paper upon which we base our statement that the leaders of P.P.P. were dominated by Communist ideas and were using all the standardised methods of Communist penetration into the machinery of Government, the public services, the police, the youth movements and the trade unions. I suggest with great earnestness that any impartial reader of the paragraph and appendix will see that these leaders looked for their inspiration to the network of Communist organisations which revolve round the W.F.T.U., and in the W.F.T.U. itself. I say to the House that we are here faced with part of the international Communist conspiracy . . .

. . . Her Majesty's Government are not prepared to tolerate the setting up of Communist states in the British Commonwealth, and I have no doubt that, in taking up that position, we have the support of the overwhelming majority of the people of this country behind us.

. . .

The right hon. Member for Ebbw Vale (Mr. A. Bevan) was reported to have said in a speech during the week-end:

"He (the Prime Minister) . . .

made a decision about British Guiana and laid down new principles for the British Commonwealth. You are free to have whatever Government you like as long as it is the kind of Government we like." . . .

It is necessary at this point . . . for me to say something about the Governor's reserve powers. It is all the more necessary to do so because an influential newspaper has suggested, as I think the hon. Lady did, that the Government of the Colony could have been carried on, without suspending the Constitution, by the continuing use of the Governor's reserve powers.

I think the House is entitled to ask me to explain Her Majesty's Government's view on this point. What would have happened if the Governor had attempted to carry on the present Constitution with the Ministers holding the offices from which they have been dismissed, by the continuing use of his reserve powers? Under those powers, the Governor could, in the interests of public safety, public order, or good government, act contrary to the advice of the Executive Council, provided that, except in urgent cases, he secured the Secretary of State's prior approval. Similarly he could ensure that a Bill which the Legislature had failed to pass should become law, provided that he had the approval of the Executive Council, or, failing that, of the Secretary of State. The Governor could also, in his absolute discretion, refuse his assent to any Bill.

In fact, a study of these reserve powers will show hon. Members, I believe, that they are intended to meet single and extraordinary cases, and cannot in any way be deemed suitable for carrying on day-to-day government. What would have happened had they been so continuously used? In the first place, there would have been a constant clash with Ministers, making the ordinary processes of government impossible. There would have been an ever-increasing tension and risk of disorder. But, even more important, if the Governor had attempted to carry on government by these means, they would in fact, have by-passed all the provisions of the Constitution.

I do not consider, and I choose my words with the greatest care, that it is constitutionally proper or seemly to set aside the provisions of the Constitution by continuous use of the Governor's reserve powers when there is a Parliamentary procedure by which the Constitution can be suspended . . .

I do not know of any legal or practical means by which we can force Ministers to do their job. I am on another point of the Amendment, and I claim that I am following the only responsible course which one of Her Majesty's Ministers could pursue, in laying an Order in Council before both Houses of Parliament which *de jure* suspends the Constitution, and not attempting to suspend it *de facto* by some juggling with the Governor's powers.

Mr. James Johnson (Rugby): Would the Minister be kind enough to tell the House why in the light of all this the Governor did not use his power to

dissolve the Assembly and to call for new elections?
Mr Lyttleton: That is again a very complicated question, into which I am quite prepared to enter if the hon. Gentleman really wants me to do so. (An hon. Member: "Yes") The Ministers did not advise dissolution. That is the last thing they wanted to do. Some strong reason would clearly have to be given for the Governor's dissolving the Assembly contrary to their advice. This is a very serious constitutional issue. The only reason that the Governor could have given was that it was impossible to work with the P.P.P. A statement of that kind would have meant a descent by the Governor into the political arena with a vengeance. Hon. Members have probably in mind the very severe consequences which have occurred from the use of the power of dissolution in other parts of the world, where the Governor publicly declared his support of one lot of Ministers against another.

(iii) Extracts from the British Guiana (Constitution) (Temporary Provisions) Order in Council, 1953. S.I. 1910/1953

PART I

3 (1) Save as is otherwise provided in this section, from the date of this Order the British Guiana (Constitution) Orders in Council, 1953 (g), shall have no effect unless and until Her Majesty, by Order in Council, shall otherwise provide. . . .

PART II
Executive Council

4 There shall be an Executive Council in and for the Colony which shall consist of three *ex-officio* Members and not more than seven Nominated Members.
5 *The ex-officio Members* of the Executive Council shall be the Chief Secretary, the Attorney-General and the Financial Secretary.
6 The Nominated Members of the Executive Council shall be such persons as the Governor, in pursuance of Instructions from Her Majesty through a Secretary of State, shall appoint by Instrument under the Public Seal:

Provided that, after Part IV of this Order comes into operation no person shall be appointed to be a Nominated Unofficial Member of the Council who is not a Nominated Unofficial Member of the Legislative Council.

(g) S.I. 1953/586; 1953/1478; and 1953/1564 (Footnote from the text of the Order in Council).

7 (1) Every Nominated Member of the Executive Council shall hold his seat in the Council during Her Majesty's pleasure . . .

8 (1) The Governor, acting in his discretion, may, by Instrument under the Public Seal, suspend any Nominated Member of the Executive Council from the exercise of his functions as such; and while such suspension is in force the person suspended shall not sit in or take part in the proceedings of the Executive Council.[10]

17 (1) The Governor may act in opposition to the advice given to him by the Members of the Executive Council, if he shall in any case consider it right so to do; but in any such case he shall report the matter to the Secretary of State, at the first convenient opportunity, with the reasons for his action.

(2) Whenever the Governor shall so act against the advice of the Executive Council it shall be competent to any Member to require that there be recorded upon the minutes any advice or opinion he may give upon the question with the reasons therefor.

18 The Governor shall alone be entitled to submit questions to the Executive Council, but if the Governor shall decline to submit any question to the Council when requested in writing by any Member so to do, it shall be competent to such member to require that there be recorded upon the minutes his written application, together with the answer returned by the Governor thereto . . .

20 The Governor, acting in his discretion, may, by directions in writing –

(a) charge any Member of the Executive Council with the responsibility for any Department or subject; and

(b) revoke or vary any directions given under this section . . .

22 If the public officer who is for the time being head of any Department shall, on any question relating to the administration of the Department, disagree with the Member of the Executive Council who is charged with the responsibility for the Department, then –

(a) the said officer may submit to the Member a statement in writing of his reasons for disagreeing with the Member and of his own recommendations on the question at issue;

(b) The Member shall send to the Governor's Secretary and Clerk to the Executive Council a copy of such statement together with any written statement which he himself may wish to make on the question at issue; and

10 Such suspension had to be reported to the Secretary of State for the Colonies and could, of course, be removed by Her Majesty on the advice of the Secretary of State.

(c) the question shall be considered at a meeting of the Executive Council and shall be disposed of as the Governor may direct . . .

PART III

Legislation enacted by the Governor

25 (1) Subject to the provisions of this Order, it shall be lawful for the Governor to make laws for the peace, order and good government of the Colony . . .

26 Subject to the provisions of this Order, the Governor shall, in the making of laws, conform as nearly as may be to the directions contained in any Instructions under Her Majesty's Sign Manual and Signet which may from time to time be addressed to the Governor in that behalf.

27 (1) Any law made by the Governor under the provisions of this Order may be disallowed by Her Majesty through a Secretary of State . . .

PART IV

Legislative Council

28 There shall be a Legislative Council in and for the Colony, which shall consist of a Speaker, three *ex-officio* Members and not more than twenty-four Nominated Members.

29 (1) The Speaker shall be a person who is not an *ex-officio* or Nominated Member of the Legislative Council and who does not hold any office of emolument under the Crown; and he shall be appointed by the Governor, acting in his discretion, by Instrument under the Public Seal.

(2) The Speaker shall hold office during Her Majesty's pleasure . . .

30 The *ex-officio* Members of the Legislative Council shall be the Chief Secretary, the Attorney-General and the Financial Secretary.

31 (1) The Nominated Members of the Council shall be such persons, qualified in accordance with the provisions of this Order, as the Governor, acting in his discretion, shall appoint by Instrument under the Public Seal.

(2) The Governor shall, without delay, report to Her Majesty, through a Secretary of State, every appointment of any person as a Nominated Member of the Council.

32 Subject to the provisions of section 33 of this Order, any person who is a British subject of the age of twenty-one years or upwards shall be qualified to be appointed a Nominated Member of the Legislative Council, and no other person shall be qualified to be so appointed or, having been so appointed, shall sit or vote in the Council.

33 No person shall be qualified to be appointed a Nominated Member of the Legislative Council, or, having been appointed thereto, shall sit or vote in the Council, who at the time of appointment –

(a) is by virtue of his own act, under any acknowledgement of allegiance, obedience or adherence to a foreign Power or State; or
(b) holds the office of Speaker; or
(c) is an undischarged bankrupt, having been adjudged or otherwise declared bankrupt under any law in force in any part of Her Majesty's dominions; or
(d) is a person adjudged to be of unsound mind or detained as a criminal lunatic under any law in force in the Colony; or
(e) has been sentenced in any part of Her Majesty's dominions to death or to imprisonment (by whatever name called) for a term exceeding twelve months, and has not either suffered punishment to which he was sentenced or such other punishment as may, by competent authority have been substituted therefor, or received a free pardon; or
(f) as, in the case of a Nominated Unofficial Member, a party to, or a partner in a firm or director or manager of a company, which is a party to, any contract with the Government of the Colony for or on account of the public service, and has not disclosed to the Governor the nature of such contract and his interest, or the interest of any such firm or company, therein.

34 (1) Every Nominated Member of the Legislative Council shall hold his seat in the Council during Her Majesty's Pleasure.

PART V

Legislation and procedure in Legislative Council

41 Subject to the provisions of this Order, it shall be lawful for the Governor, with the advice and consent of the Legislative Council, to make laws for the peace, order, and good government of the Colony.

42 Subject to the provisions of this Order, the Governor and the Council shall, in the transaction of business and the making of laws, conform as nearly as may be to the directions contained in any Instructions under Her Majesty's Sign Manual and Signet which may from time to time be addressed to the Governor in that behalf . . . .

44 The Governor may address the Legislative Council at any time while it is in session after giving previous notice to the Speaker or other Member presiding . . . .

Appendix A

(iv) Extracts from the Royal Instructions to the Governor of British Guiana, dated 22nd December, 1953. (Instruments, Not S.I., Appendix to S.I./1953.)

10 The Governor shall not, without having previously obtained Our Instructions through a Secretary of State, enact any Ordinance within any of the following classes, unless such Ordinance shall contain a clause suspending the operation thereof until the signification of Our pleasure thereon, that is to say –

(a) any Ordinance for the divorce of married persons;
(b) any Ordinance whereby any grant of land or money or other donation may be made to himself;
(c) any Ordinance affecting the currency of the Colony or relating to the issue of bank notes;
(d) any Ordinance establishing any banking association or amending the constitution, powers or privileges of any banking association;
(e) any Ordinance imposing differential duties;
(f) any Ordinance the provisions of which shall appear to him to be inconsistent with obligations imposed upon Us by treaty;
(g) any Ordinance the provisions of which shall appear to him to be likely to be harmful or unfair to the Amerindians;
(h) any Ordinance whereby persons of any racial or religious community may be subjected or made liable to any disabilities or restrictions to which persons of other such communities are not subjected or made liable or may be granted advantages which are not enjoyed by persons of other such communities;
(j) any Ordinance affecting the discipline or control of Our naval, military or air forces;
(k) any Ordinance of an extraordinary nature and importance whereby Our prerogative, or the rights or property of Our subjects not residing in the Colony, or the trade or transport or communications of any part of Our dominions may be prejudiced.
(l) any Ordinance containing provisions which have been disallowed by Us:

Provided that the Governor may, without such instructions, as aforesaid and although the Ordinance contains no such clause as aforesaid, enact any Ordinance falling within any of the clauses described in his clause (except an Ordinance with any obligations imposed upon Us by reaty), if he shall have satisfied himself that an urgent necessity exists equiring that the Ordinance be brought into immediate operation; but in any uch case he shall forthwith transmit to Us the Ordinance which he shall have nacted together with his reasons for so enacting it.

11 The Governor shall not, without having previously obtained Our instructions through a Secretary of State, assent to any Bill within any of the following classes, unless such Bill shall contain a clause suspending the operation thereof until the signification of Our pleasure thereon.[11] . . .
13 When any Ordinance shall have been enacted, the Governor shall forthwith transmit to Us, through a Secretary of State, for the signification of Our pleasure, a transcript in duplicate of the Ordinance, duly authenticated under the Public Seal of the Colony and by his own signature, together with an explanation of the reasons and occasion for the enactment of the Ordinance . . . .

(v) Extracts from the Report of the British Guiana Constitutional Commission, 1954.[12] *(Cmnd. 9274/1954.)*

CHAPTER 1
IV CONCLUSION

61 To sum up, in trying to convey a general picture of the present position in British Guiana, as we have seen it during our enquiries, we cannot but stress as main features the difficult and unpromising nature of the country: the undoubted dissatisfaction and "frustration" of the people generally at their social and economic environment: and their strong desire to speedy changes and improvements. We must couple with this the past attempts, some successful and some unsuccessful, to develop the country and to safeguard its assets. We were impressed by the friendliness and cheerfulness of people we met, but also by their naiveté and lack of appreciation of the economic realities of the situation . . . .

11 The classes of Bills from which the Governor should withhold his assent, and the procedure to be followed where he felt that the need to assent was urgent, were the same as in the case of his non-enactment of Ordinances.
12 The Commission was boycotted by the P.P.P. – although some sympathisers did give evidence. In paragraph 5 of the Report the commissioners rejected the P.P.P.'s given reasons for the boycott and assumed that the leadership of the party feared the embarrassment they would be caused by having to answer questions. The P.P.P.'s reasons for the boycott were that the terms of reference of the commission virtually committed it to some curtailment of the Constitution, and that the commission was not likely to give an impartial report, given its membership.

CHAPTER 2
THE WADDINGTON CONSTITUTION

63 Before we come to our examination of the events which led to the suspension of the 1953 Constitution we propose to describe its main features and to consider whether it might reasonably have been held by the People's Progressive Party, fresh from success at the polls, to place undue restrictions upon the fulfilment of the policies for which it stood. . . .

67 These powers (the executive powers available under the Constitution) reposed essentially in the Executive Council which comprised a majority of elected ministers. The Governor was bound, in the normal exercise of his duties, to consult with the Council and to act in accordance with its advice, and the Constitution provided that it should be the "principal instrument of policy". The Council was thus the forum in which policy and all matters of importance in the executive and legislative fields were discussed and settled. The P.P.P., having a clear majority in the House of Assembly, was able to elect six of its number to the ministerial posts in the Council and to dominate its proceedings. The three official members and the Minister without Portfolio chosen by the State Council could, of course, seek to influence matters in discussion, but their advice could be ignored by the elected Ministers who by their voting strength could decide every issue as they wished. In executive matters such decisions were final and, as we shall see, the enactment of any legislative measure decided upon in Council could be checked finally only by the interposition of the Governor's veto after passage through both houses. Thus, unless the Governor used the powers reserved to him, the Ministers were in control of the effective policy-making body and were virtually the Government. Under the Constitution Ministers could be removed from the Executive Council only by resolution of the Council itself upon the proposal of the Governor[13] or by resolution of the House of Assembly supported by at least two-thirds of the members. The elected Ministers were, therefore, in an impregnable position so long as party solidarity continued.

13 This is the view upon which Her Majesty's Government acted and to which they adhered in the debate in the House of Commons on the 7th December, 1953, when some Members suggested that under Section 11 of the British Guiana Constitution Order in Council, 1953, the Governor could have removed a Member of the Executive Council at his discretion without the approval of the Council. In any case, even if the Governor had been able to remove a Minister, the House of Assembly acting in accordance with Section 12 of the Order in Council could at once have re-elected him. (Footnote in text of Report).

68 The allocation of Portfolios to the Ministers (and their withdrawal) was a matter for the Governor in his discretion, but in fact Dr. Jagan, the Leader of the House, was consulted beforehand. It follows from the previous paragraph that Ministers could secure the endorsement of the Executive Council for such policies as they proposed for the departments under their charge. Their power to secure the observance of any directions they might give to the heads of departments for the execution of their policies was circumscribed only by the provision in the Constitution which laid down that any disagreement between a Minister and a head of department should be considered in Executive Council and disposed of as the Governor might direct. No such disagreement was referred to the Executive Council.

69 It was true that a number of important departments and subjects were the responsibility of the three official members and thus not susceptible to day-to-day control by the elected Ministers. These subjects were not however "reserved" in the constitutional sense; that is to say, they were not the exclusive responsibility of the official members, or subject to special control by the Governor – except that control of the Public Service was vested in the Governor, acting in his discretion. It appeared from what happened that matters affecting official members' portfolios could be raised by elected Ministers, discussed and decided as they wished. For example, although immigration and internal security were the responsibility of the Chief Secretary, the P.P.P. Ministers insisted on the removal of the ban on the entry into the Colony of certain well-known West Indian communists.

70 In the Legislature it was provided, as the Waddington Commission had recommended, that the elective chamber – the House of Assembly – should have the primacy. Here, as we have seen, the P.P.P. had control by virtue of its majority and the elected Ministers could rely on the passage by the House of such legislation as they might introduce in pursuance of decisions reached in Executive Council. The presence in the House of the three *ex-officio* members, and the appointment by the Governor in his discretion of a Speaker from outside it, were objected to by the Party but cannot properly be said to have constituted an impediment to its will.[14]

71 It was true that the State Council could impose some check on measures coming forward from the lower house. This is, however, the normal and proper function of the upper house in any bi-cameral legislature and is not peculiar to colonial constitutions. The delaying powers of the State Council were in fact no greater than those usually accorded to the upper chamber of a

14 At the same time an appointed Speaker and *ex-officio* members would be intolerable in any really independent, democratic legislature.

bi-cameral legislature in a fully developed democratic community.[15] Moreover, no money bill could be originated in the State Council, and the Council could not proceed upon any measure affecting public funds without the consent of the Governor, who in this matter was constitutionally bound to consult with the Executive Council.

72 The provision in the Constitution whereby the Governor in his discretion could summon joint sessions of both houses to consider measures of major concern which had been passed by one chamber but rejected by the other was not used. It is clear, however, that it could have imposed no check on the P.P.P. so far as votes go, since, with the assistance of its two nominees in the State Council, it would have commanded a majority in joint session. Indeed, the device would have operated to the Party's advantage since in joint session it could have insisted upon the passage of any measure which had been rejected by the State Council and thus have obviated the delay of three months or a year which might otherwise have been imposed. There can be no doubt that the P.P.P. Ministers would have pressed the Governor very strongly to summon a joint session to consider any important Government measure rejected by the State Council, and on crucial issues his refusal to do so would probably have precipitated a constitutional crisis.

73 In the above examination of the Constitution we have not thought it necessary to refer at each point to the powers reserved to the Governor, in both the executive and legislative fields, and the overriding powers of the Crown. These powers admittedly incompatible with fully responsible self-government are nevertheless necessary so long as that goal has still to be reached and ultimate responsibility for the welfare of a territory and its people remains with Her Majesty's Government. In point of fact in British Guiana during the period up to the suspension of the Constitution no recourse was made to the Governor's reserved powers and there can, therefore, be no suggestion that the P.P.P. was goaded by their use into extreme paths.

74 On close examination of the Constitution, therefore, we do not find its provisions, taken singly or in combination, irksome or such as would in practice render them unworkable. "Checks and balances" – a much over-worked phase in British Guiana – were certainly included in it, but none of these were in themselves so severe as to prevent a party, which was prepared to work the Constitution constructively, from carrying out a programme of radical social reform . . . .

15 The State Council's powers were rather in excess of those of the House of Lords at the time.

CHAPTER 3
THE ELECTIONS

82 With regard to the method of election, it was held by many witnesses that the system whereby a party supported by 51 per cent, of those who actually voted, and by only 37 per cent of the whole electorate, obtained 75 per cent of the seats in the House of Assembly was far from satisfactory, and it was suggested that some form of proportional representation should be adopted in future. We would not pretend to have studied in any detail the many different electoral systems which exist elsewhere, such as the second ballot, the alternative vote and the various forms of proportional representation. The merits and demerits of these systems may be argued extensively on both theoretical and practical grounds. So far as we are aware, however, until the 1953 elections there was no substantial body of opinion in British Guiana in favour of a change in the present system – of the simple election of a single member for each constituency – on the ground that that system is unsuited to the circumstances of the country; and we ourselves would hesitate to support a proposal based on an assumption of that kind. Certainly no convincing case for a change can be argued from the results of a single general election and if some system of proportional representation were not introduced it could hardly be represented as other than a device to mitigate the present dominance of the P.P.P. To enshrine in the constitution such a device would in our view be wrong and we, therefore, recommend no change in the present electoral system . . . .

CHAPTER 4
THE PUBLIC SERVICE

148 Until 1953 there had been no ministerial system in British Guiana and the administrative functions of government had been carried out under the Governor alone. We do not think that the introduction of a ministerial system into the organisation and the development of ministerial responsibility and initiatives for policy could have been affected even in the most favourable circumstances without some friction and disorganisation.

149 The British conception of the Civil Service as a body of state officials outside politics, carrying out the policy decided by political ministers, but themselves free of all political influences, is obviously an ideal to be arrived at rather than a conclusion which can be automatically achieved. In order to assist the Colonial territories in working towards this ideal, it has become customary to appoint a Public Service Commission in each territory to ensure against political influence in appointments, promotions, dismissals and discipline in the Public Service. In British Guiana the Constitutional Order in

Council of the 1st April, 1953, gave the Governor discretionary powers in all matters concerning the Public Service and set up a Public Service Commission to advise him on them.[16]

150 This provision was the subject of sustained criticisms by the elected Ministers who saw in it a formidable brake upon their power and attacked it publicly. Mr. King (Minister of Communications and Works) in "Thunder" (May issue, 1953) advocated "agitation for ultimate democratic control of the Public Service"; Mr. Martin Carter (a P.P.P. Executive Committee member), writing in the June issue of the same periodical, said:

> "This Public Service Commission is nothing but the body which controls the State. This Public Service Commission is not controlled by the representatives of the people . . . . Although the P.P.P. has won the majority of the seats at the last General Election, and, allegedly controls the Government yet staff and state power still remain in the hands of those who have ruled us for centuries",

and Dr. Jagan in a speech on the 26th July, said:

> "They have appointed a Civil Service Commission because they do not want us to have anything to do with the appointment of civil servants. We would like to have power to appoint our own people, who would be able to do our work."

151 It is clear to us that the P.P.P. Ministers either intentionally or in ignorance quite failed to appreciate the purpose of the Commission and had they remained longer in power, these threats against the Public Service Commission would have become more insistent. Indeed the Ministers had made clear their intention of refusing to vote the necessary financial provision.

152 It may well be that some senior officials were unsympathetic to the policies of the Party and there is no doubt that the Ministers genuinely suspected the loyalty of some officials working in close association with them.[17] In the atmosphere of mutual suspicion which arose in the Executive Council between the *ex-officio* Ministers and the elected Ministers it became impossible for what otherwise would have been treated as ordinary staff difficulties to be adjusted in friendly discussion between the Chief Secretary and the individual Minister concerned. The Chief Secretary and Heads of Departments were suspicious of the interest which P.P.P. Ministers were showing in civil service matters and of the reason why they did not always work through the proper departmental channels. The P.P.P. Ministers were

16 Note that this Public Service Commission was not exercising independent powers.

17 The seriousness of these charges against the Civil Service, completely undermining the British idea of loyal service to elected ministers, irrespective of political affiliation, seems to have escaped the Commission.

inclined to take action without any departmental consultation, and indeed we had evidence of occasions when they completely ignored the heads of departments or without their knowledge took junior officials into consultation on matters of departmental policy. The Minister of Education, for example, decided, and announced his intention, to abolish the system of dual control of denominational schools without prior consultation or discussion with the Director of Education, and the Minister of Labour gave the Commissioner of Labour only a few hours notice of his intention to introduce the Labour Relations Bill in the Executive Council.

MAIN ISSUES WHICH AROSE

Payment of Salaries to Members of the State Council

153 The Waddington Commission had recommended that members of the State Council should not receive salaries as such but only expenses. As against this the former Governor, in his comments on the Waddington Report, had said that members of the State Council should be renumerated on the same scale as members of the House of Assembly. The Secretary of State for the Colonies (then Mr. James Griffiths) had agreed with the former Governor's view. The previous Legislative Council had accordingly voted a sufficient sum in the 1953 Estimates to cover payment of salaries to members of both Houses, but since no specific authority for the payment had been included in the Constitution Order in Council it was necessary for special legislation to be enacted by the new Legislature. In this way the issue came up for decision. In the Executive Council the Minister without Portfolio urged that salaries should be paid to State Council members (of which he was one, though as Minister he was not financially affected by the proposal), but the P.P.P. Ministers would not agree to this. Their views were sustained by the Executive Council, and the Minister without Portfolio was alone in dissenting from the proposal not to include provision for the payment of salaries to State Council members in a Bill dealing with the payment of remuneration and subsistence allowances, etc. to members of the legislative bodies.

154 When this Bill came before the House of Assembly the three official Ministers voted with the P.P.P. majority. The State Council never dealt with the Bill as such: it did, however, debate a motion moved by the Minister without Portfolio, who was also President of the Council, recommending that Government should introduce legislation authorising the payment of remuneration to State Councillors on the same scale as Members of the House of Assembly.[18]

18 This would be regarded as a serious breach of collective responsibility in the British system.

Undesirable Publications (Prohibition of Importation) (Repeal) Bill

161 The old Legislative Council had passed a law which enabled the Governor-in-Council, i.e. the Executive Council, to forbid the importation into British Guiana of any literature which the Governor in Council declared to be undesirable. This measure had arisen from a motion in the old Council, moved by Mr. Lionel Luckhoo who had been worried at the extent to which communist literature imported by the P.P.P. was being circulated in British Guiana.

162 The measure obviously was directed against that type of literature, and there was no doubt in anybody's mind that the P.P.P. leaders would do away with this law once they had power to do so. Repeal as such was hardly an urgent and immediate necessity on practical grounds since the P.P.P. majority in the Executive Council could quite simply refuse to operate the measure or could decide that it would operate as they wished. Nevertheless the P.P.P. Ministers decided on immediate and formal repeal of the law, and there was no opposition from the official Ministers when the proposal was brought before the Executive Council. In the repeal Bill that was introduced the P.P.P. Ministers included a clause to the effect that certain acts declared valid by a section in the original law were now declared never to have been validated. The acts in question were those of the Comptroller of Customs in confiscating certain literature which Dr. Jagan had attempted to bring into the colony before the law was passed and which the Comptroller had confiscated on the grounds that Dr. Jagan had not declared the literature to the customs as he ought to have done. Apparently there was some doubt as to whether the confiscation had been legally justified and the old legislature therefore included a section in the original Ordinance validating the Comptroller's action. The object of the particular clause inserted in the repeal Bill by the P.P.P. Ministers was to remove the immunity, or rather to declare that the Comptroller had never had the immunity, which the original measure had sought to provide. The *ex-officio* Ministers did not oppose the Bill. They had no enthusiasm for it and said so, but they were not prepared to oppose it. The Attorney-General did, however, say that the particular clause to which we have referred was constitutionally and legally improper. Mr. Burnham, who is a lawyer, refused to accept this view and it may be that this incident is held by the P.P.P. Ministers to be an example of an attempt by an *ex-officio* Minister to mislead them. They insisted on retaining the clause in the Bill and it was for the reason that this particular clause was objectionable in law that the *ex-officio* Ministers voted for a motion in the Assembly to delete it. They did not vote against the other clauses of the Bill.[19]

19 This is another breach of collective responsibility pointing to the difficulty, if not the impossibility, of abiding by the conventions of Cabinet government where the Executive Council is mixed in its membership.

163 The Bill came before the State Council on the 10th August. Though on the second reading some members of the Council indicated their dislike of the Bill's intentions they also said that they did not propose to vote against the Bill as a whole. The Archbishop of the West Indies, a nominated Member, expressed his keen support of the Bill's intention. When the Council resolved itself into Committee a motion was made to amend the Bill by deletion of the clause relating to the action of the Comptroller of Customs, on the ground that it was legally and constitutionally improper. When this amendment was put to the vote it was agreed to without a division and the Bill, as amended, was read a third time and passed. When the Bill was returned to the House of Assembly the P.P.P. majority refused to accept this amendment, despite the fact that it did not defeat their ostensible object of repealing the Ordinance. They preferred to use the State Council's amendment as evidence of conflict between the two chambers.

Rice Farmers (Security of Tenure) (Amendment) Bill

164 A situation very similar to that which developed in connection with the Undesirable Publications (Repeal) Bill arose about the Rice Farmers (Security of Tenure) (Amendment) Bill. For some years there had been in force a law designed to give security of tenure to rice farmers and to prevent the landlords of rice farms from increasing rents. Even before the elections it had been recognised that this measure was inadequate and out-of-date and indeed a Committee had been set up by the old Legislature to go into the whole question of security of tenure for rice farmers. Dr. Jagan was a member of this Committee until his appointment as a Minister. Without waiting for the Committee's report and without any consultation with the Rice Producers' Association the P.P.P. Ministers decided to introduce to the legislature a bill to amend the old measure in certain respects. According to the P.P.P. Ministers the need for an immediate amendment to use the law was made urgent during August by a prolonged drought; and so far as we know, there was no opposition in the Executive Council to a proposal to make an immediate amendment to the existing law without waiting for a full-scale review in the light of the Committee's report.

165 The P.P.P. Ministers wanted to include in the amending Bill authority for a District Commissioner to enter upon rice lands and to order the landlord to make improvements, failing which the District Commissioner was himself to see that improvements were made as he thought necessary. The object of this clause was ostensibly to enable District Commissioners to take immediate steps to get landlord's irrigation ditches cleaned so that water could flow freely to the rice fields. The Ministers also proposed to include in the bill a provision that the costs due from the landlord in respect of work done under the directions of the District Commissioner should be recoverable if necessary by

a procedure known as "parate execution". This swift and drastic procedure, a remnant in British Guiana of the Roman Dutch system and unknown to English Law, is one whereby on a certificate by a public officer that money is due to the Government the Court issues summary execution against the property of the debtor, which may then be sold to discharge the debt.

166 Though the official Ministers did not oppose the general intention of the P.P.P. Ministers to introduce a bill they did object to the clause giving authority to District Commissioners to decide what work was necessary and, on the failure of the landlord to do the work, to carry it out themselves and finally to the adoption of the procedure known as "parate execution" if the landlord failed to meet the cost. It was for these reasons that they opposed the bill in the Executive Council and that subsequently in the House of Assembly the Attorney-General spoke against the provision for parate execution. The clause to which the official Ministers objected undoubtedly conferred wide and arbitrary powers on the Minister and his officials, and it is clear that drought was not the only or even the principal reason why this particular clause was retained in the measure because by the time the bill came up for consideration in the State Council the drought was at an end. *Anyone knowing the P.P.P. Ministers and realising the possible implications of various provisions in this bill was bound to wonder what were the real objectives of the measure.*[20] As introduced, and as passed by the P.P.P. majority in the House of Assembly, it could have been used by a Minister unreasonably to dispossess landlords of rice-lands. Even so the *ex-officio* Ministers voted with the Majority Party for the second reading of the Bill as a whole, and when the sub-clauses to which they had objections came up for discussion during the committee stage they abstained from voting. We cannot, therefore, see in the attitude of the official Ministers towards this measure any evidence of political hostility; rather does it seem to us that in endeavouring in the Executive Council to guide the P.P.P. Ministers in these directions they were doing exactly what they were intended to do, i.e. to try to stop the inexperienced elected Ministers from making serious blunders.

167 The Bill as passed by the House of Assembly was brought before the State Council on the 21st September. The President of the Council moved that it be read a first time and after a short discussion further debate was deferred to the 23rd September in order to enable the Rice Producers' Association to make representations as to the amendments that the Association would wish to be made to the Bill. During the debate on the second reading the bill was heavily criticised by several members of the State Council, on account of the provisions in the Bill enabling District Commissioners to undertake work on rice lands and to recover the costs by

20 Italics added.

the method of parate execution. Furthermore it was acknowledged by the P.P.P. representatives in the State Council that by this time the drought which had been given as the main justification for the Bill had passed. On the second reading the Bill was rejected by six votes to two, only the P.P.P. Members voting for the Bill.

Trades Disputes (Essential Services) (Repeal) Bill

168 The official Ministers opposed in the Executive Council the proposal of the P.P.P. Ministers to repeal a law passed by a previous legislature during the war restricting the right of workers engaged in essential services to come out to strike. The P.P.P. Ministers argued that this law was exclusively concerned with the war-time emergency and that it was therefore redundant and offensive in peace-time. The official Ministers would not have disagreed with proposals designed to amend the law and to bring it more into line with the post-war situation, but they thought that its simple repeal would be going too far. Clearly the *ex-officio* Ministers had in mind the need for a measure substantially like that in effect in Great Britain where the workers in specified public services such as gas, water, sanitation and so on, are required to give 10 days' notice before coming out on strike. We have no doubt that the official Ministers were the more inclined to maintain this view by reason of the situation which had developed in the colony during the months of August and September as a consequence of the dispute on the sugar estates. But we do not see in that evidence of political hostility to the P.P.P. Rather did the Bill provide evidence of the recklessness of the P.P.P. Ministers. The attitude of the official Ministers is to us evidence only of their determination to do their duty as responsible officials and members of the Executive Council even in the face of the tremendous pressure that was being exerted upon them in the Executive Council and in public at that time.[21] The Bill was introduced and read a first time in the House of Assembly but no further action was taken on it before the suspension of the Constitution.

Labour Relations Bill

169 In July, 1952, Dr. Jagan tabled a motion in the old Legislative Council calling attention to a "multiplicity of trade unions and in recent years an increase in the incidence of jurisdictional disputes among trade unions" in British Guiana and inviting the Legislative Council to recommend the then Government to enact legislation similar to that in force in the U.S.A. and in Canada for the avoidance of such disputes. The motion was not carried and the P.P.P. election manifesto spoke of the intention of the Party, if elected, to

21 This might well be, but it also illustrates that the Executive Council was not a political collectivity and therefore could not operate as such.

adopt legislation based upon the American Labour Relations Act to require employers to recognise and to bargain with trade unions "which have the confidence of the majority of workers in an industry or service". The P.P.P. Ministers point to these facts as proof of a long standing intention and as evidence that their decision to introduce a Labour Relations Bill and to have the Bill carried through all its stages in the House of Assembly in one day, was not made in retaliation on the sugar producers for the failure of the strike on the sugar estates, or in a determination to exploit the opportunity offered to them by the excitement and the antagonisms created by the strike and its collapse to make an immediate and serious issue of their constitutional conflict with the Governor, the *ex-officio* Ministers and the State Council.
170 It is, therefore, necessary for us to describe the nature of the inter-union disputes which lay behind the strike on the sugar estates, and which are put forward by the P.P.P. as the main reason for the Labour Relations Bill, before we deal with the contents of the Bill and with the manner in which it was hurried through the Executive Council and introduced to the House of Assembly on the 24th September.[22]

185 Though supposed to have been based upon the U.S. Labor Relations Act the Bill as passed by the House of Assembly bears hardly any resemblance to that Act. Trade unions in Great Britain would find the Bill objectionable in principle, and the trade unions of any democratic country would find most of its details totally unacceptable. For example, the Bill specifically empowers the Minister to decide in his unfettered discretion who shall be classed as a worker for the purpose of taking part in a ballot in any "industry, trade, or undertaking". The Bill does not specifically define an "industry, trade or undertaking" but authorises the Minister to make regulations "prescribing the manner of holding any ballot . . . and generally for the due carrying out" of the Bill's provisions. In other words the Act would have enabled the Minister to decide by himself whether any particular ballot should cover a whole industry or service or merely a section of it or simply a single undertaking or only a part of an undertaking, and to decide also whether all the separate categories of workers in any particular industry, etc. should be lumped together for the purpose of the ballot or should vote strictly according to some division related to craft or status as determined by him. Any trade unionist will see at once that with such powers a Minister would be able, if he was so minded, to ensure in the great majority of cases that the result of a

22 In paragraph 174 the Report states that the recognised union, the M.P.C.A., was weak and inefficient and that it had "accepted money from sugar companies for some special purpose". And further, in paragraph 181 the Report gives evidence that the G.I.W.U. could paralyse the sugar industry.

ballot was a foregone conclusion. Again, the Bill provides for the appointment *by the Minister*[23] of *ad hoc* committees to consider applications from trade unions or employers for an enquiry to be held under its provisions. But, in addition to the power of the Minister to select the members of the committees, the Bill also empowers him to dispense with a committee in any particular case and without a formal enquiry to direct that a ballot shall be taken . . .

198 . . . We were given direct evidence of several instances of stone throwing and of steps taken by shopkeepers to protect their property. Moreover it is impossible to discount the evidence of witnesses who told [*sic*] us of ugly incidents in which they themselves had been concerned with P.P.P. supporters and of remarks made to them or in their hearing about what would soon happen to the "whites"; all this goes to show that the general situation was deteriorating very rapidly and that it might at any time have got completely out of hand.

199 We have no doubt that the insolence shown by P.P.P. Ministers towards the Governor and the *ex-officio* Ministers had a bad effect upon the general position in the colony. Whatever the real intentions of the P.P.P leaders, if they did not deliberately incite the people to violence they were certainly not willing to go out of their way to discourage violence if it should develop more or less spontaneously. In our view it had become necessary to resolve the impossible position that had developed in the Executive Council, to put an end to the general anxiety and uncertainty in the Colony and in one way or another to remove the distinct danger of real trouble. The question as to whether this could have been done by measures short of suspension of the Constitution is one that was fully debated in the British House of Commons. Insofar as the answer to the question involves consideration of the various powers open to the Governor under the Constitution Order in Council, we do not think that we can add much to the Commons' debate. What we can say is that the fear of violence was real enough, that the Executive Council had come nowhere near to fulfiling its constitutional role and that if there was no certain way of resolving the situation short of suspension of the Constitution, then there was no option but to suspend the Constitution . . . .

231 We are, therefore, driven to the conclusion that so long as the P.P.P. retains its present leadership and policies there is no way in which any real measure of responsible government can be restored without the certainty that the country will again be subjected to constitutional crisis.

23 Italics in the original.

(vi) The Statement by the Secretary of State for the Colonies on British Guiana (Constitution, Amendment) on 25th April 1956. (Parliamentary Debates (Commons) Vol. 551, 1956, cc. 1779-80.)

Briefly, there will be a Legislative Council of twelve elected members, four officials, and not more than eight nominated members.[24] The Executive Council under the Governor will normally consist of four officials, one nominated and five elected members of the Legislative Council.

Preparations will be put in hand forthwith for the necessary amendments to the Constitution and for setting up the election machinery. The Governor will settle a suitable date for the elections. This will probably be some time next year but may have to be even later.

Her Majesty's Government hope that this substantial step forward will encourage healthy political development and enable experience to be gained upon which further progress can be based. Until more of the people understand the dangers of Communist leadership which could only bring a second collapse like that of 1953, we cannot run the risk of restoring the type of constitution which was suspended.

Meanwhile, the development programme will be pushed ahead, and whatever is necessary will be done to prevent counter activities promoted by a handful of Communist-trained agents, who are causing interruption of constitutional progress.[25]

(vii) Extracts from the British Guiana (Constitution) (Temporary Provision) (Amendment) Order in Council, 1956. (S.I. 2030/1956.)

9 (1) Section 28 of the Principal Order[26] is hereby revoked and the following Section is substituted therefor –

28 (1) There shall be a Legislative Council in and for the Colony, which, subject to the provisions of this Order, shall consist of a Speaker, three *ex-officio* members and not more than twenty-five other members, being either Nominated Members, or, if it is so prescribed by any Proclamation for the time being having effect under subsection (2) of this section, being not more

24 See next document for the actual composition, although numbers were increased the principle of balance was maintained.

25 The P.P.P. did win a majority of seats but this time had split into the P.P.P. led by Dr. Jagan, largely Indian supported, and the P.N.C. led by Mr. Burnham, largely Afro-Guyanese supported.

26 That is the British Guiana (Constitution) (Temporary Provisions) Order in Council, 1953. S.I. 1910/1953.

than eleven Nominated Members and not less than fourteen Elected Members.[27]

(2) If Her Majesty shall so direct by instructions given through a Secretary of State, the Governor acting in his discretion by Proclamation published in the Gazette shall, in pursuance of subsection (1) of this section, prescribe, with effect from any dissolution of the Council under section 55 of this Order, the number of Nominated and Elected Members to be comprised in the Legislative Council in accordance with such instructions; and any such Proclamation may be amended or revoked in like manner by the Governor, in pursuance of instructions given as aforesaid, with effect from any subsequent dissolution of the Council.

(3) The Governor, acting in his discretion, may, by Proclamation published in the Gazette, make provision for the establishment of electoral districts (by whatever name called) for the purpose of returning Elected Members to the Legislative Council, and the division of electoral districts for any purpose connected with elections; and any such Proclamation may be amended or revoked in like manner by the Governor.

9 (2) The Governor, acting in his discretion, shall prescribe by Proclamation made under section 28 of the principal Order, as amended by subsection (1) of this section, that with effect from the first dissolution of the Council after the commencement of this Order, there shall be in the Legislative Council eleven Nominated Members and fourteen Elected Members, and accordingly in their application to the making of that Proclamation the provisions of that subsection shall have effect as if the references therein to instructions given by Her Majesty through a Secretary of State were deleted.

27 In the event the Governor did make provision for fourteen elected members, and in the newly constituted Legislative Council of 1957 he only appointed six nominated members. This left the elected members in the majority but the P.P.P. in an overall minority.

The composition of the Council after the general elections was as follows: Speaker, three *ex-officio* members, six nominated members, and fou elected members (9 P.P.P., 3 P.N.C., 1 United Democratic Party, 1 National Labour Front).

APPENDIX B

THE SUSPENSION OF THE CONSTITUTION OF GRENADA 1962

(i) Statement by the Secretary of State for the Colonies on the Situation in Grenada, 26th June, 1962.
(Parliamentary Debates (Commons) Vol. 661, 1962. cc. 947–49.)

Mr. Maudling: I am circulating in the OFFICIAL REPORT a statement issued by the Colonial Office on the 18th June.

I have taken this action with very great regret and only because the Chief Minister of Grenada left me with no alternative. Not only did he do all in his power to prevent the inquiry being held: but his comments on the Report also showed that he completely failed to appreciate the seriousness of its findings. The only conclusion I could draw, therefore, was that if he remained in office under the constitution then in force, the same financial malpractices and the same threats against the Civil Service would continue. This is a situation which I cannot accept as long as I am responsible for good government in Grenada and for the proper expenditure of United Kingdom moneys provided for the territory.

I very much hope, however, that it will be possible to hold fresh elections in Grenada in the fairly near future and that the normal course of constitutional development can shortly be resumed . . .

Following is the statement:

The Grenada (Constitution) Order in Council, 1962, provides with effect from today, and until the next General Election is held in the territory, for the dissolution of the Legislative and Executive Councils and for the suspension of those provisions of the existing constitution relating to the Executive Council and to the functions of Ministers. During this period the Administrator will have the sole responsibility for the government of the territory. The Order in Council also provides that after the next General Election the constitution which came into effect on the 1st January, 1969 (the Grenada (Constitution) Order in Council, 1959) will be re-introduced subject to a number of changes. The main changes will be to give the Administrator wider reserved powers to act contrary to the advice of his Ministers than he possessed under the former constitution; and to empower the Administrator, acting in his discretion, to appoint an official Minister of Finance. It is hoped, subject to future developments, to arrange for a general election to be held within the reasonably near future.

The Report of the Commission of Inquiry into the Control of Public Expenditure in Grenada During 1951 and Subsequently was published as a White Paper on 22nd May, 1962 (Cmnd. 1735). This was an independent Commission, of which the Chairman was a West Indian Judge. Its main findings were as follows:–

(1) The Minister of Finance (Mr. E.M. Gairy who is also Chief Minister) had disregarded and contravened the laws and regulations governing the control of expenditure;

(2) Expenditure had been incurred wastefully or unnecessarily through failure by Ministers to seek or refusal to accept the advice of the civil servants;

(3) The Executive had deliberately destroyed the morale of the civil service by an undesirable interference with administrative duties and by improper threats against the security of office;

(4) The Civil Service had been induced by this interference and these threats to commit or condone improprieties or irregularities in the expenditure of public funds.

After considering Mr. Gairy's comments on the report, the Secretary of State has decided that firm measures must be taken to remedy the situation. As a first step the Ministers concerned will be relieved of their offices and the existing constitution will be temporarily suspended. From now and until a new general election can be held the Administrator will have the sole responsib for the Government of the territory.

It clearly will not be possible immediately after the next general election tc restore the same constitution as existed before and under which these disturbi events occurred. There must for a trial period be adequate safeguards to preve any future recurrence of the malpractices revealed by the Commission of Inquiry, in particular in regard to the expenditure of public funds. In the constitution which will take effect after the next general election, therefore, the Administrator will have a wider reserved executive power than he has possessed in the immediate past: he will be empowered to act contrary to the advice of his Ministers if he considers it necessary to do so in the interests of public order, public faith or good government. He will also be given a reserved power enabling him to ensure the enactment of legislation which the

Legislative Council has failed to pass if he considers that its enactment is necessary in the interests of public order, public faith or good government. As already stated he will also be empowered to appoint an official Minister of Finance.

On receipt of the Report, the Secretary of State found it necessary as he had already announced in Parliament, to suspend any further issues of grant-in-aid or Colonial Development and Welfare funds for the time being. Now that the necessary constitutional safeguards have been introduced to ensure that proper control is exercised over the expenditure of public money, the issue of United Kingdom funds to the territory on the normal basis will be resumed.

The Secretary of State regrets the necessity to take these measures, and he hopes that it will be possible to hold a new General Election in the island within a short time.

(ii) Extracts from the Report of the Commission of Enquiry into the Control of Public Expenditure in Grenada during 1961 and subsequently, 1962. (Cmnd. 1735/1962.)

FINANCIAL CONTROLS

17 We interpret our terms of reference into the control of public expenditure to mean an enquiry into the control of public expenditure as exercised by the executive or administrative authority having regard to the relevant substantive law, financial rules and general orders and to the financial instructions given by the Federal Government in respect of grant aided territories.

18 Our terms of reference also include enquiry into matters incidental thereto. We have avoided any enquiry which could be regarded as questioning the authority of the Legislature to appropriate funds and to direct their limits and purposes. Similarly, we were not concerned with investigating the financial or other policy of the Government which is subject to the sanction of the Legislature. Our enquiry has been directed into the supervision and management of public funds when being applied to purposes which may form part of the policy of Government . . .

CONCLUSIONS AND RECOMMENDATIONS

General conclusions

57 As a result of our enquiry we have reached the following general conclusions:—

(1) The Minister of Finance has disregarded and contravened the laws and regulations governing the control of expenditure;

(2) Expenditure has been incurred wastefully or unnecessarily through

failure by Ministers to seek or refusal to accept the advice of the civil servants;
(3) The Executive has deliberately destroyed the morale of the civil service by an undesirable interference with administrative duties and by improper threats against the security of office;
(4) The civil service has been induced by this interference and these threats to commit or condone improprieties or irregularities in the expenditure of public funds.

Discipline

58 We think it essential that the morale of the civil service should be restored and that civil servants should be permitted and encouraged to perform their proper functions without fear or favour. We therefore recommend that:–

(1) the Grenada (Constitution) Order in Council should be amended so as to provide for the appointment of members of the Public Service Commission by the Administrator acting in his discretion and not after consultation with the Chief Minister;
(2) public officers should be left in no doubt that appointment, dismissal, and all disciplinary proceedings are matters for consideration by the Public Service Commission alone and are in no way the concern of the Executive Council, and that this be made clear in regulations regarding the Public Service Commission to be made under Section 54 of the Constitution;
(3) if difficulty is experienced or anticipated in selecting from the small population of Grenada a sufficient number of Public Service Commissioners in whose impartiality public officers can feel full confidence, consideration should be given to the desirability of having a Public Service Commission in respect of senior officers which, like the Legal and Judicial Service Commission, will include persons resident outside Grenada and will have jurisdiction over Grenada and over any other territories with which Grenada is associated.

Surcharge

59 As a corollary we think that gross negligence or irregularity by public officers in the collection, custody, or payment of public funds should attract pecuniary penalties and we therefore recommend amendment of the Finance and Audit Ordinance so as to provide:–

(1) that in circumstances described in the Ordinance the Financial Secretary be required and not merely permitted to initiate proceedings for surcharge;
(2) that the initiation of such proceedings should not be dependent on a report made by the Principal Auditor;
(3) that surcharge should be levied by the Financial Secretary with the

right of appeal to the Public Service Commission; or alternatively that the irregularity etc. should be reported by the Financial Secretary to the Public Service Commissioners for decision by them with right of appeal to the Administrator acting in his discretion; and in any event that the proceedings and decisions are at no stage referred to the Executive Council or to any Minister;

(4) that if the Financial Secretary neither imposes surcharge nor reports to the Public Service Commission, as the case may be, the Principal Auditor may present the case directly to the Public Service Commissioners for consideration by them.

In our opinion surcharge is essentially a disciplinary matter and as such should not be the concern of the Executive; on the contrary, any interference by the Executive in the enforcement of discipline is an improper activity which is likely seriously to impair the efficiency of the public service.

Financial Rules

60 Certain financial irregularities have apparently been frequent for some time and we think that they denote an incomplete understanding by accounting officers of what is required of them. We therefore recommend an early revision of the Financial and Store Rules with a view to clarifying them, amending them in the light of constitutional changes, and expanding them so as to regulate procedures newly introduced. For instance, we have learned with surprise that no officer outside the Audit Department records the total amount of the expenditure authorised by special warrant in anticipation of a supplementary appropriation law, in order to ensure that it does not at any time exceed $50,000. We also consider that the machinery of control would be more easily operated if a clear distinction were drawn between a virement warrant, authorising the transfer of provision within a Head of expenditure, and a special warrant which authorises expenditure in addition to that appropriated for the Head. Accounting Officers need also to be made to understand that a decision taken in Executive Council cannot in itself convey any authority whatsoever for the incurring of expenditure.

We further recommend that consideration be given to the desirability of amending the Finance and Audit Ordinance so as to provide for giving these revised Financial Rules the force of law by some simple process such as tabling them, and any amendments to them, in the Legislative Council.

Method of Communication

61 The need to record decisions and instructions in writing might be thought too obvious to merit mention in this report but there is no doubt that Ministers and civil servants alike have failed lamentably in this respect. It becomes all the more important that there should be some written record when there is any suggestion that officers are being instructed to act contrary to regulations or

where personal relationships are strained. On many of the matters brought to our attention there has been a significant absence of anything in writing and our enquiries have been made more difficult in consequence.

Public Accounts Committee

62 We understand that a Public Accounts Committee has recently been established and we have considered whether it is likely to impose any effective check on public expenditure. We are inclined to the view that, with the present composition of the Legislative Council, its value may prove to be slight but we recommend none the less that the Standing Rules and Orders of the Legislative Council should be amended so as to provide for its constitution and conduct.

Other Matters

63 Finally, we wish to touch on two matters which may perhaps fall somewhat outside our terms of reference.

Disunity in the civil service has in our view been a potent factor in producing a state of affairs which we deplore and we have therefore interested ourselves in inquiring as to the strength and purpose of the Civil Service Association. We understand that the Association is under the vice-presidency of the Chief Minister's Principal Secretary, that its meetings are very infrequent, and that its membership is not representative of the senior ranks of Government. We think that much good would follow if the Association could be enlarged and revitalised and, while we recognise that such a revival is not likely to be lasting unless the morale of the service has first been restored by the measures which we have recommended above, we think that the Association should receive encouragement from all who are concerned to see good government in Grenada.

64 The second of these two matters concerns the periodical known as 'The Star'. We understand that the publication and free distribution of political propaganda at public expense was undertaken before the present Government came into power and we wish to record our view that such activity is always open to the strongest objections. We have not had the opportunity of seeing the previous periodical which was issued under the name of 'The Citizens' Wee but our perusal of the 'The Star' (of which extracts appear in three appendices to this report) induces us to say that it is an instrument which has been used in a manner calculated to inflict great injury on the public service. We consider that its continued publication in its present form can do nothing but harm.

(iii) Extracts from the Grenada (Constitution) Order in Council, 1962. (S.I. 1244/1962.)

2 The Legislative Council constituted at the date of commencement of this Order in accordance with the provisions of the principal Order[1] is hereby dissolved, and the provisions of the principal Order and of any other law in force in Grenada immediately before that date shall have effect as if the dissolution of the Council by virtue of this action were a dissolution of the Council under section 46(2) of the principal Order.

3(1) The Executive Council constituted at the date of commencement of this Order in accordance with the provisions of the principal Order[1] is dissolved, and, without prejudice to anything previously done thereunder and until the appointed day:–

(a) the operation of sections 12 to 21 of the principal Order is suspended.[2]

(b) the operation of subsections (1) to (5) of section 6 of the principal Order[3] and, to the extent that it requires the Administrator in the exercise of any function to act in accordance with the advice of, or after consultation with, the Executive Council or any Minister of the Government of Grenada, of any other provision of that Order or of any other law in force in Grenada is suspended; and

(c) any provision of any law in force in Grenada that confers any power or imposes any duty on any Minister of the Government of Grenada shall, subject to any modification or adaptation made under the next following subsection, be construed as if it conferred that power or imposed that duty on the Administrator . . .

4 As from the apponted day the provisions of the principal Order shall, without prejudice to anything previously done, thereunder, be amended in the manner specified in the schedule to this Order.

5 For the purposes of the two last foregoing sections 'the appointed day' means such day as the Administrator may by proclamation published in the Gazette, appoint for the purposes of those sections, which day shall not be

1 S.I. 2200/1959.

2 Sections 12 to 21 of S.I. 2200/1959 established the Executive Council and made provision for the appointment of members, their tenure of office, the appointment of the Chief Minister and the performance of the functions of that office when the office falls vacant, the appointment of temporary members of the Executive Council, the assignment of portfolios, the summoning of the Council, its procedure and the summoning of public officers to the Council.

3 The subsections set out the circumstances under which the Administrator was required to act on the advice of the Executive Council.

earlier than the day after that on which a general election of elected members of the Legislative Council is next held in accordance with the provisions of the principal Order.

THE SCHEDULE (Section 4)

Amendments to the principal Order

1 The insertion at the end of paragraph (c) of section 6(2) of the words 'and the power conferred by section 40A of this Order'.[4]

2 In section 6(4) (as modified by article 15(2) of the West Indies (Dissolution and Interim Commissioner) Order in Council 1962) the substitution for paragraphs (a) to (d) of the words 'in the interests of public order, public faith or good government (which expressions shall, without prejudice to their generality, include the responsibility of Grenada as a territory within the Commonwealth and all matters relating to the creation or abolition of any public office or to the salary or other conditions of service of any public officer)'.[5]

3 In section 12 the insertion immediately after the words 'subject to' of the words 'the next following subsection and', and the insertion immediately after subsection (1) of the following subsection:–

> '(1A) The Administrator, acting in his discretion may, by instrument under the public seal, appoint one other person, being a person who holds a public office, to be a member of the Executive Council in addition to the members aforesaid.'[6]

4 The insertion immediately after section 14(4) of the following sub-section:–

> (5) A member of the Executive Council appointed under subsection (1A) of section 12 of this Order shall vacate his office as a member if he ceases to hold a public office or if his appointment is revoked by the Administrator, acting in his discretion, by instrument under the public seal.'

4 Section 6 (2) sets out when the Administrator shall not have to obtain and ac on the advice of the Executive Council The effect of this amendment was to exclu the reserved powers of the Administrator from being exercised on advice.

5 Section 6(4), as modified, allowed the Administrator to act contrary to the advice of the Executive Council in certain circumstances. The effect of this amendment is to substitute this general clause for more specific conditions under which he could act counter to the Executive Council.

6 The effect of this amendment was to give the Administrator the discretion of adding to the Executive Council an additional nominated official member. This member, as can be seen from Section 5 of this Order, would serve as Minister of Finance. In the event the Administrator did not use his discretionai power to make this appointment.

5 In section 17(1) the insertion immediately after the words 'Provided that' of '(a)' and at the end of the proviso of the following paragraph:–

'(b) whenever there is a subsisting appointment of a member of the Executive Council under subsection 1(A) of section 12 of this Order, the Administrator, acting in his discretion, shall by directions in writing, charge that member with responsibility for finance and for any department of finance (by whatever name called) and references to the Ministers responsible for finance in any provision of this Order or of any other law in force in Grenada that confers any power or imposes any duty on that Minister shall be construed as if they were references to that member.'

6 The insertion immediately after the word 'Composition' at the beginning of Part IV of the words 'of the Legislative Council', and the substitution for section 23 of the following section:–

'23 There shall be a Legislative Council in and for Grenada constituted in accordance with the provisions of this Order.'[7]

7 In section 24 the substitution for the words and figure 'subsection (2)' in subsection (1) of the words 'the following provisions' and the insertion immediately after subsection (2) of the following subsection:–

'(3) Any person appointed to be a member of the Executive Council under subsection (1A) of section 12 of this Order shall, by virtue of being a member of the Executive Council, be a member of the Legislative Council in addition to the members aforesaid.'

8 The substitution for section 33 of the following section:–

'33 Subject to the provisions of this Order, it shall be lawful for the Administrator, with the advice and consent of the Legislative Council, to make laws for the peace, order and good government of Grenada'.[8]

9 The insertion immediately after section 40(2) of the following subsection:–

7 The previous reading of this section was: 'There shall be a Legislature for Grenada, which should consist of Her Majesty and a Legislative Council'.

8 The previous reading of this section was: 'Subject to the provisions of the West Indies (Federation) Order in Council, 1957, and of this Order, the Legislature shall have power to make laws for the peace, order and good government of Grenada'.

The effect of this amendment, taken together with the amendment to section 23 and the amendment adding a new section 40A, was to return Grenada to a less developed form of colonial constitution where the law-making power of the Legislative Council is subordinate to the Administrator's will.

'(3) The Administrator, acting in his discretion, may –

(a) send by message to the Speaker the draft of any Bill or motion which he considers should be introduced or proposed in the Legislative Council; and

(b) in the same or a later message require that the Bill or motion shall be introduced or proposed not later than a date specified in the message:

and if that requirement is not compiled with, the Bill or motion shall be deemed for all purposes to have been introduced or proposed in the Council on the date so specified.'

10 The insertion immediately after section 40 of the following section:–

'40A (1) If the Administrator considers that it is expedient in the interests of public order, public faith or good government (which expressions shall, without prejudice to their generality, include the responsibility of Grenada as a territory within the Commonwealth, and all matters pertaining to the creation or abolition of any public office or to the salary or other conditions of service of any public officer), that any Bill introduced, or any motion proposed, in the Legislative Council shall have effect, then, if the Council fails to pass the Bill or to carry the motion within such time and in such form as the Administrator thinks reasonable and expedient, the Administrator may, at any time he thinks fit, and not-withstanding any provisions of this Order or of any Standing Orders of the Council, declare that the Bill or motion shall have effect as if it had been passed or carried by the Council either in the form in which it was introduced or proposed or with such amendments as the Administrator thinks fit that have been moved or proposed in the Council, including any committee thereof; and the Bill or motion shall be deemed thereupon to have been so passed or carried, and the provisions of this Order, and in particular the provisions relating to assent to Bills and disallowance of laws, shall have effect accordingly.

(2) The Administrator shall not make any declaration under this section except in accordance with the following conditions:–

(a) the question whether the declaration should be made shall be submitted in writing by the Administrator to the Executive Council, and if the Council advises that the declaration should be made, the Administrator may make the declaration;

(b) if, when the question is submitted to it, the Council does not within such time as the Administrator may think reasonable and expedient, advise that the declaration should be made, then –

(i) the Administrator may submit the question to a Secretary of State and, if the Secretary of State so authorizes him, may make the declaration; or

(ii) the Administrator may make the declaration without submitting the question to a Secretary of State if, in his judgment, urgent necessity requires him to make the declaration before he can obtain the authority of a Secretary of State; in which case he shall, when he makes the declaration, so certify in writing.

(3) (a) Whenever the Administrator, in accordance with the provisions of the last foregoing subsection, submits to a Secretary of State the question whether a declaration should be made, or makes a declaration without submitting the question to a Secretary of State, he shall inform the Executive Council in writing of his reasons for so doing.

(b) Whenever the Administrator makes a declaration under this section, other than a declaration made with the authority of a Secretary of State, he shall forthwith report to a Secretary of State the making of, and the reasons for, the declarations and, in the case of a declaration made under sub-paragraph (ii) of paragraph (b) of the last foregoing subsection, the grounds of urgency.

(4) If any member of the Legislative Council objects to any declaration made under this section, he may, within seven days of the making thereof, submit to the Administrator a statement in writing of his reasons for so objecting; and, if he furnishes a copy of that statement and requests the Administrator to do so, the Administrator shall, as soon as practicable, forward the copy to a Secretary of State.

(5) Any declaration made under this section that relates to a motion may be revoked by a Secretary of State, and the Administrator shall cause notice of the revocation to be published in the Gazette; and from the date of such publication any motion that is deemed to have been carried by virtue of the declaration shall cease to have effect, and section 38 (2) of the Interpretation Act 1889 (a) shall apply to the revocation as it applies to the repeal of an Act of Parliament.' . . .

12 The deletion from section 46 (1) of the words 'acting in accordance with the advice of the Chief Minister'.[9]

13 In section 51 (2) the substitution for the words 'after consultation with the Chief Minister' of the words 'in his discretion'.[10]

14 The deletion of paragraph (a) of the proviso to section 52.[11]

9 The effect of this amendment was to give the Administrator discretionary power to prorogue the Legislative Council. Under the principal Order, and unchanged by this Order, the Administrator had to consult the Chief Minister before dissolution, but with this amendment did not have to accept the advice given.

10 This gave discretionary power to the Administrator to appoint the members of the Public Service Commission.

11 The proviso, deleted by this Order, had made it obligatory for the Administrator to consult (but not act on the advice of) the Chief Minister before making appointments to the Office of Permanent Secretary of a Ministry or Head or Deputy Head of a Department of Government.

(iv) Despatch from the Secretary of State for the Colonies regarding the Report of the Commission of Inquiry into Expenditure in Grenada, to the Administrator of Grenada, dated 23rd July 1962.

Sir,

I have the honour to refer to the conclusions and recommendations of the Commission of Inquiry into the control of public expenditure in Grenada during 1961 and subsequently (Cmnd. 1735).

The abuses disclosed by the Commission of Inquiry struck at the roots of good Government in that they concerned the control of public expenditure and the morale of the Civil Service. As regards the former, the Commission found that the former Minister of Finance had disregarded and contravened the laws and regulations governing the control of expenditure; and that expenditure had been incurred wastefully or unnecessarily through failure by Ministers to seek or refusal to accept the advice of the civil servants. It cannot too strongly be emphasized that the observance of proper controls over the expenditure of public funds is essential to enable a Government to maintain the confidence of the public both at home and abroad. As I am responsible to Parliament for the proper expenditure of United Kingdom funds provided for Grenada, I have felt obliged to take steps to ensure that I am in a position more effectively to discharge that responsibility. A large proportion of the funds available for Grenada is however derived from local revenues and it is therefore of direct concern to the people of Grenada themselves that there should be an effective system of control over the expenditure of public monies and that the system should be faithfully observed. Indeed this is of importance not only to the people of Grenada but to the other British territories in the area, particularly if they should decide to join together in a new federation; since financial instability in one unit would inevitability affect the financial stability of the other territories with whom it was associated.

I have, therefore, decided that special steps must in the interest of Grenada be taken to ensure that there can be no recurrence of the financial malpractice disclosed by the Commission of Inquiry. First among these is the provision in the revised constitution which will come into effect at the time of the next general election giving you the power to appoint an official as Minister of Finance. Secondly, it will be necessary to review the Finance and Audit Ordinance with the object of ensuring that it adequately safeguards public funds. I shall shortly be addressing a futher communication to you suggesting desirable amendments to your Finance and Audit Ordinance including provisions in regard to surcharge on the lines recommended by the Commissi in paragraph 59 of their report. Thirdly, I should be grateful if you would put in hand an early revision of the Financial and Store Rules on the lines recommended in paragraph 60 of the Commission's Report. Lastly, I agree with the Commission (paragraph 62 of their Report) that the Standing Rules and Orders of the Legislative Council should in due course be amended so as to provide for the constitution and conduct of the Public Accounts Committee which should have a permanent place in the machinery of Government.

As regards the Civil Service, the Commission of Inquiry found that the Executive had deliberately destroyed its morale by an undesirable interference with administrative duties and by improper threats against security of office; and that the Civil Service had been induced by this interference and these threats to commit or to condone improprieties or irregularities in the expenditure of public funds. These are very grave findings. It is essential to good government to ensure that individual public servants are in a position to perform their duties without fear or favour. This state of affairs can only come about by protecting the independence of the Civil Service from political interference. Much damage has been done to the morale of the Civil Service of Grenada by the policy of threats intimidation [*sic*] exercised by the Government now dismissed from office. In the interests of good government in Grenada, I must express the earnest hope that in time this damage will be repaired by scrupulous observance of the proper principles and tradition governing the relationship of Ministers and Civil Servants.

The Commission of Inquiry made certain recommendations in regard to the control of the Public Service in paragraph 58 of their Report. In accordance with the recommendation in paragraph 58 (1) the revised constitution which will come into effect at the time of the next general election will provide for the appointment of members of the Public Service Commission by you acting in your discretion and not after consultation with the Chief Minister as before (though in this connection I should point out that even under the former constitution the final decision on the selection of members of the Public Service Commission rested with you since you were not constitutionally required to act in accordance with the Chief Minister's advice in this particular matter). As regards the Commission's recommendation in paragraph 58 (2), it should perhaps be stated for the record that under the Grenada (Constitution) Order in Council, 1959, the power to appoint, promote, transfer, dismiss and exercise disciplinary control over public servants was clearly vested in you acting after consultation with the Public Service Commission. As you know, the effect of these provisions is to place control over individual members of the Public Service and firmly in your hands. (The phrase 'acting after consultation with the Public Service Commission' means that you are required to consult the Public Service Commission before exercising the powers but that you are not bound to follow its advice). As you are aware, these provisions will remain in the revised constitution to be introduced at the time of the next general election, but will be modified by the deletion of Section 52(a) of the Grenada (Constitution) Order in Council which required you to consult with the Chief Minister before making an appointment to the office of any permanent Secretary of a Ministry or Head or Deputy Head of a Department of Government on transfer from another such office carrying the same salary (though again, having regard to the definition in Section 6(6) of the phrase 'acting after consultation', it was not necessary for you to follow the Chief Minister's advice given under Section 52(a). Due consideration will be given at the appropriate time to the recommendation in paragraph 58(3) of the Commission's Report, though it should perhaps be made clear that the present constitutional provision regarding membership of the Public Service Commission [sic] does not exclude the appointment of members resident outside of Grenada.

Before leaving the subject of the Public Service I should like to endorse the views expressed in paragraph 63 of the Commission's Report which relates to the Civil Service Association in Grenada. A properly organised Association will receive every official encouragement in the future and that senior members of the Service will be encouraged to join and to make a useful contribution to its activities.

I would also draw attention to paragraph 61 of the Commissions' Report which emphasised the importance of recording decisions and instructions in writing. This is a matter which relates to all aspects of Government activity. As the Commission themselves pointed out, the need to record decisions and instructions in writing might be thought too obvious to require mention. I share the Commission's disquiet on learning that both the former Ministers and civil servants in Grenada failed to observe this elementary but essential procedure. I trust that suitable instructions will now be issued to ensure that it is faithfully observed in future.

Finally, I wish strongly to endorse the criticisms voiced by the Commission in paragraph 64 of their Report against the publication and free distribution of party political propaganda at public expense. There are the strongest objections of principle to this type of activity, and indeed to any similar activities by which public funds are used for strictly party political purposes (e.g. the financing from public funds of a constituency office). I am, therefore glad to note that you have now stopped the use of public funds for the publication of the party journal entitled 'The Star'.

APPENDIX C

THE DELAY IN THE GRANT OF ASSOCIATE STATEHOOD TO ST VINCENT

(i) Extracts from the Report of Discussions on Constitutional Progress in St. Vincent, 1967. (Cmnd. 3219/1967.)

The White Paper Cmnd. 3021 described the arrangements agreed with a delegation from St. Vincent at the Windward Islands Constitutional Conference in May, 1966, under which St. Vincent would become an Associated State.

2 At the time of the Conference it was known that the statutory life of the St. Vincent Legislature was about to expire and that a general election would have to be held before the new constitutional arrangements could be introduced.

3 General agreement could not be reached at the Conference on two features of the proposed constitution. These related to the establishment of a second Chamber in the Legislature and the voting age. The Secretary of State for the Colonies accordingly stated at the Conference that these questions could be re-examined if the election resulted in a change of government.

4 The general election was held in August, 1966. It resulted in the ruling Government party (the People's Progressive Party, led by Mr. E.T. Joshua, the Chief Minister) gaining five of the nine elected seats, the remaining four being won by the St. Vincent Labour Party, led by Mr. R.M. Cato.

5 Following the election two election petitions were entered by each party, in respect of which various procedural and legal difficulties later developed. It became clear towards the end of 1966 that the petitions would not be determined by the end of February, 1967, when it had been expected that six West Indian territories including St. Vincent (the others being Antigua, Dominica, Grenada, St. Kitts and St. Lucia), would proceed to Associated Statehood.

6 Although the British Government were anxious to see St. Vincent proceed to Associated Statehood as early as possible, the situation resulting from the elections posed a number of difficulties in relation to the timing of the introduction of the new constitution. A major difficulty was the proposed transitional provision referred to in paragraph 12 of Appendix III to Cmnd. 3021, by which the St. Vincent Legislature would have been authorised by the constitution to provide for four additional elected members to be elected in existing constituencies during the life of the first Legislature. It would not have been appropriate to have invoked this far-reaching provision while the issue of the election petitions was still in doubt, yet the British Government were unwilling to delay the grant of Statehood to the people of St. Vincent longer than was absolutely necessary.

7 Apart from the questions of the establishment of a second Chamber and the voting age, a number of other advantages were to be gained by the Government in office from the powers to be given to the Premier under the proposed constitution. Of particular relevance in the context of the electoral uncertainty were the provisions for the appointment of members of the Constituency Boundaries Commission by the Governor on the advice of the Premier and the appointment of a Supervisor of Elections by the Public Service Commission acting after consultation with the Premier.

8 In an endeavour to reach general agreement on measures to resolve these difficulties in a way which would not unduly delay St. Vincent's constitutional progress, the Secretary of State for the Colonies invited the Chief Minister and the Leader of the Opposition to meet him in London in mid-January . . . .

10 After detailed study and discussion of a number of alternative solutions with the Government and Opposition delegations, the difficulties referred to in paragraphs 6 and 7 above were resolved, by both delegations agreeing to the appointment of a Constituency Boundaries Commission by the British Government whose task would be to prepare for fresh general elections on revised electoral rolls for 13 (instead of 9) constituencies not later than the end of 1968; and the general acceptance by all parties of a date not later than 1 June 1967 by which the processes of conferring Associated Statehood on St. Vincent should be completed.

11 The following is the text of the document signed on 1 February by the Minister of State for Commonwealth Affairs, Mrs. Judith Hart, and for the St. Vincent delegations by the Chief Minister, the Minister for Trade, Production, Labour and Tourism, the Leader of the Opposition and the Opposition Member for the Grenadines . . . :

"A number of possible courses of action were fully and frankly discussed and eventually, because of the wish of all the delegations to find a solution, and in a spirit of compromise, it was agreed that St. Vincent would become an Associated State not later than the 1st June 1967, and that the constitutional proposals set out in Appendix III of Cmnd. 3021 should be modified in the following manner:–

(a) The Secretary of State, after consultation with the Administrator, would appoint a Boundary Commission to delimit 13 constituencies.

(b) The Government of St. Vincent and the Opposition would undertake to accept the report of the Boundary Commission.

(c) The Secretary of State would appoint a Supervisor of Elections to prepare new electoral rolls on the basis of 13 constituencies.

(d) A general election on the basis of 13 constituences would be held not later than the 31st December, 1968. Until this general election there will be no increase in the size of the Legislature.

(e) If the Supervisor of Elections appointed under (c) above was no longer available, the Secretary of State would appoint a new Supervisor of Elections to carry out any revision of the electoral rolls and to supervise the general election. The Premier of St. Vincent would inform the Secretary of State, in confidence, two months in advance of the proposed date for the dissolution of the legislature to enable the Secretary of State to make the necessary appointment in time.

(f) The new constitution would contain dormant provisions to permit the establishment of a Senate and the lowering of the voting age to 18 years, by a simple majority of the votes of the elected members of the legislature.

(g) There will be a Public Service Board of Appeal whose function will be to hear and determine appeals from decisions of the Public Service Commission in discipline cases. The Board will consist of a Chairman appointed by the Governor in his discretion, one member who is or has been an officer in the St. Vincent Civil Service on the recommendation of the St. Vincent Civil Service Association and one member appointed on the advice of the Premier.

The provisions listed from (a) to (e) above would be transitional provisions in the new constitution, while those in (f) and (g) would be permanent provisions."

(ii) Statement by the Secretary of State for Commonwealth Affairs on the political situation in St. Vincent, 12th April, 1967. (Parliamentary Debates (Commons) Vol. 744, 1967, cc. 207-208.)

Mrs. Hart: The present difficulties in St. Vincent arose when an elected minister crossed the Floor on 16th March. The Government Party previously held a 5-4 majority of the elected members. As the situation developed, it appeared that the correct first step in resolving the situation was that the elected members should be asked to show whether or not they retained confidence in the Government. It appeared from an exchange of messages with the Chief Minister that the business of the Legislature was unlikely to be arranged so that a motion of no confidence would be given priority. An Order in Council was made on 5th April empowering the Administrator to summon a meeting of the Legislature for the purpose of hearing such a motion. On the same day a message was received from the Chief Minister advising the immediate dissolution of the Legislature to be followed as soon as possible by fresh elections on the existing nine-constituency basis. I agree that this was the right solution and the Legislature was dissolved on 7th April. I considered it right, however, that in the circumstances there should be complete political impartiality in the administration of the territory during the election period. An Order in Council has been made today dissolving the Executive Council and conferring sole responsibility for the administration of St. Vincent on the Administrator. He will retain these powers until a new Government is formed immediately after the election, which is expected to be held on 16th May, but will consult with the leaders of both parties represented in the last Legislature on all significant matters within the responsibilities hitherto allocated to Ministers.

In the Agreement signed with the Chief Minister and Leader of the Opposition of St. Vincent on 1st February, published as a White Paper (Cmnd. 3219), it was envisaged that Associated Statehood would be conferred on St. Vincent not later than 1st June this year, and provisional arrangements had in fact been made for Statehood Day on 29th May. While it remains our objective that St. Vincent should become an Associated State as soon as circumstances permit, it is now clear that it will not be practicable to keep to this date.[1]

1 The general election of May 1967 was won by Mr. Cato's St. Vincent Labour Party, with six seats, to M. Joshua's People's Progressive Party with three seats.

However, certain political difficulties remained and at the Marlborough House Conference, June 1969, there was still no agreement between the two parties as to whether there should be a general election before associated statehood was achieved and if so how many constituencies there should be: nine or thirteen.

Mr. Joshua refused to sign the agreement and the Secretary of State ruled that the St. Vincent House should have a normal lifespan (that is dissolution no later than 1972) and that at the next election there should be thirteen seats in the House, but that until then the number should remain at nine.

(iii) Extracts from the St. Vincent (Electoral Provisions) Order, 1967. (S.I. 240/1967.)

2 (1) The Administrator, acting in his discretion, may by regulation make provision, for the purposes of the election of members of the proposed House of Representatives, for –

(a) the division of Saint Vincent into thirteen constituencies;
(b) the qualification of electors;
(c) the registration of electors; and
(d) any matter that appears to him to be incidental thereto or consequential thereon.

(2) Without prejudice to the generality of the preceding subsection, regulations made thereunder may make provision –

(a) for the division of Saint Vincent into constituencies to be carried out by a Commissioner or Commissioners appointed for that purpose;
(b) for the registration of electors to be carried out under the supervision of a Supervisor appointed for that purpose;
(c) for applying the provisions of any law in force in Saint Vincent for the purposes of the regulations with such adaptations, modifications and exceptions as may be specified in the regulations; and
(d) for charging any expenditures required for the purposes of the regulations upon the revenue or public funds of Saint Vincent.

(iv) Extracts from the St. Vincent (Constitution) (Amendment No. 2) Order in Council, 1967. (S.I. 547/1967.)

5 The following section shall be inserted in the principal Order[2] immediately after Section 40 –

"40A (1) If –

(a) the Administrator is satisfied that a motion of no confidence given in accordance with the Standing Orders of the Legislative Council has been received by the Clerk of the Council; or
(b) the Administrator is given notice in writing by any elected member of the Council that that member proposes a motion of no confidence for debate in the Council in terms specified in the notice,

and the Administrator is satisfied that the public interest requires that

The St. Vincent (Constitution) Order in Council, 1959. S.I. 220/1959.

the motion should be debated in the Council as a matter of urgency, the Administrator may, if he shall think fit, by Proclamation summon a special meeting of the Council at such time and place as may be specified in the Proclamation for the purpose of debating and disposing of the motion:

Provided that the Council may be so summoned notwithstanding that it stands prorogued.

(2) Where the Legislative Council meets, in pursuance of a Proclamation under subsection (1) of this Section, for the purposes of debating and disposing of a motion of no confidence, the following provisions shall apply –

(a) such member of the Council (not being an elected member) as may be specified by the Administrator by writing under his hand shall preside at the meeting;

(b) no business shall be transacted at the meeting other than debating and disposing of the motion (including an amendment to the motion);

(c) no person who is not an elected member of the Council shall vote in any proceedings at the meeting;

(d) the Standing Orders of the Council shall apply in relation to any proceedings at the meeting with such adaptations, modifications, and exceptions as may be prescribed by the Administrator by Order;

(e) if at the meeting a motion of no confidence is duly passed by a majority of all elected members of Council in accordance with the provisions of this Section, the member presiding shall transmit to the Administrator a certificate in writing under his hand to that effect; and, for the purposes of Section 14 (1) of this Order, the certificate shall be conclusive evidence that the motion was so passed and shall not be questioned in any Court.

(3) In this Section "motion of no confidence" means a motion that the Legislative Council should declare a lack of confidence in the Government of Saint Vincent.

(4) In the exercise of the powers conferred upon him by this Section the Administrator shall act in his discretion."

(v) Extracts from the St. Vincent (Constitution) (Amendment No. 3) Order, 1967. (S.I. 587/1967.)

2 (1) The Executive Council constituted at the commencment of this Order in accordance with the provisions of the principal Order is hereby dissolved.

(2) Without prejudice to anything previously done thereunder and until such day (being after the holding of the poll in the general election of elected members of the Legislative Council next following the commencment of this Order) as the Administrator may appoint by proclamation published in the Gazette –

(a) the operation of sections 12 to 21 of the principal Order is suspended;[3]

(b) the operation of subsections (1) to (5) of Section 6 of the principal Order and, to the extent that it requires the Administrator in the exercise of any function to act in accordance with the advice of, or after consultation with, the Executive Council or any Minister, of any other provision of that Order or of any other law in force in Saint Vincent is suspended; and

(c) any provision of any such law that confers any power or imposes any duty upon any Minister shall be construed as if it conferred that power or imposed that duty upon the Administrator.

(3) Until the day appointed under the last foregoing subsection, the Administrator shall exercise his functions after consultation with the persons who, in his opinion, are the leaders of the political parties which were represented in the Legislative Council last dissolved before the commencement of this Order:

Provided that –

(a) he shall not be obliged to consult with those persons –

(i) in the exercise of any function conferred upon him by the principal Order which is expressed to be exercisable by him in his discretion or in accordance with the advice of, or after consultation with, any person or authority other than the Executive Council or a Minister;

(ii) in the exercise of any function conferred upon him by any other law in terms which authorise him to exercise that

3 These sections make provisions relating to the establishment, composition and constitution of the Executive Council; the Chief Minister and other Ministers.

function without obtaining the advice of the Executive Council or a Minister;

(iii) in the exercise of the powers conferred upon him by the Emergency Powers Order in Council 1939, as from time to time amended;

(iv) concerning any matter which, in his judgment, is a matter relating to the maintenance of law and order in Saint Vincent or to the judiciary or the public service;

(v) in any case in which, in his judgment, the urgency of the matter requires him to act before those persons can be consulted or the question for decision is too unimportant to require such consultation;

(vi) in any case in which, in his judgement, it would not be in the public interest to consult those persons.

3 The following section shall be inserted in the principal Order immediately after section 47:–

"47A Whenever any person vacates his seat as an elected member of the Legislative Council for any reason other than a dissolution of the Council or whenever the election of any person as an elected member of the Council is determined under section 48 to be invalid the Administrator, acting in his discretion, shall, unless the Council is sooner dissolved, issue a writ for the election of a member to fill the vacancy returnable within sixty days from the vacation of the seat or the determination, as the case may be."

4 (1) Section 48 of the principal Order is amended by renumbering subsection (2) as subsection (7) and by substituting the following subsections for subsection (1):–

"(1) The High Court shall have jurisdiction to hear and determine any question whether –

(a) any person has been validly elected as a member of the Legislative Council;

(b) any elected member of the Council has vacated his seat therein or is required by virtue of section 29 (4) of this Order to cease to perform his functions as a member; or

(c) any person has been validly elected as a member of the Council from among persons who are not members of the Council or, having been so elected, has vacated the office of Speaker.

(2) An application to the High Court for the determination of –

(a) any question under paragraph (a) of the last foregoing subsection may be made by any person entitled to vote in the election to which the application relates or by any person who was a candidate in that election or by the principal law officer;

(b) any question under paragraph (b) of that subsection may be made by any elected member of the Council or by any person registered in some electoral district as a voter in elections of elected members of the Legislative Council or by the principal law officer;

(c) any question under paragraph (c) of that sub-section may be made by any elected member of the Council or by the principal law officer;

and if such an application is made by a person other than the principal law officer, the principal law officer may intervene and may then appear or be represented in the proceedings.

(3) The Administrator acting in his discretion may by regulation make provisions with respect to –

(a) the circumstances and manner in which and the imposition of conditions upon which any application may be made to the High Court for the determination of any question under this section;

(b) the powers and practice and procedure of the High Court in relation to any such application; and

(c) the powers and practice and procedure of the Court of Appeal in proceedings under the next following subsection.

(4) An appeal shall lie as of right to the Court of Appeal from any final decision of the High Court determining such a question as is referred to in subsection (1) of this section.

(5) No appeal shall lie from any decision of the Court of Appeal in exercise of the jurisdiction conferred by the last foregoing subsection and no appeal shall lie from any decision of the High Court in proceedings under this section other than a final decision determining such a question as is referred to in subsection (1) of this section.

(6) In the exercise of his functions under this section the principal law officer shall not be subject to the direction or control of any other person or authority." . . .

5 The Administrator, acting in his discretion, may by regulation provide that any law relating to the election of persons as members of the Legislative Council (whether enacted before or after the commencement of this order) shall have effect with such adaptations, modifications or exceptions as may be specified in the regulations; and the provisions of the principal Order shall have effect subject to the provisions of this section.

APPENDIX D

BIBLIOGRAPHY OF CONSTITUTIONAL DOCUMENTS OF THE WEST INDIES 1922-1968

The following bibliography is arranged primarily under territorial and subject headings, but with the documents listed under the headings being then arranged chronologically.

All documents listed are official publications and, except where indicated, the publishers are the government printing offices of the territories, and H.M.S.O. for the United Kingdom publications. Also, except where indicated the Gazettes referred to under territorial headings are the Government Gazettes of the respective territories.

Primary, but unofficial, documents are not included, and for the most part the only references to verbatim records of proceedings in the legislatures are references to the official record of the United Kingdom Parliament when the Secretary of State for the Colonies made official statements on policy.

The only despatches, exchanged between various Secretaries of State and officers administering the territories, which are included are those which were made public in the territories at the time.

LIST OF ABBREVIATIONS

C.L.	:	Consolidated Laws.
Cmnd.	:	House of Commons, Paper by Command, or Command Paper.
Col. No.	:	Colonial Number.
Commons (Debates)	:	Official Report. Fifth Series. Parliamenatry Debates. Commons.
G.N.	:	Government Notice.
S.I.[1]	:	Statutory Instruments.
S.R. & O.[1]	:	Statutory Rules and Orders.

1 Instruments, not registered as statutory instruments, but normally published in appendixes to annual volumes of statutory instruments are: " . . . Those Orders in Council, issued under the royal prerogative, or otherwise outside the definition of a statutory instrument, those Letters Patent, under the Great Seal, and those Instructions passed under the Royal Sign Manual and Signet, which relate to the constitutions or currency of overseas territories, or to appeals to the Judicial Committee of the Privy Council". (See H.M.S.O. annual volumes of Statutory Instruments).

A statutory instrument is an exercise of delegated legislative power by the executive authority (which in the case of colonies would be H.M. in Council) where that power is granted by Act of Parliament.

CONSTITUTIONAL DOCUMENTS OF THE WEST INDIES, 1922-68

ANGUILLA

See also: St. Christopher/Nevis/Anguilla.

Statement by Minister of State for Commonwealth Affairs on St. Kitts, Nevis and Anguilla, 27th June 1967. *Parliamentary Debates (Commons)*, Vol. 749, 1967, c. 246.

The Anguilla "White Paper". *N.Y. Times*, Monday, 14th August 1967.

Report of the Commonwealth Conference on Anguilla, 1967. *Cmnd. 3433/1967.*

Statement by Minister of State for Commonwealth Affairs on St. Kitts, Nevis and Anguilla, 30th January 1968. *Parliamentary Debates (Commons)*, Vol. 757, 1968, c. 1074.

Statement by the Secretary of State for Commonwealth Affairs on Anguilla and St. Kitts, 14th March 1968. *Parliamentary Debates (Commons)*, Vol. 760, 1968, c. 355.

ANTIGUA

See also: Leeward Islands. Associated States.

Constitutional position in 1922. *Colonial Office List, 1922,* pp. 253-4. H.M.S.O.

Address by His Excellency the Acting Governor to the Legislative Council of Antigua, on the 26th April 1923. *Leeward Islands Gazette, 1923,* p. 111.

Constitution Ordinance, 1910, Amendment Ordinance No. 2 of 1924. *Laws of Antigua.*

Constitution Ordinance, 1910, Amendment Ordinance No. 6 of 1930. *Laws of Antigua.*

Constitution Ordinance, 1910, Amendment Ordinance No. 4 of 1931. *Laws of Antigua.*

Petition of Representatives of Antigua for revision of the Constitution, etc. 1934. *Colonial Office, West Indies Pamphlet No. 623,* folio.

Constitution Validating Ordinance No. 8 of 1934. *Laws of Antigua.*

Constitution Ordinance No. 20 of 1936. *Laws of Antigua.*

ANTIGUA (cont.)

Constitution (Amendment) Ordinance No. 15 of 1948. *Laws of Antigua.*

Constitution (Amendment) Ordinance No. 8 of 1949. *Laws of Antigua.*

Antigua Constitution and Elections Ordinance No. 10 of 1951. *Laws of Antigua.*

Constitution and Elections (Amendment) Ordinance No. 5 of 1952. *Laws of Antigua.*

Constitution and Elections (Amendment) Ordinance No. 13 of 1954. *Laws of Antigua.*

Crown Proceedings Ordinance No. 19 of 1954. *Laws of Antigua.*

Public Service Commission Ordinance No. 15 of 1955. *Laws of Antigua.*

Constitutions and Elections (Amendment) Ordinance No. 16 of 1955. *Laws of Antigua.*

Leeward Islands Letters Patent, dated 20th June 1956. *Instruments not S.I., appendix to S.I./1956.*

Royal Instructions to the Governor of the Leeward Islands, dated 20th June 1956. *Instruments not S.I., appendix to S.I./1956.*

Constitution and Elections (Amendment) Ordinance No. 6 of 1956. *Laws of Antigua.*

Crown Proceedings (Amendment) Ordinance No. 15 of 1956. *Laws of Antigua.*

Constitution and Elections (Amendment No. 2) Ordinance No. 17 of 1956. *Laws of Antigua.*

Address by the Governor to the Legislative Council of Antigua, 5th November 1956 and the reply by the Hon. Mr. V.C. Bird. *Antigua, Montserrat and Virgin Islands Gazette, 1956,* p. 93 et. seq.

Constitution and Elections (Amendment) Ordinance No. 3 of 1958. *Laws of Antigua.*

Police Service Commission Ordinance No. 21 of 1959. *Laws of Antigua.*

Constitution and Elections (Amendment) Ordinance No. 25 of 1959. *Laws of Antigua.*

ANTIGUA (cont.)

Public Service Commission Ordinance No. 28 of 1959. *Laws of Antigua.*

Legal Officers (appointment, dismissal and disciplinary control) Ordinance No. 30 of 1959. *Laws of Antigua.*

Senior Law Officer (Powers) Ordinance No. 32 of 1959. *Laws of Antigua.*

Report of the Leeward and Windward Islands Constitutional Conference, 1959. *Cmnd. 804/1959.*

Letters Patent, dated 22nd December, 1959. *Instruments not S.I. appendix to S.I./1959.*

Royal Instructions, dated 22nd December 1959. *Instruments not S.I., appendix to S.I./1959.*

Constitution and Elections (Amendment) Ordinance No. 4 of 1960. *Laws of Antigua.*

Legal Officers (appointment, dismissal and disciplinary control) (Amendment) Ordinance No. 8 of 1960. *Laws of Antigua.*

Antigua (Constitution) Order in Council 1960. *S.I./1960.*

Public Service Commission (Amendment) Ordinance No. 3 of 1967. *Laws of Antigua.*

The Antigua Constitution and Elections Ordinance 1951. (Amendment) Order, 1956. *S.I.2014/1965.*

Constitutional Proposals for Antigua, St. Christopher/Nevis/Anguilla, Dominica, St. Lucia, St. Vincent, Grenada, 1965. *Cmnd. 2865/1965.*

Despatch (No. 429) from Secretary of State for the Colonies to the Administrator of Antigua, dated 17th December 1965. *Antigua, Montserrat and Virgin Islands Gazette, 1966,* p.3.

Report of the Antigua Constitutional Conference 1966. *Cmnd. 2963/1966.*

The West Indies Act, 1967. *U.K. Public General Acts, 1967,* c. 4.

Secretary of State for Commonwealth Affairs: "Delegation of authority in external affairs". Letter dated 16th February 1967. Bound in *Laws of Antigua, 1967.*

The Antigua Agreement 1967. Bound in *Laws of Antigua, 1967.*

Antigua Constitution Order 1967. *S.I.225/1967.*

ANTIGUA (cont.)

Constitution and Elections (Amendment) Ordinance No. 28 of 1967. *Laws of Antigua.*

ASSOCIATED STATEHOOD

Motion on the process of decolonization: the problem of the smaller territories. *Parliamentary Debates (Commons),* Vol. 603, 1959, c.c. 1283-369.

ASSOCIATED STATES

See also: Individual territories: Antigua, St. Christopher/Nevis/Auguilla, Dominica, St. Lucia, St. Vincent and Grenada.

Constitutional proposals for Antigua, St. Kitts/Nevis/Anguilla, Dominica, St. Lucia, St. Vincent, Grenada, 1965. *Cmnd. 2865/1965.*

Report of the Antigua Constitutional Conference, 1966. *Cmnd. 2963/1966.*

Report of the Windward Islands Constitutional Conference, 1966. *Cmnd. 3021/1966.*

Report of the St. Christopher/Nevis/Auguilla Constitutional Conference, 1966. *Cmnd. 3031/1966.*

Statement by the Prime Minister on Dependent Territories, 15th December 1966. *Parliamentary Debates (Commons),* Vol. 738, 1966, c. 151.

Speech by the Minister of State, Commonwealth Affairs, on the second reading of the West Indies Bill, 31st January 1967. *Parliamentary Debates (Commons),* Vol. 740, 1967, cc. 335-45.

The West Indies Act, 1967. *U.K. Public General Acts,* 1967 c.4.

The West Indies Act, 1967 (Appointed Days) Order 1967. *S.I. 222/1967.*

West Indies Associated States Supreme Court Agreement 1967. Bound in *Laws of Antigua, 1967.*

West Indies Associated States Supreme Court Order 1967. *S.I. 223/1967.*

West Indies Associated States (Appeals to Privy Council) Order 1967. *S.I.224/1967.*

BAHAMA ISLANDS

Constitutional position 1922. *Colonial Office List, 1922,* p. 99. H.M.S.O.

Notes on the Constitutions of the British West Indies, Bermuda, British Guiana and British Honduras, 1933. *Colonial Office, West Indies Pamphlet No. 585,* 1933, folio.

Additional Instructions to the Governor and Commander-in-Chief, dated 7th April 1937. *Instruments not S.R. & O., appendix to S.R. & O./1937.*

Report of Commission to Inquire into the disturbances of 1942 (Chairman: Sir Alison Russell) (and the proposals of the Governor). *Colonial Office, West Indies Pamphlet No. 770,* June 1942, folio.

Report of Commission to Inquire into the Franchise, 1943. *Nassau, Bahama Islands, 1943.*

Message from the Governor to the House of Assembly, 22nd January 1945. *Minutes of the House of Assembly,* 22nd January 1945.

Report of the Select Committee of the House of Assembly on the secret ballot, 1945. *Nassau, Bahama Islands, 1945.*

General Assembly Elections Act, No. 41 of 1946. *Laws of the Bahama Islands.*

General Assembly Elections (Amendment) Act, No. 17 of 1947. *Laws of the Bahama Islands.*

General Assembly Elections (Amendment) Act, No. 3 of 1948. *Laws of the Bahama Islands.*

Statement by the Secretary of State for the Colonies on the Bahamas (Constitution), 27th April 1950. *Parliamentary Debates (Commons),* Vol. 474, 1950, cc. 140-41.

House of Assembly Officers (Amendment) Act, No. 24 of 1955. *Laws of the Bahama Islands.*

Civil Service Commission Act, No. 3 of 1956. *Laws of the Bahama Islands.*

Report of the Select Committee of the House of Assembly on the reform of the Constitution, 1957. *Nassau, Bahama Islands.*

Statement by the Secretary of State for the Colonies on the Bahamas (Constitution), 26th November 1957. *Parliamentary Debates (Commons),* Vol. 578, 1957, cc. 100-101.

Statement by the Secretary of State for the Colonies on the Bahamas (Constitution), 17th April 1958. *Parliamentary Debates (Commons),* Vol. 586, 1958, cc. 343-45.

BAHAMA ISLANDS (cont.)

General Assembly Elections Act, No. 39 of 1959. *Laws of the Bahama Islands.*

Letters Patent dated 17th January 1959. *Instruments not S.I., appendix to S.I./1959.*

Statement by the Secretary of State for the Colonies on Bahamas (Constitution), February 1959. *Nassau, Bahama Islands.*

Additional Instructions to the Governor and Commander-in-Chief, dated 22nd December 1959. *Instruments not S.I., appendix to S.I./1959.*

General Assembly Elections Act, No. 1 of 1960. *Laws of the Bahama Islands.*

Votes for Women Act, No. 22 of 1961. *Laws of the Bahama Islands.*

General Assembly Elections (Amendment) Act, No. 9 of 1962. *Laws of the Bahama Islands.*

Report of the Bahamas Constitutional Conference 1963. *Cmnd. 2048/1962-63.*

Civil Service Commission Repeal Act, No. 68 of 1963. *Laws of the Bahama Islands.*

Crown Proceedings Act, No. 35 of 1963. *Laws of the Bahama Islands.*

Bahama Islands (Constitution) Act 1963. *U.K. Public General Acts,* 1963 c. 56.

(Constitution) Order in Council, 1963. *S.I. 2084/1963.*

Royal Instructions, dated 20th December 1963. *Instruments not S.I., appendix to S.I./1963.*

Court of Appeal Act, No. 48 of 1964. *Laws of the Bahama Islands.*

(Constitution) (Amendment) Order in Council 1964. *S.I. 2041/1964.*

House of Assembly Elections Act, No. 14 of 1965. *Laws of the Bahama Islands.*

Court of Appeal (Amendment) Act, No. 62 of 1965. *Laws of the Bahama Islands.*

BARBADOS

Constitutional position 1922. *Colonial Office List, 1922,* p. 105. H.M.S.O.

West Indian Court of Appeal Act, No. 4 of 1920. *Laws of Barbados.*

BARBADOS (cont.)

Letters Patent Amending Letters Patent of 4th June 1914, constituting the office of Governor and Commander-in-Chief of the Island of Barbados and its Dependencies, 1937. *S.R. & O./1937.*

Additional Instructions to the Governor and Commander-in-Chief, dated 22nd February 1937. *S.R. & O./1937.*

Additional Instructions to the Governor and Commander-in-Chief, dated 4th January 1939. *S.R. & O./1939.*

Report of the Select Committee of the House of Assembly on a bill to amend the Representation of the People Act, 1943. *Bridgetown, Barbados, 1943.*

Letters Patent dated 26th August 1943, amending Letters Patent of 1914. *S.R. & O./1943.*

Additional Instructions to the Governor and Commander-in-Chief, dated 26th August 1943. *S.R. & O./1943.*

Representation of the People (Amendment) Act, No. 48 of 1943. *Laws of Barbados.*

The Barbados Executive Committee: An Experiment in Government, 1944. *Colonial Office, Barbados Pamphlet No. 24, 1944.*

Statement by the Secretary of State for the Colonies on Barbados (Government), 6th November 1946. *Parliamentary Debates (Commons).* Vol. 248, 1946, cc. 1381-82.

Governor's Message: *Official Gazette, Vol. LXXI, No. 91,* 14th November 1946.

Governor's Address on the Prorogation of the Legislature, 1st October 1946. *Minutes of the Proceedings of the Barbados Ligislature, 1944-46.*

Governor's Address on the Prorogation of the Legislature, 23rd November 1948. *Minutes of the Proceedings of the Barbados Legislature, 1947-48.*

Representation of the People Act 1950, No. 40 of 1950. *Laws of Barbados.*

Public Service Commission Act, No. 42 of 1951. *Laws of Barbados.*

Governor's Address: *Official Gazette (Extraordinary),* 1st February 1954.

Letters Patent amending the Barbados Letters Patent, 1914. *Instruments not S.I., appendix to S.I./1954.*

Additional Instructions to the Governor and Commander-in-Chief, dated 8th March 1954. *Instruments not S.I., appendix to S.I./1954.*

BARBADOS (cont.)

Crown Proceedings Act, No. 5 of 1955. *Laws of Barbados.*

Judicial and Legal Service Commission Act, No. 34 of 1956. *Laws of Barbados.*

Supreme Court of Judicature Act, No. 56 of 1956. *Laws of Barbados.*

Letters Patent, dated 14th July 1959. *Instruments not S.I. appendix to S.I./1959.*

Additional Instructions to the Governor and Commander-in-Chief, dated 9th July 1959. *Instruments not S.I., appendix to S.I./1959.*

Letters Patent, dated 27th April 1961. *Instruments not S.I., appendix S.I./1961.*

Additional Instructions to the Governor and Commander-in-Chief, dated 27th April 1961. *Instruments not S.I., appendix to S.I./1961.*

Letters Patent (No. 2) dated 26th June 1961. *Instruments not S.I., appendix to S.I./1961.*

Executive Committee (Amendment) Act, No. 19 of 1961. *Laws of Barbados.*

Supreme Court of Judicature (Amendment) Act, No. 22 of 1961. *Laws of Barbados.*

Attorney-General (appointment, conditions of service and dismissal) Act, No. 23 of 1961. *Laws of Barbados.*

Auditor-General (appointment, conditions of service and dismissal) Act, No. 24 of 1961. *Laws of Barbados.*

Public Service Commission Act, No. 25 of 1961. *Laws of Barbados.*

Judicial and Legal Service Commission Act, No. 26 of 1961. *Laws of Barbados.*

Police Service Commission Act, No. 51 of 1961. *Laws of Barbados.*

Supreme Court of Judicature (Amendment) (No. 2) Act, No. 55 of 1961. *Laws of Barbados.*

Boundaries Commission Act, No. 41 of 1962. *Laws of Barbados.*

Attorney-General (appointment, conditions of service and dismissal) (Repeal) Act, No. 37 of 1963. *Laws of Barbados.*

Director of Public Prosecutions Act, No. 38 of 1963. *Laws of Barbados.*

BARBADOS (cont.)

Barbados (Letters Patent Consolidation) Order 1964. *S.I. 491/1964.*

Royal Instructions, dated 26th March 1964. *Instruments not S.I., appendix to S.I./1964.*

The Federal Negotiations, 1962-1965, and Constitutional Proposals for Barbados. *Barbados White Paper, Bridgetown, Barbados, 1965.*

Report of Constitutional Conference 1966. *Cmnd. 3058/1966.*

Barbados Independence Act 1966. *U.K. Public General Acts,* 1966 c. 37.

Barbados Order 1966. *S.I. 1403/1966.*

Barbados Independence Order 1966. *S.I. 1455/1966.*

Supreme Court of Judicature (Amendment) (No. 2) Act, No. 17 of 1966. *Laws of Barbados.*

Judicial and Legal Service Commission (Amendment) Act, No. 18 of 1966. *Laws of Barbados.*

Supreme Court of Judicature Act, No. 39 of 1966. *Laws of Barbados.*

Barbados (Procedure in Appeals to Privy Council) Order 1967. *S.I. 1456/1967.*

Barbados Citizenship Act, No. 50 of 1967. *Laws of Barbados.*

BRITISH CARIBBEAN

British Caribbean Court of Appeal Order in Council, 1962. *S.I. 1086/1962.*

British Caribbean (Appeals to Privy Council) Order in Council 1962. *S.I. 1087/1962.*

British Caribbean Court of Appeal (Amendment) Order in Council 1962. *S.I. 1245/1962.*

British Caribbean Court of Appeal (Amendment) (No. 2) Order in Council, 1962. *S.I. 1870/1962.*

BRITISH GUIANA (See also: Guyana)

Constitutional position in 1922. *Colonial Office List, 1922,* p. 115. H.M.S.O.

BRITISH GUIANA (cont.)

Report of the Visit of the Hon. E.F.L. Wood, M.P., to the West Indies and British Guiana, 1921-22. *Cmnd. 1679/1922.*

Despatch from Secretary of State to the Colonies (Circular), dated 29th June 1922. *Leeward Islands Gazette,* notice No. 239 of 1922.

Report of the British Guiana Commission, April 1927. *Cmnd. 2841/1927.*

Report of the British Guiana Constitutional Commission. *Cmnd. 2985/1927.*

Despatch from the Secretary of State for the Colonies to the Governor, dated 25th May 1927. *Colonial Office Papers.*

Memoranda prepared by the elected members of the Combined Court of British Guiana in reply to the Report of the British Guiana Commission. *Cmnd. 3047/1927.*

Statement by Secretary of State for the Colonies on the new constitution, 1st March 1928. *Parliamentary Debates (Commons),* Vol. 214, 1928, c.604.

British Guiana Bill: Speech on Second Reading by the Secretary of State for the Colonies, 6th March 1928. *Parliamentary Debates (Commons),* Vol. 214, 1928, cc. 989-99.

British Guiana Act 1928. *U.K. Public General Acts,* 1928 c.5.

(Constitution) Order in Council, 1928. *S.R. & O./1928.*

Proclamation by His Excellency the Governor abolishing the Court of Policy and the Combined Court of the Colony and establishing the Legislative Council for the Colony, 18th July 1928. *Laws of British Guiana, Revised edition, 1930,* cap. 2.

Message from the Secretary of State for the Colonies to H.E. the Governor of the Colony of British Guiana. *British Guiana, Royal Gazette,* 18th July 1928.

Letters Patent, dated 20th July 1928, constituting the Office of Governor and Commander-in-Chief of the Colony of British Guiana. *S.R. & O./1928.*

Royal Instructions, dated 20th July 1928. *S.R. & O./1928.*

Notes on the Constitutions of the British West Indies, Bermuda, British Guiana and British Honduras, 1933. *Colonial Office, West Indies Pamphlet, No. 585,* 1933, folio.

Report of the Franchise Commission, 1935. *Legislative Council Paper No. 4 of 1935.*

(Constitution) (Amendment) Order in Council 1935. *S.R. & O. 801/1935.*

BRITISH GUIANA (cont.)

Statement by the Secretary of State for the Colonies on the British Guiana Constitution, 22nd April 1943. *Parliamentary Debates (Commons),* Vol. 388, 1943, c. 1858.

(Constitution) (Amendment) Order in Council 1943. *S.R. & O. 1792/1943.*

Letters Patent, dated 23rd March 1943. *S.R. & O./1943.*

Report of the Franchise Commisson. 1941-44. *Legislative Council Paper No. 10 of 1944* (folio).

Statement by the Secretary of State for the Colonies on British Guiana (Franchise), 4th October 1944. *Parliamentary Debates (Commons),* Vol. 403, 1943-44, cc. 923-27.

(Constitution) (Amendment) Order in Council 1945. *S.R. & O. 990/1945.*

Legislative Council (Elections) Ordinance, No. 13 of 1945. *Laws of British Guiana.*

(Constitution) (Amendment) Order in Council, 1949. *S.I. 2200/1949.*

Report of the Constitutional Commission, 1950-51 (Chairman: Sir E.J. Waddington, G.B.E., K.C.M.G., K.C.V.O.) and Despatch from the Secretary of State for the Colonies to the Governor of British Guiana, dated 6th October 1951. *Col. No. 280/1951.*

Legislative Council (Elections) (Amendment) Ordinance, No. 202 of 1952. *Laws of British Guiana.*

Despatches exchanged between Secretary of State for the Colonies and the Governor regarding constitutional reform in that Colony, 1952. *Legislative Council Paper,* No. 2 of 1952.

Letters Patent, dated 1st April 1953, constituting the office of Governor and Commander-in-Chief of the Colony of British Guiana. *Instruments not S.I., appendix to S.I./1953.*

Royal Instructions, dated 1st April 1953. *Instruments not S.I., appendix to S.I./1953.*

(Constitution) Order in Council 1953. *S.I. 586/1953.*

Message from Secretary of State for the Colonies to the Governor of British Guiana, dated 2nd May 1953. Message No. 343, British Guiana, in *Rules, Regulations, By-Laws and Orders in Council, 1953,* pp. xlviii-l.

(Constitution) (No. 2) Order in Council 1953. *S.I. 1478/1953.*

BRITISH GUIANA (cont.)

(Emergency) Order in Council 1953. *S.I. 1479/1953.*

Additional Instructions, dated 4th October 1953. *Instruments not S.I., appendix to S.I./1953.*

Suspension of the constitution ordered on 8th October 1953. *Cmnd. 8980/1953.*

Debate on the suspension of the constitution of British Guiana, 22nd October 1953. *Parliamentary Debates (Commons),* Vol. 518, 1953, cc. 2159-280.

(Constitution) (Amendment) Order in Council 1953. *S.I. 1564/1953.*

(Constitution) (Temporary Provisions) Order in Council 1953. *S.I. 1910/1953.*

Instructions, dated 22nd December 1953. *Instruments not S.I., appendix to S.I./1953.*

Representation of the People Ordinance, No. 5 of 1953. *Laws of British Guiana.*

Supreme Court Ordinance, cap. 7. *Laws of British Guiana,* revised edition, 1953.

Report of the British Guiana Constitutional Commission (Chairman: Sir James Robertson, K.C.M.G., K.B.E.), 1954. *Cmnd. 9274/1954.*

Legislative Council. Address on the report of the British Guiana Constitutional Commission, in the Council Chamber, Tuesday, 2nd November 1954. *British Guiana Sessional Paper, No. 9.*

Supreme Court of Judicature (Amendment) Ordinance, No. 23 of 1955. *Laws of British Guiana.*

Statement by the Secretary of State for the Colonies on British Guiana (Constitution, Amendment), 25th April 1956. *Parliamentary Debates (Commons),* Vol. 551, 1956, cc. 1779-80.

(Electoral Provisions) Order in Council, 1956. *S.I. 1206/1956.*

(Constitution) (Temporary Provisions) (Amendment) Order in Council 1956. *S.I. 2030/1956.*

(Appeals) Order in Council 1957. *S.I. 1527/1957.*

Representation of the People Ordinance, No. 3 of 1957. *Laws of British Guiana.*

Federal Supreme Court (Appeals) Ordinance, No. 19 of 1958. *Laws of British Guiana.*

BRITISH GUIANA (cont.)

Report of the Constitutional Committee and records of the proceedings of the meetings, 1959. *Georgetown, 1959.*

Report of the Constitutional Conference, 1960. *Cmnd. 998/1960.*

(Constitution) Order in Council 1961. *S.I. 1188/1961.*

Representation of the People (Amendment) Ordinance, No. 21 of 1961. *Laws of British Guiana.*

Legislature (Appointment, Election and Membership Controversies) Ordinance, No. 34 of 1961. *Laws of British Guiana.*

Royal Instructions to the Governor and Commander-in-Chief of the Colony of British Guiana, dated 26th June 1961. *Instruments not S.I., appendix to S.I./1961.*

Report of Commission of Enquiry into disturbances in British Guiana in February, 1962. *Col. No. 354/1962.*

Report of the Independence Conference 1962. *Cmnd. 1870/1962.*

Report of the British Guiana Independence Conference, 1963. *Cmnd. 2203/ 1963-64.*

Statement by the Secretary of State for the Colonies on British Guiana, 17th July 1963. *Parliamentary Debates (Commons),* Vol. 681, 1963, cc. 525-28.

(Emergency Provisions) Order, 1964. *S.I. 776/1964.*

(Constitution) Order, 1964. *S.I. 921/1964.*

(Constitution) (No. 2) Order, 1964. *S.I. 1970/1964.*

(Constitution) (NO. 3) Order, 1964. *S.I. 2040/1964.*

Report by the Commonwealth Team of Observers on the Election in December 1964. 1965. *Col. No. 359/1965.*

Report of the British Guiana Constitutional Conference, 1965. *Cmnd. 2849/ 1965.*

(Constitution) Order, 1965. *S.I. 587/1965.*

(Constitution) (No. 2) Order, 1965. *S.I. 979/1965.*

(Constitution) (No. 3) Order, 1965. *S.I. 2161/1965.*

Report of the Independence Conference, 1965. *Cmnd. 2849/1965.*

Appendix D

BRITISH HONDURAS

Constitutional position in 1922. *Colonial Office List, 1922,* p. 124. H.M.S.O.

Privy Council Appeals Ordinance, Ch. 155, C.L. 1924. *Laws of British Honduras.*

Constitution (Amendment) Ordinance, No. 18 of 1926. *Laws of British Honduras.*

Supreme Court Ordinance, No. 24 of 1926. *Laws of British Honduras.*

Letters Patent, dated 31st January 1927, constituting office of Governor and Commander-in-Chief of the Colony of British Honduras. *S.R. & O/1927.*

Supreme Court (Amendment) Ordinance, No. 13 of 1929. *Laws of British Honduras.*

Constitution (Amendment) Ordinance, No. 17 of 1932. *Laws of British Honduras.*

Notes on the Constitutions of the British West Indies, Bermuda, British Guiana and British Honduras, 1933. *Colonial Office, West Indies Pamphlet No. 585,* 1933, folio.

Constitution Ordinance, No. 13 of 1935. *Laws of British Honduras.*

Constitution (Amendment) Ordinance, No. 18 of 1935. *Laws of British Honduras.*

Electoral Qualifications and Regulations (Amendment) Ordinance, No. 19 of 1935. *Laws of British Honduras.*

Royal Instructions, dated 11th January 1936. *S.R. & O./1936.*

Constitution and Electoral Qualifications and Regulations (Amendment) Ordinance, No. 21 of 1938. *Laws of British Honduras.*

Letters Patent constituting the office of Governor and Commander-in-Chief of British Honduras, 1940. *S.R. & O./1940.*

Constitution (Amendment) Ordinance, No. 5 of 1945. *Laws of British Honduras.*

Electoral Qualifications and Regulations (Amendment) Ordinance, No. 5 of 1945. *Laws of British Honduras.*

Letters Patent Amending Letters Patent of 30th April 1940, 1945. *S.R. & O./1945.*

Royal Instructions, dated 30th April 1945. *S.R. & O./1945.*

BRITISH HONDURAS (cont.)

Declaration by H.M. Government relating to boundaries of British Honduras. *Cmnd. 6934/1946.*

Texts of Notes exchanged between His Majesty's Minister and the Government of Guatemala from January 1948 to May 1949. *Council Paper No. 24 of 1949.*

Renewal by H.M. Government . . . of declaration accepting the jurisdiction of the International Court of Justice concerning the . . . boundaries of British Honduras. *Cmnd. 8206/1951.*

Report of Commission of Inquiry on Constitutional Reform. *Council Paper No. 10 of 1951.*

Note from H.M. Government to Guatemalan Government, 19th February 1952. (Text published in *B.H. Monthly Bulletin,* issued by P.R.O., Belize, British Honduras).

Report of the Select Committee of the Legislative Council on constitutional reform, 1952. *Council Paper No. 40 of 1952.*

Crown Proceedings Ordinance, No. 34 of 1952. *Laws of British Honduras.*

Despatch from the Secretary of State for the Colonies, dated 17th January 1953 on the subject of Constitutional development in British Honduras. *Council Paper No. 5 of 1953.*

Crown Proceedings (Amendment) Ordinance, No. 12 of 1953. *Laws of British Honduras.*

Representation of the People Ordinance, No. 13 of 1953. *Laws of British Honduras.*

Report of an Inquiry held by Sir Reginald Sharpe, Q.C., into Allegations of Contacts between the People's United Party and Guatemala. *Cmnd. 9139/1954*

Association of Members of the Executive Council with the administration of Departments of Government. *British Honduras Council Paper No. 37 of 1954.*

Letters Patent, dated 14th June 1954. *Instruments not S.I., appendix to S.I./1954.*

Royal Instructions to the Governor and Commander-in-Chief, dated 15th July 1954. *Instruments not S.I., appendix to S.I./1954.*

(Constitution) Order in Council, 1954. *S.I./1954.*

Constitution Ordinance, No. 13 of 1954. *Laws of British Honduras.*

BRITISH HONDURAS (cont.)

Despatch from the Secretary of State for the Colonies to the Governor of British Honduras, dated 14th December 1954. *Colonial Office Papers.*

Resolution of Legislative Assembly reaffirming the House's allegiance to the Crown and rejecting any other Government's claim to sovereignty over British Honduras. *Legislative Assembly Debates,* 17th December 1957.

Supreme Court of Judicature (Amendment) Ordinance, No. 15 of 1960. *Laws Honduras.*

Privy Council Appeals Ordinance, Ch. 9, C.L. 1958. *Laws of British Honduras.*

Message from Secretary of State for Colonies in reply to Memorial of the People's United Party. British Honduras, 15th December 1958. Text appears in the *British Honduras Monthly Newsletter* for January 1959.

Report of Sir Hilary Blood, Constitutional Commissioner for British Honduras, 1959. *Belize, British Honduras, 1959.*

Report of Conference on the Constitution of British Honduras, 1960. *Cmnd. 984/1959-60.*

Letters Patent, dated 16th November 1960. *Instruments not S.I., appendix to S.I./1960.*

Additional Instructions to the Governor and Commander-in-Chief, dated 17th November 1960. *Instruments not S.I., appendix to S.I./1960.*

Representation of the People (Amendment) Ordinance, No. 8 of 1960. *Laws of British Honduras.*

Constitution (Amendment) Ordinance, No. 12 of 1960. *Laws of British Honduras.*

Supreme Court of Judicature (Amendment) Ordinance, No. 15 of 1960. *Laws of British Honduras.*

Constitution (Amendment) (No. 2) Ordinance, No. 16 of 1960. *Laws of British Honduras.*

(Constitution) Order in Council 1961. *S.I./1961.*

Report of the British Honduras Constitutional Conference, 1963. *Cmnd. 2124/1963.*

Constitution (Amendment) Ordinance, No. 6 of 1963. *Laws of British Honduras.*

Constitution Ordinance, No. 33 of 1963. *Laws of British Honduras.*

BRITISH HONDURAS (cont.)

Representation of the People (Amendment) Ordinance, No. 13 of 1964. *Laws of British Honduras.*

Supreme Court of Judicature (Amendment) Ordinance, No. 15 of 1964. *Laws of British Honduras.*

(Constitution) Order in Council 1964. *S.I./1964.*

Letters Patent, dated 1st January 1964. *Instruments not S.I., appendix to S.I./1964.*

Additional Instructions, dated 2nd January 1964. *Instruments not S.I., appendix to S.I./1964.*

Constitution (Amendment) Ordinance, No. 23 of 1966. *Laws of British Honduras.*

Court of Appeal Ordinance, No. 18 of 1967. *Laws of British Honduras.*

Privy Council Appeals (Amendment) Ordinance, No. 19 of 1967. *Laws of British Honduras.*

COLONIAL EMPIRE

Report on the Colonial Empire, 1939-47. *Cmnd. 7167/1946-47,* and *Cmnd. 7433/1947-48.*

Progress Report on Colonial Territories, 1948-49. *Cmnd. 7715/1948-49.*

British Dependencies in the Caribbean and North Atlantic, 1939-52. *Cmnd. 8575/1951-52.*

Colonial Regulations, 1951. *Col. No. 270 of 1951.*

DOMINICA

See: Associated States. Windward Islands after 1938. Leeward Islands before 1938.

Constitutional position in 1922. *Colonial Office List, 1922,* p. 261. H.M.S.O.

Secretary of State's Despatch No. 218 of 1922. *Leeward Islands Gazette,* Notice No. 239 of 1922.

Constitution Ordinance No. 21 of 1924. *Ordinances of Dominica.*

Letters Patent, dated 18th February 1925. *S.R. & O./1925.*

DOMINICA (cont.)

Constitution (Amendment) Ordinance, No. 6 of 1926. *Ordinances of Dominica.*

The Constitution (Validating) Ordinance, No. 9 of 1930. *Ordinances of Dominica.*

The Constitution (Amendment) Ordinance, No. 7 of 1931. *Ordinances of Dominica.*

Constitution Ordinance No. 8 of 1936. *Ordinances of Dominica.*

Resume of representations and recommendations in connection with the separation of Dominica from the Leeward Islands Federation and attachment to the Windward Islands group, 1937. *Colonial Office, West Indies Pamphlet, No. 681,* 1937.

Debate on the Dominica Bill (Second Reading), 1st February 1938. *Parliamentary Debates (Commons),* Vol. 331, 1937-38, cc. 179-91.

Dominica Act 1938. *U.K. Public General Acts,* 1938 c. 10.

Transfer of Dominica to Windward Islands – postponed until 1st January 1940. *St. Vincent Government Gazette,* No. 64 1st December 1938.

Letters Patent, dated 28th December 1939, amending Letters Patent of 13th November 1936 constituting the office of Governor and Commander-in-Chief of the Windward Islands, 1939. *S.R. & O./1939.*

Address by the Governor to the General Legislative Council of the Leeward Islands, on Wednesday, 29th November 1939. *Leeward Islands Gazette,* Supplement to Gazette No. 75 of 1939.

Dominica Order in Council, 1939. *S.R. & O. 1896/1939.*

Dominica (Adaptation of Laws) Order in Council, 1939. *S.R. & O. 1897/1939.*

Constitution (Amendment) Ordinance, No. 6 of 1943. *Ordinances of Dominica.*

Windward Islands Conference on Constitutional Reform, 1945. *Colonial Office, West Indies Pamphlet No. 803,* 1945, folio.

Windward Islands Letters Patent, dated 11th May 1945, Amending Letters Patent of 13th November 1936, 1945. *S.R. & O./1945.*

Windward Islands Letters Patent, dated 27th August 1951. *Instruments not S.I., appendix to S.I./1951.*

DOMINICA (cont.)

Dominica (Legislative Council) Order in Council, 1951. *S.I. 1392/1951.*

Dominica (Legislative Council) (Electoral Provisions) Order in Council, 1951. *S.I. 330/1951.*

Legislative Council Elections Ordinance, No. 14 of 1951. *Ordinances of Dominica.*

Windward Islands Additional Instructions, dated 22nd February 1952. *Instruments not S.I., appendix to S.I./1952.*

Supreme Court (Amendment) Ordinance, No. 9 of 1952. *Ordinances of Dominica.*

Windward Islands, Additional Instructions, dated 22nd February 1952 1953. *Instruments not S.I., appendix to S.I./1953.*

(Legislative Council) (Amendment) Order in Council, 1953. *S.I. 399/1953.*

Crown Proceedings Ordinance, No. 8 of 1953. *Ordinances of Dominica.*

Windward Islands, Letters Patent, Amending Windward Islands Letters Patent, 1951, dated 10th September 1954. *Instruments not S.I., appendix to S.I./1954.*

Windward Islands, Additional Instructions, dated 10th September 1954. *Instruments not S.I., appendix to S.I./1954.*

(Legislative Council) (Amendment) Order in Council, 1954. *S.I. 1037/1954.*

Supreme Court (Amendment) Ordinance, No. 24 of 1954. *Ordinances of Dominica.*

(Legislative Council) (Amendment) Order in Council, 1955. *S.I. 1815/1955.*

Windward Islands, Additional Instructions, dated 28th December 1955. *Instruments not S.I., appendix to S.I./1955.*

Windward Islands, Letters Patent, dated 29th December 1955. *Instruments not S.I., appendix to S.I./1955.*

(Legislative Council) (Amendment) Order in Council, 1956. *S.I. 1580/1956.*

Public Service Commission Ordinance, No. 1 of 1956. *Ordinances of Dominica*

Windward Islands, Additional Instructions, dated 23rd October 1957. *Instruments not S.I., appendix to S.I./1957.*

(Legislative Council) (Amendment) Order in Council, 1957. *S.I. 1742/1957.*

DOMINICA (cont.)

Windward Islands, Letters Patent, dated 8th May 1958. *Instruments not S.I., appendix to S.I./1958.*

Proposals for constitutional reform. See Windward and Leeward Islands, 1959.

Report of the Leeward and Windward Islands Constitutional Conference, 1959. *Cmnd. 804/1959.*

(Constitution) Order in Council, 1959. *S.I. 2199/1959.*

Royal Instructions to the Administrator, dated 22nd December 1959. *Instruments not S.I., appendix to S.I./1959.*

(Constitution) (Amendment) Order in Council, 1960. *S.I. 202/1960.*

Public Service Commission (Remuneration, Privileges and Offences) Ordinance, No. 10 of 1960. *Ordinances of Dominica.*

Legislative Council (Contracts with Government) (Disqualification) Ordinance, No. 12 of 1960. *Ordinances of Dominica.*

Report by the Leeward Islands and Windward Islands Constitutional Conference, held in London in June 1961. *Cmnd. 1434/1961.*

Constitutional Proposals for Antigua, St. Christopher/Nevis/Anguilla, Dominica, St. Lucia, St. Vincent, Grenada, 1965. *Cmnd. 2865/1965.*

Windward Islands Constitutional Conference, 1966. *Cmnd. 3021/1966.*

The West Indies Act, 1967. *U.K. Public General Acts,* 1967 c. 4.

Dominica (Constitution) Order 1967. *S.I. 226/1967.*

Public and Police Service Commissions (Remuneration, Privileges and Offences) Ordinance, No. 4 of 1967. *Ordinances of Dominica.*

House of Assembly (Disqualification) Ordinance, No. 6 of 1967. *Ordinances of Dominica.*

House of Assembly (Disqualification (Amendment) Act, No. 28 of 1967. *Laws of Dominica.*

FEDERATION AND FEDERAL EXPERIMENTS

See also: Wood Commission and Moyne Commission

Secretary of State's Despatch No. 419 of 1921: Establishment of Council or Conference of West Indian Colonies. *Leeward Islands Gazette,* 1921, pp. 269 et seq.

FEDERATION AND FEDERAL EXPERIMENTS (cont.)

Hon. E.F.L. Wood: Constitutional Development and Federation, 1922. *Colonial Office, West Indies Pamphlet, No. 39,* 1922.

Statement by His Excellency the Governor of the Windward Islands to the Legislative Council of Grenada, on Mr. Wood's proposals for the confederation of the Windward Islands with the Government of Trinidad. *Minutes of the Legislative Council of Grenada,* 1922, pp. 6-8.

Indefinite postponement of West Indian Conference at Trinidad. See *Leeward Islands, Gazette Notice,* No. 318/1921.

Colonial Office Vote: Speech by Mr. Ormsby-Gore (Under-Secretary of State for the Colonies) in Committee of Supply, 25th July 1923. *Parliamentary Debates (Commons),* Vol. 167, 1923, cc. 491-94.

Correspondence referring to the proposed association of the Windward Islands with Trinidad, 1923. *Council Paper No. 103* of 1923. (Trinidad & Tobago).

Resolution on establishment of a Standing Conference on common affairs of the British West Indies, passed by the Legislative Council of Jamaica on 15th May 1923. *Minutes of Legislative Council of Jamaica,* 15th May 1923.

Proposed establishment of a Standing Conference to deal with common affairs of the British West Indies – Despatch from the Secretary of State for the Colonies, 1925. *Council Paper No. 13* of 1925. (Trinidad & Tobago).

Report of the West Indies Conference, 1926. *Cmnd. 2672/1926.*

Report of the West Indies Sugar Commission, 1930. *Cmnd. 3517 and Col. No. 49, 1930.*

Closer Union between Trinidad, the Windward and the Leeward Islands. Despatch from the Secretary of State for the Colonies, dated 4th March 1931. *Colonial Office Papers.*

Address by the Governor to the General Legislative Council of the Leeward Islands, on 28th April 1931. *Leeward Islands Gazette, Supplement to Gazette No. 20 of 1931.*

Reply to the Address by the Governor to the General Legislative Council of th Leeward Islands, on 28th April 1931. *Leeward Islands Gazette, Supplement to Gazette No. 21 of 1931.*

Colonial Office Vote: Speech by Sir P. Cunliffe-Lister (Secretary of State for the Colonies) in Committee of Supply, 11th February 1932. *Parliamentary Debates (Commons),* Vol. 261, 1931-32, cc. 1133-34

West Indian Conference Report, Roseau, Dominica, October-November 193 *The Voice Printery, Castries, St. Lucia.*

FEDERATION AND FEDERAL EXPERIMENT (cont.)

Report of the Closer Union Commission (Leeward Islands, Windward Islands, Trinidad & Tobago), April 1933. *Cmnd. 4383/1932-33.*

Despatch from the Secretary of State for the Colonies to the Governor, Leeward Islands, dated 21st September 1934, regarding the recommendations of the Closer Union Commission. *Supplement to the Leeward Islands Gazette of 25th October 1934.*

Address by the Governor to the General Legislative Council of the Leeward Islands. *Leeward Islands Gazette, Supplement to Gazette No. 12 of 1934.*

Report of Conference for the purpose of considering the Financial Implications of the scheme for Closer Union of the Leeward and Windward Islands, 1934. *Colonial Office, West Indies Pamphlet, No. 611,* 1934, folio.

Statement by Secretary of State for the Colonies on West Indies (Closer Union Proposals), 31st October 1934. *Parliamentary Debates (Commons),* Vol. 293, 1933-34, cc. 192-93.

Address by the Governor to the General Legislative Council of the Leeward Islands, on Wednesday, 29th November 1939. *Leeward Islands Gazette, Supplement to Gazette No. 75 of 1939.*

Reply to the Unofficial Members to the Address by the Governor to the General Legislative Council of the Leeward Islands on Wednesday, 29th November 1939. *Leeward Islands Gazette, Supplement to Gazette No. 76 of 1939.*

Statement by His Majesty's Government on colonial development policy, and including a statement on the recommendations of the West Indies Royal Commission. *Leeward Islands Gazette, Supplement to Gazette No. 14 of 1940.*

Report of the West Indian Conference held in Barbados, 1944. (Chairman: Sir Frank Stockdale, K.C.M.G., C.B.E.). *Col. No. 186/1944.*

Despatch from the Secretary of State for the Colonies on a West Indian Federation, dated 14th March 1945. *Minutes of the St. Vincent Legislative Council, 1946,* pp. 62-63.

Report of Windward Islands Conference held in Grenada in 1945. *Government Printers, St. George's, Grenada.*

Despatch from the Secretary of State for the Colonies to the Governor of the Windward Islands and the Governor of the Leeward Islands, dated 14th March 1946. *Leeward Islands Gazette, Supplement to Extraordinary Gazette No. 35 of 1946.*

FEDERATION AND FEDERAL EXPERIMENTS (cont.)

Address by the Governor of the Windward Islands to the Legislative Councils of the Windward Islands. "Federation of the Windward and Leeward Islands", *Council Paper No. 3, Grenada, 1946.*

Report of the Committee of Unofficial Members. "Federation of Windward and Leeward Islands", *Council Paper No. 8, Grenada, 1946.*

Resolution of the General Legislative Council of the Leeward Islands on the despatch, dated 14th March 1946, from the Secretary of State for the Colonies. *Leeward Islands Gazette,* 1946, p. 146.

Government Notice. Closer Union, Leeward Islands and Windward Islands. *Leeward Islands Gazette,* 1946, p. 177.

Address by the Governor to the General Legislative Council of the Leeward Islands, on Tuesday, 26th November 1946 and the reply by Unofficial Members. *Leeward Islands Gazette, Supplement to Gazette No. 130 of 1946.*

Agenda for Conference on Closer Union of Windward and Leeward Islands to be held at St. Kitts on 27th January 1947. *Leeward Islands Gazette, Supplement to Gazette No. 130 of 1946.*

Conference on Closer Union of the Windward and Leeward Islands held in St. Kitts during January and February 1947. See Council Paper No. 3 of 1947, *Legislative Council of Grenada.*

Despatch from the Secretary of State for the Colonies and Memorandum on Closer Association of the British West Indian Colonies, dated 14th February 1947. *Colonial Office Papers.*

Despatch from the Secretary of State for the Colonies on the proposal for Closer Union of the Windward and Leeward Islands, dated 22nd July 1947. *Colonial Office Papers.*

Memorandum on the Closer Association of the British West Indian Colonies, 1947. *Cmnd. 7120/1946-47.*

Conference on the Closer Association of the British West Indian Colonies, Montego Bay, Jamaica, 11th – 19th September 1947. Part I: Report. *Cmnd. 7291/1948.* Part II: Proceedings. *Col. No. 218/1948.*

Report of the British Caribbean Standing Closer Association Committee (Chairman: Major General Sir Hubert Rance, G.C.N.G., G.B.E., C.B.), 1948-49, *Col. No. 255/1950.*

Report of the Commission on the Unification of the Public Services in the British Caribbean Area, 1948-49. *Col. No. 254/1950.*

FEDERATION AND FEDERAL EXPERIMENTS (cont.)

Report of the Commission on the Establishment of a Customs Union in the British Caribbean area, 1948-50. *Col. No. 268/1951.*

Despatch from the Secretary of State for the Colonies to the Governors of the West Indian territories on the question of Federation, dated 27th February 1952. *Colonial Office Papers.*

British Dependencies in the Caribbean and North Atlantic, 1939-52. *Cmnd. 8575/1952.*

Report by the Conference on the West Indian Federation held in London in April 1953. *Cmnd. 8837/1952-53.*

The plan for a British Caribbean Federation: Agreed on by the Conference on West Indian Federation held in London in April 1953. 1953. *Cmnd. 8895/1953.*

Statement by Secretary of State for the Colonies on the proposed Federation of the British West Indies, 2nd February 1955. *Parliamentary Debates (Commons),* Vol. 536, 1955, cc. 1093-96.

Movement of Persons within a British Caribbean Federation. Report of the Conference held in Port of Spain, Trinidad, from 14th March to 17th March 1955. *Col. No. 315/1955.*

The plan for a British Caribbean Federation 1955. Reports of the Fiscal, Civil Service and Judicial Commissioners. *Cmnd. 9618-9620/1955.*

Report of the Conference on British Caribbean Federation 1956. *Cmnd. 9733/1956.*

Statement by the Secretary of State for the Colonies on the British Caribbean Federation (Conference Report), 29th February 1956. *Parliamentary Debates (Commons),* Vol. 549, 1956, cc. 1183-84.

Report of the British Caribbean Federal Capital Commission 1956. Recommendation of Barbados, Jamaica, and Trinidad (in that order) as sites for the federal capital, based on various criteria. *Col. No. 328/1956.*

Report of the Chaguaramas Joint Commission, 25th September 1956. *Col. No. 328/1956.*

British Caribbean (Federation) Act, 1956. *U.K. Public General Acts,* 1956, c. 63.

West Indies (Federation) Order in Council, 1957. *S.I. 1364/1957.*

FEDERATION AND FEDERAL EXPERIMENTS (cont.)

Royal Instructions to the Governor-General and Commander-in-Chief, dated 20th August 1957. *Instruments not S.I., appendix to S.I./1957.*

West Indies (Federation) (Amendment) Order in Council, 1958. *Instrument not S.I., appendix to S.I./1958.*

Constitution of the West Indies (Amendment) Order in Council., 1960. *Instruments not S.I., appendix to S.I./1959.*

Constitution of the West Indies (Amendment) Order in Council, 1960. *Instrument not S.I., appendix to S.I./1960.*

Constitution of the West Indies (Amendment No. 2) Order in Council, 1960. *Instrument not S.I., appendix to S.I./1960.*

Jamaica Legislature. House of Representatives. Jamaica's proposals for the W.I. Federation. *Ministry Paper No. 3/1960.*

Report of the West Indies Constitutional Conference 1961. *Cmnd. 1417/1961.*

Decisions of Conference of Chief Ministers of Leeward and Windward Islands and Premier of Barbados, 1962. *St. Vincent Council Paper No. 14 of 1962.*

The West Indies Act, 1962. *U.K. Public General Acts,* 1962, c. 19.

The West Indies (Dissolution and Interim Commissioner) Order in Council 1962. *S.I. 1084/1962.*

West Indies (Constitution) (Amendment) Order in Council, 1962. *Instruments not S.I., appendix S.I./1962.*

West Indies (Constitution) (Amendment No. 2) Order in Council, 1962. *Instruments not S.I., appendix to S.I./1962.*

The West Indies (Retirement and Compensation) Order in Council, 1962. *S.I. 1085/1962.*

Statement by the Secretary of State for the Colonies on the West Indies, 6th February 1962. *Parliamentary Debates (Commons),* Vol. 653, 1962, cc. 230-35.

Report of the Conference on the East Caribbean, 1962. *Cmnd. 1946/1962.*

Statement by the Secretary of State for the Colonies on West Indies, 22nd January 1963. *Parliamentary Debates (Commons),* Vol. 670, 1963, cc. 13-14.

Statement by the Secretary of State for the Colonies on the East Caribbean (Federation Conference), 2nd July 1963. *Parliamentary Debates (Commons),* Vol. 680, 1963, cc. 27-28.

FEDERATION AND FEDERAL EXPERIMENTS (cont.)

The West Indies (Retirement Compensation) (Amendment No. 2) Order in Council, 1963. *S.I. 790/1963.*

Report of the Fiscal Commissioner on Federation of the East Caribbean territories, 1963. *Cmnd. 1991/1963.*

Report of Civil Service Commissioner on Federation of the East Caribbean territories, 1963. *Cmnd. 1992/1963.*

Draft Federal Scheme and Certain Correspondence between the Secretary of State and Chairman Regional Council of Ministers and between Chairman and Governments concerned in 1963 and 1964. 1965. Published with *St. Vincent Government Gazette,* 10th February 1965.

Despatch from Secretary of State for the Colonies to the governments of the East Caribbean territories, dated 22nd March 1965. *Colonial Office Papers.*

Proposals for a Federation of East Caribbean territories, 1965. *Col. No. 360/1965.*

Federal negotiations 1962-65. *Government Printing Office, Bridgetown, Barbados, 1965.*

GREAT BRITAIN

COLONIAL OFFICE Papers. See: individual territories.

See: Regulations for H.M.'s Colonial Service 1922. *Colonial Office List, 1922.* H.M.S.O.

Notes on the Constitutions of the British West Indies, Bermuda, British Guiana and British Honduras, 1933. *Colonial Office, West Indies Pamphlet, No. 585,* 1933, folio.

DEBATES Official Report. Fifth Series. Parliamentary Debates. Commons.

PARLIAMENT Papers by command.
The following is a list, in chronological order, of command papers relating to the British West Indian territories, and some of the more important papers relating to the Empire and Commonwealth as a whole.

(1) Imperial Conference 1921. Summary Proceedings and Documents. *Cmnd. 1474/1921.*

(2) Report by the Parliamentary Under-Secretary of State for the Colonies on a Visit to the West Indies and British Guiana, 1921-22. *Cmnd. 1679/1922.*

GREAT BRITAIN (cont.)

PARLIAMENT (cont.)

(3) Imperial Conference, 1923. Summary of Proceedings. *Cmnd. 1987/1923.*

(4) Report of the West Indies Conference, 1926. *Cmnd. 2672/1926.*

(5) Imperial Conference, 1926. Summary of proceedings. *Cmnd. 2768/1926.*

(6) Report of the British Guiana Commission, April 1927. *Cmnd. 2841/1927.*

(7) Report of the British Guiana Constitutional Commission. *Cmnd. 2985/1927.*

(8) Memorandum prepared by the elected members of the Combined Court of British Guiana in reply to the report of the British Guiana Commission. *Cmnd. 3047/1927.*

(9) Report of the Conference on Dominion Legislation and Merchant Shipping Legislation, 1929. *Cmnd. 3479/1929-30.*

(10) Imperial Conference, 1930. Summary of Proceedings. *Cmnd. 3717/1930-31.* Appendices. *Cmnd. 3718/1930-31.*

(11) Report of the Closer Union Commission (Leeward Islands, Windward Islands, Trinidad & Tobago), April 1933. *Cmnd. 4383/1932-33.*

(12) Jamaica. Despatch from the Secretary of State for the Colonies to the Governor of Jamaica, dated 10th February 1945. *Cmnd. 6427/1942-43.*

(13) Report of the West India Royal Commission, 1938-39. *Cmnd. 6607/1945.* (See also Recommendations. *Cmnd. 6174/1940;* and Statement of Action Taken on Recommendations. *Cmnd. 6656/1945.*)

(14) Memorandum on the Closer Association of the British West Indian Colonies, 1946-47. *Cmnd. 7120/1946-47.*

(15) Report of the Conference on the Closer Association of the British West Indies Colonies (Part I), 1947-48. *Cmnd. 7291/1948.*

(16) Report on the Colonial Empire. 1939-47. *Cmnd. 7167/1946/47* and *Cmnd. 7433/1947-48.*

(17) Progress Report on Colonial Territories. 1948-49. *Cmnd. 7715/1948-49.*

(18) British Dependencies in the Caribbean and North Atlantic, 1939-52. *Cmnd. 8575/1951-52.*

(19) Report by the Conference on the West Indian Federation held in London in April 1953. *Cmnd. 8837/1952-53.*

(20) British Guiana. Suspension of the Constitution. *Cmnd. 8980/1952-53.*

GREAT BRITAIN (cont.)

PARLIAMENT (cont.)

(21) The Plan for a British Caribbean Federation agreed by the Conference on the West Indian Federation held in London in April 1953. *Cmnd. 8895/1952-53.*

(22) Report of the British Buiana Constitutional Commission, 1954. *Cmnd. 9274/1953-54.*

(23) Report of the Fiscal Commissioner, 1955-56. *Cmnd. 9618/1955-56.*

(24) Report of the Civil Service Commissioner, 1955-56. *Cmnd. 9619/1955-56.*

(25) Report of the Judicial Commissioner, 1955-56. *Cmnd. 9620/1955-56.*

(26) Report on the Conference on the British Caribbean Federation held in London in February 1956. *Cmnd. 9733/1956.*

(27) Report on the Leeward and Windward Islands Constitutional Conference. *Cmnd. 804/1959.*

(28) Report of the British Honduras Conference held in February 1960. *Cmnd. 984/1959-60.*

(29) Report of the British Guiana Constitutional Conference, held in London in March 1960. *Cmnd. 998/1959-60.*

(30) Report of the Trinidad & Tobago Constitutional Discussions, held in Trinidad in June 1960. *Cmnd. 1123/1959-60.*

(31) Report of the West Indies Constitutional Conference, 1961, held in London, May and June 1961. *Cmnd. 1417/1960-61.*

(32) Report by the Leeward Islands and Windward Islands Constitutional Conference, held in London in June 1961. *Cmnd. 1434/1960-61.*

(33) Report of the Jamaica Independence Conference, 1962, held in London in February 1962. *Cmnd. 1638/1961-62.*

(34) Report of Commission of Inquiry into the control of Public Expenditure in Grenada during 1961-62. *Cmnd. 1735/1962.*

(35) Report of the East Caribbean Conference, 1962. *Cmnd. 1946/1961-62.*

(36) Report of the Trinidad & Tobago Independence Conference, 1962. *Cmnd. 1757/1961-62.*

(37) Report of the British Guiana Independence Conference, 1962. *Cmnd. 1870/1962-63.*

GREAT BRITAIN (cont.)

PARLIAMENT (cont.)

(38) Eastern Caribbean Federation –

(a) Report of the Fiscal Commissioners. *Cmnd. 1991/1962-63.*

(b) Report of the Civil Service Commissioners. *Cmnd. 1992/1962-63.*

(39) Report of the Bahamas Constitutional Conference, 1963. *Cmnd. 2048/1962-63.*

(40) Report of the British Honduras Constitutional Conference, 1963. *Cmnd. 2124/1962-63.*

(41) Report of the British Guiana Independence Conference, 1963. *Cmnd. 2203/1963-64.*

(42) Report of the British Guiana Constitutional Conference, 1965. *Cmnd. 2849/1965.*

(43) Constitutional Proposals for Antigua, St. Kitts/Nevis/Auguilla, Dominica, St. Lucia, St. Vincent, Grenada, 1965. *Cmnd. 2865/1965.*

(44) Report of the Antigua Constitutional Conference, 1966. *Cmnd. 2963/1965-66.*

(45) Report of the Windward Islands Constitutional Conference, 1966. *Cmnd. 3021/1966.*

(46) Report of the St. Kitts/Nevis/Anguilla Constitutional Conference, 1966. *Cmnd. 3031/1966.*

(47) Report of the Barbados Constitutional Conference, 1966. *Cmnd. 3058/1966.*

(48) Report of the British Virgin Islands Constitutional Conference, 1966. *Cmnd. 3129/1966.*

(49) Report on the discussions on the constitutional progress of St. Vincent, 1966. *Cmnd. 3219/1966.*

(50) Report of the Commonwealth Conference on Anguilla, 1967. *Cmnd. 3433/1967.*

SOVEREIGNS For Royal Instructions and Letters Patent extending to individual territories, see under territorial headings.

STATUTES Some of the more important statutes extending to the colonies and defining colonial status (mentioning only the original statutes and not subsequent amendments).

1833 Judicial Committee Act 1833 c. 41.

GREAT BRITAIN (cont.)

SOVEREIGNS (cont.)

1865 Colonial Laws Validity Act 1865 c. 63.

1866 Jamaica Act 1866 c. 12.

1870 Imperial Act 31 & 32 Vict. c. 72.

1870 Extradition Act 1870 c. 52.

1870 Foreign Enlistment Act 1870 c. 90.

1871 Leeward Islands Act 1871 c. 107.

1876 Customs Consolidation Act 1876 c. 36.

1876 St. Vincent & Grenada Constitution Act 1876 c. 47.

1877 Colonial Fortifications Act 1877 c. 23.

1878 Territorial Waters Jurisdiction Act 1878 c. 73.

1881 Fugitive Offenders Act 1881 c. 69.

1887 Trinidad & Tobago Act 1887 c. 44.

1887 British Settlements Act 1887 c. 54.

1890 Colonial Courts of Admiralty Act 1890 c. 27.

1890 Foreign Jurisdiction Act 1890 c. 37.

1894 Merchant Shipping Act 1894 c. 60.

1900 Colonial Stock Act 1900 c. 62.

1908 Appellate Jurisdiction Act 1908 c. 51.

1909 Naval Establishments Act 1909 c. 18.

1911 Pensions (Governors of Dominions etc.) Act 1911 c. 24.

1911 Naval Discipline Act 1911 c. 47.

1914 British Nationality and Status of Aliens Act 1914 c. 17.

1919 West Indian Court of Appeal Act 1919 c. 47.

1920 Administration of Justice Act 1920 c. 81.

1926 Indian and Colonial Divorce Jurisdiction Act 1926 c. 40.

1928 British Guiana Act 1928 c. 5.

1931 Statute of Westminster 1931 c. 4.

1931 Colonial Naval Defence Act 1931 c. 9.

1933 Foreign Judgments (Reciprocal Enforcement) Act 1933 c. 13.

1938 Dominica Act 1938 c. 10.

GREAT BRITAIN (cont.)

SOVEREIGNS (cont.)

1939 Ships and Aircraft (Transfer Restrictions) Act 1939 c. 70.

1945 Colonial Development and Welfare Act 1945 c. 20.

1948 British Nationality Act 1948 c. 56.

1952 Visiting Forces Act 1952 c. 67.

1953 Royal Styles and Titles 1953 c. 9.

1955 Army Act 1955 c. 18.

1955 Air Force Act 1955 c. 19.

1956 Leeward Islands Act 1956 c. 23.

1956 British Caribbean (Federation) Act 1956 c. 63.

1962 West Indies Act 1962 c. 19.

1962 Jamaica Independence Act 1962 c. 40.

1962 Trinidad & Tobago Independence Act 1962 c. 54.

1963 Bahama Islands (Constitution) Act 1963 c. 56.

1966 Guyana Independence Act 1966 c. 14.

1966 Barbados Independence Act 1966 c. 37.

1967 West Indies Act 1967 c. 4.

STATUTORY INSTRUMENTS See individual territories for Statutory Rules and Orders and Statutory Instruments extending to them.

GRENADA

See also: Associated States. Windward Islands.

Constitutional position, 1922. *Colonial Office List, 1922,* pp. 442-43. H.M.S.O.

Statement by His Excellency the Governor of the Windward Islands to the Legislative Council on Mr. Wood's proposals for the confederation of the Windward Islands with the Government of Trinidad. *Minutes of the Legislative Council of Grenada, 1922,* pp. 6-8.

Despatch from the Secretary of State for the Colonies to the Governor of the Windward Islands, 1922. *Grenada Legislative Council Minutes, 1922.*

(Legislative Council) Order in Council 1924. *S.R. & O./1924.*

GRENADA (cont.)

Windward Islands Letters Patent, dated 9th April 1924. *S.R. & O./1924.*

Legislative Council (Registration of Voters) Ordinance, No. 10 of 1925. *Ordinances of Grenada.*

Supreme Court (Amendment) Ordinance, No. 20 of 1927. *Ordinances of Grenada.*

(Legislative Council) (Amendment) Order in Council 1930. *S.R. & O. 1142/ 1930.*

Despatch from the Secretary of State for the Colonies to the Governor of the Windward Islands, 1934. *Colonial Office Papers.*

Despatch from Secretary of State for the Colonies, dated 2nd June 1935, to the Governor of the Windward Islands re Constitution of Grenada. *Grenada Legislative Council Minutes, 1935.*

Winward Islands Letters Patent, dated 13th November 1936. *S.R. & O./1936.*

Grenada (Legislative Council) Order in Council, 1936. *S.R. & O. 1371/1936.*

Supreme Court (Amendment) Ordinance, No. 22 of 1936. *Ordinances of Grenada.*

Report of Select Committee on Amendment of the Legislative Council (Elections) Ordinance, 1939. *Council Paper No. 13 of 1939.*

Windward Islands Letters Patent, amending Letters Patent, 1936, dated 28th December 1939. *S. R. & O./1939.*

Report of the Select Committee on the Legislative Council (Amendment) Ordinance, 1940. *Council Paper No. 7 of 1940.*

Grenada (Legislative Council) (Amendment) Order in Council, 1944. *S.R. & O. 939/1944.*

Windward Islands Conference on Constitutional Reform. *Colonial Office, West Indies Pamphlet, No. 803,* 1945, folio.

Windward Islands Letters Patent, amending Letters Patent, 1936, dated 11th May 1945. *S.R. & O./1945.*

Grenada (Legislative Council) (Amendment) Order in Council, 1945. *S.R. & O. 403/1945.*

Report of Committee on Federation, 1946. *Council Paper No. 8 of 1946.*

GRENADA (cont.)

Windward Islands Letters Patent, 1951. *Instruments not S.I., appendix to S.I./1951.*

Windward Islands Royal Instructions 1951. *Instruments not S.I., appendix to S.I./1951.*

Grenada (Legislative Council) (Electoral Provision) Order in Council, 1951. *S.I. 328/1951.*

Grenada (Legislative Council) Order in Council, 1951. *S.I. 1393/1951.*

Legislative Council (Elections) Ordinance, No. 10 of 1951. *Ordinances of Grenada.*

Message from His Excellency the Governor of the Windward Islands to the Grenada Legislative Council, dated 21st December 1951. *Minutes of Legislative Council, 1951,* pp. 23-4.

Windward Islands Additional Instructions, 22nd February 1952. *Instruments not S.I., appendix to S.I./1952.*

Windward Islands Additional Instructions, dated 19th March 1953. *Instruments not S.I., appendix to S.I./1953.*

(Legislative Council) (Amendment) Order in Council, 1953. *S.I. 400/1953.*

Announcement by President of Council to Grenada, Legislative Council, on 20th December 1954. *Minutes of Legislative Council, 1954,* pp. 19-21.

Windward Islands Letters Patent, 1954. *Instruments not S.I., appendix to S.I./1954.*

Windward Islands Additional Instructions, dated 10th September 1954. *Instruments not S.I., appendix to S.I./1954.*

(Legislative Council) (Amendment) Order in Council, 1954. *S.I. 1038/1954.*

Public Announcement on Constitutional Reform in the Colonies of Grenada, St. Lucia and St. Vincent. Windward Islands, 1955. See *Minutes of the Legislative Council of Grenada,* 7th January 1955 (appendix I to Address by the Acting Administrator).

(Legislative Council) (Amendment) Order in Council, 1955. *S.I. 1816/1955.*

Public Service Commission Ordinance, No. 31 of 1955. *Ordinances of Grenada.*

Crown Proceedings Ordinance, No. 33 of 1955. *Ordinances of Grenada.*

GRENADA (cont.)

Windward Islands Letters Parent. 28th December 1955. *Instruments not S.I., appendix to S.I./1955.*

Windward Islands Royal Instructions. 28th December 1955. *Instruments not S.I., appendix to S.I./1955.*

(Legislative Council) (Amendment) Order in Council, 1956. *S.I. 1581/1956.*

Windward Islands Additional Instructions, 23rd October 1957. *Instruments not S.I., appendix to S.I./1957.*

(Legislative Council) (Amendment) Order in Council, 1957. *S.I. 1743/1957.*

Windward Islands Letters Patent, dated 8th May 1958. *Instruments not S.I., appendix to S.I./1958.*

Report of the Select Committee appointed to consider an Advanced Constitution for Grenada. 1959. *Council Paper No. 5 of 1959.*

Report of the Leeward and Windward Islands Constitutional Conference, 1959. *Cmnd. 804/1959.*

Windward and Leeward Islands (Courts) Order in Council, 1959. *S.I. 2197/1959.*

Windward and Leeward Islands (Police Service Commission) Order in Council, 1959. *S.I. 2198/1959.*

(Constitution) Order in Council, 1959. *S.I. 2200/1959.*

Royal Instructions to the Administrator, dated 22nd December 1959. *Instruments not S.I., appendix to S.I./1959.*

Legislative Council (Contracts with Government) (Disqualification) Ordinance, No. 18 of 1960. *Ordinances of Grenada.*

Report of Commission of Inquiry into the Control of Public Expenditure in Grenada during 1961, 1962. *Cmnd. 1735/1962.*

Despatch from Secretary of State for the Colonies regarding reports of commission of inquiry into expenditure in Grenada, dated 23rd July 1962. *Grenada Government Gazette,* Vol. 8, No. 44, 28th July 1962.

Statement by Secretary of State for the Colonies on the Suspension of the Grenada Constitution, dated 18th June 1962. *Parliamentary Debates (Commons),* Vol. 661, 1962, cc. 948-949.

Grenada (Constitution) Order in Council 1962. *S.I. 1244/1962.* (To be taken together with Grenada (Constitution) Order in Council. *S.I. 2200/1959).*

GRENADA (cont.)

Additional Royal Instructions, dated 14th June 1962. *Instruments not S.I., appendix to S.I./1962.*

Telegrams exchanged between Chief Minister of St. Vincent and Secretary of State for the Colonies on Suspension of the Grenada Constitution, June 1962. *St. Vincent Government Gazette,* Vol. 95, No. 37, 1962.

Legal and Constitutional Commission on the Question of Unitary Statehood of Grenada and Trinidad & Tobago. *Government Printers, Port of Spain, Trinidad, 1963.*

Constitutional proposals for Antigua, St. Christopher/Nevis/Anguilla, Dominica, St. Lucia, St. Vincent, Grenada. *Cmnd. 2867/1965.*

(Constitution) Order, 1965. *S.I. 2162/1965.*

Windward Islands Constitutional Conference 1966. Report, general conclusions and Grenada appendix. *Cmnd. 3021/1967.*

The West Indies Act, 1967. *U.K. Public General Acts,* 1967 c. 4.

(Constitution) Order, 1967. *S.I. 227/1967.*

House of Representatives (Elections) (Amendment) Act, No. 8 of 1968. *Laws of Grenada.*

Legislative (Privileges, Immunities and Powers) Act, No. 24 of 1968. *Laws of Grenada.*

GUYANA

For pre-independence (1966) see British Guiana.

Independence Act 1966. *U.K. Public General Acts,* 1966 c. 14.

Independence Order, 1966. *S.I. 575/1966.*

National Security (Miscellaneous provisions) Act, No. 7 of 1966. *Laws of Guyana.*

(Procedure in Appeals to Privy Council) Order 1967. *S.I. 576/1967.*

Guyana Citizenship Act, No. 14 of 1967. *Laws of Guyana.*

Ombudsman Act, No. 17 of 1967. *Laws of Guyana.*

National Registration Act, No. 24 of 1967. *Laws of Guyana.*

Appendix D

IMPERIAL CONFERENCES

Conference 1921. Summary of Proceedings and Documents. *Cmnd. 1474/ 1921.*

Conference, 1923. Summary of Proceedings. *Cmnd. 1987/1923.*

Conference, 1926. Summary of Proceedings. *Cmnd. 3717/1930-31.* Appendices. *Cmnd. 3718/1930-31.*

JAMAICA

Constitutional position in 1922. *Colonial Office List, 1922,* pp. 230-31. H.M.S.O.

Address by the Governor to the Legislative Council, 28th February 1922. *Legislative Council Minutes, 1922.*

Address by the Governor to the Legislative Council, 21st November 1922. *Legislative Council Minutes, 1922.*

Petition to His Majesty the King on the subject of a change in the Political Constitution from the Elected and certain Nominated (Unofficial) Members of the Council, 1922. *Appendix XXX, Legislative Council Minutes, 1922.*

Despatch from the Secretary of State for the Colonies re petition for a change in the Political Constitution of the Colony, dated 15th May 1922. *Appendix L, Legislative Council Minutes, 1922.*

Despatch from the Secretary of State for the Colonies re Report of Major Wood, 29th June, 1922. *Appendix LIX, Legislative Council Minutes, 1922.*

Correspondence re formation of Executive Committee. *Appendix VI, Legislative Council Minutes, 1923.*

Despatch from the Governor to the Secretary of State for the Colonies, re Political Constitution, March 1923. *Appendix XXXI, Legislative Council Minutes, 1923.*

Despatch from the Governor to the Secretary of State for the Colonies, re Political Constitution, 14th April 1923. *Appendix XXXII, Legislative Council Minutes, 1923.*

Despatch from the Governor to the Secretary of State for the Colonies, re Political Constitution, 29th March 1923. *Appendix XLIII, Legislative Council Minutes, 1923.*

JAMAICA (cont.)

Report re Amendments to Constitution as amended and adopted by Council on 5th December 1923. *Appendix LIII, Legislative Council Minutes, 1923.*

Letter from the Governor to the Secretary of State for the Colonies re proposed Reform of the Constitution, 28th December 1923. *Appendix XX, Legislative Council Minutes, 1924.*

Constitution of Jamaica, clause in regard to the proposed reform. (Statement on procedure). *Appendix XXI, Legislative Council Minutes, 1924.*

Constitution of Jamaica, Draft Clauses sent to the Secretary of State for the Colonies, 28th April 1924. And Message re alteration of the Constitution from the Governor to the Legislative Council, 28th April 1924. *Appendix XXX, Legislative Council Minutes, 1924.*

Reply of Secretary of State for the Colonies in regard to the Governor's overriding power in the new Constitution 1st January 1925. *Appendix III, Legislative Council Minutes, 1925.*

Despatch from the Secretary of State for the Colonies to the Governor, 25th August 1925. *Appendix XXXVI, Legislative Council Minutes, 1925.*

Despatch from the Secretary of State for the Colonies to the Governor, re proposed new Constitution, 29th June 1926. *Appendix XXXIII, Legislative Council Minutes, 1926.*

Judicature (Amendment) Law, No. 16 of 1929. *Laws of Jamaica.*

Court of Appeal Law, No. 9 of 1935. *Laws of Jamaica.*

Judicature (Amendment) Law, No. 28 of 1935. *Laws of Jamaica.*

(Appeals to Privy Council) (Amendment) Order in Council 1936, 24th July 1936. *S.R. & O./1936.*

Registration of Voters (Amendment) Law, No. 11 of 1937. *Laws of Jamaica.*

Report of the Select Committee of the Legislative Council re Political Constitution for Jamaica. *Minutes of Legislative Council of Jamaica, 1939.* Appendix No. XXXII.

Minority Report on Select Committee on Political Constitution for Jamaica. (Report). *Minutes of Legislative Council, 1939.* Appendix No. XXXIV.

Judicature (Amendment) Law, No. 29 of 1939. *Laws of Jamaica.*

Despatch (No. 42) from the Secretary of State to the Governor, dated 7th March 1941. *Minutes of the Jamaican Legislative Council.* 12th March 1941.

JAMAICA (cont.)

Statement by the Under-Secretary of State for the Colonies on the Jamaican Constitutions, 12th March 1941. *Parliamentary Debates Commons),* Vol. 369, 1940-41, cc. 1265-6.

Court of Appeal (Amendment) Law, No. 59 of 1941. *Laws of Jamaica.*

Despatch (No. 1A) from the Secretary of State to the Governor, dated 5th January 1942. *Proceedings of the Jamaican Legislative Council.* Spring Session, pp. 1-2, 1942.

Despatch from the Governor to the Secretary of State, dated 5th November 1942. *Colonial Office Papers.*

Despatch from the Secretary of State for the Colonies to the Governor of Jamaica, dated 10th February 1943. *Cmnd. 6427/1942-43.*

Governor's Address to the Legislative Council, 1st June 1943. *Proceedings of the Legislative Council 1st June,* 1943, p. 250.

Proposals for new Constitution of Jamaica, 20th July 1944. *Kingston, Jamaica, 1944.*

Governor's Message No. 52 re Constitution – Comments of Secretary of State re further amendments proposed. *Minutes of Legislative Council of Jamaica, 1944,* p. 273.

Governor's Message No. 57 re Constitution – final draft proposals. *Minutes of Legislative Council of Jamaica, 1944,* p. 273.

(Constitution) Order in Council, 1944. *S.R. & O. 1215/1944.*

Letters Patent constituting the office of Captain-General and Governor-in-Chief of the Island of Jamaica and its Dependencies, dated 27th October 1944. *S.R. & O./1944.*

Instructions, dated 27th October 1944. *S.R. & O./1944.*

Representation of the People Law, No. 44 of 1944. *Laws of Jamaica.*

Despatch No. 207 from the Secretary of State for the Colonies to the Governor of Jamaica, 31st August 1948; His Excellency's Despatch No. 48 of the 14th March 1948, to the Secretary of State for the Colonies with its enclosures. *Colonial Office Papers.*

Judicature (Amendment) Law, No. 22 of 1948. *Laws of Jamaica.*

Report of Select Committee of House of Representatives re the Political Constitution, 1949. *Government Printer, Kingston.*

JAMAICA (cont.)

Jamaica (Constitution) Order in Council, 1949. *S.I. 1436/1949.*

Jamaica (Constitution) (No. 2) Order in Council, 1949. *S.I.2201/1949.*

Report of the Commission to enquire into the Public Service (Mr. E. Mills, sole Commissioner). 1950. *Government Printer, Kingston.*

Public Service Commission Law, No. 48 of 1951. *Laws of Jamaica.*

Report on Ministries, by D.C. MacGillivray, Colonial Secretary, 1951. *Government Printer, Kingston.*

Governor's Address to House of Representatives, 29th April 1952. *Proceedings of House of Representatives,* Vol. 1, 1952, pp. 145-47.

Statement by the Secretary of State for the Colonies on Jamaica (Constitution), 29th April 1952. *Parliamentary Debates (Commons),* Vol. 499, 1952, cc. 79-80.

(Constitution) Order in Council, 1953. *S.I. 747/1953.*

Report of the Select Committee of the House of Representatives re Internal Self-Government, September 1954. *Government Printer, Kingston.*

(Constitution) Order in Council, 1955. *S.I. 1214/1955.*

(Constitution) Order in Council, 1956. *S.I. 1209/1956.*

Report of the Select Committee of the House of Representatives on proposals for constitution reform, dated 19th June 1957. *Government Printer, Kingston, 1957.*

Report of the Committee of Unofficial Members of the Legislative Council on proposals for constitutional reform, 1957. *Government Printer, Kingston, 1957.*

Despatch from Secretary of State for the Colonies to the Governor of Jamaica, 24th September 1957. *Colonial Office Papers.*

(Constitution) Order in Council, 1957. *S.I. 1744/1957.*

Letters Patent, dated 31st October 1957 to amend Jamaica Letters Patent, 1944. *Instruments not S.I., appendix to S.I./1957.*

Additional Instructions, dated 31st October 1957. *Instruments not S.I., appendix to S.I./1957.*

Judicial Service Commission Law, No. 45 of 1957. *Laws of Jamaica.*

JAMAICA (cont.)

Report of the Select Committee of the House of Representatives on constitutional changes. April 1958. *Minutes of the House of Representatives, 1958.* Appendix XII.

Crown Proceedings Law, No. 68 of 1958. *Laws of Jamaica.*

Despatch from Secretary of State for the Colonies to the Governor of Jamaica, dated 13th May 1959. *Colonial Office Papers.*

(Constitution) Order in Council, 1959. *S.I. 862/1959.*

(Constitution) (Amendment) Order in Council, 1959. *S.I. 2202/1959.*

Royal Instructions to the Captain-General and Governor-in-Chief, dated 19th May 1959. *Instruments not S.I., appendix to S.I./1959.*

Judicature (Supreme Court) (Amendment) Law, No. 10 of 1960. *Laws of Jamaica.*

Referendum (Federation) Law, No. 53 of 1960. *Laws of Jamaica.*

(Constitution) (Amendment) Order in Council, 1961. *S.I. 571/1961.*

Report of the Committees of the Legislature re Independence Constitution, 1962. *Government Printer, Kingston.*

Report of the Independence Conference, 1962. *Cmnd. 1638/1962.*

Ministry Paper No. 3 re Jamaica Independence Constitution, London, 1962.

Judicature (Appellate Jurisdiction) Law, No. 15 of 1962. *Laws of Jamaica.*

Independence Act 1962. *U.K. Public General Acts,* 1962 c. 40.

(Constitution) Order in Council 1962. *S.I. 1550/1962.*

(Consequential Provisions) Order in Council 1962. *S.I. 1647/1962.*

Parliament (Membership Questions) Act, No. 8 of 1963. *Acts of Jamaica.*

Judicature (Supreme Court) (Amendment) Act, No. 50 of 1963. *Acts of Jamaica.*

Representation of the People (Amendment) Act, No. 54 of 1963. *Acts of Jamaica.*

JUDICIAL AND LEGAL SERVICE COMMISSION

See constitutions of individual territories.
Windward Islands and Leeward Islands (Courts) Order in Council 1959.

LEEWARD ISLANDS

See also: Federation and Federal Experiments, and the individual territories: Antigua, Dominica, (up to 1938), Montserrat, St. Christopher/Nevis/Anguilla, Virgin Islands.

Constitutional position in 1922. *Colonial Office List, 1922,* p. 251. H.M.S.O.

The (Colonial) West Indian Court of Appeal Act, No. 3 of 1921. *Acts of the Leeward Islands.*

An Act to amend the Privy Council Appeal Act, 1909. No. 1 of 1922. *Acts of the Leeward Islands.*

Secretary of State's Despatch No. 218 of 1922. *Leeward Islands Gazette Notice No. 239 of 1922.*

Secretary of State's Despatch No. 241 of 1922. *Leeward Islands Gazette Notice No. 291 of 1922.*

Leeward Islands Act, 1871, Amendment Act, 1923. No. 6 of 1923. *Acts of the Leeward Islands.*

General Legislative Council (composition of elective membership). Proclamation by Governor of Leeward Islands. *Leeward Islands Gazette, 1923,* p. 219.

Leeward Islands Act, 1871, Amendment Act No. 5 of 1924. *Acts of the Leeward Islands.*

The (Colonial) West Indian Court of Appeal (Amendment) Act, 1925. *Acts of the Leeward Islands.*

The (Colonial) West Indian Court of Appeal Act, No. 7 of 1931. *Acts of the Leeward Islands.*

The Supreme Court (Amendment) Act, No. 14 of 1931. *Acts of the Leeward Islands.*

The (Colonial) West Indian Court of Appeal (Amendment) Act, No. 22 of 1932. *Acts of the Leeward Islands.*

Closer Union of Trinidad, the Windward Islands and the Leeward Islands. Despatch from the Secretary of State for the Colonies, dated 4th March 1931. *Colonial Office Papers.*

LEEWARD ISLANDS (cont.)

Report of the Closer Union Commission (Leeward Islands, Windward Islands, Trinidad & Tobago), April 1933. *Cmnd. 4383/1932-33.*

Address by the Governor to the General Legislative Council of the Leeward Council. *Leeward Islands Gazette,* Supplement to Gazette No. 12 of 1934.

Address by Governor to the General Legislative Council of the Leeward Islands on 2nd March 1935. *Leeward Islands Gazette,* Supplement to Gazette No. 10 of 1935.

Leeward Islands (Amendment) Act, No. 10 of 1936. *Acts of the Leeward Islands.*

Leeward Islands (Amendment) Act, No. 5 of 1937. *Acts of the Leeward Islands.*

Address by the Governor to the Legislative Council of Antigua on 19th June 1936. *Leeward Islands Gazette, 1936.*

Precis of the Governor's Address to the General Legislative Council of the Leeward Islands on 18th November 1936. *Leeward Islands Gazette,* Supplement to Gazette No. 60 or 1936.

Letters Patent, dated 17th November 1936, constituting the Office of Governor and Commander-in-Chief of the Leeward Islands 1936. *S.R. & O./ 1936.*

Instructions passed under the Royal Sign Manual and Signet to the Governor and Commander-in-Chief of the Leeward Islands, 17th November 1936. *S.R. & O./1936.*

Notes on discussions and resolutions passed by General Legislative Council on 23rd November 1937. *Leeward Islands Gazette,* Supplement to Gazette No. 16 of 1938.

Address by the Governor to the General Legislative Council of the Leeward Islands on Friday, 18th November 1938. *Leeward Islands Gazette,* Supplement to Gazette No. 56 of 1938.

Address by the Governor to the General Legislative Council of the Leeward Islands, on Wednesday, 29th November 1939. *Leeward Islands Gazette,* Supplement to Gazette No. 75 of 1939.

Courts Act 1939. *Acts of the Leeward Islands.*

Leeward Islands and Windward Islands (Courts) Order in Council, 1939. *S.R. & O. 1898/1939.*

LEEWARD ISLANDS (cont.)

Letters Patent, dated 28th December 1939, passed under the Great Seal of the Realm amending the Letters Patent of the 17th November 1936, constituting the office of Governor and Commander-in-Chief of the Leeward Islands. *S.R. & O./1939.*

Additional Instructions passed under the Royal Sign Manual and Signet to the Governor and Commander-in-Chief of the Leeward Islands. *S.R. & O./1940.*

Windward and Leeward Islands (Appeal to Privy Council) Order in Council, 1942. *S.R. & O./1942.*

Letters Patent, dated 12th July 1943, Amending Letters Patent of 17th November 1936, 1943. *S.R. & O./1943.*

Leeward Islands (Amendment) Act, 1943. No. 9 of 1943. *Acts of the Leeward Islands.*

Leeward Islands (Amendment) Act, 1944. *Acts of the Leeward Islands.*

Government Notice. Constitutional Reform. Windward and Leeward Islands. *Leeward Islands Gazette, 1949,* p. 87.

Government Notice. Constitutional Reform..*Leeward Islands Gazette, 1949,* p. 267.

Leeward Islands and Windward Islands (Courts) (Amendment) Order in Council 1949. *S.I. 600/1949.*

Leeward Islands (Amendment) Act, 1950. No. 2 of 1950. *Acts of the Leeward Islands.*

Address by the Governor to the General Legislative Council of the Leeward Islands, on 15th October 1951. *Leeward Islands Gazette,* Supplement to Gazette No. 57 of 1951.

Additional Instructions passed under the Royal Sign Manual and Signet to the Governor and Commander-in-Chief, Leeward Islands, dated 30th December 1950. *S.R. & O./1951.*

Letters Patent amending Letters Patent of 1936, constituting the office of Governor and Commander-in-Chief of the Leeward Islands, dated 15th January 1951. *S.R. & O./1951.*

Leeward Islands (Amendment) Act, 1951. No. 13 of 1951. *Acts of the Leeward Islands.*

Additional Instructions to the Governor of the Leeward Islands, dated 22nd February 1952. *Instruments not S.I., appendix to S.I./1952.*

LEEWARD ISLANDS (cont.)

Address by the Governor to the General Legislative Council of the Leeward Islands on 6th January 1953. *Leeward Islands Gazette, 1953,* p. 15.

Leeward Islands (Amendment) Act 1953. *Acts of the Leeward Islands.*

Letters Patent, dated 21st December 1953. *Instruments not S.I., appendix to S.I./1954.*

Royal Instructions, dated 21st December 1954. *Instruments not S.I., appendix to S.I./1954.*

The Leeward and Windward Islands (Courts) (Amendment) Order in Council, 1954. *S.I. 1040/1954.*

Statement by the Secretary of State for the Colonies on proposed abolition of the Leeward Islands Federation, 21st December 1954. *Parliamentary Debates (Commons),* Vol. 535, 1954, c. 271.

Address by the Governor to the General Legislative Council of the Leeward Islands, 5th January 1955 and the reply of the Unofficial Members. *Leeward Islands Gazette,* Supplement to Gazette No. 3 of 1955.

Leeward Islands (Amendment) Act No. 19 of 1955. *Acts of the Leeward Islands.*

Letters Patent passed 28th December 1955. *Leeward Islands Gazette,* Supplement to Gazette No. 3 of 1956 and *Instruments not S.I., appendix to S.I./1955.*

Additional Royal Instructions passed on 28th day of December 1955. *Leeward Islands Gazette,* Supplement to Gazette No. 3 of 1956 and *Instruments not S.I., appendix to S.I./1955.*

Address by the Governor to the General Legislative Council of the Leeward Islands on 28th January 1956. *Leeward Islands Gazette, Supplement to Gazette No. 7 of 1956.*

Letters Patent, dated 20th June 1956. *Leeward Islands Gazette,* Supplement to Gazette No. 30 of 1956 and S.I./1956.

Royal Instructions, dated 20th June 1956. *Leeward Islands Gazette,* Supplement to Gazette No. 30 of 1956 and *Instruments not S.I., appendix to S.I./1956.*

Leeward Islands Act 1956. *U.K. Public General Acts,* 1956 c. 23.

Leeward Islands (Miscellaneous Provisions) Order, 1956. *S.I. 833/1956.*

LEEWARD ISLANDS (cont.)

Leeward Islands and Windward Islands (Courts) Order in Council, 1957. *S.I. 2167/1957.*

Letters Patent, dated 8th May 1958. *Instruments not S.I., appendix to S.I./ 1958.*

Additional Royal Instructions, dated 5th May, 1958. *Instruments not S.I., appendix to S.I./1958.*

(Emergency Powers) Order in Council, 1958. *S.I. 591/1958.*

Proposals for constitutional reform in the Territories of Antigua, Dominica, Grenada, Montserrat, St. Christopher/Nevis/Anguilla, St. Lucia, and St. Vincent, agreed to at the Conference convened by the Federal government at Federal House, Port of Spain, Trinidad, from 23rd March to 26th March 1959. *Federal Government Publication, Port of Spain, Trinidad.*

Report of the Leeward and Windward Islands Constitutional Conference 1959. *Cmnd. 804/1959.*

Leeward Islands and Windward Islands (Courts) Order in Council, 1959. *S.I. 2197/1959.*

(Police Service Commission) Order in Council 1959. *S.I. 2198/1959.*

(Emergency Powers) Order in Council, 1959. *S.I. 2206/1959.*

Report by the Leeward Islands and Windward Islands Constitutional Conference held in London in June, 1961. *Cmnd. 1434/1960-61.*

MONTSERRAT

See also: Leeward Islands.

Constitutional Position 1922. *Colonial Office List, 1922,* p. 263. H.M.S.O.

An Ordinance to amend the Montserrat Constitution Ordinance 1909. No. 18 of 1922. *Laws of Montserrat.*

Constitution Ordinance No. 16 of 1936. *Laws of Montserrat.*

Constitution (Extension of Duration) Ordinance No. 3 of 1948. *Laws of Montserrat.*

Address by the President to the Montserrat Legislative Council, Tuesday, 19 December 1950. *Leeward Islands Gazette,* Supplement to Gazette No. 3 of 1951.

MONTSERRAT (cont.)

Legislative Council (Registration of Voters) Ordinance, No. 8 of 1951. *Laws of Montserrat.*

Constitution and Elections Ordinance, No. 1 of 1952. *Laws of Montserrat.*

Constitution and Elections (Amendment) Ordinance No. 9 of 1954. *Laws of Montserrat.*

Crown Proceedings Ordinance, No. 12 of 1954. *Laws of Montserrat.*

Constitution and Elections (Amendment) Ordinance No. 9 of 1955. *Laws of Montserrat.*

Public Service Commission Ordinance, No. 1 of 1956. *Laws of Montserrat.*

Crown Proceedings (Amendment) Ordinance No. 10 of 1956. *Laws of Montserrat.*

Assignment passed under the Public Seal of Montserrat to the Administrator of the Colony of Montserrat of certain powers and authorities vested in the Governor of the Leeward Islands by the Leeward Islands Letters Patent, 1956. *The Antigua, Montserrat and Virgin Islands Gazette, 1956.* p. 59.

Constitution and Elections (Amendment) Ordinance No. 11 of 1957. *Laws of Montserrat.*

Constitution and Elections (Amendment) Ordinance 1958. No. 18 of 1958. *Laws of Montserrat.*

Constitutional Conference, 1959. *Cmnd. 804/1959.*

The Police Service Commission Ordinance No. 25 of 1959. *Laws of Montserrat.*

Letters Patent, dated 22nd December, 1959. *Instruments not S.I., appendix to S.I./1959.*

Royal Instructions to the Administrator, dated 22nd December, 1959. *Instruments not S.I., appendix to S.I./1959.*

Constitution and Elections (Amendment) Ordinance, 1960. No. 1 of 1960. *Laws of Montserrat.*

Public Service Commission Ordinance, 1960. No. 8 of 1960. *Laws of Montserrat.*

The Crown Attorney (Powers) Ordinance, 1960. No. 9 of 1960. *Laws of Montserrat.*

MONTSERRAT (cont.)

Legal Officers (Appointment, dismissal and disciplinary control) Ordinance, No. 10 of 1960. *Laws of Montserrat.*

Constitution and Elections (Amendment No. 2) Ordinance, No. 11 of 1960. *Laws of Montserrat.*

Legal Officers (Appointment, dismissal and disciplinary control) (Amendment) Ordinance No. 17 of 1960. *Laws of Montserrat.*

(Constitution) Order in Council 1960. *S.I./1960.*

Constitutional Conference, 1961. *Cmnd. 1434/1961.*

Despatch from Secretary of State for the Colonies to the Administrator of Montserrat, dated 8th November, 1962. No. 194. *The Antigua, Montserrat and Virgin Islands Gazette, 1962,* p. 265.

Constitution Order 1962. *S.I. 1084/1962.*

Public Service Commission (Amendment) Ordinance No. 2 of 1967. *Laws of Montserrat.*

(Appeals to Privy Council) Order 1967. *S.I. 223/1967.*

Montserrat Order 1967. *S.I. 230/1967.*

West Indies Associated States Supreme Court (Montserrat) Ordinance, No. 1 of 1968. *Laws of Montserrat.*

Public Service Commission (Amendment) Ordinance, No. 17 of 1968. *Laws of Montserrat.*

MOYNE COMMISSION REPORT

West India Royal Commission 1938-39.

Report *Cmnd. 6607/1945.*

Recommendations. *Cmnd. 6174/1940.*

Statement of action taken on the recommendations. *Cmnd. 6656/1945.*

REGULATIONS FOR H.M.'s COLONIAL SERVICE

See Colonial Office List, 1922. H.M.S.O. and subsequent Lists.

Appendix D

ST. CHRISTOPHER/NEVIS/ANGUILLA

See also: Leeward Islands. Associated States.

Constitutional position in 1922. *Colonial Office List, 1922,* p. 256. H.M.S.O.

St. Christopher-Nevis (Amendment) Act, No. 9 of 1923. *Acts of the Leeward Islands.*

Constitution Ordinance No. 14 of 1936. *Laws of St. Christopher/Nevis.*

Constitution (Amendment) Ordinance No. 3 of 1949. *Laws of St. Christopher/Nevis.*

St. Christopher and Nevis (Change of Title) Act No. 7 of 1949. *Acts of the Leeward Islands* (Change to St. Christopher, Nevis and Anguilla).

Constitution and Elections Ordinance No. 5 of 1952. *Laws of St. Christopher/Nevis/Anguilla.*

Crown Proceedings Ordinance No. 6 of 1955. *Laws of St. Christopher/Nevis/Anguilla.*

Constitution and Elections (Amendment) Ordinance No. 2 of 1956. *Laws of St. Christopher/Nevis/Anguilla.*

Public Service Commission Ordinance No. 3 of 1956. *Laws of St. Christopher/Nevis/Anguilla.*

Crown Proceedings (Amendment) Ordinance No. 12 of 1956. *Laws of St. Christopher/Nevis/Anguilla.*

Letters Patent passed 20th June 1956. *Leeward Islands Gazette,* Supplement to Gazette No. 30 of 1956 or *Instruments not S.I., appendix to S.I./1956.*

Royal Instructions, dated 20th June 1956. *Instruments not S.I., appendix to S.I./1956.*

Constitutional Conference 1959. *Cmnd. 804/1959.*

Letters Patent, dated 22nd December 1959. *Instruments not S.I., appendix to S.I./1959.*

Royal Instructions to the Administrator, dated 22nd December 1959. *Instruments not S.I., appendix to S.I./1959.*

Public Service Commission Ordinance No. 10 of 1959. *Laws of St. Christopher/Nevis/Anguilla.*

Attorney-General (Powers) Ordinance, No. 11 of 1959. *Laws of St. Christopher/Nevis/Anguilla.*

ST. CHRISTOPHER/NEVIS/ANGUILLA (cont.)

Police Service Commission Ordinance, No. 12 of 1959. *Laws of St. Christopher/Nevis/Anguilla.*

Legal Officers (Appointment, dismissal and disciplinary control) Ordinance, No. 15 of 1959. *Laws of St. Christopher/Nevis/Anguilla.*

(Constitution) Order in Council 1960. *S.I./1960.*

Constitution and Elections (Amendment) Ordinance, No. 2 of 1960. *Laws of St. Christopher/Nevis/Anguilla.*

Legal Officers (appointment, dismissal and disciplinary control) (Amendment) Ordinance, No. 12 of 1960. *Laws of St. Christopher/Nevis/Anguilla.*

Constitutional Conference, 1961. *Cmnd. 1434/1961.*

Constitution and Elections (Amendment) Ordinance, No. 3 of 1961. *Laws of St. Christopher/Nevis/Anguilla.*

Public Service Commission (Amendment) Ordinance, No. 22 of 1961. *Laws of St. Christopher/Nevis/Anguilla.*

Constitution and Elections (Amendment) Ordinance, No. 5 of 1962. *Laws of St. Christopher/Nevis/Anguilla.*

Supreme Court Act (Amendment) Ordinance, No. 15 of 1963. *Laws of St. Christopher/Nevis/Anguilla.*

Constitutional Proposals for Antigua, St. Christopher/Nevis/Anguilla, Dominica, St. Lucia, St. Vincent, Grenada, 1965. *Cmnd. 2865/1965.*

The West Indies Act, 1967. *U.K. Public General Acts,* 1967 c. 4.

Report of the St. Christopher/Nevis/Anguilla Constitutional Conference, 1966 *Cmnd. 3031/1966.*

Constitution Order 1967. *S.I. 228/1967.*

Director of Public Prosecutions Act, No. 12 of 1967. *Acts of St. Christopher/Nevis/Anguilla.*

Emergency Powers Act, No. 15 of 1967. *Acts of St. Christopher/Nevis/Anguilla.*

The Anguilla White Paper. *N.Y. Times,* Monday, 14th August 1967.

Report of the Commonwealth Conference on Anguilla, 1967. *Cmnd. 3433/1967.*

ST. LUCIA

See: Associated States. Windward Islands.

Constitutional position, 1922. *Colonial Office List, 1922,* p. 446. H.M.S.O.

(Legislative Council) Order in Council 1924. *S.R. & O./1924.*

Windward Islands Letters Patent, dated 9th April 1924. *S.R. & O./1936.*

Windward Islands Royal Instructions, dated 9th April 1924. *S.R. & O./1924.*

Legislative Council (Elected Members) Ordinance, No. 12 of 1925. *Laws of St. Lucia.*

(Legislative Council) (Amendment) Order in Council, 1931. *S.R. & O./1931.*

Legislative Council (Elected Members) (Amendment) Ordinance, No. 10 of 1935. *Laws of St. Lucia.*

Legislative Council (Elected Members) (Amendment No. 2) Ordinance, No. 16 of 1935. *Laws of St. Lucia.*

St. Lucia (Legislative Council) Order in Council, 1936. 27th October. *S.R. & O./1936.*

Windward Islands Letters Patent, dated 18th December 1936. *S.R. & O./1936.*

Windward Islands Additional Instructions, dated 13th November 1936. *S.R. & O./1936.*

Legislative Council (Elected Members) Order in Council, 1936. *St. Lucia, Rules and Orders, No. 70 of 1936.*

St. Lucia (Legislative Council, (Amendment) Order in Council, 1937. 25th March. *S.R. & O./1937.*

Windward Islands Letters Patent, amending Letters Patent, 13th November, 1936, dated 28th December 1939. *S.R. & O./1939.*

Windward Islands Additional Instructions, dated 28th December 1939. *S.R. & O./1939.*

Legislative Council (Elected Members) Ordinance, No. 26 of 1939. *Laws of St. Lucia.*

St. Lucia (Legislative Council) (Amendment) Order in Council, 1941. 4th April. *S.R. & O./1941.*

St. Lucia (Legislative Council) (Amendment) Order in Council, 1944. 10th August. *S.R. & O./1944.*

ST. LUCIA (cont.)

Windward Islands Letters Patent amending Letters Patent, 13th November, 1936, dated 11th May 1945. *S.R. & O./1945.*

Windward Islands Additional Instructions, dated 11th May 1945. *S.R. & O./ 1945.*

Legislative Council (Elected Members) (Amendment) Ordinance, No. 2 of 1945. *Laws of St. Lucia.*

St. Lucia (Legislative Council) (Amendment) Order in Council, 1947. 19th December. *S.R. & O./1947.*

St. Lucia (Legislative Council) Order in Council, 1951. 1st August. *S.I./1951.*

Windward Islands, Letter Patent, dated 27th August 1951. *Instruments not S.I., appendix to S.I./1951.*

Windward Islands, Royal Instructions, dated 10th August 1951. *Instruments not S.I., appendix to S.I./1951.*

(Legislative Council) (Electoral Provisions) Order in Council, 1951. *S.I./1951.*

Legislative Council (Elections) Ordinance, No. 13 of 1951. *Laws of St. Lucia.*

(Legislative Council) (Amendment) Order in Council, 1952. 30th January 1952. *S.I./1952.*

Windward Islands, Additional Instructions, dated 22nd February, 1952. *Instruments not S.I., appendix to S.I./1952.*

St. Lucia (Legislative Council) (Amendment) Order in Council, 1954. 30th July. *S.I./1954.*

Windward Islands Letters Patent, dated 10th September 1954. *Instruments not S.I., appendix to S.I./1954.*

Windward Islands Additional Instructions, dated 10th September 1954. *Instruments not S.I., appendix to S.I./1954.*

Public Announcement on Constitutional Reform in the Colonies of Grenada, St. Lucia and St. Vincent. Windward Islands. 1955. See *Minutes of the Legislative Council of Grenada, 7th January 1955.* (Appendix I to Address by the Acting Administrator).

(Legislative Council) (Amendment) Order in Council, 1955. *Instruments not S.I., appendix to S.I./1955.*

Supreme Court Ordinance, No. 30 of 1955. *Laws of St. Lucia.*

ST. LUCIA (cont.)

Public Service Commission Ordinance, No. 37 of 1955. *Laws of St. Lucia.*

Windward Islands Letters Patent, dated 14th March 1955. *Instruments not S.I., appendix to S.I./1955.*

Windward Islands Royal Instructions, dated 28th December 1955. *Instruments not S.I., appendix to S.I./1955.*

(Legislative Council) (Amendment) Order in Council, 1956. *Instruments not S.I., appendix to S.I./1956.*

Crown Proceedings Ordinance, No. 27 of 1956. *Laws of St. Lucia.*

(Legislative Council) (Amendment) Order in Council, 1957. *Instruments not S.I., appendix to S.I./1957.*

Windward Islands Additional Instructions, dated 23rd October 1957. *Instruments not S.I., appendix to S.I./1957.*

Statement by the Under-Secretary of State for the Colonies on St. Lucia (Constitution) 31st October 1957. *Parliamentary Debates (Commons)* Vol. 575, 1957, cc. 78-79.

Windward Islands Letters Patent, dated 8th May 1958. *Instruments not S.I., appendix to S.I./1958.*

Constitutional Conference 1959. *Cmnd. 804/1959.*

Windward Islands and Leeward Islands (Police Service Commission) Order in Council, 1959. *S.I. 2198/1959.*

(Constitution) Order in Council, 1959. *Instruments not S.I., appendix to S.I./ 1959.*

Royal Instructions to the Administrator, dated 22nd December 1959. *Instruments not S.I., appendix to S.I./1959.*

(Constitution) Order in Council 1960. *S.I./1960.*

Constitutional Proposals for Antigua, St. Christopher/Nevis/Anguilla, Dominica, St. Lucia, St. Vincent, Grenada, 1965. *Cmnd. 2865/1965.*

Report of Select Committee on Constitutional Advancement, 1966. *S.R. & O./ No. 13 of 1966.*

The West Indies Act, 1967. *U.K. Public General Acts,* 1967 c. 4.

Constitution Order 1967. *S.I. 229/1967.*

ST. VINCENT

See also: Windward Islands. Associated States.

Constitutional position, 1922. *Colonial Office List, 1922,* p. 450. H.M.S.O.

Windward Islands Letters Patent, dated 9th April 1924. *S.R. & O./1936.*

Windward Islands Royal Instructions, dated 9th April 1924. *S.R. & O./1924.*

(Legislative Council), Order in Council 1924. *S.R. & O. 1575/1924.*

Legislative Council (Elected Members) Ordinance, No. 14 of 1925. *Laws of St. Vincent.*

Supreme Court of Judicature (Amendment) Ordinance, No. 7 of 1926. *Laws of St. Vincent.*

(Legislative Council) (Amendment) Order in Council 1931. *S.R. & O. 910/1931.*

Windward Islands Additional Instructions, dated 13th November 1936. *S.R. & O./1936.*

Windward Islands Letters Patent, dated 18th December 1936. *S.R. & O./1936.*

St. Vincent (Legislative Council) Order in Council 1936. *S.R. & O. 1372/1936.*

Windward Islands Letters Patent, dated 28th December 1939. *S.R. & O./1939.*

Windward Islands Additional Instructions, dated 28th December 1939. *S.R. & O./1939.*

Supreme Court Ordinance, No. 5 of 1941. *Laws of St. Vincent.*

St. Vincent (Legislative Council) (Amendment) Order in Council 1941. *S.R. & O. 2150/1941.*

St. Vincent (Legislative Council) (Amendment) Order in Council 1944. *S.R. & O. 940/1944.*

Windward Islands Letters Patent, dated 11th May 1945. *S.R. & O./1945.*

Windward Islands Additional Instructions, dated 11th May 1945. *S.R. & O./1945.*

Report of a Select Committee appointed to consider Proposals for the Closer Union of the Leeward and Windward Islands. *St. Vincent Council Paper No. 22 of 1946.*

St. Vincent (Legislative Council) (Amendment) Order in Council, 1947. *S.R. & O. 2916/1947.*

ST. VINCENT (cont.)

Report of a committee appointed to consider constitutional reform held at Government Office on Monday 8th August 1949. *Minutes of the Legislative Council for the half year ended 31st December, 1949,* pp. 24-25.

St. Vincent (Legislative Council) (Electoral Provisions) Order in Council, 1951. *S.I. 329/1951.*

Legislative Council (Elections) Ordinance, No. 13 of 1951. *Laws of St. Vincent.*

St. Vincent (Legislative Council) Order in Council 1951. *S.I. 1394/1951.*

Windward Islands Royal Instructions, dated 10th August 1951. *Instruments not S.I., appendix to S.I./1951.*

Windward Islands Letters Patent, dated 27th August 1951. *Instruments not S.I., appendix to S.I./1951.*

Message from the Governor of the Windward Islands to the Administrator of St. Vincent, dated 3rd January 1952. *Minutes of Legislative Council of St. Vincent, 3rd and 4th January 1952,* pp. 1-2.

Crown Proceedings Ordinance, No. 37 of 1952. *Laws of St. Vincent.*

Report of the Constitutional Reform Committee, 1953. *Government Printers, Kingstown, St. Vincent.*

(Legislative Council) (Amendment) Order in Council, 1953. *S.I. 401/1953.*

Public Announcement on Constitutional Reform in St. Vincent, dated 29th December 1954. Government Notice No. 625. *St. Vincent Government Gazette, 29th December, 1954,* pp. 507-10.

(Legislative Council) (Amendment) Order in Council, 1954. *S.I. 1039/1954.*

ublic Announcement on Constitutional Reform in the Colonies of Grenada, t. Lucia and St. Vincent. Windward Islands, 1955. *See Minutes of the egislative Council of Grenada, 7th January 1955.* (Appendix I to Address by he Acting Administrator).

Legislative Council) (Amendment) Order in Council, 1955. *S.I. 1817/1955.*

indward Islands Additional Instructions, dated 28th December 1955. *struments not S.I., appendix to S.I./1955.*

indward Islands Letters Patent, amending the Letters Patent of 27th August 51, dated 28th December 1955. *Instruments not S.I., appendix to S.I./1955.*

ST. VINCENT (cont.)

(Legislative Council) (Amendment) Order in Council 1956. *S.I. 1582/1956.*

Public Service Commission Ordinance, No. 2 of 1956. *Laws of St. Vincent.*

Supreme Court (Amendment) Ordinance, No. 18 of 1956. *Laws of St. Vincent.*

(Legislative Council) (Amendment) Order in Council, 1957. *S.I. 1745/1957.*

Constitutional Conference, 1959. *Cmnd. 804/1959.*

(Constitution) Order in Council, 1959. *S.I. 2201/1959.*

Royal Instructions to the Administrator, dated 22nd December 1959. *Instruments not S.I., appendix to S.I./1959.*

Report of the Commission of Inquiry into the Public Works Department, 1963. *Kingstown, St. Vincent, 1963.*

Statement by Secretary of State for the Colonies on St. Vincent (Commission of Inquiry – Report), 11th February 1964. *Parliamentary Debates (Commons),* Vol. 689, 1964, cc. 201-2.

Constitutional Proposals for Antigua, St. Christopher/Nevis/Anguilla, Dominica, St. Lucia, St. Vincent, Grenada, 1965. *Cmnd. 2865/1965.*

Report of Committee to consider Constitutional Proposals for St. Vincent, 1966. *Government Printers, Kingstown, St. Vincent.*

Report of the Windward Islands Constitutional Conference, 1966. *Cmnd. 3021/1966.*

Supreme Court (Amendment) Ordinance, No. 20 of 1966. *Laws of St. Vincent.*

The West Indies Act, 1967. *U.K. Public General Acts,* 1967 c. 4.

Report of Discussions on Constitutional Progress 1967. *Cmnd. 3219/1967.*

(Constitution) (Amendment) Order 1967. *S.I. 232/1967.*

St. Vincent Electoral Provisions Order, 1967. *S.I. 240/1967.*

(Constitution) (Amendment No. 2) Order 1967. *S.I. 547/1967.*

(Constitution) (Amendment No. 3) Order 1967. *S.I. 587/1967.*

Statement by the Secretary of State for Commonwealth Affairs on St. Vincent (Political Situation), 12th April 1967. *Parliamentary Debates (Commons),* Vol. 744, 1967, cc. 207-8.

ST. VINCENT (cont.)

Constitution (Amendment) Order 1968. *S.I. 1098/1968.*

TRINIDAD AND TOBAGO

Constitutional position in 1922. *Colonial Office List, 1922,* p. 417. H.M.S.O.

Secretary of State's Instructions. *Council Paper No. 126 of 1922.*

Additional Royal Instructions 1923. 5th February 1923. *Instruments not S.I., appendix to S.I./1923.*

Report of the Franchise Commission, 1923. *Council Paper No. 90 of 1923.*

Correspondence referring to the proposed association of the Windward Islands with Trinidad, 1923. *Council Paper No. 103 of 1923.*

(Legislative Council) Order in Council, 1924. *S.R. & O./1924.*

Letters Patent, dated 6th June 1924, constituting the office of Governor and Commander-in-Chief of the Colony of Trinidad & Tobago. *S.R. & O./1924.*

Royal Instructions to the Governor and Commander-in-Chief of Trinidad & Tobago, dated 6th June 1924. *S.R. & O./1924.*

Legislative Council (Elections) Ordinance, 1925. (Cap. 2, No. 2, C.L. 1940). *Laws of Trinidad & Tobago.*

Reference of measures to Secretary of State for the Colonies. Question and reply in Legislative Council of Trinidad & Tobago, 1st May 1925. *Legislative Council Debates, 1925.*

Proposed establishment of a Standing Conference to deal with common affairs of the British West Indies. Despatch from the Secretary of State for the Colonies, 1925. *Council Paper No. 13 of 1925.*

Civil Service Committee – reply of Colonial Secretary to a motion in the Legislative Council, 16th March 1928. *Legislative Council Debates, 1928.*

(Legislative Council) (Amendment) Order in Council 1928. *S.R. & O./1928.*

Closer Union between Trinidad, the Windward and the Leeward Islands. Despatch from the Secretary of State for the Colonies, dated 4th March 1931. *Council Paper No. 32 of 1931.*

Report of the Closer Union Commission (Leeward Islands, Windward Islands, Trinidad & Tobago), April 1933. *Cmnd. 4383/1932-33.*

TRINIDAD AND TOBAGO (cont.)

Announcement on new constitution by the Governor to the Legislative Council, 20th December 1940. *Legislative Council Debates, 1940.*

Letters Patent, dated 5th May 1941, amending Letters Patent of 1924. *S.R. & O./1941.*

Royal Instructions to the Governor and Commander-in-Chief, dated 5th May 1941. *S.R. & O./1941.*

(Constitution) (Amendment) Order in Council 1941. *S.R. & O./1941.*

(Legislative Council) (Amendment) Order in Council, 1942. *S.R. & O./1942.*

Legislative Council (Elections) (Amendment) Ordinance, No. 28 of 1942. *Laws of Trinidad & Tobago.*

Judicature (Amendment) Ordinance, No. 38 of 1944. *Laws of Trinidad & Tobago.*

Report of the Committee to examine the extension of the franchise, 1944. *Trinidad & Tobago Council Paper, No. 35 of 1944.*

(Constitution) (Amendment) Order in Council 1945. *S.R. & O./1945.*

Legislative Council (Elections) Ordinance, No. 10 of 1946. *Laws of Trinidad & Tobago.*

Report of the Committee on Constitutional Reform 1948. *Port of Spain, Trinidad, 1948.*

The New Constitution. Full text of the Secretary of State's Despatch, (Despatch dated 7th January 1949) the Governor's Message to the People of the Colony. *Port of Spain, Trinidad, 1949.*

Letters Patent, dated 16th March 1950. *Instruments not S.I., appendix to S.I./1950.*

Royal Instructions to the Governor and Commander-in-Chief, dated 31st March 1950. *Instruments not S.I., appendix to S.I./1956.*

(Constitution) Order in Council, 1950. *S.I. 510/1950.*

Trinidad & Tobago (Constitution) (Amendment) Order in Council, 1951. *S.I. 1944/1951.*

Legislative Council (Powers & Privileges) Ordinance, No. 3 of 1953. *Laws of Trinidad & Tobago.*

TRINIDAD AND TOBAGO (cont.)

The New Constitution, 1956: report of the Constitution Reform Committee, 1955, and despatches exchanged with the Secretary of State. *Council Paper No. 16 of 1956.*

(Constitution) Order in Council, 1956. *S.I. 835/1956.*

(Electoral Provisions) Order in Council, 1956. *S.I. 415/1956.*

Additional Instructions to the Governor and Commander-in-Chief, dated 20th June 1956. *Instruments not S.I., appendix to S.I./1956.*

Legislative Council (Qualification of Electors) Ordinance, No. 16 of 1957. *Laws of Trinidad & Tobago.*

Legislative Council (Removals of Certain Disqualifications) Ordinance, No. 19 of 1957. *Laws of Trinidad & Tobago.*

Judicature (Amendment) Ordinance, No. 28 of 1957. *Laws of Trinidad & Tobago.*

Resolution of Legislative Council requesting the Secretary of State to recommend to Her Majesty in Council certain constitutional reforms, passed 20th September 1957. *Legislative Council Debates, 1957.*

Resolution of Legislative Council approving the recommendation of additional constitutional amendments, passed 13th June 1958. *Legislative Council Debates, 1958.*

Statement by the Secretary of State for the Colonies on Trinidad & Tobago (Constitutional Changes), 3rd November 1958. *Parliamentary Debates (Commons),* Vol. 594, 1958, cc. 18-22.

(Constitution) Order in Council, 1958. *S.I. 428/1958.*

Report of the Select Committee on the New Constitution, 1959. *Council Paper, No. 11 of 1959.*

(Constitution) (Amendment) Order in Council 1959. *S.I. 1044/1959.*

Additional Instructions to the Governor and Commander-in-Chief, dated 15th June 1959. *Instruments not S.I., appendix to S.I./1959.*

Letters Patent, dated 14th July 1959. *Instruments not S.I., appendix to S.I./1959.*

Exchequer and Audit Ordinance, No. 20 of 1959. *Laws of Trinidad & Tobago.*

Report of the Trinidad & Tobago Constitutional Discussions, held in London in November 1959 and in Trinidad in June 1960. *Cmnd. 1123/1960.*

TRINIDAD AND TOBAGO (cont.)

Representation of the People Ordinance, No. 33 of 1960. *Laws of Trinidad & Tobago.*

(Constitution) Order in Council 1961. *S.I. 1192/1961.*

Royal Instructions to the Governor and Commander-in-Chief of the Colony of Trinidad & Tobago, dated 26th June 1961. *Instruments not S.I., appendix to S.I./1961.*

Constitutional Adviser to the Cabinet (Special Post) Order, 1961. *Trinidad & Tobago, Subsidiary Legislation, G.N. No. 169/1961.*

Verbatim notes of proceedings of the meeting on the draft constitution held at the Queen's Hall, Port of Spain, 1962. *Port of Spain, Trinidad, 1962.*

Report of the Joint Select Committee to consider proposals for an independence constitution for Trinidad & Tobago. 1962. *House Paper No. 2/1962.*

Report of the Conference on Trinidad & Tobago Independence, 1962. *Cmnd. 1957/1962.*

Trinidad & Tobago (Procedure in Appeals to Privy Council) Order in Council 1962. *S.I./1962.*

Trinidad & Tobago Independence Act 1962. *U.K. Public General Acts,* 1962 c. 54.

(Constitution) Order in Council 1962. *S.I. 1875/1962.*

Trinidad & Tobago Citizenship Act, No. 11 of 1962. *Laws of Trinidad & Tobago.*

Supreme Court of Judicature Act, No. 12 of 1962. *Laws of Trinidad & Tobago.*

Legal and Constitutional Commission on the question of Unitary Statehood of Grenada and Trinidad & Tobago. *Port of Spain, Trinidad, 1963.*

Trinidad & Tobago Constitution (Amendment) Act, No. 13 of 1964. *Laws of Trinidad & Tobago.*

Supreme Court of Judicature Act, No. 14 of 1964. *Laws of Trinidad & Tobago.*

Trinidad & Tobago Constitution Ordinance, (Amendment) Act, No. 22 of 1965. *Laws of Trinidad & Tobago.*

TRINIDAD AND TOBAGO (cont.)

Representation of the People (Amendment) Act, No. 4 of 1966. *Laws of Trinidad & Tobago.*

Crown Liability and Proceedings Act, No. 17 of 1966. *Laws of Trinidad & Tobago.*

Representation of the People Act, No. 41 of 1967. *Laws of Trinidad & Tobago.*

Supreme Court of Judicature (Amendment) Act, No. 29 of 1968. *Laws of Trinidad & Tobago.*

Trinidad & Tobago Constitution (Amendment) Act, No. 25 of 1968. *Laws of Trinidad & Tobago.*

VIRGIN ISLANDS

See also: Leeward Islands.

Constitutional position in 1922. *Colonial Office List, 1922,* p. 265. H.M.S.O.

Report of the Committee to consider the composition of a Legislative Council and allied questions. *Leeward Islands Gazette, 1950.*

The Virgin Islands Constitution Act, No. 1 of 1950. *Acts of the Leeward Islands.*

Voters Registration and Election Ordinance No. 3 of 1950. *Laws of the Virgin Islands.*

Constitution and Elections Ordinance, No. 7 of 1954. *Laws of the Virgin Islands.*

Crown Proceedings Ordinance No. 4 of 1955. *Laws of the Virgin Islands.*

Crown Proceedings (Amendment) Ordinance No. 8 of 1956. *Laws of the Virgin Islands.*

Virgin Islands (Appeals) Order in Council, 1957. *S.I. 1746/1957.*

Constitution and Elections (Amendment) Ordinance No. 2 of 1958. *Laws of the Virgin Islands.*

Police Service Commission Ordinance No. 20 of 1959. *Laws of the Virgin Islands.*

Legal Officers (appointment, dismissal and disciplinary control) Ordinance No. 21 of 1959. *Laws of the Virgin Islands.*

VIRGIN ISLANDS (cont.)

Virgin Islands Letters Patent, dated 22nd December 1959. *Instruments not S.I., appendix to S.I./1959.*

Royal Instructions to the Administrator, dated 22nd December 1959. *Instruments not S.I., appendix to S.I./1959.*

Letters Patent, dated 12th May 1960. *Instruments not S.I., appendix to S.I./1960.*

Legal Officers (appointment, dismissal and disciplinary control) (Amendment) Ordinance No. 6 of 1960. *Laws of the Virgin Islands.*

Report of the Constitutional Commissioner, 1965. *Col. No. 361/1965.*

Report of the British Virgin Islands Constitutional Conference, 1966. *Cmnd. 3129/1966.*

(Courts) Order 1967. *S.I. 231/1967.*

(Appeals to Privy Council) Order 1967. *S.I. 234/1967.*

(Constitution) Order 1967. *S.I. 471/1967.*

WEST INDIES

See also: Federation and Federal Experiments.

Summary of constitutional position, 1922, in Colonial Regulations 1922. *Colonial Office List, 1922.* H.M.S.O.

Report of the Visit of the Hon. E.F.L. Wood, M.P., to the West Indies and British Guiana, 1921-22. *Cmnd. 1679/1922.*

Notes on the Constitution of the British West Indies, Bermuda, British Guiana and British Honduras, 1933. *Colonial Office, West Indies Pamphlet, No. 585, 1933,* folio.

Report of the West India Royal Commission, 1938-39. *Cmnd. 6607/1945.*

Report of the West Indies Constitutional Conference, 1961. *Cmnd. 1417/196*

West Indies Act 1962. *U.K. Public General Acts,* 1962 c. 19.

West Indies (Dissolution and Interim Commission) Order in Council 1962. *S.I. 1084/1962.*

Constitutional Proposals for Antigua, St. Christopher/Nevis/Anguilla, Dominica, St. Lucia, St. Vincent, Grenada, 1965. *Cmnd. 2865/1965.*

WEST INDIES (cont.)

The West Indies Act 1967. *U.K. Public General Acts,* 1967 c. 4.

West Indies Associated States Supreme Court Order, 1967. *S.I. 223/1967.*

WINDWARD ISLANDS

See also: Federation and Federal Experiments. Associated States, and individual territories, Dominica (after 1938), Grenada, St. Lucia, St. Vincent.

Constitutional position, 1922. *Colonial Office List, 1922,* p. 441. H.M.S.O.

Despatch (No. 95 of 1922) from the Secretary of State for the Colonies to the Governor of the Windward Islands, 1922. *Grenada Legislative Council Minutes, 1922.*

Circular Despatch from Secretary of State for the Colonies (Despatch No. 241 of 1922). See: *Leeward Islands Gazette Notice No. 291 of 1922.*

Correspondence referring to the proposed association of the Windward Islands with Trinidad, 1923. *Council Paper No. 103 of 1923 (Trinidad & Tobago).*

Letters Patent, dated 9th April 1924, constituting the office of Governor and Commander-in-Chief of the Windward Islands comprising the Islands of Grenada, St. Vincent and St. Lucia and the Dependencies thereof. *S.R. & O./ 1924.*

Closer Union between Trinidad, the Windward and the Leeward Islands. *Despatch from the Secretary of State for the Colonies, dated 4th March 1931.*

Report of the Closer Union Commission (Leeward Islands, Windward Islands, Trinidad & Tobago), April 1933. *Cmnd. 4383/1932-33.*

Despatch (No. 149 of 1934) from the Secretary of State for the Colonies to the Governor of the Windward Islands.

Letters Patent, dated 13th November 1936, constituting the Office of Governor and Commander-in-Chief of the Windward Islands 1936. *S.R. & O./ 1936.*

Windward Islands and Dominica Conference, 1939.

(1) Precis of Findings, *Grenada Council Paper No. 8 of 1939.*

(2) Despatch from Secretary of State. *Grenada Council Paper No. 12 of 1939.*

Leeward Islands and Windward Islands (Courts) Order in Council, 1939. *S.R. & O. 1898/1939.*

WINDWARD ISLANDS (cont.)

Letters Patent, dated 28th December 1939, amending Letters Patent of 13th November 1936 constituting the Office of Governor and Commander-in-Chief of the Windward Islands. 1939. *S.R. & O./1939.*

Windward and Leeward Islands (Appeal to Privy Council) Order in Council, 1942. *S.R. & O./1942, 5th March.*

Windward Islands and Leeward Islands (Appeal to Privy Council) Order in Council, 1943. *S.R. & O./1943, 11th March.*

Windward Islands Conference on Constitutional Reform. *Colonial Office, West Indies Pamphlet No. 803, 1945, folio.*

Letters Patent, dated 11th May 1945, amending Letters Patent of the 13th November 1936, 1945. *S.R. & O./1945.*

Government Notice. Constitutional Reform. Windward and Leeward Islands. *Leeward Islands Gazette, 1949,* p. 87.

Government Notice. Constitutional Reform. *Leeward Islands Gazette, 1949,* p. 267.

Leeward Islands and Windward Islands (Courts) (Amendment) Order in Council 1949. *S.I. 600/1949.*

Letters Patent, dated 27th August 1951. *Instruments not S.I., appendix to S.I./1951.*

Royal Instructions, dated 10th August 1951. *Instruments not S.I., appendix to S.I./1951.*

Additional Instructions to the Governor and Commander-in-Chief, dated 19th March 1953. *Instruments not S.I., appendix to S.I./1953.*

Additional Instructions to the Governor and Commander-in-Chief, dated 19th March 1953. *Instruments not S.I., appendix to S.I./1953.*

Letters Patent amending Windward Islands Letters Patent, 1951. *Instruments not S.I., appendix to S.I./1954.*

Additional Instructions to the Governor and Commander-in-Chief, dated 10th September 1954. *Instruments not S.I., appendix to S.I./1954.*

Public Announcement on Constitutional Reform in the Colonies of Grenada, St. Lucia and St. Vincent. Windward Islands, 1955. See: *Minutes of the Legislative Council of Grenada, 7th January 1955* (Appendix I to Address by the Acting Administrator).

WINDWARD ISLANDS (cont.)

The Leeward and Windward Islands (Courts) (Amendment) Order in Council 1954. *S.I. 1040/1954.*

Additional Royal Instructions, dated 28th December 1955. *Instruments not S.I., appendix to S.I./1955.*

Letters Patent, dated 29th December 1955. *Instruments not S.I., appendix to S.I./1955.*

Additional Instructions to the Governor and Commander-in-Chief, dated 23rd October 1957. *Instruments not S.I., appendix to S.I./1957.*

Leeward Islands and Windward Islands (Courts) Order in Council, 1957. *S.I. 2167/1957.*

Letters Patent, dated 8th May 1958. *Instruments not S.I., appendix to S.I./ 1958.*

Proposals for constitutional reform in the Territories of Antigua, Dominica, Grenada, Montserrat, St. Christopher/Nevis/Anguilla, St. Lucia, and St. Vincent, agreed to at the Conference convened by the Federal Government at Federal House, Port of Spain, Trinidad, from 23rd March to 26th March 1959. *Federal Government Publication, Port of Spain, Trinidad.*

Report of the Leeward and Windward Islands Constitutional Conference, 1959. *Cmnd. 804/1959.*

Windward Islands and Leeward Islands (Courts) Order in Council 1959. *S.I. 2197/1959.*

Windward Islands and Leeward Islands (Police Service Commission) Order in Council 1959. *S.I. 2198/1959.*

Windward Islands and Leeward Islands (Courts) (Amendment) Order in Council, 1960. *S.I. 1658/1960.*

Report by the Leeward Islands and Windward Islands Constitutional Conference, held in London in June, 1961. *Cmnd. 1434/1960-61.*

Admiralty Jurisdiction (St. Christopher, Nevis and Anguilla) Order 1964. *S.I. 1663/1964.*

Windward Islands Constitutional Conference, 1966. Report, general conclusions and Grenada appendix. *Cmnd. 3021/1966.*

Supreme Court of the Windward Islands and Leeward Islands (Judges' Remuneration and Terms and Conditions of Office) Order, 1967. *S.I./1967.*

WINDWARD ISLANDS (cont.)

Windward Islands and Leeward Islands (Courts) Order 1967. *S.I. 162/1967.*

WOOD COMMISSION

Report of the Hon. E.F.L. Wood, M.P., on his visit to the West Indies and British Guiana, 1922 *Cmnd. 1679/1922.*

Index